Microprocessor Technology

John D. Kershaw

Component Engineer
ITT North Electric Company

Breton Publishers
A Division of Wadsworth, Inc.
Boston, Massachusetts

Breton Publishers
A Division of Wadsworth, Inc.
20 Providence Street
Boston, Massachusetts 02116

Library of Congress Cataloging in Publication Data

Kershaw, John D
Microprocessor technology.

Includes index.
1. Microprocessors. 2. Microcomputers. I. Title.
TK7895.M5K47 621.3819'5 79-26246

ISBN 0-534-00748-1

This book and its cover were designed by John Servideo. The type was set and the art was rendered by Jay's Publishers Services, Inc. Printing and binding were done by Interstate Book Manufacturers, Inc.

Contents

Chapter 3

Chapter 4

Chapter 5

Chapter 6

Chapter 7

Chapter 8

Preface

This text is for the reader who is familiar with digital electronics and who would like to step into the rapidly expanding field of microprocessors.

The benefits to be derived from microprocessor-controlled electronics are so great that these devices have already been designed into a wide variety of equipment. The list of automated control tasks to which the microprocessor has been applied is rapidly growing and has all but propelled us into the age of the robot. The resulting demand for microprocessor circuits has encouraged most manufacturers of integrated circuits either to develop their own microprocessors or to become suppliers of one of several popular models. At the present time a wide variety of microprocessor circuits are on the market. The circuits may differ by number of bits in address and data bus, by type of interrupt system, and by instruction set, but fortunately for the student they are more alike than they are different. It is also fortunate that the bulk of the market for microprocessor components (not counting those sold in calculators and other assemblies) is supplied by only a few models.

At this writing the Intel 8080A and the Motorola M6800 represent the bulk of those in use. Each of these devices is manufactured by three or more integrated circuit manufacturers. For this reason I have included chapters on the hardware and programming of both.

Several promising contenders, such as, the Zilog Z80, RCA 1800, the MOS Technology 6500, and the Texas Instrument 9900 have definite advantages, but I have reserved coverage of these for future editions depending on their success.

There is a wealth of information available in the form of data sheets and application manuals from each microprocessor manufacturer. The manufacturers' primary interest is in the sale of microprocessors and complex peripheral devices. The information supplied is directed at design engineers and engineering managers who in most cases are designing these devices into very complex systems. The object of this text is to present simple yet meaningful applications of the microprocessor in systems that use elementary peripheral devices. In this way, the reader can master the microprocessor before being confronted with peripheral devices that rival the microprocessor in complexity.

The world of computers and microprocessors is rich in vocabulary, expanding beyond that used in basic and digital electronics. To introduce this new language, Chapter 2 gives a complete overview of the organization of computer and microprocessor systems. New words are defined, in the Key Terms sections, as they are introduced.

A review of number systems is also included because hexadecimal code has taken on a new importance and there is frequent need to convert between decimal, hexadecimal, and binary.

Chapters 4 through 6 are designed to provide a gradual growth in hardware complexity as a backgound for introducing the total microprocessor hardware system.

Professionals concerned with computers generally divide into the two specialties of hardware or software. The student learning about microprocessors is putting a foot in both camps. Functional success of a microprocessor system is as dependent on software as it is on hardware. When a microprocessor system malfunctions, it is often difficult to determine whether the fault is with hardware or software. At this point the need for people who understand both aspects of the problem becomes acute.

A standard microprocessor with 8 data bits and 16 address bits (if used to the limits of its capacity) could handle a program of over 10,000 instructions requiring a printout of several hundred pages. On the other hand, because of its low cost, it is still economical to use this same device in a dedicated application requiring only a few dozen instructions.

The programs I have used are designed to be short but meaningful, and they are arranged to provide piecemeal and progressive introduction of the instruction sets. The selection of programs provides examples of typical programming techniques such as interrupts, subroutines, counter, timer and sequencer routines, and the use of lookup tables. The same programs are used both for the 8080 and for the M6800. Therefore, students learning both devices need to familiarize themselves with the problem conditions only once.

Although it may appear from the presentation of these programming problems that one of the two microprocessors might be more efficient in the given application, a minor change in approach might well alter this appearance. I emphasize that these programs were written for simplicity and clarity. They are not intended as benchmark programs for comparing the efficiency of the two microprocessors.

Not every reader will choose to learn both microprocessors or choose to learn them in the order that they appear in this book. Therefore, the chapters on the M6800 and the 8080A are independent of each other. The explanation of the 8080A is not dependent on any supporting background information in the chapter on the M6800.

In the advanced application of microprocessors, programs are developed on assembly systems or on development systems that are purchased or rented from microprocessor vendors. Because rental fees are presently $20 to $35 per hour, I did not feel that many readers would have access to such systems. The assembly system adds to the program format numerous instructions and coding that increase the complexity of program listings. I have given some explanation of assembly systems in the appendix, but I have chosen to use a simpler format for program listing in the text.

John D. Kershaw

To my daughters Linda and Lisa—
their self-reliance and helpfulness made
this effort possible.

Chapter 1

The Microprocessor: A Brief Introduction

1.1 The Robots Are Coming...

We cannot predict how much the microprocessor will change our lives, but we can be sure that the changes will be nothing less than revolutionary. The microprocessor brings us one step closer to the universal robot—a machine that looks and acts like a human being. Such a machine will perform difficult, routine, and tedious labor for us. To do this the machine must be able to duplicate all forms of human motion. It must have sensors to detect what is happening around it. It must be able to communicate with its human masters, and above all, it must be able to think, learn, remember, and make decisions. In short, it must have a brain.

Developing an artificial brain suitable for controlling the useful activities of a robot has long been a dream of science fiction writers. Machines that duplicate human motion are as old as the machine age. But machines that think, remember, learn, and make decisions, even to a limited extent, are new.

The relay and vacuum tube computers developed during the 1950s had the necessary brain power, but they were many times too large to fit into the head of a robot. The million-dollar price tag of the computer of that day certainly made their use in every home unthinkable. Even the cost of electricity for the operation of such a brain would have been too much for the average household. Today, however, that same brain power can be provided by a set of integrated circuits small enough to hold in the palm of one hand. Furthermore, these circuits can be produced for less than a hundred dollars, and the power required for their operation is no more than is needed to operate a simple flashlight. The artificial brain is no longer unattainable—it is here!

1.2 Microprocessor Versus Medium-Scale Integrated Circuits (MSI)

Although the microprocessor seems to bring forth a new generation in electronics, it does not provide any new functions. The functions to which microprocessors are presently applied have for many years been available to us through the use of small computers or the same functions have been possible by the assembly of small- and medium-scale integrated logic circuits. However, the microprocessor provides a new approach which, for most applications, proves to have several advantages over older techniques. The advantages may be in flexibility, smaller size, standardization, lower cost, or expandability.

The microprocessor and its peripheral building blocks represent a third generation in digital integrated circuits. Small-scale integrated logic circuits, the first generation of integrated circuit logic building blocks, became available in production quantities as early as 1964. These provided several logic gates* per integrated circuit and more complex logic functions were fabricated by the interconnection of these small-scale devices on circuit boards. By 1970 a second generation of building blocks became available in the form of medium-scale integrated circuits (MSI). The logic functions that are available in MSI form are quite numerous, but each can be classified as one of the following:

- adders
- counters
- registers
- latches
- encoders
- decoders
- multiplexers
- comparators.

When this list is compared with the hardware and software functions available from a microprocessor system, the flexible nature of the microprocessor becomes apparent: It has an arithmetic logic unit and it can add or subtract. The registers in it can be incremented and decremented like a counter. Numbers in its registers can be shifted left or right to provide all register functions. Data can be latched in registers or RAM. The parallel logical instructions can be used to provide all forms of coding and decoding. Data can be multiplexed or demultiplexed at its I/O ports. Although the microprocessor is capable of providing all these

*In this introductory chapter, the reader will encounter some terms that might be unfamiliar. These terms will be defined in the proper context, in later chapters.

functions, it does not perform them simultaneously. It performs such operations one at a time and must be instructed on the order in which they are to be executed, on what data it is to operate, and where to store the results. The microprocessor receives its instructions from a program stored in the program memory. Herein lies its shortcoming. The MSI circuit provides an output within a short propagation delay after the proper inputs arrive. The microprocessor, on the other hand, in doing the same function must fetch and decode one or more instructions, read the data, perform the operation, and move the results out of the way so that the next operation can be executed. All of this takes much more time than is required by the MSI circuit. Although the microprocessor system may have the means to supply any needed logic function, it may not be fast enough for some and it may not be economical enough for others. A digital system that would require only about 20 SSI/MSI circuits may be too small to warrant implementing it with a microprocessor system. (The number 20 is based on today's cost of a minimum microprocessor system of three or four LSI circuits.) In the near future, microcontrollers that contain microprocessor, ROM, RAM, and I/O interface in a single circuit may have a hardware cost cheaper than 20 SSI/MSI circuits.

Hardware cost alone is not sufficient for comparing the relative merits of a microprocessor and selecting it over standard digital logic. Software is more often a determining factor. For the hobbyist, the time spent working on software may be part of the fun, but to the manufacturer, the labor cost for writing, assembling, and debugging programs can be staggering. Also, cost for software is difficult to estimate accurately. However, software is an initial fixed cost and once the program has been perfected that cost can be divided by the number of systems that are produced.

1.3 Types of Microprocessors

There are millions of microprocessors manufactured each year. They come from several dozen integrated circuit manufacturers who make a multitude of variations. Most are of MOS technology, but a few are CMOS, and recently TTL and I^2L devices have been added to the list. They vary in size of both address and data bus, in size of instruction set, and in number of registers. Most are processing units which must be used with external memory, but some are microcontrollers, containing CPU, ROM, RAM, and I/O ports on a single chip. The typical microprocessor is a 40-pin dual-in-line integrated circuit as Figure 1.1(a) shows. The 40-pin circuit in itself seems small considering the many remarkable functions it can perform. Yet the actual active element within the 40-pin circuit as seen by the circuit with the lid removed is a chip of silicon only .160″ × .160″ in size. This chip of silicon contains arrays of minute transistors precisely connected to produce all of the needed logic functions. Figure 1.2 shows a photograph of the chip of the 8080A microprocessor. Of the many microprocessors produced each year, a

FIGURE 1.1 (a) The 9440 Microflame CPU, a 16-bit bipolar microprocessor. The 40-pin package is 2 inches long and 0.6 inches wide. The die photograph, shown as background, is magnified 30 times.

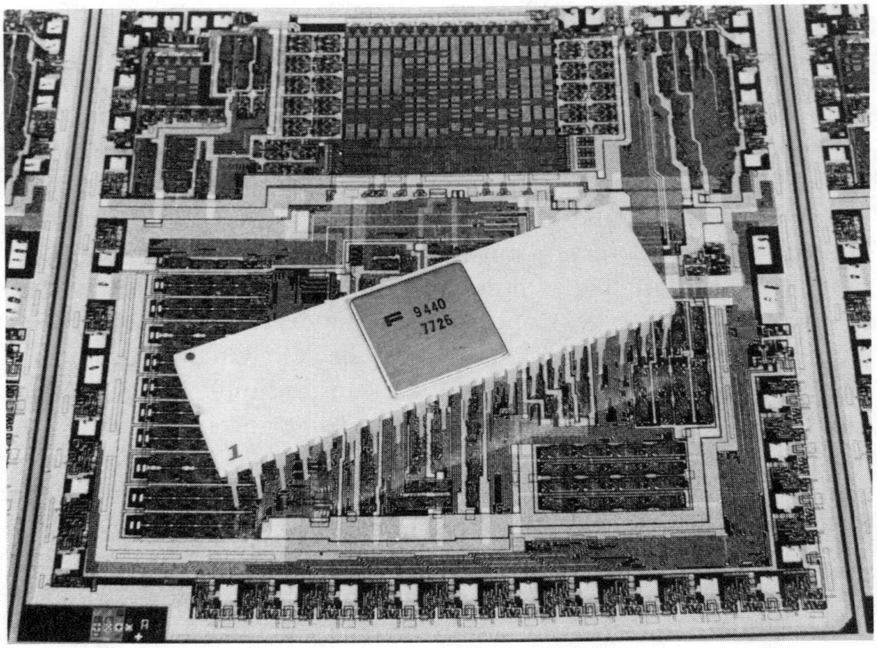

(b) Similar microprocessor unit with metal lid removed showing bond wire connections between the die and the 40-pin package. *(Courtesy of Fairchild Camera & Instrument Corp.)*

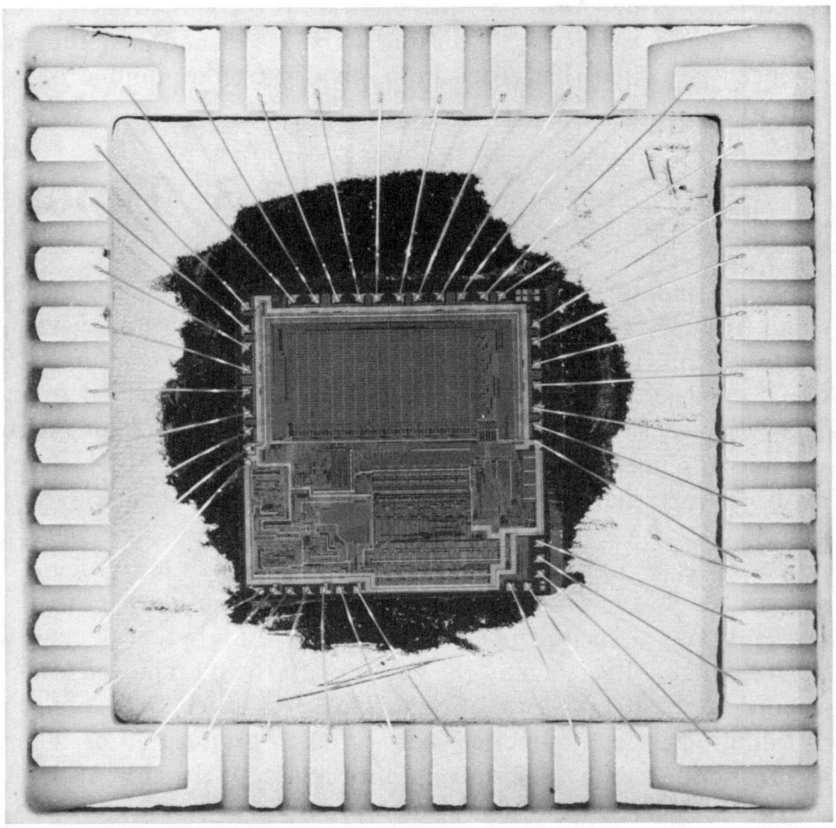

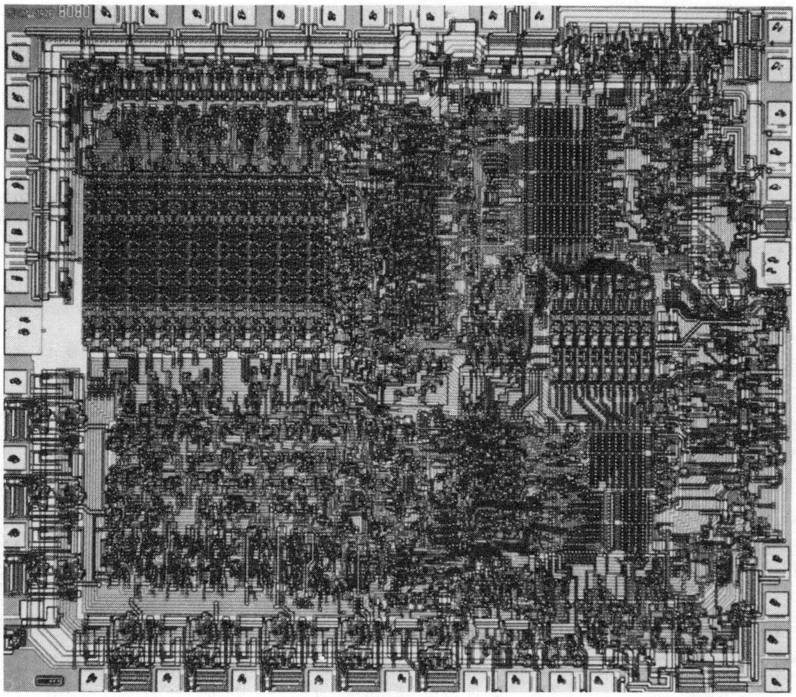

FIGURE 1.2 Silicon chip (die) of the 8085 Microprocessor. (*Courtesy of Intel Corp.*)

substantial number are assembled into calculators and similar devices. Of primary concern to us, however, are those sold to private users or equipment manufacturers as integrated circuits. Table 1.1 lists some widely used microprocessors, their characteristics, and their sources.

Table 1.2 lists the microcontrollers which differ from microprocessors in that they contain internal RAM, ROM, or I/O ports and are often considered single chip microcomputers. The amount of onboard RAM or ROM is usually small, but it is enough to allow these devices to perform dedicated functions which require only short programs such as the control of household appliances.

At the other end of the scale are the microprocessor building blocks such as the 1-bit and 4-bit slice devices listed in Table 1.3. The heart of a microprocessor is the arithmetic logic unit (ALU). This unit combined with an accumulator is involved in all instructions performed by a microprocessor other than the move, store, and transfer instructions. A 1-bit microprocessor slice is essentially a 1-bit arithmetic logic unit. Microprocessor slices can be paralleled to develop a microprocessor of any needed data-bit size. Five 4-bit slices can be paralleled to develop a microprocessor of 20 data bits. As the list of 2900 devices in Table 1.3 shows, numerous other circuits are required to provide functions other than ALU. Developing microprocessors from these building blocks is not a task for beginners. It is more difficult than employing a standard design device. These circuits however are TTL and can provide systems with limited instructions but of much higher speed than is available from standard devices.

TABLE 1.1 Microprocessor characteristics and manufacturers.

MODEL	DATA BITS	ADDRESS BITS	TECHNOLOGY	POWER SUPPLIES	PINS PER CKT	ORIGINATOR	OTHER SOURCES	REMARKS
4040	4	6	PMOS	-15V	24	INTEL		
PPS-4	4		PMOS	-17V	42	ROCKWELL		
F-8	8	16	NMOS	+12 +5	40	FAIRCHILD	MOSTEK	
8080A	8	16	NMOS	+5V -5V +12V	40	INTEL	AMD NATIONAL T.I. NEC	
8085	8*	16*	NMOS	+5V	40	INTEL	AMD	
6800	8	16	NMOS	+5V	40	MOTOROLA	FAIRCHILD AMI	
650X	8	16	NMOS	+5V	40	MOS TECHNOLOGY	SYNERTEK ROCKWELL	
SC/MP	8*	16*	NMOS	-12V or +5 -7	40	NATIONAL		4 AD/DATA USE +5V -7V FOR TTL COMPOUT
Z80	8	16	NMOS	+5V	40	ZILOG	MOSTEK	
1802	8	16	CMOS	+10V	40	RCA	SOLID STATE SCIENTIFIC	
2650	8	15	NMOS	+5V	40	SIGNETICS		
6100	12	12	CMOS	+5V or +10V	40	INTERSIL	HARRIS	EMULATES PDP-8
8086	16*	20*	NMOS	+5V	40	INTEL	MOSTEK	
1600	16*	16*	NMOS	+5V +12V -3V	40	GENERAL INSTRUMENT		PDP-II TYPE INSTRUCTIONS
PACE	16*	16*	NMOS	+5V -12V +3V	40	NATIONAL		
9440	16*	15	BIPOLAR	+5V	40	FAIRCHILD		(MICROFLAME™)
TMS 9900	16	15	NMOS	+5V -5V +12V	64	TEXAS INSTRUMENT	AMI	AVAILABLE IN I^2L
68000	16	23	NMOS	+12V	64	MOTOROLA		

*Multiplexed address and data.

TABLE 1.2 Microcontrollers. (Sometimes called single chip microcomputers.)

NUMBER (MFG.)	INTERNAL			EXTERNAL BUS EXPANSION	OTHER FEATURES
	RAM	ROM	I/O		
8048 (INTEL)	64 X 8	1K X 8	27 LINES 3 8-BIT PORTS +3	1 8-BIT PORT USED AS HIGH ADDRESS BYTE 1 8-BIT PORT USED AS MULTIPLEXED ADDRESS LOW BYTE WITH DATA BYTE	ON BOARD CLOCK TIMER/COUNTER
6801E (MOTOROLA)	128 X 8	2K X 8	33 LINES + SERIAL	8-BIT DATA (PORT3) 8-BIT ADR (PORT4) OR 8-BIT DATA } PORT3 8-BIT ADRL } MUX. 8-BIT ADRH (PORT4)	ON BOARD CLOCK TIMER/COUNTER
6500/1 (MOS TECHNOLOGY) (ROCKWELL)	64 X 8	2K X 8	32 LINES (4 PORTS)		ON BOARD CLOCK TIMER/COUNTER FIVE INTERRUPTS
3870 (MOSTEK) (FAIRCHILD)	64 X 8	2K X 8	32 LINES (4 PORTS)		ON BOARD CLOCK TIMER/COUNTER EXTERNAL INTERRUPT

TABLE 1.3 2900 4-bit slice Microprocessor series. These circuits are high speed building blocks which can be assembled to provide microprocessors of varied size.

CIRCUIT NUMBER	NAME	CONTENT-DESCRIPTION	PIN NO.
2901	4-BIT BIPOLAR MICROPROCESSOR SLICE	4-BIT ARITHMETIC LOGIC UNIT STATUS FLAGS WORKING REGISTERS	40
2902	HIGH-SPEED CARRY LOOK-AHEAD	SPEED UP ARITHMETIC BY ANTICIPATING CARRY IN ADVANCE	16
2909	MICROPROGRAM SEQUENCER	CONTROLS ADDRESSING WITHIN A 2900 SYSTEM	28
2911			20
2913	PRIORITY INTERRUPT EXPANDER	EXPANDS 2914	20
2914	VECTORED PRIORITY INTERRUPT ENCODER	CONTROL 2900 MICROPROCESSOR VECTORED INTERRUPT SYSTEM	40
2905	QUAD BUS TRANSCEIVERS	OPEN COLLECTOR	24
2906		OPEN COLLECTOR WITH PARITY	24
2907		3-STATE WITH PARITY	20
2915		3-STATE W/INTERFACE LOGIC	24
2916		" " PLUS PARITY	24
2917		" " "	20
2918	QUAD D REGISTER	3-STATE OUTPUTS	16
29700	64-BIT RAM	NONINVERTING	16
29702		INVERTING	
29704	16-WORD BY 4-BIT RAM	2-PORT RAM	28
29750	PROM	32-WORD BY 8-BIT	16
29760		256-WORD BY 4-BIT	16
29790	FPLA	FIELD PROGRAMMABLE LOGIC ARRAY	28

1.4 Hardware Development

Enhancing the growth of microprocessor applications has been a parallel development of larger and better memory circuits for use with microprocessors. Fusible link programmable read only memories have advanced from as few as 256 bits per circuit in 1973 to as many as 8192 bits per circuit in 1978. Equally important has been the development of static RAMS of higher density, from 1024 bits per circuit in 1973 to the 8192 bits per circuit available in 1979. Growing even more rapidly than the memory circuits is the development of special peripheral devices designed to facilitate numerous microprocessor applications. A list of these and their functions is given in Table 1.4.

TABLE 1.4 Microprocessor Peripheral Circuits

The circuits listed are designed to facilitate microprocessor control of numerous peripheral devices.

CIRCUIT NUMBER	DESCRIPTION	MFG.	PINS
6821 8255	PERIPHERAL INTERFACE ADAPTER	MOTOROLA INTEL	40 40
6840 8253	PROGRAMMABLE TIMER	MOTOROLA INTEL	24 24
6843 8271	FLOPPY DISK CONTROLLER	MOTOROLA INTEL	40 40
6844 8257	DIRECT MEMORY ACCESS CONTROLLER	MOTOROLA INTEL	40 40
6845 8275	CRT CONTROLLER	MOTOROLA INTEL	40 40
6850 8251	COMMUNICATIONS INTERFACE	MOTOROLA INTEL	24 28
6828 8259	PRIORITY INTERRUPT CONTROLLER	MOTOROLA INTEL	24 28
8279	PROGRAMMABLE KEYBOARD/ DISPLAY CONTROLLER	INTEL	40

1.5 Software Development Tools

Short, dedicated microprocessor programs are relatively easy to write and are seldom difficult to debug, but an 8-bit microprocessor with 16-bit address bus may be used in a system having thousands of instructions. Figure 1.3 shows a Micro Control Co. memory tester designed to provide both production and development test of memory and other LSI circuits. It is controlled by a single 8080A microprocessor. It communicates with the operator through either a teletype or a CRT terminal. A minimum system uses 16,000 bytes of memory and communicates with 200 I/O ports within the system. A microprocessor system of this magnitude requires a program of such length that a computer program is needed to assist in assembling and editing it. Figure 1.4 shows a development system for the Intel 8080/8085 microprocessor. Large

FIGURE 1.3 Memory Tester Microprocessor Controlled. (*Courtesy of Micro Control Co.*)

programs are generally developed in modules of small routines and segments. These are entered on the CRT terminal of a development system and edited. An editor program within the system recognizes certain types of errors, computes conditional jumps, and provides for the insertion of missing instructions. After each program module is edited it is assembled. The assembler converts the alphabetical mnemonic code used by the programmer into the machine code used by the microprocessor. It assigns consecutive addresses to each instruction. Upon completion of assembly, the program segments can be stored in a library on floppy disk. Programs or segments of software can be debugged by execution of the program in a simulated system, stopping the program at critical points (breakpoints) to allow the examination of data in microprocessor registers and key memory locations. On completion of all

FIGURE 1.4 The Intellec® Development System.
From left to right: High Speed Paper Tape Reader, Universal PROM Programmer, Printer, Floppy Dukette Operating System, CRT Terminal and Keyboard, In-Circuit Emulator. (*Courtesy of Intel Corp.*)

segments or modules of a given program, a link and locate feature in the development system connects the segments and locates them correctly in memory. At any time during or after development of a program, a printed program listing can be obtained through the RS232C teletype adapter. The final program can be loaded into a PROM for installation into the user's system. Finally an in circuit emulator can be connected in place of the 8080 microprocessor. In this way the debug routines such as breakpoints and register display can be used to troubleshoot the user's system.

1.6 The Challenge

How does a beginner learn all of the hardware and software features of so many microprocessors, and at the same time cope with the growing number of peripheral devices that are used to enhance their applications? Add to this a need to know the operating commands and characteristics of the development systems. Combine all this with the feeling that new and improved devices are reaching the market faster than one can master the use of older models. Knowing the capabilities and features of all the microprocessors as well as keeping up with new developments presents a formidable learning task. On the other hand, microprocessors of different models are more alike than they are different, and fortunately one of two models are used in nearly 90% of present-day applications.

Figure 1.5 shows an operating model of a traffic light. A microprocessor supplies the timing and the sequencing of the red, yellow, green, and left turn signals. It requires a microprocessor system of only four circuits or as few as two circuits with a microcontroller. It has a program of fewer than 70 instructions. It is not formidable at all. It is quite simple. It works, and there are thousands of applications like it. This is where we begin.

FIGURE 1.5 Traffic light model connected to a microprocessor system.

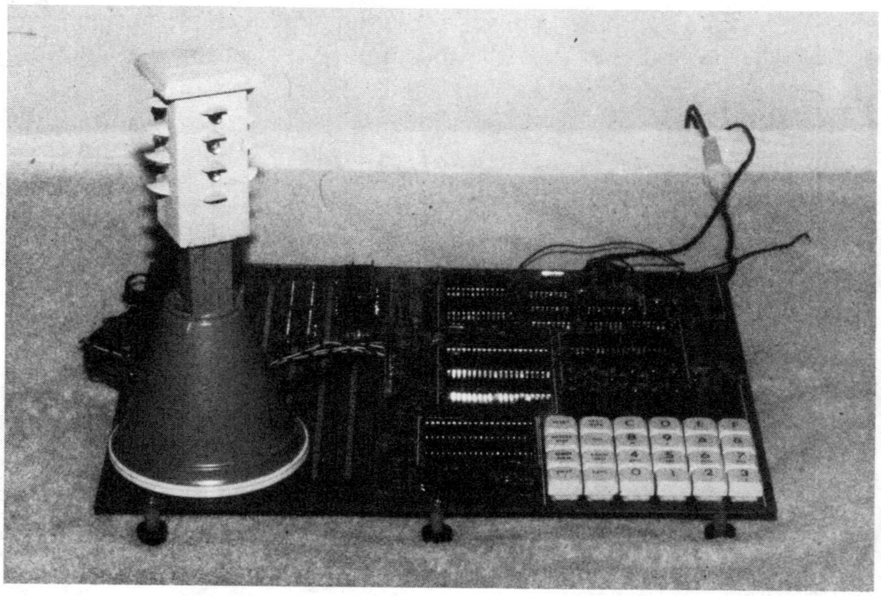

Chapter 2

Computer Organization and Routines

Objectives

On completion of this chapter you will be able to:

- Identify the numerous functions of a microprocessor and its associated components.
- Use the vocabulary peculiar to microprocessor and computer systems.
- Use the vocabulary associated with microprocessor software.
- Read and assemble a microprocessor program listing.
- Recognize the addressing modes of microprocessor instructions.

2.1 Systems Components

Any computer, regardless of its size, is made up of an input device, a timing and control unit, an arithmetic logic unit, a memory unit, and an output device. See Figure 2.1.

The timing and control circuit combined with the arithmetic unit is called a **central processor** or **central processing unit**, (**CPU**). When these units are provided in a single integrated circuit, that circuit is called a **microprocessor**, (**MPU**). In addition to the arithmetic unit, the processor contains sets of **registers**, counters, and **decoding circuits**. Using these logic circuits, the processor can respond to a variety of simple **instructions**. The list of instructions that a processor can execute is known as an **instruction set**. Processors may have instruction sets with

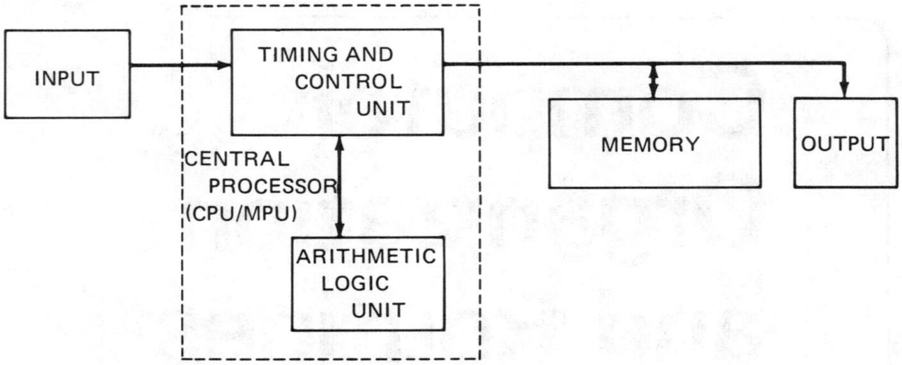

FIGURE 2.1 Block diagram of a digital computer. The combined timing, control, and arithmetic logic unit is called a central processor. If supplied in a single integrated circuit, it is called a microprocessor.

as few as 50 or as many as 150 instructions. A processor that has a small instruction set usually can perform the same functions as one that has a large instruction set, but it normally requires more memory locations and machine cycles.

Table 2.1 is a partial instruction set for the 8080 microprocessor. Note that each instruction is expressed both as a **mnemonic** which is convenient for the programmer, and as a **machine code**. After the user writes a program with the mnemonics, it must be converted first to the machine code before being written into the computer memory as a **stored program**. The machine code instruction tells the computer which operation is to be executed. With a few expeptions, the complete program instructions must also tell the processor where in memory the number to be operated on is located. This portion of the instruction is called the **operand**.

The following instruction tells the computer to add 04 to the accumulator with carry.

$$\text{Opcode} \longrightarrow \overbrace{\text{ACI} \qquad\qquad 04}^{\text{Instruction}} \longleftarrow \text{Operand}$$

TABLE 2.1 Typical instructions from 8080 microprocessor instruction set.

MNEMONIC	MACHINE CODE	DESCRIPTION
MOV M,B	01110000	Move data from register B to memory.
MOV B,M	01000110	Move data from memory to register B.
INR C	00001100	Increment register C.
DCR C	00001101	Decrement register C.
ADD M	10000110	Add memory to accumulator.
ACI	11001110	Add operand to accumulator with carry.
CPI	11111110	Compare operand with accumulator.
JMP	11000011	Jump unconditional
JC	11011010	Jump on carry
JNC	11010010	Jump on no carry
JZ	11001010	Jump on zero
JNZ	11000010	Jump on no zero

It contains two terms. The **operation code** or **opcode** (ACI) and the operand (04). Both opcode and operand are converted to binary form before being stored in program memory. In this form, the opcode is called a machine code. For the programmers convenience; however, the opcodes are generally listed in mnemonic form while the operands are listed in a higher number system, such as, octal, decimal, or hexadecimal.

Key Terms

Central Processing Unit (CPU) That portion of a computer which contains the necessary timing and control circuits needed to execute a program. It includes the arithmetic logic unit, the instruction decoder, program counter, and other register counter circuits.

Decoding Circuit A circuit that receives binary coded signals on its input lines. A different output line or set of lines becomes active for each combination of binary levels at the inputs.

Instruction A signal transmitted to the processor in the form of a machine code that will cause it to begin executing a specific operation such as arithmetic or logic operation or the movement of data.

Instruction Set Every processor or microprocessor has a specific set of instructions that it can execute. Each instruction in the set is specified as both a mnemonic and a machine code.

Machine Code The operation code expressed in the mnemonics of the instruction set must first be translated into binary form before being entered in computer memory as a stored program. For each opcode mnemonic there is a corresponding binary number called the machine code.

Microprocessor (MPU) An integrated circuit of usually 40 pins, originally developed to control the arithmetic processes of a digital calculator and later applied as a universal control circuit for medium-sized digital systems.

Mnemonic An operation code expressed in three or more letters that sound or look similar to the operation being performed. For example, STA for store the accumulator in memory, or BEQ for branch on equal.

Operand The data word on which the operation is performed. For some instructions, the operand will be already located in the processor. For other instructions, it will be necessary for the processor to read the operand from memory.

Operation Code (Opcode) The portion of the instruction that determines the operation to be performed. It may fall short of being a complete instruction in that it may not provide the operands. The opcode may be in mnemonic form for the programmer's convenience, but it must be converted to machine code (binary) before being stored in program memory.

Register A logic circuit used to store digital numbers. It consists of flip-flops or binaries that can be placed in recognizable 1 or 0 state. The size of the register is measured in bits. Register circuits in a processor can shift numbers to right or left, and like counter circuits, they can increment or decrement.

Stored Program A list of instructions that tell the processor what to perform. The program contains both opcodes and operands stored in successive memory locations such that the processor can fetch and execute them in correct order.

2.2 Inside the Processor

Figure 2.2 shows a simple block diagram of a processor. For simplicity we will assume that the computer has the same number of bits in the data and address **bus**.

FIGURE 2.2 Typical block diagram of a microprocessor having address and data bus of equal size.

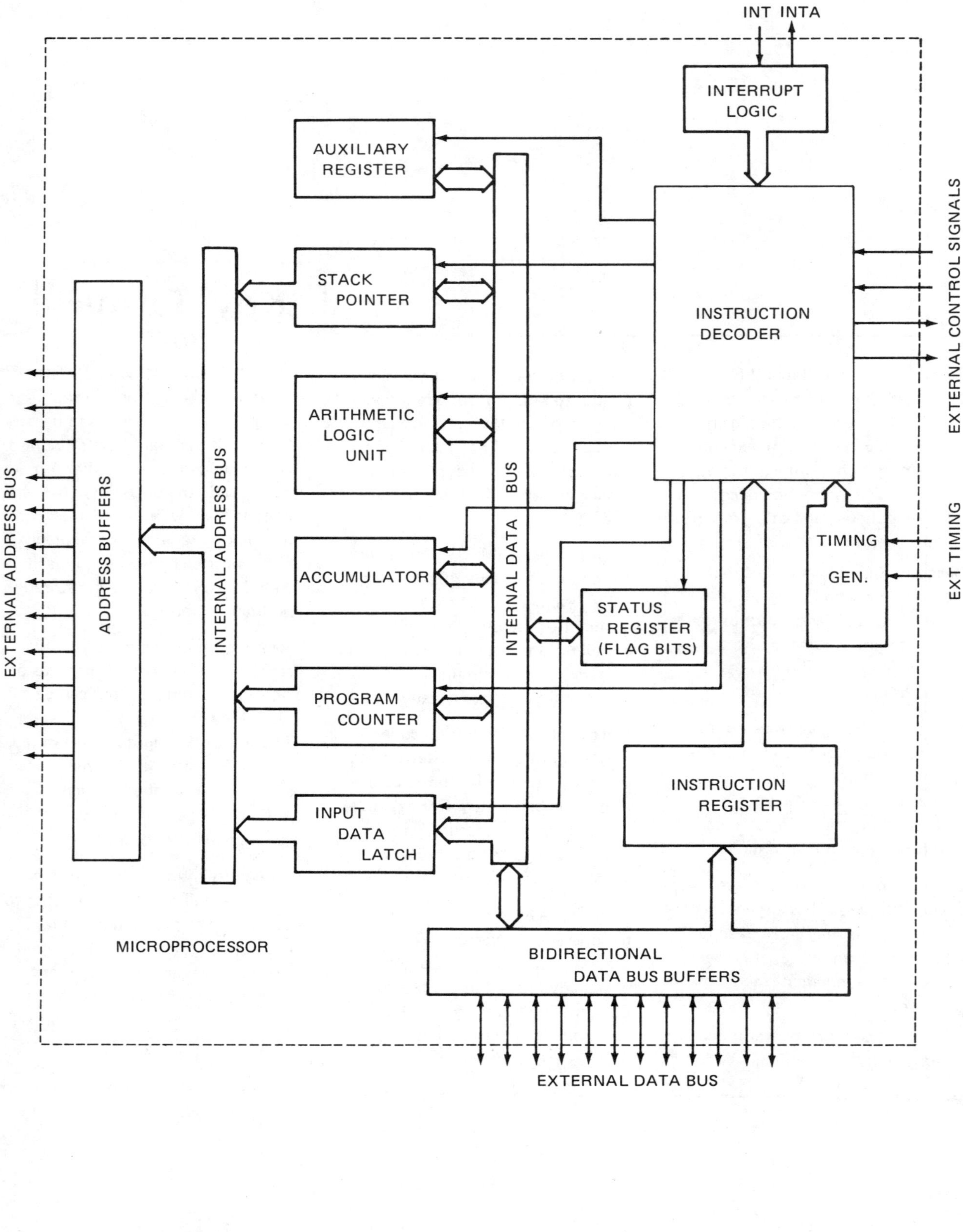

2.2.1 The Program Counter

At the beginning of a program, the **program counter** is set to the memory address of the first opcode. The contents of the program counter are momentarily connected to the address bus to fetch the first opcode. At the same time that the first opcode is strobed into the **instruction register**, the program counter is incremented. From the opcode in the instruction register, the instruction decoder determines whether an operand must be read from memory using the new address in the program counter or if the operand is already in the processor. After each **instruction fetch** or reading of an operand from program memory, the program counter is incremented. For very simple programs, the program counter merely counts through each step of the program; but for most programs, there are **loops**, **jumps**, and **branches** which require that the contents of the program counter be set back or ahead to specific points in the program. Table 2.2 shows a program containing both a jump instruction and a branch instruction. The program says that if the number in the accumulator is equal to 4, advance the program counter 5 counts. If not, the program counter will be incremented as usual. A few instructions later, an unconditional jump sets the program counter back to instruction 0302. This table illustrates the three methods of affecting the program's movement. Each is a manipulation of the program counter. The usual movement is determined by the incrementing of the program counter, but it can be moved ahead or back by adding or subtracting a value to the number in the program counter, or it can be jumped ahead or back as the result of replacing the current value in the program counter with a new one specified by the jump instruction.

STATEMENT NUMBER	OPCODE	OPERAND
0304	CPX	04
0306	BEQ	05
0308	INX	
0309	JMP	0203

TABLE 2.2 Typical program listing (6500).

2.2.2 Input Data Latch

Inputs from the data bus, which are not opcodes, are stored in the input data **latch**. If it is recognized by the processor as an operand, it will be transferred to the arithmetic unit or to the accumulator or auxiliary registers where it will be operated on as called for by the preceding opcode. If, however, it is recognized as a memory address of the true operand, it is transferred to the address bus so that the operand stored in memory can be read.

2.2.3 The Accumulator

The accumulator is the work horse register of the processor. When a program is loaded, each **byte** is first loaded in the accumulator and from there stored in successively higher memory locations. The terms and the results of arithmetic operations are stored in the accumulator. Numbers in the accumulator can be incremented, they can be shifted left or right, and they can be compared with other numbers in memory or in other registers. On completion of such operations, the results can be moved from the accumulator and stored in memory or in auxiliary registers.

2.2.4 Arithmetic Unit

In most microprocessors the arithmetic unit is either a 1s or 2s complement parallel adder with provisions for decimal correction. The adder may also provide compare, OR, AND, exclusive OR, and similar logic functions between numbers in the accumulator and those from operand memory locations.

2.2.5 Processor Status Register (Flags)

The **status register** contains the independent **flag** bits. The Z flag is set only when the accumulator is zero. The carry flag, C, is used as the carry bit of the arithmetic unit. The overflow flag, V, indicates an overflow in the arithmetic unit. The N flag indicates a negative result to an arithmetic operation. The I flag indicates that the interrupt is disabled. A variety of other flags may be found in various processors. Most branch or conditional jump instructions are based on the condition of one of the flag bits.

2.2.6 Auxiliary Registers

In using the accumulator, intermediate results of an operation must often be stored to clear the accumulator for other uses and then be brought back again for additional operations with the accumulator. Moving an operand from the accumulator to a register within the processor requires fewer instruction **words** than moving it to memory and back. The auxiliary registers may also be used as counters, sequencers, or timers. In these functions they are often called index registers.

2.2.7 The Stack Pointer

The **stack pointer** is used in all programs that have **subroutines** and in all operations that involve **interrupts**. These operations cause the program to leave the normal sequence of instructions. To accomplish this the contents of the program counter must be changed in the same fashion that it is changed for a branch or jump instruction, but the operations differ in that at the end of a subroutine or interrupt, the program counter must be returned to the count of the program it was on prior to the subroutine or interrupt. This previous program count is stored in a memory location called the **stack**. The stack pointer keeps track of the memory location in which the return to main program counts are stored. In addition to the program count, at the programmer's direction, the contents of accumulator and status register may also be stored on the stack. The program counter and the stack pointer function in a similar fashion: They both keep track of a memory address. The program counter tracks the program memory while the stack pointer tracks a section of memory called a stack. The program counter increments after each fetch from program memory. The stack pointer may be **decremented** each time an address or data is pushed onto the stack (when a jump to subroutine or interrupt occurs). The stack pointer is **incremented** each time an address or data is popped from the stack (when a return from subroutine or return from interrupt occurs).

Key Terms

Auxiliary Register A logic circuit used to store digital numbers. It consists of flip-flops or binaries that can be placed in recognizable 1 or 0 state. The size of the register is measured in bits. Register circuits in a processor can shift numbers to right or left, and like counter circuits, they can increment or decrement.

Branch Instruction (Conditional Jump) A branch instruction is like a jump instruction except that the jump occurs only if certain conditions are satisfied, such as, the equality of two numbers.

Bus A set of parallel signal lines to which are connected one or more transmitting devices and a number of receiving devices. A bidirectional bus allows the devices connected to it to transmit and receive on the same signal lines.

Byte The organization of binary cells or bits into small groups. In microprocessors the byte is eight bits in length (two hexadecimal digits).

Decrement The act of decreasing the count of a digital counter or register by one.

Flag A single bit of the status register. signal device

Increment The act of increasing the count of a digital counter or register by one.

Index Register A decrementing register used to control the number of times a program routine or loop is executed. A number is stored in the index register prior to starting the routine (entering the loop). Each time the routine is completed, the index register is checked for zero. If the index register is not zero, it is decremented and the routine is repeated. If the index register is zero, the processor moves ahead (exits the loop) in the program.

Instruction Fetch A memory read function differing from other read functions in that the processor will interpret the data read as an opcode. Most microprocessors provide some control or syncronizing signal during the instruction fetch.

Instruction Register A register inside a processor which stores the opcode for the period of time needed to complete execution of the instruction.

Interrupt A control line through which a peripheral device signals the processor that it needs to be serviced.

Jump Instruction Program instructions are normally executed one at a time starting at the lowest address of the program memory. A jump instruction tells the processor to either skip ahead in the program or to return to a previous statement. The address to jump to is identified by its statement number. The jump is accomplished by setting the program counter to the statement number being jumped to.

Latch A circuit which stores the digital signal level applied at its input only during a trigger or clock time. Level changes on the signal inputs that occur before or after the clock have no effect on the logic level (1 or 0) in storage.

Loops Loops exist when a program branches back repeatedly through the same program statements and continues doing so until a condition is satisfied.

(Continued on the next page.)

Key Terms

Memory A circuit used to store digital numbers. The circuit must have a large number of binary cells that can be set to binary 1 or 0 state. To be useful the cells must be organized into bytes or words. Each word must have an addressable location in the memory.

Pointer A register or counter used to keep track of or point to the next address to be used in a particular section of memory. Modern processors contain at least two pointers, the program counter and the stack pointer. In some processors an additional register is designated a pointer to point to address locations in read/write memory where variable data is to be stored.

Program Counter A counter-register inside the processor which counts through the program. Each fetch of an opcode or read of an operand is accomplished by outputting the contents of the program counter onto the address bus. After each fetch the program counter is incremented. The continued incrementing of the program counter causes the execution of instructions in the order of their address in program memory. Jumps and branches in the program are accomplished by setting a new number into the program counter.

Stack A section of read/write memory used to keep track of the program address to be returned to after an interrupt or jump to subroutine.

Stack Pointer A counter used to keep track of the address in the stack memory that is currently in use.

Status Register A register of independent flag bits indicating such things as Z-zero in the accumulator, C-carry bit, V-overflow bit.

Subroutines A section of program that is needed in numerous places throughout the overall program. At the point in the program where it is needed, the processor jumps to the subroutine and returns to the normal program sequence after the subroutine is completed. The result is a substantial saving in memory.

Word The organization of memory bytes into complete units. A word may contain one or more bytes.

2.3 The Program

A computer program is a list of program statements. Each statement contains three essential parts, the **statement number**, the opcode, and the operand. Looking again at the program in Table 2.2, the left-hand column contains the statement number, the second column contains the opcode, the third column contains the operand.

The statement numbers are the memory addresses taken by the opcodes when the program is stored in memory. Note that the statement numbers are in numerical order but after statements which contain operands a number is skipped. The numbers skipped are the addresses of the operands. Statement 0309 is a jump instruction; the operand of that statement is actually the statement number the program is jumping to. The statement numbers are listed primarily so that the programmer can keep track of and identify statements to be jumped or branched to. When the program is executed the program counter within the processor is set to the first statement number. After each opcode or operand is fetched the program counter is incremented. When a jump instruction is executed, the program counter is set to the statement number to which the program is jumping. The statement numbers can also be described as the number in the program counter at the time an opcode is being fetched.

The opcode or mnemonic in the second column must be one of those selected from the processor's instruction set. It tells the processor what operation is to be performed. These operations add, compare, move, and store data. Taken separately they are very simple. It is the task of the programmer to arrange these in a sequence that will perform the complex operations for which computers are famous. A program may contain hundreds of statements along with jumps, loops, and subroutines. The opcodes in Table 2.2 are in mnemonic form. Prior to storing them in program memory they will be converted to the equivalent machine codes.

The third column containing operands is blank for some statements because for these instructions the operand is implied by the opcode and is already in the processor. In this case, it is not necessary for the processor to read it from memory. The numbers or symbols in the third column are either operands or they are the memory addresses where the operands are located.

Figure 2.3 shows the program of Table 2.2 as it would be stored in **program memory.**

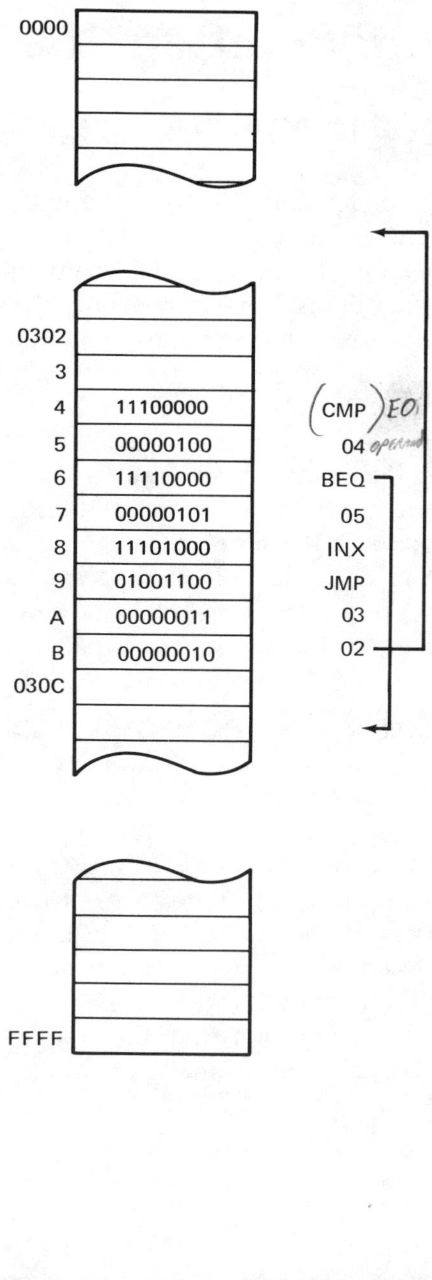

FIGURE 2.3 Memory map showing the program of Table 2.3 stored in the specified memory addresses.

Key Terms

Constant Operand An operand whose numberical value is known at the time the program is written and, therefore, can be stored in program memory immediately following the opcode. For this reason constant operands are often called immediate operands.

Statement Number Statements in a computer program are usually given statement numbers. The statements are numbered in numerical order with the numbers being identical to the memory addresses of the opcode. As a result they are identical to the number in the program counter at the time the opcode is being fetched from memory.

Program Memory That section of memory in which the program is stored. It normally contains opcodes and operands which are constants. Variable operands are usually stored in addresses outside the program memory.

Program Statement One line of a computer program describing a single instruction complete with statement number, opcode and operand.

Variable Operand An operand whose value is computed during the program and, therefore, is unknown when the program is written. The variable operand is usually stored outside of program memory at a designated RAM address. The effective address of the variable operand is then stored in program memory immediately following the opcode.

2.4 Hardware for Executing the Program

2.4.1 The External Buses

To understand how the computer executes the program, let's look first at its external bus organization. As Figure 2.4 shows, the processor connections to memory and to **input/output interfaces** can be divided into three buses: the address bus, the data bus, and the control bus. Note that the address bus transmits addresses from the processor to either memory or input/output interfaces. The data bus, on the other hand, is bidirectional and data travels to and from the processor. The control bus contains an assortment of control signals, such as, a ready signal through which an output device tells the processor that it is ready to accept a data character, an interrupt request through which an input device asks the processor to temporarily halt what it is doing and accept a data character, or the read-write signal that tells the memory whether the processor is reading a data byte from the memory location on the address bus or writing new data into that location.

2.4.2 Loading a Program

If a computer or a portion of its total address is dedicated to a single program that is not likely to need change, that program can be loaded into a read only memory, **ROM** or **PROM**. To start an execution of such a program, the processor need only be directed to the lowest address of the program which, in the usual case, is the zero address of the **PROM**. When the power is first turned on, the processor addresses a specific memory location. This memory location is called a **reset vector**. At this memory location, the computer operator inserts the address of the first statement of the program the computer is to execute.

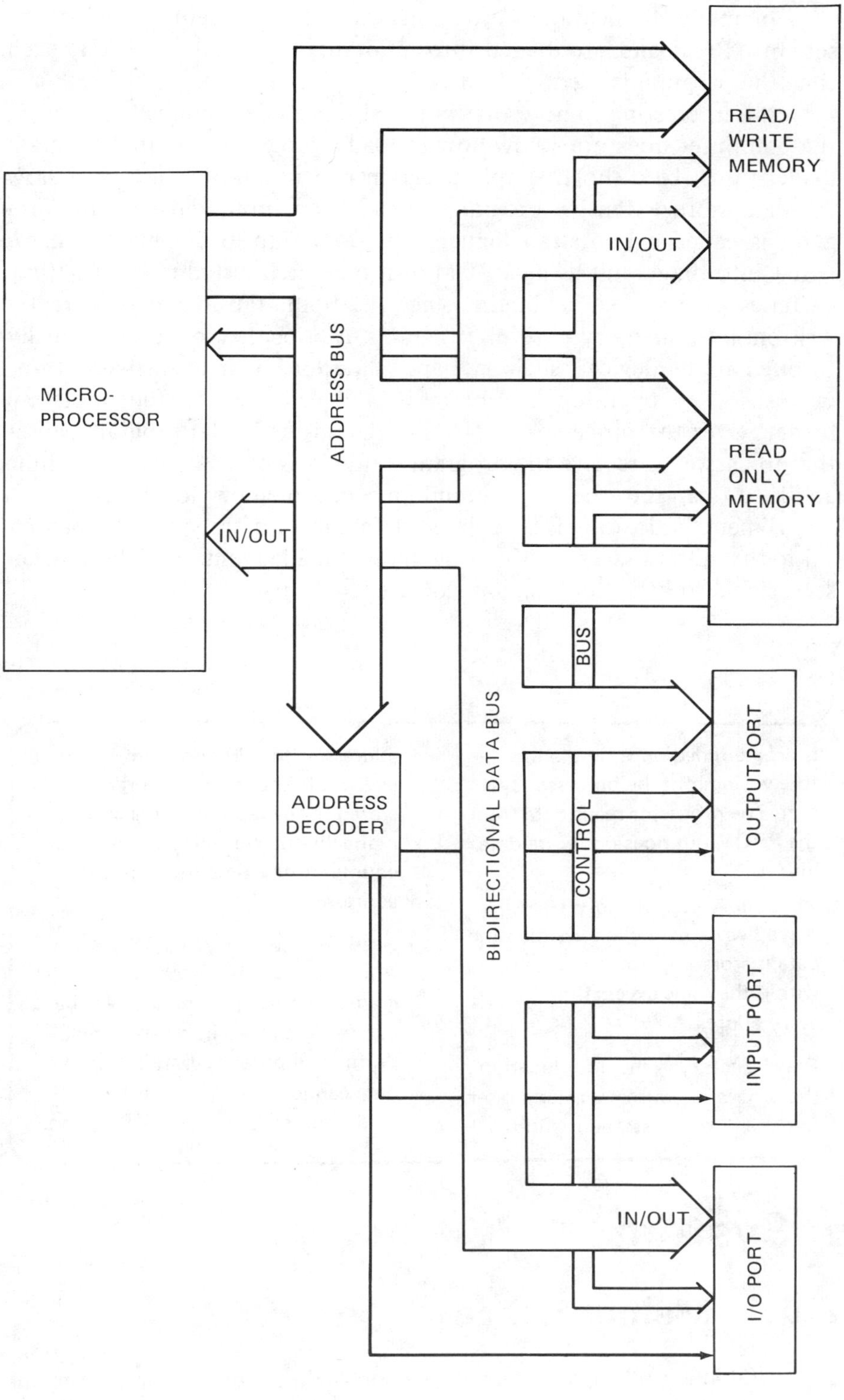

FIGURE 2.4 Microprocessor configuration showing typical connection of memory and I/O ports to the address, control, and data buses.

In many applications, programs are not permanent enough to be set into ROM and are loaded into **random access money (RAM)** each time the program is used.

It is interesting to note that in the absence of programs in memory, the computer does not know how to load a program. The first program loaded must be a short, simple program instructing the processor how to load more extensive programs through an input device. This program is called a **bootstrap loader**. The bootstrap loader may be hardwired into the circuit using a ROM or it may be inserted manually using switches or a simple keyboard. Once the bootstrap loader is correctly written into memory, useful programs can be loaded automatically through input devices, such as, paper tape reader or by magnetic tape or disks. The operator merely resets the processor to the bootstrap loader, gives the processor a start signal, and the loader program causes the processor to receive the program statements one data byte at a time and load them into the correct random access memory locations.

When the loading is complete, the operator merely sets the processor to the initial address of the program just loaded and provides another start signal to have the program executed.

Key Terms

Bootstrap Loader In the absence of programs in its memory, a computer cannot load data into memory from a complex input device such as a tape reader or magnetic disk. A short, simple program telling the computer how to input more complicated programs can be loaded manually through switches or keyboard. This program is called a bootstrap loader.

Programmable Read Only Memory (PROM) A read only memory that is programmed once by the user before wiring into the processor system. The processor reads data from the PROM but does not write data into it.

Random Access Memory (RAM) A read-write memory for which the data is stored or becomes available within the same access time for every address.

Reset Vector A memory location the processor addresses after a reset. In this address is stored the initial address of the first program to be executed. The starting address stored in the reset vector is automatically transferred to the program counter at the time the vector is addressed.

Read Only Memory (ROM) A memory circuit which is programmed during manufacture. The data programmed in it can be read during computer operation but the data cannot be changed. It has a read function but no write function.

2.5 The Memory System

2.5.1 Memory Size

The total memory bus of the processor or microprocessor system includes all connections to RAM, ROM and, in some cases, I/O interfaces. A microprocessor with a 16-bit address bus can address a total of 2^{16} or 65536 memory locations. For small computers or for microprocessors dedicated to control functions, that amount of memory is usually more than is needed. In any case, it is a problem for the systems designer to see that the memory bus is correctly organized and it is a problem for the programmer to select and direct the processor to the correct memory locations. Sections of the memory system may be divided into several unique functions: the program memory, **variable storage, look-up tables, I/O ports,** the stack, and **vectors.**

2.5.2 The Program Memory

The program memory is that portion of memory into which the program is loaded. The first statement of the program is in the lowest address of this section. With the exception of branches, jumps, and subroutines, the statements are stored in the order executed—in the order that the incrementing program counter, modified where needed by branch and jump instructions can address them in correct sequence. In most cases, subroutines occupy addresses above the remainder of the program. Once the program is entered, addresses are read but not written. The lack of the need to write into program memory during the program execution makes this an application for ROM or PROM. A RAM, however, can be used for programs which are not permanent enough for the use of PROM.

2.5.3 Program Variables

Variables which are computed during the execution of the program must be stored for use later on in the program. This requires both read and write functions and a RAM must be used. It may occupy addresses above or below the program memory.

2.5.4 Look-up Tables

Look-up tables can often be used to shorten a program in which several variable conditions call for branches in the program. The addresses can be computed from the variables and the response or branch conditions can be taken from the data in the tables. As the tables are read only, a ROM or PROM can be used. Standard mathematical tables may also be included as part of the memory system.

2.5.5 Vectors

A few memory addresses must be alloted for vectors. The usual vector addresses are the reset vectors and the **interrupt vectors.** The reset vector address is a memory address that appears on the address bus when the processor is reset. In this address, the programmer writes the address of the first program the processor is to run. The interrupt vector contains the beginning address of the program used to service the interrupt. The actual address of the vectors is built into the processor. The address stored in these vector locations is determined by the systems designer if ROM is used, or by the programmer if the vectors are in RAM. The contents of a vector are transferred to the program counter where the vector is addressed.

2.5.6 The Stack

Another portion of random access memory must be allocated to the stack. As explained in Section 2.2, the stack is used to keep track of the return addresses to be used in directing the processor back to the main program after completion of a subroutine or **interrupt service routine.** A subroutine may be used more than once during the execution of a program. The address of the subroutine is the same each time it is used; but, because it occurs at different points in the program, the return address will be different for each point in the program that the subroutine is used. Therefore, it is necessary for the computer to remember which of these numerous addresses to return to. As Figure 2.5 shows, when the jump to subroutine **(call) instruction** is executed, the next main program instruction address is stored on the stack at the same instant that the first address of the subroutine is loaded into the program counter. The last instruction of the subroutine is a return from subroutine which causes the address on the stack to be transferred to the program counter resulting in a return to main program. During an interrupt, the stack functions in a similar but more complicated manner. Instead of being initiated by the program, an interrupt may occur at any point in the program even during the execution of an instruction. The interrupt occurs not as a result of a decoded instruction but as a signal on the control line. It occurs as the act of an input device signaling the processor that it is ready to be serviced. If the processor is in the midst of executing an instruction it will not acknowledge or react to the interrupt until it has completed that instruction. Instead of fetching the next instruction, it will store the present program count on the stack then take the address stored in the interrupt vector and transfer it to the program counter. The address taken from the vector contains the first instruction of the interrupt service routine. The last instruction of the interrupt service routine is a return from interrupt. This instruction causes the address stored on the stack to be transferred to the program counter resulting in a return to main program.

The location of the stack in the **memory map** is, for most processors, determined by a register called the stack pointer. The loading of the stack address into the stack pointer is an initial instruction of the program.

The stack must have more than a single memory address. Considering the fact that subroutines may occur within subroutines, interrupts may occur during subroutines, and subroutines may be written into interrupt service routines; the stack may be required to store a substantial number of return addresses. In addition to return addresses, the programmer may recognize a need to store the contents of the accumulator or the status flags. This data may also be written on the stack at the beginning of a subroutine or interrupt program and moved back to the processor registers just prior to a return from subroutine or interrupt. Figure 2.6 describes the stack functions of a processor which receives an interrupt request when it is in the midst of a **nested subroutine.**

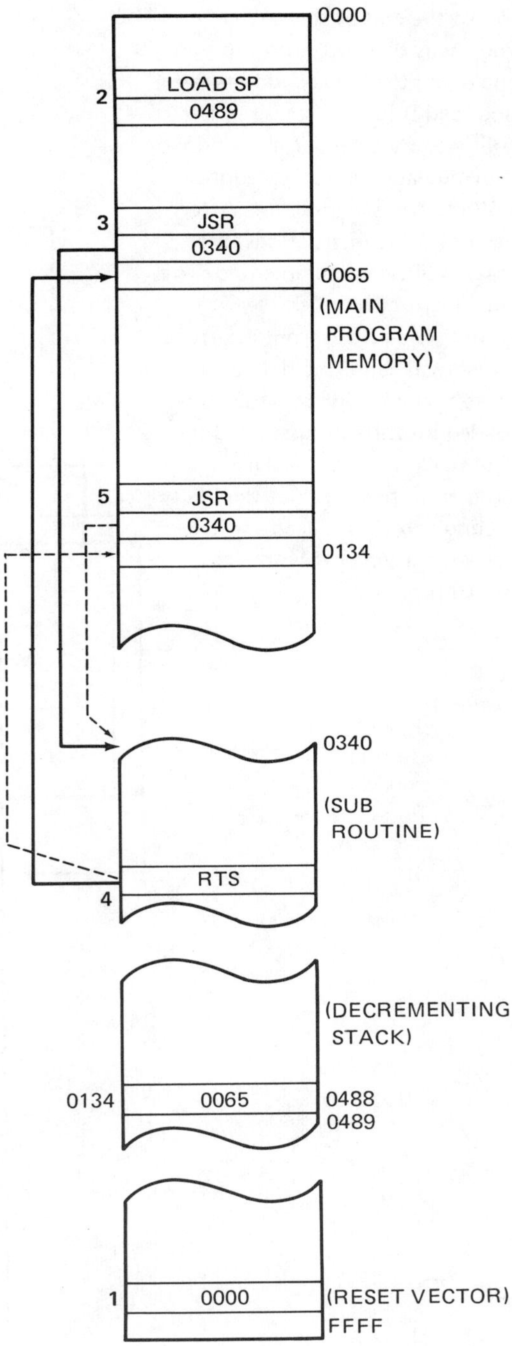

FIGURE 2.5 Memory map for a program using a subroutine with a stack located at address 0489. Note that each time the subroutine is called, a different return address is pushed onto the stack.

1 When the processor is reset for execution of a program, the address that the programmer has placed in the reset vector is transferred to the program counter.

2 One of several initializing instructions the programmer must provide to the processor is the memory location to be used for the stack. This memory address is loaded into the stack pointer.

3 As the program progresses a subroutine is called just before address 0065. The stack pointer is decremented. The contents of the program counter +1 (0065) is pushed onto the stack. The program counter is changed to the first address of the subroutine.

4 The last instruction of the subroutine is a return from subroutine. This causes the program counter to be loaded with the contents of the current stack address. The stack pointer is incremented.

5 The same subroutine is called again before address 0134 and the process is repeated. The program moves as shown by the dotted lines. The address (0134) is stored on the stack and the program returns to this address.

FIGURE 2.6 Memory map for a program having a nested subroutine showing the typical stack operation when an interrupt occurs during the execution of the second subroutine.

1 2 3 The execution of the program proceeds as explained in **1** through **3** of Figure 2.5.

4 Within the running of the first subroutine, a second subroutine is called just before address 0371. The stack pointer is decremented. The contents of the program counter +1 (0371) is pushed onto the stack. The program count is changed to the first address of the second subroutine (0300).

5 During the running of the second subroutine, the processor receives an interrupt request. The processor completes the instruction it was in the process of executing. Prior to fetching another opcode at 0328, it jumps to an interrupt service routine. The stack pointer is decremented. The program count +1 (0328) is pushed onto the stack. The address written in the interrupt vector (0380) is transferred to the program counter. The processor begins execution of the interrupt service routine.

6 The first instructions of the service routine are to push the current contents of accumulator and status register (flags) onto the stack. This is in realization of the fact that the contents of these registers may be vital to the subroutine program and unless moved to memory they will be lost during the service routine.

7 At the end of the service routine is the instruction to pop the data off of stack address 0484 and load it in the status register followed by a similar instruction moving data from stack address 0485 to the accumulator. After each of these instructions, the stack pointer is incremented. The final instruction of the service routine is a return from interrupt which will cause the data at the current stack address 0486 to be loaded into the program counter. The stack increments. The program is now back at the second subroutine ready to take up where it left off before the interrupt.

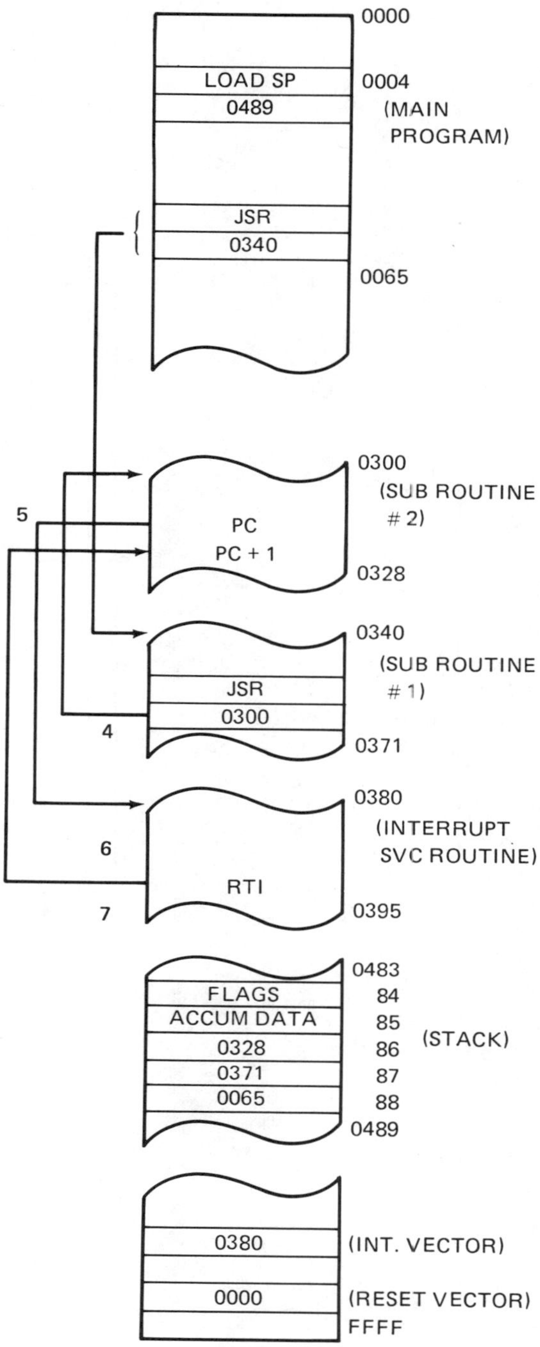

The stack functions as a **last in first out memory, LIFO**. This is accomplished in either of two methods: incrementing the stack pointer each time data is written on the stack and decrementing the stack pointer each time the stack is read, or by decrementing when the stack is written and incrementing when it is read. Either method produces the necessary LIFO memory function.

2.5.7 Address Pages

It is sometimes convenient to think in terms of address pages of 256 address words to a page. A processor with a 16-bit address bus has a capacity of 256 pages of 256 words each. This organization became popular in conjunction with the use of memory circuits with 256 word addresses. As larger memory circuits become available, it may become more convenient to think in terms of larger but fewer pages.

2.5.8 ROMS, PROMS, or RAMS

For a dedicated computer function that has a fixed program, the read only memory (ROM) is ideal for program storage. The ROM is mask programmable with a mask charge of about one thousand dollars. It is, therefore, economical only for tried and proven programs used in systems that are reproduced in reasonable quantities. In a one of a kind system or for a program that may require occasional changes, the programmable (program once) read only memory such as a fusible link or electrically programmable memory may be used. In addition to program memory, the ROM or PROM is ideal for use as look-up tables. This applies not only to arithmetic tables but also to programs where the computer must vary its output in response to two or more input variables.

2.5.9 A Typical Memory System

Figure 2.7 shows a microprocessor system used to control a model railway switching. The program uses only a trivial portion of the available address capacity of this microprocessor. For that reason two bits of the address bus are devoted solely to addressing the I/O interface.

Key Terms

Call Instruction Another name for a subroutine jump—a subroutine call.

Input/Output Ports A circuit used to interface between the computer data bus and an electronic input/output device whose bus is not compatible in power, impedance or synchronization with the computer bus.

Interrupt Service Routine A routine which tells the processor how to service a peripheral or I/O port. The service routine is executed in response to an interrupt signal.

Interrupt Vector A memory location the processor addresses after acknowledging an interrupt. The address which is stored in the interrupt vector is automatically transferred to the program counter thus directing the processor to the interrupt service routine.

Last in First Out Memory (LIFO) A memory from which the stored data can be read only in the reverse order that it has been written.

Look-up Tables A read only memory designed to function like a mathematical table.

Memory Map A pictorial drawing of the sections of memory indicating the memory spaces occupied by the main program, subroutines, service routine, stack, vectors, and variables used in the execution of a program or set of programs.

Nested Subroutine A subroutine within a subroutine.

Variable Storage A section of memory used to store data that is generated during the running of the program. RAM must be used for this function.

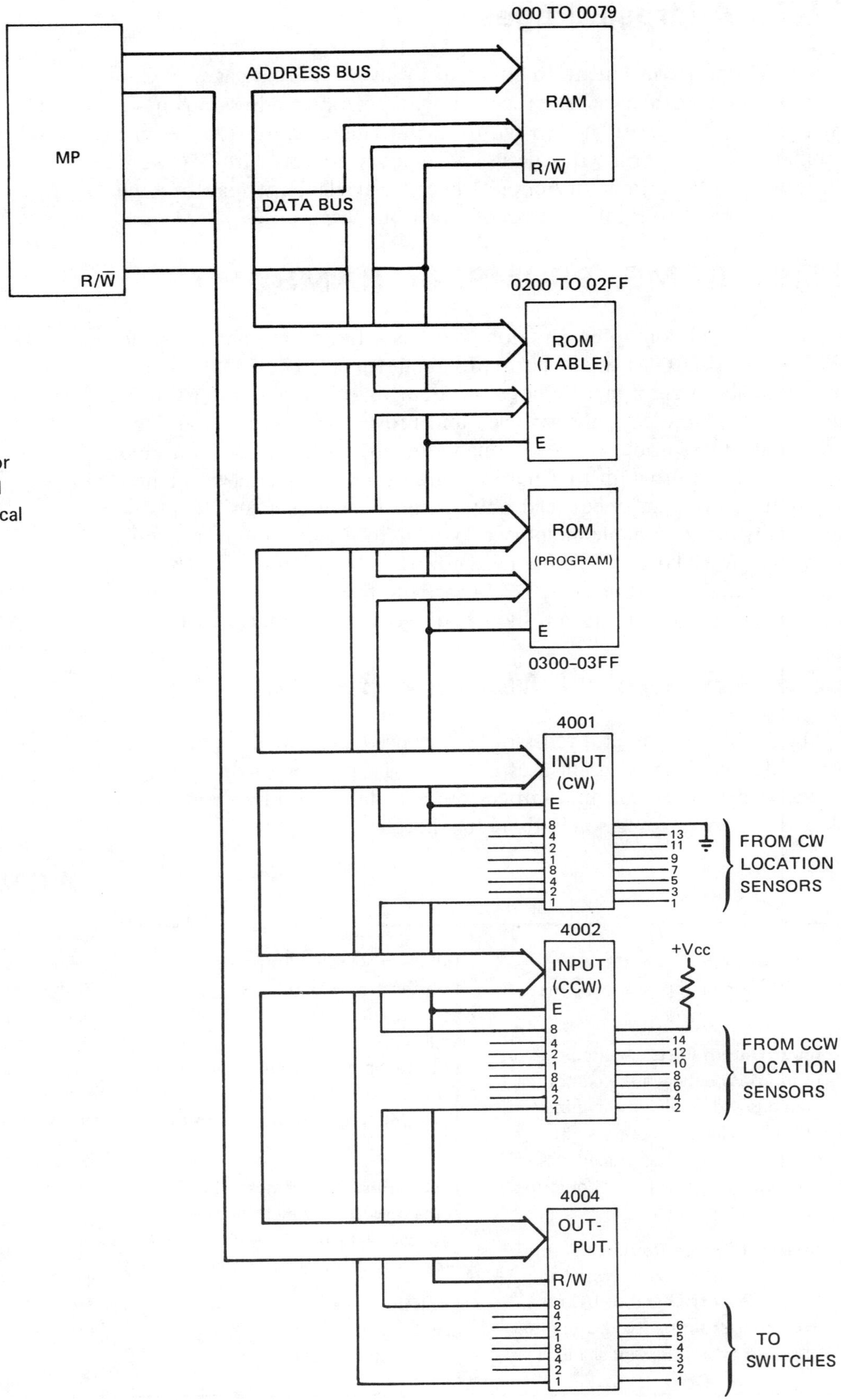

FIGURE 2.7 Microprocessor configuration used for model railway control showing typical connection of circuits.

2.6 Input/Output Interfaces

2.6.1 The Need for Interface Circuits

The connection of input/output devices to the processor system is usually a more difficult problem to deal with than the connection of memory circuits. Memory circuits specifically designed for connection to the microprocessor address, data, and control buses are readily available. Keyboards, printers, displays, sensors, actuators, and similar candidates for computer control, on the other hand, often require additional **interface circuits.**

Many inputs to a computer control system are not even electrical in nature. A transducer is usually employed to convert such physical quantities as temperature, pressure, strain, and weight to analog voltages. The analog voltages of many transducers are too low a level for further conversion and linear amplifiers must then be used to bring them to a suitable level. Analog voltages can then be converted to digital signals of compatible bit size using analog-to-digital converters which are presently available in both hybrid and monolithic integrated circuit form. Many useful input devices such as teletype and other keyboard terminals have digital outputs but are serial rather than parallel. In this case, a serial-to-parallel conversion is needed to input and a parallel-to-serial conversion is required to output. A standard integrated circuit, such as, the **Universal Asynchronous Receiver Transmitter (UART)** can be used to effectively make the conversion.

Microprocessor systems are presently available in data bus sizes of 4, 8, 12, and 16 bit. Where the bit size of the input device exceeds that of the processor data bus, the input may need to be **multiplexed.**

Once the signal is converted to correct digital form, it must be connected to the data bus through an input port that is addressable. A number of integrated circuit devices known as **peripheral interface adapters (PIA)** are available for this purpose. They are essentially parallel latch circuits which store the input data bits and output them to the data bus only when the PIA is addressed.

The operating speed of microprocessors and their associated memory circuits may be many times faster than the input devices they are likely to be controlling. A teletype terminal can input only 10 to 30 characters per second; a high speed paper tape reader may input 300 characters per second. A thermocouple that is monitoring a process temperature may have a thermal time constant of a tenth of a second and reading it more often than that would be valueless. A processor with an address cycle time of several microseconds is capable of monitoring dozens of such slow speed input devices while at the same time using the input data in an elaborate program. To take advantage of the processor's high speed, some method must be devised so that the various input ports can be serviced in a timely fashion without disrupting the other extensive operations which are going on in the processor. Two methods of doing this are widely used. The simplest of these is called poling.

2.6.2 Poling

Poling is primarily a software solution to servicing an interface. The program periodically directs the processor to address each input port in turn and inquire about the existence of *new* data to be processed or transferred to memory. There is an emphasis here on new data because the slower input devices may be poled several times before the data at the port is changed. The processor must have some means of distinguishing new data so that it can avoid unwanted repetitions. The solution to this problem may require both hardware and software provisions.

2.6.3 Interrupts

Another method of handling the input ports is to allow the input device to interrupt the processor whenever it needs to be serviced. A provision for this is built into most processors. On receipt of a signal on its interrupt request line, the processor will complete the instruction it is working on. It will record the contents of the program counter in a memory location called the stack, then it will proceed to a subroutine where it is instructed how to service the input port. Where a number of input ports are serviced by the same processor having a single interrupt request line, a circuit must be used to allow the input ports to interrupt the processor in accordance with an established priority. This circuit, known as a priority interrupt encoder, can even be used to notify the processor of the correct service subroutine to be used for the particular port causing the interrupt.

2.7 The Instruction Set

2.7.1 Description

Now that we have reviewed the hardware elements that are interconnected to form a computer, let us take a more thorough look at the software and how it controls the activities of the machine.

The fundamental element of software is the instruction set. In machine language, instruction sets are actually sets of binary codes which an **instruction decoder** within the central processor of the computer decodes into individual levels. These levels are used to enable the occurance of the correct set of functions needed to cause the execution of the instruction. To make programming easier, each machine code instruction is assigned a mnemonic—a code of three or four letters. The mnemonic generally sounds like the functions or an abbreviation of the functions that are caused by the instruction. For example, CLA stands for clear the accumulator, and DEC stands for decrement the accumulator.

There is virtually no standardization of machine codes. Each processor or microprocessor is likely to have a unique set, but the mnemonics have fortunately reached a reasonable level of similarity so that they are more alike than they are different. In spite of any mnemonic identities that exist between processors, the machine codes are not identical. Again we must keep in mind that the instruction mnemonic is only part of the program listing. The program list has two or three essential parts. Table 2.3 shows a typical program list.

STATEMENT NUMBER	OPCODE	OPERAND	COMMENTS
3C7F	MVI	E, 00	
3C81	MOV	A, E	
3C82	OUT	OFOH	
3C84	OUT	OF1H	
3C86	MOV	A, C	
3C87	OUT	OFOH	
3C89	MOV	A, D	
3C8A	OUT	OF1H	
3C8C	DCR	C	
3C8D	JNZ	863CH	
3C90	MOV	C, B	
3C91	INR	E	
3C92	JZ	A43CH	

TABLE 2.3 Typical program listing (8080 microprocessor). The left-hand column contains statement numbers. The second column lists the opcodes. The third column contains operands. Move instructions require two operands known as the destination and the source. They are listed in the operand column in that order. The individual letters A through E represent registers within the microprocessor. They are designated in the opcode and do not occupy addresses in program memory. The far right column is reserved for comments used as an aid to debugging the program.

In the left column is the statement number. The statement number corresponds to the address of the opcode when it is stored in the program memory. The second column is the mnemonic. The third column contains the operand or the address of the operand. The right-hand column is generally reserved for comments that help the programmer keep track of what the program is doing. The comments are useful when it comes time to debug the program.

2.7.2 Classes of Instructions

Data Moves Data moves include the movement of data between registers within the processor and the movement of data between registers and memory. Load and store instructions are examples of data moves. Generally, two operands are defined in a data move: the source operand and the destination operand.

Arithmetic-Logic Operations The arithmetic operation includes operations as simple as incrementing and decrementing registers or as complex as addition and subtraction of numbers. In microprocessors, the more complicated arithmetic operations like multiplication and division are accomplished by programs of the simpler arithmetic instruction. Logic operations include AND-OR-Complement and Exclusive OR functions between numbers in the accumulator and numbers in memory. Arithmetic-logic operations affect the flag bits, such as the zero, carry, sign, and overflow flags.

Jump or Branch Instructions The unconditional jump instruction merely jumps the program to a new location by inserting a new address in the program counter instead of permitting it to increment as usual. The branch or conditional jump instruction is a reaction to a decision. The processor looks at the condition of a status flag and either increments the program counter as usual or moves out of sequence depending on whether the flag is set or reset. Conditional jump or branch instructions are always found at points in a program where the flow diagram shows a decision diamond. They must be preceded by an arithmetic or logic operation which affects the flags. The power of modern day computers is heavily dependent on these combined instructions. The arithmetic-logic instruction makes the decision. The conditional jump or branch instruction allows a choice of action based on that decision. Table 2.4 shows a list of jump or branch instructions from the instruction sets of several microprocessors.

TABLE 2.4 Typical branch or jump instructions from the instruction sets of several microprocessors.

MICROPROCESSOR			
9900	**6500**	**8085**	**DESCRIPTION**
JNC	(BCC)	JNC	Jump (Branch) on carry clear
JOC	(BCS)	JC	Jump (Branch) on carry set
	(BEQ)	JZ	Jump (Branch) on result zero
	(BMI)	JM	Jump (Branch) on minus
	(BNE)	JNZ	Jump (Branch) on not zero
	(BPL)	JP	Jump (Branch) on plus
JNO	(BVC)		Jump (Branch) on overflow clear
JOP		JPO	Jump on odd parity
JMP	JMP	JMP	Jump unconditional

Note: Each of the above microprocessors has ten or more jump or branch instructions. Those listed above were selected for their similarity.

Shift and Rotate Instructions Numbers in registers and in memory can be shifted left or right. In the rotate instruction, the leftmost bit is shifted into the rightmost bit or the rightmost bit into the leftmost bit. The carry bit may or may not be included in the shift or rotate. Figure 2.8 illustrates some typical microprocessor shift and rotate instructions.

Input/Output Instructions For some microprocessors, the I/O devices are memory mapped and therefore require no special I/O instruction. The ports are addressed as though they were memory addresses. For others, the address bus fractions differently when addressing I/O ports as compared to addressing memory. This requires special input-output instructions.

Control Instruction A variety of control instructions may be required by particular microprocessors. These include instructions, such as, no operation (which does nothing), break instructions, and return from subroutine, or interrupt.

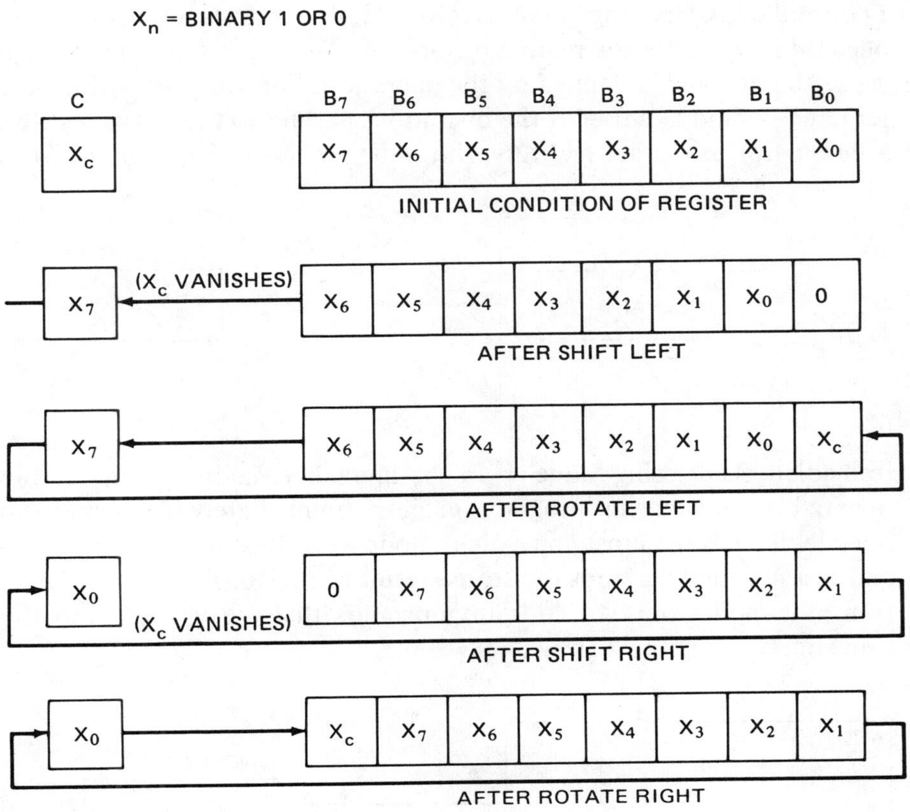

FIGURE 2.8 Change in register bits resulting from shift and rotate instructions.

2.7.3 Address Modes

The concept of address modes is another factor the programmer must master. As can be seen from the program list of Table 2.2, some instruction steps require more memory locations than others. This variation usually exists in the addressing of the operand. The effective address is the memory or register address which contains the actual operand. Often, one or more intermediate addresses must be used to point the way to the effective address. This leads to a variation in the number of memory locations and the number of machine cycles required to complete the execution of an instruction. If the operand is located in the processor, the instruction may require only an opcode. If the operand is stored in memory in the address following the opcode, then the instruction requires two memory locations. But, if the address following the opcode contains, instead of the operand, the address of the operand, then the processor must make additional trips to memory to complete the instruction. Each of these conditions is a different address mode. Although processors and microprocessors do not have identical addressing modes, there are a few modes which are common to most of them. We will discuss these now and cover the others in our discussion of specific microprocessors.

The Implied Addressing Mode (Register Mode) Instructions with implied addressing do not require an operand from program memory because the operand is implied by the operation. For some processors, the term register mode is used if the operations pertain to the status register, accumulator, and other registers within the processor. See Figure 2.9(a).

FIGURE 2.9 Addressing Modes

(a) The implied addressing mode requires only an opcode in the program memory. The operand is a register within the processor.

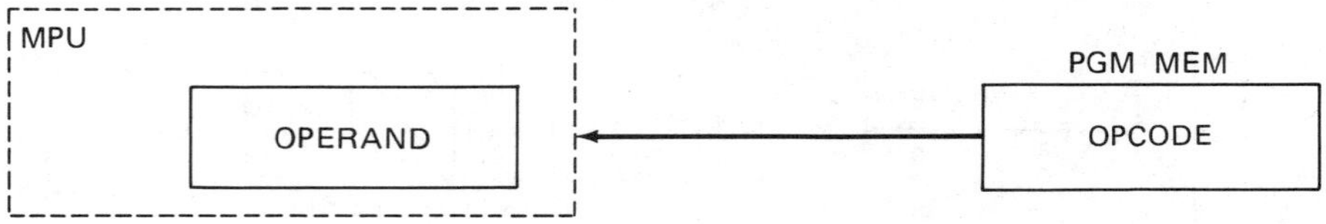

(a)

Immediate Addressing Mode In the immediate addressing mode the operand is located in program memory immediately following the opcode. This is the most convenient mode of addressing when the operand is a constant and not the stored result of previous program calculations. It applies only to constant operands that are written into the program. See Figure 2.9(b).

(b) The immediate addressing mode requires only two bytes of program memory. The opcode is in memory address PC while the operand is in PC+1. The operand in this mode must be a constant.

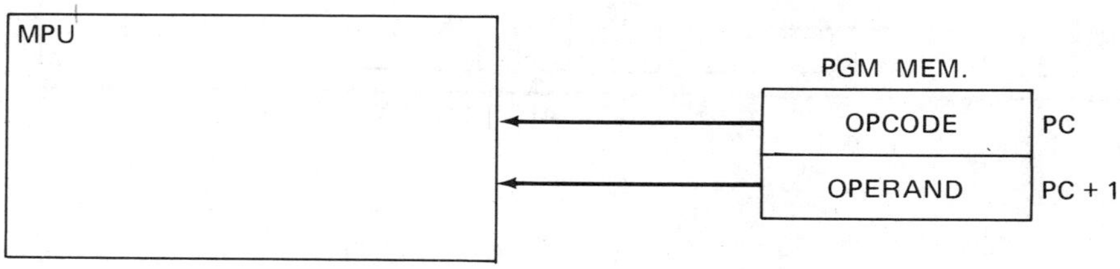

(b)

Register Indirect Addressing Mode To use this mode the address of the operand must first be loaded into a pointer register within the processor. The pointer register can point to an operand in variable storage. See Figure 2.9(c).

(c) The register indirect mode uses a previously loaded register in the processor to point to the memory location. In this mode the operand can be a variable.

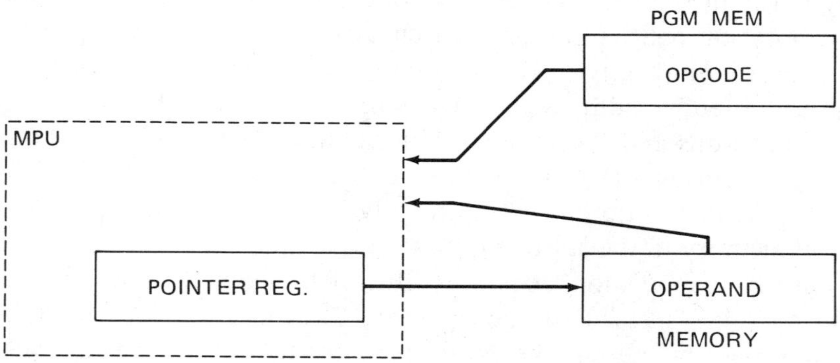

(c)

Direct Addressing Mode Direct addressing uses the byte or bytes following the opcode in the program memory as the address of the true operand. This allows for the use of variables computed during the program and stored in predetermined memory addresses located outside of program memory. See Figure 2.9(d).

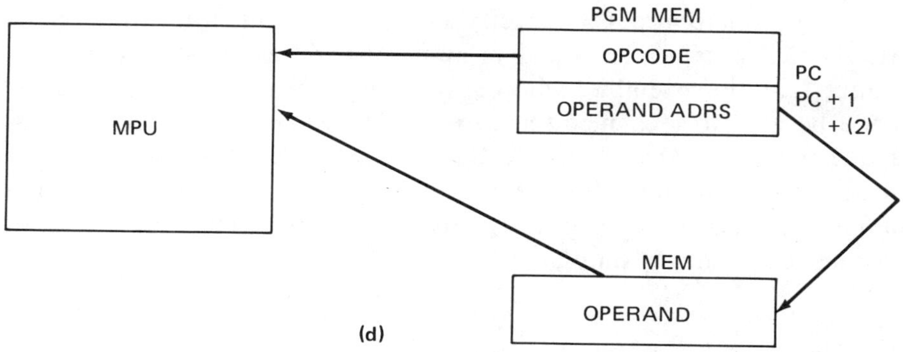

(d)

(d) The direct addressing mode uses the byte or bytes following the opcode in program memory to supply the address of the operand.

Indexed Addressing Mode The indexed addressing mode computes successive adjacent operands by incrementing or decrementing a register each time it is added to a fixed value from program memory. This mode, used in conjunction with loops in the program in which the index register is incremented or decremented, can bring into use an array of computed data from successive memory locations outside of program memory. It can also be used to store an array of computed data in successive, adjacent memory locations. See Figure 2.9(e). Some processors provide automatic incrementing or decrementing with the indexed addressing mode. These modes are commonly called auto-increment or auto-decrement.

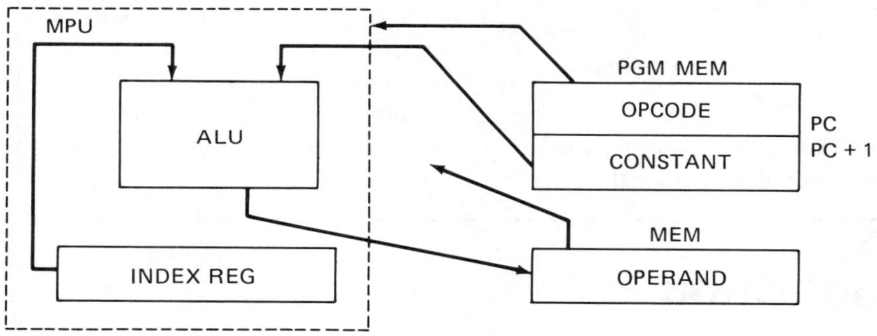

(e)

(e) The indexed addressing mode uses the sum of a constant from program memory and the contents of an index register to compute the address of the operand. This mode combined with the incrementing or decrementing of the index register permits the use of complete blocks of adjacent memory locations.

The Relative Addressing Mode This mode is used in branch or conditional jump instructions. The address to branch or jump to is computed by adding an offset value to the current contents of the program counter. See Figure 2.9(f).

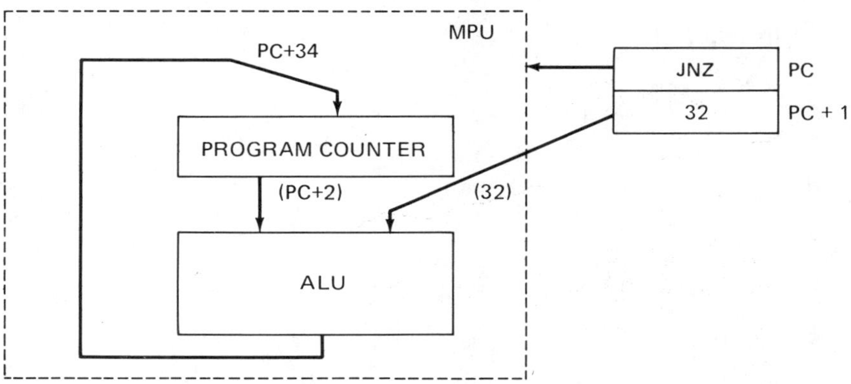

(f)

(f) The relative addressing mode is used in branch or conditional jump instructions. A constant is added or subtracted from the current contents of the program counter.

Some microprocessors specify a single mnemonic for a given operation which can be performed in numerous addressing modes. This requires that the assembler who converts the mnemonic to the machine code be able to recognize the correct address mode. For each address mode, a given mnemonic has a different machine code. For other microprocessors, both operation and address mode are distinguished by a unique mnemonic designator. This requires a larger mnemonic set, but it is less confusing to translate.

Key Terms

Instruction Decoder The instruction decoder receives the opcode on its input and decodes it into the control signal or signals used to enable the circuits that will cause the instruction to be executed.

Interface Circuits Digital signals must often be transferred between buses having differences in logic levels, bit size, or timing. The special circuits used to convert the signals to compatible form are known as interface circuits.

Peripheral Interface Adaptor (PIA) A special I/O port designed to interface between the computer bus and a peripheral device, such as, a teletype, mag tape reader, etc.

Poling A software method for servicing slow speed I/O ports. The processor periodically pauses in the running of the program and interrogates the ports to determine their need for service.

Pop Instruction A memory read instruction that calls for the transfer of data from the current stack memory address to a register within the processor.

Push Instruction A memory write instruction that calls for the transfer of data from a processor register to the current stack memory address.

Universal Asynchronous Receiver-Transmitter (UART) A circuit specially designed to interface the computer bus with a teletype terminal. The transmitter part of the circuit converts the parallel computer output data to serial-level train transmission, inserting the necessary start, stop, and parity bits required for each character. The receiver part of the circuit converts the serial input from the teletype to parallel bits compatable with the computer bus.

Questions

2.1 What section of a computer is a microprocessor most like?

2.2 Which of the following would be considered hardware?

- CPU
- opcode
- instruction
- RAM
- pointer
- operand
- counter
- mnemonic
- I/O port
- flag

2.3 Name three types of pointers. How do their functions differ?

2.4 Which of the following may be located in RAM?

- program instructions
- stack
- vectors
- program constants
- program variables

2.5 Which of the preceding cannot be stored in ROM?

2.6 What is the function of the accumulator?

2.7 What information is normally found in the status register?

2.8 What is a statement number? How is it used?

2.9 What is the primary difference between the bus structure of the address and data bus of a microprocessor?

2.10 What name is given to the addressing mode in which the operand is read from program memory immediately following the opcode?

2.11 Explain why the indexed addressing mode is useful in reading or writing blocks of date in memory.

2.12 In the absolute or direct addressing mode, from where is the effective address of the operand obtained?

2.13 Explain why the stack memory may be considered a LIFO memory.

2.14 What name is given to a short program that controls the loading of larger programs?

2.15 If a stack pointer is incremented prior to each stack write, what happens to the stack pointer during a stack read?

2.16 With which program operations is the stack used?

2.17 What is the last instruction of a subroutine?

2.18 What is the last instruction of an interrupt service routine?

2.19 What determines the location of the stack in a computer memory system?

2.20 A processor receives an interrupt request during a nested subroutine. What is the number of return addresses stored in the stack during execution of the interrupt service routine?

2.21 An 8-bit microprocessor with a 16-bit memory bus would have how many pages of memory? How many memory bytes would there be to a page?

2.22 What is the main advantage of ROM or PROM as a microprocessor program memory?

2.23 For the construction of a one of a kind microprocessor system, what is the main disadvantage of a MASK programmable ROM?

2.24 Explain the relative merits of poling as compared to interrupt for servicing I/O devices.

2.25 Why are mnemonics used in place of machine codes?

2.26 Name two distinct operands existing in a data move instruction.

2.27 How do conditional jump instructions relate to a flow diagram of the program?

Chapter 3

Number Systems for Microprocessors

Objectives

Upon completion of this chapter you will be able to:

- Identify numerical quantities in five different number systems.
- Convert quantities from one number system to another.
- Compute microprocessor address offsets in hexadecimal numbers.
- Compute the number of memory bytes available between memory addresses listed in hexadecimal notation.

3.1 Number Systems

At least three number systems are used in the hardware and software applications of a given microprocessor. The decimal system, which is the mathematical language of humans; the binary system, which is the language of digital machines; and an auxiliary number system, which has some of the advantages of decimal, but is easier to convert from binary. The auxiliary number system used may be either octal or hexadecimal. Table 3.1 shows an identical quantity represented in four basic number systems.

TABLE 3.1

HEXADECIMAL (BASE 16)	DECIMAL (BASE 10)	OCTAL (BASE 8)	BINARY (BASE 2)
3124_H	12580_{10}	30444_8	11000100100100_2

Note that the subscripts H, 10, 8, and 2 are written to indicate which number system is being used. Subscripts are used only where the possibility of confusion exists. Normally, a number written completely in ones and zeros is accepted as binary. If it is not binary, a subscript will be used. A number with integers higher than 1 is understood to be decimal unless a subscript indicates otherwise. In a program listing it may be understood that all addresses are in hexadecimal. In this case subscripts are not used. In the operand column, hexadecimal and decimal numbers may be mixed and numbers are understood to be decimal unless the subscript H identifies them as hexadecimal.

3.2 The Binary Number System

3.2.1 Binary Base and Integers

In the binary number system quantities are represented by a series of ones and zeros. Each binary place is called a bit. The bit represents a power of two. The powers of two are in ascending order, the highest value necessary on the left and the least value 2^0 on the right. The decimal quantity 237 is represented in binary as 11101101. Only the integers 1 and 0 are needed when representing quantities in binary. This accounts for its usefulness in digital machines which function at two distinct voltage levels designated as binary 1 and 0. The machine codes of the microprocessor and all the high speed functions controlled by them are functions of these two voltage levels.

Most of the numerical data that are input to a microprocessor system for processing originate in decimal form. The results will output from the microprocessor in binary form and must be converted to decimal so they can be easily understood by the user. For this reason, conversions from decimal to binary and conversions from binary to decimal are important operations. Table 3.2 compares binary and decimal numbers to the count of 22.

TABLE 3.2 Binary and decimal numbers compared to the count of 22.

DECIMAL	BINARY
1	1
2	10
3	11
4	100
5	101
6	110
7	111
8	1000
9	1001
10	1010
11	1011
12	1100
13	1101
14	1110
15	1111
16	10000
17	10001
18	10010
19	10011
20	10100
21	10101
22	10110

3.2.2 Decimal to Binary Conversion

There are two commonly used methods of converting from decimal to binary numbers. The most straightforward method is to determine the most significant binary bit first by finding the highest power of two in the decimal number. Let us take for example the decimal number 163_{10}. The highest power of 2 in 163 is

$$2^7 = 128$$

This means that the binary number will have 8 bits to the left of the binary point (2^0 through 2^7). Each of these binary places and its decimal value are shown in Table 3.3.

TABLE 3.3

BINARY PLACE VALUE	2^7	2^6	2^5	2^4	2^3	2^2	2^1	2^0
DECIMAL VALUE	128	64	32	16	8	4	2	1

Finding the binary number equal in magnitude to the decimal number 163 is a matter of finding the sum of successively smaller powers of 2 needed to equal 163 and writing a 1 for the binary places needed and a 0 for those not needed.

For example:

$2^7\ 2^6\ 2^5\ 2^4\ 2^3\ 2^2\ 2^1\ 2^0$

1 0 1 0 0 0 1 1

The highest power of 2 in 163 is $2^7 = 128$.

$$\begin{array}{r} 163 \\ -128 \\ \hline 35 \end{array}$$

The highest power of 2 in 35 is $2^5 = 32$.

$$\begin{array}{r} 35 \\ -32 \\ \hline 3 \end{array}$$

The highest power of 2 in 3 is $2^1 = 2$.

$$\begin{array}{r} 3 \\ -2 \\ \hline 1 \end{array}$$

The highest power of 2 in 1 is $2^0 = 1$.

$$\begin{array}{r} 1 \\ -1 \\ \hline 0 \end{array}$$

Therefore, $163_{10} = 10100011_2$

This method determines the most significant bit (MSB) first.

A second method divides the decimal quantity successively by 2 and uses the remainders as the binary integers. This method determines the least significant bit (LSB) first. For example:

For example:

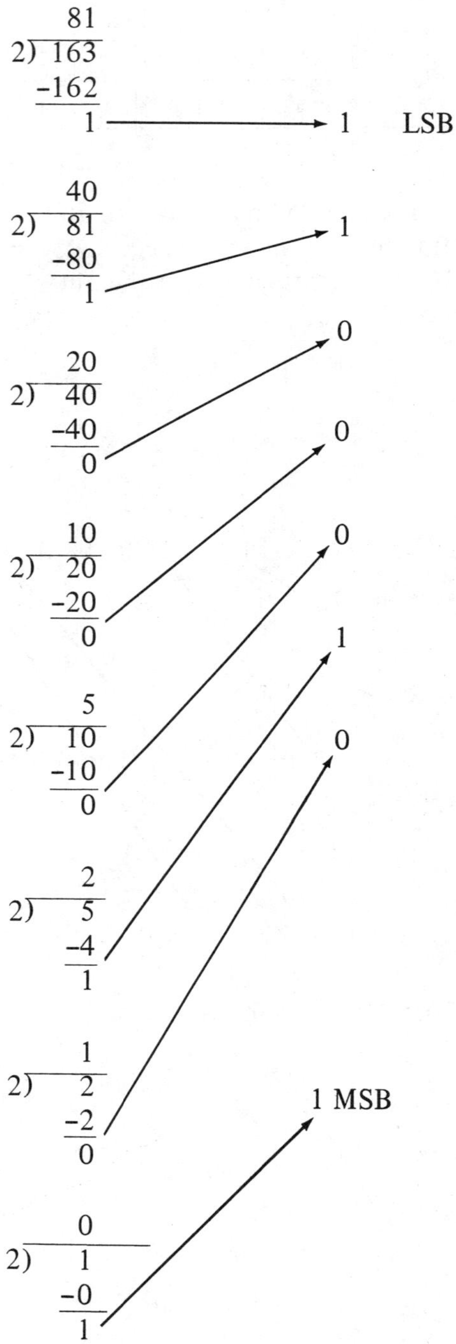

MSB ↓ LSB ↓

$10100011_2 = 163_{10}$

Problem 3.1

Convert the following decimal numbers to binary.

511, 375, 1024, 227, 573,
195, 675, 500, 105, 144

3.2.3 Binary to Decimal Conversion

Converting a binary number to decimal is a simple matter of adding up the powers of two represented by the ones in the binary number.

For example:

$$
\begin{array}{ccccccccc}
2^8 & 2^7 & 2^6 & 2^5 & 2^4 & 2^3 & 2^2 & 2^1 & 2^0 \\
1 & 1 & 0 & 1 & 0 & 1 & 0 & 0 & 1_2
\end{array}
$$

$$
\begin{array}{r}
1 \\
8 \\
32 \\
128 \\
\underline{256} \\
425_{10}
\end{array}
$$

Problem 3.2

Convert the following binary numbers to decimal.

1100101, 1111, 1001011, 10011001, 1001001,

1100101, 10101010, 1001001, 1101101, 11100111

3.3 The Hexadecimal Number System

3.3.1 Hexadecimal Base and Integers

Converting large numbers from decimal to binary or binary to decimal is difficult for a computer operator or programmer, it cannot be done at a glance. It requires some degree of scratch pad calculation. If, on the other hand, the numbers can be separated into small groups and converted piecemeal it becomes quite easy. There are several number systems for which this piecemeal conversion is possible. The auxiliary number system most widely used with microprocessors is hexadecimal which is a number system with a base of 16. The advantage of this system is that exactly four binary bits are required for each hexadecimal digit, and today's microprocessors have address and data bus bit sizes that are divisible by four.

Although hexadecimal is different from the decimal system, it has some of the same advantages. For example, the number of digits for a given quantity is small in comparison to the equivalent binary number. Also, uniqueness, relative magnitude, and numerical order of hexadecimal numbers can be recognized much more easily than equivalent binary numbers. Its advantage over decimal notation is the ease and economy of conversion because a binary number need only be separated into groups of four bits, and each group can be converted individually to a hexadecimal digit.

The number of numerals needed to express any quantity is always equal to the base number of a particular system. In the decimal system (base 10), the numerals zero through nine are used. In the binary system (base 2), the numerals used are zero and one.

The hexadecimal system requires 16 numerals to express any quantity. But, because the decimal system has only 10 numerals, we have to invent symbols to represent the quantities 10, 11, 12, 13, 14, and 15. In the past, various symbols were used. Today, the letters A, B, C, D, E, and F are used to represent these values.

Table 3.4 compares decimal, hexadecimal, and binary numbers to the count of 32.

TABLE 3.4 Decimal, hexadecimal, and binary numbers compared to the count of 32.

DECIMAL	HEXADECIMAL	BINARY
1	1	1
2	2	10
3	3	11
4	4	100
5	5	101
6	6	110
7	7	111
8	8	1000
9	9	1001
10	A	1010
11	B	1011
12	C	1100
13	D	1101
14	E	1110
15	F	1111
16	10	10000
17	11	10001
18	12	10010
19	13	10011
20	14	10100
21	15	10101
22	16	10110
23	17	10111
24	18	11000
25	19	11001
26	1A	11010
27	1B	11011
28	1C	11100
29	1D	11101
30	1E	11110
31	1F	11111
32	20	100000

3.3.2 Binary to Hexadecimal Conversion

To convert a binary number to hexadecimal notation, it is necessary to separate the binary number into four-bit groups starting at the right (the binary point).

Problem 3.3

Convert the 16-bit number 1111001101101101_2 to a hexadecimal number. This separates into groups.

(15)			(13)
1 1 1 1	0 0 1 1	0 1 1 0	1 1 0 1
F	3	6	D

Therefore, $1111001101101101_2 = F36D_H$

Now consider the binary number

$$1111011011011001_2$$

At a glance it is difficult to say whether this is a larger binary number than the binary number given in Problem 3 3. If we take the trouble to count the number of bits in each, and they are not the same, we would know which is the larger. If they have the same number of bits, we would have to compare successively smaller significant bits until we found the first to differ. We could then state that the number having the 0 bit is the smaller of the two. On the other hand, the second binary number converted to hexadecimal is $F6D9_H$. At a glance we can tell that $F6D9_H$ is a larger number than $F36D_H$.

Problem 3.4

Convert the following 8080 microprocessor machine codes, taken from Table 2.1, to their equivalent hexadecimal codes. Then convert the same machine codes to decimal, and note how much more difficult it is.

MACHINE CODE	
01110000	11111110
01000110	11000011
00001100	11011010
00001101	11010010
10000110	11001010
11001110	11000010

3.3.3 Hexadecimal to Binary Conversion

Converting hexadecimal numbers to binary is a simple matter of converting each digit to its equivalent four-bit binary number.

$$\underbrace{1\,0\,1\,0}_{A}\ \underbrace{0\,1\,1\,1}_{7}\ \underbrace{1\,1\,0\,0}_{C}\ \underbrace{0\,0\,1\,1}_{3}$$

$$A7C3_H = 1010011111000011_2$$

Problem 3.5

Convert the following statement numbers, taken from the program of Table 2.2, to their binary equivalents.

STATEMENT NUMBERS

0304
0306
0308
0309

3.3.4 Hexadecimal to Decimal Conversion

On rare occasions it is useful to convert hexadecimal numbers to their equivalent decimal values. The place values of hexadecimal numbers are given in Table 3.5. Conversion is accomplished by multiplying the place value by the integer in each place and adding them to get the decimal equivalent.

TABLE 3.5 Place values of hexadecimal numbers.

MSD			LSD
16^3	16^2	16^1	16^0
4096	256	16	1

Problem 3.6

Convert the number $B43E_H$ to its equivalent decimal value.

$$(B \times 16^3) + (4 \times 16^2) + (3 \times 16) + E =$$

$$(11 \times 4096) + (4 \times 256) + (3 \times 16) + 14 =$$

$$45{,}056 + 1024 + 48 + 14 = 46{,}142$$

Problem 3.7

The main program in Figure 2.6 ends with memory address 023B. You are planning to expand the program to include several new subroutines. You may use any open addresses below $04FF_H$. Determine the size (in decimal) of each open memory slot.

Note: In spite of the absence of integers A through F, the memory map is labeled in hexadecimal.

3.3.5 Decimal to Hexadecimal Conversion

Converting decimal numbers to hexadecimal can be accomplished by dividing the decimal number by 16 successively, and using the remainder as the hexadecimal digits. Continue dividing until the quotient is zero and the remainder is less than 16.

```
     2,883
16)46,142
   46,128
       14   = E (LSD)

       180
16) 2,883
    2,880
        3   = 3 (2ND SD)

        11
   16) 180
       176
         4  = 4 (3rd SD)

         0
    16) 11
        -0
        11  = B (MSD)
```

$46{,}142_{10} = \text{B43E}_H$

Problem 3.8

Determine the equivalent decimal numbers for the address labels in the memory map of Figure 2.5.

3.4 The Octal Number System

3.4.1 Octal Base and Integers

The octal number system is widely used with some minicomputers and microprocessors. Its application is like that of hexadecimal in that conversions between octal and binary are much easier than conversions between decimal and binary. Conversion from binary is accomplished by dividing the binary number into groups of 3 bits and converting each group separately into octal digits. Octal provides advantages over binary similar to those provided by decimal and hexadecimal. The uniqueness of numbers can be quickly recognized. The relative magnitude and numerical order can be recognized more quickly than for a binary number of similar magnitude. It has a considerable advantage over hexadecimal in that it uses the integers 0 through 7, and new integers did not need to be adopted for its use. Table 3.6 compares octal numbers with the equivalent binary and decimal numbers to the count of 16.

TABLE 3.6 Decimal, Octal, and Binary numbers compared to the count of 16.

DECIMAL	OCTAL	BINARY
1	1	1
2	2	10
3	3	11
4	4	100
5	5	101
6	6	110
7	7	111
8	10	1000
9	11	1001
10	12	1010
11	13	1011
12	14	1100
13	15	1101
14	16	1110
15	17	1111
16	20	10000

3.4.2 Binary to Octal Conversion

Conversion of binary numbers to octal is accomplished by dividing the binary number into 3-bit groups starting with the LSB. Let us convert the binary number 110111011001 separated into groups of three bits.

$$\begin{array}{cccc} 110 & 111 & 011 & 001 \\ 6 & 7 & 3 & 1 \end{array}$$

The octal digits can be determined at a glance.

$$110111011001_2 = 6731_8$$

Problem 3.9

Table 3.7 is a partial list of the instruction set of the 6100 microprocessor. Convert the machine codes to octal.

TABLE 3.7 Partial list of instructions from 6100 microprocessor instruction set.

MNEMONIC	MACHINE CODE	OPERATION
SRQ	110000000011	Skip if interrupt request.
CLA	111110000001	Clear accumulator.
SZA	111100100000	Skip on zero accumulator.
CMA	111000100000	Complement accumulator.
STA	111010100000	Set the accumulator.
SPA	111101001000	Skip on positive accumulator.
CAF	110000000111	Clear all flags.
HLT	111100000010	Halt.

3.4.3 Octal to Binary Conversion

Converting octal numbers to binary is an easy matter of converting each octal integer to its 3-bit binary equivalent.

Problem 3.10

Convert the octal number 137215_8 to binary.

1	3	7	2	1	5
001	011	111	010	001	101

$$137215_8 = 1011111010001101_2$$

Problem 3.11

Table 3.8 is a bootstrap loader program for the PDP-11 computer. Convert both addresses and instructions to binary.

TABLE 3.8 PDP-11 bootstrap loader. (*Courtesy of Digital Equipment Corporation*).

ADDRESS	DATA	REMARKS
37744	016701	(24 K Memory)
46	000026	
50	012702	
52	000352	
54	005211	
56	105711	
60	100376	
62	116162	
64	000002	
66	137400	
70	005267	
72	177756	
74	000765	
37776	177560	(LSR)

3.4.4 Octal to Decimal Conversion

Conversion of octal numbers to decimal can be accomplished by multiplying each place value by its integer and adding up the total, as shown in Table 3.9. Convert 153742_8 to decimal.

TABLE 3.9

PLACE VALUE	8^5	8^4	8^3	8^2	8^1	8^0
INTEGER	32768	4096	512	64	8	1

$$\begin{aligned}
1 \times 8^5 &= 32{,}768 \\
5 \times 8^4 &= 20{,}480 \\
3 \times 8^3 &= 1{,}536 \\
7 \times 8^2 &= 448 \\
4 \times 8^1 &= 32 \\
2 \times 8^0 &= \underline{\quad 2} \\
& 55{,}266
\end{aligned}$$

$$153{,}742_8 = 55{,}266_{10}$$

Problem 3.12

Convert the following octal numbers to decimal:

177564,	5210,
16700,	5710,
764,	100376,
224,	22021,
17601,	17550,

3.4.5 Decimal to Octal Conversion

Decimal numbers can be converted to octal numbers by dividing the number by 8 successively, using the remainders as the octal integers. Continue dividing until the quotient is zero and the remainder is less than 8.

Problem 3.13

Convert the decimal number 7184 to octal.

```
    898
 8)7184
   7184
      0    0    LSD

    112
 8) 898
    896
      2    2    2nd SD

     14
 8) 112
    112
      0    0    3rd SD

      1
 8)  14
      8
      6    6    4th SD

      0
 8)   1
      0
      1    1    MSD
```

$7184_{10} = 16020_8$

Problem 3.14

Convert the following decimal numbers to octal.

310,	572,
255,	675,
2100,	99,
9628,	8,888
31,975,	121

3.5 Binary Coded Decimal Numbers (BCD)

Binary coded decimal numbers are formed by converting each individual digit of a decimal number to its 4-bit binary equivalent. BCD numbers have a similar appearance to binary numbers but are different for quantities higher than nine as can be seen for the value 10.

$$10_{10} = 1010_2 \quad \text{but} \quad 10_{10} = 10000_{BCD}$$

BCD numbers provide the dual state requirement of a digital system equally as well as binary does, but, for a given value, require a larger number of bits. Its single advantage over binary is the ease of conversion.

BCD numbers are not widely used in either the logic or programming of microprocessors. However, to accommodate BCD systems which may input to the microprocessor, the arithmetic units of most microprocessors have provisions for decimal correction which makes BCD arithmetic programs possible.

Problem 3.15

Convert the decimal number 4095 to BCD.

4	0	9	5
0100	0000	1001	0101

$$4095_{10} = 0100000010010101_{BCD}$$

Problem 3.16

Convert the decimal numbers listed below to both BCD and binary notation.

1247
6356
4830
2475
3752

BCD to decimal conversion is accomplished by dividing the BCD number into 4-bit groups and decoding each group into a decimal digit. (**Note**: if any digit in the group exceeds 9, either the groups were incorrectly separated or the number is not BCD).

Problem 3.17

Convert the BCD number 1001011001010011 to decimal notation. Separated into four bit groups

1001	0110	0101	0011
9	6	5	3

$$1001011001010011_{BCD} = 9653_{10}$$

Problem 3.18

There are 5 quantities listed below in both binary and BCD. Determine which are BCD. Convert the BCD to decimal and match each with its equivalent binary number.

100101010110	1110111100
11010000111	1010101111
10110011000	1001010110
100001100000	1101011100
10010000110	111100110

3.6 Comparison of Number Systems

Table 3.10 shows the five number systems most widely used with microprocessors. The advantage of fewer places for a high value number favors hexadecimal, but the need for six additional integers is a serious disadvantage. In spite of the confusion caused by extra integers, the hexadecimal number system has become the most popular auxiliary number system used with microprocessors. This may be partly due to the fact that it decodes from binary in 4-bit groups, which is compatible with the fact that today's microprocessors tend to have address and data bus bit sizes that are divisible by four. Octal, on the other hand, is easier to use than hexadecimal particularly for beginners because there are no unfamiliar digits. Octal has been widely used for some time and still has many proponents. However, there is no reason for both octal and hexadecimal to be used together in the same program or software system. Software development systems offered by most microprocessor manufacturers generally use hexadecimal, but recently, test equipment manufacturers have been offering systems with a choice of either hexadecimal or octal.

HEXADECIMAL	DECIMAL	OCTAL	BINARY	BCD
1	1	1	1	1
2	2	2	10	10
3	3	3	11	11
4	4	4	100	100
5	5	5	101	101
6	6	6	110	110
7	7	7	111	111
8	8	10	1000	1000
9	9	11	1001	1001
A	10	12	1010	1 0000
B	11	13	1011	1 0001
C	12	14	1100	1 0010
D	13	15	1101	1 0011
E	14	16	1110	1 0100
F	15	17	1111	1 0101
10	16	20	10000	1 0110
11	17	21	10001	1 0111
12	18	22	10010	1 1000
13	19	23	10011	1 1001
14	20	24	10100	10 0000
15	21	25	10101	10 0001
16	22	26	10110	10 0010
17	23	27	10111	10 0011
18	24	30	11000	10 0100
19	25	31	11001	10 0101
1A	26	32	11010	10 0110
1B	27	33	11011	10 0111
1C	28	34	11100	10 1000
1D	29	35	11101	10 1001
1E	30	36	11110	11 0000
1F	31	37	11111	11 0001
20	32	40	100000	11 0010

TABLE 3.10 Comparison of the five number systems to the count of 32.

3.7 Number System Conversions with a Calculator

Number system conversions can be made easier by the use of a simple 4-function calculator. Most calculators will provide a constant and repeat function. This function may exist as a normal state or may require a switch position or push button labeled K. With this function the second number entered in an operation is retained as a constant and each time the = button is depressed, the operation with the constant is repeated. Table 3.11 shows this function used to determine the powers of 2 from 2^2 to 2^{10}. The constant and repeat function works equally well for octal or hexademical.

TABLE 3.11 Powers of 2 (binary place values) obtained using the constant and repeat calculator function. To convert from binary numbers to decimal, list only the values which are 1 in the binary number and add them. Include 2^0 and 2^1 values if they are 1 in the number being converted.

KEY DEPRESSIONS	DISPLAY	POWER OF 2
[ON]	0	
(K) if needed	0	
[2] [×] [2] [=]	4	2^2
[=]	8	2^3
[=]	16	2^4
[=]	32	2^5
[=]	64	2^6
[=]	128	2^7
[=]	256	2^8
[=]	512	2^9
[=]	1024	2^{10}

Table 3.12 shows the operation used to determine the powers of 16^2 to 16^5.

TABLE 3.12 Powers of 16 (hexadecimal place values) obtained using the constant and repeat calculator function. To convert, multiply each place value by the place digit and add these products. Include the LSD multiplied by 1 and the 2nd significant digit multiplied by 16.

KEY DEPRESSIONS	DISPLAY	POWERS OF 16
[ON]	0	
K (If needed)	0	
[1] [6] [×] [1] [6] [=]	256	16^2 (3rd significant digit)
[=]	4096	16^3
[=]	65536	16^4
[=]	1048576	16^5

The calculator is equally useful in converting from decimal to other number systems. The divide-by-2 method of decimal to binary conversion has the advantage that it can be done very easily using the constant and repeat function. Table 3.13 shows the steps needed to obtain the conversion of 81.

TABLE 3.13 Decimal to binary conversion aided by constant and repeat calculator function. If the number is odd, the LSB is 1; if even, the LSB is 0. Each time the calculator [=] button is depressed, another bit of the binary number is determined by whether the whole number portion is odd or even. When the whole number of the display is one, the conversion is complete.

KEY DEPRESSIONS	DISPLAY	BITS DETERMINED
[ON]	**0**	
[8] [1]	**81**	Odd = 1 (LSB)
[÷] [2] [=]	**40**.5	Even = 0
[=]	**20**.25	Even = 0
[=]	**10**.125	Even = 0
[=]	**5**.0025	Odd = 1
[=]	**2**.53125	Even = 0
[=]	**1**.265625	Odd = 1 (MSB)
$81_{10} = 1010001_2$		

Conversions from decimal to number systems greater than 2 are a little more awkward but still much easier than a totally manual conversion. Table 3.14 shows the steps used to convert $46{,}142_{10}$ to hexadecimal. Divide repeatedly by sixteen, until the display reads less than 16.

KEY DEPRESSIONS	DISPLAY	RECORD
ON		
4 6 1 4 2	46142	
÷ 1 6 =	2883.875	.875
=	180.24218	.2421
=	11.265136	.2651
		MSD = B
. 2 6 5 1 × 1 6 =	4.24	4
. 2 4 2 1 × 1 6 =	3.872	3
. 8 7 5 × 1 6 =	14	LSD = E
$46142_{10} = B43E_H$		

TABLE 3.14 Decimal to hexadecimal conversion aided by constant and repeat calculator function. Divide the decimal number successively by 16 until the dividend is less than 16. Use the whole number value of the final dividend as the MSB of the hexadecimal number. Record the first four digits to the right of the decimal point after each depression of the equal button. Determine the remaining digits by multiplying the recorded decimal values by 16. Use only the whole number portion of the products as the hexadecimal digits.

After each depression of the equal button, record the first 4 digits to the right of the decimal point. When a number less than 16 is displayed, use the whole number of that display as the MSB of the hexadecimal number. The remaining digits are determined by multiplying each recorded decimal value by 16, using only the whole number of these products as the hexadecimal digits. The decimal portion of that product is discarded regardless of how close it approaches a whole number.

Questions

3.1 What are the advantages of using an auxiliary number system like octal or hexadecimal?

3.2 Why does hexadecimal seem more advantageous for use with today's microprocessors?

3.3 What major disadvantage does hexadecimal have with regard to integers?

3.4 What is the lowest power of 2 which exceeds 1000_{10}?

3.5 Why is the binary number system used for machine code?

3.6 Which place value has an equal weight in all number systems?

3.7 What is the highest power of 2 in an 8-bit number?

3.8 What is the highest decimal value that can be expressed with an 8-bit number?

3.9 What is the total number of whole number decimal values that can be expressed by an 8-bit binary number including zero?

3.10 By how much does the value FF_H differ from 2^8?

3.11 What is a disadvantage of using the BCD number system?

3.12 Which binary and hexadecimal place values are of equal weight (for values less than $100{,}000_{10}$)?

Problems

3.1 Convert the following decimal numbers to binary.

2, 526, 11, 243, 58, 87, 36, 176, 1

3.2 Convert the numbers given for Problem 3.1 to hexadecimal.

3.3 Convert the following decimal numbers to binary.

7, 1023, 513, 63, 129, 31, 255, 65, 535

3.4 Convert the numbers given for Problem 3.3 to octal.

3.5 Convert the following decimal numbers to binary.

24, 27, 127, 511, 65, 33, 257

3.6 Convert the numbers given for Problem 3.5 to hexadecimal.

3.7 Convert the following binary numbers to decimal.

110011, 1001001, 11000, 1111011, 11011, 1001, 11111, 1

3.8 Convert the numbers given for Problem 3.7 to hexadecimal.

3.9 Convert the following numbers to decimal.

111111, 1000001, 10100101, 110011000101

3.10 Convert the numbers given for Problem 3.9 to octal.

3.11 Convert the following numbers to decimal.

1011, 10001, 1001, 11011, 1001001, 110011, 11111111

3.12 Convert the numbers given for problem 3.11 to hexadecimal.

3.13 Listed below are numbers in decimal, octal, and hexadecimal (three of each). Express all nine in binary and hexadecimal.

C376	1897	1066
9672	37E0	7320
6535	7896	3B28

3.14 Listed below are numbers in binary and in BCD (four of each). Convert the BCD numbers to decimal and convert the binary numbers to hexadecimal.

100100101000	101010010100
111001010011	100001100011
1101110110	10010110111
100111010011	11001111001

3.15 Table 3.15 is a partial listing of the Z80 microprocessor instruction set. Convert the opcodes to hexadecimal.

TABLE 3.15 General purpose arithmetic and CPU control groups instructions for the Z80 microprocessor. (*Courtesy of Zilog*)

Notes: IFF indicates the interrupt enable flip-flop. CY indicates the carry flip-flop.
Flag Notation: • = flag not affected, 0 = flag reset, 1 = flag set, X = flag is unknown,
‡ = flag is affected according to the result of the operation.

MNEMONIC	SYMBOLIC OPERATION	FLAGS C	Z	P/V	S	N	H	OPCODE 76 543 210	NO. OF BYTES	NO. OF M CYCLES	NO. OF T STATES	COMMENTS
DAA	Converts acc. content into packed BCD following add or subtract with packed BCD operands	‡	‡	P	‡	•	‡	00 100 111	1	1	4	Decimal adjust accumulator
CPL	$A \leftarrow \bar{A}$	•	•	•	•	1	1	00 101 111	1	1	4	Complement accumulator (ones complement)
NEG	$A \leftarrow 0 - A$	‡	‡	V	‡	1	‡	11 101 101 01 000 100	2	2	8	Negate acc. (twos complement)
CCF	$CY \leftarrow \overline{CY}$	‡	•	•	•	0	X	00 111 111	1	1	4	Complement carry flag
SCF	$CY \leftarrow 1$	1	•	•	•	0	0	00 110 111	1	1	4	Set carry flag
NOP	No operation	•	•	•	•	•	•	00 000 000	1	1	4	
HALT	CPU halted	•	•	•	•	•	•	01 110 110	1	1	4	
DI	$IFF \leftarrow 0$	•	•	•	•	•	•	11 110 011	1	1	4	
EI	$IFF \leftarrow 1$	•	•	•	•	•	•	11 111 011	1	1	4	
IM 0	Set interrupt mode 0	•	•	•	•	•	•	11 101 101 01 000 110	2	2	8	
IM 1	Set interrupt mode 1	•	•	•	•	•	•	11 101 101 01 010 110	2	2	8	
IM 2	Set interrupt mode 2	•	•	•	•	•	•	11 101 101 01 011 110	2	2	8	

3.16 Table 3.16 is a partial listing of the 6500 microprocessor instruction set. Convert the hexadecimal codes to binary. Convert the binary codes to octal.

TABLE 3.16 Partial listing of the 6500 Microprocessor instruction set.

MNEMONIC	OPCODES	DESCRIPTION
ADC	69	Add with carry (IMM)
CMP	CD	Compare (ABS)
JMP	4C	Jump (ABS)
LDX	A2	Load X (IMM)
STX	8E	Store X (ABS)
BEQ	FO	Branch on Carry (REL)
BPL	10	Branch on Plus (REL)
SEC	38	Set Carry (IMP)
EOR	45	Exclusive Or (0 Page)
SEI	78	Set I Flag (IMP)
TAY	AB	Transfer A to Y (IMP)

3.17 A 512-X-8 PROM supplies microprocessor memory from 0300 to 04FF. This memory has vacant address slots between and including the following addresses.

03A1	and	03B9	041A	and	0436
0317	and	032F	047C	and	04A6
033C	and	0376	04E0	and	04FF

(a) How many memory bytes are available in each vacant slot? Answer in decimal.

(b) List in hexadecimal the memory segments in use, and determine the number of memory bytes in each.

3.18 The 8080 Microprocessor has restart addresses as listed. Convert the hexadecimal addresses to decimal.

RST 0	0000_H
RST 1	0008_H
RST 2	0010_H
RST 3	0018_H
RST 4	0020_H
RST 5	0028_H
RST 6	0030_H
RST 7	0038_H

How many memory bytes exist between each restart address?

3.19 A 32-X-8-bit memory is connected to a microprocessor memory bus so that its lowest address is at 0100_H, what is its highest address?

3.20 Construct a table like Table 3.12, but show key depressions, displays, etc., for octal place values to 8^6.

3.21 Construct a table like Table 3.13 for the conversion of 179_{10} to binary.

3.22 Construct a table like that of Table 3.14 for the conversion of 46142_{10} to octal.

3.23 In the conversion of Table 3.14, the value 3.872 is almost 4, why is the hexadecimal digit not rounded off to a 4? Is this method an approximation or is it exact (for whole numbers)?

3.24 Construct a table like Table 3.14 for the conversion of $65{,}535_{10}$ to hexadecimal.

Chapter 4

Microprocessor Buses

Objectives:

On completion of this chapter you will be able to:

- Assemble TTL circuits to form an open collector bus.
- Select and assemble circuits to form a 3-state bus.
- Interface CMOS logic systems to a TTL bus.
- Provide correct interface circuits for a bidirectional bus.
- Use the available 74S and 74LS octal buffers and latches for interfacing with a microprocessor bus.
- Provide correct timing and latch circuits for a multiplexed bus.

4.1 Standard Logic Lines

The standard logic circuit TTL or CMOS is designed to have only one output or driver circuit connected to a logic line. That single driver can supply sink or source currents to a number of inputs depending on its unit load rating. In the case of standard 74 series TTL, an output can drive 10 input circuits. The connection of two standard outputs to the same logic line should not occur because of the likelihood that one output may be driving the line high and the other driving it low. As shown in Figure 4.1, a short circuit results.

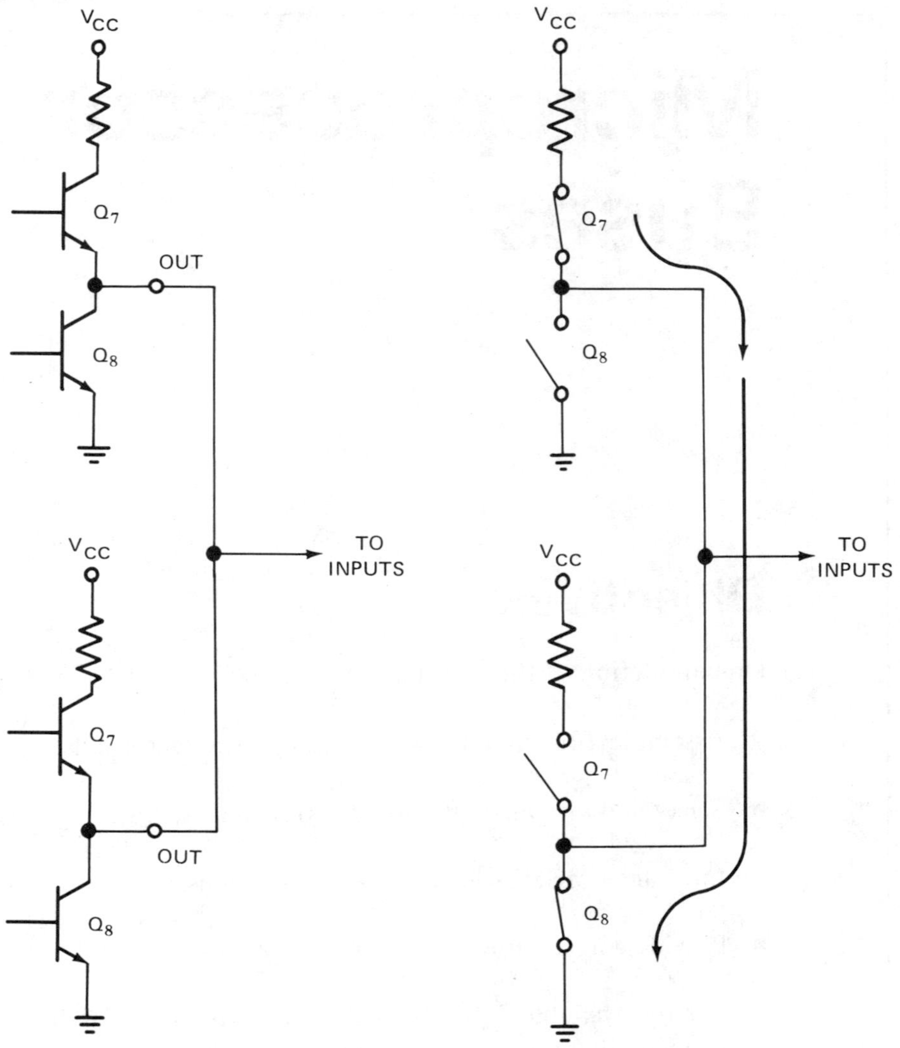

FIGURE 4.1 Connecting standard TTL totem pole output circuits to the same signal line can result in excessive current draw as one circuit seeks to drive the line high while the other tries to drive it low.

To drive the same set of inputs with more than one standard logic output requires the use of an OR gate (assuming the **inactive state** of the drivers to be low or logic 0). If the signal is active low, the AND gate can be used as indicated by its alternate symbol as an OR gate for logic 0. These solutions are shown in Figure 4.2.

4.2 The Open Collector Bus

A convenient solution for connecting numerous logic drivers to the same set of logic inputs is the **open collector bus.** Figure 4.3 shows the schematic diagram of several open collector drivers connected to a single pullup resistor. For the **bus** to go high, the output transistors of all drivers must be turned off (logic 1). The output of any one driver can cause the bus to go low by turning on and grounding the end of the pullup resistor through its output transistor. To function correctly, the inactive state of the drivers must be high, and only one driver should be using the bus at any given time. Many TTL circuits, including ROMS

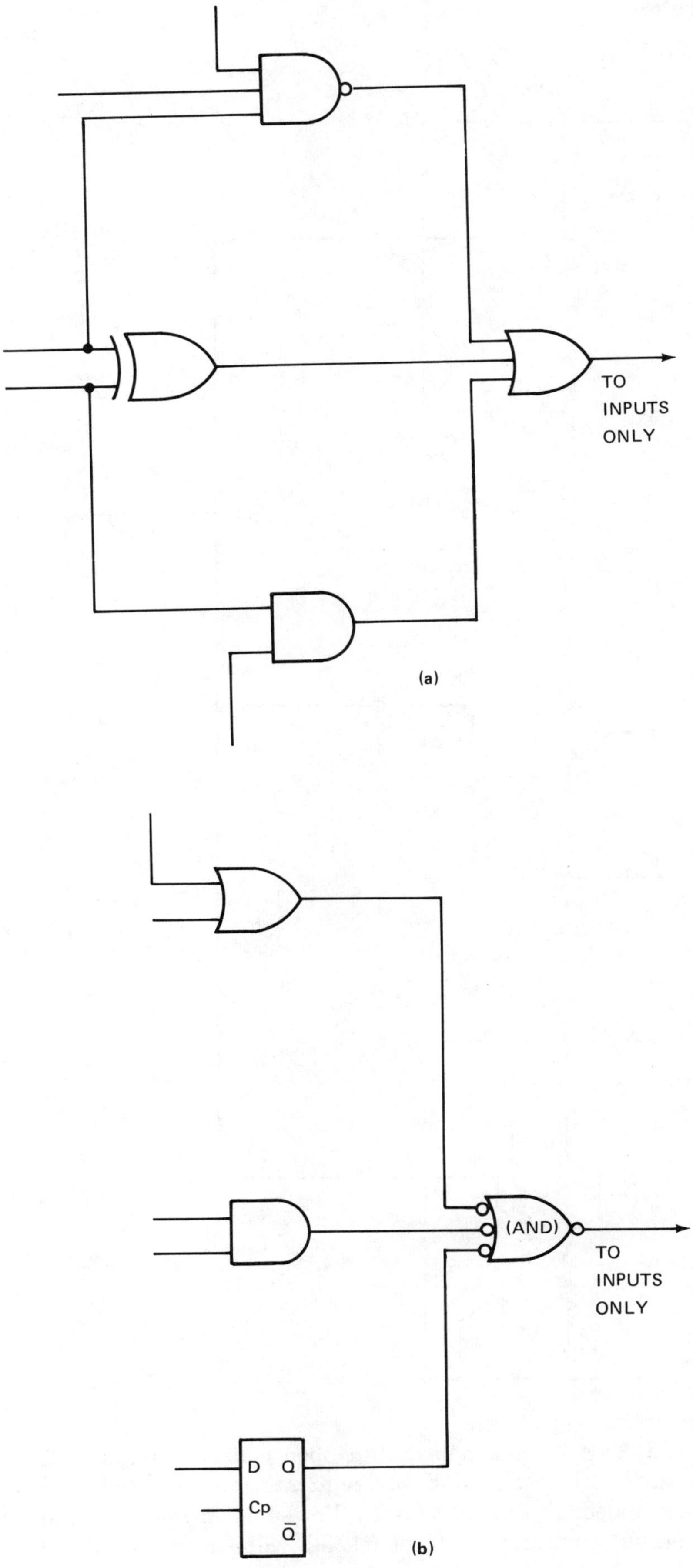

FIGURE 4.2 To allow several standard output circuits to drive the same logic line, (a) an OR gate is used if the active state of the signal is high; (b) an AND gate is used if the active state of the signal is low.

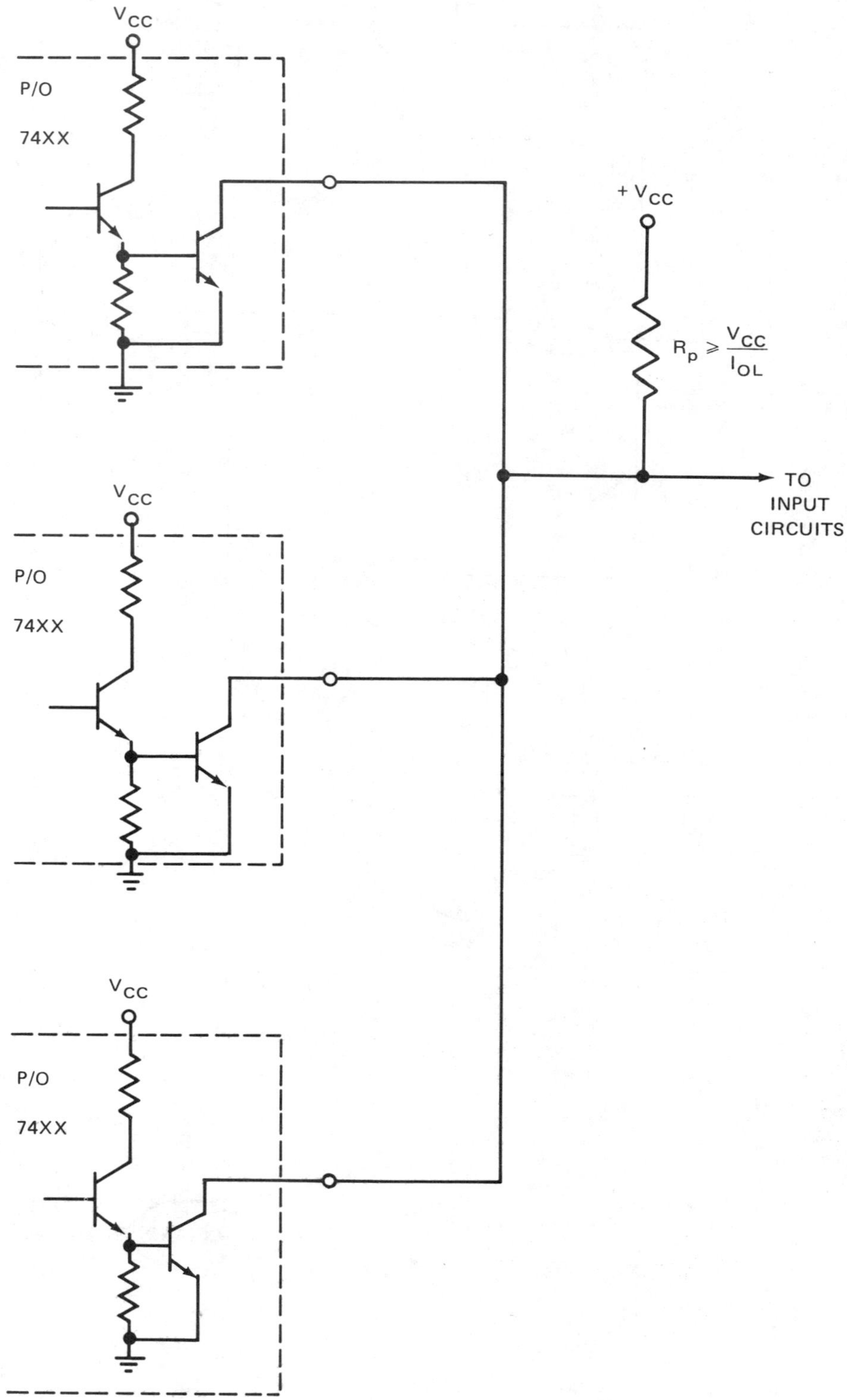

FIGURE 4.3 TTL open collector output circuits connected to the same bus line. A single pullup resistor is needed. Only one output should be controlling the bus at any given time. The inactive state of the open collector driver is high (output transistor turned off).

and RAMS, are supplied with open collector outputs. This output is particularly useful when the address size of a memory circuit is being expanded. Figure 4.4 shows a 32- X 8-bit memory with open collector output connected to form a 128- X 8-bit memory. The chip select in-

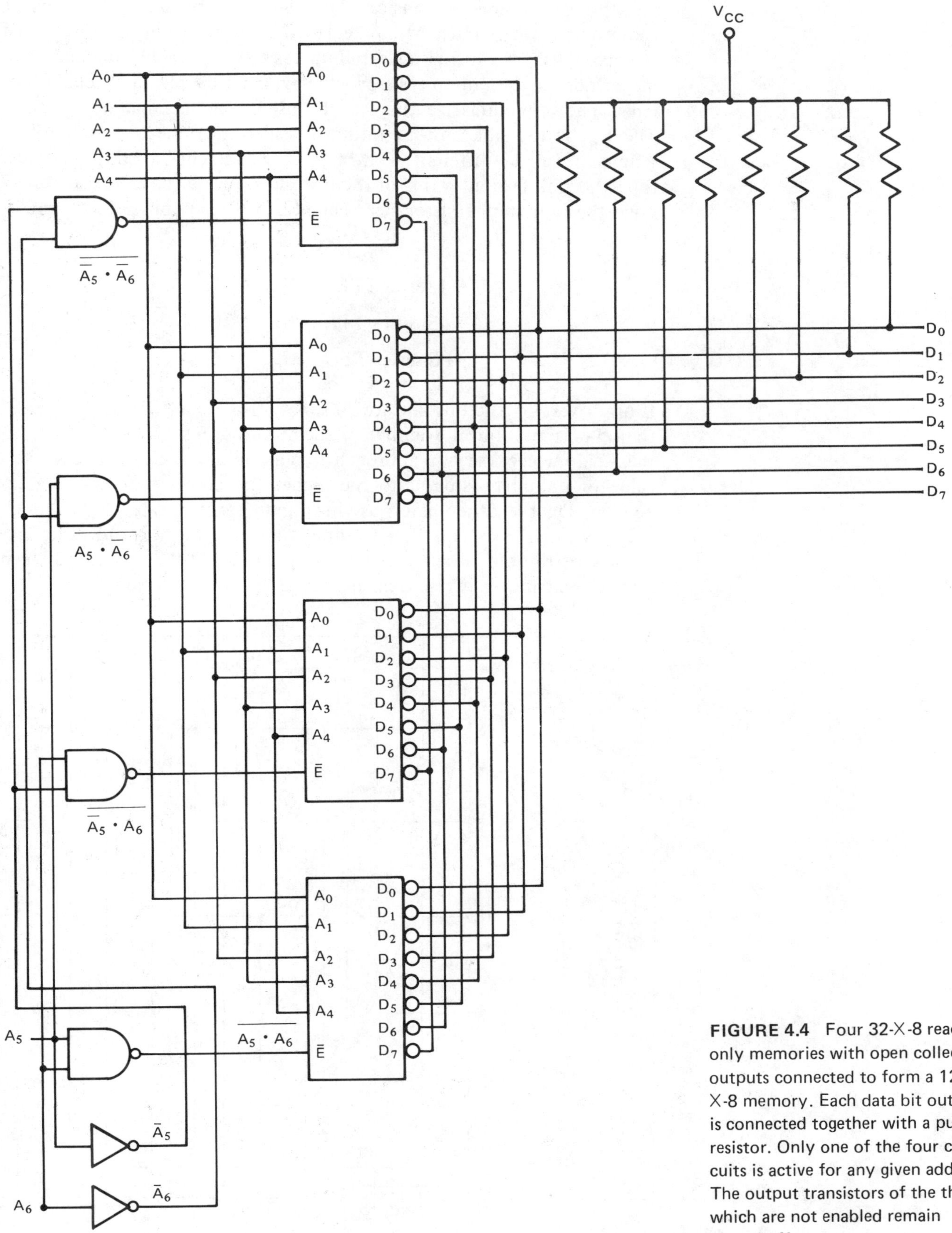

FIGURE 4.4 Four 32-X-8 read only memories with open collector outputs connected to form a 128-X-8 memory. Each data bit output is connected together with a pullup resistor. Only one of the four circuits is active for any given address. The output transistors of the three which are not enabled remain turned off.

puts provide address expansion. The eight data outputs from each of the four memories must be connected to the same 8-bit data bus. This is accomplished with a single pullup resistor for each data line. The magnitude of the pullup resistor is determined by several circuit problems. The minimum size that can be used is approximately V_{CC}/I_{OL}. The I_{OL} is the sink current rating of a driver connected to the line. Where drivers of different TTL families are attached to the same bus, then the sink current rating of the lowest power device is used to determine the minimum resistor size. The I_{OL} of three popular TTL families are:

74 series TTL	$I_{OL} = 16mA$
74S series TTL	$I_{OL} = 20mA$
74LS series TTL	$I_{OL} = 8mA$

If all drivers on the bus line are 74 series TTL, then R_P must be greater than 5V/16mA, but if even one of them is a 74LS then $R_P > 5V/8mA$. It is seldom necessary to approach this minimum value. The lower the value of pullup resistor used, the higher the power that must be expended. On the other hand, as the pullup resistor value is increased. there is an increase in the switching time limiting the operating frequency of the bus. Figure 4.5 shows the trade off that occurs between power dissipation and rise time as the pullup resistor is varied.

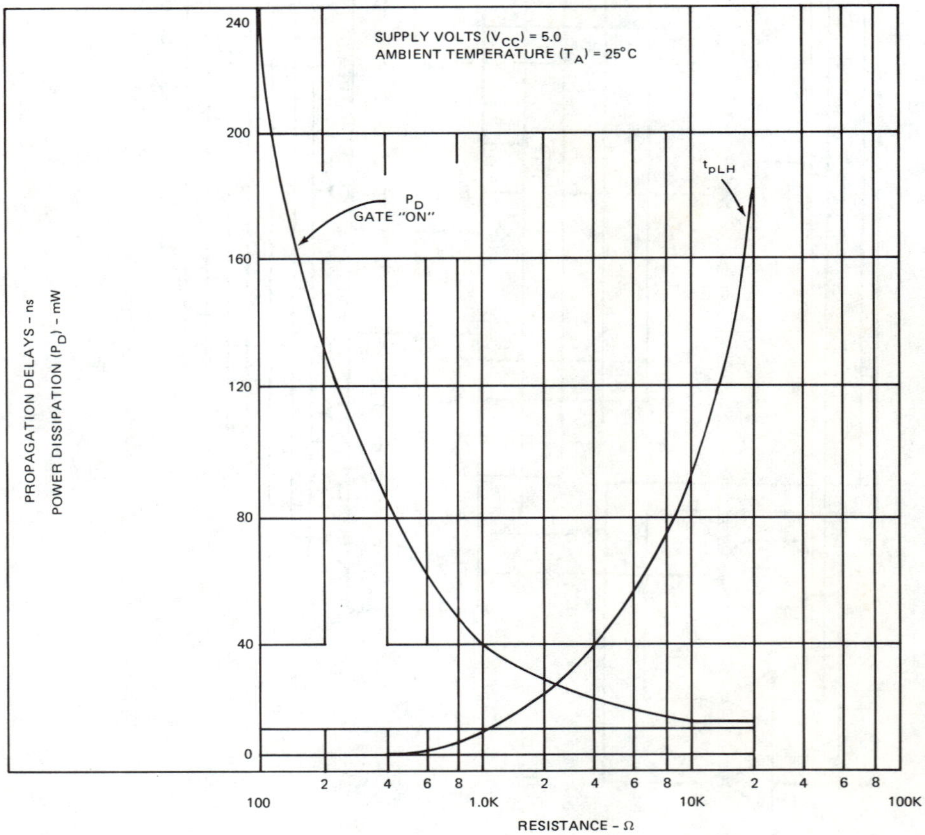

FIGURE 4.5 As the value of the pullup resistor is decreased, the power expended in the gate and resistor increases. As the value of the pullup resistor is increased, the propagation delay of the signal through the gate is increased.

4.3 The Three-State Bus

The typical totem pole TTL output circuit, as shown in Figure 4.6(a), functions by having either upper or lower transistor turned on at any given time. To produce a logic 1 or high output, Q_1 is turned on and Q_2 is turned off. To produce a logic 0 or low output, Q_1 is turned off and Q_2 is turned on. As compared to a pullup of the open collector circuit in Figure 4.4, the transistor Q_1 is an active pullup and is a high resistance during a logic 0 out and a low resistance during logic 1 output. This provides the best of both worlds for both high speed and minimum power dissipation, but as previously mentioned, totem pole outputs cannot be connected together on the same bus. With a minor change to the TTL circuit, however, a third state can be created during which both transistors of the totem pole are turned off together. This third state produces a high impedance output. The **3-state** or **tri-state®** bus allows a large number of outputs to be connected to a single bus line as long as all but one of these outputs is in the high impedance state (disabled) at any given time. Figure 4.6(c) shows the modification to a TTL circuit used to produce a 3-state output. Note that an enable/disable control must be held in the enable state when this driver is outputting to the bus. It must be switched to the disable state when the bus is relinquished to another driver. The number of 3-state drivers that may be connected to a bus is limited by the operating frequency.

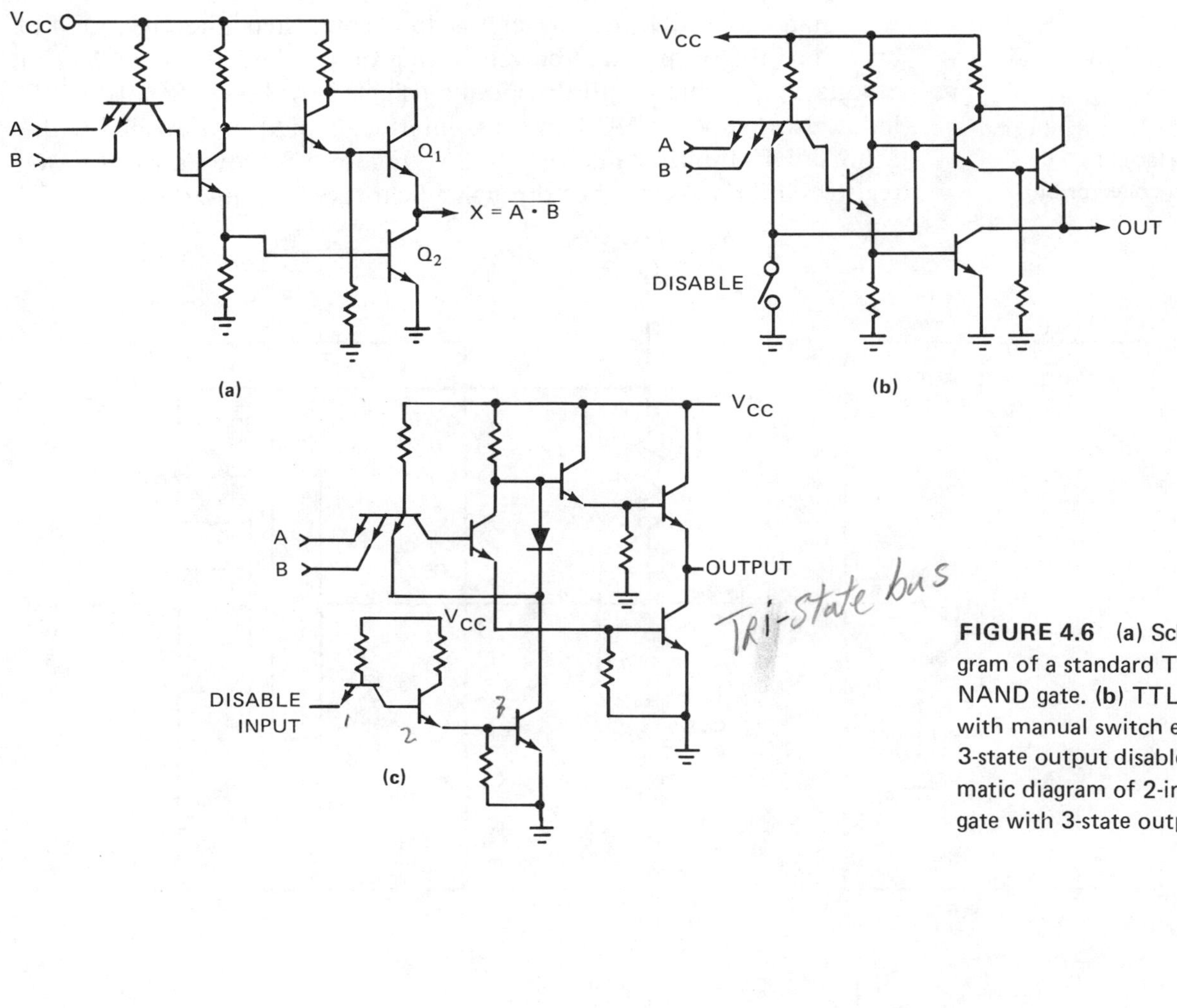

FIGURE 4.6 (a) Schematic diagram of a standard TTL 2-input NAND gate. **(b)** TTL NAND gate with manual switch equivalent of 3-state output disable. **(c)** Schematic diagram of 2-input NAND gate with 3-state output.

4.4 Loading the Bus

Each disabled driver adds from 3 to 8 pf to the overall bus capacitance. At low switching frequencies, over a hundred 3-state drivers may be connected to a single bus. The number of input circuits on that same bus is limited by the sink or source current rating of the weakest driver on the bus. For TTL inputs, the source load is seldom significant. The sink load amounts to 1.6 mA for a standard 74 series input and only 400μA for each 74LS input.

CMOS inputs, however, cause no significant current load, but they add a capacitance to the bus of up to 7.5 pf per input. Although CMOS circuits are seldom bused together with TTL devices, there may be occasions where it can be done. If the switching speed is low enough, CMOS circuits operating with a V_{DD} of 5 volts may be connected to a TTL bus provided the V_{OH} level of the bus can be maintained at 3.5 volts or higher. On a 3-state bus, pullup resistors may be required to do this, because V_{OH} ratings of tri-state drivers are 2.4 volts minimum. It is more convenient with an open collector bus because pullup resistors are already employed. CMOS circuits using V_{DD} higher than 5 volts require special **interface** circuits between them and the bus. The TTL open collector **buffers** 7405 or 7406 can be used for this purpose. The output transistors of these devices are rated for 30V. The V_{CC} of the buffer connects to +5V, but the pullup resistor connects to the V_{DD} supply of the CMOS circuit, as shown in Figure 4.7.

Standard CMOS drivers are seldom connected directly to a TTL bus, since the output sink current rating of standard B series CMOS at 5 volts V_{DD} is enough to drive only a single Low Power Schottky TTL input. Normally a CMOS to TTL interface would be provided with a Schottky TTL buffer like the (8T26). Figure 4.8 shows a set of CMOS registers interfaced to a bus through a Schottky TTL interface.

FIGURE 4.7 CMOS circuit using $V_{DD} > 5V$ interfaced to TTL through an open collector buffer.

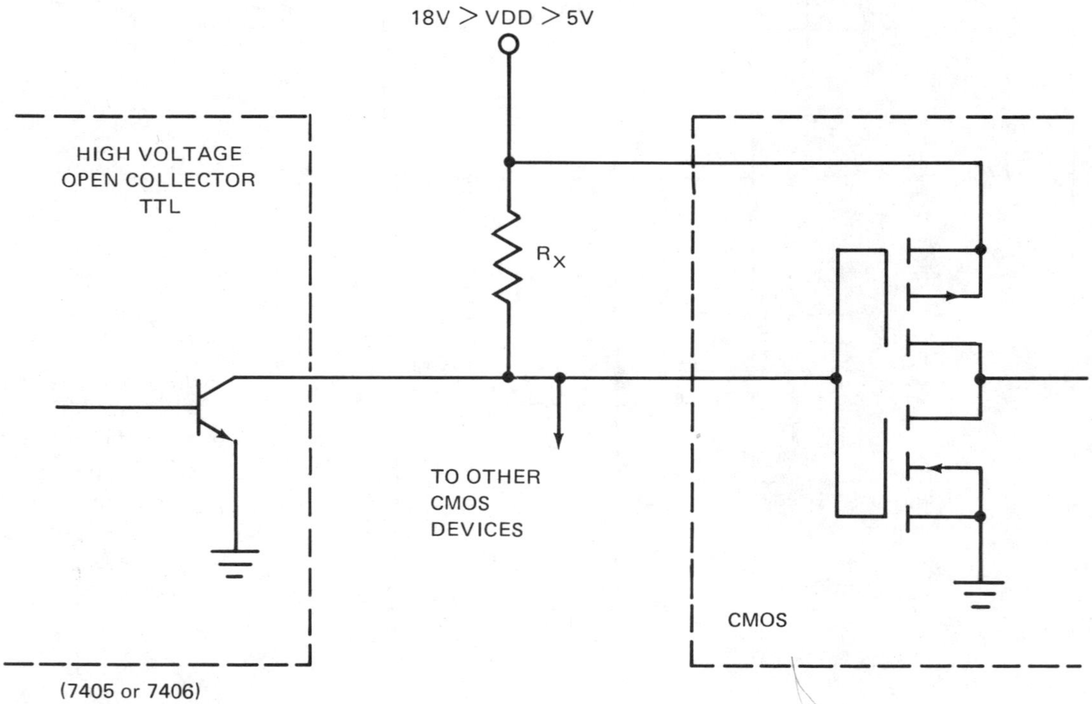

36

FIGURE 4.8 CMOS register interfaced to a TTL bus through a Schottky bus transceiver. A B-series CMOS can sink only 400 μ amps sufficient to drive only one low-power Schottky load. The 8T26 requires only 200 μ amps sink current on its driver inputs and can supply up to 10mA current to the microprocessor bus.

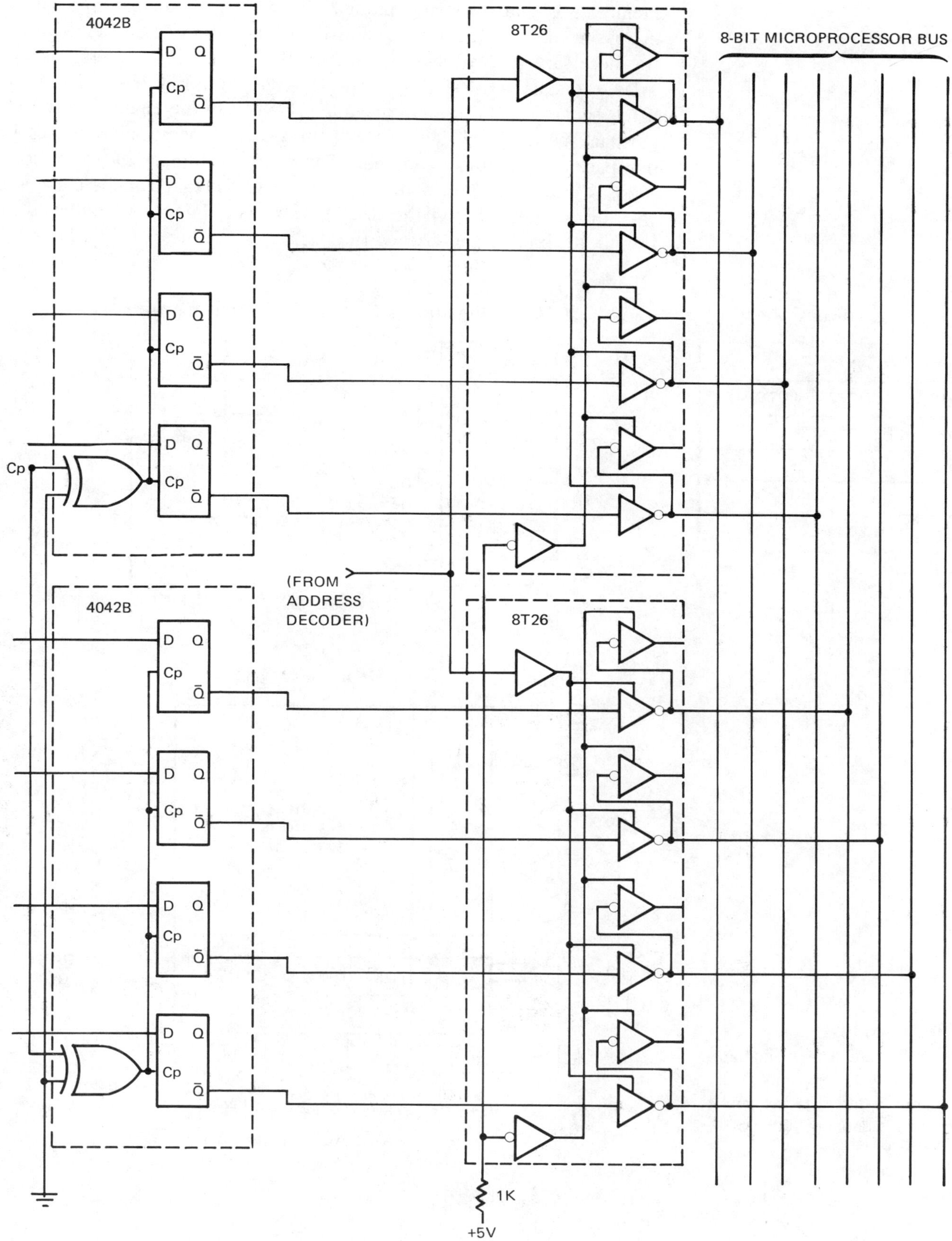

4.5 The Bidirectional Bus

One of the problems encountered by designers of integrated circuit memories is that of having enough pins on the circuit package for the increasing number of address and data bits without sacrificing any of the necessary control signals. One of the older more successful memories, the static 1K-X-1 RAM, (2102), is shown in Figure 4.9. Note that it has separate data in and data out pins. It is in the highly favored 16-pin package. It has a single CE. At this point in memory circuit design, our package has run out of pins. There are no unnecessary functions, such as extra chip select or chip enable leads, that can be dispensed with in order to expand the size of address or data. One obvious solution is to expand the size of the package. Another is to combine the

PIN NAMES

D_{IN}	DATA INPUT
A_0–A_9	ADDRESS INPUTS
R/W	READ/WRITE INPUT
$\overline{CE}$	CHIP ENABLE
D_{OUT}	DATA OUTPUT
V_{CC}	POWER (+5V)

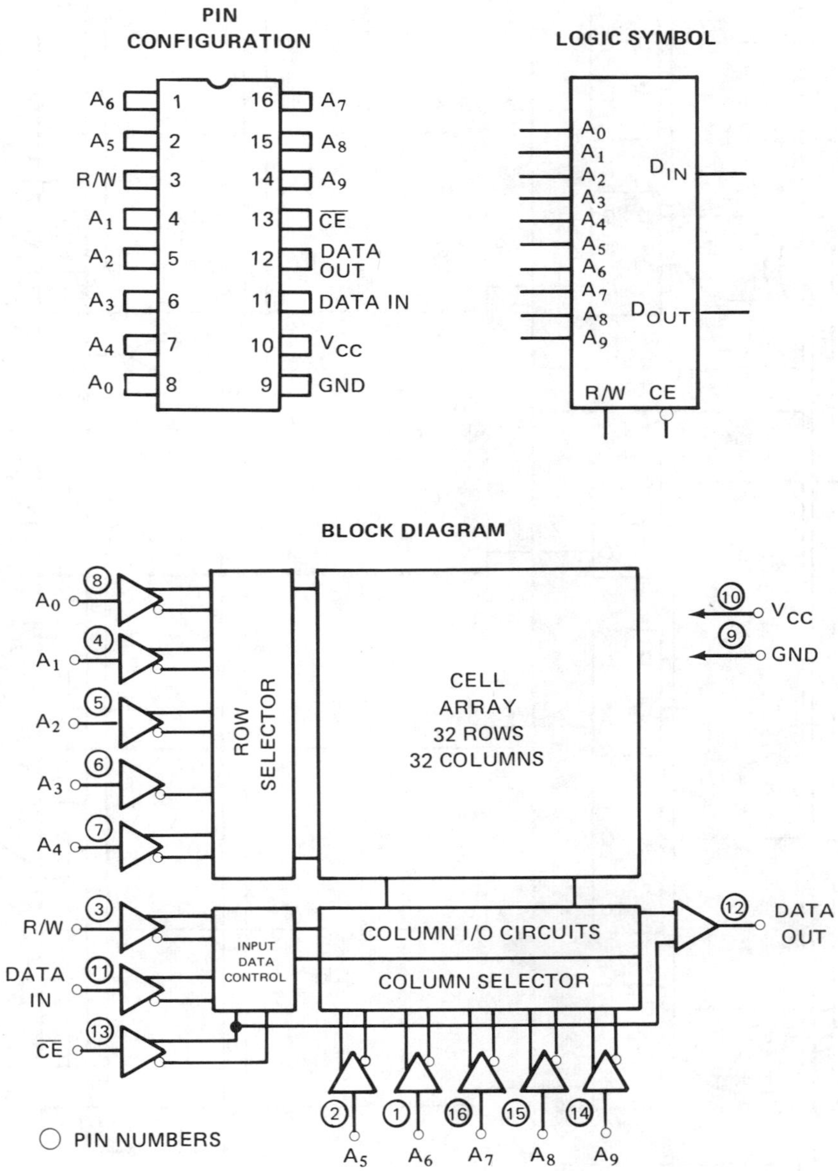

FIGURE 4.9 2102 Static 1K-x-1 RAM has separate data in and data out. If memory system timing is suitable, the 3-state data out can be shorted to the data in to form a common I/O.

input and output pins for a common I/O. The 2102 memory, in fact, can function with its input and output pins shorted together to form a common I/O. The output driver is 3-state and remains in high impedance during the write enable, while the data in is inhibited during the read cycle. If these functions were shorted together internally, one pin could be saved. Figure 4.10 shows the 2114 static RAM. It has a 1024-bit address like the 2102, but it has 4 data bits. Had separate I/O leads been used, it would have required 6 additional pins, but with common I/O only 2 additional pins were needed for this expansion. The same saving of pins by use of common I/O pins appears in microprocessors. The microprocessor data bus is bidirectional. All devices connected to

PIN CONFIGURATION

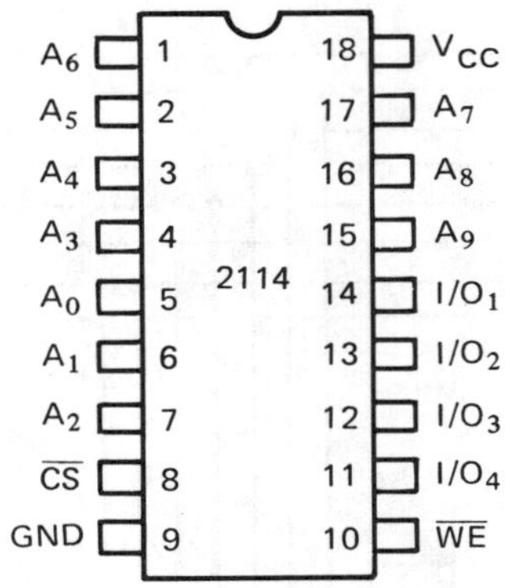

BLOCK DIAGRAM

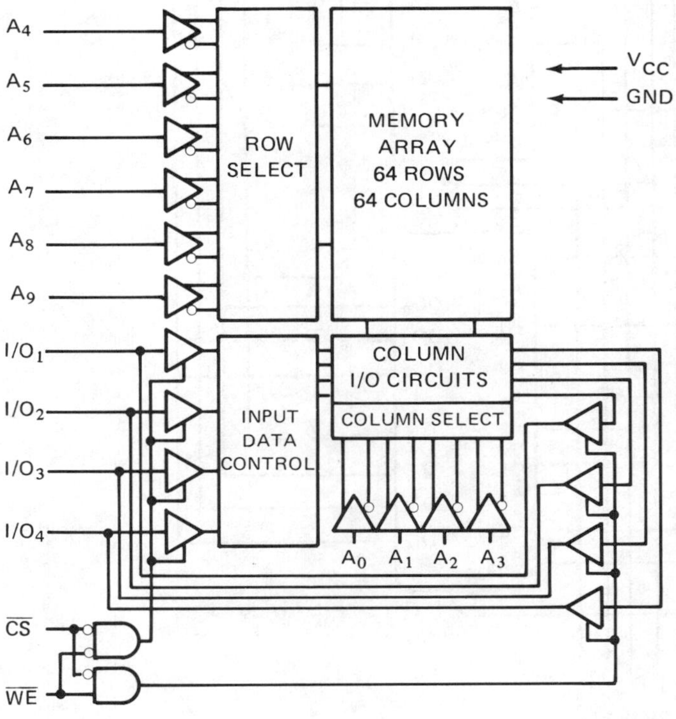

FIGURE 4.10 2114 Static 1K-x-4 RAM with common I/O comes in an 18-pin package.

the bidirectional bus do not have to be bidirectional. As Figure 2.4 shows, the microprocessor and the RAM are bidirectional while the ROMS are not.

Combining input and output data on the same bus is convenient, but at some point these respective data must be separated. For most devices connected to the bidirectional bus, the separation is performed internally.

Three-state RAMS which do not have common I/O can usually be connected to a bidirectional data bus by merely connecting each data in and data out bit together on the same bus line. The device data sheet should be checked carefully before doing this. Figure 4.11 shows a 256-X-4 random access memory having separate I/O, connected to a bidirectional data bus. For some RAMS the **chip enable, CE (chip select, CS)**

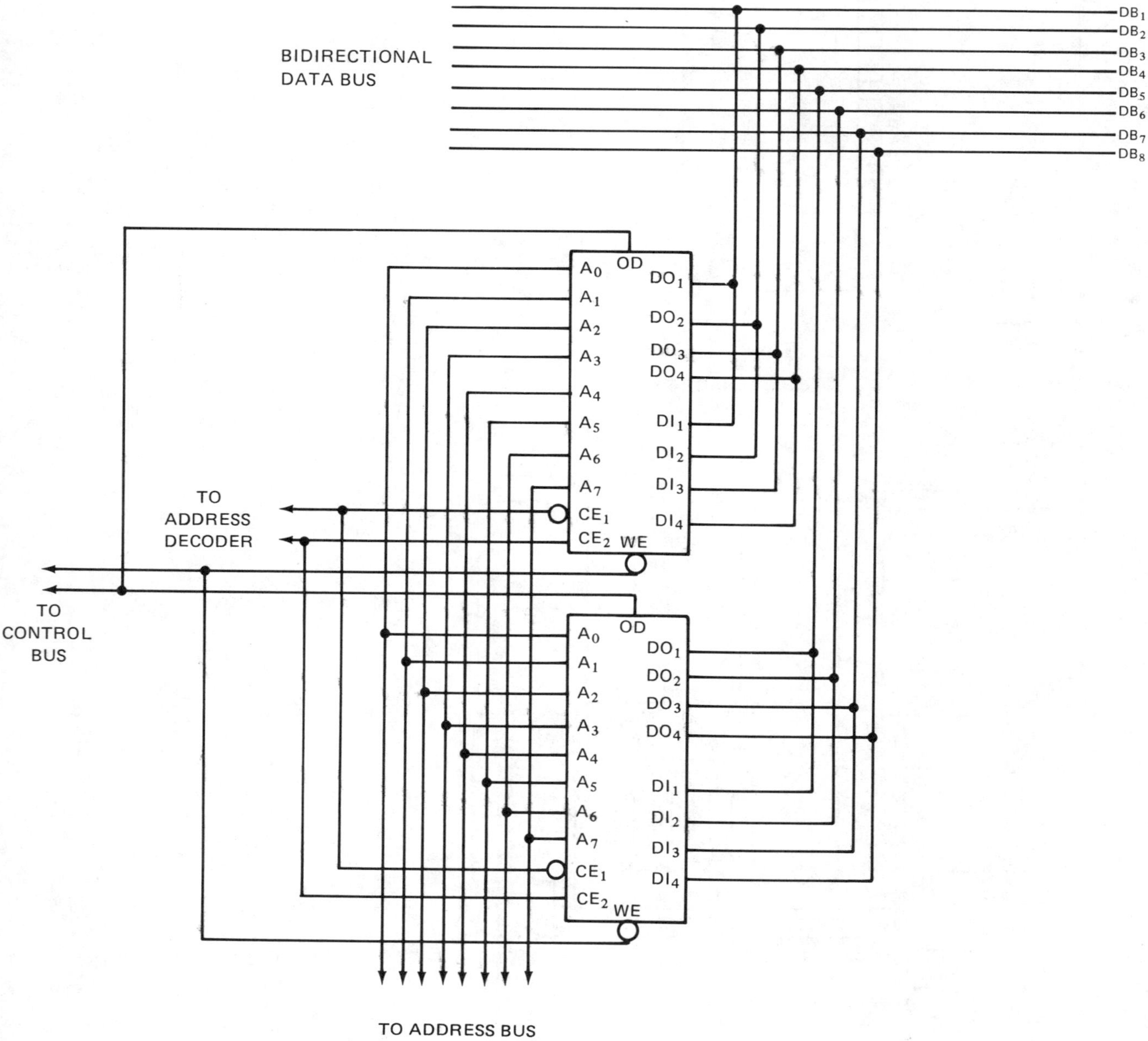

FIGURE 4.11 2101 Static 256-x-4 RAM connected to a bidirectional data bus. During a write cycle, the output disable (OD) goes active prior the chip enable and insures that the output drivers do not turn on and interfere with the incoming data.

inputs along with the write enable (WE) are all the controls supplied for switching between high impedance, data in, and data out. When the device is deselected, the data out drivers are in high impedance and the receiver inputs are turned off. When it is selected the data out drivers are switched on but will be switched off when the write enable becomes active. If the system timing is such that the write enable is delayed for a substantial period after the device is selected, then for a time during the write cycle two sets of drivers will be on the bus simultaneously. To avoid this problem, an additional control signal may be supplied which is used to disable the output drivers prior to the device being selected for a write cycle. The **output disable (OD)** supplied with the 2101 memory in Figure 4.11 is used for this purpose. During a write cycle, this signal becomes active prior to the chip enable (chip select). Where an output disable function is not supplied, the WE (write enable) should come as early as possible during the write cycle.

Where memory or other circuits require separation of the bidirectional data bus into separate input and output (receive and transmit) buses, the 8T28 bus transceiver can be used as shown in Figure 4.12.

4.6 External Buses

Many digital devices, which can be controlled or serviced by microprocessors, cannot be connected directly to the microprocessor bus, for various reasons. They may operate at different logic levels, they may require more power than the microprocessor can provide, they may be too slow in speed, or they may not be 3-state. Whatever the reason, an interface is needed between the microprocessor bus and the bus of these peripheral devices. The circuits used for the interface may be referred to as I/O ports, peripheral interface adapters (PIA), or communications interface adapters. They may be as simple as the 16-pin 8T26 Quad Three-State Bus Transceiver or they may rival the microprocessor in size and complexity. The interface adapter may provide one or more of the following functions:

1. conversion between bidirectional and separate receive-transmit bus
2. increased drive levels
3. addressability
4. conversion to other logic levels
5. interrupt request signals
6. parallel-to-serial conversion
7. serial-to-parallel conversion
8. storage latches
9. change in speed or clock rate
10. synchronization

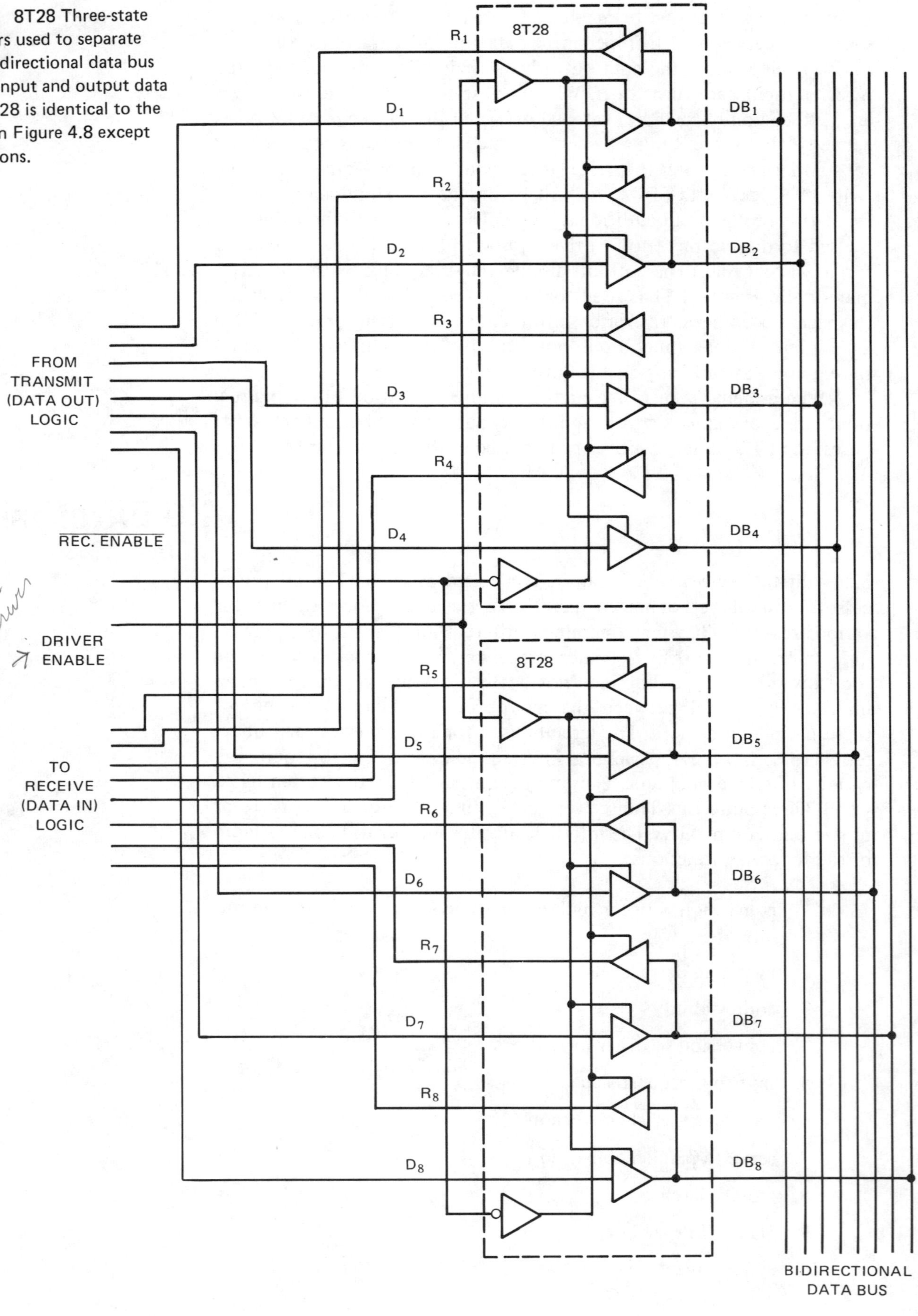

FIGURE 4.12 8T28 Three-state bus transceivers used to separate data from a bidirectional data bus into separate input and output data buses. The 8T28 is identical to the 8T26 shown in Figure 4.8 except for the inversions.

The 8T26 or 8T28 Quad Three-State Bus Transceiver, as applied in Figures 4.8 and 4.12 provide only a few of the functions mentioned. It can, however, be used in conjunction with other logic circuits to provide any of the functions listed. Another relatively simple I/O port is the 8212 shown in Figure 4.13. As an input or output port it provides a full 8 bits in a single 24-pin package. It is reversible and it can be configured in either direction, or a pair of 8212S can be paralleled for bidirectional transmission in each direction. It has provisions for generating an interrupt. Data can be stored in the latches and strobed through the output drivers at the proper time or the high level can be maintained on the clock (C) causing the data to pass directly through the latches from input to the drivers.

full duplex and half duplex

A number of octal buffers and latches ideal for use on 8-bit microprocessor data buses have been introduced to the integrated circuit

LOGIC DIAGRAM

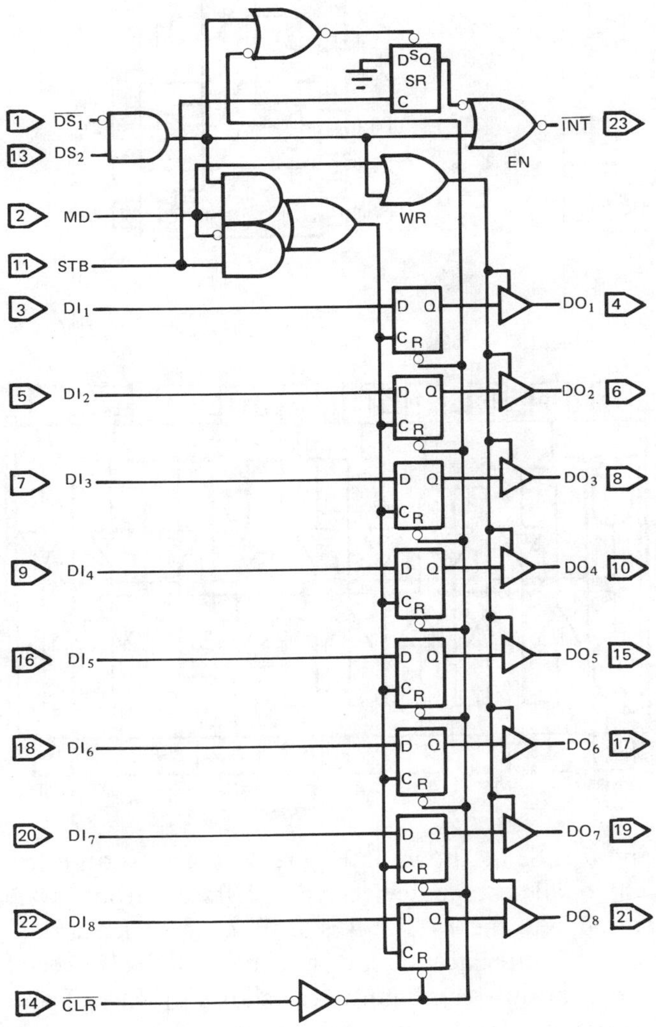

PIN CONFIGURATION

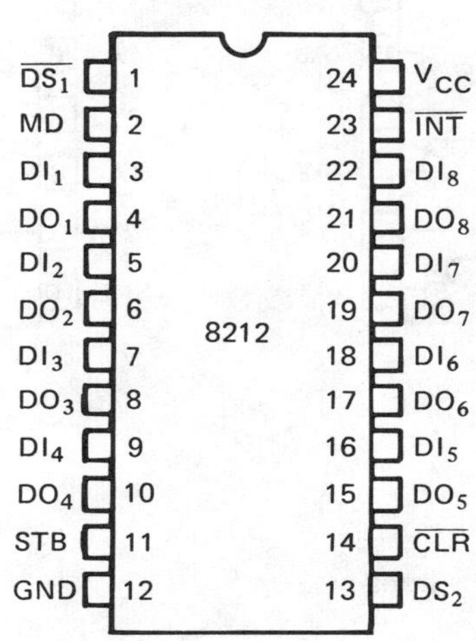

PIN NAMES

$DI_1 \cdot DI_8$	DATA IN
$DO_1 \cdot DO_8$	DATA OUT
$\overline{DS_1} \cdot DS_2$	DEVICE SELECT
MD	MODE
STB	STROBE
$\overline{INT}$	INTERRUPT (ACTIVE LOW)
$\overline{CLR}$	CLEAR (ACTIVE LOW)

FIGURE 4.13 Versatile 8-bit input/output port, the 8212 in addition to either input or output interface, provides an 8-bit storage latch and generates an interrupt signal. (*Courtesy of Intel Corporation*)

market recently. These include the octal buffer series shown in Figure 4.14. They are 3-state and are available in either Schottky or low power Schottky. Note that the buffers differ only by inversions of the buffers or the enable inputs. The 74SL241 can be used as a quad transceiver by connecting E and $\bar{E}$ and tieing input and outputs of respective buffers together. The 74LS245 shown in Figure 4.15 is an octal bus transceiver. It does not, however, provide separate receive and transmit buses as does the 8T26 and 8T28 bus transceivers.

FIGURE 4.14 Microprocessor Interface Buffers. These three buffer circuits are available in both Schottky and Low Power Schottky. The outputs are at high impedance when the drivers are turned off.

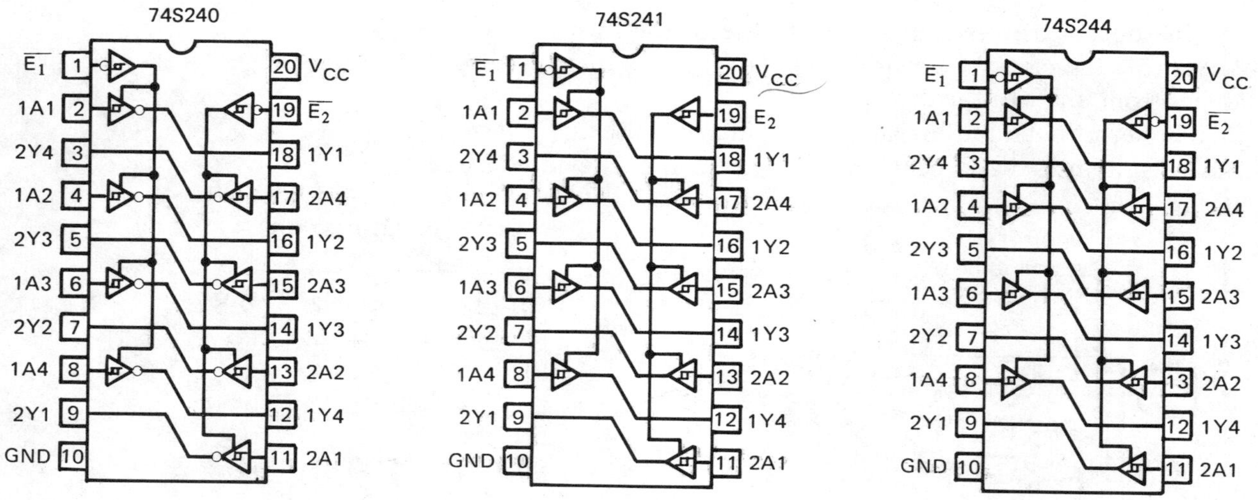

FIGURE 4.15 Octal bus transceiver (74LS245).

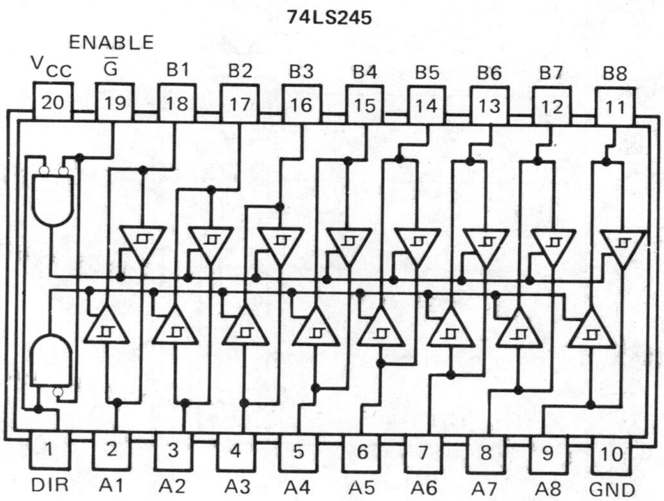

FUNCTION TABLE

ENABLE $\bar{G}$	DIRECTION CONTROL DIR	OPERATION
L	L	B data to A bus
L	H	A data to B bus
H	X	Isolation

H = high level, L = low level, X = irrelevant

The 74LS373 and 74LS374 shown in Figure 4.16 are useful interface circuits. They are octal storage devices with 3-state outputs. The 74LS373 is level operated, and the 74LS374 is leading-edge triggered.

Another widely used interface circuit is the UART (Universal Asynchronous Receiver Transmitter). Figure 4.17 shows the UART and a block diagram of its function. It contains both receiver and transmitter sections. The receiver section receives a serial-level train from the input, and it outputs 8-bit parallel data bytes to the microprocessor interface. The transmitter section accepts 8-bit parallel data from the micropro-

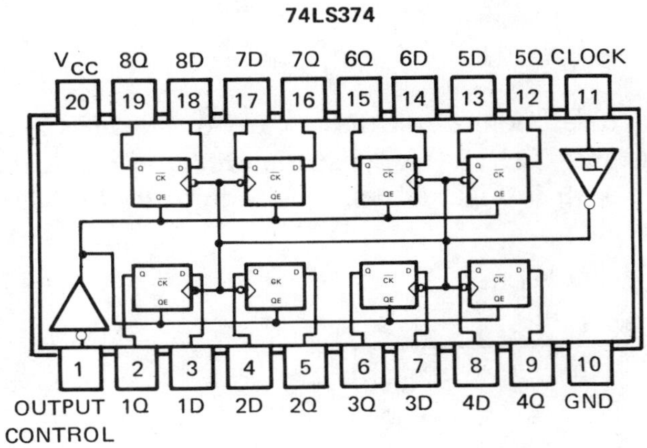

FUNCTION TABLE

OUTPUT CONTROL	CLOCK	D	OUTPUT
L	↑	H	H
L	↑	L	L
L	L	X	Q_0
H	X	X	Z

(a)

FIGURE 4.16 Octal interface circuits with storage. (a) octal edge-triggered flip-flops (74LS274), (b) octal D latches (74LS273).

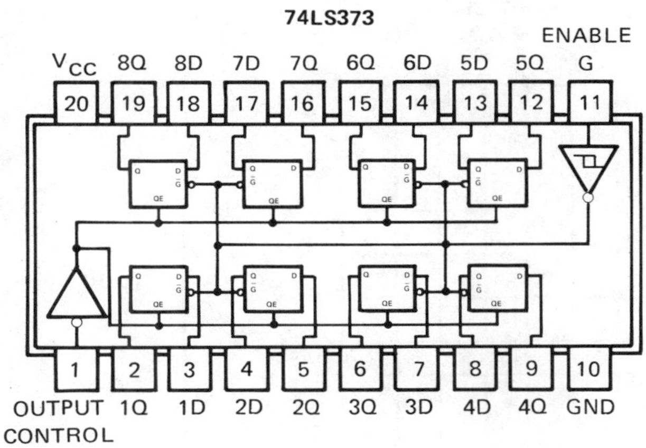

FUNCTION TABLE

OUTPUT CONTROL	ENABLE G	D	OUTPUT
L	H	H	H
L	H	L	L
L	L	X	Q_0
H	X	X	Z

(b)

FIGURE 4.17 The UART (Universal Asynchronous Receiver Transmitter) connected to a microprocessor interface to provide serial transmission and reception between the microprocessor and a peripheral device.

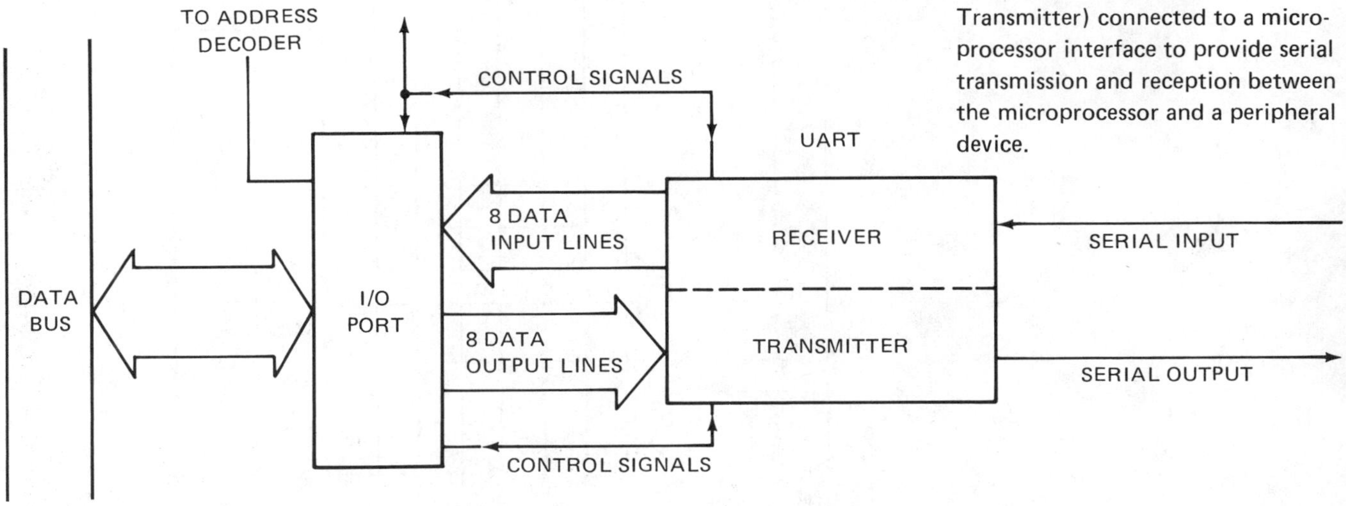

cessor interface, and converts it to an equivalent serial-pulse train which transmits over a single-output bus line. In addition to providing serial-to-parallel and parallel-to-serial conversions, the UART provides parity, parity check, and stop and start bits to properly time the transmission and reception of data.

4.7 The Multiplexed Bus

Another method used to economize on the number of bus lines is to multiplex information onto the bus. A typical **multiplexed bus** is the 8085 microprocessor shown in Figure 4.18. This circuit uses the same

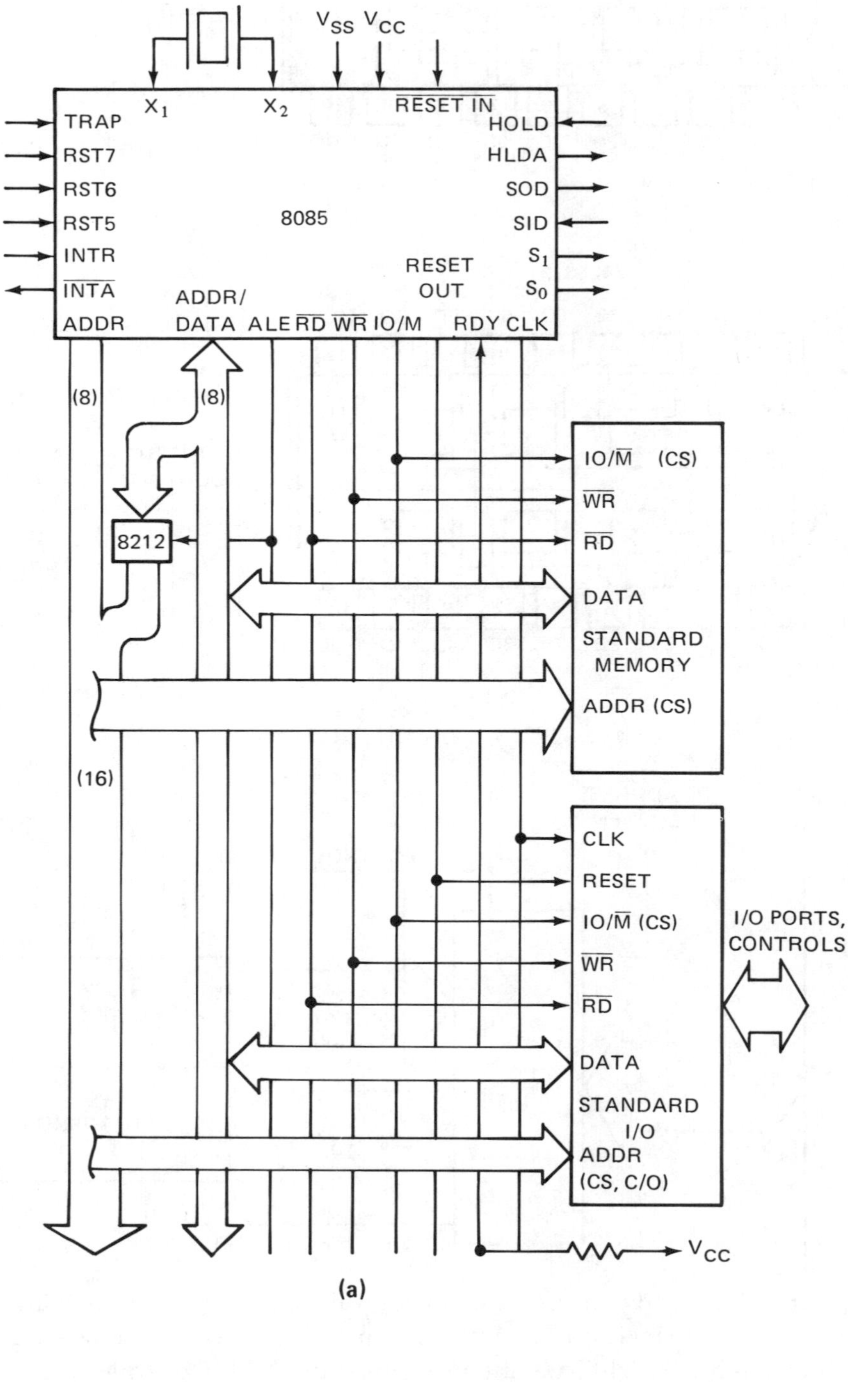

FIGURE 4.18 (a) 8085 Microprocessor using an 8212 as a latch circuit to latch the low order 8 bits of address. (*Courtesy Intel Corporation.*)

FIGURE 4.18 (b) Interconnections between 8085 microprocessor and the 8212 used as an address latch.

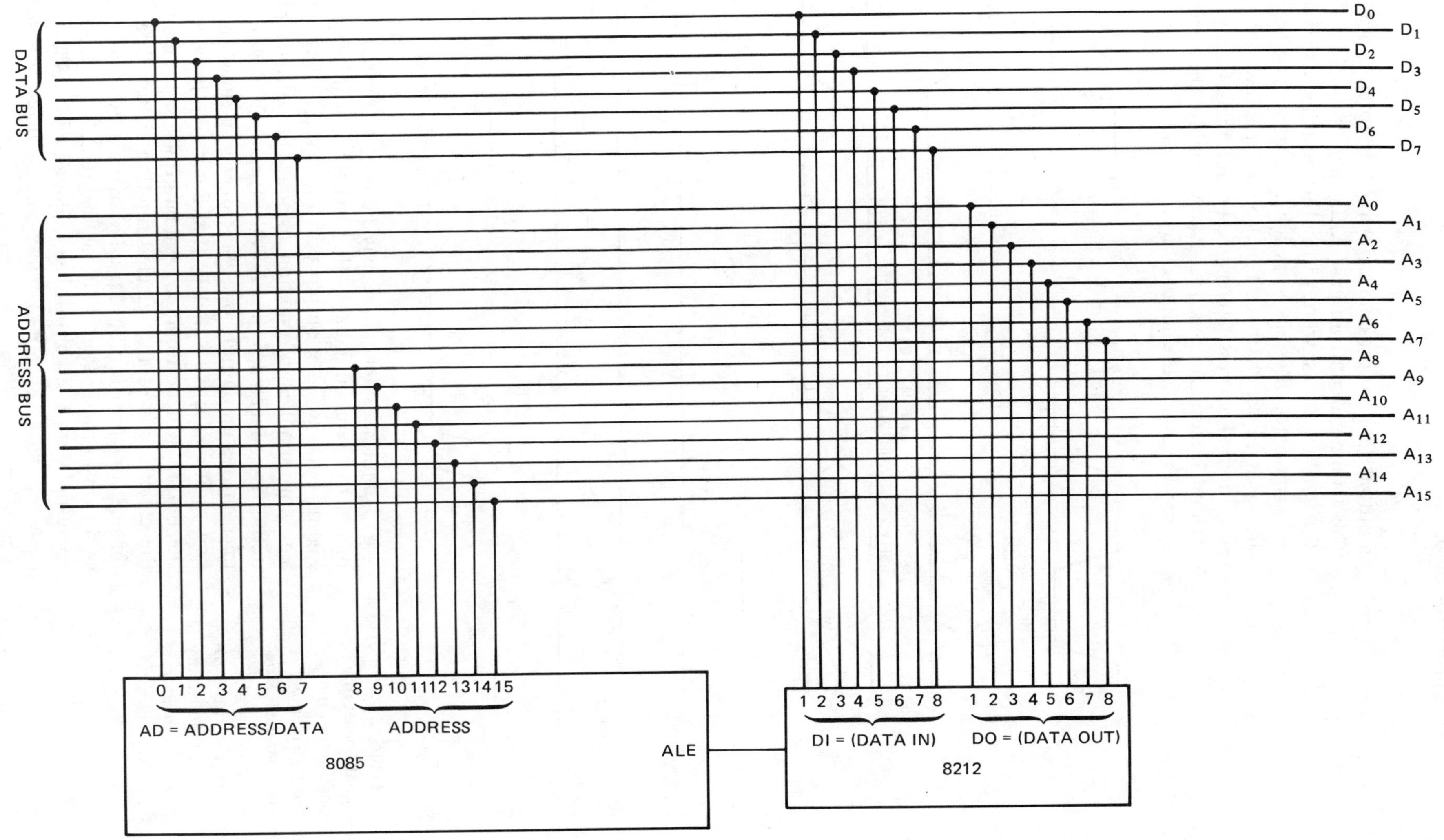

(b)

8 output pins for the data as for the low order eight bits of the address. This requires a control signal ALE (address latch enable) which is used to latch the address word within the receiving device during the address time and before the bus is switched to data. The timing for this bus is shown in Figure 4.19. To function on this bus, memory circuits must have internal address latches. To permit memory and peripheral devices without internal address latches to be employed, a separate latch circuit is used to expand the address bus to 16 bits.

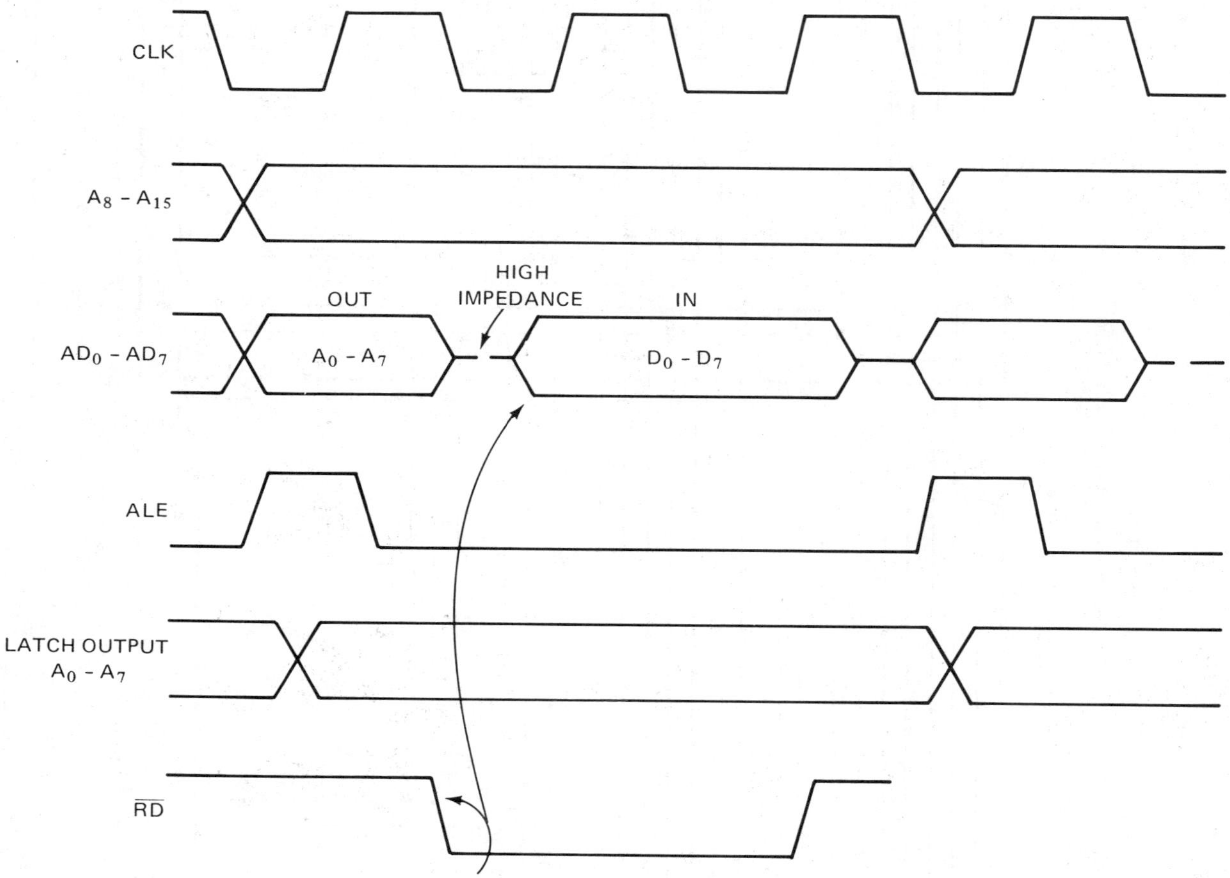

FIGURE 4.19 Timing diagram of the address and data buses of a 8085 microprocessor and the 8212 address latch during a memory read cycle. During the read cycle, the AD_0 - AD_7 address-data bus receives address from the microprocessor and data from the memory. During a write cycle both address and data are from the microprocessor.

A multiplex technique may be used to output a larger number of bits in the external data bus than exists in the microprocessor data bus. Figure 4.20 shows an output port on an 8-bit microprocessor data bus. The port supplies information to four, BCD flip-flops. Each data bit output is connected to an equivalent input of each quad flip-flop. The microprocessor outputs one 4-bit digit at a time; and with each digit, two additional bits (A and B) that determine to which set of flip-flops the output will be directed. A demultiplexer routes the R/W pulse to the clock input of the selected flip-flop circuit. The number of digits through this port can be expanded to eight by connecting the 74LS155 as shown in the bottom table of Figure 4.21 to form a 1-line to 8-line demultiplexer. The control bits included with each output would now be A, B, and C. Such a system would be using one 74LS155 device to replace three additional output ports. The saving in hardware is not

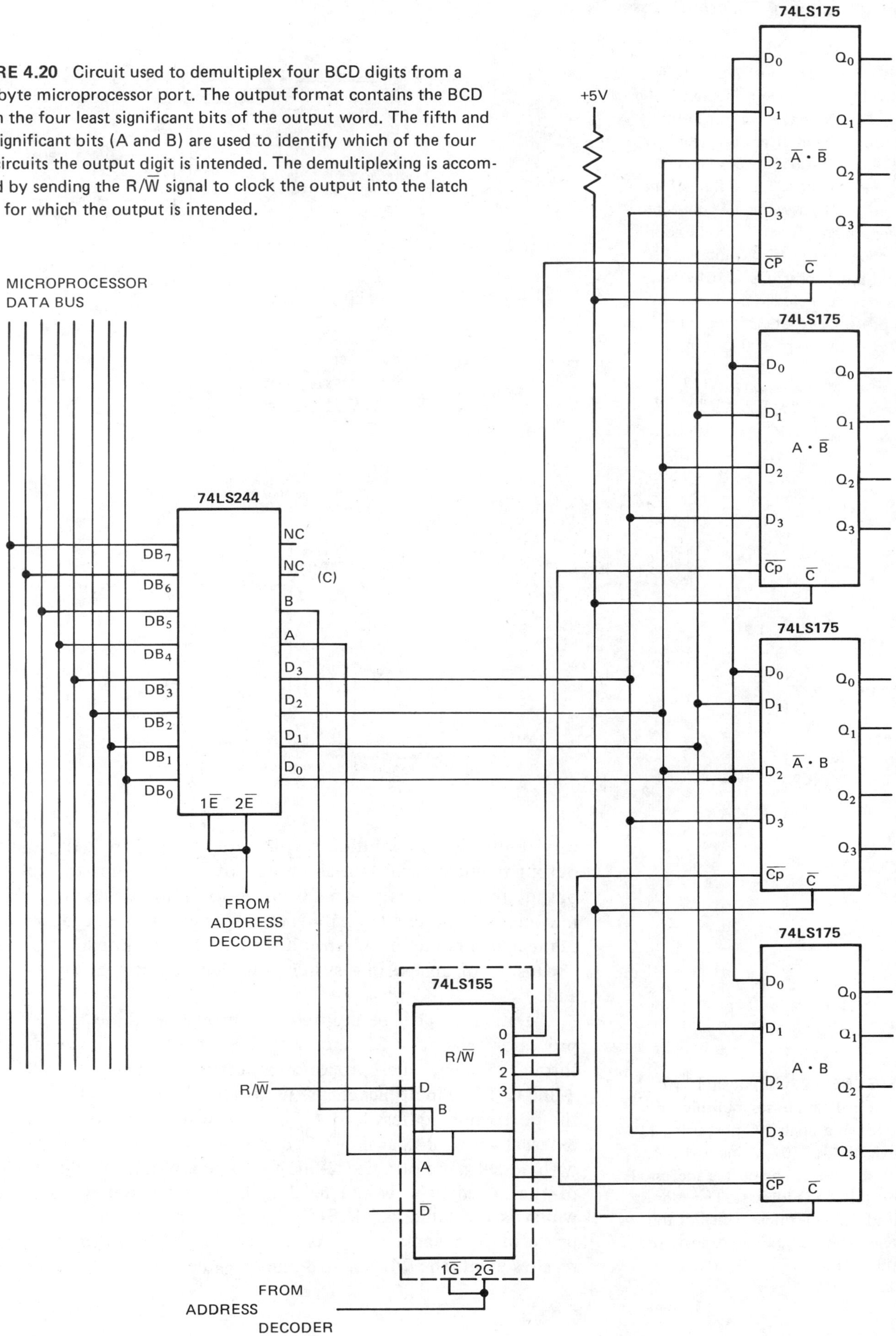

FIGURE 4.20 Circuit used to demultiplex four BCD digits from a single byte microprocessor port. The output format contains the BCD digit in the four least significant bits of the output word. The fifth and sixth significant bits (A and B) are used to identify which of the four latch circuits the output digit is intended. The demultiplexing is accomplished by sending the R/$\overline{W}$ signal to clock the output into the latch circuit for which the output is intended.

FIGURE 4.21 Dual 2-Line to 4-Line Decoder/Demultiplexer. If the eight BCD digits were to be output through the interface of Figure 4.20, the 74LS155 would be connected for the 1-line to 8-line function. The R/W would be connected through an OR gate with the address decoder to the 1G–2G inputs. An additional control level (C) would have to be included in the microprocessor output. This would connect to the combined D $\bar{D}$ inputs.

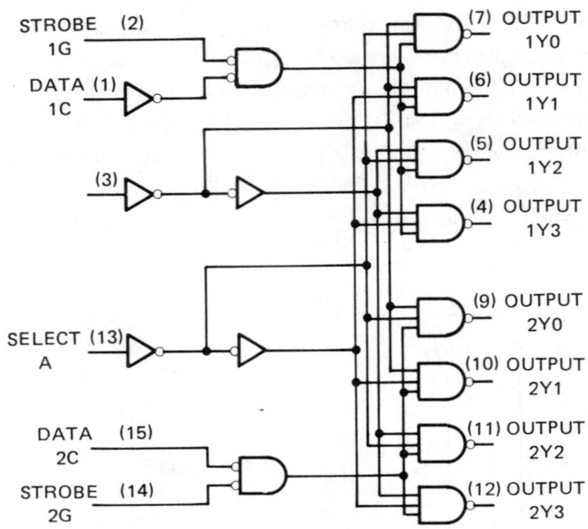

FUNCTION TABLES
2-LINE-TO-4-LINE DECODER
OR 1-LINE-TO-4-LINE DEMULTIPLEXER

INPUTS				OUTPUTS			
SELECT		STROBE	DATA	1Y0	1Y1	1Y2	1Y3
B	A	1G	1C				
X	X	H	X	H	H	H	H
L	L	L	H	L	H	H	H
L	H	L	H	H	L	H	H
H	L	L	H	H	H	L	H
H	H	L	H	H	H	H	L
X	X	X	L	H	H	H	H

INPUTS				OUTPUTS			
SELECT		STROBE	DATA	2Y0	2Y1	2Y2	2Y3
B	A	2G	2C				
X	X	H	X	H	H	H	H
L	L	L	L	L	H	H	H
L	H	L	L	H	L	H	H
H	L	L	L	H	H	L	H
H	H	L	L	H	H	H	L
X	X	X	H	H	H	H	H

FUNCTION TABLE
3-LINE-TO-8-LINE DECODER
OR 1-LINE-TO-8-LINE DEMULTIPLEXER

INPUTS				OUTPUTS							
SELECT			STROBE OR DATA	(0)	(1)	(2)	(3)	(4)	(5)	(6)	(7)
C†	B	A	G‡	2Y0	2Y1	2Y2	2Y3	1Y0	1Y1	1Y2	1Y3
X	X	X	H	H	H	H	H	H	H	H	H
L	L	L	L	L	H	H	H	H	H	H	H
L	L	H	L	H	L	H	H	H	H	H	H
L	H	L	L	H	H	L	H	H	H	H	H
L	H	H	L	H	H	H	L	H	H	H	H
H	L	L	L	H	H	H	H	L	H	H	H
H	L	H	L	H	H	H	H	H	L	H	H
H	H	L	L	H	H	H	H	H	H	L	H
H	H	H	L	H	H	H	H	H	H	H	L

†C = inputs 1C and 2C connected together
‡G = inputs 1G and 2G connected together
H = high level, L = low level, X = irrelevant

very impressive. In addition to the hardware required, the multiplexed output requires a substantial amount of programming to condition the output bytes correctly. An advantage to multiplexing must usually be in something other than hardware cost, such as, the need to reduce the number of lines used to transmit the data to a remote location or in the expansion of an existing system to which additional ports cannot be added.

Data may also be multiplexed through an input port of a microprocessor. Figure 4.22 shows two 8-bit external buses multiplexed through a single microprocessor input port. A pair of 74LS157 Quad 2-line to 1-line multiplexers are used. The I/O address decoder addresses the port while address lead A_0 is used to select between the two 8-bit external buses. Expansion to additional buses could be accomplished with added pairs of Quad 2-line to 1-line multiplexers, but the outputs of the added pairs would need to be ORed together. The 74LS256, which is the same as 74LS157 except for being 3-state output, might prove more advantageous. As the number of buses to be multiplexed reaches eight, the 74LS151, 8-line to 1-line multiplexers could be used.

FIGURE 4.22 (opposite) Two external data buses multiplexed through a single I/O port using a pair of 74LS157, 2-line to 1-line multiplexers. The port is addressed by adjacent addresses. The address lead A_0 determines which of the two external buses are transferred through the port.

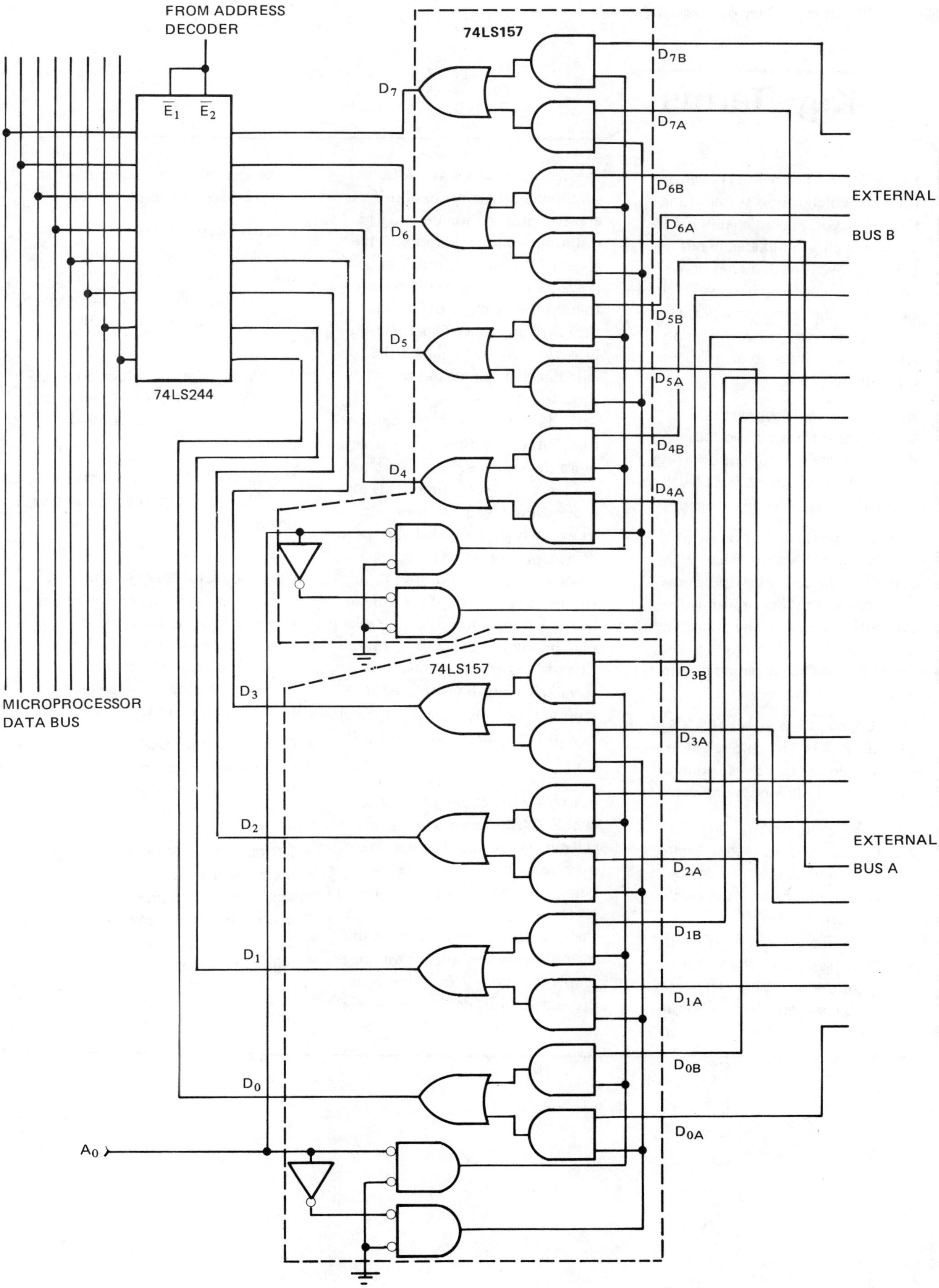

FROM ADDRESS DECODER
$\overline{E}_1$
$\overline{E}_2$
74LS244
MICROPROCESSOR DATA BUS
74LS157
D_7
D_6
D_5
D_4
D_3
D_2
D_1
D_0
D_{7B}
D_{7A}
D_{6B}
D_{6A}
D_{5B}
D_{5A}
D_{4B}
D_{4A}
D_{3B}
D_{3A}
D_{2A}
D_{1B}
D_{1A}
D_{0B}
D_{0A}
74LS157
A_0
EXTERNAL BUS B
EXTERNAL BUS A

Key Terms

Active State The high (1) or low (0) state which causes system functions to occur. A chip enable (CE) is active high. A chip enable not ($\overline{CE}$) is active low. A digital signal line may be changing between high and low in the active state but will return to a steady state of high or low when it is inactive or the signal is complete.

Buffer A circuit connected between transmitting and receiving devices for the purpose of boosting current drive, changing logic levels, or providing addressing control.

Bus A logic signal line or set of parallel signal lines to which numerous inputs and outputs are connected. Only one transmitter (output) is active on the bus at any given time. Not all receivers (input) need be (enabled) listening on the bus at any given time.

Chip Enable, Chip Select (CS, $\overline{CS}$, CE, $\overline{CE}$, E, $\overline{E}$) The chip select or chip enable can be used for one or more of the following functions.

(1) Address decoding: differs from an address lead in that it selects the entire memory device but no particular address within the memory.

(2) To prevent erratic output (glitches) during the switching of the address. When addresses are being changed, changes on different address leads will not occur simultaneously because of differences in propagation delays. The resulting erratic conditions at the edges of the data outputs can be prevented by using a chip select to hold the memory off during the switching time. This function is particularly important if the data lines are connected to edge activated devices.

(3) To prevent bus contention. Bus contention occurs when more than one device outputs to the bus at the same time. This may occur during read cycles on a bus to which high speed and low speed devices are connected. The high speed memory may output prior to the end of the hold time of the low speed memory. The chip select may be used to delay the outputting of the high speed memory. A less likely solution is to use the chip select of the slow speed memory to speed up the turnoff of its outputs.

Bus contention often occurs during a write cycle if the write enable (WE) becomes active late in the cycle. The data to be written may be on the bus but the memory being addressed functions as though it is being read and will output to the bus also between the time the memory is addressed and the time it sees the active WE. This can be prevented by using the chip select to deselect the memory until after the WE becomes active.

Inactive State The state of a digital signal driver when it is turned off. The open collector driver is inactive high. The 3-state driver is high impedance in the inactive state.

Interface A buffer which connects distinct systems or subsystems such as a computer and its peripheral devices.

Multiplexed Bus A bus which is shared by two or more instruments or functions on a time division basis.

Open Collector Bus A digital bus on which all outputs or drivers are open collector (See Figure 4.3) except that 3-state drivers may also function on an open collector bus. A pullup resistor is connected between the bus and V_{CC}.

Output Disable (OD) A control signal which places drivers of a 3-state device in the high impedance state.

3-State Bus (Tri-State)® A digital bus on which all outputs or drivers are 3-state. Only one driver may control the bus at any given time. The inactive drivers are held in the high impedance state.

Questions

4.1 Why should standard logic drivers not be tied to the same signal line?

4.2 How does the open collector output differ from the standard TTL totem pole output?

4.3 If the I_{OL} of each driver on an open collector bus is 20 mA, what is the minimum size of the pullup resistor?

4.4 What is the disadvantage of using the minimum size pullup resistor?

4.5 What is the disadvantage of having too high a value for a pullup resistor?

4.6 What additional control signal is needed for the operation of a 3-state logic circuit?

4.7 What is the state of the totem pole output transistors when a 3-state device is disabled?

4.8 If an open collector device is to be added to a tri-state bus, what added components must the bus have?

4.9 What conditions on a bus with all tri-state drivers would call for the addition of pullup resistors?

4.10 How does a chip select differ in function from an address lead?

4.11 What limits the number of drivers that can be connected to a 3-state bus?

4.12 How many low power Schottky (74LSXX) inputs can be driven on a bus on which all drivers are (74SXX)?

4.13 How many low power Schottky inputs can a B series CMOS circuit drive?

4.14 A memory circuit with common I/O and no output disable depends on what two inputs to switch the outputs to high impedance? What disadvantage is created by this?

4.15 What functions are performed by interface adapters?

4.16 List three standard circuits that can be used as bidirectional interface adapters.

4.17 List three standard circuits that are most advantageous for interface adapters in a single direction.

4.18 List three standard circuits that provide storage in addition to acting as interface adapters.

4.19 What is a UART?

4.20 What is the function of the ALE control signal of the 8085 microprocessor?

Problems

In Figure 4.8 two 8T26 bus transceivers are used to act as transmitters for a pair of CMOS quad latches.

4.1 Draw the circuit using a single 74LS240 as the buffers.

4.2 Draw the circuit as a receiver using the 74LS244 as the interface and the 4042B as latches at $V_{DD} = 5V$.

4.3 Draw the 2114 memory circuit connected to an 8T28 bus transceiver for the purpose of providing separate data in and data out.

4.4 Draw a timing diagram for the control signals used with the 2101 memory shown in Figure 4.11. Show relative timing of OD, CE, $\overline{CE}$, address, DI and DO needed to avoid decode glitches and bus contention.

4.5 Draw an output interface to an 8-bit bus which provides for parallel-to-serial conversion. Use 74LS165.

4.6 Draw an input interface to an 8-bit bus which provides serial-to-parallel-conversion. Use 74LS164.

4.7 Repeat Problem 4.2 with $V_{DD} = 12V$.

Chapter 5

Random Access Memories

Objectives

On completion of this chapter you will be able to:

- Match the correct RAM timing to a given microprocessor.
- Assemble a random access memory to a microprocessor address and data bus.
- Determine which segments of a memory map are occupied by a given memory connection.
- Design a decoder to prevent two or more memories from occupying duplicate segments of the address map.
- Connect memory circuits with fewer than eight data bits such that they provide a full data byte per address.
- Select from the available semiconductor memory devices the one most advantageous for a given microprocessor application.
- Connect a CMOS RAM for a battery backup memory system.
- Assemble a hexadecimal keyboard with the necessary debouncing and storage latches.
- Connect 7-segment display with multiplexers to read the data being entered and verified in a memory circuit.
- Use a counter to increment the address to a memory being loaded or verified.

5.1 Types of Memories

Any form of memory designed for use with digital computers can be used with microprocessors. These include not only the semiconductor memories connected directly to the microprocessor bus, but also magnetic tape, floppy discs, and other bulk storage auxiliary memories connected through interface adapters. The most important of these memories are the random access memory and the read only memory. Both of these memories are in fact random access. The important differences between them are that the RAM is a volatile read/write memory while the ROM is a nonvolatile read only memory. A **volatile memory** (RAM) loses the data stored in it whenever the power is removed. The **nonvolatile memory** (ROM) does not. In most microprocessor applications all but a small portion of memory is devoted to the storage of the program. Once the program is stored in memory, the running of the program can be repeated over and over as a read only operation. This means that ROM is ideal for program storage in a dedicated system or for a fixed routine within a general purpose system. ROM cannot be used where the program is subject to change.

A system using RAM for program storage has flexibility in application and is practical if supported by an auxiliary memory system such as magnetic tape or disc. The loading of programs into RAM through a keyboard prior to execution is a laborious job. Once it is loaded, however, it can be transferred to magnetic (nonvolatile) storage. If, at any time, the program is lost due to a power offage, it can be very quickly written back into RAM using the magnetic reader. Although a microprocessor system organized using only RAM is feasible, the use of only ROM rarely is, as both the storage of variables generated during the program and operation of the stack require read/write memory. Most practical systems contain both ROM and RAM.

5.2 RAM Specifications

When selecting a random access memory for use with a microprocessor, a careful comparison of the timing specifications of both devices is necessary. Figure 5.1 shows a portion of the timing diagrams of the 6800 microprocessor and a static RAM memory, which might be a candidate for connection to its bus. Note that during a memory read, the microprocessor outputs an address shortly after the leading edge of the ϕ_1 clock. Within the time ^tA (peripheral access time), the memory circuit must have the data on the bus and the data must remain for the period ^tDSR (data setup time) to be sure that the microprocessor will input it correctly.

To work with the 6800 microprocessor, a memory must have an **address access time** of less than 540 nanoseconds (nsec). For today's memory technology this is not a difficult specification to meet. Figure 5.1(a) shows the timing of the read cycle of a 2114 (1K-X-4 Static RAM). It indicates that from the time the address becomes stable until

SYMBOL	CHARACTERISTIC	MIN	TYP	MAX	UNIT
t_{AD}	Address Delay	–	220	300	ns
t_A	Peripheral Read Access Time $t_A = t_{ut} - (t_{AD} + t_{DSR})$	–	–	540	ns
t_{DSR}	Data Set-up Time (Read)	100	–	–	ns
t_H	Input Data Hold Time	10	–	–	ns
t_H	Output Data Hold Time	10	25	–	ns
t_{AH}	Address Hold Time (Address, R/W, VMA)	50	75	–	ns

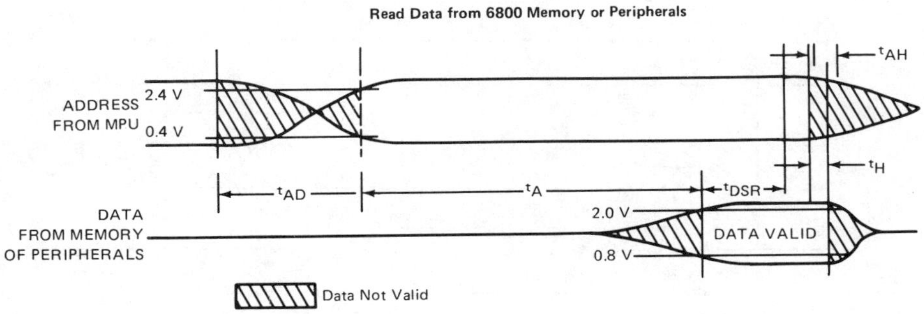

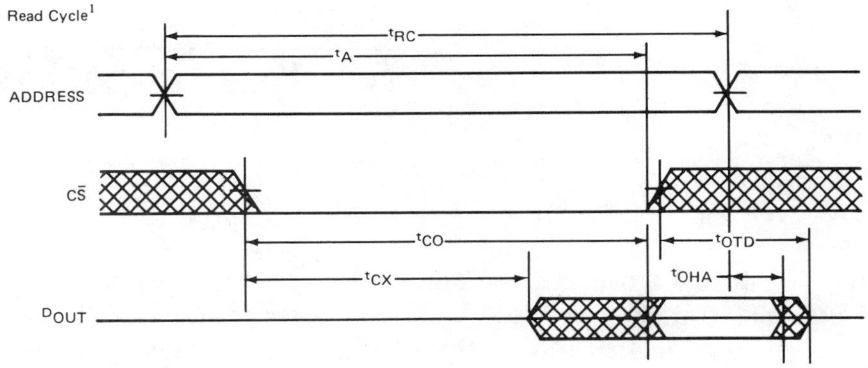

Note: 1 $\overline{WE}$ is high for a Read Cycle

SYMBOL	PARAMETER	2114, 2114L MIN	2114, 2114L MAX	UNIT
READ CYCLE				
t_{RC}	Read Cycle Time	450		nsec
t_A	Access Time		450	nsec
t_{CO}	Chip Select to Output Valid		150	nsec
t_{CX}	Chip Select to Output Enabled	0		nsec
t_{OTD}	Chip Deselect to Output Off	0	100	nsec
t_{OHA}	Output Hold From Address Change	10		nsec

FIGURE 5.1 (a) Comparison of 6800 microprocessor read data timing with the read cycle timing of the 2114 RAM proves them to be compatible.

FIGURE 5.1 (b) The write cycle timing of the 2114 RAM.

Data Storage When $\overline{WE}$ is high, the data input buffers are inhibited to prevent erroneous data from being written into the array. As long as $\overline{WE}$ remains high, the data stored cannot be affected by the Address, Chip Select, or Data I/O logic levels or timing transitions.

Data storage also cannot be affected by $\overline{WE}$, Addresses, or the I/O ports as long as $\overline{CS}$ is high. Either $\overline{CS}$ or $\overline{WE}$ or both can prevent extraneous writing due to signal transitions. Data within the array can only be changed during Write time — defined as the overlap of $\overline{CS}$ low and $\overline{WE}$ low. The addresses must be properly established during the entire Write time plus t_{WR}.

Internal delays are such that address decoding propagates ahead of data inputs and therefore no address setup time is required. If the Write time precedes the addresses, the data in previously addressed locations, or some other location, may be changed. Addresses must remain stable for the entire Write cycle but the Data Inputs may change. The data which is stable for t_{DW} at the end of the Write time will be written into the addressed location.

SYMBOL	CHARACTERISTICS	MIN	MAX	UNIT
t_{WC}	Write Cycle Time	450		nsec
t_{AW}	Address to Write Setup Time	0		nsec
t_{W}	Write Pulse Width	200		nsec
t_{WR}	Write Release Time	0		nsec
t_{OTW}	Write to Output Off	0	100	nsec
t_{DW}	Data to Write Overlap	200		nsec
t_{DH}	Data Hold	0		nsec

Write Cycle

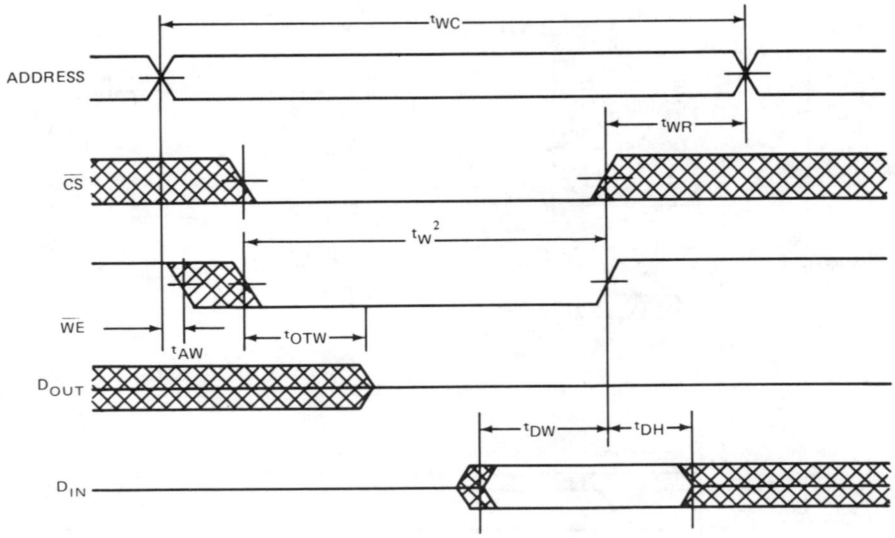

Note: 2 t_{W} is measured from the latter of CS or $\overline{WE}$ going low to the earlier of CS or WE going high.

the time the data becomes valid (address access time) requires a maximum of 450 nsec, well ahead of the 540 nsec required by the 6800. The t_{OHA} parameter tells us that the data will remain valid until at least 10 nsec after the address changes. This meets the 100 nsec data setup time (t_{DSR}) requirement and the input data hold t_{H} of the 6800 microprocessor.

In addition to the address to data timing, the chip select or chip enable timing must be considered. Usually chip select access times are shorter than address access times. For most microprocessor applications the chip select is tied to an address bus line and the address-to-data times are the limiting parameters. This may not be the case for all memories or even for all applications of this memory. In spite of the fact that the chip selects are often connected to an address bus line, there is an important functional difference between the chip select and an address. When the memory is deselected the output is turned off. On the other hand, the address access time does not mean that the data output is turned off prior to the access time. It specifies only that the output may not be valid until after the access time. For applications, such as a multiplexed bus in which the bus is not available for some time after the address becomes stable, the chip select must be used to hold the memory output buffers off until the data bus becomes available. In these applications, the microprocessor usually provides a correctly timed control signal (data bus enable, ϕ_2 clock, etc.) to which the chip select or chip enable can be connected.

Comparing the write cycles is slightly more difficult in that there is an additional signal from which timing must be considered. In addition to a stable address and chip select, the memory must receive a properly timed write enable. The write enable remains in the inactive state during the read cycle. The question being considered is whether the memory will write the data in response to the address and control signals received from the microprocessor at the time the microprocessor data output is valid. Will it do so in spite of any fluctuating conditions on the bus before and after the valid data period and will the memory output drivers be turned off in time to avoid interfering with the incoming data? Figure 5.1(b) shows the write cycle timing diagrams of the 2114 static RAM.

The write to output off (^{t}OTW) requires a maximum of 100 nsec. If having data on the bus during this period creates a problem, the write enable ($\overline{WE}$) can precede the $\overline{CS}$ (but not the address) by 100 nsec. The write pulse width (^{t}W) is the period during which both the $\overline{CS}$ and $\overline{WE}$ are active. This total time must be at least 200 nsec. The correct data in must be on the bus during the final 200 nsec of the write time.

5.3 RAM Size and Organization

As most widely used microprocessors have an 8-bit data bus, it would seem that random access memories with 8-bit data I/O would be the most practical to use. This is true for small blocks of RAM where a circuit like the 128- X 8-bit memory shown in Figure 5.2 can be used. The address pins A_0 through A_6 connect to these respective address bus lines. The chip select leads (CS or $\overline{CS}$) may connect either to one of the higher address lines or the CS leads may be selected (enabled) by a fixed 1 and the $\overline{CS}$ leads selected by a fixed 0. Address and select leads are both involved in the addressing scheme. The select leads either enable or inhibit the entire memory chip while the state of A_0 through A_6 determines which single address byte within the chip is read or written. The total number of combined address and select bits is 13. Unless some auxiliary decoding circuits are used to involve the additional 3 bits of the 16-bit address, this chip will occupy more than a single 128-word block within the total 64K word memory map.

If we think in terms of address pages, this single circuit connected as shown in Figure 5.3 will occupy the lower half of each **memory page** and only the upper halves of each page would be available for other uses. This means that the data byte stored in address 05_H of this mem-

FIGURE 5.2 The 6810 TTL RAM has 128 8-bit bytes. This requires only 7 address leads, but there are 6 chip select (enable) inputs which are useful for selecting or deselecting the chip. (*Courtesy of American Microsystems Incorporated*)

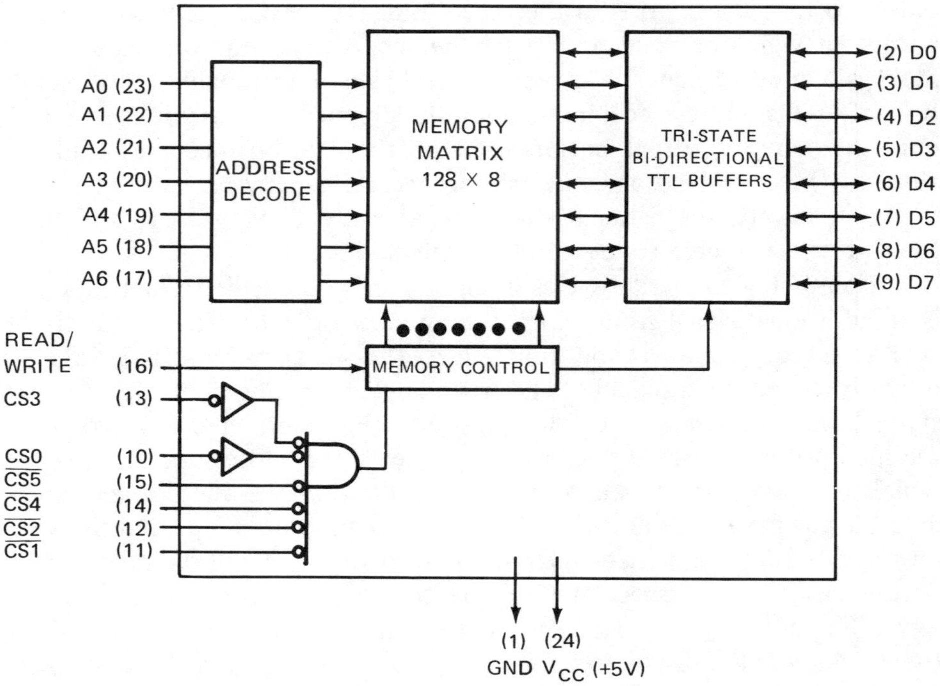

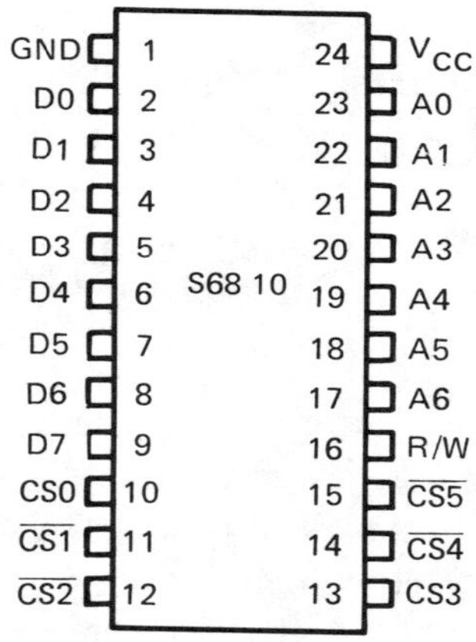

BLOCK DIAGRAM

Features

- Organized as 128 Bytes of 8 Bits
- Static Operation
- Bi-Directional Three-State Data Input/Output
- Six Chip Enable Inputs (Four Active Low, Two Active High)
- Single 5-Volt Power Supply
- TTL Compatible
- Maximum Access Time = 1.0μs for S6810
  575 ns for S6810-1

FIGURE 5.3 The 6810 connected as shown will occupy the lower half of each page in the entire 64K memory map.

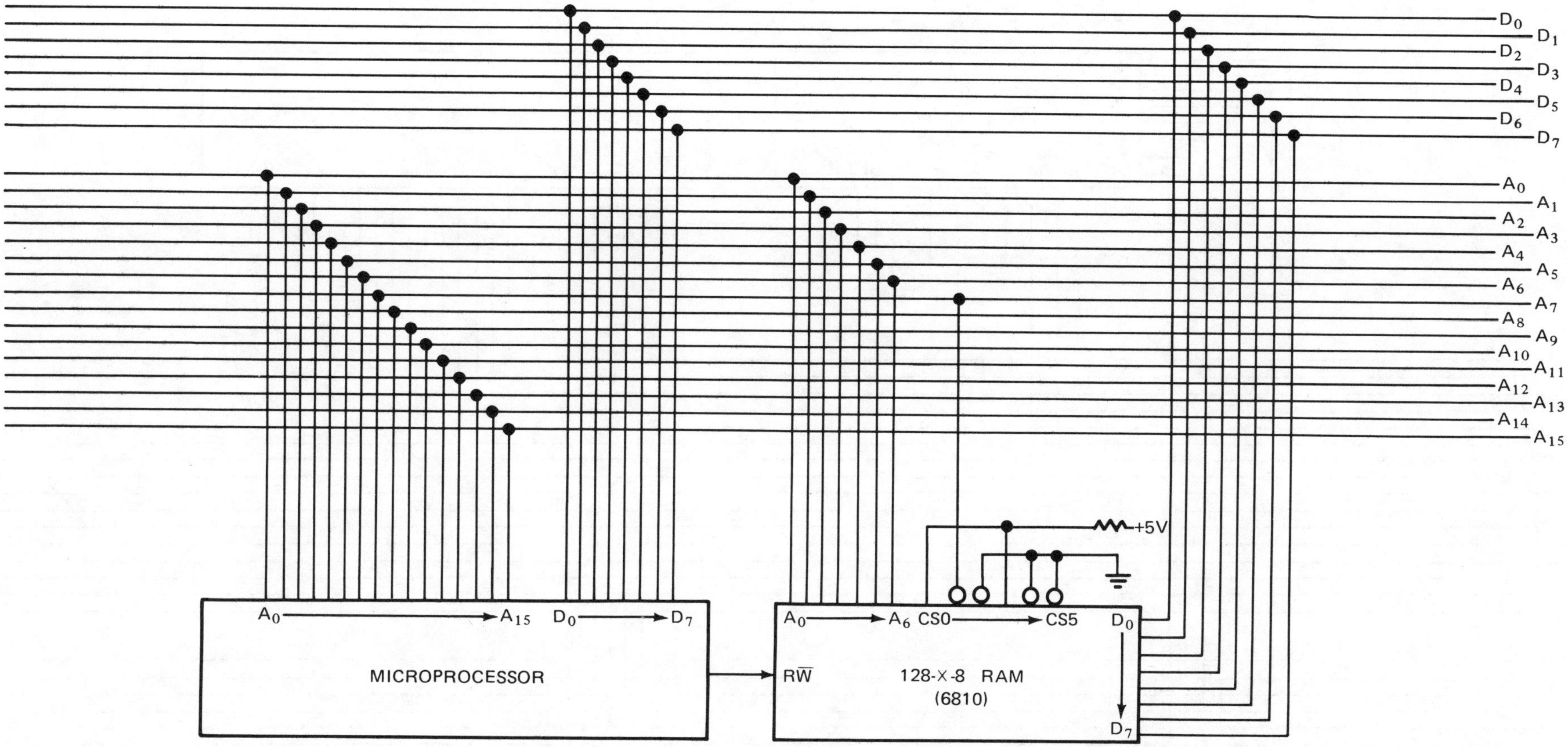

Address of this memory is EEEE EEEE 0XXX XXXX

X = Will be 1 or 0 depending on byte being addressed.
0 = Memory will be selected only when this bit is 0 (low).
E = Memory will be selected for either 1 or 0 in this bit (causes duplication of addresses within the memory map).

FIGURE 5.4 (a) The 6810 with its four $\overline{CS}$ leads connected as shown will occupy memory blocks as shown in the memory map, **(b)**. **(c)** Connecting the two CS leads to A11 and A12 will reduce the memory map occupancy to the lower half of eight pages.

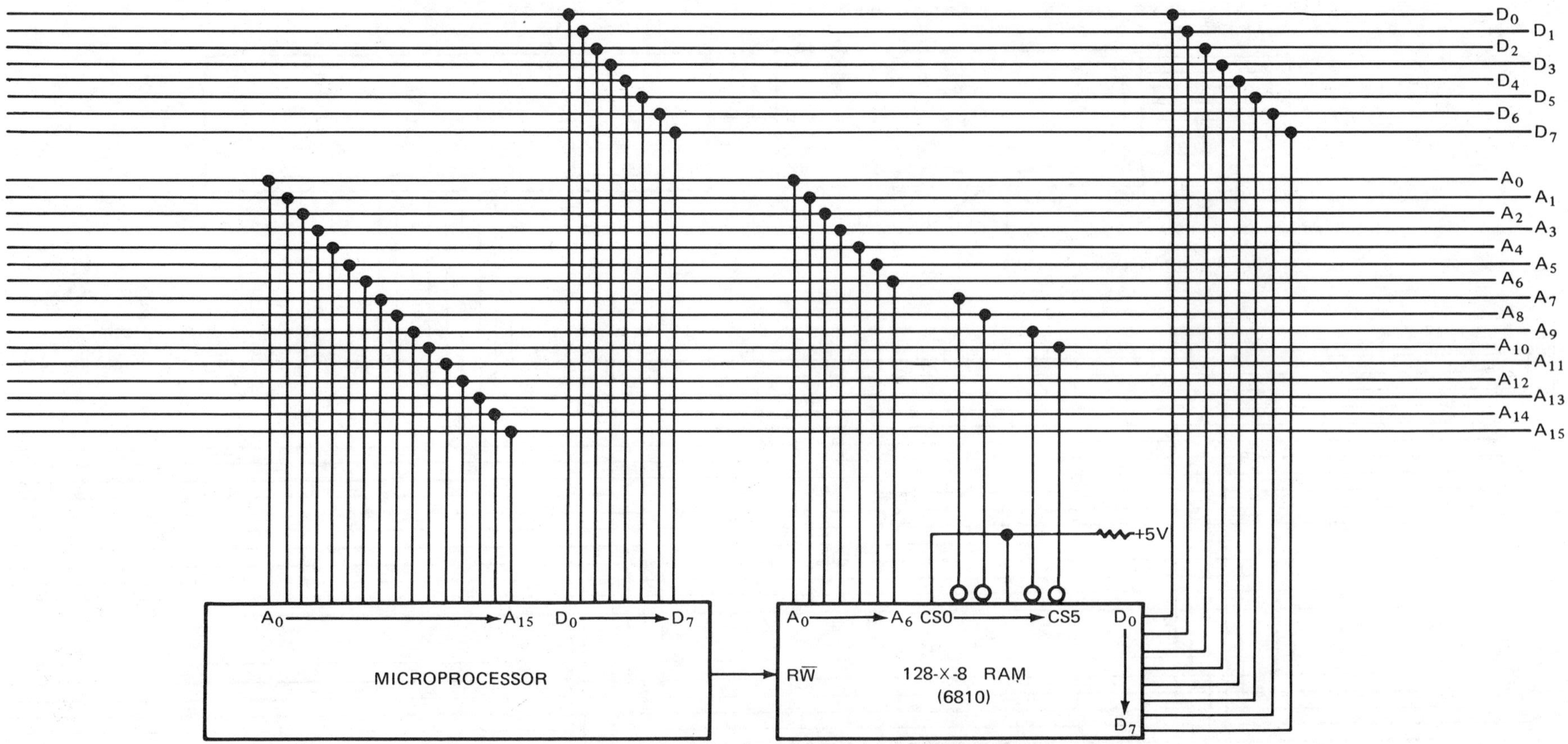

Address of this memory is EEEE E000 0XXX XXXX

X = Will be 1 or 0 depending on byte being addressed.
1 = Memory will be selected only when this bit is 1 (high).
0 = Memory will be selected only when this bit is 0 (low).
E = Memory will be selected for either 1 or 0 in this bit (causes duplication of the addresses within the memory map).

ory will appear on the data bus any time the microprocessor reads addresses 0005_H or 0105_H or 0205_H or for address 05_H with any page address from 00_H to FF_H. We only need one address for each memory byte, but because the higher order address bits are not connected to it, we will be addressing each location in this memory with 256 of the microprocessor's addresses. Even though half of the microprocessor's 64K memory map is occupied by this small RAM, we are only getting practical use equal to half a page of memory. We can connect the remaining chip select pins to address leads and recover more of the available memory map for other use. The connection shown in Figure 5.4(a) will occupy the memory map as shown in 5.4(b).

FIGURE 5.4 (b) Addresses in hexadecimal.

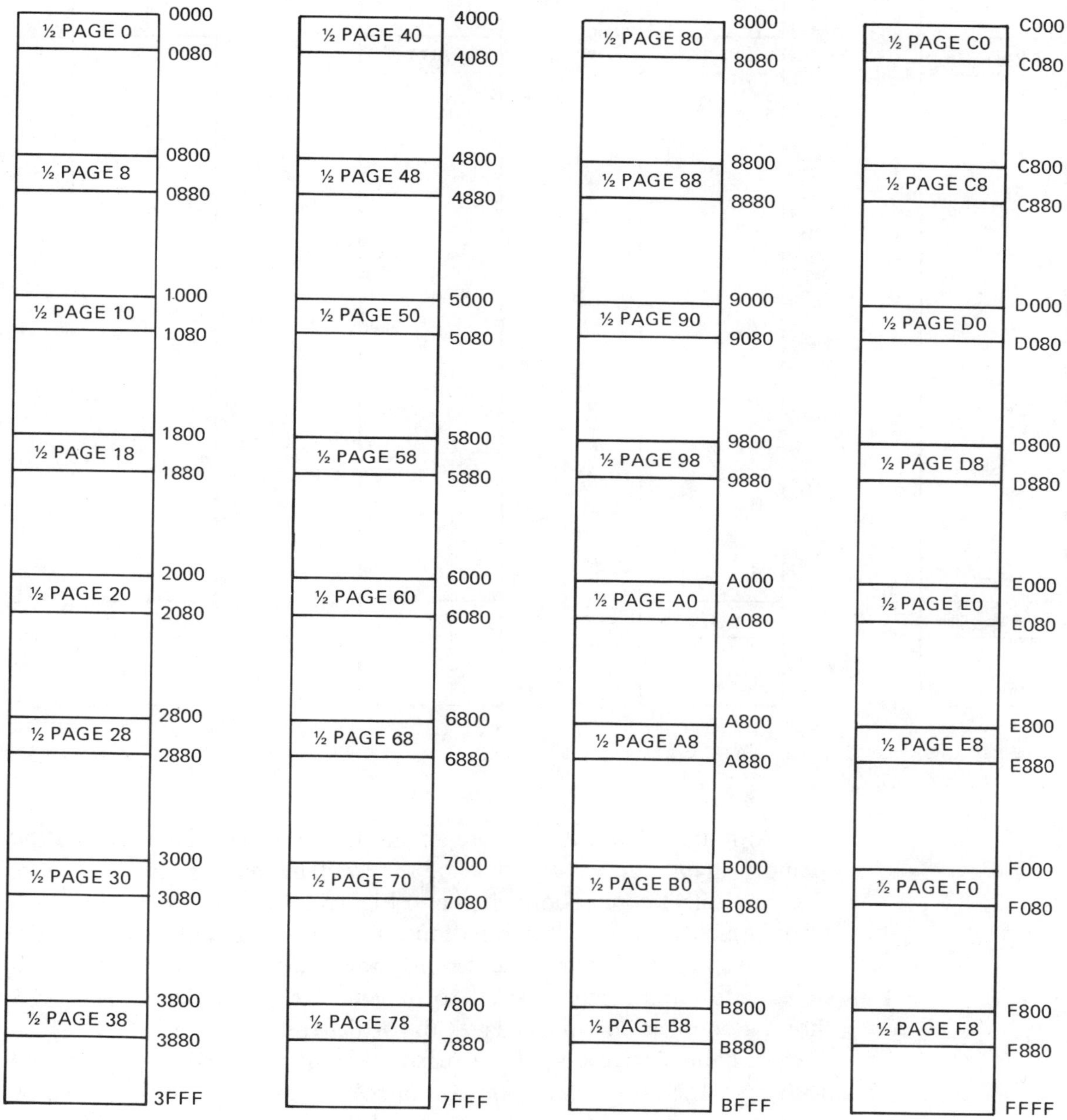

(b)

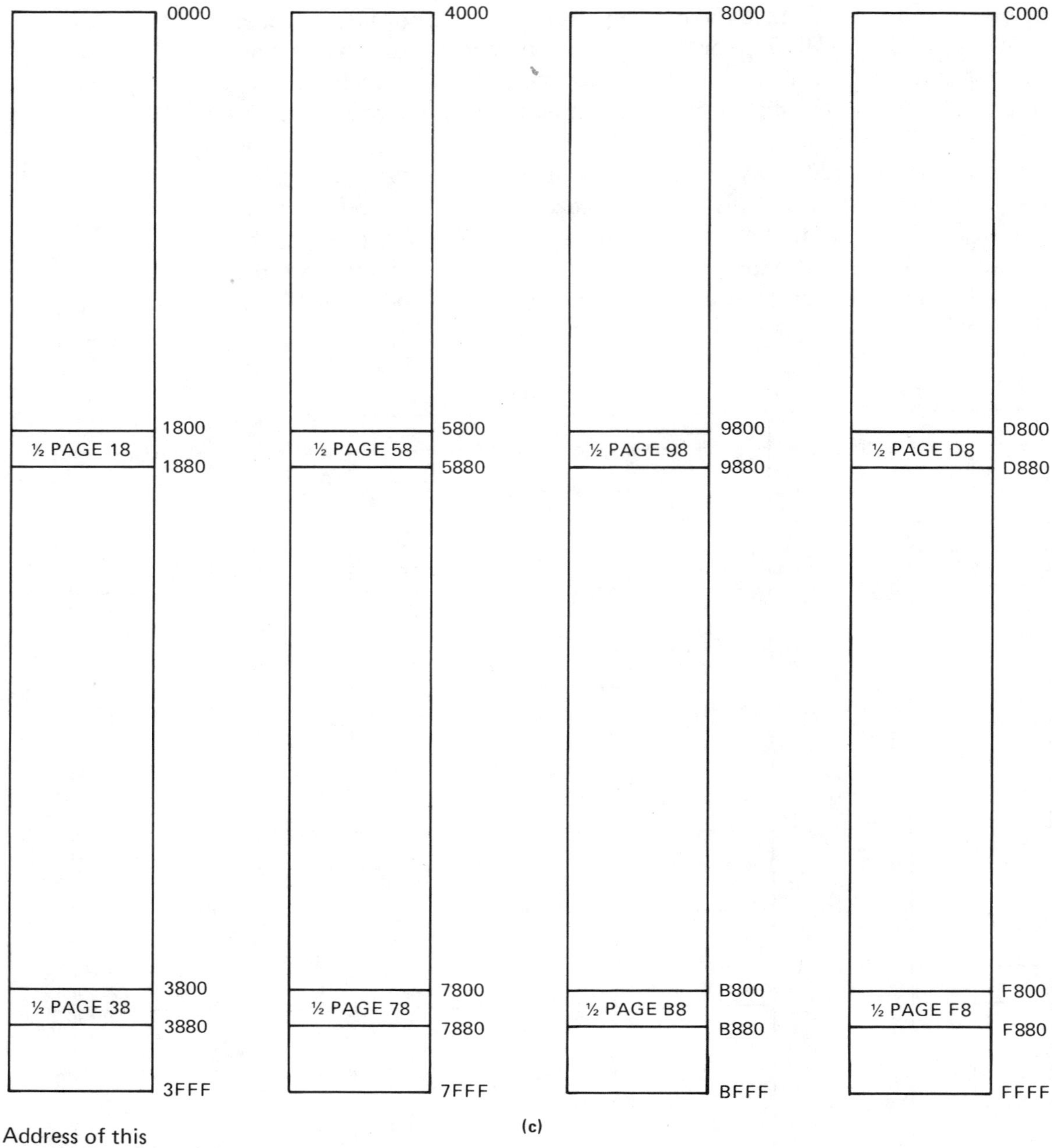

FIGURE 5.4 (c) Address of this memory is: EEE1 1000 0XXX XXXX.

Although it occupies more than the necessary 128 bytes of the memory map, it leaves the bulk of the available address for other use. The chip select connections shown in Figure 5.4 are only one of numerous combinations. Each combination results in a different memory map. For a system in which the entire memory map must be put to use, a single gate circuit can be used to expand the chip select. Figure 5.5 shows a connection which places the 128 bytes of this memory on the bottom half of page 03_H. By a rearrangement of the address leads connected to the chip selects and the auxiliary gates, the system can be structured to locate the 6810 on any of the 256 pages of the microprocessor's 16-bit address system.

FIGURE 5.5 6810 memory connected to the microprocessor so that the addresses are not repeated elsewhere in the memory map. The OR gate is used to expand one of the chip selects so that all 16 address leads are involved in the addressing. The memory is connected to occupy the lower half of memory page 03_H.

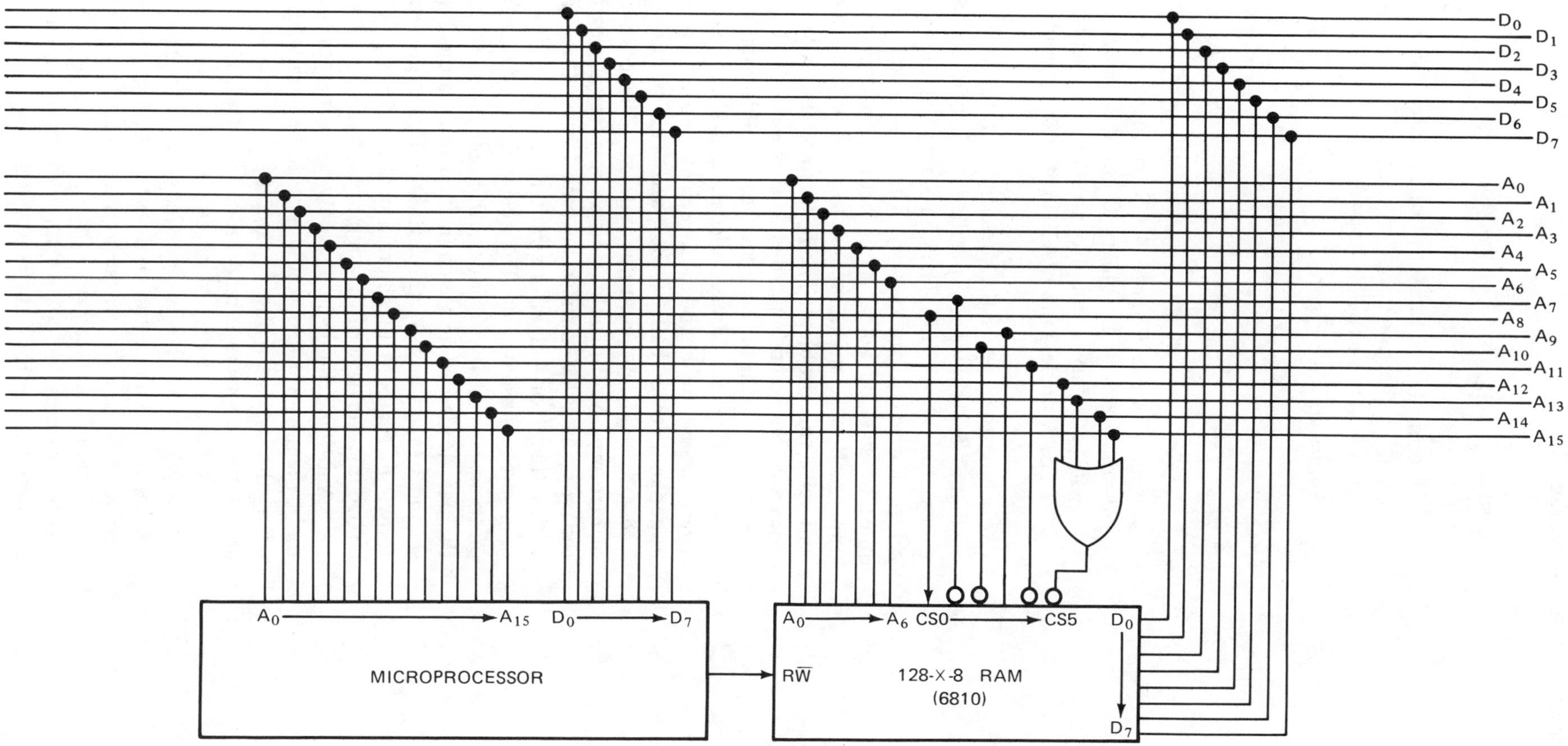

Address of this memory is 0000 0011 0XXX XXXX

X = Will be 1 or 0 depending on byte being addressed.

1 = Memory will be selected only when this bit is 1 (high).

0 = Memory will be selected only when this bit is 0 (low).

Example

Reconnect the address bus of the circuit in Figure 5.5. To place the 6810 in the upper half of page 63_H use either a quad NOR or quad AND to expand the address.

Solution: See Figure 5.6.

For the address $63XX_H$ = 0110 0011 1XXX XXXX_2
↑
upper half of page

Needed are 5 CS and 4 $\overline{CS}$. If there were enough selects, those leads that will be binary 0 could connect to $\overline{CS}$ and those that will be binary 1 could connect to CS, but there are only 4 $\overline{CS}$ and 2 CS. A single 4 input AND gate can expand the CS sufficiently.

Expanding the size of the memory to a full page can be accomplished, as Figure 5.7 shows, by paralleling all of the address and select leads except for the A7 bus. The 6810 used for the lower half page must be selected when A7 is low (0). The 6810 used for the upper half page must be selected when A7 is high (1). Connecting A7 to a CS of the upper half page memory and to a $\overline{CS}$ of the lower half page memory will solve this problem. The D_0 through D_7 data leads of the two memories are connected in parallel to the respective D_0 to D_7 data bus lines. The memory can be expanded to an additional page using four 6810s by paralleling all address and data and select leads except A7 and A8. These would be encoded to select between pages and between the upper and lower half of the page. The memory expansion using the 128-X-8 RAM may continue until at 8 devices we would have 4 pages of memory. At this point a larger memory is worth considering. Unfortunately, as RAM devices become larger, they are generally supplied with either 1 or 4 data bits rather than the 8 that are needed to fill the microprocessor data bus. The device with 4 data bits requires that a pair of them be wired with identical connections to the address bus, while the data leads of one are connected to data bus D_0 through D_3 and the second to data bus D_4 through D_7. This type data bus connection was shown in Figure 4.11 where a pair of 256-X-4 RAMS were connected to occupy one page of the memory map.

Another reliable and widely used memory device is the 1K X 1. Eight memory devices would have to be paralleled to the address bus in using the 1K X 1, but 4 pages of memory would result. Figure 5.8 shows the connection of 8 1K-X-1 devices. Here again an auxiliary decoder is needed to select the memory for only 1024 addresses of the memory map. Unlike the previous two devices we discussed, the 2102 has separate data in and data out pins. A check of the microprocessor timing indicates that these may be connected together to the bidirectional data bus. This causes no difficulty with the 2102 as the output driver is in high impedance state whenever the input is enabled (during a write cycle). A look at the 6800 microprocessor timing shows that the

FIGURE 5.6 6810 (128-X-8 memory) connected to occupy the upper half of memory page 63_H.

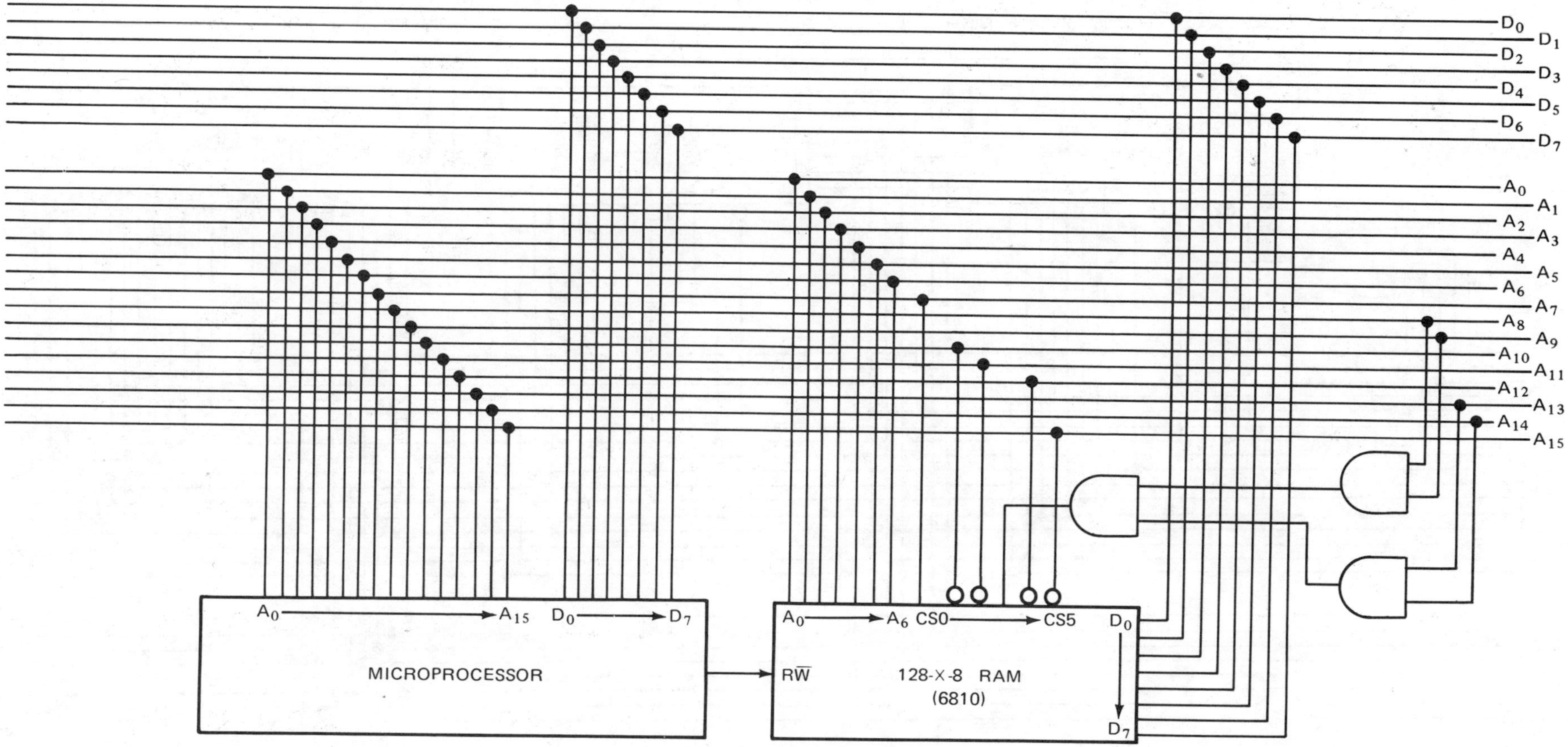

Address of this memory is $\overbrace{0110}^{6}\ \overbrace{0011}^{3}$ 1XXX XXXX

X = Will be 1 or 0 depending on byte being addressed.

1 = Memory will be selected only when this bit is 1 (high).

0 = Memory will be selected only when this bit is 0 (low).

FIGURE 5.7 Two 6810 memories connected to the microprocessor bus to form a 256-X-8 memory. The data outputs of both are connected in parallel to the data bus. Address and chip select leads with the exception A_7 are connected in parallel to the address bus. One 6810 is selected for the lower half page when A_7 is 0. The other 6810 is selected for the upper half page when A_7 is 1.

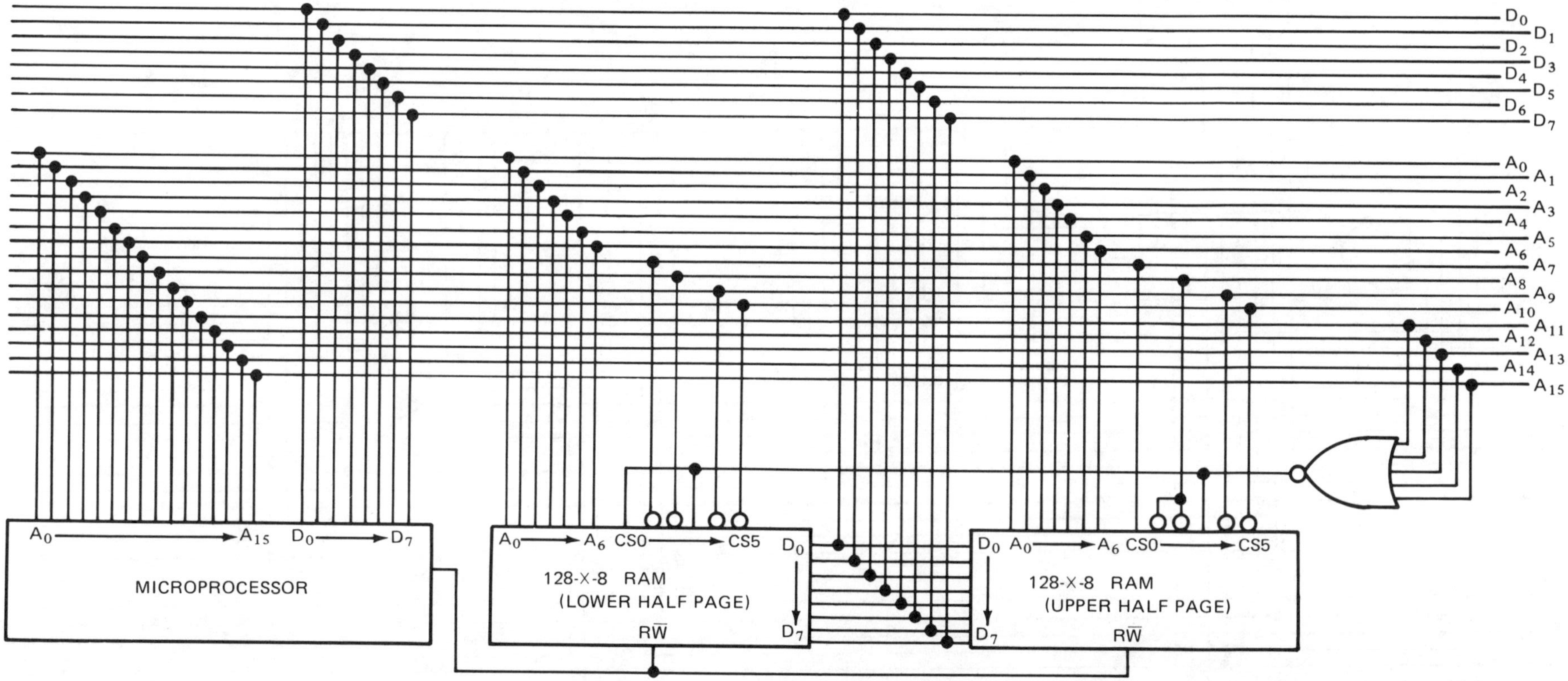

Address of this memory is 0000 0000 [X] XXX XXXX

X = Will be 1 or 0 depending on byte being addressed.

[X] = Byte will be addressed in chip or chips selected by 1 or 0 in this bit.

0 = Memory will be selected only when this bit is 0 (low).

FIGURE 5.8 Eight 2102 1K-X-1 memories must be connected with their address leads in parallel. The data in and data out leads are shorted and each chip data lead is connected to a different address bus line. This forms a 1K-X-8 memory. The 1 of 8 decoder (binary to octal) is useful in restricting the occupancy of this 1K block of memory. As connected it will occupy the lower 4 pages and due to a lack of connection to the A_{15} address line it will occupy a duplicate 1K block from 8000_H to 83FF. **Note:** The term 1K is loosely used in description of memory size in that 1K is used to indicate 1024. This abbreviated description also applies to multiples of 1K in that a 4K RAM is really a 4096-bit RAM, a 16K-RAM is 16,384 bits.

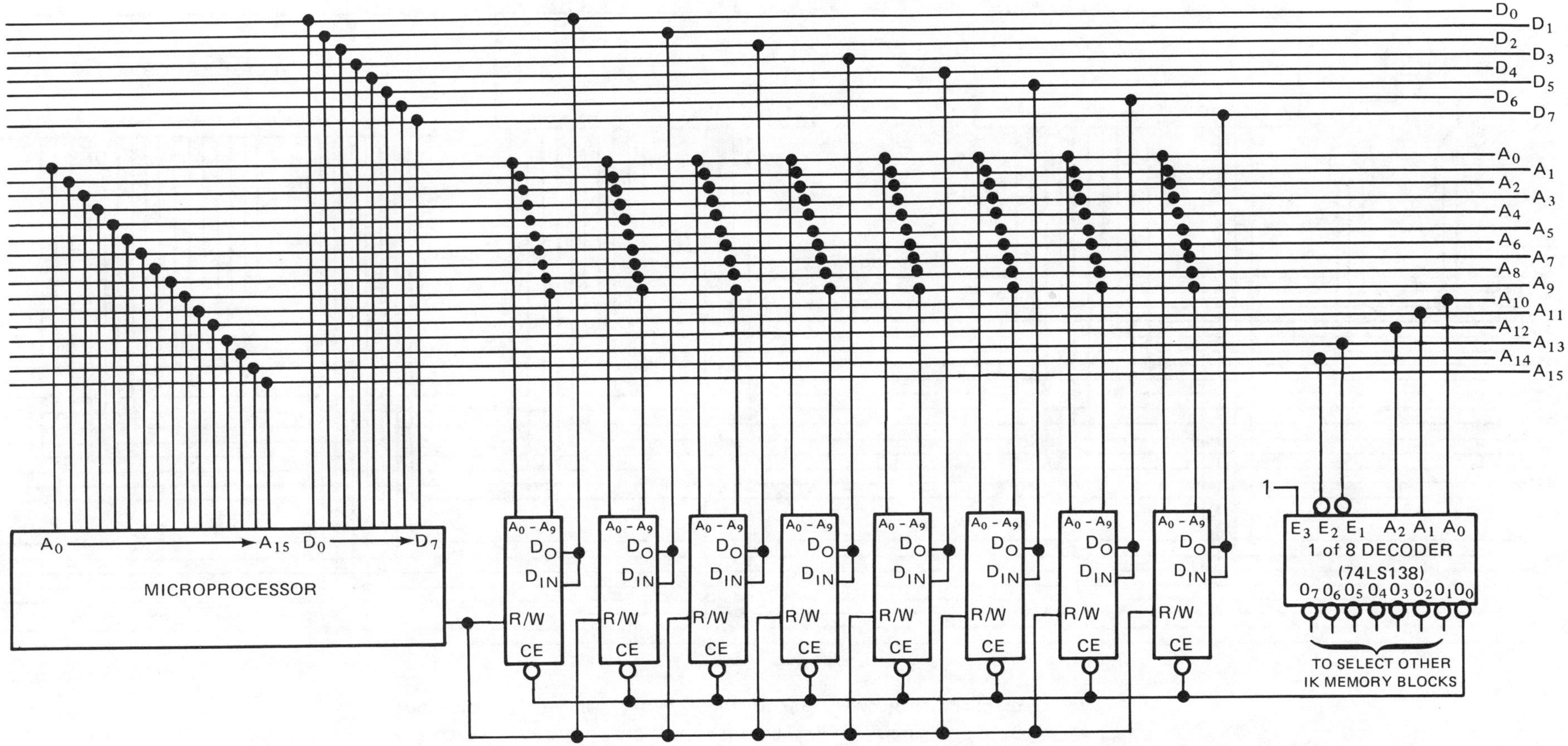

Address of this memory is E000 00XX XXXX XXXX

X = Will be 1 or 0 depending on byte being addressed.
0 = Memory will be selected only when this bit is 0 (low).
E = Memory will be selected for either 1 or 0 in this bit (causes duplication of the addresses within the memory map).

FIGURE 5.9 Two 1K-X-4 Static RAMS (2114) can provide four pages of microprocessor memory by connecting the addresses in parallel. The four data bits of one device connect to data bus D_0 through D_3. The data leads of the other device connect to D_4 through D_7. A triple 3-input OR gate provides expansion of the chip select.

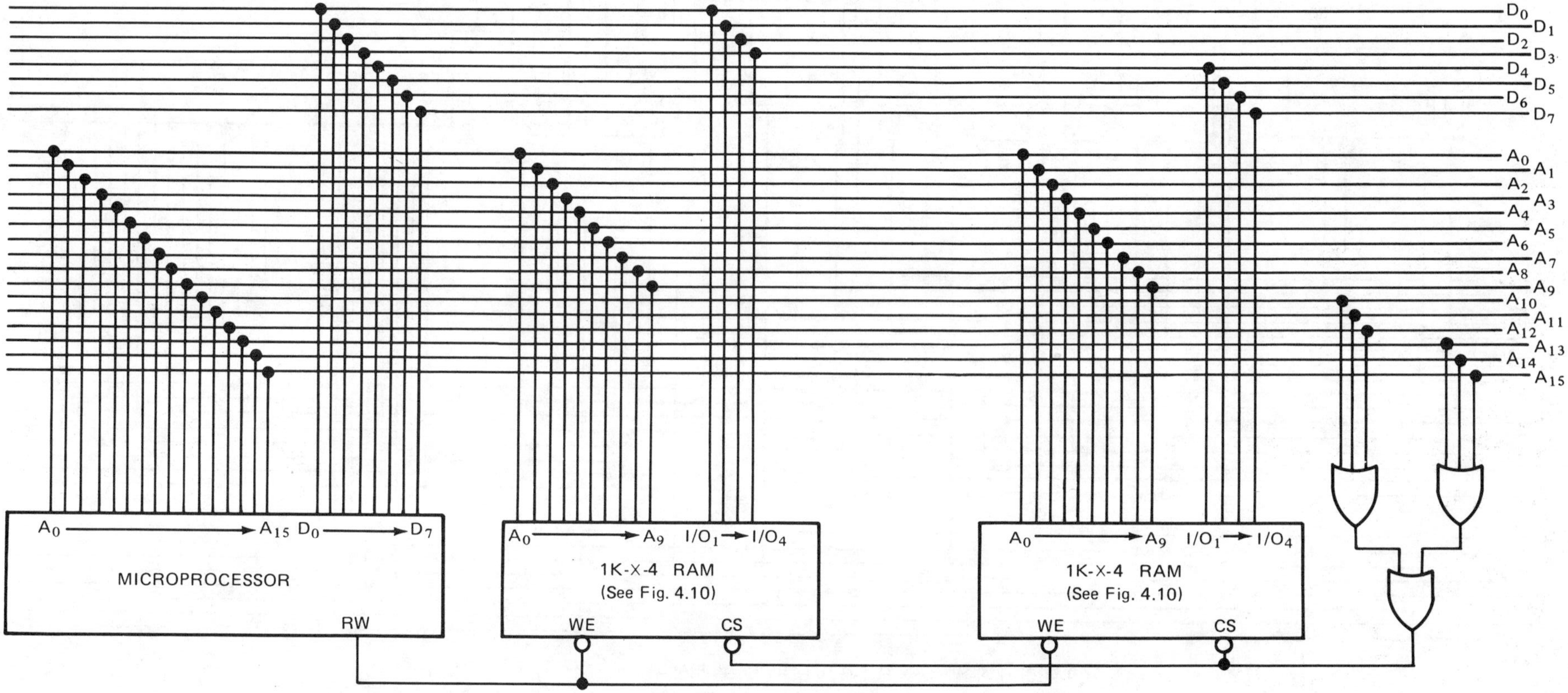

Address of this memory is 0000 00XX XXXX XXXX

X = Will be 1 or 0 depending on byte being addressed.

0 = Memory will be selected only when this bit is 0 (low).

read/write line to the 2102 goes low (turning off the 2102 output drivers) a sufficient time before the microprocessor outputs data to the bus. A similar check of timing would be advisable for use of the 2102 with other microprocessors. Use of the single chip select lead of the 2102s would cause this 1024 block of memory to occupy additional blocks of memory totaling a full half of the memory map. If there is no intention to use some of the blocks either for additional RAM, ROM, or I/O interfaces, there would be no purpose to deselect the memory at these blocks. A useful device for select decoding is the 1 of 8 decoder used in Figure 5.8. Note that the decoder can be used with a total of 8 such memory blocks. The single E and two $\bar{E}$ leads permit considerable flexibility in the placement of these eight 1K memory blocks within the 64K memory map.

For the 3 RAMS thus far described, 8 individual devices are required to provide 4 pages of memory totaling 1024 addressable bytes. An improvement over this occurs in using the 4K static RAM. This RAM exists in both 1K-X-4 and 4K-X-1 organization. Using the 1K-X-4, 4 pages of memory can be obtained with only 2 18-pin memory devices. Figure 5.9 shows a pair of 1K-X-4 memory devices connected to provide random access memory from 0000_H to memory address $03FF_H$. Figure 5.10 shows a 4K-X-1 static RAM. Figure 5.11 shows the assembly

Connection Diagram
Dual-In-Line Package

Logic Symbol

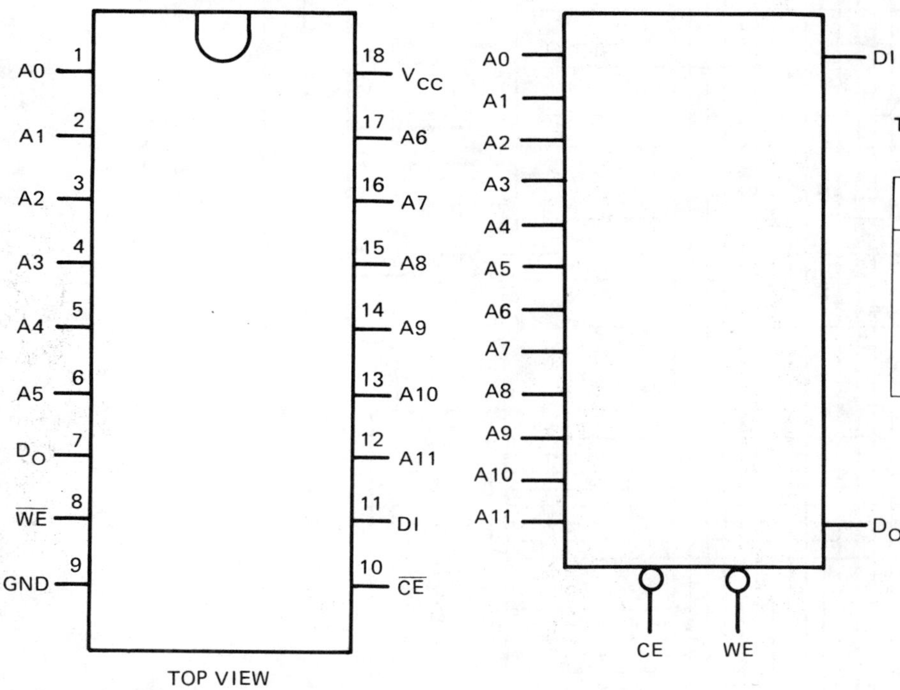

FIGURE 5.10 A 4K Static RAM organized as a 4K × 1. *(Courtesy of National Semiconductor Corporation)*

Truth Table

$\overline{CE}$	$\overline{WE}$	DI	D_{OUT}	MODE
H	X	X	Hi-Z	Not Selected
L	L	H	Hi-Z	Write 1
L	L	L	Hi-Z	Write 0
L	H	X	D_{OUT}	Read

MM5257 4096-X-1 Static Random Access Memory

Features

- All inputs and outputs directly TTL compatible
- Static operation—no clocks or refreshing required
- Low power—200 mW typical
- High speed—250 ns typical
- TRI-STATE output for bus interface
- Separate Data In and Data Out pins
- Single +5V supply
- Standard 18-pin Dual-In-Line Package

FIGURE 5.11 Using the 4K-X-1 static RAM with the microprocessor requires one device for each data bit. The twelve address leads of each device are connected in parallel to the address bus. The single 1 of 8 decoder divides the lower half of the memory map into eight 4K blocks.

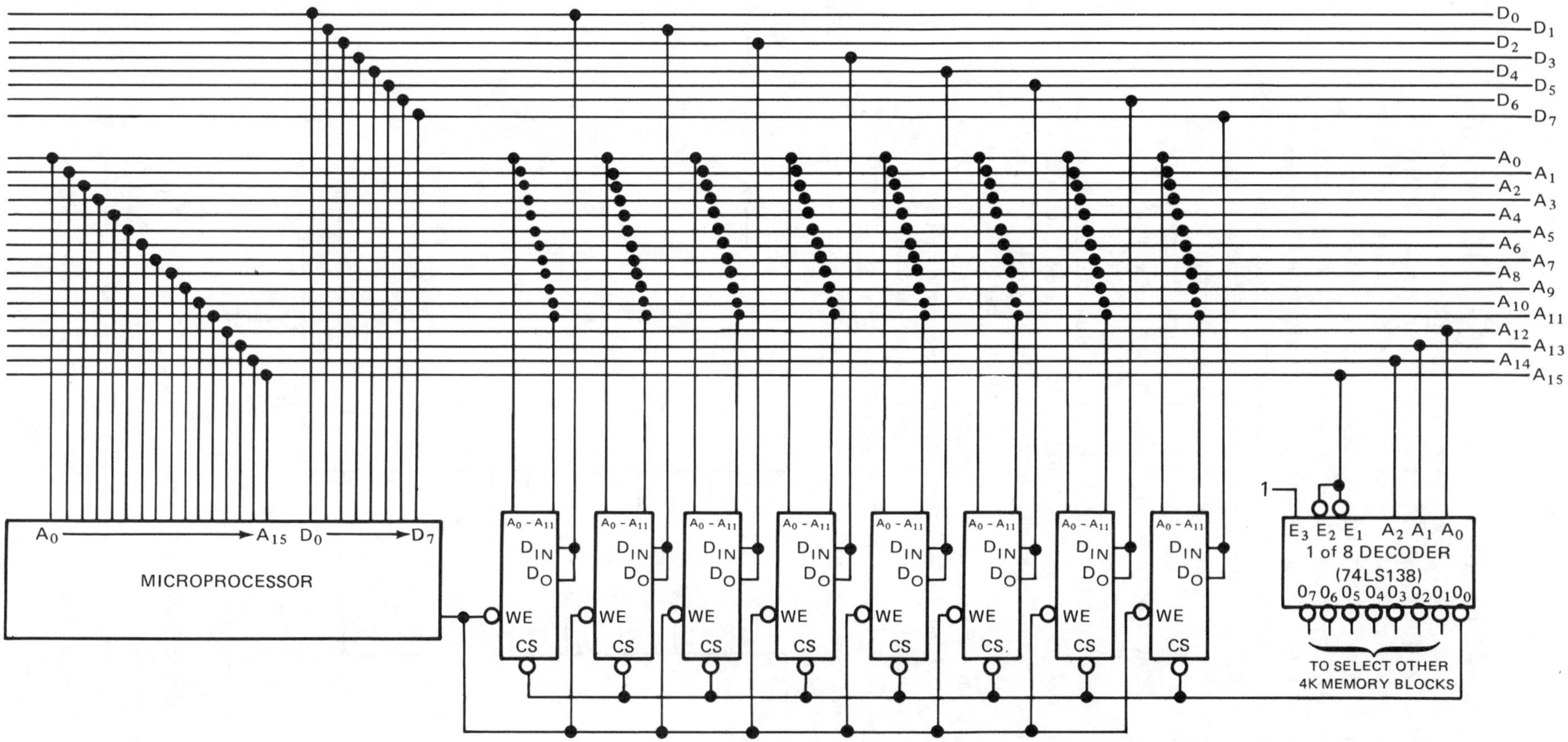

Address of this memory is 0000 XXXX XXXX XXXX

X = Will be 1 or 0 depending on byte being addressed.

0 = Memory will be selected only when this bit is 0 (low).

of 8 4K-X-1 static RAM circuits to form 4096 bytes of microprocessor memory. The one of eight select decoder can be used to locate this 4096 bytes at any location within the 64K memory map, as connected in Figure 5.10. It occupies the lower 4K of the memory map.

5.4 The CMOS RAM and Battery Backup

The RAMS discussed thus far were bipolar or NMOS devices, either version being TTL compatible. TTL compatible implies:

$$V_{CC} = 5V$$
$$V_{OL} = 0.4V \text{ max}$$
$$V_{OH} = 2.4V \text{ min}$$
$$V_{IL} = 0.8V \text{ max}$$
$$V_{IH} = 2.0V \text{ min}$$

However, variations will exist in the input and output currents.

On the other hand, CMOS operating voltage level may vary. CMOS devices may be designed for a supply voltage range (V_{DD}) of from 4V to 18V, and the input and output voltages are specified as a percentage of V_{DD}. A number of CMOS RAMS have been designed for use with CMOS microprocessors. The CMOS RAM has a major advantage in its low quiescent power dissipation. When the device is deselected it requires less than a milliwatt of power as compared to as high as 200 milliwatts for an equivalent NMOS memory.

One solution to the volatility of semiconductor memories is the use of battery backup, a system in which a battery voltage is used to maintain a minimum voltage to the memory circuit for the purpose of retaining the data when the system power is turned off. The low quiescent power dissipation of the CMOS RAM makes it ideal for use in a battery backup system. If a CMOS RAM with standard CMOS inputs were used, a considerable disadvantage would exist in the need for pullup resistors on the inputs. Fortunately, a TTL compatible CMOS RAM is available which will retain data with a V_{CC} level as low as 2 volts. At this level the power drain from the battery will be in microamps. Figure 5.12 shows a 5101, CMOS RAM memory connected for battery backup in an otherwise TTL system. The +5V V_{CC} to the CMOS devices is connected through a diode which is forward biased when V_{CC} is on, and reversed biased when V_{CC} is turned off. However, the 3V-battery is connected through a diode which is forward biased when V_{CC} is turned off.

A diode with low forward voltage drop is ideal for use between the system V_{CC} line and the RAM V_{CC} line. A Schottky or gerniamium diode, or a transistor with base and collector shorted, may be used for this application. In addition to the diodes and batteries, a resistor of 10K to 100K in size should be connected between CE2 and ground to keep the RAM in standby mode when the normal V_{CC} is turned off.

FIGURE 5.12 Two TTL compatible CMOS RAMS connected to form one page (256 × 8) of microprocessor memory. The CMOS RAM is ideal for battery backup because of its capacity to retain data with a V_{CC} as low as 2V along with the fact that its quiescent current at this voltage is only microamps.

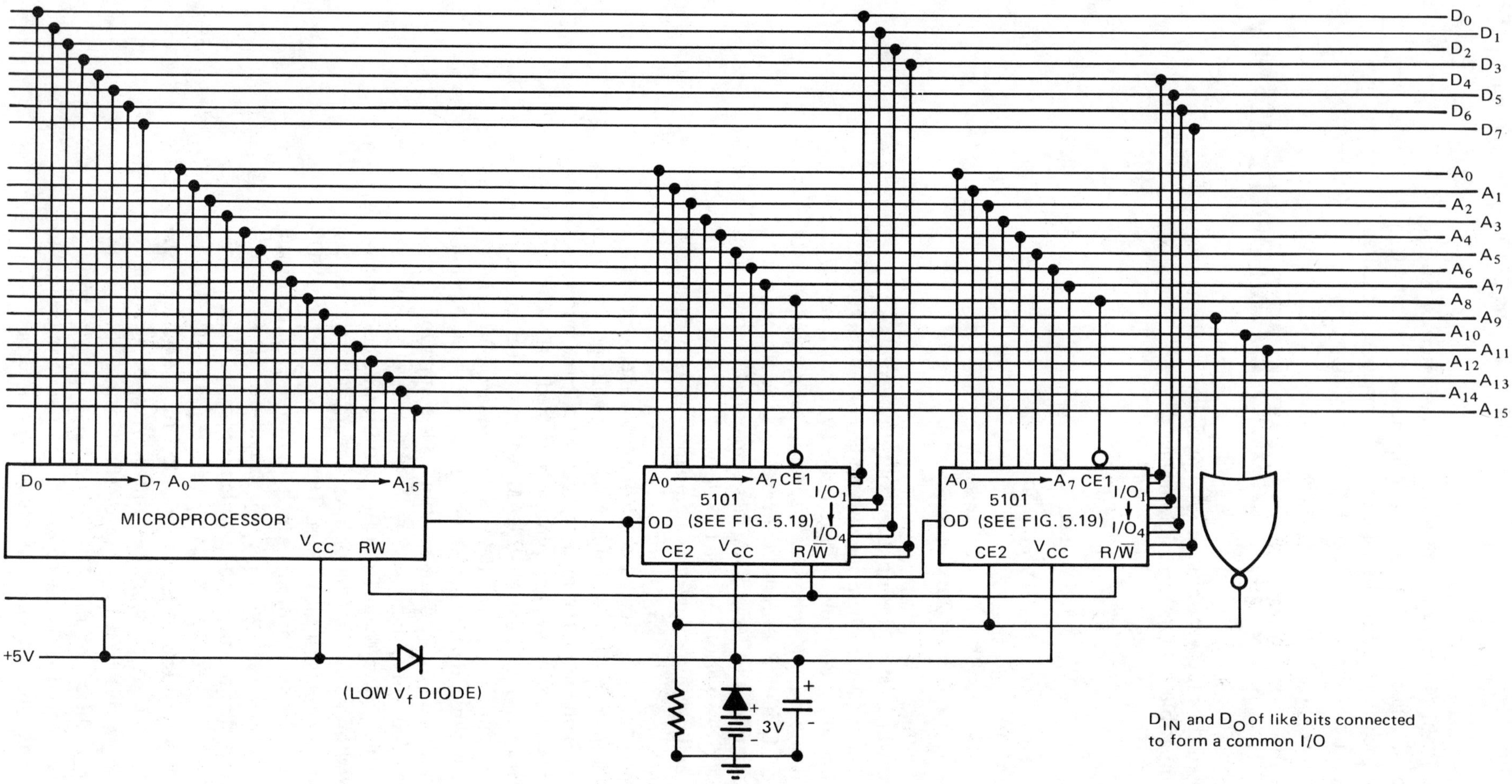

Address of this memory is EEEE 0000 XXXX XXXX

X = Will be 1 or 0 depending on byte being addressed.
0 = Memory will be selected only when this bit is 0 (low).
E = Memory will be selected for either 1 or 0 in this bit (causes duplication of the addresses within the memory map).

5.5 Loading and Verifying Random Access Memory

In keeping with our bootstrap philosophy of learning the microprocessor system, let us consider separately the loading of data into a random access memory. The simplest method would be to connect switches to each input and light emitting diodes to each output. But for a memory of any size this would be too slow and awkward. A reasonable compromise would be a simple hexadecimal keyboard to enter the data and a counter to increment through the addresses. Figure 5.13 is a block diagram of such a system. The step-for-step functioning of this system is given by the flow diagrams in Figure 5.14.

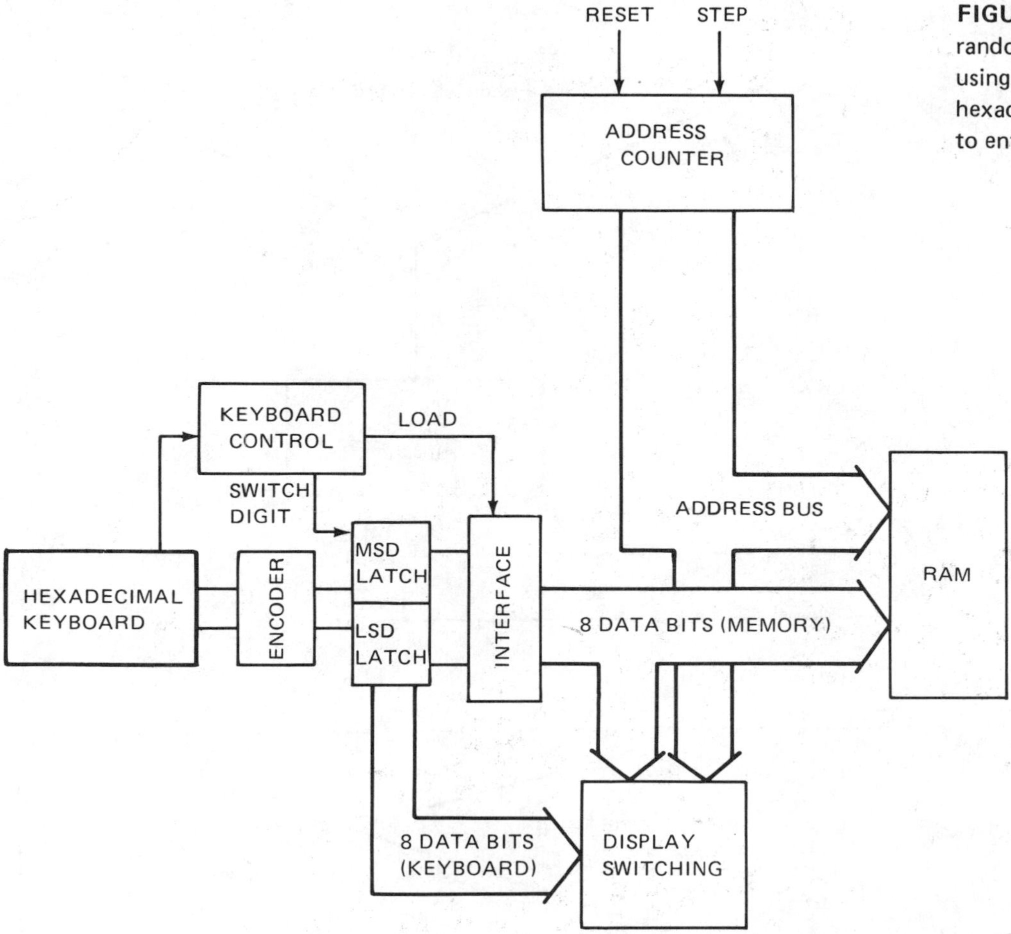

FIGURE 5.13 Block diagram of a random access memory system using an address counter and a hexadecimal keyboard with which to enter the data.

Hexadecimal keyboards may be supplied with as many as 9 contact closures per key, but a single contact closure is the most common and is easy to use. Figure 5.15 shows the hexadecimal keyboard and the logic circuits used to encode the 16 contact closures into a 4-bit binary code. An additional output is needed to indicate a contact closure including zero, which cannot be identified at the encoder outputs. The necessary logic functions for the encoder indicate a need for four 8-input OR gates. An OR gate with this many inputs is not readily available in TTL circuits and various alternatives may have to be considered for implementing these functions. One is the use of the 7430, 8-input NAND gate.

FIGURE 5.14 Flow diagram of the operation of the memory system of Figure 5.13 (**a**) Load operation. (**b**) Verify operation.

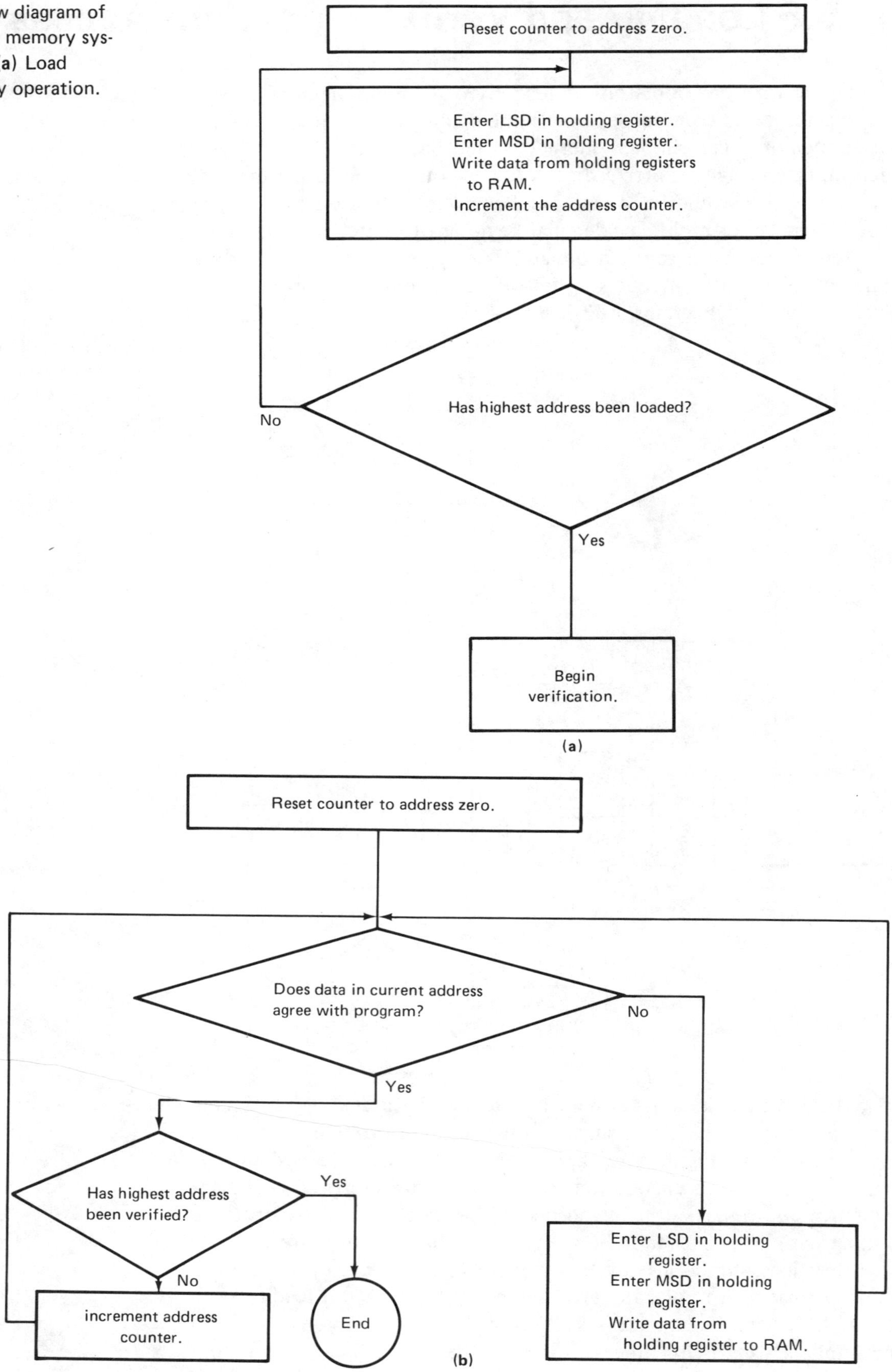

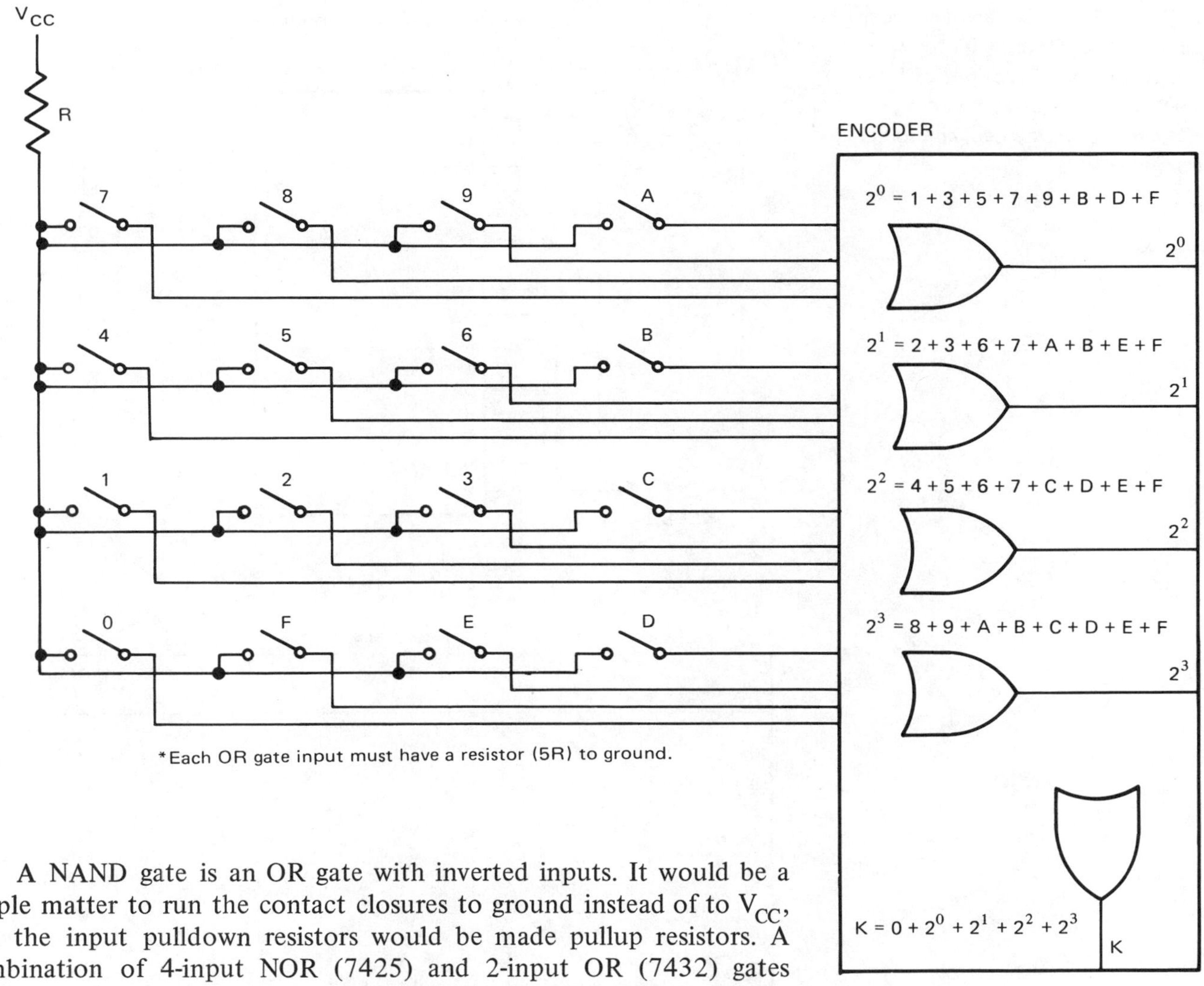

FIGURE 5.15 Schematic diagram of the hexadecimal keyboard and wiring to the encoder circuit. The encoder circuit must produce the logic OR functions given in the encoder diagram.

A NAND gate is an OR gate with inverted inputs. It would be a simple matter to run the contact closures to ground instead of to V_{CC}, and the input pulldown resistors would be made pullup resistors. A combination of 4-input NOR (7425) and 2-input OR (7432) gates could be used to create the output functions in an inverted form. The inversion could be cancelled at the output of the storage flip-flops. Another solution is the use of the Harris HD-0165 Keyboard Encoder shown in Figure 5.16. It provides the necessary functions and, in addition, a key roll over function that cancels the output in event that more than one key is depressed at a time.

The timing pulse needed to strobe the digits into the correct holding latches (MSD or LSD) is supplied by a pair of monostable multivibrators. As the K waveform in Figure 5.17(b) shows, the key depression is preceded by a period of contact bounce that may last from 5 to 50 milliseconds depending on the quality of the switches. The first rise in the contact bounce fires multivibrator 1. The C_1R_1 combination is selected to provide a pulse whose duration exceeds the contact bounce time. Multivibrator number 2 is triggered by the trailing edge of MV1 Q output. The C_2R_2 combination must be selected for a pulse wide enough to strobe the digits into latches. This pulse width would not be critical from several microseconds to several milliseconds. The pulse from MV2 will be gated through whichever AND gate is enabled by the digit flip-flop. This will result in the digit being latched

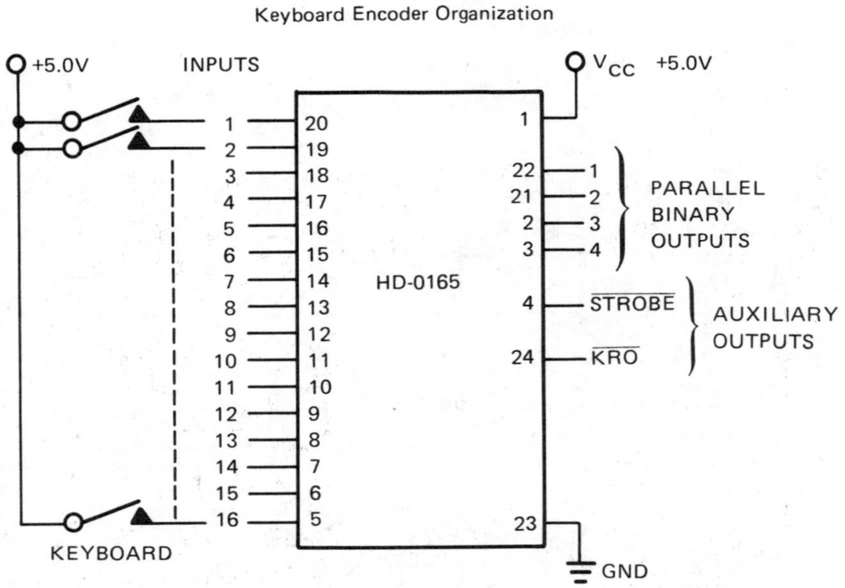

FIGURE 5.16 Keyboard encoder circuit HD-0165 provides the required encoding functions within a single 24-pin integrated circuit. (*Courtesy of Harris Semiconductor Company*)

TRUTH TABLE, HD-0165

INPUTS 1	2	3	4	5	6	7	8	9	10	11	12	13	14	15	16	OUTPUTS 1	2	3	4	St.	K_{RO}
L	L	L	L	L	L	L	L	L	L	L	L	L	L	L	L	H	H	H	H	H	H
H	L	L	L	L	L	L	L	L	L	L	L	L	L	L	L	H	H	H	H	L	H
L	H	L	L	L	L	L	L	L	L	L	L	L	L	L	L	L	H	H	H	L	H
L	L	H	L	L	L	L	L	L	L	L	L	L	L	L	L	H	L	H	H	L	H
L	L	L	H	L	L	L	L	L	L	L	L	L	L	L	L	L	L	H	H	L	H
L	L	L	L	H	L	L	L	L	L	L	L	L	L	L	L	H	H	L	H	L	H
L	L	L	L	L	H	L	L	L	L	L	L	L	L	L	L	L	H	L	H	L	H
L	L	L	L	L	L	H	L	L	L	L	L	L	L	L	L	H	L	L	H	L	H
L	L	L	L	L	L	L	H	L	L	L	L	L	L	L	L	L	L	L	H	L	H
L	L	L	L	L	L	L	L	H	L	L	L	L	L	L	L	H	H	H	L	L	H
L	L	L	L	L	L	L	L	L	H	L	L	L	L	L	L	L	H	H	L	L	H
L	L	L	L	L	L	L	L	L	L	H	L	L	L	L	L	H	L	H	L	L	H
L	L	L	L	L	L	L	L	L	L	L	H	L	L	L	L	L	L	H	L	L	H
L	L	L	L	L	L	L	L	L	L	L	L	H	L	L	L	H	H	L	L	L	H
L	L	L	L	L	L	L	L	L	L	L	L	L	H	L	L	L	H	L	L	L	H
L	L	L	L	L	L	L	L	L	L	L	L	L	L	H	L	H	L	L	L	L	H
L	L	L	L	L	L	L	L	L	L	L	L	L	L	L	H	L	L	L	L	L	H
ANY TWO OR MORE HIGH																X	X	X	X	L	L

INPUTS: L = Open Circuit or < +1.0V H = > +4.5V Current Source
OUTPUTS: L = > +0.4V H = > +2.4V X = Erroneous Data

FIGURE 5.17 (a) opposite Both the binary and the K (keydepressed) outputs of the encoder will contain a period of contact bounce at the beginning and ending of a key depression. Monostable multivibrator 1 will output a pulse on the first bounce C_1, and R_1 should be selected to provide a pulse that lasts longer than the contact bounce. Monostable multivibrator 2 will trigger on the trailing edge of Q1. C_2 R_2 may be selected for a pulse wide enough to strobe the encoder outputs into the digit latches. The digit flip-flop triggers on the trailing edge of Q_3 switching the strobe output between LSD and MSD latches after each key depression.

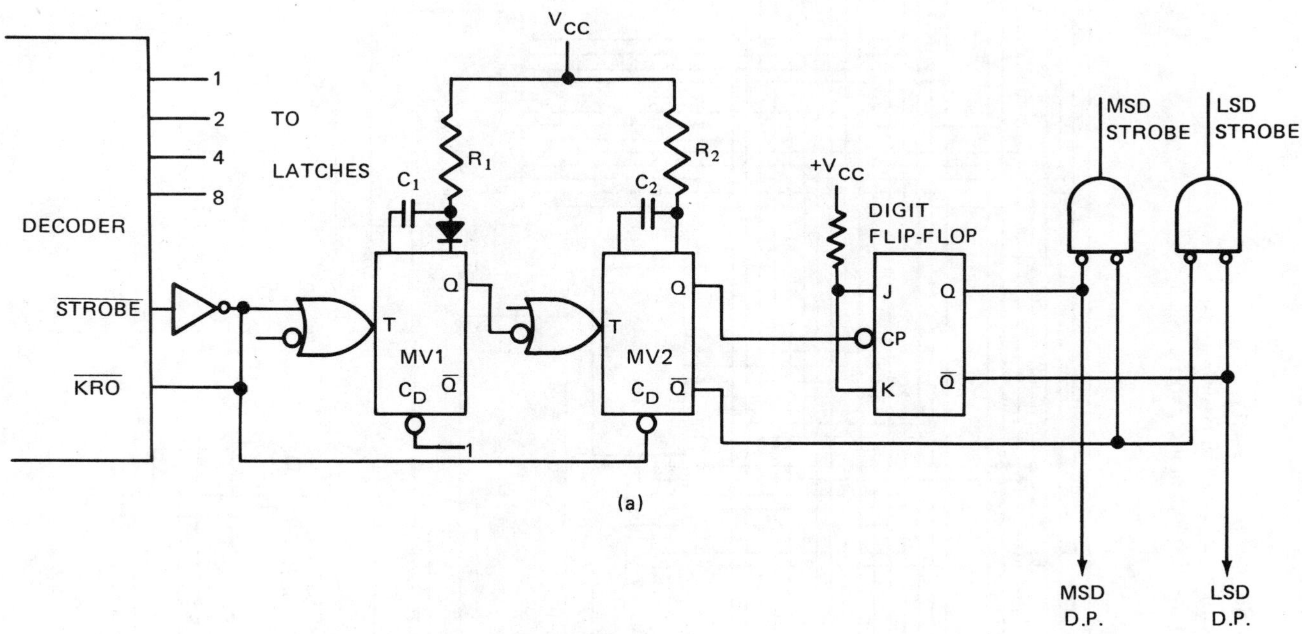
VCC
1
2
4
8
TO
LATCHES
DECODER
STROBE
KRO
R1
C1
R2
C2
+VCC
DIGIT
FLIP-FLOP
MSD
STROBE
LSD
STROBE
T
MV1
Q
CD
T
MV2
J
CP
K
MSD
D.P.
LSD
D.P.

(a)

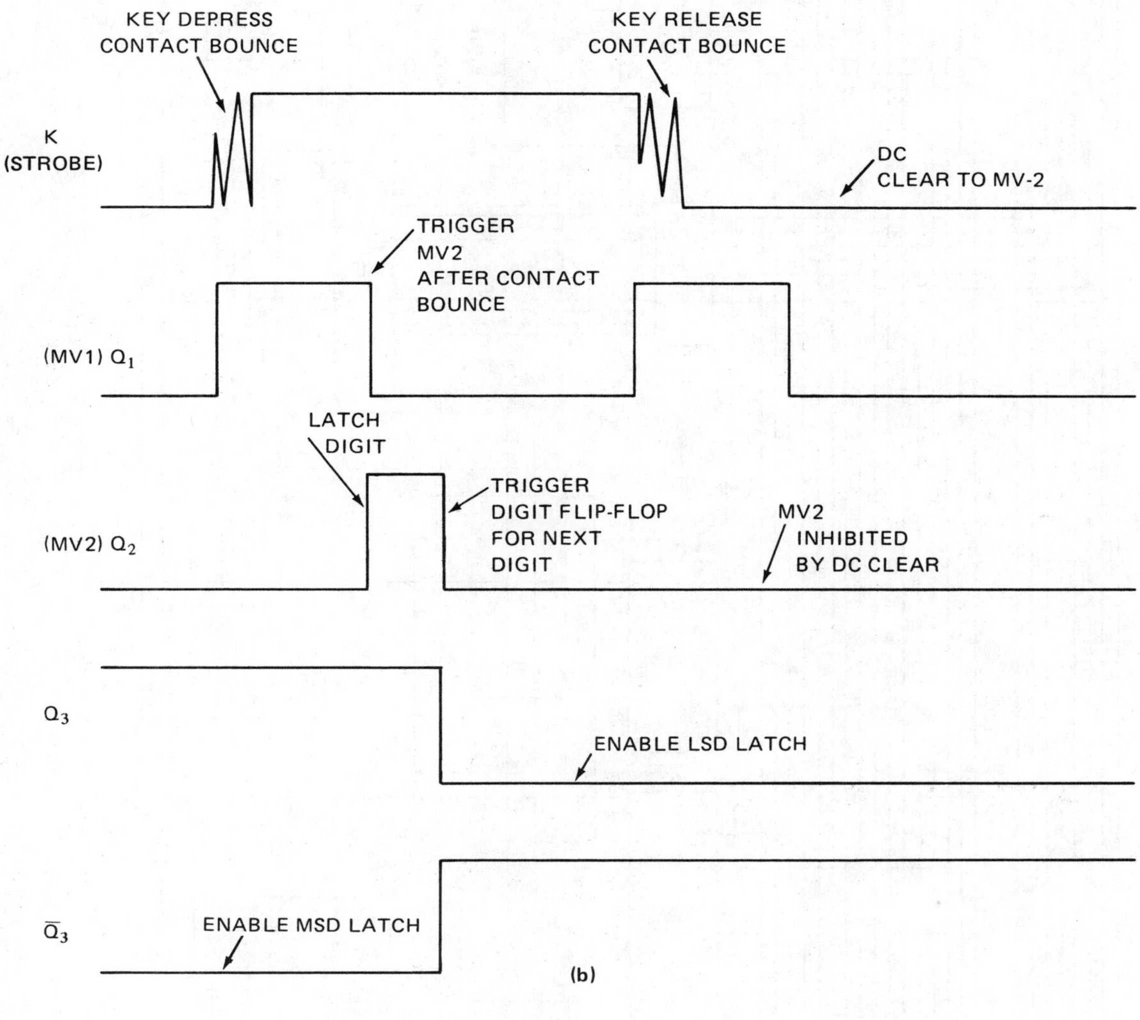
KEY DEPRESS
CONTACT BOUNCE
KEY RELEASE
CONTACT BOUNCE
K
(STROBE)
DC
CLEAR TO MV-2
TRIGGER
MV2
AFTER CONTACT
BOUNCE
(MV1) Q1
LATCH
DIGIT
TRIGGER
DIGIT FLIP-FLOP
FOR NEXT
DIGIT
MV2
INHIBITED
BY DC CLEAR
(MV2) Q2
Q3
ENABLE LSD LATCH
ENABLE MSD LATCH

(b)

FIGURE 5.18 Complete random access memory system using hexadecimal keyboard as an entry device. This system uses two 5101 TTL compatible CMOS RAMS and can be modified for nonvolatile operation by wiring in the battery, diodes, and resistors as shown in Figure 5.12.

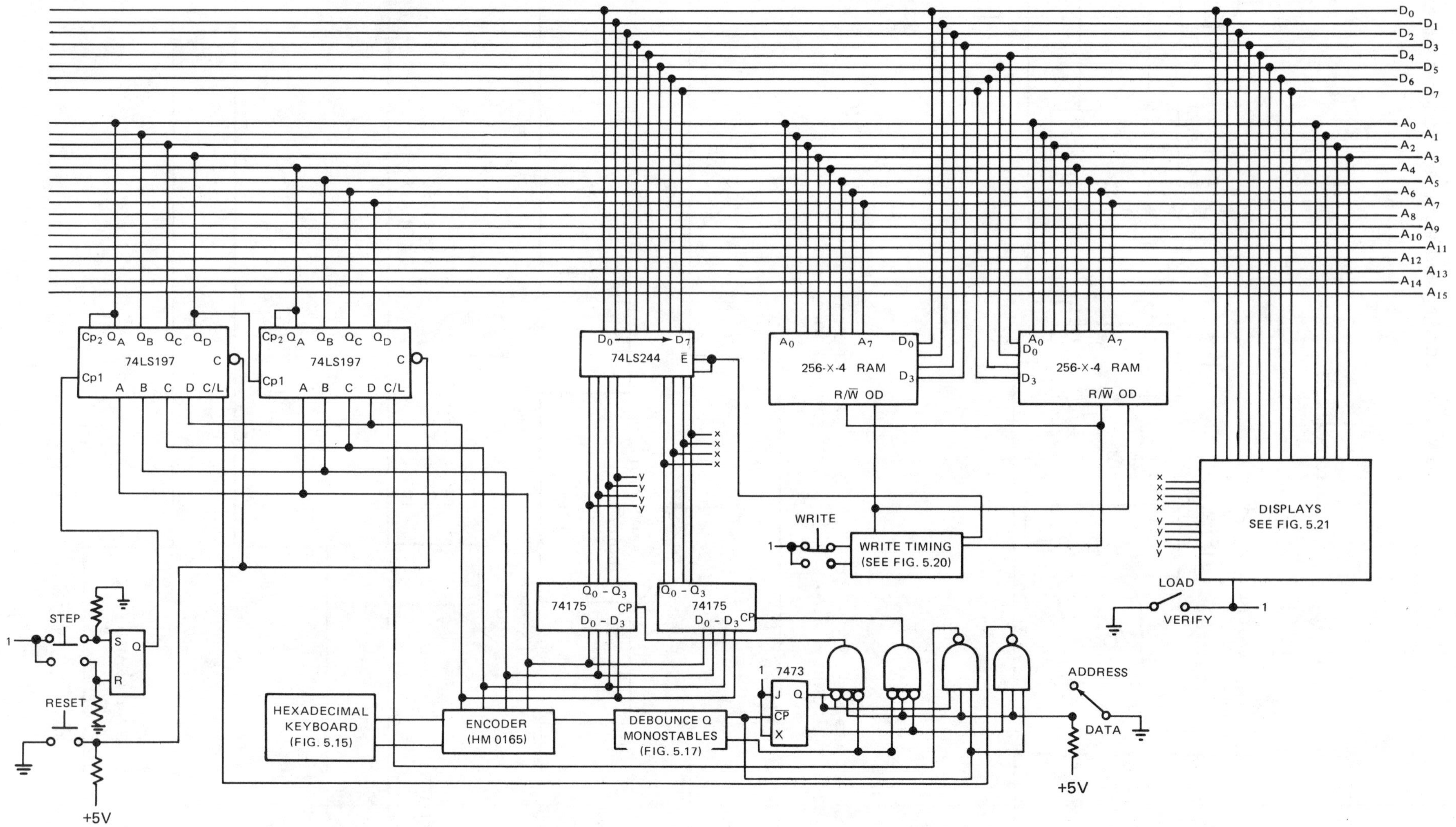

into the register indicated by the illuminated decimal point. As the MV2 waveform indicates, the MV2 pulse must occur during a period free from contact bounce. When the key is released, another period of contact bounce occurs but manages to trigger MV1 only. By the time the MV2 trailing edge occurs, the K output is a steady zero level which as a result of being applied to the MV2 $\overline{CD}$ input keeps MV2 from firing. The digit latches are leading-edge triggered. However, the digit flip-flop triggers on the trailing edge of the MV2 pulse, thus preparing the circuit to enter the opposite digit. Interconnection of these circuits with the keyboard is shown in Figure 5.18.

In Section 5.2 we discussed the high-speed timing needed to interface correctly a semiconductor RAM with a microprocessor. Even at the low operating speed of a switchboard, timing must be considered. Figure 5.19 is the AC characteristics and the timing diagram of the 5101 CMOS RAM. The read function is a simple matter of insuring that the address and the four control inputs will statically enable the memory and the output will appear continuously on the data bus. The CE2 and the R/W inputs must be high while the $\overline{CE1}$ and OD inputs are held low. The memory will under these conditions be outputting the data

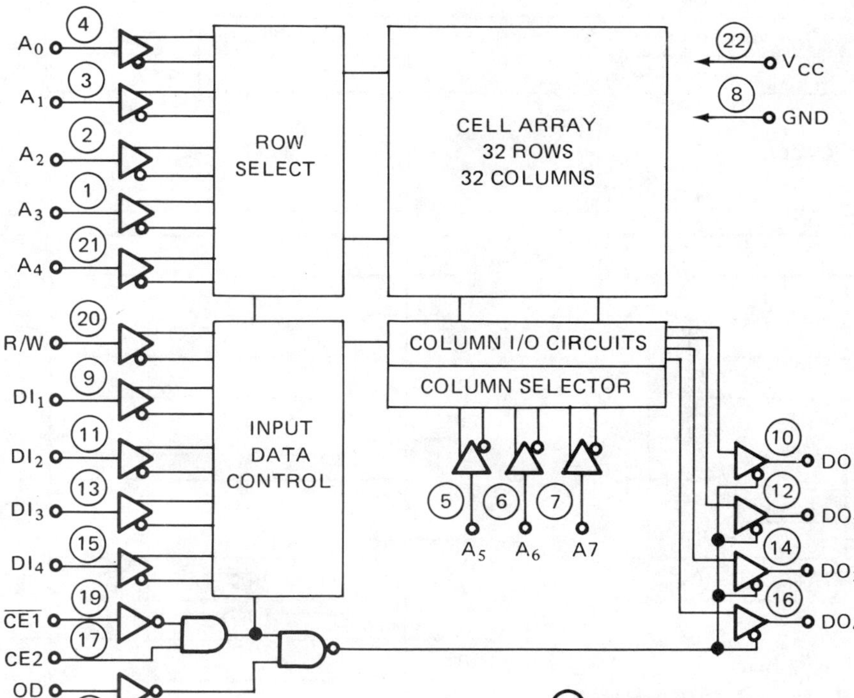

FIGURE 5.19 SY5101 TTL compatible CMOS RAM. (*Courtesy of Synertek.*)

Features

- Very Low Power — 100mW operating
  — 50μW standby
- Pin compatible with SY2101 RAM-operates in same sockets
- Standby operation whenever chip is not selected
- Single +5V power supply
- Power Down (2 volt) memory retention
- Totally TTL compatible—inputs and outputs
- 3-state output

FIGURE 5.19 (continued).

A.C. CHARACTERISTICS $T_A = 0°C$ to $70°C$, $V_{CC} = 5V \pm 5\%$ unless otherwise specified.

READ CYCLE

Symbol	Parameter	5101L-1 Limits (ns) Min.	5101L-1 Max.	5101L and 5101L-3 Limits (ns) Min.	Max.	5101-8 Limits (ns) Min.	Max.
t_{RC}	Read Cycle	450		650		800	
t_A	Access Time		450		650		800
t_{CO1}	Chip Enable ($\overline{CE\ 1}$) to Output		500		600		800
t_{CO2}	Chip Enable (CE 2) to Output		500		700		850
t_{OD}	Output Disable to Output		250		350		450
t_{DF}	Data Output to High Z State	0	130	0	150	0	200
t_{OH1}	Previous Read Data Valid with Respect to Address Change	0		0		0	
t_{OH2}	Previous Read Data Valid with Respect to Chip Enable	0		0		0	
WRITE CYCLE							
t_{WC}	Write Cycle	450		650		800	
t_{AW}	Write Delay	130		150		200	
t_{CW1}	Chip Enable ($\overline{CE\ 1}$) to Write	350		550		650	
t_{CW2}	Chip Enable (CE 2) to Write	350		550		650	
t_{DW}	Data Setup	250		400		450	
t_{DH}	Data Hold	50		100		100	
t_{WP}	Write Pulse	250		400		450	
t_{WR}	Write Recovery	50		50		100	
t_{DS}	Output Disable Setup	130		150		200	

TIMING DIAGRAMS **READ CYCLE**

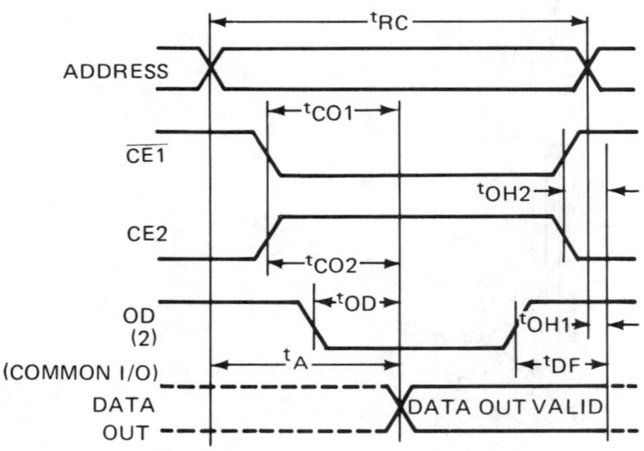

WRITE CYCLE

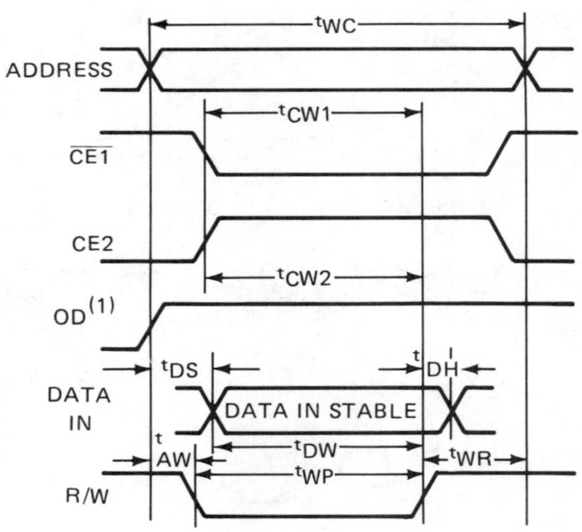

NOTES:
1. During the write cycle, OD is a logical 1 for common I/O and "don't care" for separate I/O operation.
2. OD may be tied low for separate I/O operation.

CAPACITANCE[3] $T_A = 25°C$, f = 1 MHz

Symbol	Test	Typ.	Max.	Unit
C_{IN}	Input Capacitance (All Input Pins) $V_{IN} = 0V$	4	8	pF
C_{OUT}	Output Capacitance $V_{OUT} = 0V$	8	12	pF

Note 3: This Parameter is periodically sampled and is not 100% tested.

stored in the current address until the write button is depressed. When the write button is depressed, the output disable should go high. Then, after 200 nsec, the R/W should go low, and the data must be enabled through the interface onto the data bus. To return to the read state, the W/R must go high at least (^tDH) 100 nsec before the data is removed. Finally the OD returns to the low state. A write push button can be connected as shown in Figure 5.20.

The set-reset latch removes the switch contact bounce in addition to supplying the necessary output disable (OD). The first monostable provides the required output disable setup time (^tDS) which is equal and concurrent with (^tAW). The second multivibrator provides the R/W input and is set for a pulse width of ^tWP. This same output ($\overline{Q}_3$) is used to enable the data through the interface and return the interface to high impedance after the write time is over and well ahead of the OD going low. Unfortunately, if Q_3 is applied directly to the interface output enable, the ^tDH (data hold) will be only the 20 nsec or so delay of the interface disable time. An additional 80 nsec may be needed to meet the 100 nsec minimum called for in the specification. Leftover circuits with RC delays can very easily provide delays of this magnitude, particularly if one of them is an open collector.

A counter with as many bits as the memory has address bits could be used. If a counter lacking preset inputs is used, then a change made at address 105 would require that the memory be reset to zero and the

FIGURE 5.20 Write pushbutton circuit. The R-S flip-flop can be made with cross NOR gates. The first monostable provides a delay of t_{DS} (200 nsec.min.) The second monostable provides the R/W control of t_{WP} (450 nsec. minimum). A delayed Q_3 can be used to strobe the data through the interface providing the correct t_{DH} (100 nsec minimum).

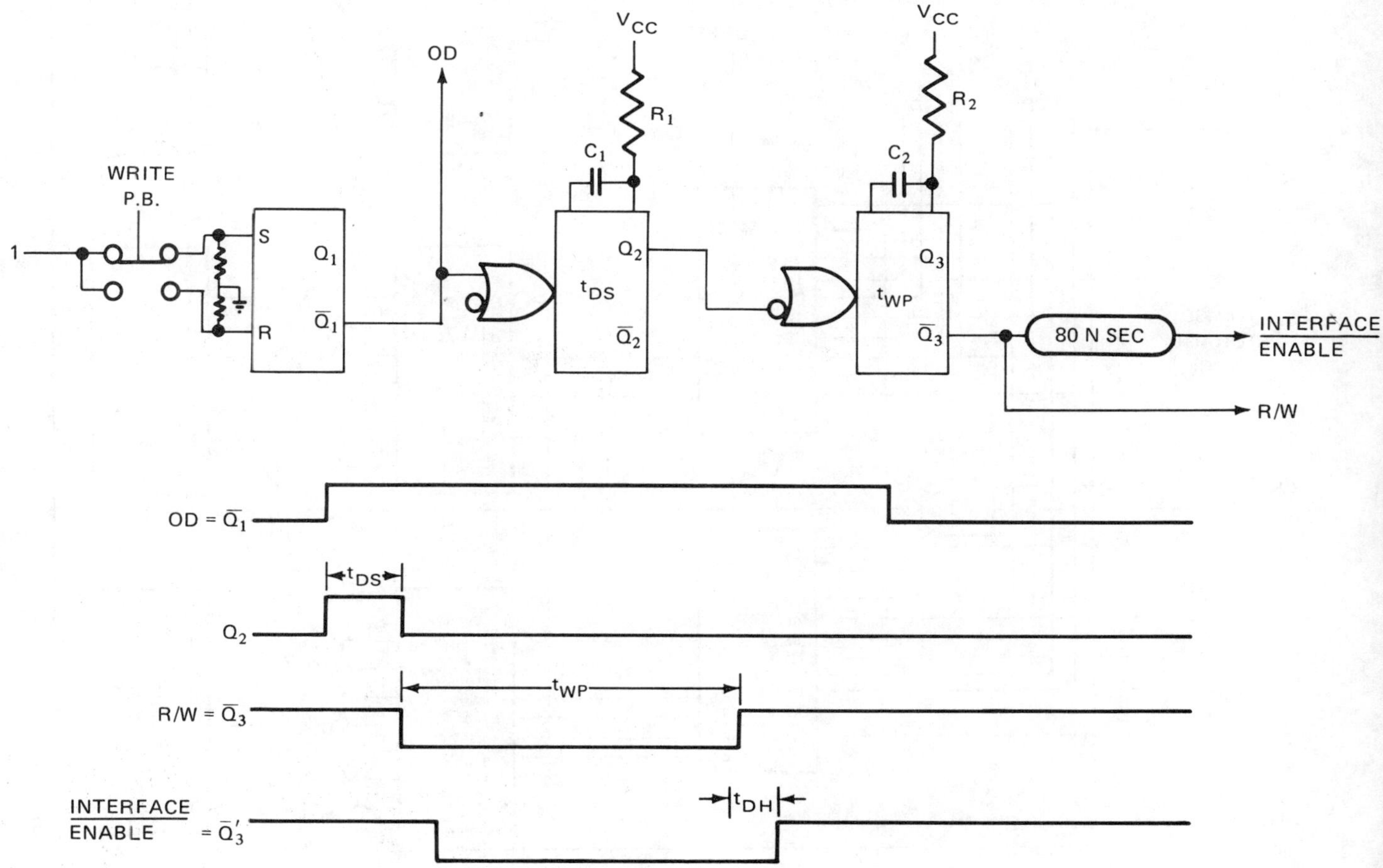

step switch be depressed 105 times. To avoid this, the 74LS197 counter was used in Figure 5.18. When the count/load input of this counter goes low, the device acts similar to the quad latch, in that the outputs are preset to the levels on the A through D inputs. The preset of the counter through the keyboard can be accomplished by throwing the address data switch to address. To provide a reset, a simple push-button switch is all that is needed. The clock (step push button), however, requires a debounce. If a double pole push button is used, then a simple latch flip-flop can be used for debounce as shown in Figure 5.18. Still to be considered are the displays. A minimum of three 7-segment display digits must be used to make the system practical: a pair which can be switched between the data storage latches and the data bus, and a third to display the lower address digit. For the sake of economy, the higher address bits can be displayed with individual LEDS.

Because the address is normally incremented, a hexadecimal display of all address digits is not so essential. Figure 5.21 is a logic diagram of the display circuit. This circuit uses three common anode,

FIGURE 5.21 Three-digit display circuit. One digit is used to display the LSD of the address. Two are used to display the data. These two are switched between the data bus and the holding latches. During load operation one of the DP elements will be lit to indicate which digit (LSD or MSD) the next key depression will affect.

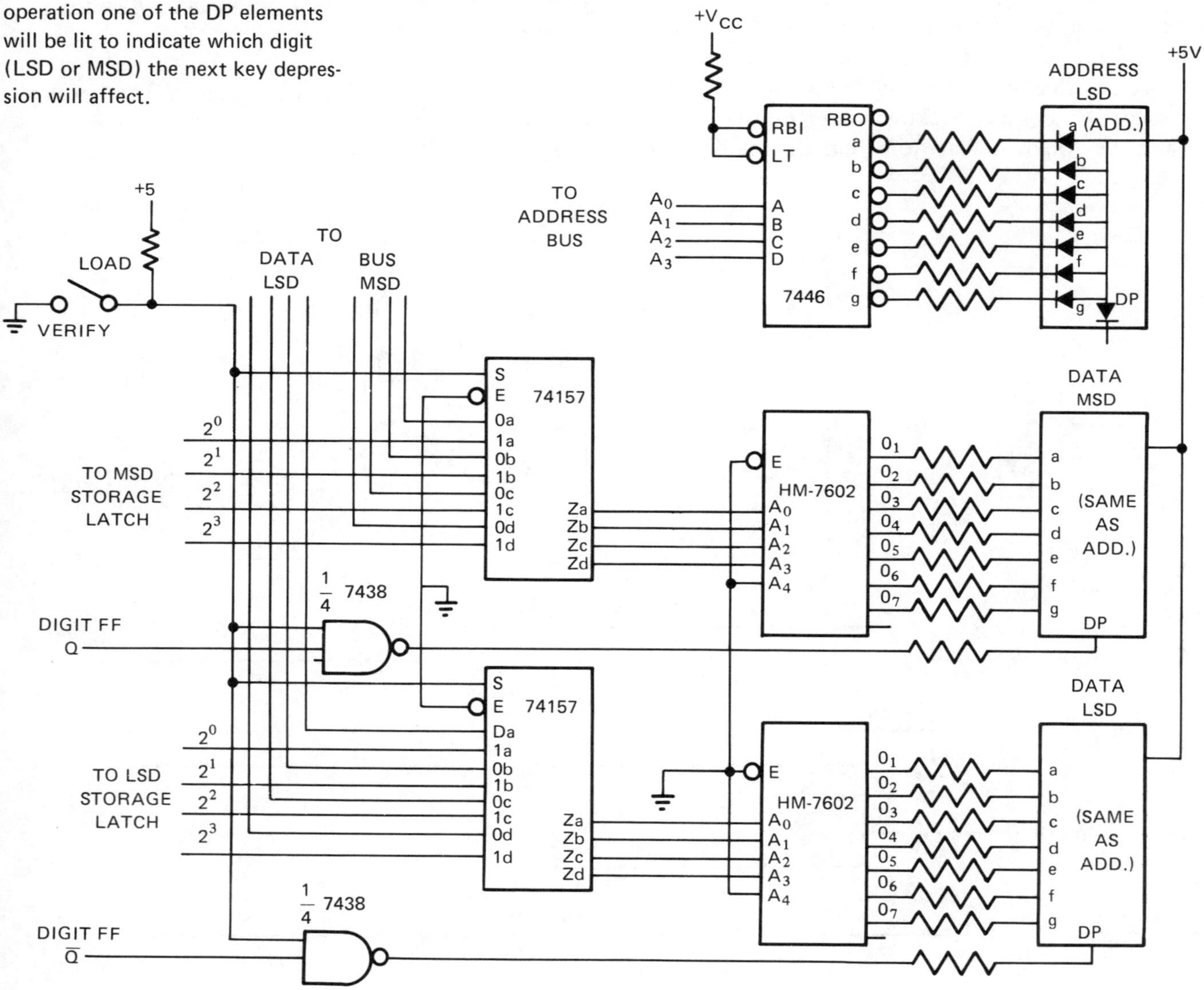

7-segment displays. These can be driven by three identical decoder drivers. The diagram, however, shows a 7446 used on one display and an HM-7602 used for the other two. This is merely to introduce the two devices to the reader. The 7446, BCD to 7-segment decoder driver does not provide the letters A through F. Figure 5.22 shows the outputs that do occur.

At the date of this writing, binary to 7-segment decoder drivers which output the letters A through F are not easy to come by. However, a decoder driver can be made by programming a 32-X-8 fusible link programmable read only memory (PROM). These can be programmed to produce the letters shown in Figure 5.22(b). The data readout can serve both to display the keyboard storage latches during the load operation

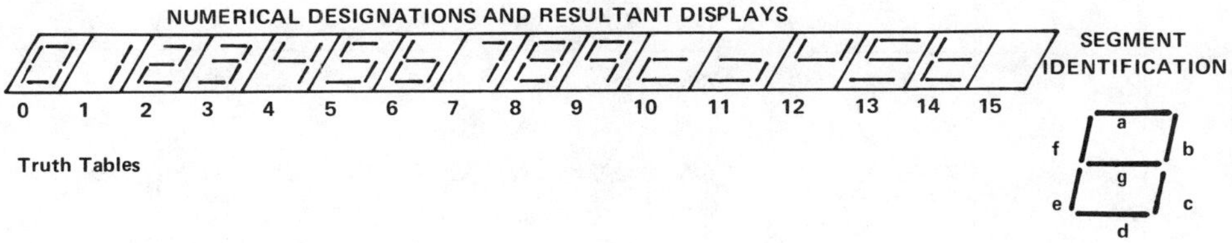

Truth Tables

46A, 47A, LS47

DECIMAL OR FUNCTION	INPUTS						BI/RBO(1)	OUTPUTS							NOTE
	LT	RBI	D	C	B	A		a	b	c	d	e	f	g	
0	H	H	L	L	L	L	H	L	L	L	L	L	L	H	
1	H	X	L	L	L	H	H	H	L	L	H	H	H	H	
2	H	X	L	L	H	L	H	L	L	H	L	L	H	L	
3	H	X	L	L	H	H	H	L	L	L	L	H	H	L	
4	H	X	L	H	L	L	H	H	L	L	H	H	L	L	
5	H	X	L	H	L	H	H	L	H	L	L	H	L	L	
6	H	X	L	H	H	L	H	H	H	L	L	L	L	L	
7	H	X	L	H	H	H	H	L	L	L	H	H	H	H	
8	H	X	H	L	L	L	H	L	L	L	L	L	L	L	(2)
9	H	X	H	L	L	H	H	L	L	L	H	H	L	L	
10	H	X	H	L	H	L	H	H	H	H	L	L	H	L	
11	H	X	H	L	H	H	H	H	H	L	L	H	H	L	
12	H	X	H	H	L	L	H	H	L	H	H	H	L	L	
13	H	X	H	H	L	H	H	L	H	H	L	H	L	L	
14	H	X	H	H	H	L	H	H	H	H	L	L	L	L	
15	H	X	H	H	H	H	H	H	H	H	H	H	H	H	
BI	X	X	X	X	X	X	L	H	H	H	H	H	H	H	(3)
RBI	H	L	L	L	L	L	L	H	H	H	H	H	H	H	(4)
LT	L	X	X	X	X	X	H	L	L	L	L	L	L	L	(5)

Notes
(1) BI/RBO is wire-AND logic serving as blanking input (BI) and/or ripple-blanking output (RBO).
(2) The blanking input (BI) must be open or held at a high logic level when output functions 0 through 15 are desired. The ripple-blanking input (RBI) must be open or high if blanking of a decimal zero is not desired.
(3) When a low logic level is applied directly to the blanking input (BI), all segment outputs are H regardless of the level of any other input.
(4) When ripple-blanking input (RBI) and inputs A, B, C, and D are at a low level with the lamp test input high, all segment outputs go H and the ripple-blanking output (RBO) goes to a low level (response condition).
(5) When the blanking input/ripple blanking output (BI/RBO) is open or held high and a low is applied to the lamp-test input, all segment outputs are L.
H = High Level, L = Low Level, X = Don't Care

(a)

FIGURE 5.22 **(a)** Truth table of the 7446 BCD to 7-segment display driver. The numbers 10 through 15 can be identified but do not conform to the letters A through F.

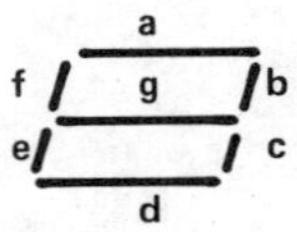

SEGMENT IDENTIFICATION

FIGURE 5.22 (b) Program truth table for the 7602 PROM and the resulting 7-segment display.

FUNCTION TABLE

DECIMAL OR FUNCTION	INPUTS						SEGMENT/OUTPUTS							DISPLAY
							0_1	0_2	0_3	0_4	0_5	0_6	0_7	
	A_4	A_3	A_2	A_1	A_0	$\bar{E}$	a	b	c	d	e	f	g	
0	X	L	L	L	L	L	ON	ON	ON	ON	ON	ON	OFF	0
1	X	L	L	L	H	L	OFF	ON	ON	OFF	OFF	OFF	OFF	1
2	X	L	L	H	L	L	ON	ON	OFF	ON	ON	OFF	ON	2
3	X	L	L	H	H	L	ON	ON	ON	ON	OFF	OFF	ON	3
4	X	L	H	L	L	L	OFF	ON	ON	OFF	OFF	ON	ON	4
5	X	L	H	L	H	L	ON	OFF	ON	ON	OFF	ON	ON	5
6	X	L	H	H	L	L	ON	OFF	ON	ON	ON	ON	ON	6
7	X	L	H	H	H	L	ON	ON	ON	OFF	OFF	OFF	OFF	7
8	X	H	L	L	L	L	ON	ON	ON	ON	ON	ON	ON	8
9	X	H	L	L	H	L	ON	ON	ON	ON	OFF	ON	ON	9
10	X	H	L	H	L	L	ON	ON	ON	OFF	ON	ON	ON	A
11	X	H	L	H	H	L	OFF	OFF	ON	ON	ON	ON	ON	b
12	X	H	H	L	L	L	ON	OFF	OFF	ON	ON	ON	OFF	C
13	X	H	H	L	H	L	OFF	ON	ON	ON	ON	OFF	ON	d
14	X	H	H	H	L	L	ON	OFF	OFF	ON	ON	ON	ON	E
15	X	H	H	H	H	L	ON	OFF	OFF	OFF	ON	ON	ON	F
INHIBIT	X	X	X	X	X	H	OFF	OFF	OFF	OFF	OFF	OFF	OFF	NONE

H = high level, L = low level, X = irrelevant
ON IS A LOW
OFF IS A HIGH

(b)

and the data bus during the verify. These inputs are switched electronically through a pair of multiplexers 74157. The multiplexers transfer levels from 0 inputs to the Z outputs when the select (S) is low and from the 1 inputs to the Z outputs when select is high. The single-pole single-throw load verify switch causes the switching of all eight levels. In addition, the select level also turns off the decimal points during verify and enables them to be used to identify the digit being loaded during the load operation.

The resistors connected to the displays are needed to limit the current through the LED segments to the specified level. The value of the resistor can be obtained by the equation

$$R = \frac{V_{CC} - (V_D + V_{OL})}{I_D}$$

I_D = Light saturation current of LED Segment

V_D = Forward voltage drop of LED Segment

V_{OL} = (0.4V)

V_{CC} = +5V

A convenient device recently introduced is the MC14495 Hexadecimal Latch/Decoder Driver. As shown in Figure 5.23, the circuit can latch the input by using a negative going clock or the CL can be held low allowing the display to respond to all input changes. The decoder produces the 16-figure alpha numeric display as shown. The segment drivers are designed for common cathode displays and contain internal resistors limiting the diode current to 7 to 10 mA per segment. The device is CMOS and may require pullup resistors on the input leads if driven by TTL compatible devices.

FIGURE 5.23 MC14495 Hexadecimal Latch/Decoder Driver. This circuit receives a 4-bit hexadecimal input and will drive a common cathode 7-segment display. (*Courtesy of Motorola Inc.*)

TRUTH TABLE

INPUTS				OUTPUTS									
D	C	B	A	a	b	c	d	e	f	g	h + i	$\overline{VCR}$	DISPLAY
0	0	0	0	1	1	1	1	1	1	0	0	Open	0
0	0	0	1	0	1	1	0	0	0	0	0	Open	1
0	0	1	0	1	1	0	1	1	0	1	0	Open	2
0	0	1	1	1	1	1	1	0	0	1	0	Open	3
0	1	0	0	0	1	1	0	0	1	1	0	Open	4
0	1	0	1	1	0	1	1	0	1	1	0	Open	5
0	1	1	0	1	0	1	1	1	1	1	0	Open	6
0	1	1	1	1	1	1	0	0	0	0	0	Open	7
1	0	0	0	1	1	1	1	1	1	1	0	Open	8
1	0	0	1	1	1	1	1	0	1	1	0	Open	9
1	0	1	0	1	1	1	0	1	1	1	1	Open	A
1	0	1	1	0	0	1	1	1	1	1	1	Open	b
1	1	0	0	1	0	0	1	1	1	0	1	Open	C
1	1	0	1	0	1	1	1	1	0	1	1	Open	d
1	1	1	0	1	0	0	1	1	1	1	1	Open	E
1	1	1	1	1	0	0	0	1	1	1	1	0	F

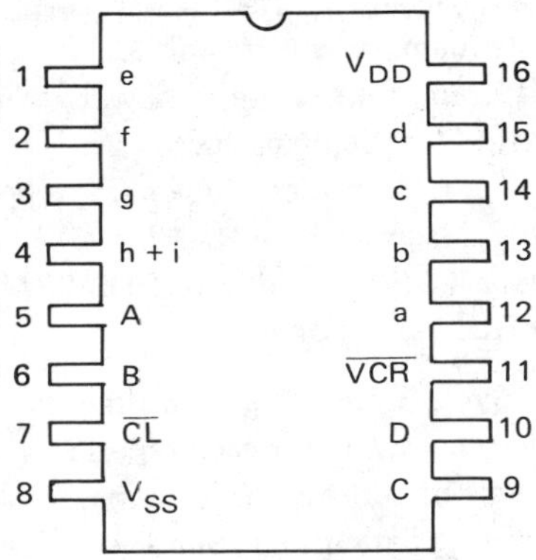

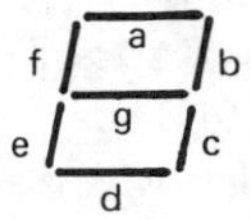

BLOCK DIAGRAM

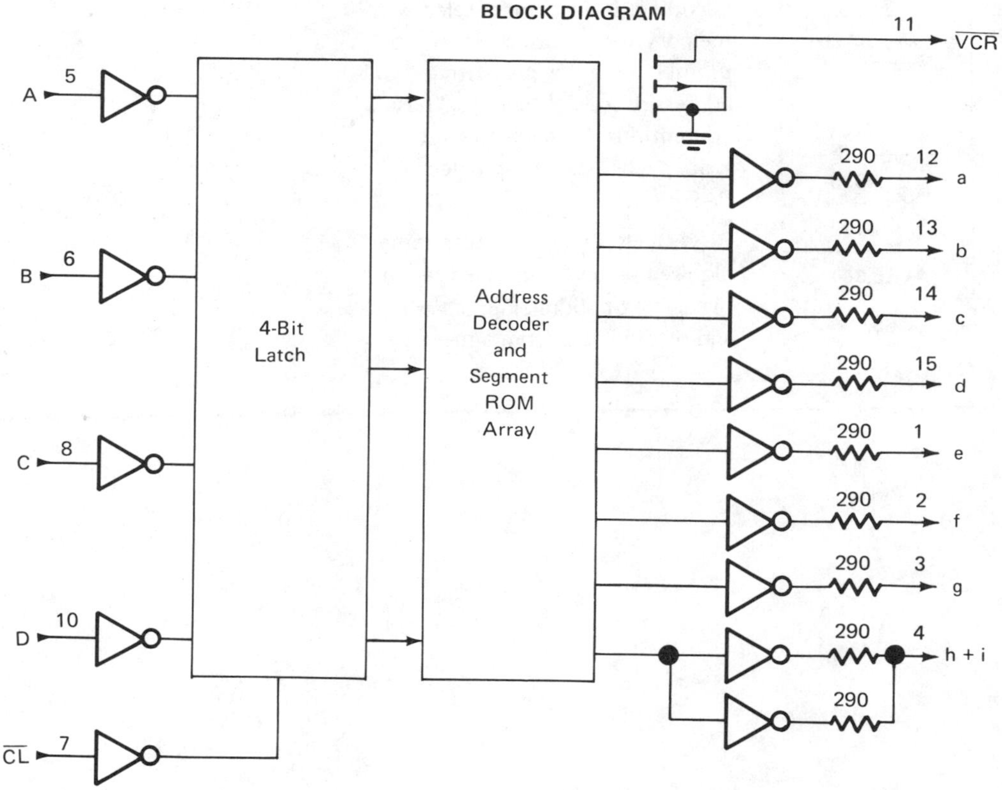

Key Terms

Address Access Time Time measured from stable address or select inputs until the output becomes valid.

Hold Time Time that an output will remain stable after the inputs that enabled it are removed.

K (Memory Size) The letter K as a reference of memory size indicates 1024 addressable locations. Because the addresses are in binary, memory sizes are generally a power of 2. A memory with address leads A_0 through A_9 has 1024 addresses. The size increases by a power of 2 with each added address lead. It is convenient to refer to the memory size as so many K of memory; it being understood that each 1K = 1024 (bits, bytes, or addresses). Table 5.1 shows the memory size references and the actual numerical size.

TABLE 5.1

K	Actual Size
1K	1024
2K	2048
4K	4096
8K	8192
16K	16,384
64K	65,536

Note that a 1K-X-4-bit memory has 1024 addresses with 4 data bits stored at each address, but it may also be called a 4K RAM when referring to its total capacity of 4096 bits.

Memory Page A convenient subdivision of microprocessor memory. A microprocessor with 16 address leads has a total of 64K memory bytes. The lower 8 bits of the memory bus provide 256 addressable bytes for each increment of the upper 8 bits of the address bus. This provides 256 address pages of 256 bytes each. The four hexadecimal digits of an address can be divided such that the upper two digits form the page address.

Output Disable (OD) Control lead supplied with some memories which have 3-state outputs. Can supply functions of a chip enable with the exception of address decoding. It does not deselect memory for a write cycle. It is a useful control for preventing address decode glitches and bus contentions during both read and write cycles. (See **Chip Select** PAGE 60.)

Read Cycle Time The total time required per cycle for each repetitive cycle of addressing, selecting, and reading data from a memory.

Setup Time Time that a specified input must be stable in advance of another input change or in advance of a valid output.

Volatile Memory A volatile memory will lose the data stored in it if the power is interrupted. A nonvolatile memory will retain the data stored in it in spite of power interruptions. Semiconductor random access memories (RAM) are volatile. Magnetic core RAMS are nonvolatile. Semiconductor ROMS and PROMS are nonvolatile.

Write Cycle Time The total time required per cycle for each repetitive cycle of addressing, selecting, and writing data into a memory.

Questions

5.1 A 6810 memory is connected to a 64K memory bus such that its addresses can be expressed as EEEE EE01 0XXX XXXX_2. An input port with address 0400_H is connected to the same bus. What connection need be added to the memory to prevent it from being addressed in coincidence with the port.

5.2 Which of the two memory devices in Figure 5.7 will output to the data bus for an address of $007F_H$? For an address of 0127_H? For an address of $00F7_H$?

5.3 How many actual memory bits are in an 8K RAM?

5.4 Why do the 2114 memory devices of Figure 5.9 have identical address connections?

5.5 The 2114 and 5257 memories are both 4K RAMS. With 8-bit microprocessors when is the 2114 more advantageous than the 5257?

5.6 Under what condition would it not be advisable to use the 5257 of Figure 5.10 as a common I/O memory?

5.7 For what application is the CMOS RAM advantageous?

5.8 Why is a resistor to ground used on the CE_2 lead in Figure 5.12?

5.9 Why is a low V_f diode used in the V_{CC} line of Figure 5.12?

5.10 What is contact bounce? When does it occur?

5.11 What shortcoming does the 7446 7-segment decoder driver have in comparison to a correctly programmed 7602?

5.12 A 1-of-8 decoder 74LS138 is connected to a microprocessor bus as shown in Figure 5.8. What blocks of memory are selected by each decoder output?

Problems

5.1 Reconnect the memory of Figure 5.3 so that it will occupy only the upper half of page 01 within the address range 0000 and 01FF. Addresses above 01FF will not occur.

5.2 Represent the address of the memory of Problem 5.1 in terms of the legend EX01.

5.3 Rewire the connection of the 6810 memory in Figure 5.6 for the memory to occupy the lower half of page 37.

5.4 Change the wiring of the decoder in Figure 5.8 to provide the 1K of memory at address pages 94 through 97 (addresses 9400 through 97FF).

5.5 Add the necessary inverters or change a single gate in the decoder of Figure 5.9 so that the 2114 memories occupy addresses 1C00 to 1FFF.

5.6 Add an additional 1K bytes of memory to the circuit of Figure 5.11. The added four pages are to occupy addresses 3000 to 3FFF. Use the existing decoder and the most convenient memory circuit described in this chapter.

5.7 Design a hexadecimal keyboard encoder using triple 3-input gate circuits.

5.8 Figure 5.24 shows four 2111 memories to be connected to the microprocessor bus. Draw in the connections needed for these memories to occupy address 0200 to 03FF. (Figure 5.24 is on page 121.)

5.9 Add the necessary logic gate decoders to the circuit of Figure 5.24 to deselect the upper addresses of the duplicated memory blocks.

5.10 In the circuit of Figure 5.3, change the address and select wiring so that the memory occupies the upper half of memory page $B4_H$. Use three input NOR gates for any necessary decoding.

5.11 Use the 74LS138 decoder with the memory of Figure 5.4 so that the memory will occupy the lower half of page 58_H.

5.12 Change the gate and select wiring in Figure 5.6 to use triple 3-input NAND gates without changing the memory select address.

5.13 The waveforms in Figure 5.25 are for the microprocessor circuit of Figure 5.8. The memory circuits are high speed and output data within 150 nsec of the address change. The WE does not go low until 250 nsec after the address. Show a correctly timed chip enable waveform to be used on E_3 that will hold the output buffers of the memory off until WE becomes active. The Enable to output delay of the 74LS138 is 25 nsec. (Figure 5.25 is on page 122.)

5.14 Redraw the circuit of Figure 5.9 to use (2102) 1K-X-1 memory in place of the 1K-X-4 memories shown. Use the same address.

5.15 Redraw the circuit of Figure 5.11 using 1K-X-4 (2114) memory in place of the 4K-X-1 memories shown. Use the same address.

5.16 The OR gates in Figure 5.15 have 8 inputs. Draw the keyboard circuit modified to use (74LS30) 8 input NAND gates.

FIGURE 5.24 Connect four 2111 memories to occupy addresses 0200 through 03FF.

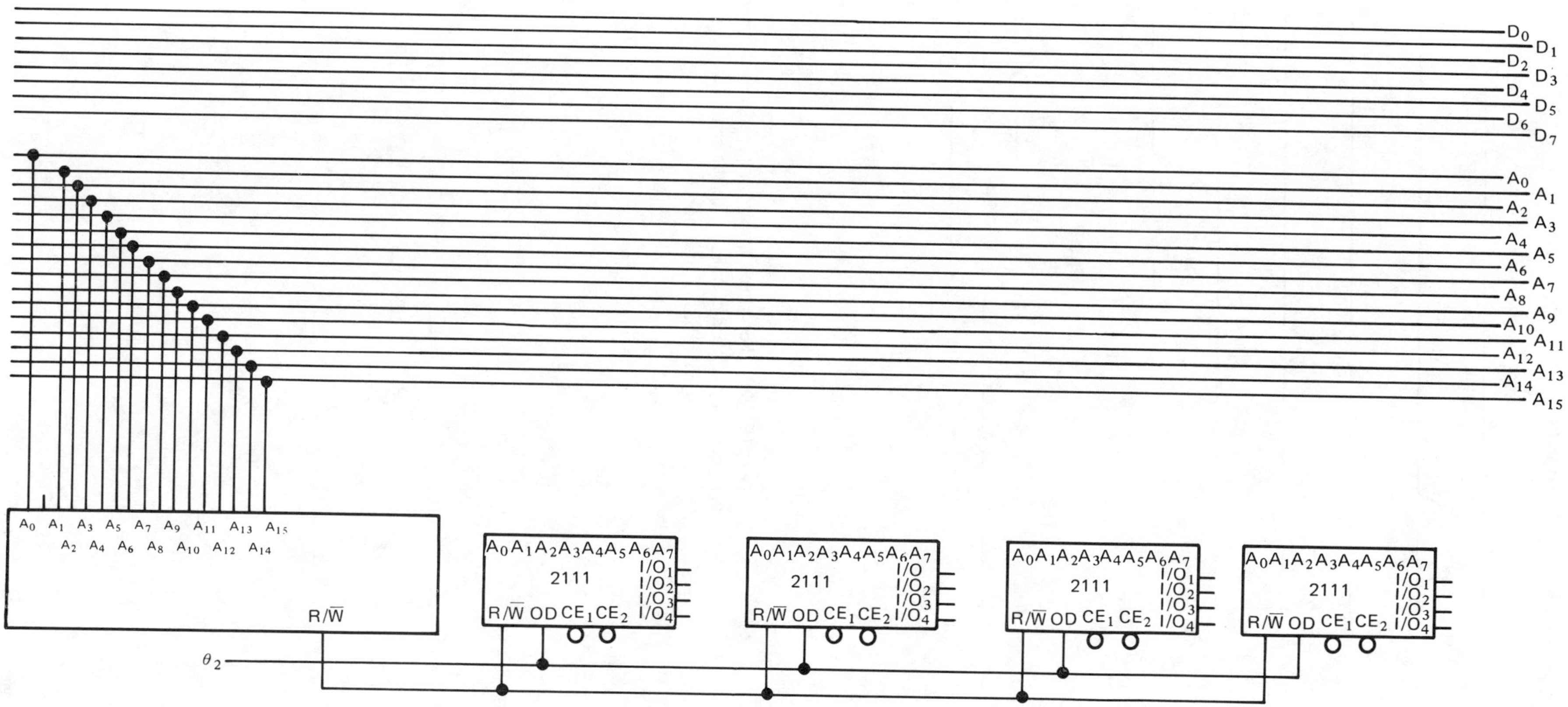

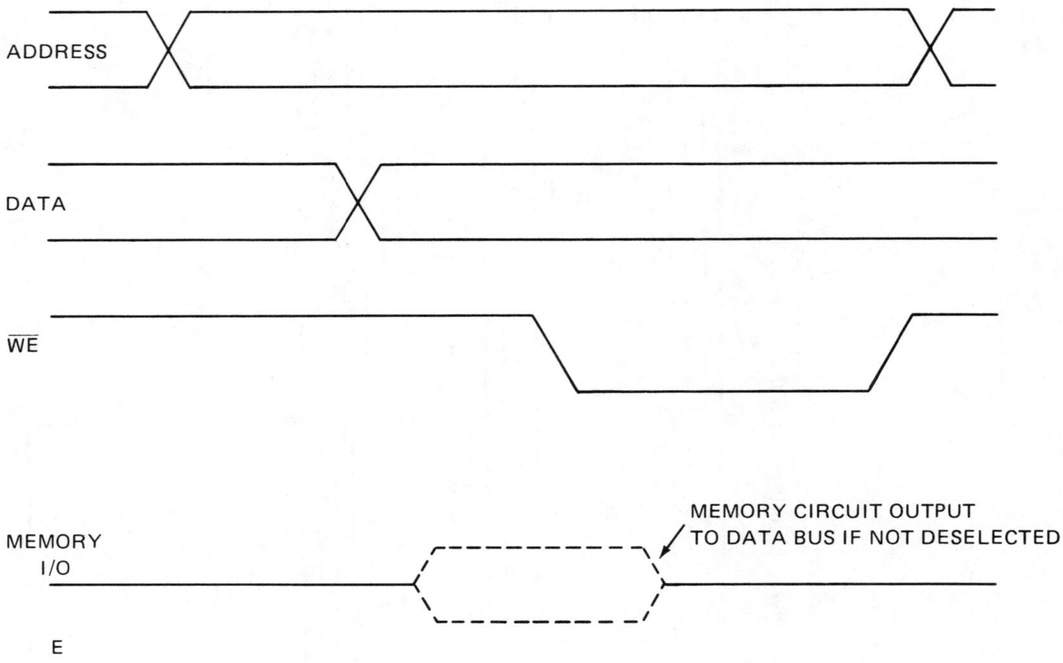

FIGURE 5.25 Top three waveforms are from the microprocessor. Microprocessor and memory I/O are connected to the same data bus. Draw the enable waveform needed to prevent bus contention.

Chapter 6

Read Only Memory

Objectives

On completion of this chapter you will be able to:

- Select from among the several ROM or PROM technologies the one most suitable for a given microprocessor application.
- Determine the most suitable size and configuration of PROM for a given microprocessor program.
- Prepare a binary format program tape for programming fusible link PROMS.
- Prepare an ASCII Tape for programming fusible link PROMS.
- Assemble a digital circuit for programming fusible link PROMS through a hexadecimal keyboard.
- Provide a PROM programmer with a comparitor circuit for verification of the programming.
- Modify the PROM programmer with socket adapters and personality boards for programming PROMS of different size and from different manufacturers.
- Program the 2708 ultraviolet erasable PROM.
- Organize a fusible link PROM memory so that corrections can be made.

6.1 Types of ROMS

The read only memory is as useful in microprocessor application as the read-write RAM. The ROM has the advantage of being nonvolatile and does not have to be loaded each time the system is started up. There are several types available which are erasable and several which are non-erasable. The mask programmable, or MROM, is programmed by the manufacturer to a program supplied by the user. The initial charge for the mask may be as high as $1000, and unless a large number of devices are purchased to a given program, it is an expensive memory. If even a minor change becomes necessary, the mask charge is repeated. The MROM has the highest long-term reliability of all the ROMS. They may be bipolar or MOS, depending on size, and they are fast enough for use with microprocessors.

The fusible link PROM, sometimes referred to as the program once memory, is programmed by blowing minute metallic fuses to produce either one or zero levels. Some manufacturers supply PROMS which are originally zero, and fuses must be blown to produce ones. Others supply PROMS which are originally one, and fuses must be blown to produce zeros. A number of standard configurations are available, such as, 256×4, 512×4, and 512×8, for which the parts supplied by different manufacturers are interchangeable once they are programmed, but the method of programming is different for each manufacturer. If programmed according to specification, the fusible link PROMS are highly reliable. They are bipolar devices having access times fast enough for present microprocessor applications.

The ultraviolet erasable EPROM can be programmed by the user. It has two operating modes: the read mode and the program mode. The voltages applied differ for the two modes. In the program mode each word is addressed and voltages are applied at the data out pins to program 1 or 0 levels. In the read mode, normal operating voltages are applied and the memory outputs the data that was programmed. The inputs and outputs are at normal TTL levels. The EPROM has a transparent lid over the silicon chip and can be erased by exposing it to ultraviolet light of the correct wavelength and intensity.

The electrically alterable or EAROMS come close to functioning like RAMS, with certain important exceptions. They are like RAMS in that they can be read and written in the same circuit, but unlike RAMS an erase mode must precede the write cycle and, equally important, the write cycle takes many times longer than the read cycle. However, they are the closest to a nonvolatile read-write semiconductor memory that the industry has thus far produced. They have many interesting applications as peripheral devices into which the contents of RAM can be transferred prior to a loss of power. In this respect they are an alternative to a battery backup system.

Table 6.1 compares the four commercially available types of ROMS with respect to programming, speed, erasability, and price.

TABLE 6.1 Four types of ROMS and their characteristics.

TYPE	PROGRAMMED	TYPICAL READ ACCESS TIMES (nsec)	ERASABLE OR NON-ERASABLE	PRICE
Mask Programmed (MROM)	During manufacture	70	Nonerasable	Highest for small quantities. Lowest for very large quantities.
Fusible Link (PROM)	After Manufacture by manufacturer, distributor, or user	70	Nonerasable	Low
Ultraviolet Erasable (EPROM)	By user out of circuit	450	Erasable	High
Electrically Alterable ROM (EAROM)	By user in circuit	650 to 950	Erasable	Highest

6.2 Mask Programmed ROMS

Mask programmed ROMS in a wide selection of sizes and configurations are available from many manufacturers of semiconductor memories. The programming is accomplished through the presence or absence of connections in the final metal mask used during circuit manufacture. The buyer supplies the manufacturer with a program usually in machine readable form, such as paper tape or IBM cards. In addition to the program, the buyer may also specify whether the select inputs are CS or $\overline{CS}$. The two conditions required to make the use of mask programmed ROMS feasible are that the program be tried, proven, and not subject to change; and that the quantities to be used with identical programming be large (at least several thousand). For microprocessor application, the user may select between bipolar or TTL compatible MOS ROMS. Table 6.2 shows a comparison of a bipolar and MOS ROM of equivalent size. The MOS ROM has the advantage of low power consumption while the TTL ROM has a higher operating speed and a higher output drive current. Figure 6.1 shows the SY2332 (4K-X-8 ROM). It is a TTL compatible NMOS IC with an I_{OL} sink current rating of 2.1 mA maximum. The timing of the ROM is much simpler than that of the RAMS dis-

TABLE 6.2 Typical TTL and MOS Mask Programmed ROMS compared.

MANUFACTURER'S NUMBER	SIZE	READ ACCESS TIME (nsec)*	POWER DISSIPATION (mw)	IC TECHNOLOGY	OUTPUT SINK CURRENT (mA)
6280	1K X 8	55	850	TTL	10
MK30000	1K X 8	450	330	MOS	3.3

*nsec = nanoseconds.

FIGURE 6.1 A 32K mask programmed ROM and its AC characteristics. (*Courtesy of Synertek*)

PIN CONFIGURATION

SY2332

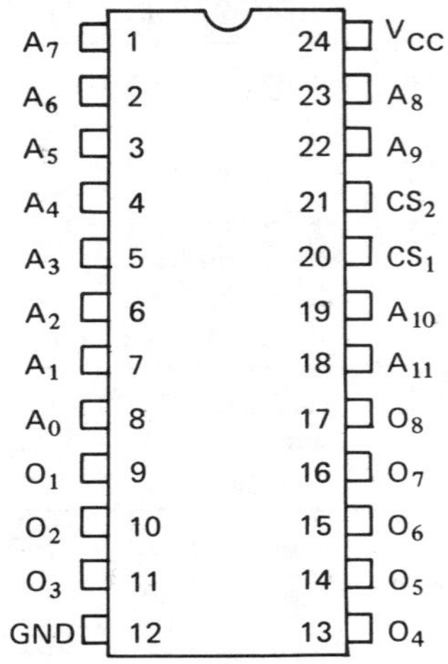

BLOCK DIAGRAM

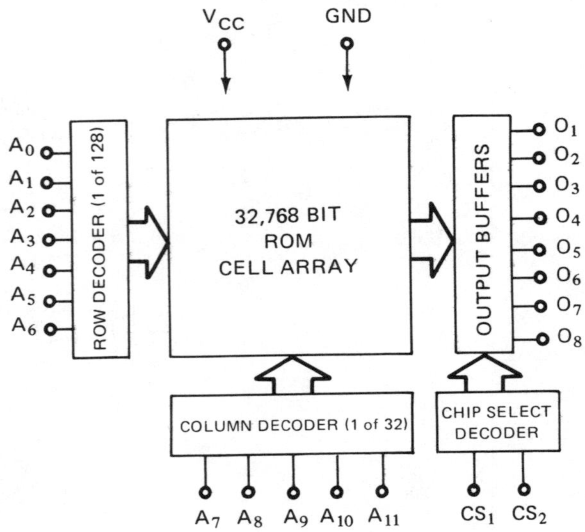

A.C. CHARACTERISTICS

$T_A = 0°C$ to $+70°C$, $V_{CC} = 5.0V \pm 5\%$ (unless otherwise specified)

Symbol	Parameter	SY2332 Min.	SY2332 Max.	Units	Test Conditions
t_{ACC}	Address Access Time		450	ns	Output load: 1 TTL load and 100pF
t_{CO}	Chip Select Delay		150	ns	Input transition time: 20ns
t_{DF}	Chip Deselect Delay		150	ns	Timing reference levels:
t_{OH}	Previous Data Valid After Address Change Delay	20		ns	Input: 1.5V Output: 0.8V and 2.2V

CAPACITANCE

$t_A = 25°C, f = 1.0MH_z$, See Note

Symbol	Parameter	Min.	Max.	Units	Test Conditions
C_I	Input Capacitance		7	pF	All pins except pin under test tied to AC ground
C_O	Output Capacitance		10	pF	

Note: This parameter is periodically sampled and is not 100% tested.

TIMING DIAGRAM

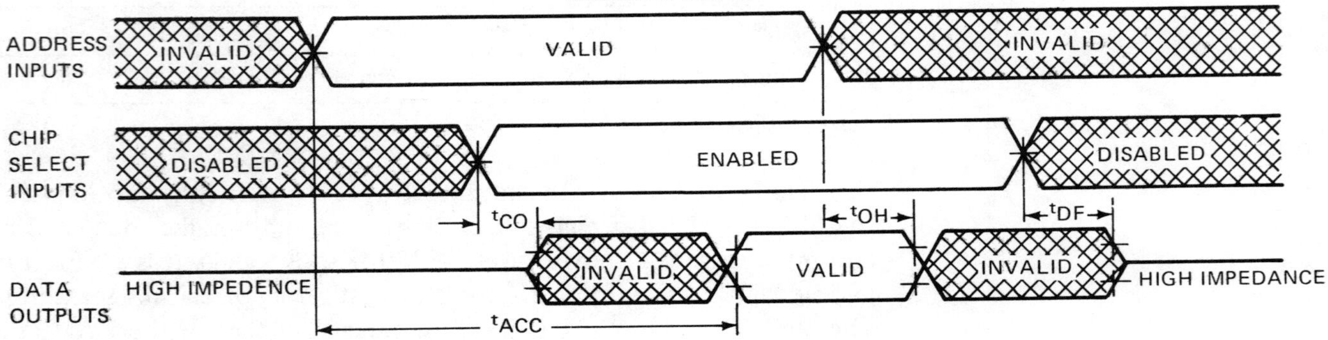

FIGURE 6.2 A 4K-X-8 ROM connected to a microprocessor bus.

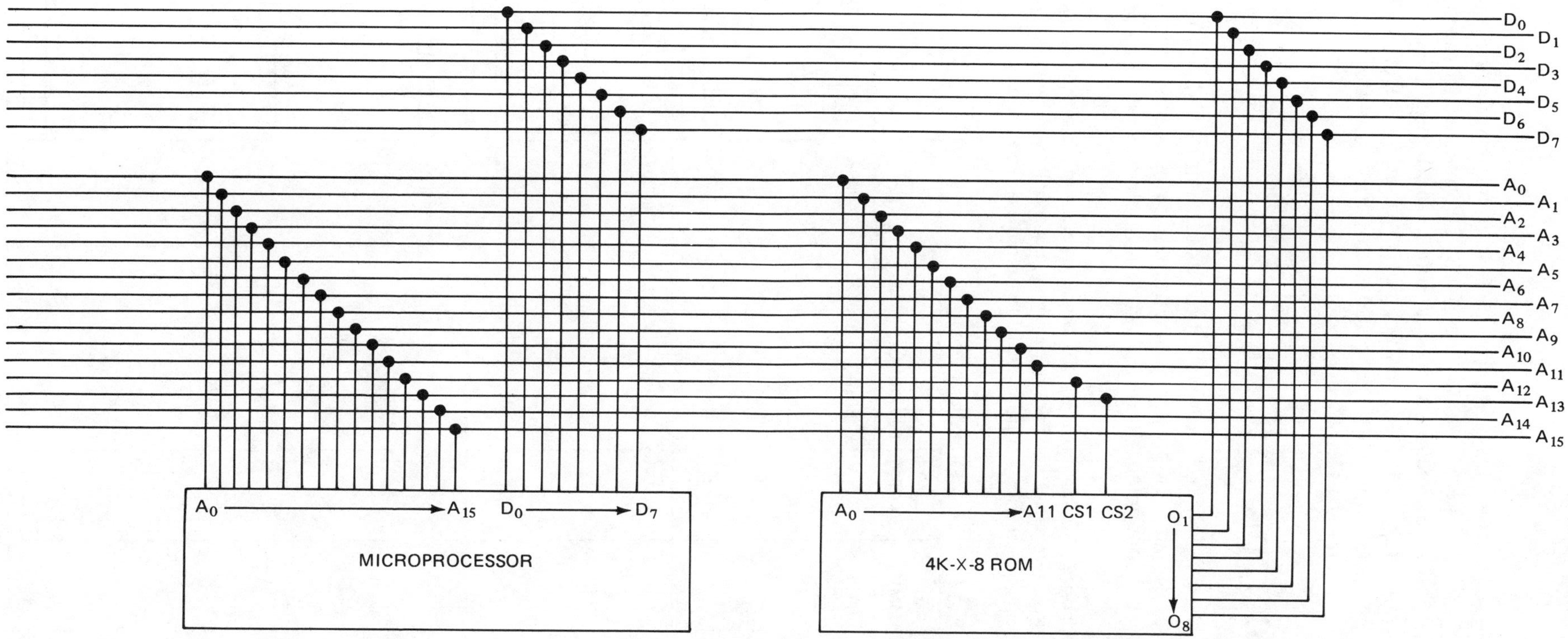

Address of this memory is EE11 XXXX XXXX XXXX

X = Will be 1 or 0 depending on byte being addressed.

1 = Memory will be selected only when this bit is 1 (high).

E = Memory will be selected for either 1 or 0 in this bit (causes duplication of addresses within the memory map).

cussed in Chapter 5 in that it has no write cycle timing to consider. Figure 6.2 shows the SY2332 connected to the microprocessor bus so as to occupy addresses 3000_H to $3FFF_H$. Because the higher 2 bits of the 16-bit address are not involved in selecting this ROM, it will also occupy addresses 7000_H to $7FFF_H$, $B000_H$ to $BFFF_H$, and $F000_H$ to $FFFF_H$.

6.3 The Fusible Link PROM

Table 6.3 shows a list of fusible link PROM configurations. Each manufacturer prescribes a different programming procedure, but once programmed, they will work interchangeably. Figure 6.3 shows the 7611

TABLE 6.3 (This page and opposite.) Fusible link PROMS come in a variety of sizes and configurations. Those from different manufacturers are interchangeable after programming, but usually program differently. Only the 3-state versions are listed. Open collector revisions are also available from these same sources.

SIZE	WORDS BY BITS	MANUFACTURER TYPE						PINOUT DIAGRAM (not to scale)
		HARRIS	MMI*	FCS†	INTERSIL	SIGNE-TICS	TI‡	
256	32 X 8	7603	6331		5610	82S123	74S288	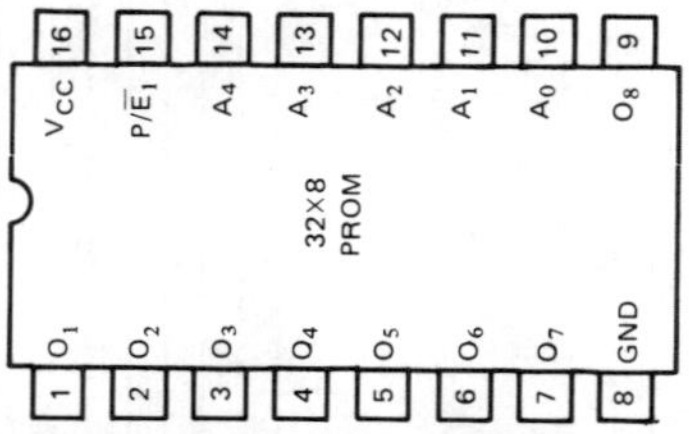
1024	256 X 4	7611	6301	93427	5623	82S129	74S287	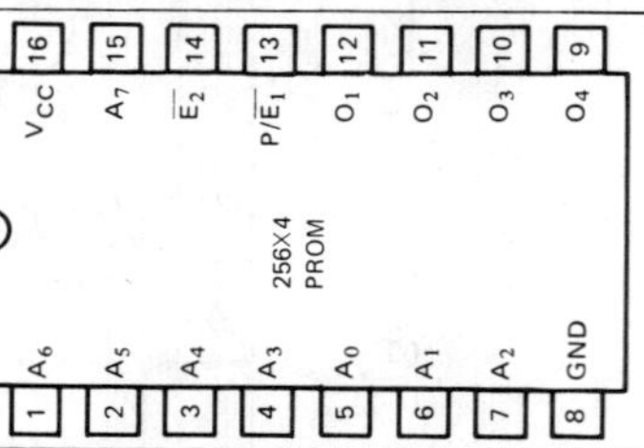
2048	256 X 8		6336			82S114	74S471	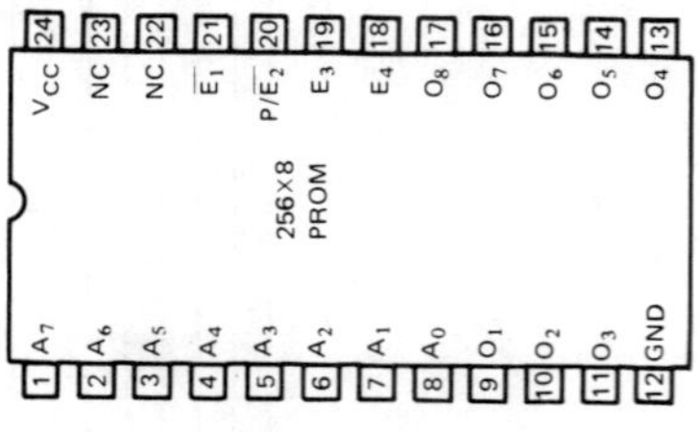
2048	512 X 4	7621	6306	93446	5624	82S131		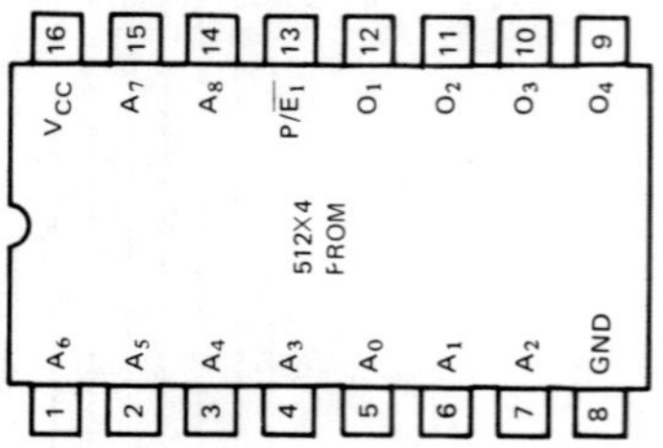

PROM. It is configured as a 256-X-4 and two must be connected to fill an 8-bit microprocessor data bus. One circuit supplies the lower four data bits, the second supplies the upper four data bits. The 7641 is a more advanced model of this memory with a 512-word X 8-bit configuration. It supplies two full pages of memory in a single 24-pin circuit. This family of fusible link memories, supplied by Harris Semiconductor Inc., is among the easiest to program because the programming voltage and average currents used are within the specifications of the 7400 series TTL high voltage open collector buffers. This means they can be programmed using standard digital logic circuits without the aid of linear or discrete components. The programming specifications are given in Table 6.4. Figure 6.4 shows a typical circuit used at the memory data pins. The open collector circuits are turned on, effectively grounding the end of the pullup resistors and dropping the 12 volts across the resistor. Those data bits to be programmed with a zero level will receive a program pulse that turns off the open collector output allowing the voltage to rise to a level that will blow the fuse. Only one data fuse can be blown at a time.

TABLE 6.3 (Continued)

SIZE	WORDS BY BITS	MANUFACTURER TYPE HARRIS	MMI*	FCS†	INTERSIL	SIGNETICS	TI‡	PINOUT DIAGRAM (not to scale)
4096	512 X 8	7641	6341	93448	5625	82S141	74S472	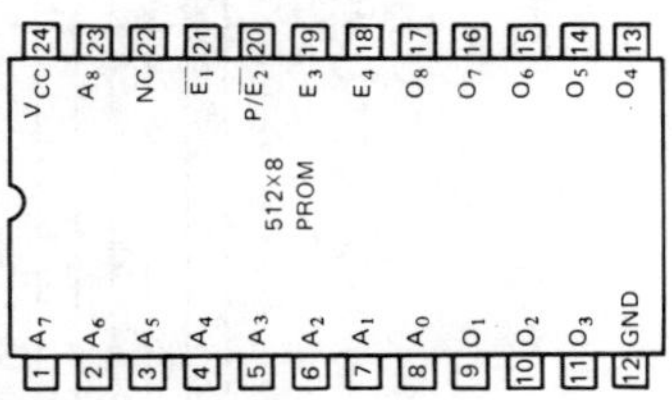
4096	1024 X 4	7643	6353	93453	5626	82S137		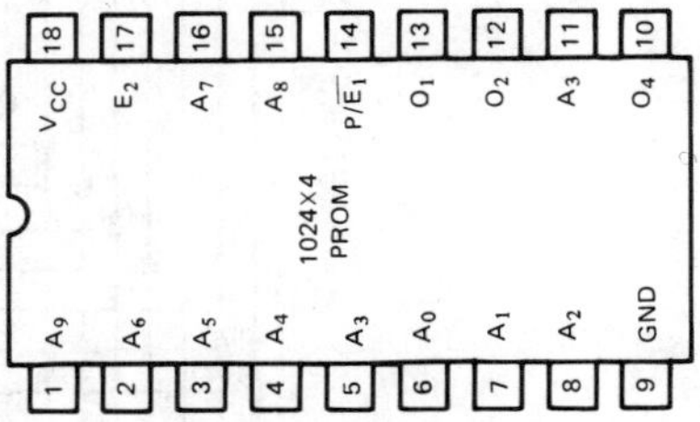
8192	1024 X 8	7681	6381	93451	5618	82S181	74S478	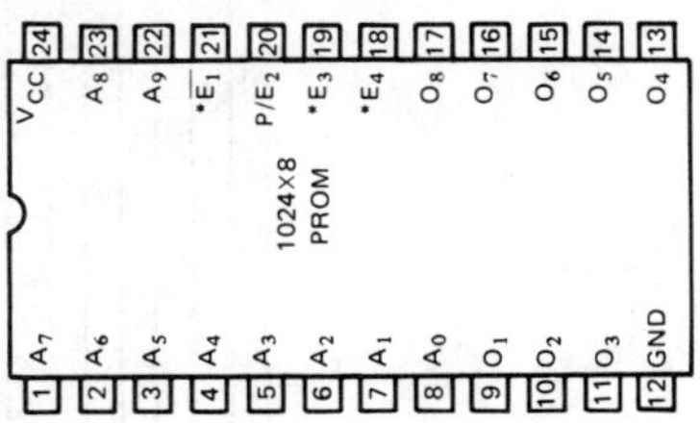

*MMI: Monolithic Memories
†FCS: Fairchild Semiconductor
‡TI: Texas Instruments

FIGURE 6.3 Two 256-X-4 PROMS connected to provide one page of ROM.

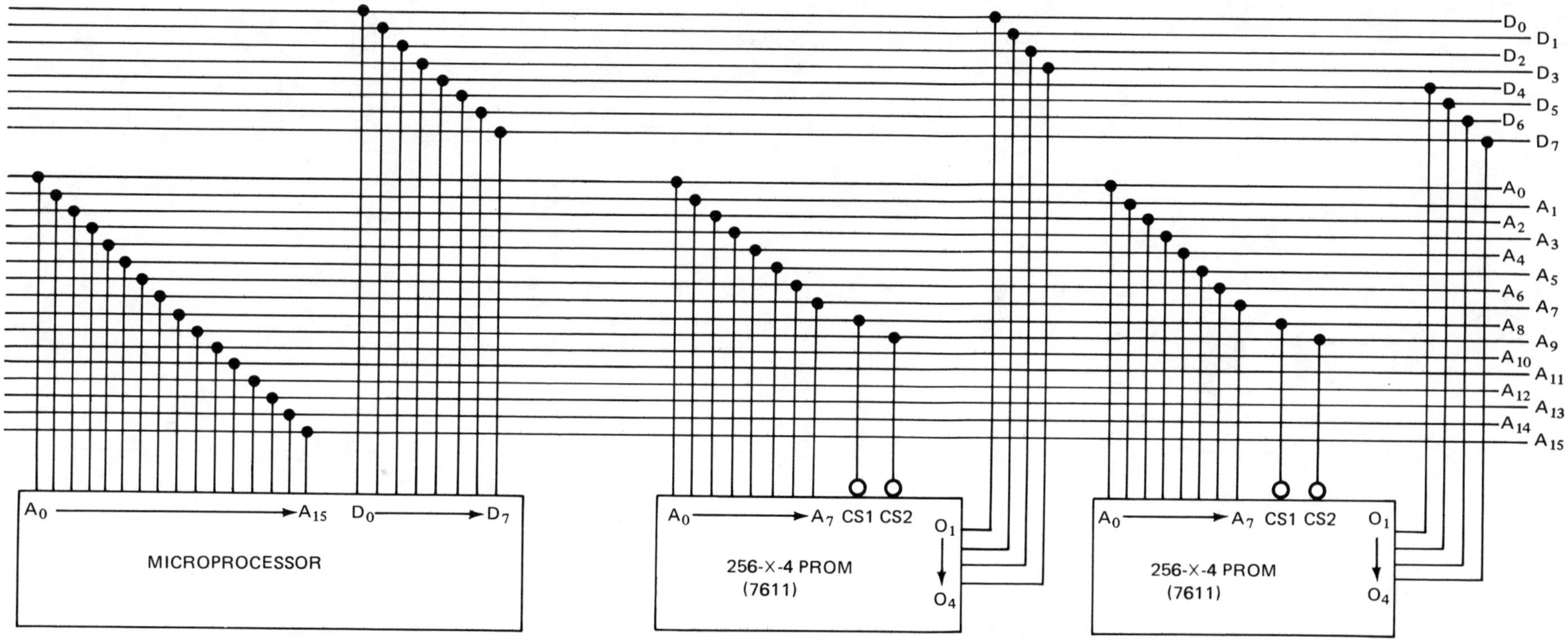

Address of this memory is EEEE EE00 XXXX XXXX

X = Will be 1 or 0 depending on byte being addressed.

0 = Memory will be selected only when this bit is 0 (low).

E = Memory will be selected for either 1 or 0 in this bit (causes duplication of addresses within the memory map).

TABLE 6.4 Voltage and timing parameters specified for the programming of the Harris 7641 PROM. Other Harris 7600 series PROMS use the same specifications. (*Courtesy of Harris Semiconductor Co.*)

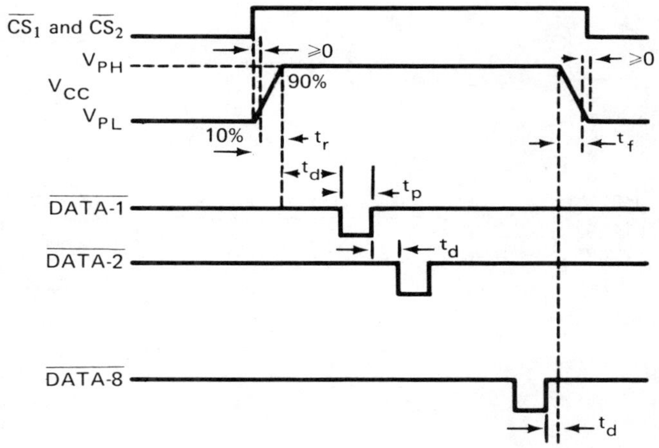

PARAMETER	SYMBOL	MIN.	RECOM-MEND VALUE	MAX.	UNITS
Address Input Voltage (1)	V_{IH} V_{IL}	2.4 0.0	5.0 0.4	5.0 0.8	V V
Programming/Verify Voltage to V_{CC} (2)	V_{PH} V_{PL}	11.5 3.75	12.0 4.0	12.5 4.25	V
Programming Voltage Current Limit	I_{CCP}			600	mA
Programming (V_{CC}) Voltage Rise and Fall Time	t_r t_f	1 1	1 1	10 10	μs μs
Programming Delay	t_d	10	10	100	μs
Programming Pulse Width—First Attempts	t_{p1}	100	100	200	μs
Programming Pulse Width—Subsequent	t_{p2}	10	10	20	ms
Programming Duty Cycle	D.C.	—	10	10	%
Output Voltage Enable Disable (3)	V_{OPE} V_{OPD}	9.5 0	10.0 .45	10.5 5.5	V V
Output Voltage Enable Current Limit	I_{OPE}			10	mA
Case Temp	T_C			75	°C

1. Address and chip select should not be left open for V_{IH}.
2. Verification at V_{CC} = 4.0 ± .25 Volts, T_A = 25°C is recommended to guardband performance over full temperature and voltage range.
3. Disable condition will be met with output open circuit.

There is no quick, simple way to transfer data from a program sheet to a PROM. There are at least four principal operations involved.

1. Render data into machine readable form.
2. Verify the machine readable data.
3. Transfer the data to the PROM.
4. Verify that the PROM is correctly programmed.

The need for verification must not be overlooked because the probability of human errors in punching a thousand or more keys to a program is very high and usually a single error is enough to make a PROM useless. Verification after programming is necessary since not all fuses blow on the first attempt. There are a number of commercial PROM blowers

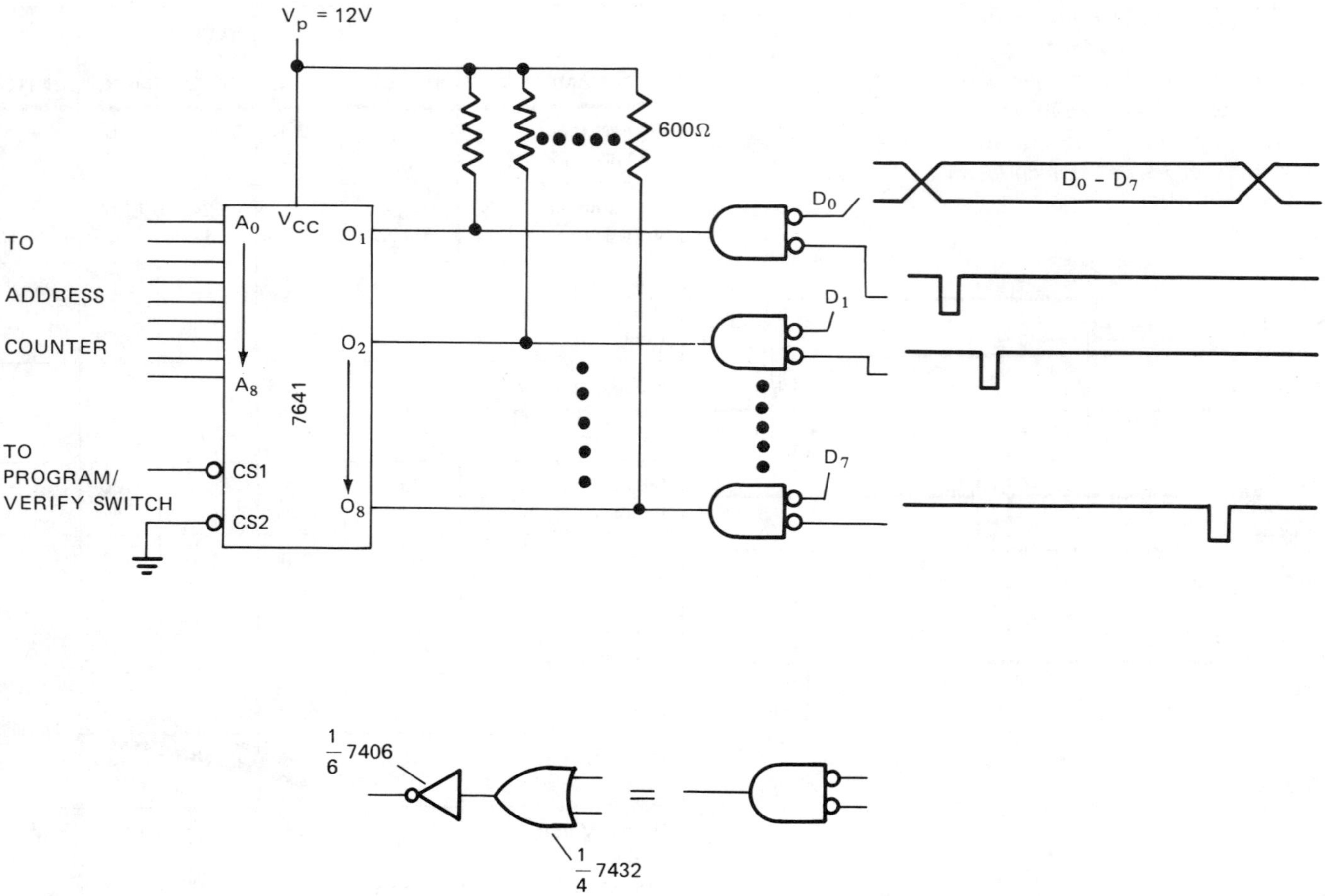

FIGURE 6.4 Fusing pulses of the correct width and timing can be applied to a Harris 7641 PROM through NOR gates as shown. The standard 7433 NOR buffer has too low a voltage rating to accommodate V_p. The NOR function can be made using a 7432 OR gate with a high voltage inverting buffer 7406.

which facilitate these four essential operations. Typical of these is the DATA I/O Model 5 Programming System shown in Figure 6.5. This system provides a random access memory of 4K bytes. The program can be loaded into RAM using the keyboard. Then it can be verified by stepping through each address and checking the display. Once the program is loaded and verified, it can be transferred automatically from RAM to PROM. The blowing of the PROM is verified as each address is blown. An optional paper tape punch can provide a tape for future use of the same program. The tape can be used not only for programming by the originator, but also, it can be sent to a PROM manufacturer or distributor for the purchase of preprogrammed PROMS. The Model 5 programs PROMS from the data stored in its RAM. The RAM can be loaded from one of three sources: the keyboard, the tape reader, or a master PROM.

For most commercial PROM blowers the program in machine readable form is a perforated paper tape. There are various formats used for the tape. The simplest of these is the binary format in Figure 6.6.

Unfortunately, paper tape equipment that provides a binary format is somewhat specialized and not readily available to all laboratories. Most PROM suppliers can program from a tape punched in ASCII hexadecimal code. A tape containing this code is shown in Figure 6.7. As the name implies, the data to be programmed is expressed

FIGURE 6.5 Data I/O Model 5 Programming System. (*Courtesy of Data I/O Corporation*)

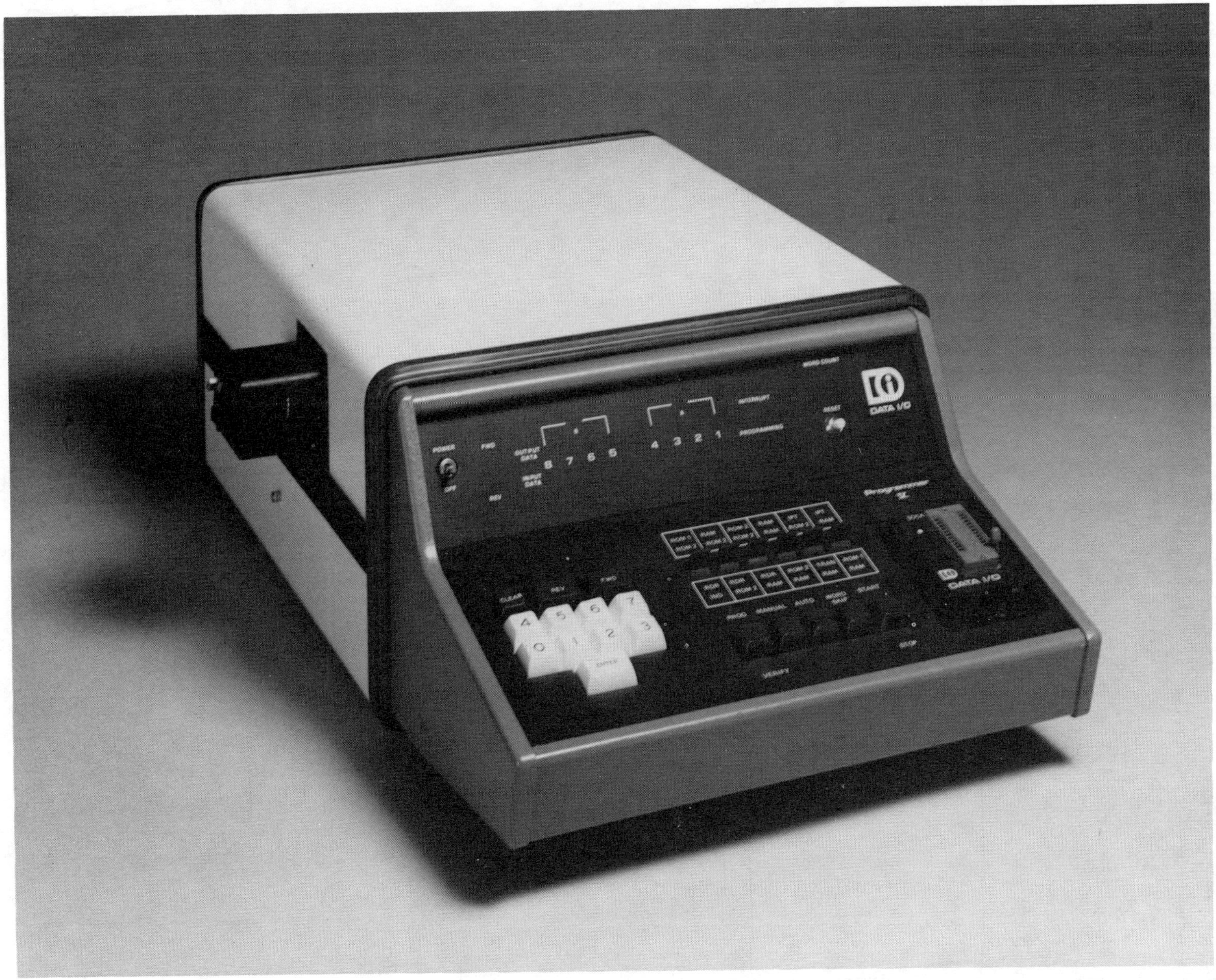

FIGURE 6.6 The simplest paper tape format is the binary format. The programmer recognizes address zero as the address following the first rubout (all holes). The tape shown is for a 512-X-8 PROM. A tape for a 512-X-4 would have no holes in channels 5 through 8 following the rubout.

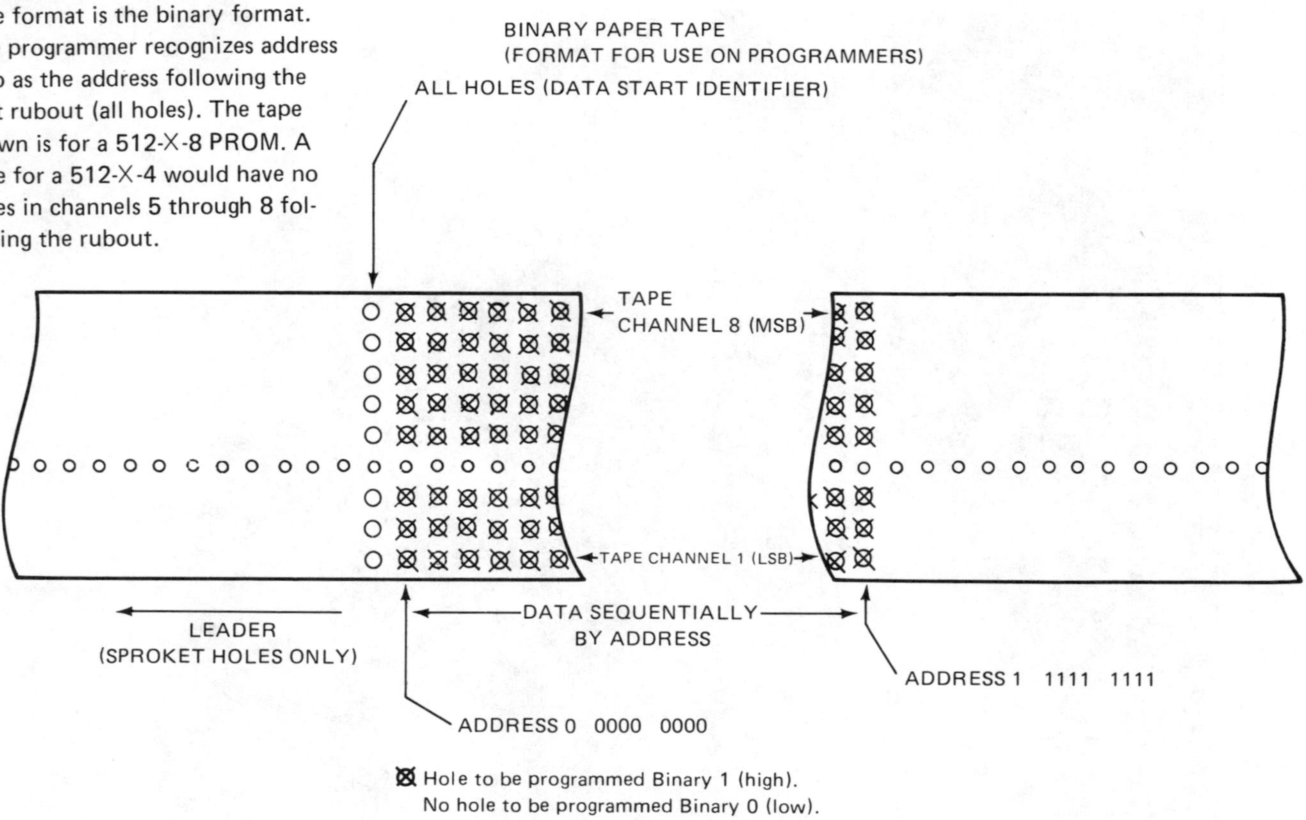

FIGURE 6.7 The ASCII hexadecimal tape requires the use of "SOH" to start the translator process. An "ETX" is used for tapes shorter than word limit. Use CR and LF to help format data for printout. (*Courtesy of Data I/O Corporation*)

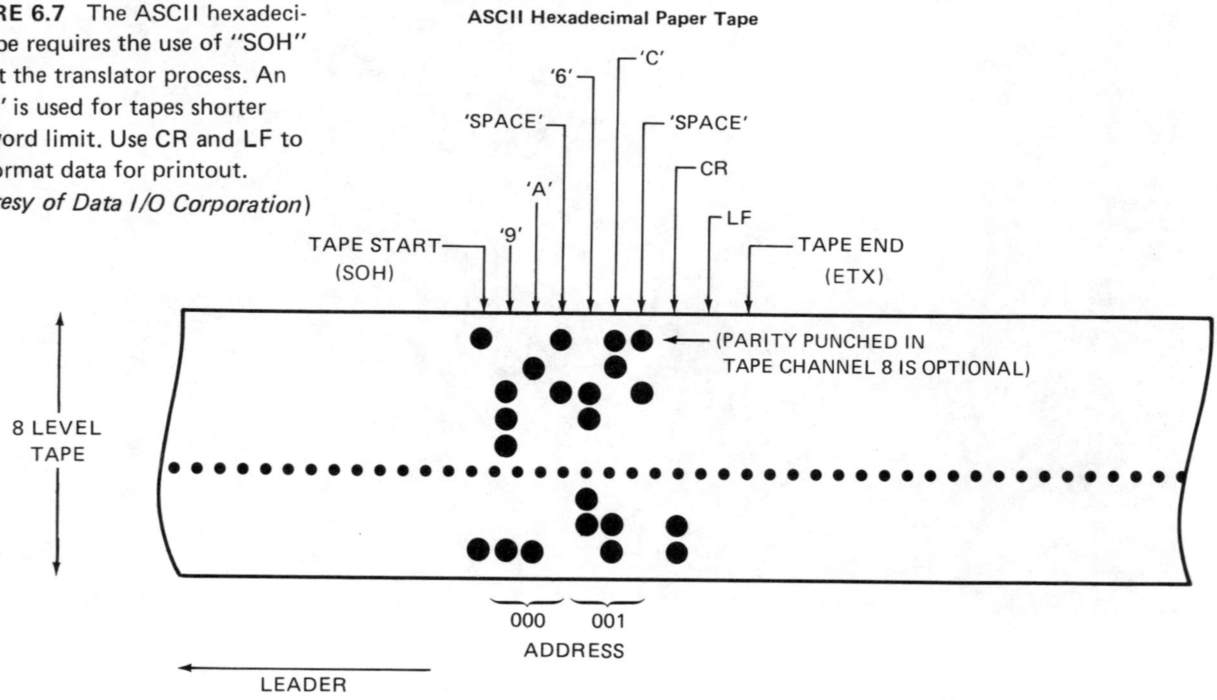

Tape Start = "SOH" or Control A.
Tape End = "ETX" or Control C.

as hexadecimal digits that are punched on the tape as ASCII characters. Using a teletype with a paper tape punch, the data bytes are typed MSD followed by LSD and then a space such that each address of an 8-bit* PROM will result in two hexadecimal characters, 0 through F, punched in ASCII code on the tape followed by a space character. If the PROM has only four data bits, then only a single character is punched before each space. A single "SOH" character (control A) is punched prior to address zero and an ETX (Control C) is typed at the end of the tape. The PROM programmer accepts the characters following the "SOH" as being address zero.

If a mistake is made in typing the hexadecimal characters, it is no problem to correct it as long as the space bar has not been depressed. The space bar is an execute command for the PROM programmer. For an 8-bit PROM, it programs the address based on two characters preceding the space bar. Additional characters preceding those are ignored. For a 4-bit PROM, additional characters preceding the one character before the space are ignored. However, if the space bar has been depressed, and a mistake exists in the one character preceding for a 4-bit PROM or either of two characters preceding for an 8-bit PROM, then the tape must be discarded and a new one started. The PROM programmer is designed to ignore the ASCII characters for carriage return and line feed. The reader function of the teletype is useful when listing the contents of the tape in a convenient format for verification. If all addresses in a PROM are not to be programmed, the ETX character after the last character to be programmed will prevent any fuses from being blown in the remaining addresses of the PROM. All addresses preceding the ETX must contain the correct hexadecimal characters plus space bar. No addresses can be skipped. If an unprogrammed section is to remain between two programmed segments of the PROM, then the addresses of the unprogrammed section must be programmed all F or all 0 depending on whether the unprogrammed device outputs all high levels or all low levels.

The price charged by distributors for programming PROMS to a user's tape is relatively low in comparison to the price of the unprogrammed PROM. This is particularly true for the large, higher priced PROMS. Table 6.5 is a distributor's step-by-step instruction for generating an ASCII hexadecimal programming tape.

For small laboratory operation where the expense of a teletype with tape punch and reader are not warranted, the data can be loaded in RAM and verified using a circuit like that developed in Figure 5.18. The content of the RAM can then be transferred to the PROM. Figure 6.8 shows a block diagram of the added circuits needed to convert the RAM circuit of Figure 5.18 to a PROM blower for 7600 family PROMS.

---

*In this discussion, PROMS which store 8 data bits per address are referred to as 8-bit PROMS; those which store 4 data bits per address are referred to as 4-bit PROMS.

TABLE 6.5 PROM programming tape generation procedure.

Step 1	Go to TWX machine, place machine on Local Loop, turn on tape punch, and turn on main power. (TWX machine–8 level Tape output)
Step 2	Press and release "HERE IS" key about 20 times to run off a 1 foot leader.
Step 3	While holding "CTRL" key down, type the letter A once. This places the programmer into the "Read Data" configuration.
Step 4	Starting with PROM address Ø, enter the data word you desire in hexadecimal code one digit at a time, MSD first.
Step 5	After typing the data digits, if no mistake has been made, hit the space bar once and only once. (If a typographical error occurs, you can correct it by typing in the correct digits before you hit the space bar. The programmer is setup to ignore all but the last two keys entered before the space bar is hit. If you have already hit the space bar, it is too late and you must begin all over again from Step 2.)
Step 6	Repeat Steps 4 and 5 for each word in the PROM. *DO NOT* skip any addresses. If you desire all output bits to be Ø: type ØØ at those locations.
Step 7	When the line you are on has run out of space, at the end of a word and after the space, you may hit "LINE FEED" and "CARRIAGE RETURN" to start a new line of paper, after which you enter the data for the next word. The programmer will ignore the 2 paper commands.
Step 8	When you have finished entering the data for all the addresses in the PROM hold the "CTRL" key depressed and type the letter C once. The CTRL C on the tape will take the programmer out of the "Read Data" configuration.
Step 9	To complete tape, press and release the "HERE IS" key 10 times to provide a trailing leader.
Step 10	If you desire, you can check your tape by playing it back and read the printout to check it for errors. Tape is now ready to be sent in for programming the PROM.

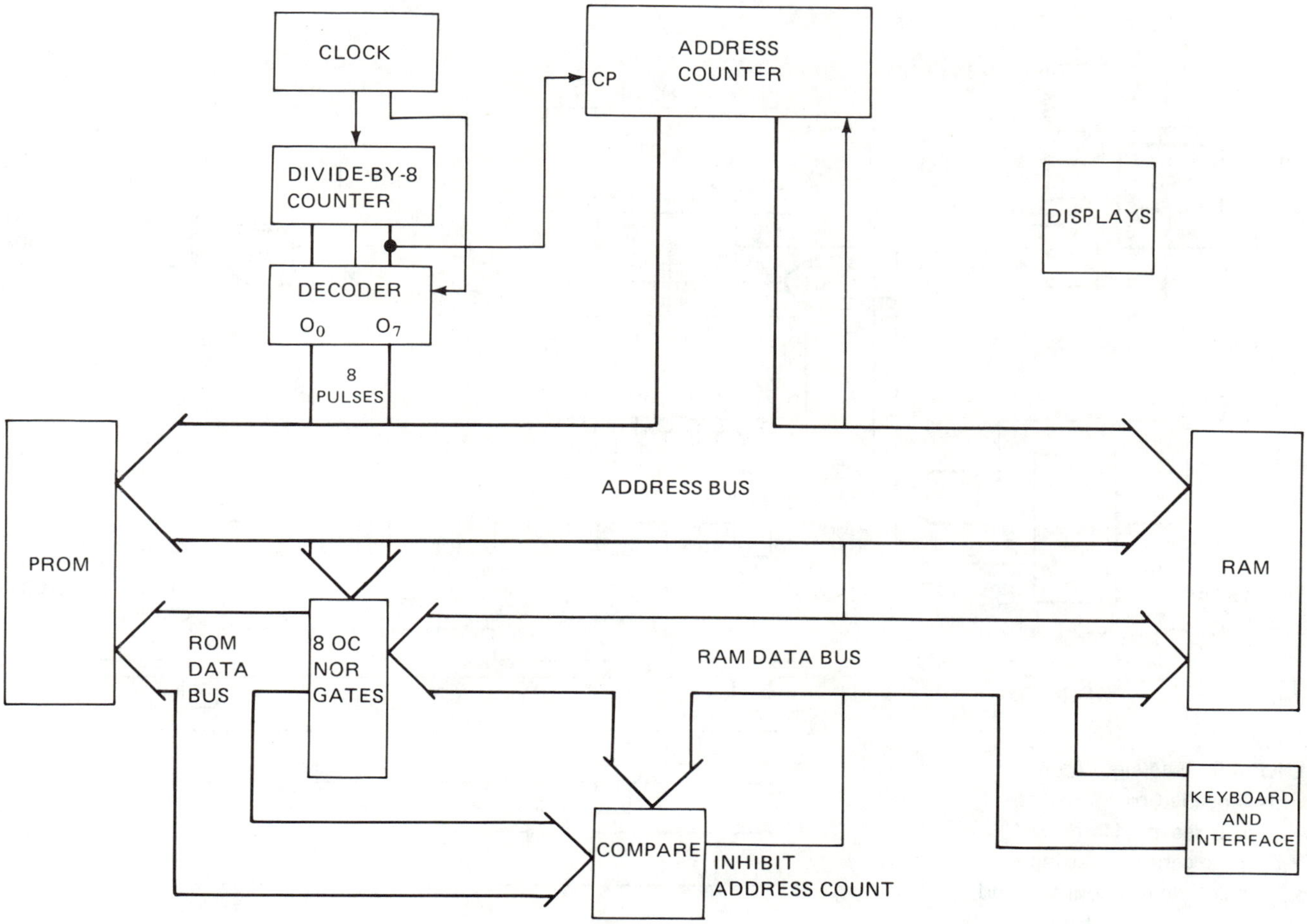

FIGURE 6.8 Block diagram of a PROM blower that uses a hexadecimal keyboard as an entry device and a RAM for storage of the program. During programming, the data is transferred from RAM to PROM one address at a time.

The clock and timing circuit is shown in detail in Figure 6.9. The requirement from this circuit is 8 parallel, consecutive pulses, 0.1 to 20 milliseconds (msec) wide, and separated in time by a minimum of 10 msec. To simplify the design we have made them 10 msec apart. The 555 timer circuit with RC values set for 10 msec pulses (f = 5KHZ), provides a suitable clock. The clock operates a divide-by-eight counter. The outputs of the counter are decoded. The D (MSD) input of the decoder is used as a strobe, and the result is a set of eight pulses, 10 msec apart, occurring one on each of eight separate lines (0 through 7). The Q_D output of the divide-by-eight counter is used to clock the address counter immediately after the eight pulse has occurred.

Another problem to be considered is stopping and starting the PROM blower at address zero. As Figure 6.9 shows, the start-stop switch causes the clock to the divide-by-eight counter to be inhibited during stop. In addition, a logic 1 on the decoder D input prevents any active output from the decoder. When the switch is placed in start, the J-K flip-flop will clock to the set condition on the negative going edge of $\overline{CP}$, removing the reset and enabling the clock to the CP_B input. The J-K flip-flop insures that the cycle starts on the trailing edge of the clock insuring a full pulse width at the decoder zero output.

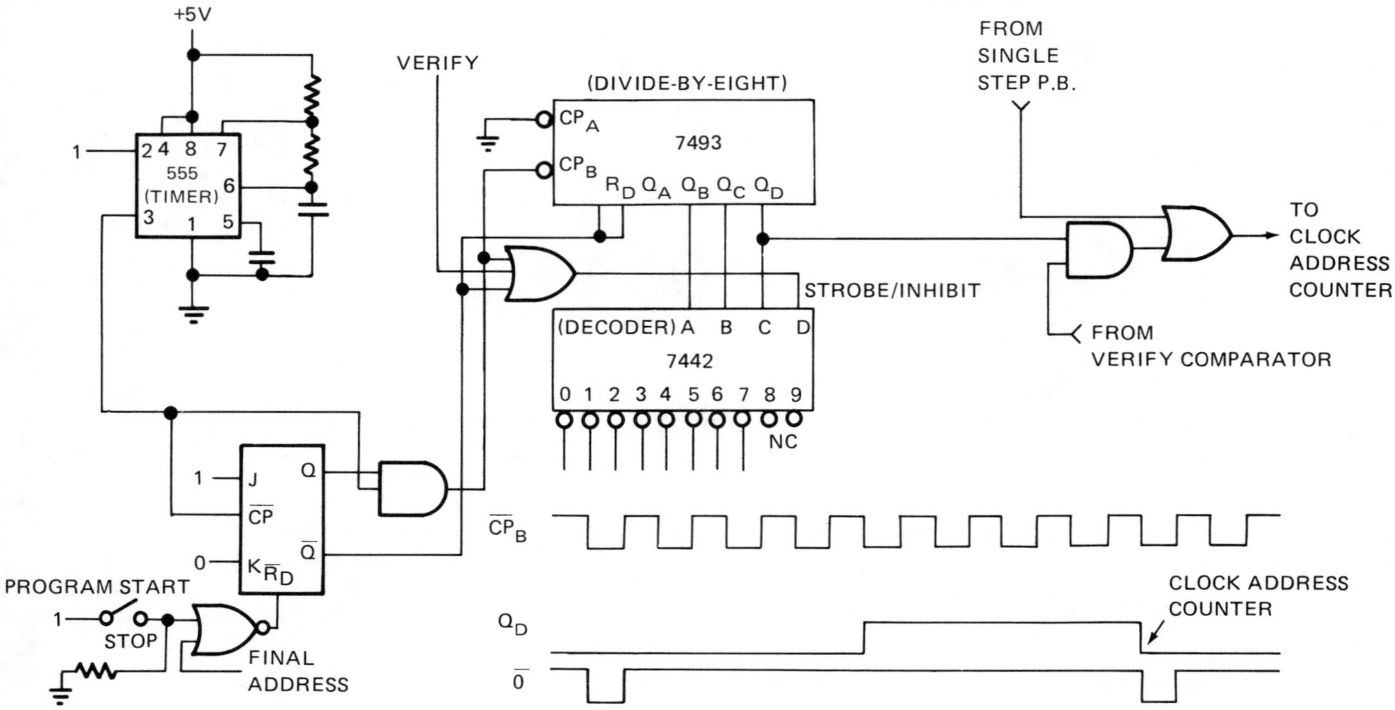

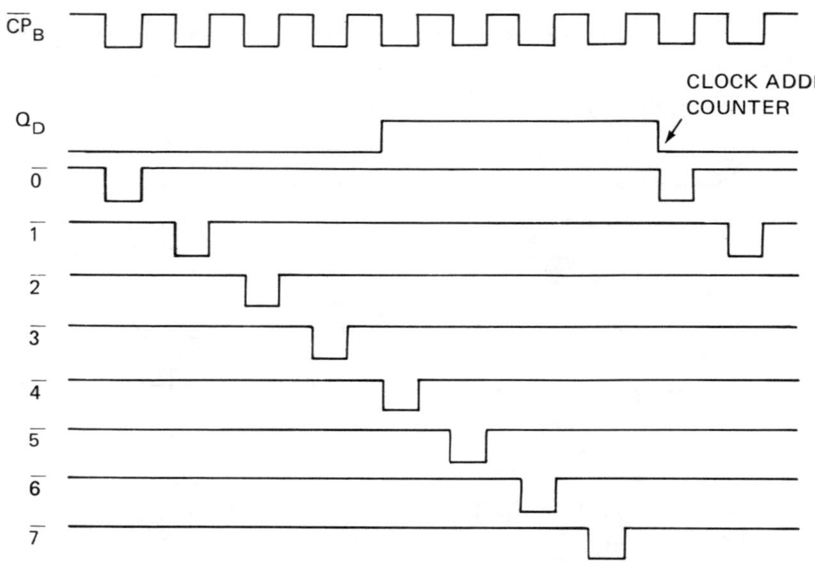

FIGURE 6.9 The eight consecutive pulses needed to control the blowing of fuses in a Harris 7641 PROM can be generated using a clock, divide-by-eight counter, and decoder. The pulse width can be adjusted by varying the resistor capacitor combination at the 555 timer. The address counter is clocked once for each set of eight pulses.

An extra bit in the address counter stops the program when the address counter passes the highest address to be programmed. Depressing the reset button will return the address counter to zero, and unless the start-stop switch has been returned to stop, the program run will be repeated. If a section of the PROM is to be reserved for future use and there is no way to avoid addressing it during a program run, these addresses in the RAM should be loaded with an FF or 00, whichever does not blow fuses in the PROM.

Yet to be added to the circuit is a provision for verifying the programming of the PROM. In the verify mode, the RAM and PROM are addressed simultaneously and the output of the RAM is compared with the output of PROM at each address. On the first address for which the data fails to compare, the clock is inhibited. If all fuses were correctly blown, the address count would continue to the MSB. If one or more fuses fail to blow, the pulse width can be switched to maximum (20 milliseconds) and the entire PROM can be programmed again. Application of the fusing pulses to addresses which have already blown correctly causes no degradation and little if any power dissipation. It is best to blow as many fuses as possible at the narrower pulse width first to avoid overheating the PROM. Figure 6.10 shows the added circuit needed to verify. The CS leads must be selected and the fuse pulses inhibited. A pair of 4-bit magnitude comparators determines if the PROM and RAM outputs are identical and either enables or inhibits the address count. The step push button (in the RAM circuit) can be used to override a no compare at any single address. The logic circuit of the complete PROM blower is shown in Figure 6.11.

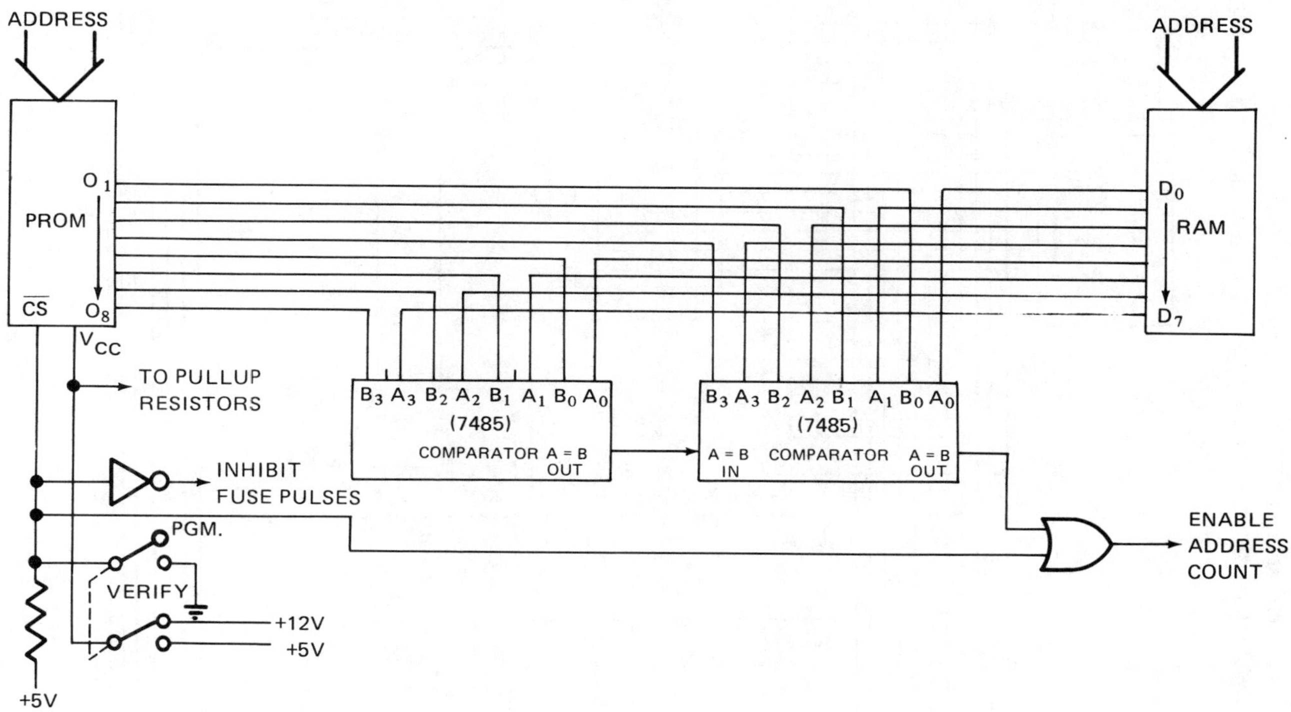

Note: Unless mechanical switches are used to disconnect the comparator B inputs during programming, an interface circuit will be needed to protect the comparator from the high voltage programming pulses.

FIGURE 6.10 A pair of 4-bit comparators are combined to compare the programmed PROM with the output of the RAM after each program run. The counter will stop on any address that failed to program. When a failure to program occurs, the programming pulse width should be increased (by reducing the frequency of the 555 timer) and the program run again. Application of programming pulses to outputs that have already been successfully programmed causes no degradation or power dissipation. The programming pulse width must not be increased beyond the specified limit.

FIGURE 6.11 Complete diagram of a PROM blower with provisions for socket adapters and personality card to allow for programming PROMS of different sizes and programming specification. The B inputs to the digital comparator are shown connected to the PROM outputs. This is to simplify the drawing. (See Note Figure 6.10.)

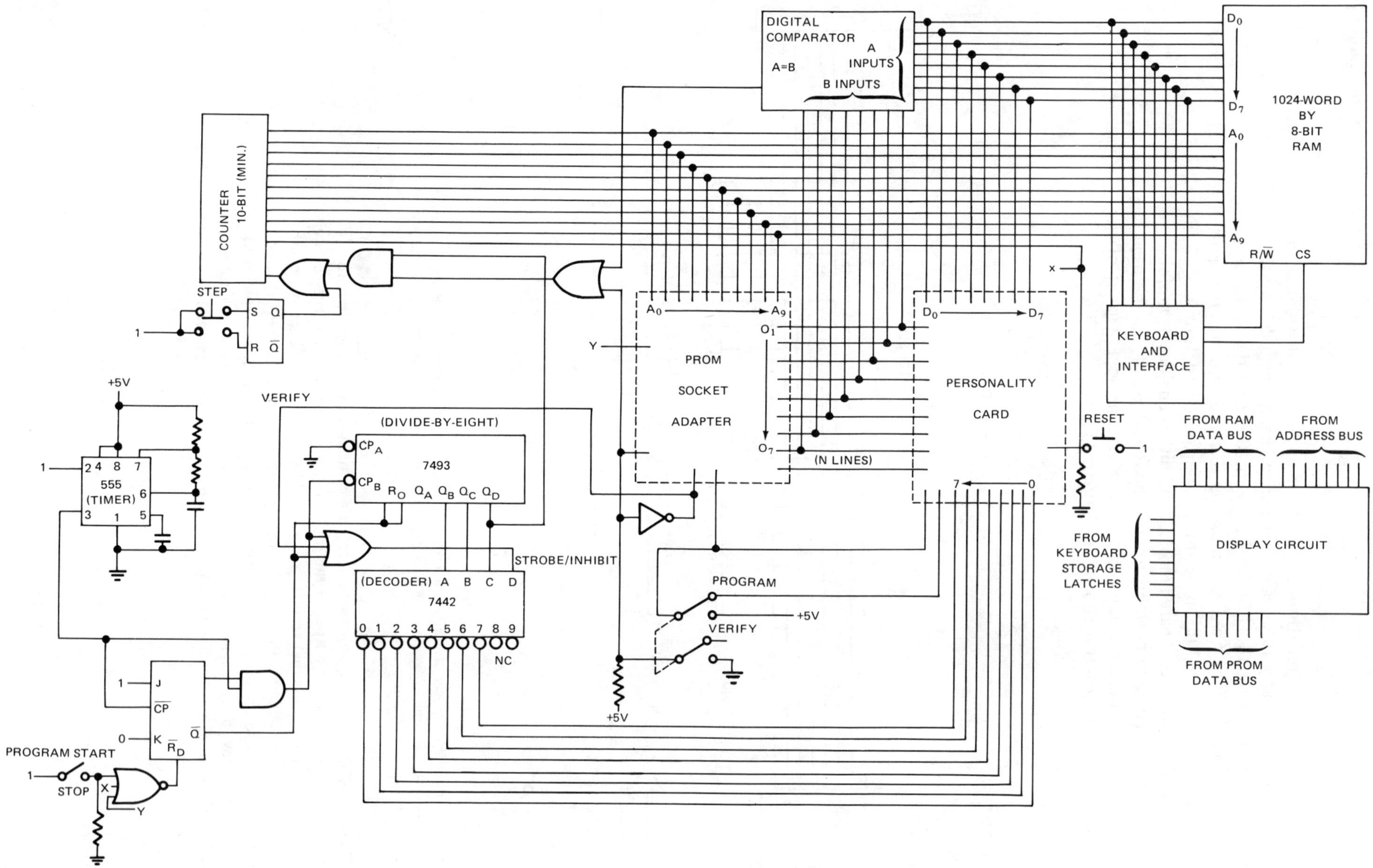

6.4 Personality Cards and Socket Adapters

PROMS are presently available in standard 16-, 18-, and 24-pin DIP circuits. To accommodate the different sizes and different pinout arrangements, the commercial PROM programmer is generally supplied with a variety of socket adaptors so that PROMS as small as 32 X 8 and as large as 2048 X 8 can all be programmed on the same basic programming system.

Programming Parameters Do not test these parameters or you may program the device.

SYMBOL	PARAMETER	TEST CONDITIONS	LIMITS MIN	TYP	MAX	UNITS
T_R	Rise Time of Program Pulse Applied Data Out or Program Pin		0.34	0.40	0.46	V/μs
V_{CCP}	V_{CC} Required During Programming		5.40	5.50	5.60	V
I_{OLV_1}	Output Current Required During Verification	Chip Enabled T_A = +25°C, V_{CC} = 4.2V	11	12	13	mA
I_{OLV_2}	Output Current Required During Verification	Chip Enabled T_A = +25°C, V_{CC} = 6.0V	0.19	0.2	0.21	mA
MDC	Maximum Duty Cycle During Automatic Programming of Program Pin and Output Pin	T_P/T_C			25	%
V_{pp}	Required Programming Voltage on Program Pin		27	27	33	V
V_{out}	Required Programming Voltage on Output Pin		20	20	26	V
I_L	Required Current Limit of Power Supply Feeding Program Pin and Output During Programming	V_{pp} = 33V, V_{out} = 26V, V_{CC} = 5.50V	240			mA
T_{D_1}	Required Time Delay Between Disabling Memory Output and Application of Output Programming Pulse	Measure at 10% Levels	70	80	90	μsec
T_{D_2}	Required Time Delay Between Removal of Programming Pulse and Enabling Memory Output	Measure at 10% Levels	100			nsec

TABLE 6.6 Voltage and timing parameters for the programming of PROMS manufactured by Monolithic Memories, Inc. (*Courtesy of Monolithic Memories Inc.*)

PROGRAMMING TIMING

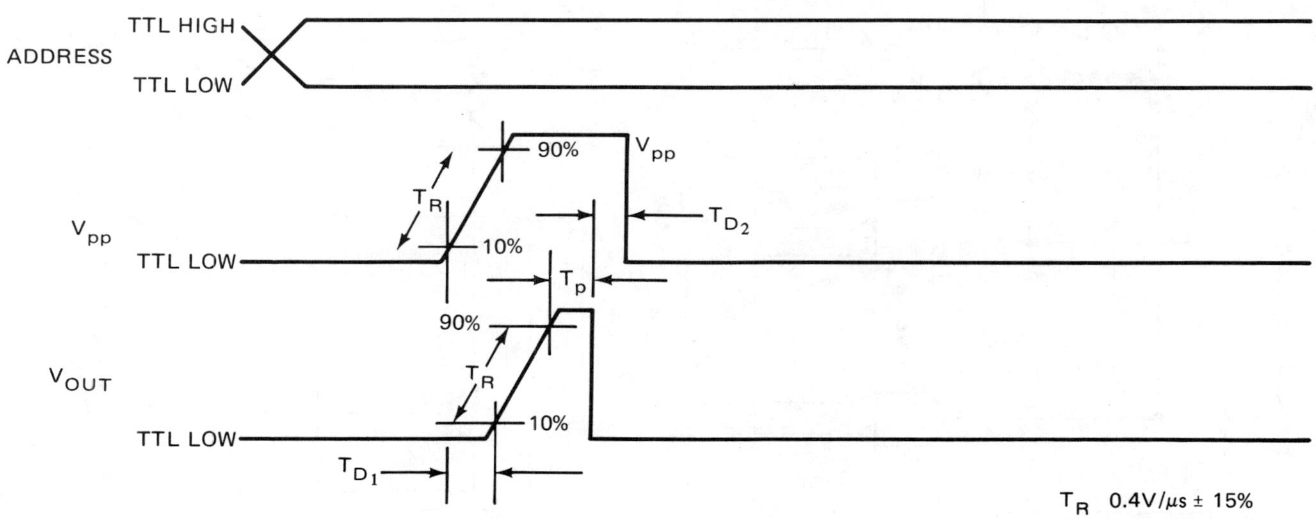

T_R 0.4V/μs ± 15%
T_P 1 μs min. 40 μs max.
T_{D_1} 80 = 10 μs
T_{D_2} 100 ns min.

*Note: Output Load = 0.2mA during 6.0V check.
Output Load = 12mA during 4.2V check.

As previously mentioned, there are some radical differences between PROM manufacturers in the specifications for programming a PROM although after programming they will function identically. The programming specification given in Table 6.4 for a Harris Semiconductor PROM differs radically from that given in Table 6.6 for Monolithic Memories, Inc. Note that the MMI procedure does not call for a higher than normal V_{CC}, but it does apply a high voltage pulse to one of the enable inputs ($\overline{E}_2$). This high voltage program pulse must bracket the narrower pulse applied to the input that is to be blown.

Note that the rise time of the V_{PP} and V_{OUT} is specified rather critically. To blow the PROM reliably, these limits must be adhered to. In the case of Harris or Fairchild PROMS the specified rise times are short enough to be provided with the use of a large capacitance. In the case of MMI and other PROMS which require long rise times, a digital-to-analog conversion technique may be used to provide the correct waveshape.

The PROM program specification given by Fairchild Semiconductor differs only slightly from the Harris program specification. The procedure is the same except that V_{CC} is kept at the normal 5V level, and the program voltage pulses are 21V with current limited to 100mA. Changing the NOR gates of Figure 6.4 to OR (7432) gates and adding a small NPN transistor to take the place of the open collector supplied by the 7402 is the only modification needed. The transistors used must be rated for an I_C maximum in excess of 100mA and a BV_{CBO} in excess of 21 volts. The personality boards for a Harris 512-X-8 PROM and a Fairchild equivalent are compared in Figure 6.12.

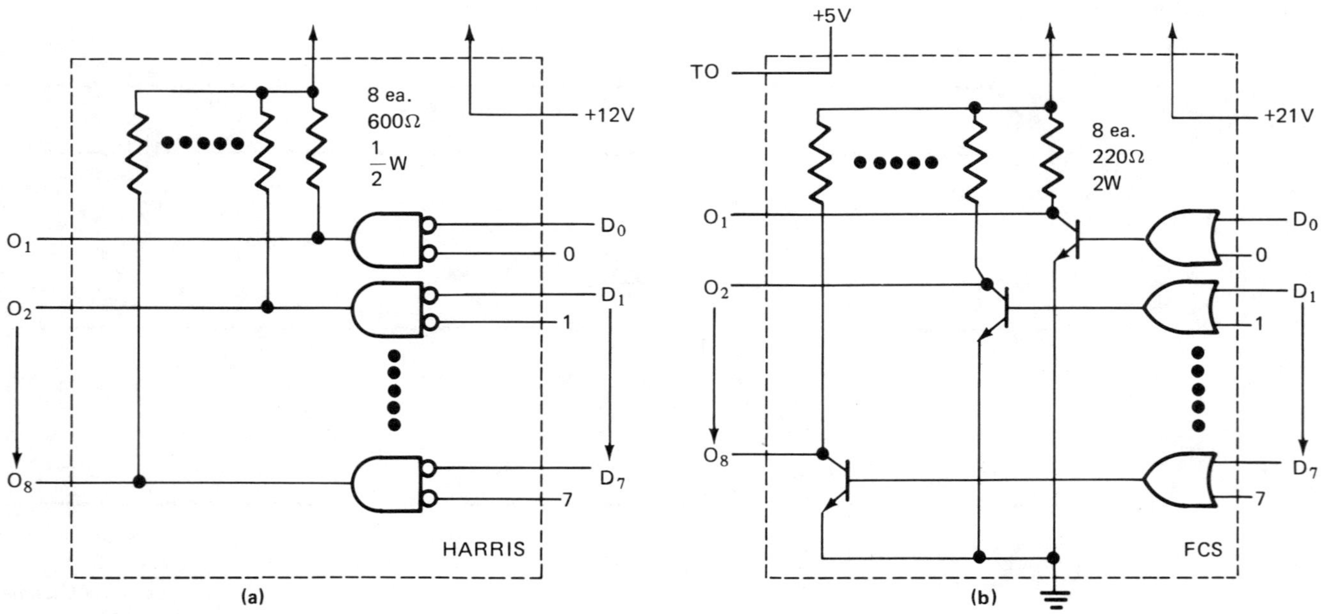

FIGURE 6.12 Diagram of personality cards for a Harris 7641 and an equivalent Fairchild Semiconductor 93448. The Fairchild PROM programs in a similar fashion to the Harris except that the voltage and currents required are too high for TTL buffers and a small transistor must be used with each of eight TTL OR gates. This provides the NOR function with greater voltage and current capacity. All wiring and circuitry subject to change between different manufacturer types must be located on the personality card. Resistor or capacitors used to change the frequency of the timer may also be located on the personality card.

6.5 The Ultraviolet Erasable EPROMS

Ultraviolet erasable EPROMS are available in several sizes, 256 X 8, 1K X 8, and a recent entry to the market, 2K X 8. Figure 6.13 shows the pin configuration of the three types. Although all three of these are TTL compatible when being read, they are not so alike when it comes to programming. The 1702 256-X-8 size is inconvenient to program due to the need for negative voltages. The 2708 1K-X-8 size programs with levels that can be handled with TTL logic circuits or buffers. Figure 6.14 gives the programming waveforms and specifications of the 2708.

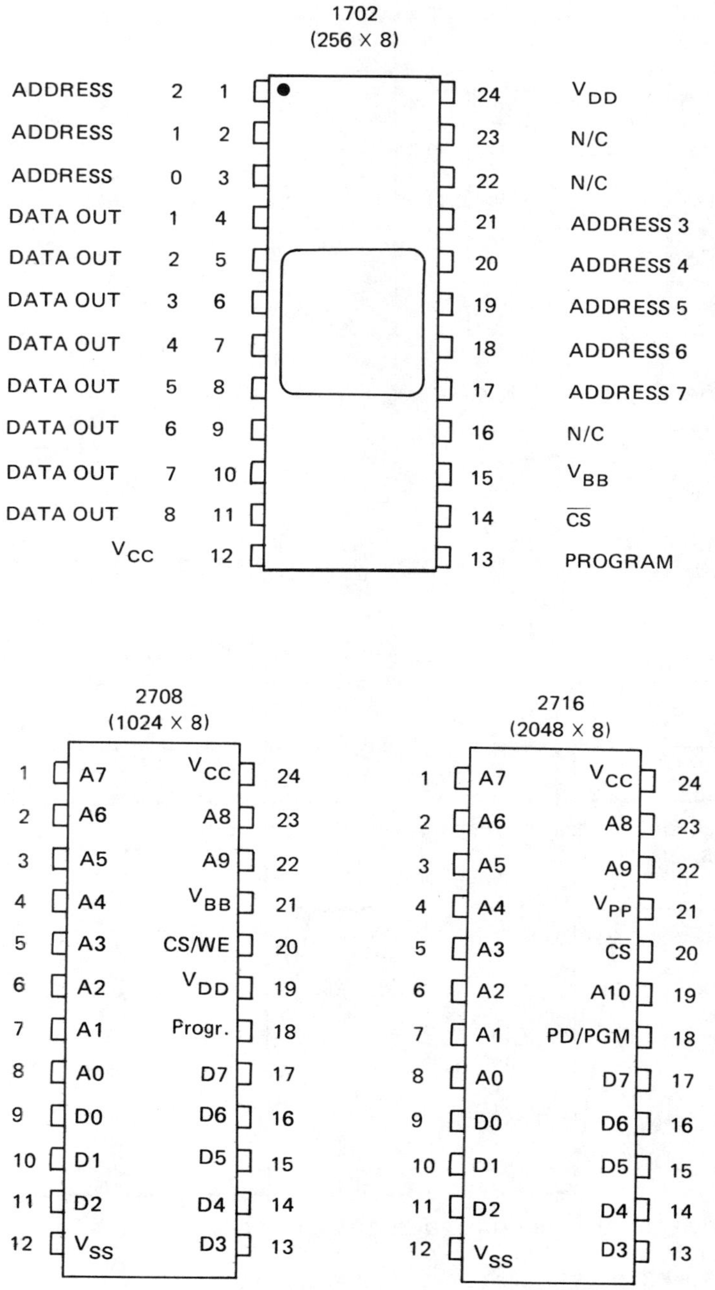

FIGURE 6.13 EPROMS. All three devices are in a 24-pin package with a transparent lid that enables erasure by exposure to ultraviolet light. The 1702 and 2708 use three supply voltages: V_{CC} = +5V, V_{BB} = -5V, V_{DD} = +12V. A programmed 2716 needs only +5V for its operation.

FIGURE 6.14 (Here and opposite.) Programming specifications for the 2708 EPROM. (*Courtesy of Intel*)

2708
PROGRAM CHARACTERISTICS
$T_A = 25°C$, $V_{CC} = 5V \pm 5\%$, $V_{DD} = +12V \pm 5\%$, $V_{BB} = -5V \pm 5\%$, $V_{SS} = 0V$, Unless Otherwise Noted.
D.C. Programming Characteristics

Symbol	Parameter	Min.	Typ.	Max.	Units	Test Conditions
I_{LI}	Address and $\overline{CS}$/WE Input Sink Current			10	μA	$V_{IN} = 5.25V$
I_{IPL}	Program Pulse Source Current			3	mA	
I_{IPH}	Program Pulse Sink Current			20	mA	
I_{DD}	V_{DD} Supply Current		50	65	mA	Worst Case Supply Currents: All Inputs High $\overline{CS}$/WE = 5V; $T_A = 0°C$
I_{CC}	V_{CC} Supply Current		6	10	mA	
I_{BB}	V_{BB} Supply Current		30	45	mA	
V_{IL}	Input Low Level (except Program)	V_{SS}		0.65	V	
V_{IH}	Input High Level for all Addresses and Data	3.0		$V_{CC}+1$	V	
V_{IHW}	$\overline{CS}$/WE Input High Level	11.4		12.6	V	Referenced to V_{SS}
V_{IHP}	Program Pulse High Level	25		27	V	Referenced to V_{SS}
V_{ILP}	Program Pulse Low Level	V_{SS}		1	V	$V_{IHP} - V_{ILP}$ = 25V min.

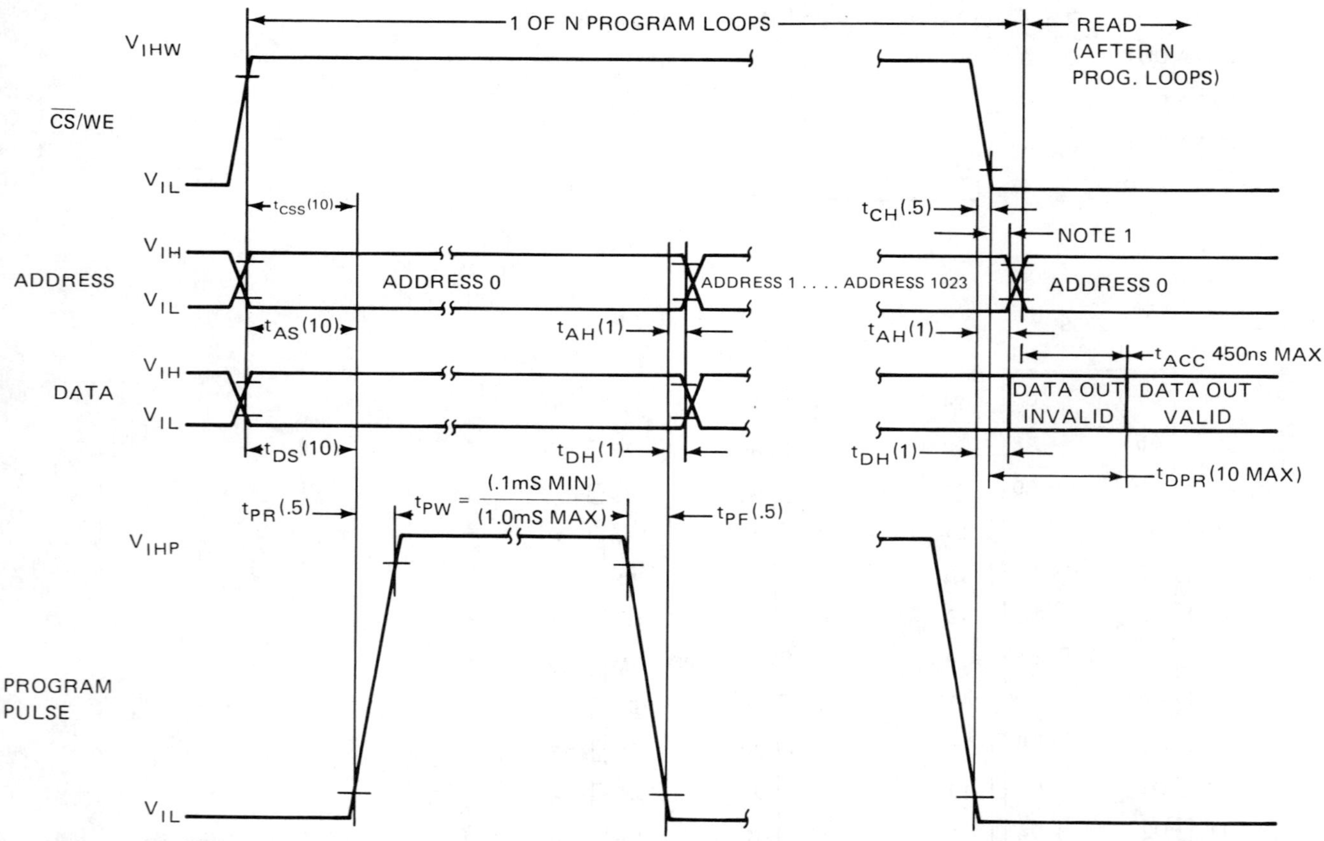

NOTE 1. THE $\overline{CS}$/WE TRANSITION MUST OCCUR AFTER THE PROGRAM PULSE TRANSITION AND BEFORE THE ADDRESS TRANSITION.
NOTE 2. NUMBERS IN ( ) INDICATE MINIMUM TIMING IN μS UNLESS OTHERWISE SPECIFIED.

A.C. Programming Characteristics

Symbol	Parameter	Min.	Typ.	Max.	Units
t_{AS}	Address Setup Time	10			μs
t_{CSS}	$\overline{CS}$/WE Setup Time	10			μs
t_{DS}	Data Setup Time	10			μs
t_{AH}	Address Hold Time	1			μs
t_{CH}	$\overline{CS}$/WE Hold Time	.5			μs
t_{DH}	Data Hold Time	1			μs
t_{DF}	Chip Deselect to Output Float Delay	0		120	ns
t_{DPR}	Program To Read Delay			10	μs
t_{PW}	Program Pulse Width	.1		1.0	ms
t_{PR}	Program Pulse Rise Time	.5		2.0	μs
t_{PF}	Program Pulse Fall Time	.5		2.0	μs

NOTE: Intel's standard product warranty applies only to devices programmed to specifications described herein.

When initially supplied or after ultraviolet erasure, the outputs are all 1 and the zero bits must be programmed. To program, the CS/WE must be raised to +12V. With each address, the standard TTL level data are applied to the data out pins and a single 26V pulse 0.1 to 1 msec wide is applied to the program input (pin 18). The entire 1024 addresses are progammed with this procedure. It is then repeated. It is repeated N times where

$$N \geqslant \frac{100 \text{ msec}}{\text{program pulsewidth}}$$

To accomplish this with the programming circuit we developed for the fusible link PROMS, an extra counter will be needed. Figure 6.15 shows a personality card used to adapt the PROM blower of Figure 6.11 to the function of programming the 2708.

The 2708 ultraviolet EPROM can be partially programmed and the remaining (unprogrammed) portion reserved for later use. This is done by programming all ls in the section of memory to be saved. When the reserved sections are put to use there is no need for an erasure, however, the previously used sections must be reprogrammed along with the newly programmed sections.

Ultraviolet Erasure The EPROMS are erased by illuminating the quartz window with ultraviolet light of the correct wavelength and intensity. Lamps for this are available from several sources. Table 6.7 gives a list of ultraviolet lamp models, their intensities, and minimum erasure times.

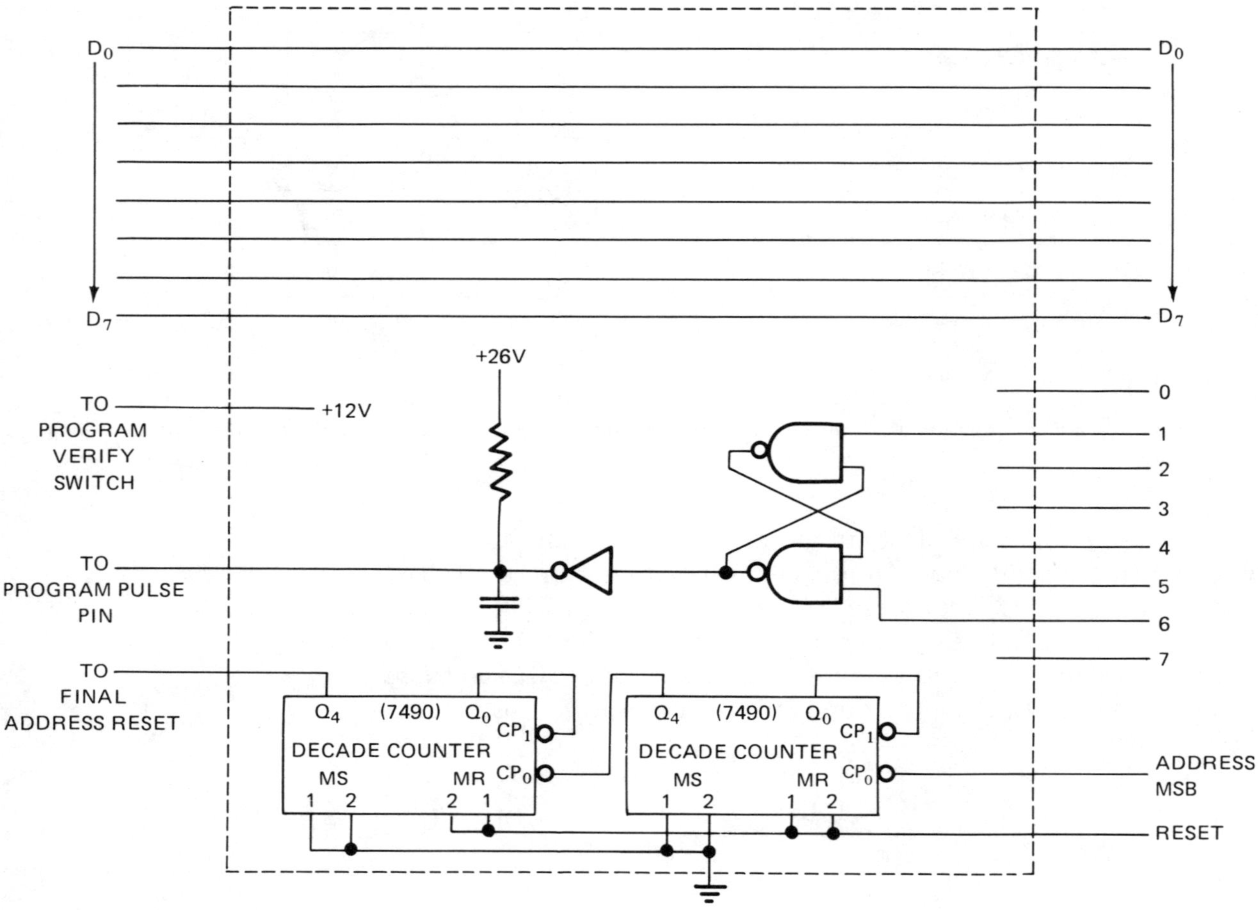

FIGURE 6.15 Personality card used to adapt the fusible link PROM blower to program a 2708 ultraviolet PROM. The standard TTL outputs of the RAM are applied directly to the PROM outputs. The eight programming pulses generated for fusible link PROMS are converted to a single pulse lasting from time 1 to time 6. The clock is adjusted to make this pulse 1 msec wide. The high voltage inverting buffer with pullup resistor to 26V provides the correct pulse amplitude. A pair of decade counters allows the programming cycle to occur 100 times.

TABLE 6.7 Standard models of ultraviolet lamps, their intensities, and erasure times.

Model	Power Rating	Minimum Erase Time for Indicated Dosage Without a Filter Over the Bulb: 6 W-sec 1702A, 4702A	15 W-sec All Intel EPROMS or EPROMS with I/O Ports Except the 1702A/4702A
R-52	13000 $\mu W/cm^2$	7.7 min	19.2 min
S-52	12000 $\mu W/cm^2$	8.3 min	20.7 min
S-68	12000 $\mu W/cm^2$	8.3 min	20.7 min
UVS-54	5700 $\mu W/cm^2$	17.5 min	43.8 min
UVS-11	5500 $\mu W/cm^2$	18.2 min	45.6 min

6.6 Programming Errors

When programming errors occur, the losses can be divided into the categories of hardware or software. The cost of converting a program to machine readable form before loading it into a PROM may be much greater than the cost of the PROM. If a text editor or some other electronic means is available to save the good portions of the program and allow the insertion of new or corrected portions, then the software loss would be minimal. If the entire program has to be reloaded from a keyboard with each new correction, then the labor loss would be more serious than the loss of PROMS.

Where ultraviolet EPROMS are used there is no hardware loss to consider. Because of this, ultraviolet EPROMS often are used in prototype systems where changes and modifications are expected.

Where fusible link PROMS are used, the probability of wasting a number of PROMS before a program is successfully entered and tested is relatively high. Most PROM manufacturers guarantee a 95% programming yield if the PROMS are programmed according to specification. The chance of human error is usually greater than this. Even if the original program is correctly entered into the PROM, minor changes are often necessary when the program is checked. A 512-X-8 PROM costs five times as much as a 32-X-8 PROM, but has 16 times as much memory. Yet a single error in a 512-X-8 circuit makes it as worthless as it does the cheaper 32-X-8 circuit. Although larger PROMS are more economical in cost per bit, there is, unfortunately, a risk of greater loss in event of error. For the small microprocessor user, a system more tolerant of errors can be devised. Such a system uses a combination of a large and a small PROM. A 512-X-8 PROM can be divided into 8 blocks of 64 bytes each, while a 32-X-8 PROM can be divided into 10 blocks of 3 bytes each.

When the program is assembled, an unconditional jump instruction is inserted in the last three bytes of each 64-byte block of the 512-X-8 PROM. The jumps executed by the microprocessor are to successive 3-byte blocks of the 32-X-8 PROM. These 3-byte blocks merely jump the processor back to the adjacent 64-byte block of the 512-X-8 PROM. Figure 6.16 shows the effect that these extra instructions will have on the movement of the program.

If everything goes well, we have managed to waste only about 10% of the available memory bytes and caused a similar increase in the execution time. Suppose in verifying the program we find an error in address 0334_H, and the program otherwise seems correct. Instead of discarding the \$20 512-X-8 PROM along with all the work of entering and verifying the program, our alternative is to discard the \$3 32-X-8 PROM. At the top of the 512-X-8 PROM where some spare memory exists, we insert a corrected segment of program.

It is not necessary to replace the entire block in which the error exists. All of the bytes above the error can still be used. When the 32-X-8 PROM is reprogrammed instead of jumping to the beginning of block

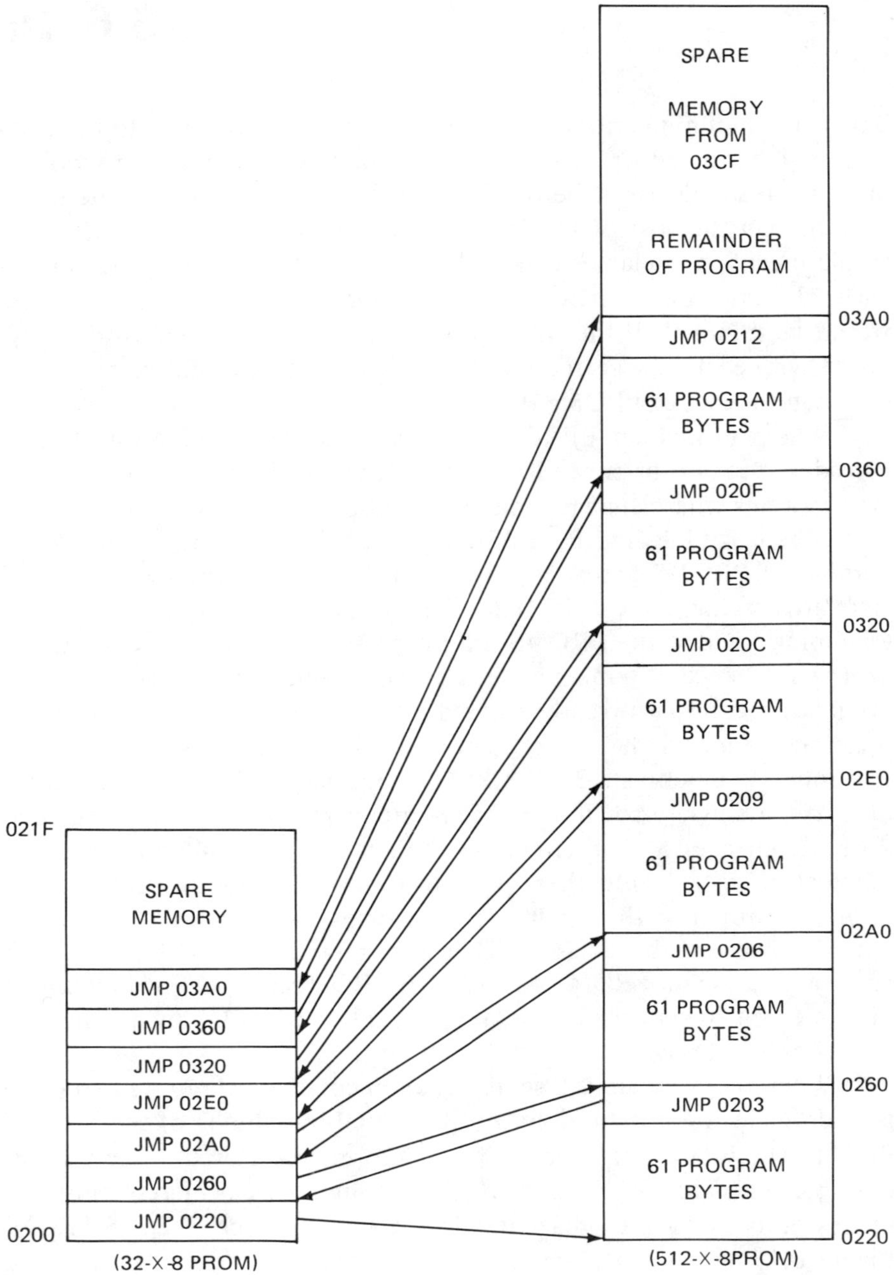

FIGURE 6.16 Memory map of a 512-X-8 PROM containing an unconditional jump to a 32-X-8 PROM at the end of each 64-byte memory block. The 32-X-8 PROM contains JMP instructions back to the next 64-byte memory block. This arrangement allows for insertion of corrections for any one of the blocks.

0320 there is a jump to the top of the memory where the corrected segment has been entered. The last three bytes of the correction comprise a jump instruction back to the remaining good segment of block 0335_H. Figure 6.17 shows the change in program movement after the correction is made.

Adding correction segments to the unprogrammed portion of a fusible link PROM requires that the PROM blower have a provision for presetting the address counter to the spare memory address. The cor-

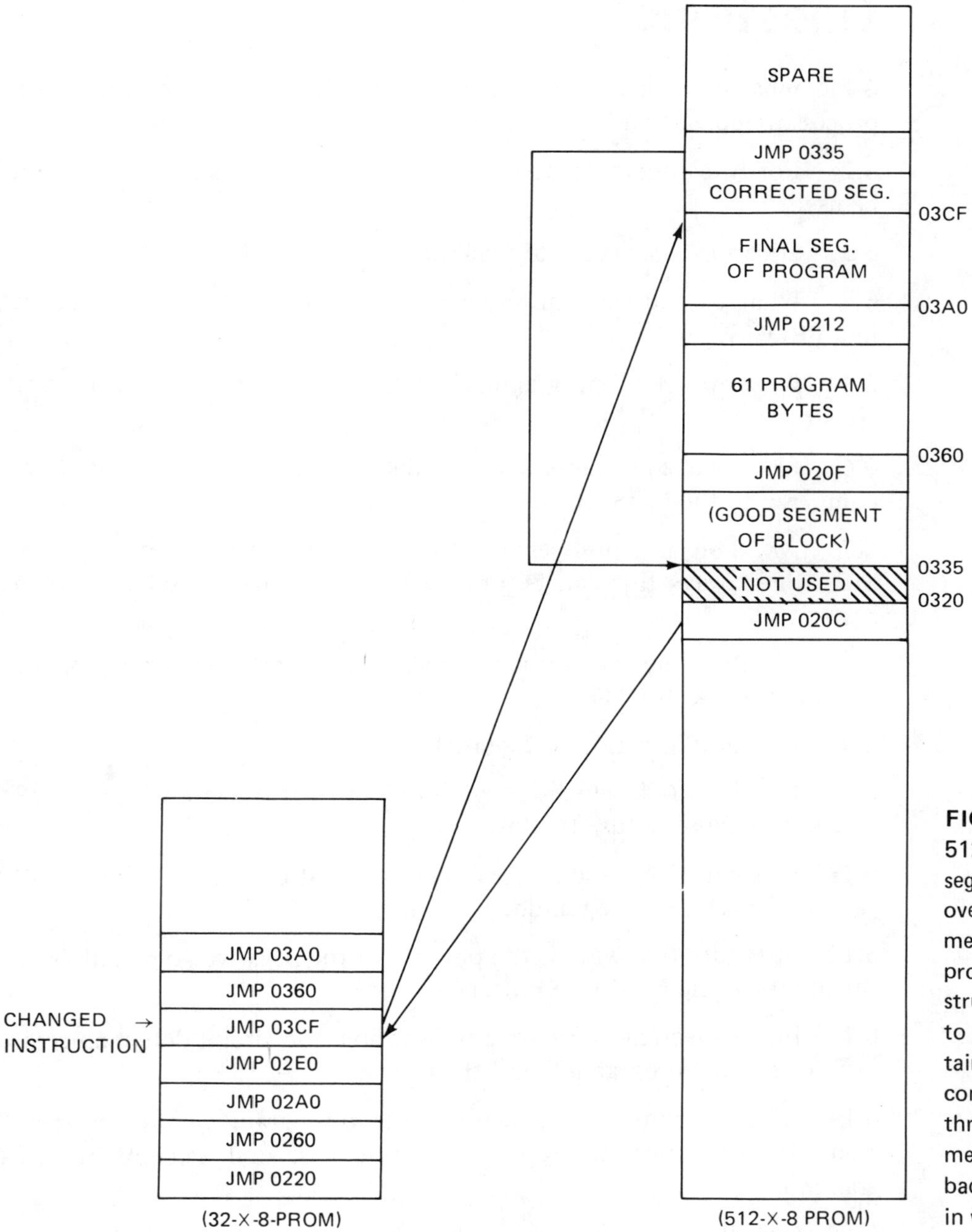

FIGURE 6.17 Memory map of 512-X-8 PROM with correction segment programmed into the left-over portion at the top of the memory. A new 32-X-8 PROM is programmed with a set of jump instructions that causes the program to jump around the segment containing the error to the segment containing the correction. The last three bytes of the correction segment comprise a jump instruction back to the remainder of the block in which the error was detected.

rected segment and its subsequent jump instruction are all that need be loaded into the RAM and subsequently transferred to PROM. Care must be taken that the PROM not be addressed in the sections of the program that are to be retained unless the RAM contains the identical data in those addresses. If the PROM blower has no provision for restricting the address count, then the RAM may be loaded with FF bytes or 00 bytes (whichever do not blow fuses) in all addresses not to be changed during the reprogramming of the correction into the PROM.

Questions

6.1 What main advantage does the read only memory have for microprocessor application?

6.2 For what microprocessor applications can read only memory not be used?

6.3 Describe three types of read only memories.

6.4 What two distinct differences exist in the fusing of the fusible link PROMS?

6.5 Why are mask programmed ROMS not suitable for prototype construction?

6.6 Give two advantages and one disadvantage of the TTL ROM as compared to the MOS ROM.

6.7 An 8-bit microprocessor system requires two pages of ROM. State three ways this can be provided using standard PROM sizes per system.

6.8 What are the four principal operations in transferring a program to a fusible link PROM?

6.9 Why is verification so essential?

6.10 In Figure 6.4, which logic level (1 or 0) at the input to the NOR gate buffer causes a fuse to blow?

6.11 In Figure 6.4, which logic level (1 or 0) at the output of the NOR gate buffer causes a programmed zero level?

6.12 In Figure 6.4, what is the purpose of the negative going pulses on the inputs to the NOR gate buffers?

6.13 In the diagram of Figure 6.6, how does the circuit detect an error or failure in the programming of the PROM?

6.14 After a failure of one or more bits to program, what changes are made in the programming circuit before a second attempt at programming?

6.15 Describe the differences in the personality cards for the 7641 and 93438. Is the logic function different?

6.16 What difference exists in programming pulses between the 1702 and the 2708 ultraviolet EPROMS?

6.17 If the upper half of a 2708 is to be reserved for future program additions, how should the unused portion be programmed?

6.18 When the unused portion of a 2708 has program added to it, what must be done about the previously programmed portion?

6.19 Why is a counter needed on the personality board for the 2708 PROM?

6.20 Can an ordinary fluorescent lamp be used to erase an ultraviolet EPROM?

6.21 Explain how an unconditional jump instruction can be used to facilitate changes in the programming of a large fusible link PROM.

Problems

6.1 Draw a microprocessor bus like that of Figure 6.2, but having 2K of PROM implemented with the 7643 or equivalent 1K-X-4 device. The PROM is to occupy addresses 0000 to 03FF. Use a 1 of 8 decoder to prevent repetition of the address above page 0F.

6.2 The 7602 is a 32-X-8 fusible link PROM with open collector outputs. Draw a microprocessor bus like that of Figure 6.2 with a 7602 occupying the lower 32 bytes of the address bus. What must be done to accommodate the fact that the outputs are open collector?

6.3 Draw a microprocessor bus, like that in Figure 6.2, with two 2708 memories connected to occupy addresses 0000 through 07FF. Use a 74LS138 to deselect for addresses above page 08.

6.4 Draw the microprocessor bus of Figure 6.3, but replace the two 7611 PROMS with a single 512-X-8 fusible link PROM.

6.5 Complete the PROM programming circuit of Figure 6.4 showing all logic gates and input programming pulses.

6.6 Figure 6.16 is a memory map for a 32-X-8 PROM. Make a list of the keys to be punched on a teletype to provide a programming tape in ASCII hexadecimal format.

6.7 Make a list of the keys to be punched on a teletype to provide a programming tape in ASCII hexadecimal format for the 32-X-8 PROM in Figure 6.16.

6.8 Draw a microprocessor bus like that of Figure 6.3. Include a 2114 RAM at address 0000_H to $03FF_H$ and two pages of PROM (512-X-8) occupying adjacent addresses. Use an 74LS138 for address decoding.

6.9 Draw a microprocessor bus like that of Figure 6.3. Use 2111 (256-X-4) RAMS to occupy address 0000_H to $00FF_H$. Include a 2708 EPROM at address 0200 to 05FF and an output port at address X8XX. Use two 8T28 as the output port and a 74LS138 as an address decoder. Note: use ϕ_2 clock for the OD control.

6.10 Reconstruct the memory maps of Figure 6.16 showing the changes needed for a correction at address 02B1.

Chapter 7

The 6800 Microprocessor

Objectives

On the completion of this chapter you will be able to:

- Assemble a microcomputer using the 6800 microprocessor.
- Use the 6800 instruction set.
- Select correct addressing modes for 6800 instructions.
- Provide for the servicing of an I/O port through the 6800 interrupt system.
- Assemble a bootstrap loader for a 6800 microprocessor system.
- Write arithmetic programs for the 6800 microprocessor.
- Write programs for the 6800 using subroutines.
- Write 6800 programs that employ counter and timer routines.
- Write 6800 programs that employ sequencer routines.
- Write 6800 programs that use look-up tables.

7.1 Description

The 6800 microprocessor is one of the more widely used 8-bit microprocessors. As Figure 7.1 shows, it is a 40-pin integrated circuit powered by a single power supply (+5v). It uses a 16-bit address bus and an 8-bit bidirectional data bus. It requires an outboard clock to provide two nonoverlapping clock phases of 100 KHZ to 1 MHZ. Figure 7.1(b) shows the registers contained within the 6800. There are two 8-bit accumulators, A and B. The program counter, stack pointer, and index register are all 16 bits corresponding to the size of the address bus. The condition code register contains the individual flags: carry (C), overflow (V), Zero (Z), negative (N), Interrupt Mask (I), and half carry (H).

FIGURE 7.1 The M6800 microprocessor. **(a)** Pin Diagram (*Courtesy of Motorola Inc.*)

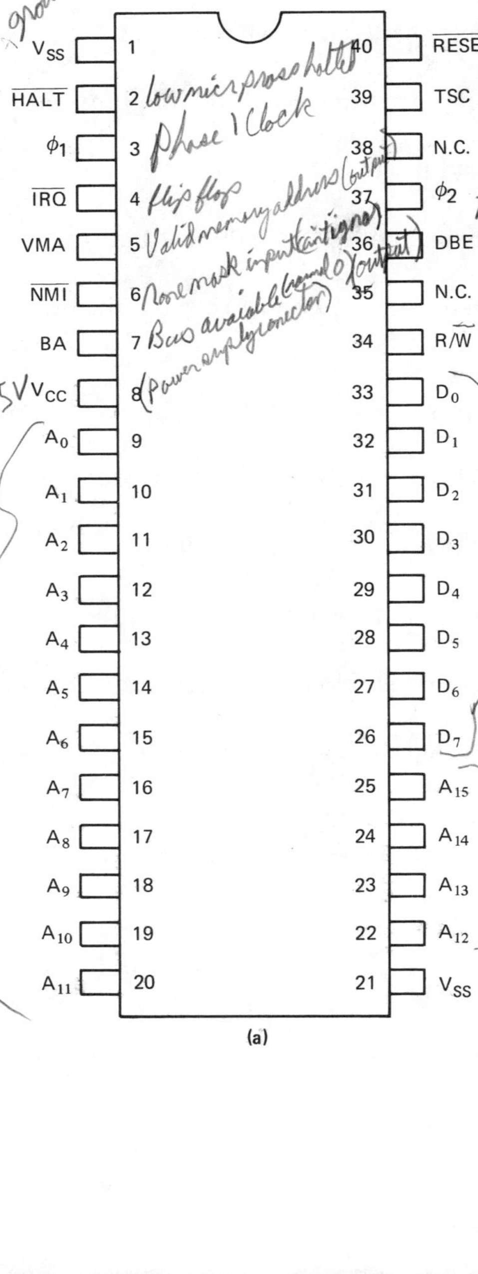

(a)

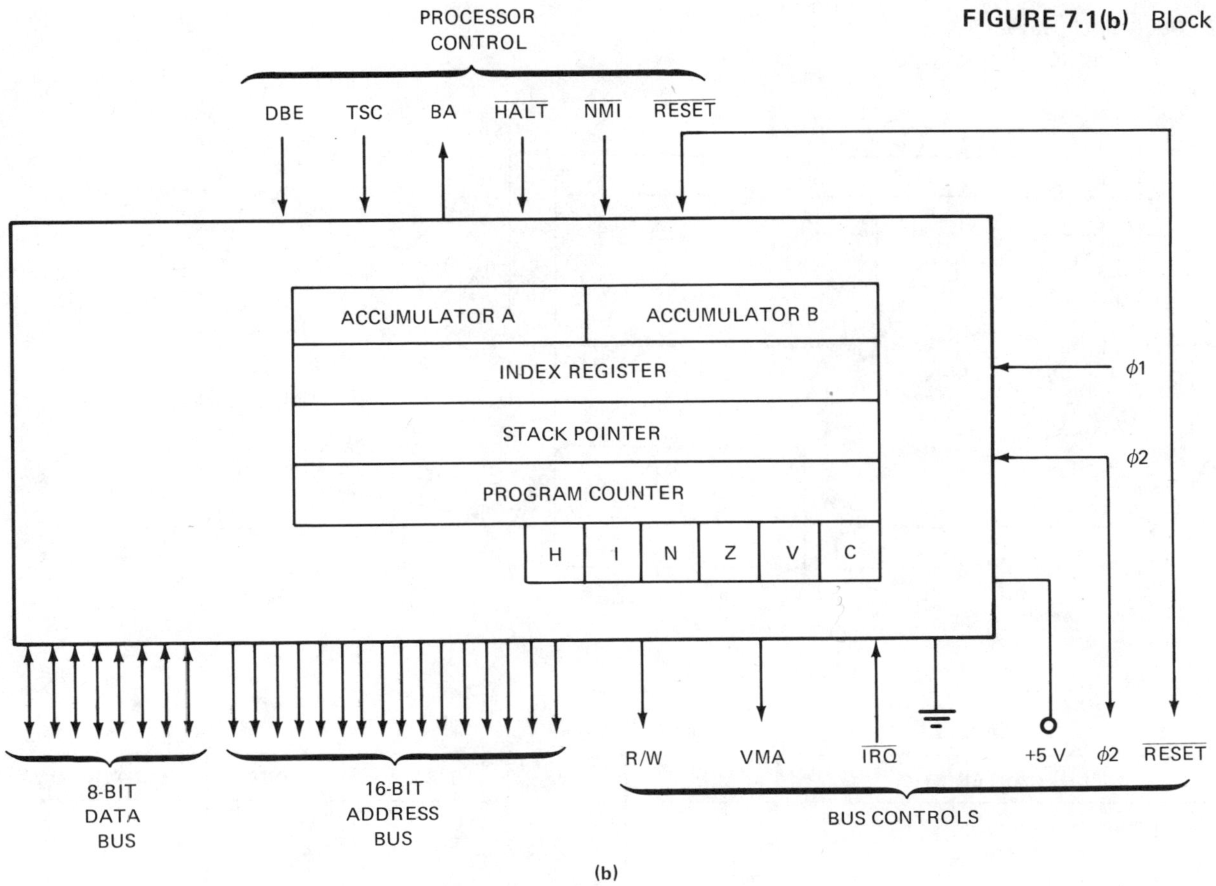

FIGURE 7.1(b) Block diagram.

7.2 Control Signals in the 6800 Microprocessor System

7.2.1 Clock Inputs

Two nonoverlapping clock pulses must be supplied to the ϕ_1 and ϕ_2 inputs. The 6800 is a dynamic device and will malfunction as the result of an interruption to the clock inputs. The minimum clock frequency is 100 KHZ. The standard model 6800 is guaranteed to operate at 1 MHZ clock. Newer models are faster. The clock inputs are not TTL compatible. The voltage and timing requirements are shown in Figure 7.2.

The Motorola MC6870 or MC6871, "Two Phase Clock" is specifically designed for this application. A CMOS clock or other clock with a CMOS interface could provide pulses with suitable V_{OLC} and V_{OHC} levels. The ϕ_2 output of this clock is also needed in the timing of other devices in the system. The system's ϕ_2 clock must have TTL drive levels.

Reset During the first 8 clock cycles of reset low, the 6800 initializes itself then begins outputting the address FFFE. The FFFE

FIGURE 7.2 6800 clock waveforms and specifications. (*Courtesy of Motorola Inc.*)

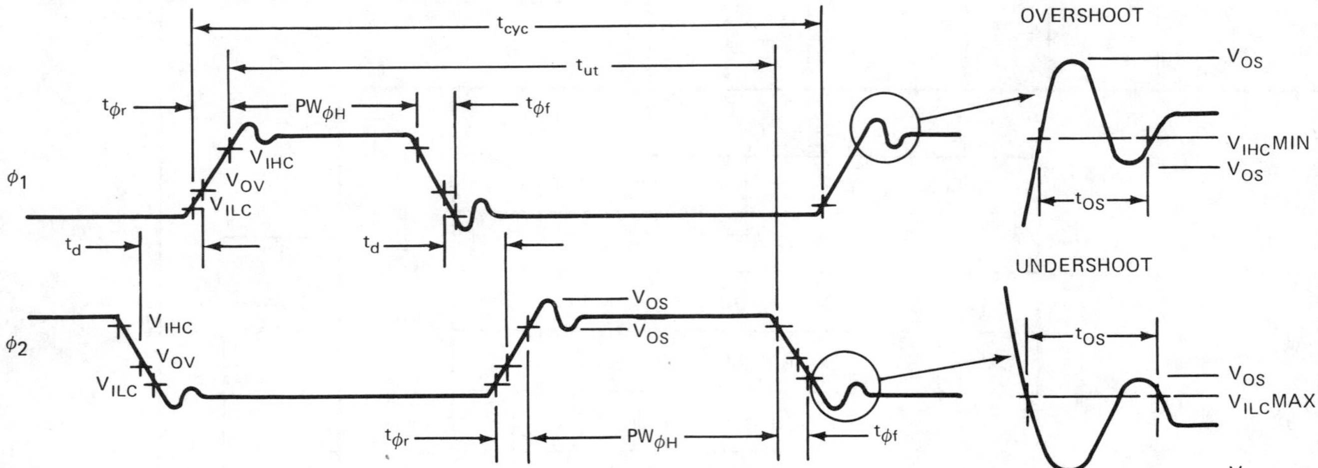

$V_{OV} = V_{SS} + 0.5$ V = Clock Overlap measurement point

SYMBOL	CHARACTERISTIC	MIN	TYP	MAX	UNIT	CONDITIONS
V_{IH} V_{IHC}	Input HIGH Voltage Logic $\phi 2$ (TTL) ϕ_1,ϕ_2	V_{SS} + 2.0 V_{CC} - 0.3	— —	V_{CC} V_{CC} + 0.1	V	
V_{IL} (TTL) V_{ILC}	Input LOW Voltage Logic $\phi 2$ (TTL) ϕ_1,ϕ_2	V_{SS} - 0.3 V_{SS} - 0.1	— —	V_{SS} + 0.3 V_{SS} + 0.3	V	
V_{OS}	Clock Overshoot/Undershoot Input HIGH Input LOW	V_{CC} - 0.5 V_{SS} - 0.5	— —	V_{CC} + 0.5 V_{SS} + 0.5	V	
I_{IN}	Input Leakage Current ϕ_1,ϕ_2	— —	—	100	μA	V_{IN} = 0 to 5.25 V, V_{CC} = MAX V_{IN} = 0 to 5.25 V, V_{CC} = 0.0 V
t_{cyc}	Clock Timing Cycle Time	1.0	—	10	μs	
$PW_{\phi H}$	Clock Pulse Width ϕ_1 ϕ_2	430 450	— —	4500 4500	ns	V_{CC} = -0.3 V
t_{ut}	Total ϕ_1 and ϕ_2 Up Time	940	—	—	ns	
$t_{\phi r}, t_{\phi f}$	Rise and Fall Times ϕ_1,ϕ_2	5.0	—	50	ns	V_{SS} + 0.3 V and V_{CC} = -0.3 V
t_d	Delay Time or Clock Separation	0	—	9100	ns	V_{OV} = V_{SS} = + 0.5 V
t_{OS}	Overshoot Duration	0	—	40	ns	

address is repeated as long as the reset remains low. When the reset line goes high, a final FFFE followed by FFFF occurs on the address bus. The memory bytes FFFE, FFFF are the reset vectors. The starting address of the first program to be executed must be stored at these memory addresses (in ROM). These two bytes are transferred automatically to the program counter within the microprocessor. A reset is normally received during a power turn-on. A simple RC network is used to hold the reset input low for some microseconds after the power is supplied to the system. This is shown in Figure 7.3. A pushbutton may be connected to the same network in order to provide a restart at the initial instruction without an interruption to the system's power.

7.2.2 Microprocessor Control Signal for Memory and PIA

Valid Memory Address (VMA) The VMA output of the microprocessor goes high and remains high whenever there is a valid memory address being output from the 6800. It will be low when the 6800 is outputting an invalid address or during (DMA), direct memory access operations. During reset and during some internal operations the 6800 may output extraneous addresses along with an indeterminate state of the R/W line. The VMA signal may be used to deselect RAM which might otherwise lose essential data through an unprogrammed write operation. It may also be needed on ROM or I/O ports where erratic outputs will have an ill effect. The VMA connects to a chip select (CS) or chip enable (CE) of all RAMS and interface adapters. It may be connected directly or by ANDing it with one or more address bus lines.

Read/Write (R/W) The memory read/write output is normally high and remains high when the microprocessor is reading data from memory or inputting from an input interface. The R/W goes low when the 6800 is writing data into RAM or when outputting through an interface adapter.

Data Bus Enable (DBE) Input The 6800 outputs data within 225 nsec of the time the DBE goes high. When DBE is low the 6800 data

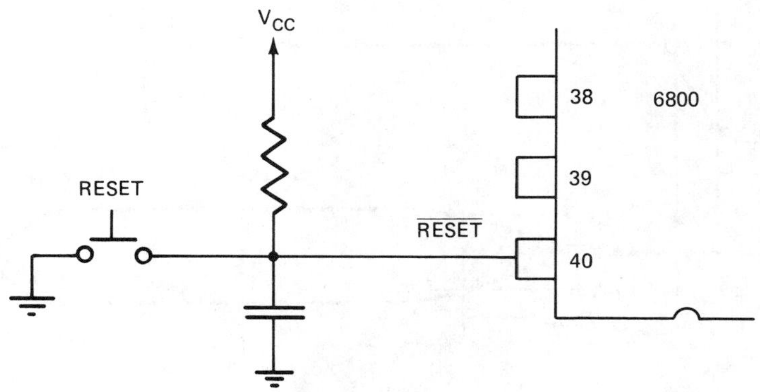

FIGURE 7.3 Provisions for reset of the 6800 microprocessor during power turn on requires only an RC network with a time constant greater than 8 clock cycles. A push-button switch provides a reset without removing power.

FIGURE 7.4 Memory write timing diagram of the M6800 showing the effect that variations of the DBE input have on the data output from the microprocessor. *(Courtesy of Motorola Inc.)*

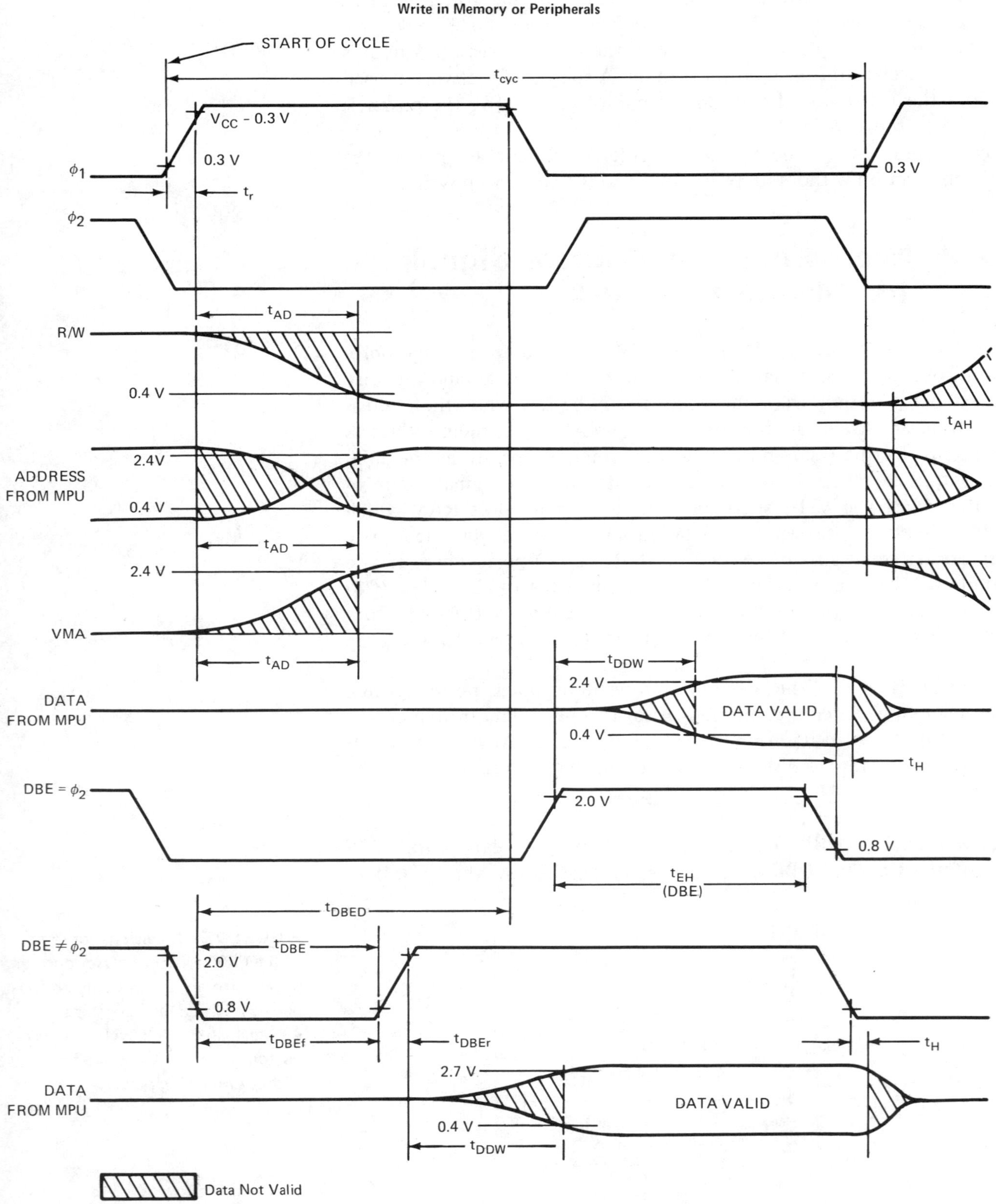

bus drivers are disabled. The DBE requires a TTL input and is normally supplied by a ϕ_2 TTL clock except where the memory or interface requires the microprocessor output earlier in the cycle. Figure 7.4 shows the effect that varying the pulse width of DBE has on the data output from the 6800.

7.2.3 Control Signals Used with Interface Adapters

Interrupt Request Input ($\overline{\text{IRQ}}$) The IRQ is a signal from an I/O device that it needs to be serviced. When this line goes low the 6800 completes the instruction that is in process then automatically it loads the contents of its registers on the stack in the order shown in Figure 7.5. The stack pointer decrements with the loading of each byte. A stack pointer containing a current stack address of m would finish an IRQ routine with an address of m – 7. After loading the stack the interrupt mask bit (I) in the condition code register is set. As long as this bit is set the 6800 will not initiate another interrupt request routine. Next, the data bytes stored at the interrupt vector FFF9 and FFF8 are transferred automatically to the program counter. Table 7.1 shows the memory map of the 6800 vectors. This vector address is the beginning address of the service routine used to service the interface that generated the interrupt request.

FIGURE 7.5 BEFORE Stack memory with current address of m. AFTER Stack memory after receipt of an IRQ is loaded with complete microprocessor status. The stack pointer has decremented to m - 7. (*Courtesy of Motorola Inc.*)

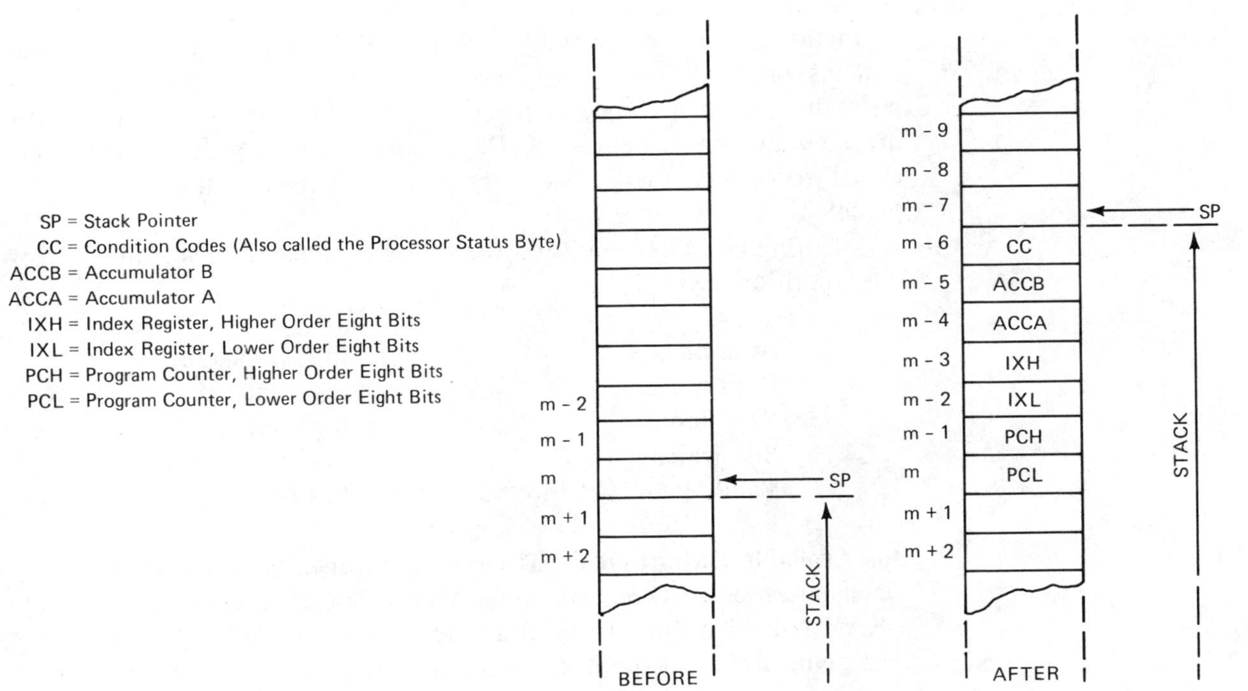

TABLE 7.1 Memory map for interrupt vectors.
(Courtesy of Motorola Inc.)

VECTOR		
MS	LS	DESCRIPTION
FFFE	FFFF	Restart
FFFC	FFFD	Nonmaskable Interrupt
FFFA	FFFB	Software Interrupt
FFF8	FFF9	Interrupt Request

Nonmaskable Interrupt Input (NMI) This input responds to a negative going edge. It generates the same interrupt routine described for the IRQ except that it will occur regardless of the state of the interrupt mask bit in the condition code register. It also uses a different interrupt vector as Table 7.1 shows. The NMI can interrupt a service routine that had previously been started by an IRQ.

7.2.4 Single Instruction and DMA Operations

$\overline{\text{HALT}}$ The Halt input is used to suspend microprocessor operations during Direct Memory Access (DMA) operations. When $\overline{\text{HALT}}$ goes low all microprocessor operations cease, but the content of registers is maintained. This would not be the case if a halt condition were accomplished by stopping the clock pulses. The $\overline{\text{HALT}}$ can be used to provide single instruction operation. The $\overline{\text{HALT}}$ must not go low during the last 250 nsec of the ϕ_1 clock. When $\overline{\text{HALT}}$ is low, all three state outputs from the microprocessor are in the high impedance state.

A circuit providing single instruction operation is shown at the top of Figure 7.14(b). When the switch is in RUN a continuous high level remains on $\overline{\text{HALT}}$ input and no halts occur in the 6800 operation. With the switch in single instruction, the $\overline{\text{HALT}}$ line is held low until the step button is depressed. Depressing the step pushbutton causes $\overline{\text{HALT}}$ to go high for a single clock period between trailing edges of the ϕ_2 clock.

During a $\overline{\text{HALT}}$ condition the following data, address, and control bus conditions exist.

Address bus	high impedance
Data bus	high impedance
R/W line	high impedance
Bus available (BA)	high (1)
Valid Memory Address (VMA)	low (0)

Bus Available Output (BA) Three State Control Input (TSC) These signals are used in Direct Memory Access (DMA), a technique in which a RAM is loaded directly from an input device without the data bytes first being stored in the microprocessor registers during the movement of the data. This is an advanced technique that will not be discussed in this chapter. For the usual system that does not use DMA, the bus available is left open and the TSC is tied to a fixed zero level.

7.3 The Instruction Set

The 72 mnemonics of the instruction set are given in Table 7.2. The mnemonics are composed of three or four letters and are suggestive of the microprocessor function they cause. The mnemonics are used by the programmer to represent the opcode portion of each instruction. Where applicable, the programmer must add the operands. As Table 7.3 indicates, these instructions may take one or more of the seven address modes. Those with dual operands will be suffixed by the letter A or B indicating operation with the A or B accumulator. The numbers in the table indicate the number of clock cycles and memory bytes needed to execute the instruction in a given address mode.

As Figure 7.6 shows, each clock cycle is the period of a ϕ_1 clock pulse. For example, the instruction LDAA (load accumulator A) may take any one of four machine codes 86, 96, A6, or B6. Likewise, LDAB (load accumulator B) may take any one of four machine codes C6, D6, E6, or F6. The programmer will select any one of the four codes depending on where he or she wishes the processor to obtain the data byte (or operand) it is to load into the accumulator. Instructions differ both in the number of memory bytes occupied and in the time to exe-

TABLE 7.2 6800 Microprocessor Instruction Set—Alphabetic Sequence

ABA	Add Accumulators	CLR	Clear	PUL	Pull Data
ADC	Add with Carry	CLV	Clear Overflow	ROL	Rotate Left
ADD	Add	CMP	Compare	ROR	Rotate Right
AND	Logical And	COM	Complement	RTI	Return from Interrupt
ASL	Arithmetic Shift Left	CPX	Compare Index Register	RTS	Return from Subroutine
ASR	Arithmetic Shift Right	DAA	Decimal Adjust	SBA	Subtract Accumulators
BCC	Branch if Carry Clear	DEC	Decrement	SBC	Subtract with Carry
BCS	Branch if Carry Set	DES	Decrement Stack Pointer	SEC	Set Carry
BEQ	Branch if Equal to Zero	DEX	Decrement Index Register	SEI	Set Interrupt Mask
BGE	Branch if Greater or Equal Zero	EOR	Exclusive OR	SEV	Set Overflow
BGT	Branch if Greater than Zero	INC	Increment	STA	Store Accumulator
BHI	Branch if Higher	INS	Increment Stack Pointer	STS	Store Stack Register
BIT	Bit Test	INX	Increment Index Register	STX	Store Index Register
BLE	Branch if Less or Equal	JMP	Jump	SUB	Subtract
BLS	Branch if Lower or Same	JSR	Jump to Subroutine	SWI	Software Interrupt
BLT	Branch if Less than Zero	LDA	Load Accumulator	TAB	Transfer Accumulators
BMI	Branch if Minus	LDS	Load Stack Pointer	TAP	Transfer Accumulators to Condition Code Reg.
BNE	Branch if Not Equal to Zero	LDX	Load Index Register	TBA	Transfer Accumulators
BPL	Branch if Plus	LSR	Logical Shift Right	TPA	Transfer Condition Code Reg. to Accumulator
BRA	Branch Always	NEG	Negate	TST	Test
BSR	Branch to Subroutine	NOP	No Operation	TSX	Transfer Stack Pointer to Index Register
BVC	Branch if Overflow Clear	ORA	Inclusive OR Accumulator	TXS	Transfer Index Register to Stack Pointer
BVS	Branch if Overflow Set	PSH	Push Data	WAI	Wait for Interrupt
CBA	Compare Accumulators				
CLC	Clear Carry				
CLI	Clear Interrupt Mask				

TABLE 7.3 Accumulator and memory instructions. (*Courtesy of Motorola Inc.*)

		ADDRESSING MODES														
	MNE-	IMMED			DIRECT			INDEX			EXTND			IMPLIED		
OPERATIONS	MONIC	OP	~	=	OP	~	=	OP	~	=	OP	~	=	OP	~	=
Add	ADDA	8B	2	2	9B	3	2	AB	5	2	BB	4	3			
	ADDB	CB	2	2	DB	3	2	EB	5	2	FB	4	3			
Add Acmltrs	ABA													1B	2	1
Add with Carry	ADCA	89	2	2	99	3	2	A9	5	2	B9	4	3			
	ADCB	C9	2	2	D9	3	2	E9	5	2	F9	4	3			
And	ANDA	84	2	2	94	3	2	A4	5	2	B4	4	3			
	ANDB	C4	2	2	D4	3	2	E4	5	2	F4	4	3			
Bit Test	BITA	85	2	2	95	3	2	A5	5	2	B5	4	3			
	BITB	C5	2	2	D5	3	2	E5	5	2	F5	4	3			
Clear	CLR							6F	7	2	7F	6	3			
	CLRA													4F	2	1
	CLRB													5F	2	1
Compare	CMPA	81	2	2	91	3	2	A1	5	2	B1	4	3			
	CMPB	C1	2	2	D1	3	2	E1	5	2	F1	4	3			
Compare Acmltrs	CBA													11	2	1
Complement, 1s	COM							63	7	2	73	6	3			
	COMA													43	2	1
	COMB													53	2	1
Complement, 2s	NEG							60	7	2	70	6	3			
(Negate)	NEGA													40	2	1
	NEGB													50	2	1
Decimal Adjust, A	DAA													19	2	1
Decrement	DEC							6A	7	2	7A	6	3			
	DECA										4A	2		4A	2	1
	DECB													5A	2	1
Exclusive OR	EORA	88	2	2	98	3	2	A8	5	2	B8	4	3			
	EORB	C8	2	2	D8	3	2	E8	5	2	F8	4	3			
Increment	INC							6C	7	2	7C	6	3			
	INCA													4C	2	1
	INCB													5C	2	1
Load Acmltr	LDAA	86	2	2	96	3	2	A6	5	2	B6	4	3			
	LDAB	C6	2	2	D6	3	2	E6	5	2	F6	4	3			
Or, Inclusive	ORAA	8A	2	2	9A	3	2	AA	5	2	BA	4	3			
	ORAB	CA	2	2	DA	3	2	EA	5	2	FA	4	3			
Push Data	PSHA													36	4	1
	PSHB													37	4	1
Pull Data	PULA													32	4	1
	PULB													33	4	1
Rotate Left	ROL							69	7	2	79	6	3			
	ROLA													49	2	1
	ROLB													59	2	1
Rotate Right	ROR							66	7	2	76	6	3			
	RORA													46	2	1
	RORB													56	2	1

TABLE 7.3 Continued.

OPERATIONS	MNEMONIC	ADDRESSING MODES														
		IMMED			DIRECT			INDEX			EXTND			IMPLIED		
		OP	~	=	OP	~	=	OP	~	=	OP	~	=	OP	~	=
Shift Left,	ASL							68	7	2	78	6	3			
Arithmetic	ASLA													48	2	1
	ASLB													58	2	1
Shift Right,	ASR							67	7	2	77	6	3			
Arithmetic	ASRA													47	2	1
	ASRB													57	2	1
Shift Right,	LSR							64	7	2	74	6	3			
Logic	LSRA													44	2	1
	LSRB													54	2	1
Store Acmltr	STAA				97	4	2	A7	6	2	B7	5	3			
	STAB				D7	4	2	E7	6	2	F7	5	3			
Subtract	SUBA	80	2	2	90	3	2	A0	5	2	B0	4	3			
	SUBB	C0	2	2	D0	3	2	E0	5	2	F0	4	3			
Subtract Acmltrs	SBA													10	2	1
Subtr. with Carry	SBCA	82	2	2	92	3	2	A2	5	2	B2	4	3			
	SBCB	C2	2	2	D2	3	2	E2	5	2	F2	4	3			
Transfer Acmltrs	TAB													16	2	1
	TBA													17	2	1
Test, Zero	TST							6D	7	2	7D	6	3			
or Minus	TSTA													4D	2	1
	TSTB													5D	2	1

LEGEND:
OP Operation Code (Hexadecimal);
~ Number of MPU Cycles;
= Number of Program Bytes;
Note Accumulator addressing mode instructions are included in the column for IMPLIED addressing.

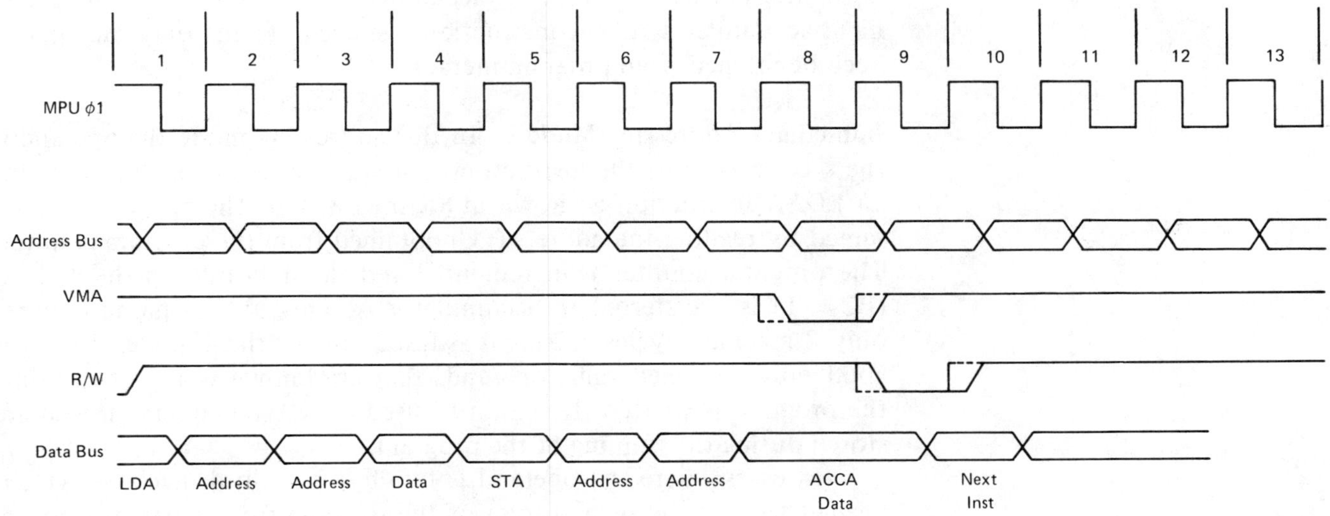

FIGURE 7.6 Typical waveforms on the address, data, and control busses. These waveforms are for the load and store instructions in the extended addressing mode. The timing is referenced to the ϕ_1 clock periods.

cute the instruction as measured in clock cycles. The most economical instructions require a single memory byte and two machine cycles to execute. These are in contrast to others requiring three memory bytes and as many as 10 machine cycles to execute. If the operand is already in the processor, then only the opcode need be fetched from program memory. If the operand is a constant (a value already known at the time the program is written), it is generally written in program memory directly following the opcode, thus forming a two-byte instruction. If, on the other hand, the value of the operand is a value computed during the program and, therefore, unknown at the time the program is written, it must be stored at a predetermined address (the effective address of the operand). In this case, a second and third byte of the instruction may be used to provide the effective address of the operand and a total of four bytes must be read from either program memory or data storage. Let us look at the specific addressing modes in detail.

Implied Addressing Mode (Inherent) The implied or inherent addressing mode applies to single-byte instructions. The operand is implied by the opcode, and no address need be used for the operand. In most cases the operand is located within the 6800. This applies to instructions like clear the carry bit (CLC), or increment the index register (INX). This mode is illustrated in Figure 7.7.

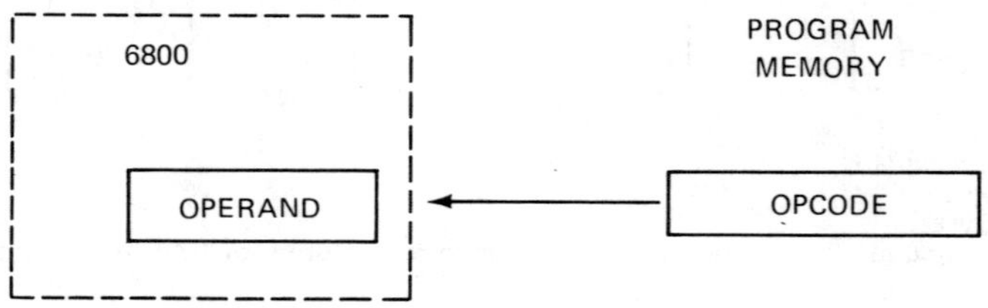

FIGURE 7.7 Implied addressing mode. The implied addressing mode requires only an opcode in the program memory. The operand is a register within the processor.

Accumulator X This mode is a specific form of the implied addressing mode. The operand is either accumulator A or B. INCA means increment accumulator A. The instruction is single-byte and only the opcode need be fetched from program memory.

Immediate Addressing Mode In this addressing mode the operand is the second byte of the instruction. The relative timing of this mode for an LDAA instruction is shown in Figure 7.8. First the opcode 86 is obtained by reading the address (PC) obtained from the program counter. The program counter is incremented and the data byte in the address (PC + 1) is transferred to accumulator A. This address mode requires only 2 machine cycles making it as fast as any of the 4 modes. But, it is good only for fixed value operands that are known values at the time the program is written. It cannot be used for variable operands that are stored during the running of the program.

In cases where the operand is two bytes, a third machine cycle is needed to read the second byte of the operand from program memory (PC + 2).

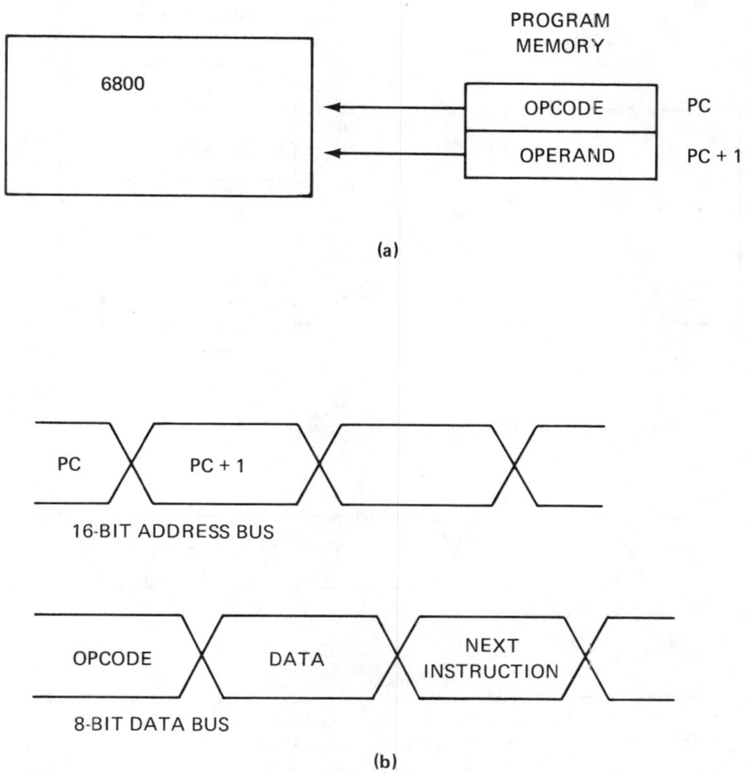

FIGURE 7.8 Immediate addressing mode. **(a)** The immediate addressing mode requires only two bytes of program memory. The opcode is in memory address PC while the operand is in PC + 1. The operand in this mode must be a constant. **(b)** In the immediate address mode, the 6800 fetches the opcode from program memory address PC. The operand (data) is obtained from program memory address (PC + 1).

Extended Addressing Mode In extended addressing the operand is obtained from storage outside of program memory. However, the address of the operand is obtained from program memory immediately following the opcode. As Figure 7.9 shows, two trips to program memory are required to obtain the address of the operand: one trip to obtain the lower significant bits, and the second trip to obtain the higher significant bits of the address. This 16-bit address is then used to obtain the operand. This mode requires at least four machine cycles, but its use is not restricted to constant, predetermined values. It can be used for variable operands computed and stored during the running of the program.

Direct Addressing Mode (Zero Page) Direct addressing is an abbreviated form of extended addressing. The lower significant bits of the effective address are obtained from the program memory address immediately following the opcode. The higher significant bits of the effective address are made zeros automatically. As Figure 7.10 shows, this address mode requires three machine cycles. It accomplishes the same advantages as the extended mode, but it saves one memory byte and one machine cycle. To take advantage of this mode, the lowest 256 bytes of memory should be reserved for the storage of variables in RAM rather than use as program memory.

Indexed Addressing Mode In the indexed addressing mode, the second byte of the instruction contains an offset value which is added to

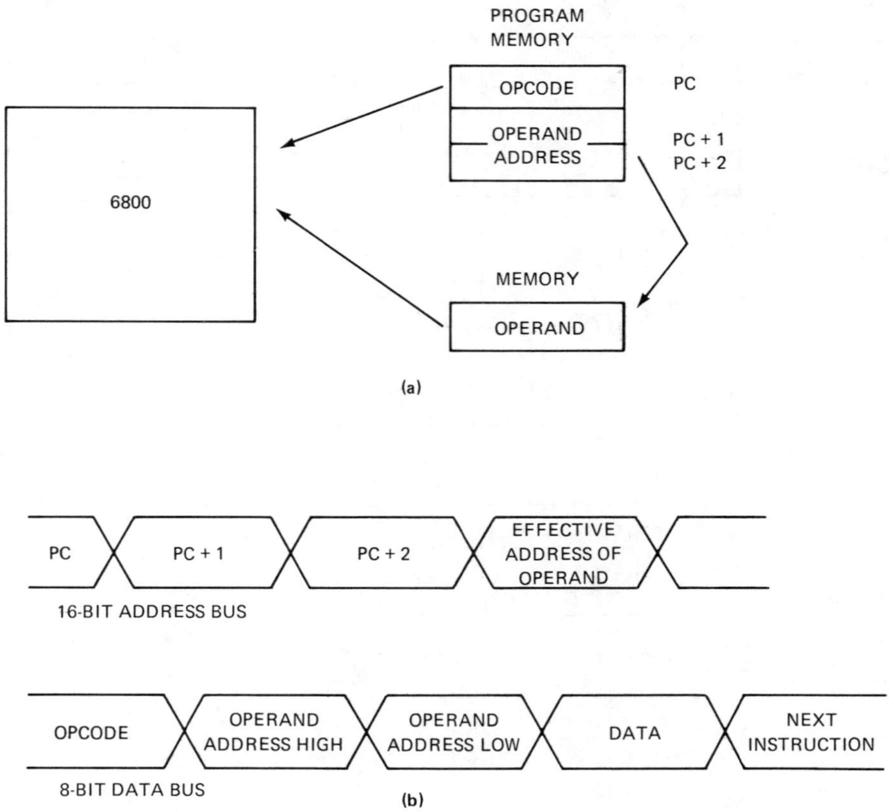

FIGURE 7.9 Extended addressing mode. **(a)** The extended addressing mode uses the bytes following the opcode in program memory to supply the address of the operand. **(b)** In the extended mode, the 6800 fetches the opcode from program memory address PC. Next the high byte of the effective address of the operand is read from (PC + 1). Then the low byte of the effective address of the operand is read from (PC + 2). The effective address is then used to read the operand (data).

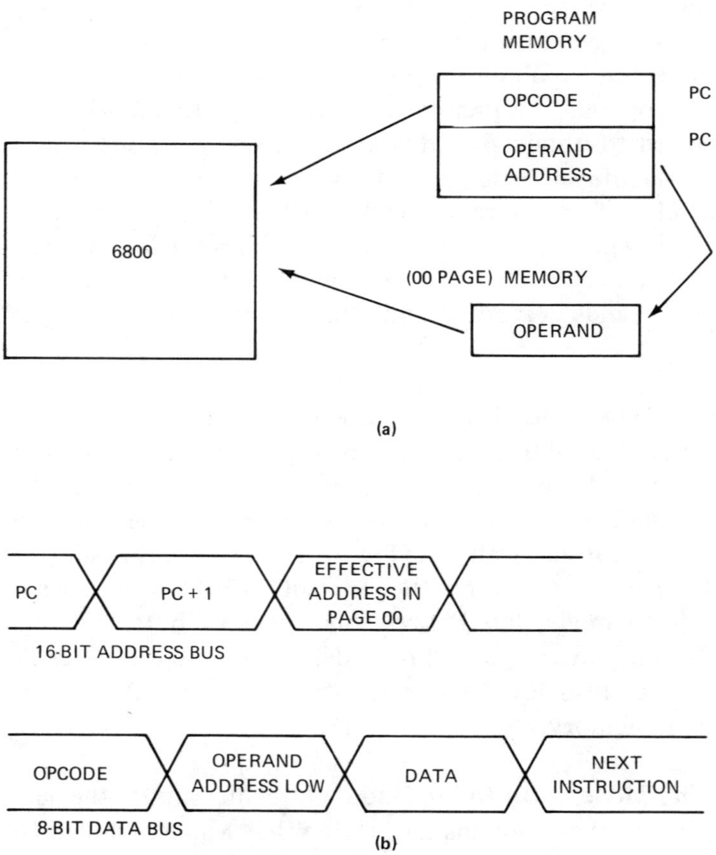

FIGURE 7.10 Direct addressing mode. **(a)** The direct addressing mode uses the byte following the opcode in program memory to supply the low byte of the operand address. The high byte of the address is zero. (This mode is often called Zero Page). **(b)** In the direct address mode, the 6800 fetches the opcode from program memory address PC. Next, the low byte of the effective address of the operand is read from (PC + 1). An effective address using 00 as the high byte is then used to locate the operand (data) in page zero of the memory.

the contents of the index register. The sum is used as the effective address. The contents of the index register are not changed. When this mode is used in a program loop containing an INX (increment the index register) or DEX (decrement the index register), a series of adjacent memory locations can be written or read. The transfer or manipulation of complete blocks of data can be accomplished. The movement of bytes for this mode is shown in Figure 7.11. The arithmetic logic unit plays a role in this mode. The LDAA instruction in this mode requires 5 machine cycles.

Relative Addressing Like indexed addressing, an offset value is obtained from the second byte of the instruction. As Figure 7.12 shows, the offset is added to the contents of the program counter. This results in a new location in program memory. Note that this mode exists for branch instructions only.

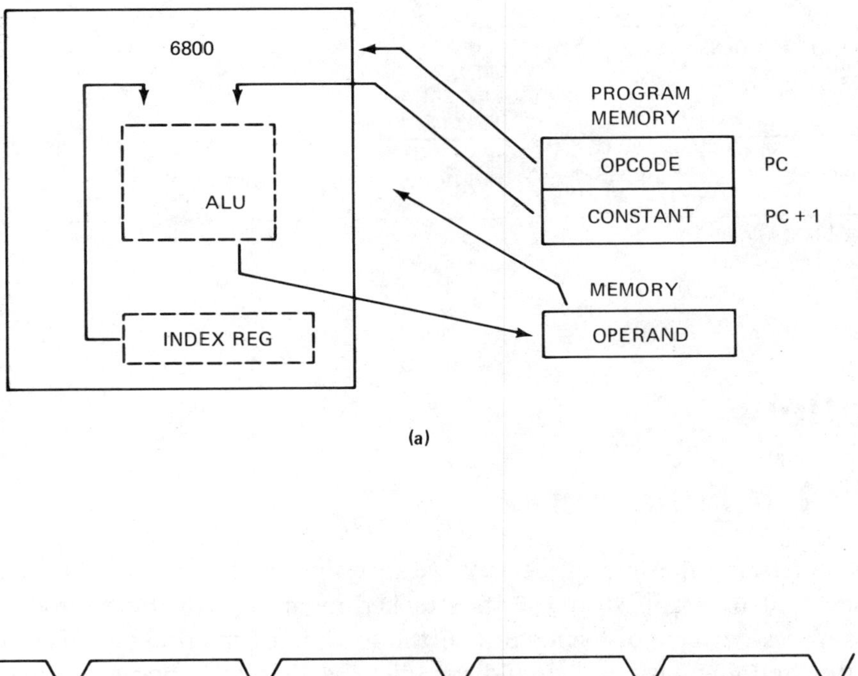

(a)

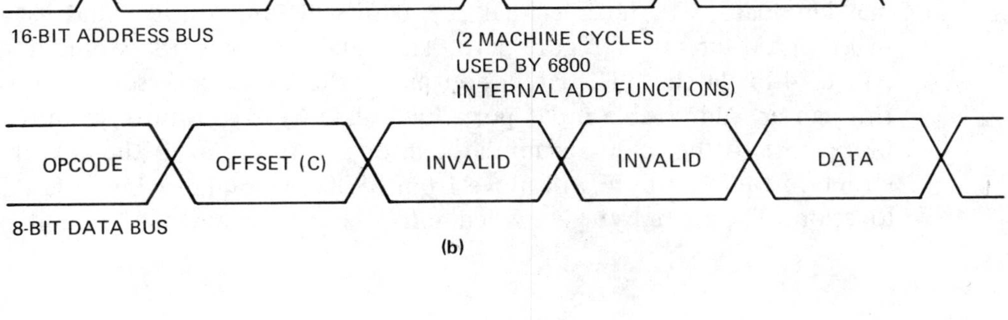

(b)

FIGURE 7.11 Indexed addressing mode. **(a)** The indexed addressing mode uses the sum of a constant from program memory and the contents of the index register to compute the address of the operand. This mode combined with the incrementing or decrementing of the index register permits the use of complete blocks of adjacent memory locations. **(b)** In the indexed address mode, the 6800 fetches the opcode from program memory address PC. Next, an offset value is read from (PC + 1). The offset is added to the value stored in the index register to form the effective address of the operand.

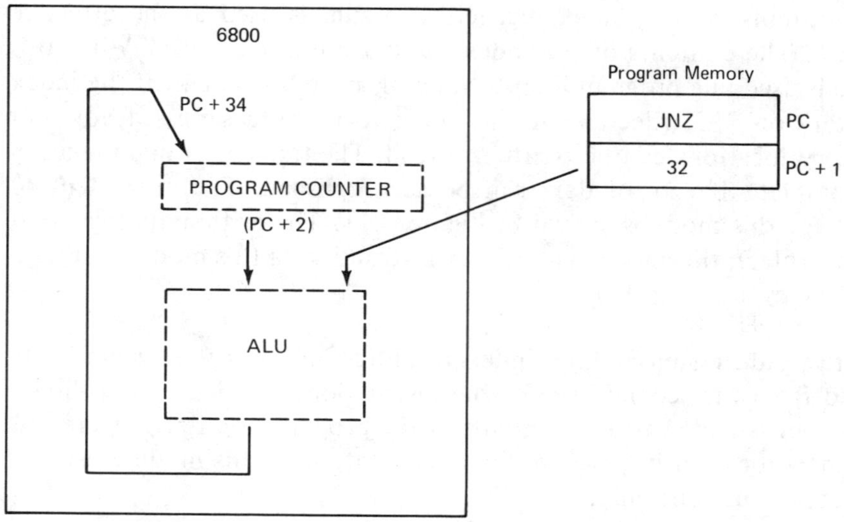

(a)

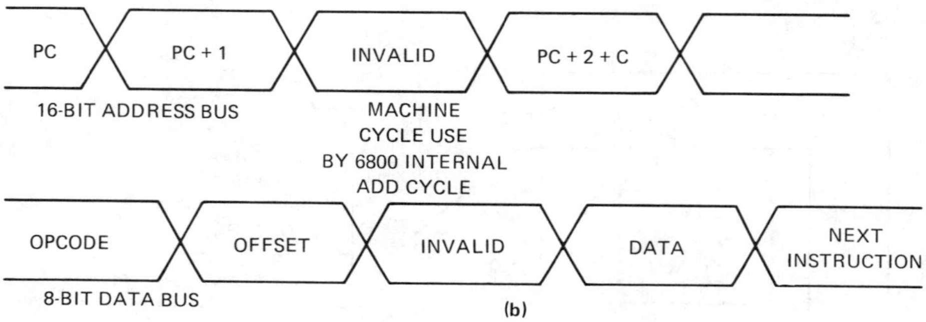

(b)

FIGURE 7.12 Relative addressing mode. **(a)** The relative addressing mode is used in branch or conditional jump instructions. A constant is added or subtracted from the current contents of the program counter. **(b)** In the relative address mode, the 6800 fetches the opcode from program memory address PC. Next, an offset value is read from (PC + 1). The offset is then added to the value in the program counter. The result being that the program branches to a new location in the program memory. This new address is (PC + 2) + (offset). This mode exists for branch instructions only. For a branch backward in program memory (PC + 1) will contain the offset in twos complement.

7.4 Bootstrap Loader

7.4.1 Function

In operating the microprocessor we face the simple fact that, in the absence of programs stored in its attached memories, the microprocessor is useless. It cannot even assist in the loading of the program. The first programming task we should complete is that of a bootstrap loader which will enable the loading of programs into RAM from a hexadecimal keyboard. The hexadecimal keyboard will function like that used in the RAM circuit of Figure 5.18. The data bytes are first stored in a pair of 4-bit latches. The latches output to the microprocessor data bus through an addressable input port. Each data byte will move from the input port to the 6800 accumulator in one instruction. In the next instruction the data byte will move from 6800 accumulator into a RAM location. The next byte is loaded into the switchboard latches and is moved to the accumulator, then to an adjacent RAM address. Before proceeding with the hardware and software design for this function, let's examine some classes of instructions needed for this type program.

7.4.2 Data Move Instructions

The most widely used instructions are the data moves. There are three groups of these: load, store, and transfer instructions. Move instructions have two operands, the destination and the source, one of which is implied by the opcode. In any move instruction, data moves from the source to the destination.

$$D \longleftarrow (S)$$

Load instructions cause data to move from memory to a microprocessor register.

$$R_D \longleftarrow (M_S)$$

Store instructions cause data to move from a microprocessor register to memory.

$$M_D \longleftarrow (R_S)$$

Transfer instructions cause data to move from one microprocessor register to another.

$$R_D \longleftarrow (R_S)$$

On completion of a move instruction, the data in the source operand has not changed. Destination and source operands will both contain the same data. The following describes 6800 data move instructions:

LDAX
ACCX $\longleftarrow$ (M) X = A or B

Load the contents of memory into either the A or B accumulator.

LDS
SPH $\longleftarrow$ (M)
SPL $\longleftarrow$ (M + 1)

Load the contents of 2 consecutive memory locations into the stack pointer (high and low bytes) used to initialize the stack address.

LDX
IXH $\longleftarrow$ (M)
IXL $\longleftarrow$ (M + 1)

Load the contents of 2 consecutive memory locations into the index register (high and low bytes).

Store instructions have a source operand implied by the opcode. The destination operand or its effective address must be given in the operand column of the program statement.

STAX X = (A or B)

M ←—— (ACCX)

Store the contents of accumulator (A or B) in memory. The contents of the accumulator remains unchanged.

STX

M ←—— (IXH)

(M + 1) ←—— (IXL)

Store the contents of the index register in 2 consecutive memory locations (high byte first).

Transfer instructions have both the source and destination of operands implied by the opcode.

TAB

ACCB ←—— ACCA

Move the contents of ACCA to ACCB. The contents of ACCA does not change.

TBA

ACCA ←—— ACCB

Move the contents of ACCB to ACCA. The contents of ACCB does not change.

7.4.3 Condition Code Register

Although most instructions are used without concern for the state of the condition code register, there are instructions which are seriously affected by the state of one or more of the condition code register bits. Figure 7.13 shows the condition code register and its individual flag bits.

- The **C bit** is the carry/borrow bit. It acts as a store for the carry during an arithmetic operation or a borrow during a subtract. It is also affected by shift and rotate instructions.
- The **V bit** is called the overflow flag. It is set after an arithmetic operation during which a carry occurs from bit 6 into the bit 7 position. It is used in conjunction with the sign and carry bits

1	1	H	I	N	Z	V	C

FIGURE 7.13 The condition code register of the 6800.
C = Carry/Borrow
V = Two's Complement Overflow Indicator
Z = Zero Indicator
N = Negative Indicator
I = Interrupt Mask
H = Half Carry

to determine the sign of the answer and the presence or absence of a carry.

- The **Z bit** is set after any instruction which ends with a value of zero in the operand accumulator or memory byte.
- The **N bit** is set after any instruction which ends with a 1 (high level) in bit 7 of the operand accumulator or memory byte.
- The **I bit** is the interrupt mask and will be set whenever an IRQ or NMI interrupt signal is received. The 6800 will not respond to an IRQ if the I bit is set. The I bit can be reset by a programmed instruction, CLI or by the reloading of a previous condition code register content that occurs as the result of a return from interrupt instruction, RTI.
- The **H bit** is a half carry bit. It is used in BCD arithmetic. It is set when there is a carry from the fourth significant digit during add instructions ABA, ADC, or ADD.
- **Bit** 6 and **bit** 7 of the condition code register are always 1 (high).

In many instances the programmer will find that a condition code register bit is in an incorrect state for the instruction he or she wishes to use. To alter the state of condition code register bits, either as a part of initializing instructions at the beginning of a program or at any point within a program, the following instructions can be used.

CLC	Clear Carry
CLI	Clear Interrupt Mask
CLV	Clear Overflow
SEC	Set Carry
SEV	Set Overflow
SEI	Set Interrupt Mask

The interrupt mask may be set to prevent the interruption of a critical section of the program. The instruction CLR can be used to clear the contents of a memory address. CLRX can be used to clear either accumulator. The CLR instruction

$$\mathrm{ACCX} \longleftarrow 00$$
$$\mathrm{M} \longleftarrow 00$$

sets the Z bit and clears the N bit of the condition code register.

7.4.4 Increment and Decrement Instructions

The Increment and Decrement instructions are used frequently in most programs. In conjunction with compare instructions (CMP, CPX) they are often used to count program cycles. In reading or writing blocks of data in consecutive memory locations, the index register used as the address pointer is incremented or decremented through the series of addresses.

Either accumulator can be incremented with the instructions INCA or INCB.

$$\text{ACCA} \longleftarrow (\text{ACCA}) + 1$$

or

$$\text{ACCB} \longleftarrow (\text{ACCB}) + 1$$

Memory can be incremented with the same instruction in the indexed or extended mode INC.

$$\text{M} \longleftarrow (\text{M}) + 1$$

In the extended mode the memory address whose content is to be incremented is obtained from the two program memory bytes following the opcode. In the indexed mode, the memory address whose content is to be incremented is obtained from the index register.

The instruction INX increments the index register. If the index register is being used as an address pointer the result is that memory addresses are incremented.

$$\text{IX} \longleftarrow (\text{IX}) + 1$$

A companion set of decrement instructions is also a part of the 6800 instruction set. These are

- Decrement accumulator A

  DECA $\quad \text{ACCA} \longleftarrow (\text{ACCA}) - 1$

- Decrement accumulator B

  DECB $\quad \text{ACCB} \longleftarrow (\text{ACCB}) - 1$

- Decrement memory

  DEC $\quad \text{M} \longleftarrow (\text{M}) - 1$

- Decrement the index register

  DEX $\quad \text{IX} \longleftarrow (\text{IX}) - 1$

7.4.5 Interrupt Handling Instructions

Although interrupts are initiated by signals from outside the microprocessor (IRQ, NMI), there are several 6800 instructions which are used in the handling of interrupts. Two of these we will use with the bootstrap loader are WAI and RTI.

Wait for Interrupt (WAI) is used when the microprocessor has completed running a program to a point where it must wait for data from an input device. In executing a WAI, the 6800 loads the microprocessor status on the stack, in the order shown in Figure 7.5, exactly as if the interrupt request had already been received. It will then cease all program operations until an active IRQ or NMI input signal is received. When either of these signals is received, during a wait for interrupt, the 6800 will proceed directly to the service routine (by loading the program counter PCL and PCH with the data bytes taken from the interrupt vectors). It will neglect the operation of loading the stack in recognition of the fact that this function has already been performed by the WAI instruction.

The Return from Interrupt Instruction (RTI) is the final instruction in every interrupt routine. It causes the 6800 to transfer microprocessor status from the stack to the microprocessor registers. This causes the program to return to the instruction one higher than the one executed prior to the receipt of the interrupt signal.

7.4.6 Bootstrap Loader Hardware

Figure 7.14(a) shows a block diagram of a microprocessor system with a bootstrap loader. The hexadecimal keyboard interface differs from that of Figure 5.12 in that it is addressed from a 16-bit comparator. A set of 16 switches attached to the B inputs of the comparator are compared with the address bus attached to the A inputs. Therefore, the keyboard interface will output to the data bus whenever the MPU outputs an address identical to that set on the switches. The compare output $A \equiv B$ is used to enable the keyboard interface. This same compare signal or its complement $A \neq B$ can be used to inhibit memory devices which might otherwise output for the same address set on the switches. With this feature, any single address in the 64K memory map can be superseded by presetting the address comparator switches. This as we will demonstrate adds considerable flexibility to the microprocessor system. At this point we face three considerations: hardware, software, and operating procedure. Either of these can be simplified at the expense of complicating the other two. As the object here is to learn the use of data move instructions, I will use a system with elaborate but straightforward hardware for the sake of keeping program and procedure simple. The keyboard hardware shown in Figure 5.18 would allow

FIGURE 7.14(a) The 6800 Microprocessor system with a hexadecimal keyboard for loading programs.

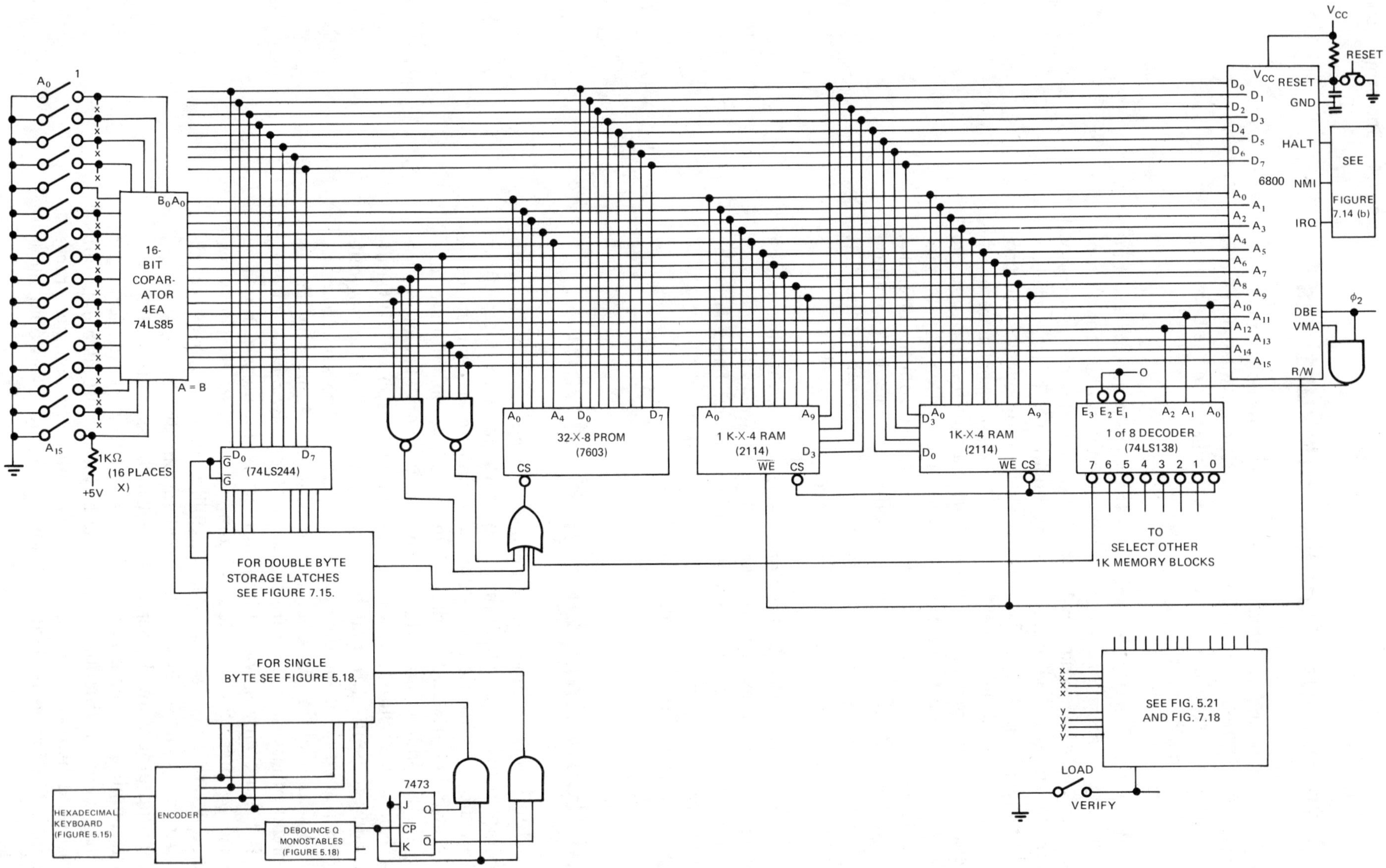

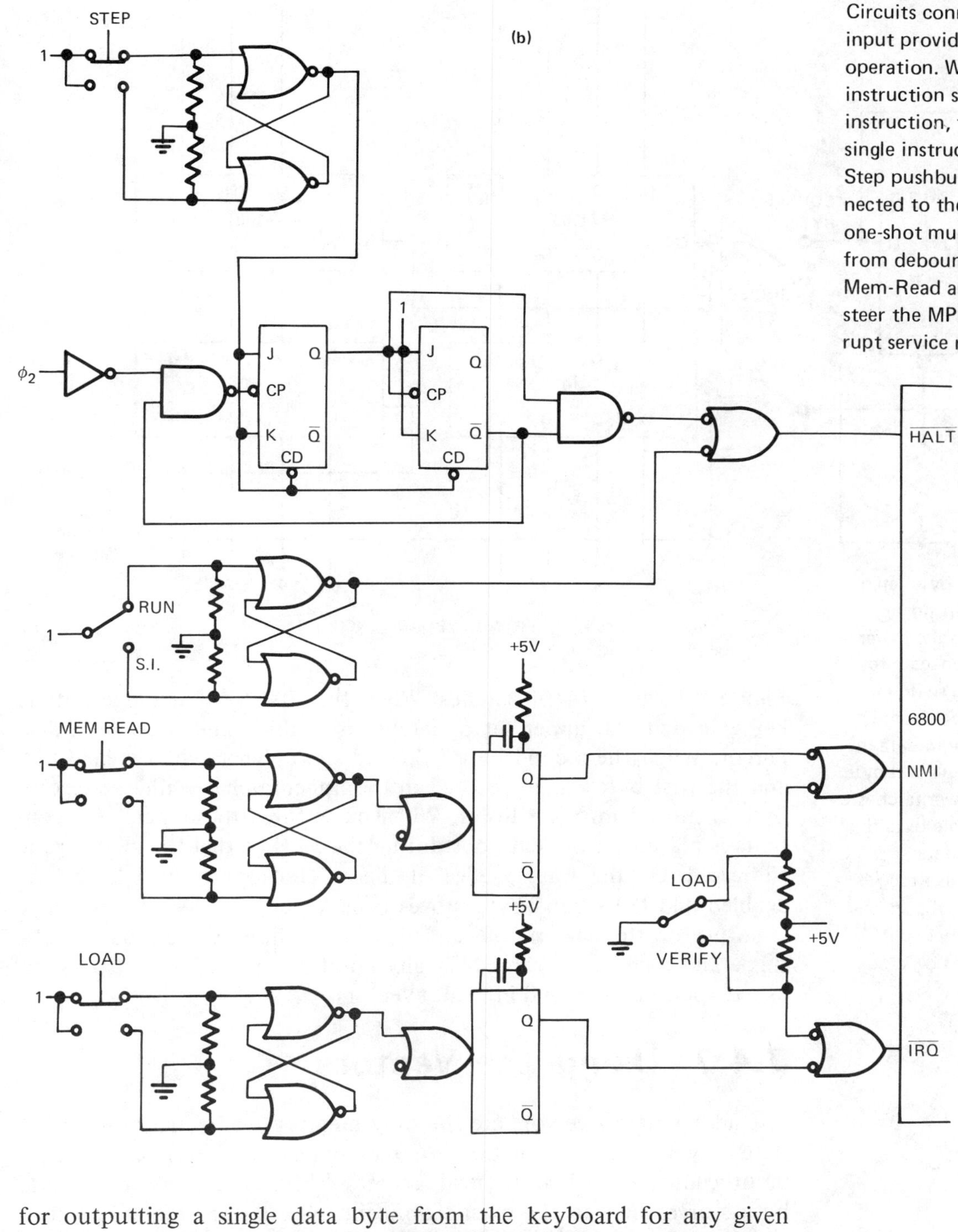

FIGURE 7.14(b) Control circuits used with 6800 bootstrap loader. Circuits connected to the $\overline{\text{HALT}}$ input provide single instruction operation. When the Run-Single instruction switch is in single instruction, the 6800 will execute a single instruction each time the Step pushbutton is depressed. Connected to the interrupt inputs are one-shot multivibrators activated from debounced pushbuttons. Mem-Read and Load pushbuttons steer the MPU to appropriate interrupt service routines.

for outputting a single data byte from the keyboard for any given address set on the switches. Although data is loaded a single byte at a time, the vectors and many operands are double byte and the ability to store and load two bytes would add greater flexibility to the system. A simple modification to the keyboard holding registers will permit two data bytes to be held in storage. These would be outputted at adjacent addresses when the keyboard is addressed. This modification shown in

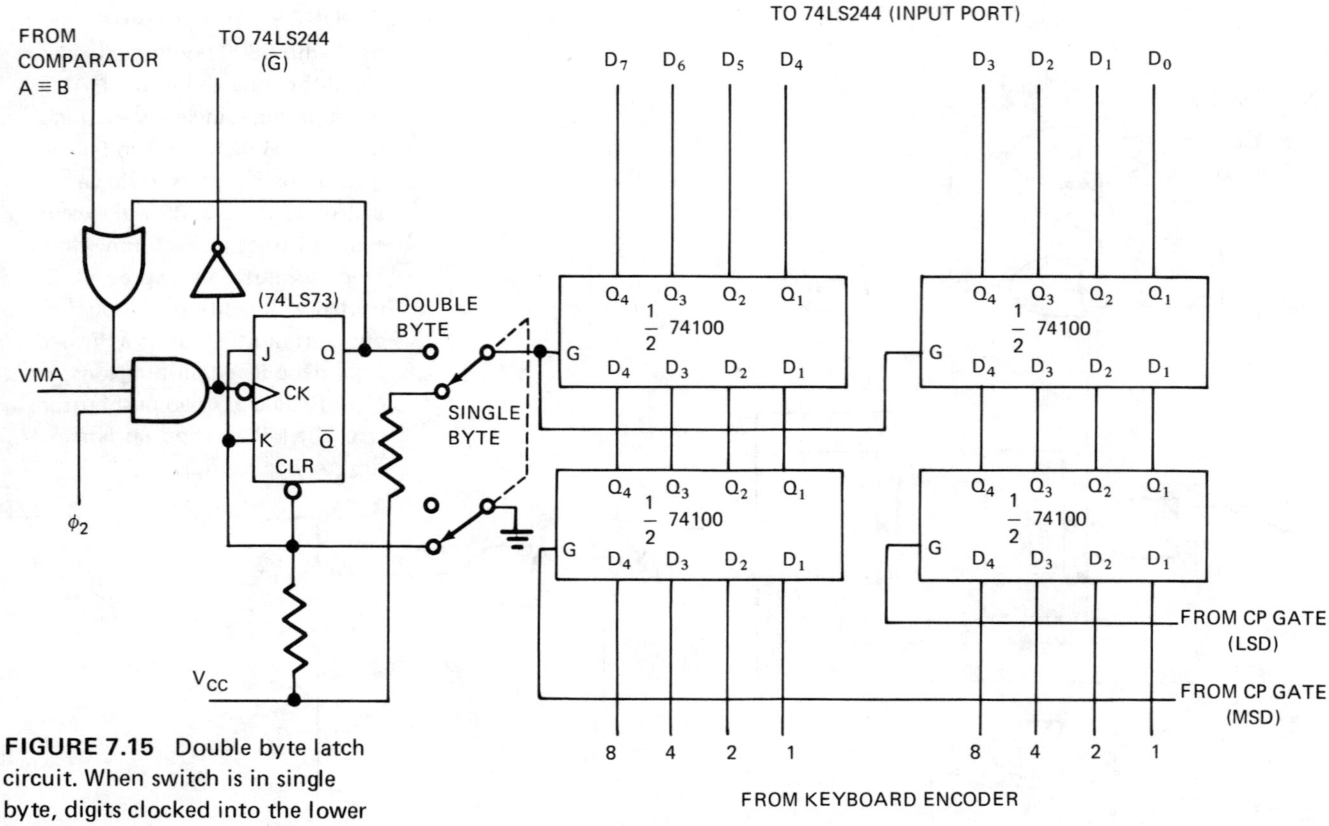

FIGURE 7.15 Double byte latch circuit. When switch is in single byte, digits clocked into the lower latches immediately propagate to the upper latches. When switch is in double byte, the low level from Q to G inhibits any change in data in the upper latches and a second byte may be stored in the lower latches. When outputting a double byte the ϕ_2 pulse which enables data through the input port also toggles the JK flip-flop enabling the second byte into the upper latches so it will output with the next ϕ_2 clock pulse.

Figure 7.15 uses 74100 latches. When the first byte or single byte is being loaded the upper set of latches is enabled and becomes transparent. When the second byte is loaded the upper latch G is held low and the first byte remains stored in the upper latches while the second byte is moved into the lower. When outputting, the upper latch contents is placed on the data bus during the ϕ_2 time that the keyboard is addressed. On the trailing edge of the ϕ_2 clock, the upper latch G is enabled and the second byte moves from lower to upper latch where it is output on the next ϕ_2 pulse. This feature allows us to modify both single and dual byte operands at any point in a program. It also allows us to supersede reset and interrupt vectors.

7.4.7 Using the Vectors

The addressing of vectors are the only memory read functions not initiated by program instructions. A momentary low level on the reset input causes the 6800 to read address FFFE and transfer the data byte stored there to the most significant byte of the program counter (PCH). This is followed by a transfer of the data byte stored at address FFFF to the least significant byte of the program counter (PCL). This function allows the programmer to steer the 6800 to the starting address of his or her choice. In many cases the 6800 is dedicated to a single program for which the starting address is always the same. For these applications, vectors FFFE and FFFF are covered by PROM. However, the keyboard register and comparator of Figure 7.14 can be used to supersede this vector. This allows the operator to start the processor at any address in the 256-page memory map. The interrupt vectors can be altered in a similar fashion by the keyboard and comparator, thus permitting a choice of service routines to be used with an interrupt. We will demonstrate how these features make it possible for us to load and verify a program. Unfortunately, it is not practical to change the address comparator switches while a program is being run. Changes to the data in the keyboard register can be made during a program run as long as the keyboard interface is not addressed by the program. The address comparator switches should be changed only prior to reset, during a wait for interrupt, or during a halt. The halt conditions occur when the 6800 is operated in single instruction mode.

7.4.8 The Bootstrap Loader Program

Table 7.4 shows a bootstrap loader program which is to be loaded into the same 32-X-8 PROM that includes the vectors. Figure 7.16 shows the address map and contents of that 32-X-8 PROM. The highest address in the 6800 memory map is $FFFF_H$. A 32-word memory occupying the highest addresses would begin at FFE0.

$$32_{10} = 20_H \qquad \begin{array}{r} FFFF_H \\ - \quad 20_H \\ \hline FFDF_H \end{array} + 1 = FFE0_H$$

If we wish to include FFFF in that memory it must begin just above FFDF, which is FFE0. The bootstrap loader program begins at address FFE1. The reset vector located at FFFF and FFFE contains an address FFE1, which means that unless the address comparator switch is set to supersede the reset vector, a reset will initialize a bootstrap loader program. Before reset, however, the address comparator switches must be set to FFE5 and the address of the program to be loaded must be stored, high byte first in the keyboard latches.

The steps for initializing the loader program are

Step 1 Place keyboard interface in single byte mode. Load the high byte of the program to be loaded. (Page Address)

Step 2 Place keyboard in double byte mode. Load the low byte address of the program to be loaded.

Step 3 Set Comparator switches to FFDF.

Step 4 Reset.

Step 5 Place keyboard interface to single byte, address comparator switches remain at FFDF.

TABLE 7.4 Bootstrap loader program. The program has three segments: initialization, load routine, and memory read. The memory read routine is also a part of the load routine. Initialization uses instructions FFE1 to FFE9. Memory read is an interrupt (NMI) service routine using instructions FFF2 through FFF7 and FEEA. Load routine is an interrupt (IRQ) service routine using instructions FFED through FFE7 and FFEA.

ADDRESS	MOVEMENT	MNE-MONIC	OPERAND	DESCRIPTION	MODE
FFE1		LDS	01FF	Load initial stack address at top of Page 1.	Immediate
E4		LDX	(FFDF)	Load starting address of program to be loaded. (Index register to be used as address pointer for loading program).	Extended
E7		DEX		Used to cancel the first INX in MEM-READ routine.	Implied
E8		CLI		Clear Interrupt flag.	Implied
E9		WAI		Wait for interrupt places the 6800 in the wait state so that a byte can be loaded into the switchboard register.	Implied
EA		JMP	FFE8	Jump back to the WAI.	Extended
ED	IRQ* (Load)	LDA A	(FFDF)	Moves byte from keyboard holding register to accumulator A.	Extended
F0		STA A	00	Byte is moved from accumulator A to the memory address pointed to by the index register (a zero offset is used).	Indexed
F2	NMI (verify)	INX		Advance to next address.	Implied
F3		LDA A	00	Load A with memory byte pointed to by index reg.	Indexed
F5		STA A	(FF)	Move byte from A to display port 00FF	Direct
FFF7		RTI		Return to WAI.	Implied

*Beginning of interrupt service routine initiated by an IRQ. The interrupt vectors FFF8 and FFF9 must contain the address FFED.

Depressing the reset button results in the execution of the initialization instructions shown in the first block of the flow diagram of Figure 7.17.

Loading the program is now a simple matter of entering each byte into the keyboard latches and pressing the load button. The instructions for initializing the loader program are FFE1 through FFE9 of Table 7.4. These accomplish the following functions.

1. The processor is directed to beginning instruction of the loader program by a reset.
2. The stack pointer is initialized.
3. The starting address of the program to be loaded is transferred from keyboard to the index register.
4. The interrupt flag is cleared and a DEX is used to cancel out the first INX in the program.

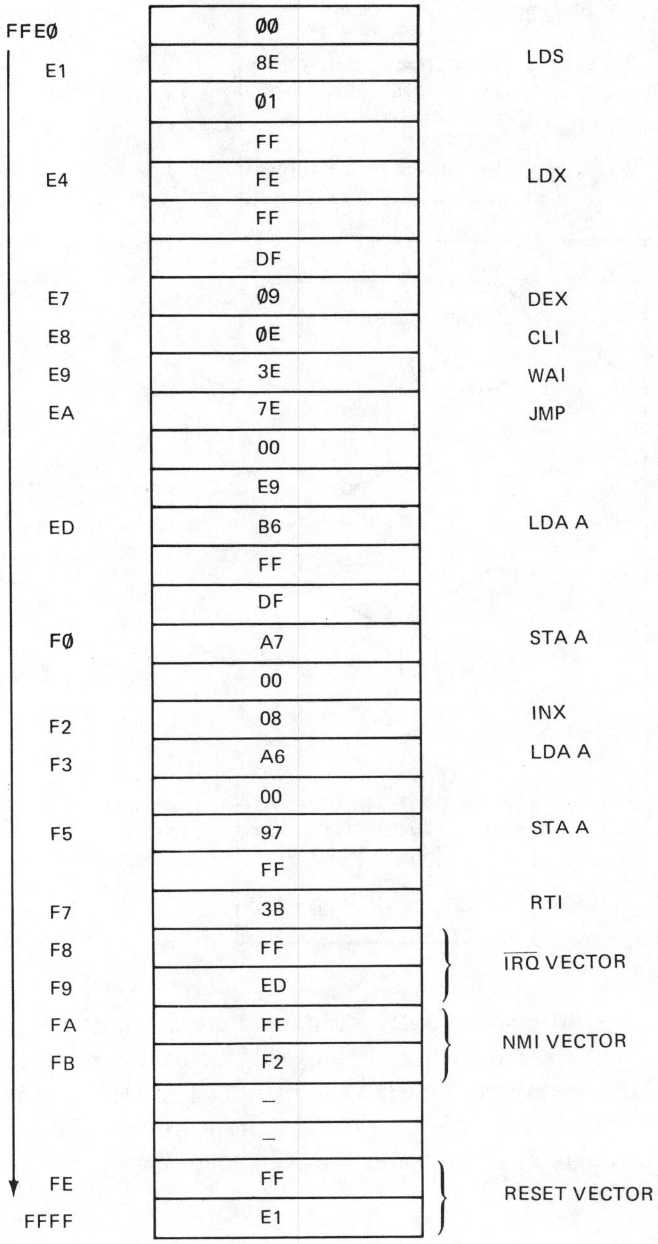

FIGURE 7.16 Memory map of 32-X-8 PROM used to contain both a bootstrap loader program and the 6800 vectors. Address and content are listed in hexadecimal.

5. The processor waits for interrupt.
6. Depressing the memory read button causes an (NMI) nonmaskable interrupt jump to service routine at FFF2.
7. The index register is incremented.
8. The contents of memory byte pointed to by the index register is moved to accumulator A and then to the display register. The program returns to a wait for interrupt, and is now at the starting address ready for the first byte to be loaded.

The WAI instruction causes a wait in the program which allows the keyboard register to be loaded with the byte that belongs in the mem-

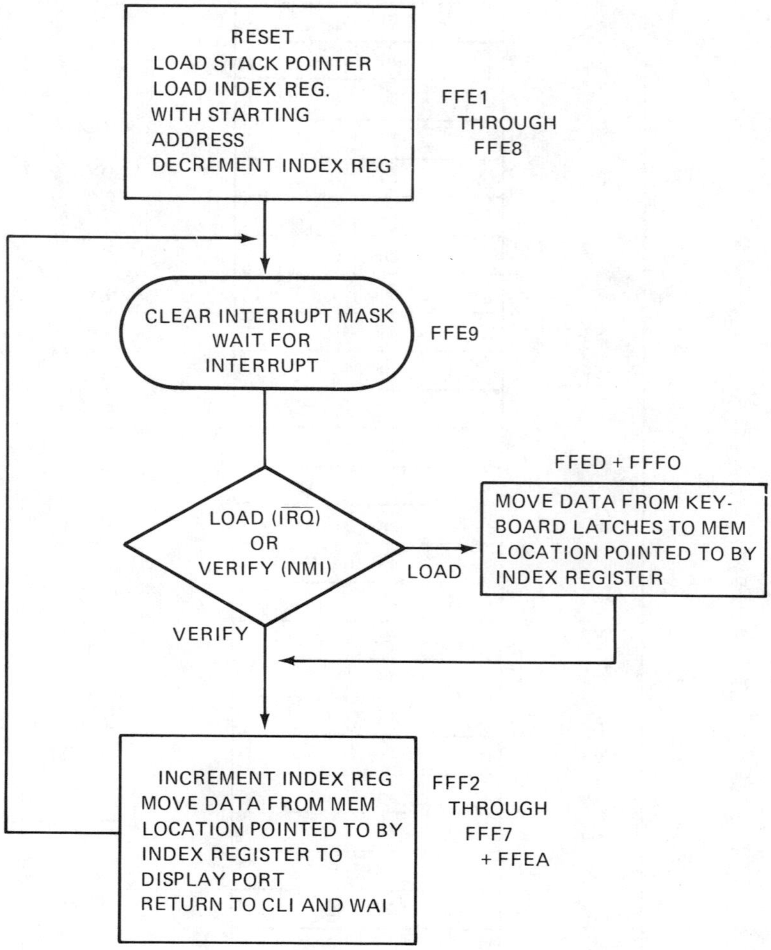

FIGURE 7.17 6800 Bootstrap loader flow diagram. The program has three segments: initialization, load routine, and verify or display routine. The pause in the program provided by the (WAI) wait for interrupt allows for the loading of each memory byte during a load operation or the examination of each memory byte during a verify operation.

ory address currently contained in the index register. The keyboard latches are loaded and the load button depressed. Depressing the load button produces an IRQ interrupt. The IRQ vector initiates the service routine beginning at FFED. This routine includes instructions FFED through FFF7 of Table 7.4. The load service routine provides functions as follows:

1. Data byte is moved from keyboard interface to accumulator.
2. Data byte is moved from accumulator to the memory location pointed to by the index register.
3. Index register is incremented in preparation for loading next byte.
4. Address and content of new memory location are moved to a display port.
5. Program returns to the WAI instruction.

After the last byte is loaded the program can be verified. The verification routine uses the same initialization instructions as the loader routine. Each address of the program loaded is verified by pressing the memory read button which causes an NMI interrupt, which starts a service routine at address FFF2. This routine includes instructions FFF2 through FFF7 in Table 7.4. It is, in fact, a segment of the load routine instructions and provides functions as follows:

1. The index register is incremented, advancing the address of program being verified.
2. The accumulator is loaded with data byte taken from address pointed to by the index register.
3. Data is moved from accumulator to a display port at address 00FF.
4. Returns to WAI instruction and waits for next interrupt.

This results in the display of the first memory byte. At this point, we examine the display to determine if it is correct; if so, we depress the memory read button (NMI) to display the next byte. The load button is not used until an error is detected. To correct an error, the correction is loaded into the keyboard latches and the load button is depressed. The load operation will load the correction and automatically display the next memory byte.

If a memory read button is depressed by mistake during a load operation, it causes an entry to be missed. If a load button is depressed by mistake during a verify operation, it would load the contents of the keyboard latches into an incorrect memory address. A load-verify switch might help to reduce the chances of these errors. The interrupt circuits including this switch are shown in Figure 7.14(b). Because of the shortness of the service routines, the interrupt pulse duration must be very short in comparison to the contact bounce of the switches. For this reason, the one-shot multivibrators are preceded by debounce flip-flops.

The operator instructions for the bootstrap loader are as follows:

To Load

1. Place keyboard interface in single byte and enter the high byte of the beginning address of program being loaded.
2. Place keyboard interface in double byte and enter the low byte of the beginning address of program being loaded.
3. Set address comparator switches to FFDF.
4. Reset.
5. Place keyboard interface to single byte and address comparator switches remain at FFDF.
6. Place verify-load switch to verify.
7. Depress memory read and verify that beginning address is correct.

8. Place verify-load switch in load.
9. Enter byte to be loaded into keyboard latches.
10. Depress load switch.
11. Repeat 9 and 10 until all bytes are loaded.

To Verify Perform 1 through 7 of load instructions.

8. Depress memory read and verify that both address and data are correct.
9. Repeat 8 until all bytes are verified.

To Enter Corrections If an error is detected, do not advance to subsequent memory addresses until a correction is loaded.

Make corrections as follows

10. Enter correction in keyboard latches.
11. Place load-verify switch in load.
12. Depress load button.
13. Before returning to verify, check to see that subsequent byte is correct, if not, continue making corrections of subsequent bytes by repeating 10, 12, and 13 until a correct byte is displayed. Then return to the verify routine by:
14. Place load verify switch in verify.
15. Return to Step 8 of the verify routine until all bytes are verified.

7.4.8 Displays

The circuits necessary for display have thus far been taken for granted in order to simplify the explanation of the bootstrap loader. Four-digit 7-segment LED displays may be used for the address and two to display the data outputted at the display port. Both address and data to the displays must be latched. As Figure 7.18 shows, the decoded address of the display port 00FF can be used to latch the data. A separate data display may be used with the keyboard latches or a single data display can be used, switching between memory data and keyboard data on a last-to-be-changed basis.

The address to be displayed must be the current content of the index register. This address is on the address bus during the fifth cycle of the indexed mode LDAA instruction. A decode of FFF3 will detect the first cycle of this instruction and enable a count of 4 to latch the address display at the proper time.

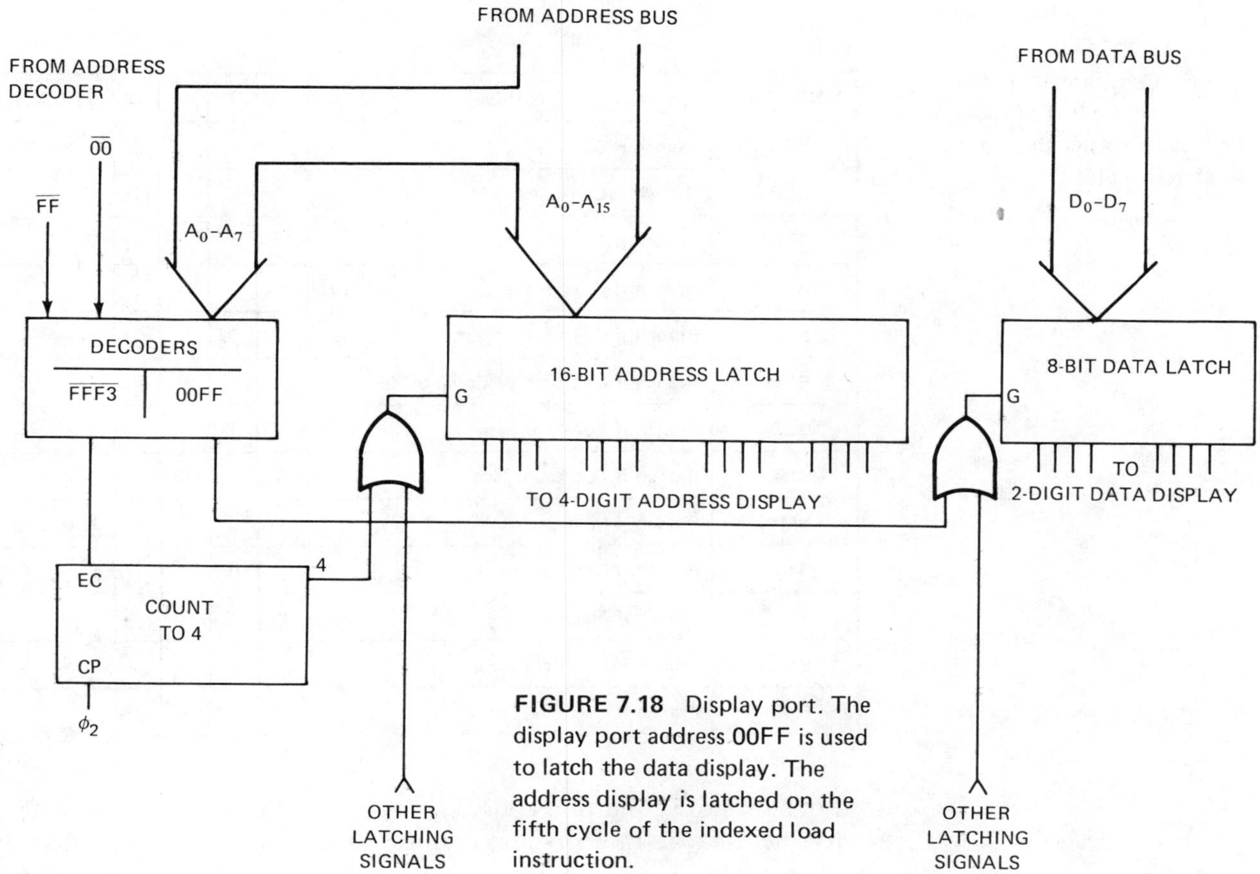

FIGURE 7.18 Display port. The display port address 00FF is used to latch the data display. The address display is latched on the fifth cycle of the indexed load instruction.

7.5 6800 Arithmetic Programs

7.5.1 Arithmetic Instructions

The provisions for arithmetic within the 6800 are numerous. They make it possible for the programmer to use any of the varied forms of binary arithmetic including BCD and binary by ones or twos complement. Arithmetic within a program can be quite simple, requiring a single instruction, or it can be very complex, requiring an extensive routine with many loops and branches. Where it is necessary for terms in an equation to have positive or negative sign and magnitude of 7 bits or greater, a lengthy program is required. To allow for algebraic addition of signed numbers, the program must examine the sign of the terms as they are read by the microprocessor and branch to the necessary routine. After every add or subtract routine, the program will branch to a selected correction routine depending on the state of the condition code register. In this respect the branch instructions are as important to an arithmetic operation as are the add and subtract instructions. The conditional branch instructions are shown in Table 7.5. The branch instruction causes the microprocessor to examine the state

TABLE 7.5 Conditional branch instructions and the bits of the condition code register that cause the branch to occur.

MNEMONIC	NAME	N	Z	V	C	EQUATION
BCC	Branch if Carry Clear				0	C = 0
BCS	Branch if Carry Set				1	C = 1
BEQ	Branch if Equal		1			Z = 1
BGE	Branch if Greater than or Equal to Zero	V		N		N = V
BGT	Branch if Greater than Zero	V	0	N		N = V Z = 0
BLE	Branch if Less than or Equal to Zero	$\bar{V}$	1	$\bar{N}$		N = V $\bar{Z}$ = 1
BLS	Branch if Lower or Same		1		1	Z = 1 C = 1
BLT	Branch if Less than Zero	$\bar{V}$		$\bar{N}$		N = $\bar{V}$
BMI	Branch if Minus	1				N = 1
BNE	Branch if Not Equal		0			Z = 0
BPL	Branch if Plus	0				N = 0
BVC	Branch if Overflow Clear			0		V = 0
BVS	Branch if Overflow Set			1		V = 1

of one or more condition code register bits and either continue with the incrementing of the program counter or it will cause a (jump) branch either ahead or back to a different routine. The branch is executed by adding an offset to the current value in the program counter.

All branch instructions use the relative addressing mode. To jump ahead, an offset value of not greater than 127 is added to the program count (of the branch instruction) plus two (PC + 2), which is the statement number of the instruction following the branch instruction. To branch backwards in the program, the twos complement of a number not greater than 127 is added to the program count plus two (PC + 2). Table 7.6 compares a program which branches from instruction 4083 forward 5 counts to one which branches backwards 8 counts.

The N and Z bits of the condition code register are set or clear depending on the state of the operand (ACCX or M) of the instruction preceding the branch instruction. If the branch is to be determined by the state of (ACCX or M) other than the preceding operand, the branch instruction can be preceded by a TST instruction.

TST (X) = Test X = ACCX or M

Sets condition code N and Z bits according to the contents of ACCX or M.

The arithmetic instructions of 6800 are:

ABA = Add Accumulator B to Accumulator A

$$\text{ACCA} \longleftarrow (\text{ACCA}) + (\text{ACCB})$$

ADC = ADD with Carry

	Address	Instruction	Operand	Comment
(a)	402D	BNE	offset value	
	402D	BNE	05	Branch forward if Z flag is zero.
	402F	INC	02	Increment memory 0002.
	4031	JMP	3C02	Jump unconditionally to instruction 3C02
	4034	CMP A	90	Is accumulator A = 90?
(b)	4027	INC A		
	4028	STA A	3F40	Store accumulator A at memory 3F40
	402B	CMP A	06	Is accumulator A = 6?
	402D	BNE	F8 (offset in 2s complement)	Branch back to 4027 if A not = six (if Z = 0)

TABLE 7.6 Branch instructions and the relative addressing mode. **(a)** A branch ahead is accomplished by adding an offset of 05 to the program count. After the BNE 05 instruction, the program counter contains the count 402F. If the conditions for a branch exist, the 05 is added to 402F causing a 4034 to be executed next. If conditions for the branch do not exist, 402F will be executed instead. **(b)** A branch backward is accomplished by subtracting the offset from the program count at the end of the branch instruction. The subtraction is accomplished by adding the twos complement of the offset. This is an 8-bit addition without carry and disregarding the carry from the eighth significant bit

```
 1
 402F     Value of PC after execu-
+ F8      tion of 402D
 4027    (carry to 3rd digit
          is dropped)
```

Adds contents of accumulator memory and carry and places the result in the accumulator. Either accumulator may be used.

$$\text{ACCX} \longleftarrow (\text{ACCX}) + (\text{M}) + (\text{C})$$

ADD = Add without Carry
Adds the contents of memory to the accumulator and places the result in the accumulator. Either accumulator may be used.

$$\text{ACCX} \longleftarrow (\text{ACCX}) + (\text{M})$$

SBA = Subtract Accumulators
Subtracts the contents of ACCB from the contents of ACCA and places the results in ACCA.

$$\text{ACCA} \longleftarrow (\text{ACCA}) - (\text{ACCB})$$

SCC = Subtract with Carry
Subtracts the contents of Memory and Carry from the contents of the accumulator and places the results in the accumulator.

$$\text{ACCX} \longleftarrow (\text{ACCX}) - (\text{M}) - (\text{C})$$

SUB = Subtract
Subtracts the contents of memory from contents of the accumulator and places the result in the accumulator.

$$\text{ACCX} \longleftarrow (\text{ACCX}) - (\text{M})$$

In addition to branch, add, and subtract instructions the complement instruction is useful for ones, twos, and nines complement arithmetic.

COM = Complement

Replaces the contents of accumulator or memory with its ones complement.

$$\begin{aligned} ACCX &\longleftarrow (\overline{ACCX}) = FF - (ACCX) \\ M &\longleftarrow (\overline{M}) \quad = FF - (M) \end{aligned}$$

NEG = Negate

$$\begin{aligned} ACCX &\longleftarrow 00 - (ACCX) \\ M &\longleftarrow 00 - (M) \end{aligned}$$

Replaces the contents of ACCX or M with its twos comment.

7.5.2 Twos Complement Algebraic Adder

As an example of an arithmetic routine, let us program for twos complement algebraic addition S = X + Y for which both X and Y may have either positive or negative signs. By the rules of algebra, if the signs are the same we add the terms X and Y. If the signs differ, the sum will be the difference between X and Y and will take the sign of the greater. If we implement this program with twos complement arithmetic, only add instructions need be used. For single precision arithmetic (single byte), the first 7 bits represent the magnitude of the binary number. The eighth bit represents the sign. A one level in the eighth bit signifies a negative number. A zero level signifies a positive number. Figure 7.19 shows some examples of twos complement arithmetic with numbers having both positive and negative signs. The sign bits are true only as the numbers input to the microprocessor.

During manipulation within the microprocessor, the program must

FIGURE 7.19 Twos complement addition, showing complements required and the state of N, V, and C bits on completion of the add cycle. Numbers in parentheses are in twos complement form.

0111 1111	+127	0001 0110	+22
0000 0101	+ 5	0100 0010	+66
1000 0100	+132	0101 1000	+88
N = 1		V = 0	
V = 1		N = 0	
C = 0		C = 0	
0111 1111	+127	(0110 1010)	-22
(0111 1011)	- 5	+0100 0010	+66
1111 1010	+122	1010 1100	+44
N = 1	-5 = 1000 0101	V = 1	-22 = 1001 0110
V = 1	2s Comp = 0111 1011	N = 1	2s Comp = 0110 1010
C = 0		C = 0	
(0000 0001)	-127	0001 0110	22
0000 0101	+ 5	(0011 1110)	-66
(0000 0110)	-122	(0101 0100)	-44
1111 1010		1010 1100	
N = 0	-127 = 1111 1111	N = 0	-66 = 1100 0010
V = 0	2s Comp = (0000 0001)	V = 0	2s Comp = (0011 1110)
C = 0		C = 0	

interpret the condition code register to determine if the sign is true or inverted. The program must also determine if a valid carry exists. The programmer must determine how the extra bit of information generated is to be handled in outputting the results. The input terms contain 8 bits of information, but because of the carry, 9 bits are needed to express the results. The two byte output format is another programmer's option.

Figure 7.20 shows the flow diagram of the twos complement adder program. The program begins with the X term being read from a memory location or input port. If X is negative, the N bit will be set as a

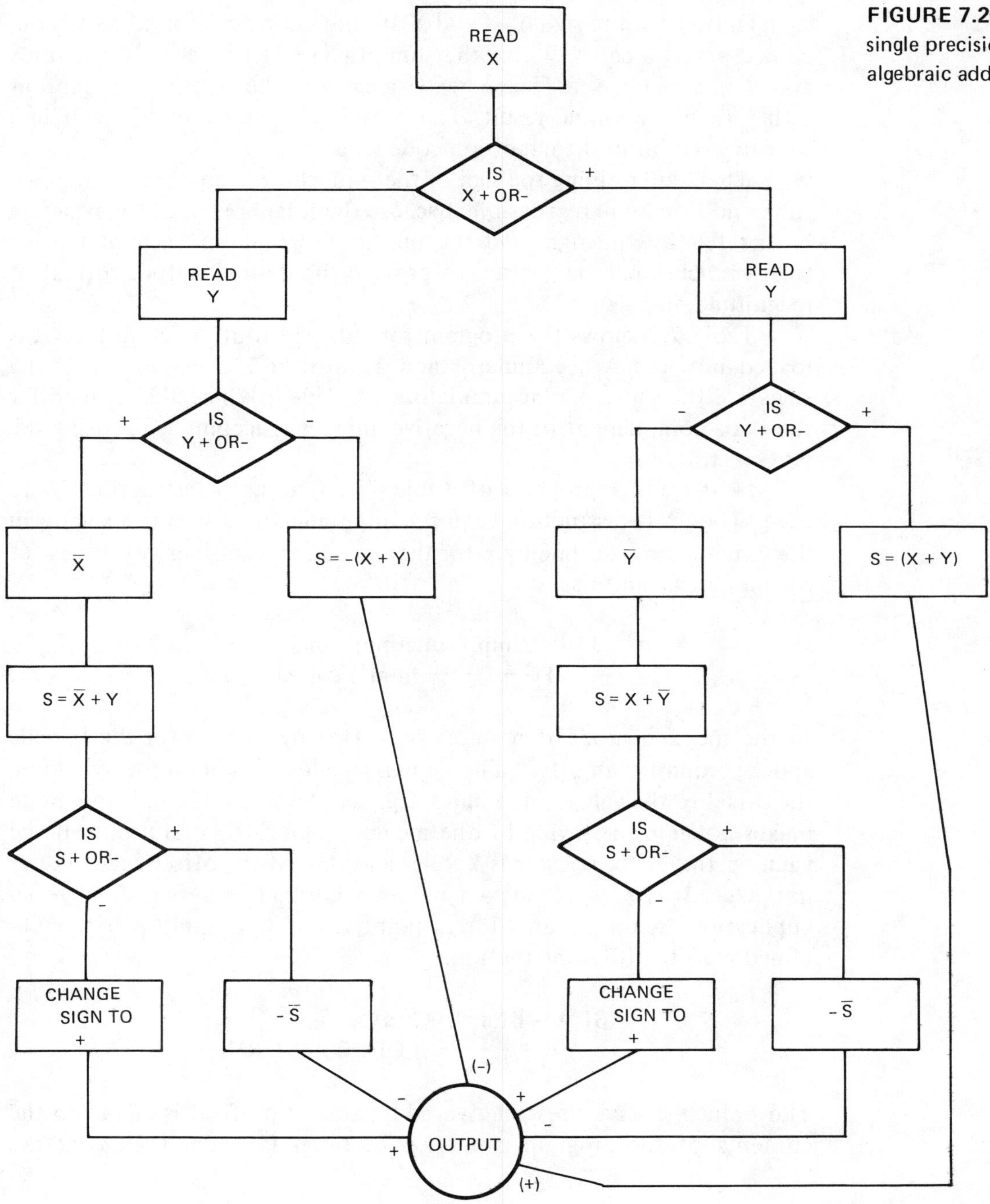

FIGURE 7.20 Flow diagram of a single precision, twos complement, algebraic adder program.

result of the load instruction. If X is positive, the program will continue ahead. The +X and –X branches of the program are very much alike. In both branches Y is read, but in one branch +Y results in a simple ADD. In the other branch –Y results in a simple add. When the signs differ, the negative term is converted to its twos complement before adding. After the adding of a positive term with the twos complement of a negative term, the N bit of the condition code register will depict whether the sum is negative or positive. Unfortunately, at this point the sign is inverted. A high or set N bit means the sum is positive and only the eighth bit need be inverted. If the N bit is clear, the sum is negative but in twos complement form and must be converted. After twos complement, the eight-bit result will be correct both in magnitude and in sign. Only when the sign of X and Y are the same do we need to be concerned about a carry. Where the sum of (X) + (Y) exceeds 127, both N and V bits will be set. This indicates a carry to the eighth significant bit rather than a negative result. The X and Y negative would result in a set carry (C) bit in the condition code register.

When determining the sign of the sum, there is no need to examine the condition code register bits because the final branch of the program is dictated by the sign, and the output program for each of the six final branches can be written to provide the desired output format of magnitude plus sign.

Table 7.7 shows the program for this add routine. Note that X is loaded into the A accumulator and Y into the B accumulator. If the signs are the same, the accumulators are added. Where the signs differ the twos complement of the negative number is accomplished using the NEG instruction.

In the adder program of Table 7.7, five jump instructions were used. The JMP instruction requires three memory bytes to execute in the extended mode: one byte for the opcode and another two bytes for the numerical address.

$$\begin{aligned} &\text{JMP} = \text{Jump (unconditional)} \\ &\quad \text{PC} \longleftarrow \text{numerical address} \end{aligned}$$

In the indexed mode it requires only two bytes: one for the opcode and a second for an offset. The numerical address is obtained by adding the offset to the value in the index register. Although the indexed mode makes possible the saving of one memory byte, it is useful only if the value in the index register is known and only if the offset needed does not exceed 127. The indexed mode is normally reserved for special applications requiring an address pointer. A 2-byte jump is better obtained with the BRA instruction.

$$\begin{aligned} &\text{BRA} = \text{Branch Always} \\ &\quad \text{PC} \longleftarrow (\text{PC}) + 0002 + \text{REL} \end{aligned}$$

The branch always uses relative addressing. An offset is added to the contents of the program counter. The program count (PC) is at the

TABLE 7.7 Single precision algebraic adder program. (See Appendix A.)

ADDRESS	MOVEMENT	MNEMONIC	OPERAND	DESCRIPTION	MODE*
0401		LDA A	(X)	Move X to accumulator A	EXT.
04		BMI	12	Branch if X is negative	REL.
06		LDA B	(Y)	Move Y to accumulator B	EXT.
09		BPL	09	Branch if Y is plus	REL.
0B		NEG B		Twos complement Y	
0C		ABA		Add X and 2s complement of Y	
0D		BMI	16	BRANCH if sum is negative	REL.
0F		NEG A		Twos complement sum	
10		JMP	0482	Jump to output (-)	EXT.
14		ABA		Add +X TO +Y	
15		JMP	048D	Jump to output (+)	EXT.
18		LDA B	(Y)	Move Y to accumulator B	EXT.
1B		BMI	0D	Branch if Y is negative	REL.
1D		NEG A		Twos complement X	
1E		ABA		Add Y plus 2s complement of X	
1F		BMI	04	Branch if negative	REL.
21		NEG A		Twos complement sum	
22		JMP	0482	Jump to output (-)	EXT.
25		ADD A	80	Change sign by adding 80	IMM.
27		JMP	0480	Jump to output (+)	EXT.
2A		ABA		Add -X to -Y	
042B		(PROGRAMMERS OPTION)		Begin output routine	

*Modes not specified are implied.

beginning of the BRA instruction or it is the address of the BRA instruction. The address of the instruction immediately following the BRA instruction is (PC) + 2. If the branch is backward in the program count, the offset value must be twos complement form. If the instruction being branched to is further removed from (PC) + 2 than ± 127, the JMP instruction should be used.

7.5.3 Double Precision Signed Arithmetic

Programs for either signed or unsigned arithmetic can be written to allow for the use of two bytes for each term. For unsigned arithmetic this permits terms of 16 bits in magnitude. For signed arithmetic only the higher byte contains a sign bit. This permits terms that can be 15 bits in magnitude. Let us compare the double precision arithmetic equivalent to the algebraic adder of Figure 7.20. For simplicity, we will begin the program with the values X and Y stored in four memory bytes which we will identify as X_L, X_H, Y_L, Y_H. Figure 7.21 shows the flow diagram of this program. The high order bytes must be examined to determine the signs. This requires a TST instruction. The low order bytes are added first. The low order bytes can be added using an add without carry. This avoids the need for a CLC instruction prior to the

FIGURE 7.21 Flow diagram of a double precision, twos complement, algebraic adder program.

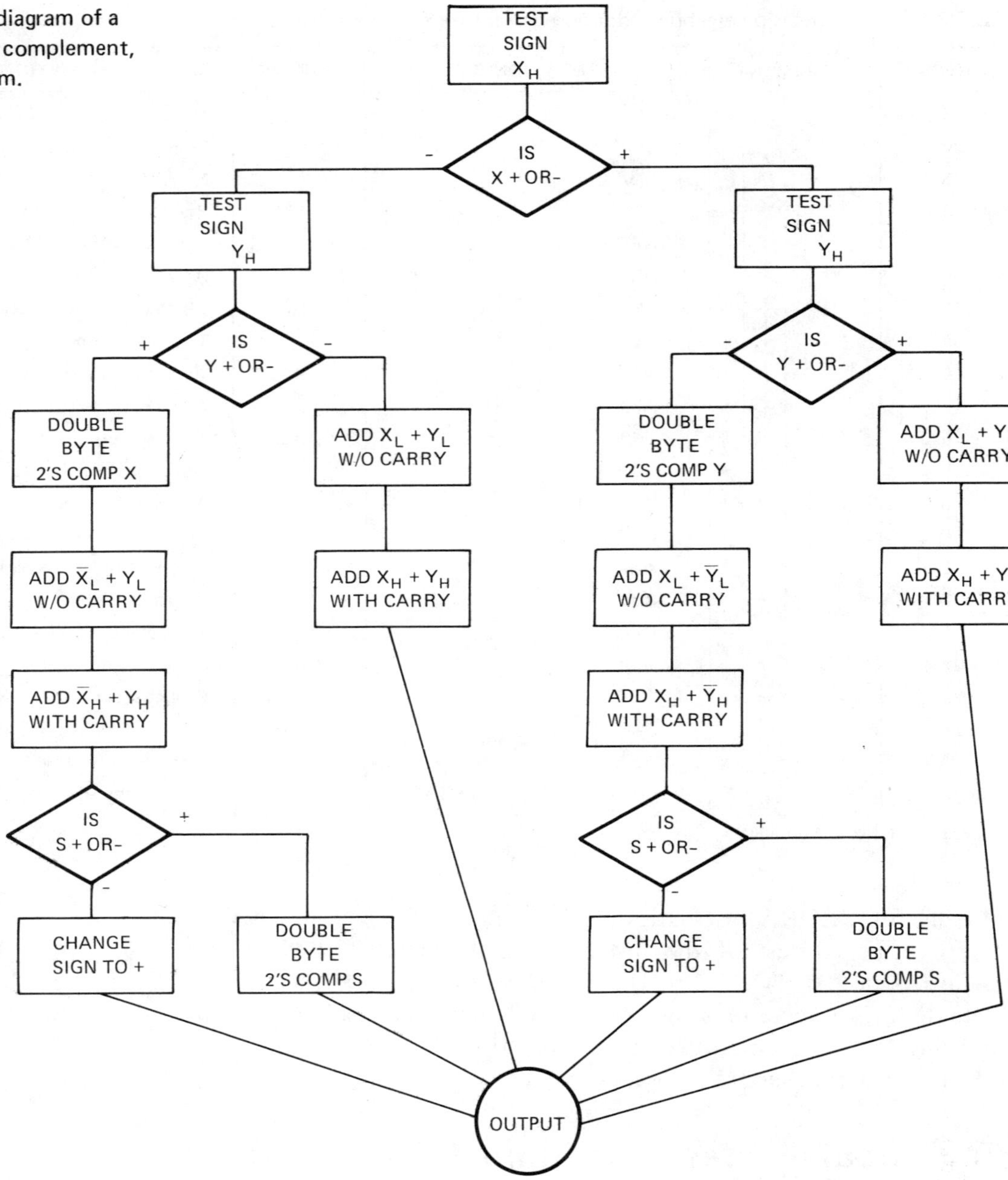

add cycle. The high order bytes must be added using the add with carry instruction. Either of the two terms X_L or Y_L is stored in accumulator A and added ADD A to the other term in memory.

$$\text{ACCA} \longleftarrow (\text{ACCA}) + (\text{M})$$

The corresponding high order byte is stored in accumulator B and added with carry ADCB to the other high order byte in memory.

$$\text{ACCB} \longleftarrow (\text{ACCB}) + (\text{M}) + (\text{C})$$

The result is a sum with the low order byte in accumulator A and a high order byte in accumulator B. The twos complement routine is more lengthy than that required for the single precision program.

A review of a method used to accomplish twos complement will give us some clue as to what is needed. A twos complement can be accomplished by a ones complement plus 1, but in dealing with separate high and low bytes, we would not be correct in adding one to both bytes. It would seem logical to add one to the low byte only and use only the ones complement of the high order byte. But, if the low order byte were zero, adding one to its complement would return it to zero and produce a carry to the high order byte. In the case of a low order byte being zero, we would be correct in leaving the low order byte unchanged and twos complement only the high order byte. As Table 7.8 shows, the twos complement routine first tests the low order byte. If it is zero, it branches to a NEG (twos complement) of the high order byte. If it is not zero, the program starts with a NEG of the low order byte followed by a COM (ones complement) of the high order byte.

TABLE 7.8 Two's complement routine for a 2-byte number.

ADDRESS	MOVEMENT	MNEMONIC	OPERAND	DESCRIPTION	MODE
0491		TST	(X_L)	Check low byte for zero	EXT.
94		BEQ	06	If zero begin 2s complement with high byte	REL.
96		NEG	(X_L)	If low byte nonzero	EXT.
99		COM	(X_H)	begin 2s complement with low byte	EXT.
9C		BRA	03		REL.
049F		NEG	(X_H)	2s complement high byte only	EXT.
					REL.

7.5.4 Use of Subroutines

In many programs, there are portions of program which are repeated in two or more locations. A saving in memory bytes can be accomplished by writing it one time as a subroutine. Each point in the program at which the routine is needed, a jump or branch to subroutine instruction is inserted. The subroutine branch differs from other branch instructions in that the program address jumped to is the same at each point in the program that it is called, but the address to which the program returns differs. Returning to the correct point in the program on completion of the subroutine is accomplished as the result of the return address being automatically pushed onto the stack when the subroutine is called and being pulled back into the program counter as the result of a return from subroutine instruction.

The 6800 subroutine instructions follow.

BSR = Branch to Subroutine The branch to subroutine uses the relative addressing mode. After the program counter content is loaded on the stack, the offset is added to the program count, changing the program count to that of the subroutine address. The BSR instruction is advantageous for branching to a subroutine within 127 of the current program count. The BSR instruction requires only two bytes, compared to three for a JSR instruction.

JSR = Jump to Subroutine The jump to subroutine uses extended or indexed addressing. After the program counter content is loaded on the stack, the program count is changed to the address of the subroutine.

RTS = Return from Subroutine The return from subroutine is the last instruction in every subroutine program. It causes the program count to be changed to the address taken from the stack.

Unlike the automatic loading of the stack that occurs on receipt of an interrupt the BSR and JSR instructions cause only the program count to be loaded on the stack. An interrupt loads the complete microprocessor status. See Figure 7.5. This happens because the point of occurrence of interrupts is not predictable while the point of occurrence of subroutines is predictable. The programmer must consider carefully at each point where a subroutine is inserted whether the content of accumulators, index register, or condition code register need be saved. The content of accumulators can be saved on the stack by using the push instruction.

PSH = Push Data onto Stack The contents of ACCX is stored in the stack pointer. The stack pointer is then decremented.

The push instructions are normally inserted as the initial instructions of the subroutine. Although the PSH instruction can be used directly to save only the accumulators, once the accumulators have

TABLE 7.9 Saving the microprocessor status on the stack requires PSH instructions at the beginning of the subroutine and PUL instructions just prior to the return from subroutine.

ADDRESS	MOVEMENT	MNEMONIC	OPERAND	DESCRIPTION
0501		PSH A		ACCA to Stack
02		PSH B		ACCB to Stack
03		TPA		CCR to ACCA
04		PSH A		ACCA to Stack
05		STX		IX to MEM
07		↕		useful portion of subroutine
38				
39		LDX		MEM to IX
3B		PUL A		Stack to ACCA
4C		TAP		ACCA to CCR
4D		PUL B		Stack to ACCB
4E		PUL A		Stack to ACCA
054F		RTS		Return to main program

been pushed onto the stack the TPA instruction can be used to transfer the condition code register to the A accumulator. This is followed by another PSH A instruction. The index register content is more conveniently saved in regular data storage rather than on the stack. At the end of the subroutine, the status is pulled from the stack and returned to the 6800 registers using the PUL instruction.

PUL = Pull Data from Stack The stack pointer is incremented. The ACCX is then loaded from the stack, from the address contained in the stack pointer.

Table 7.9 shows the list of instructions needed to push and pull

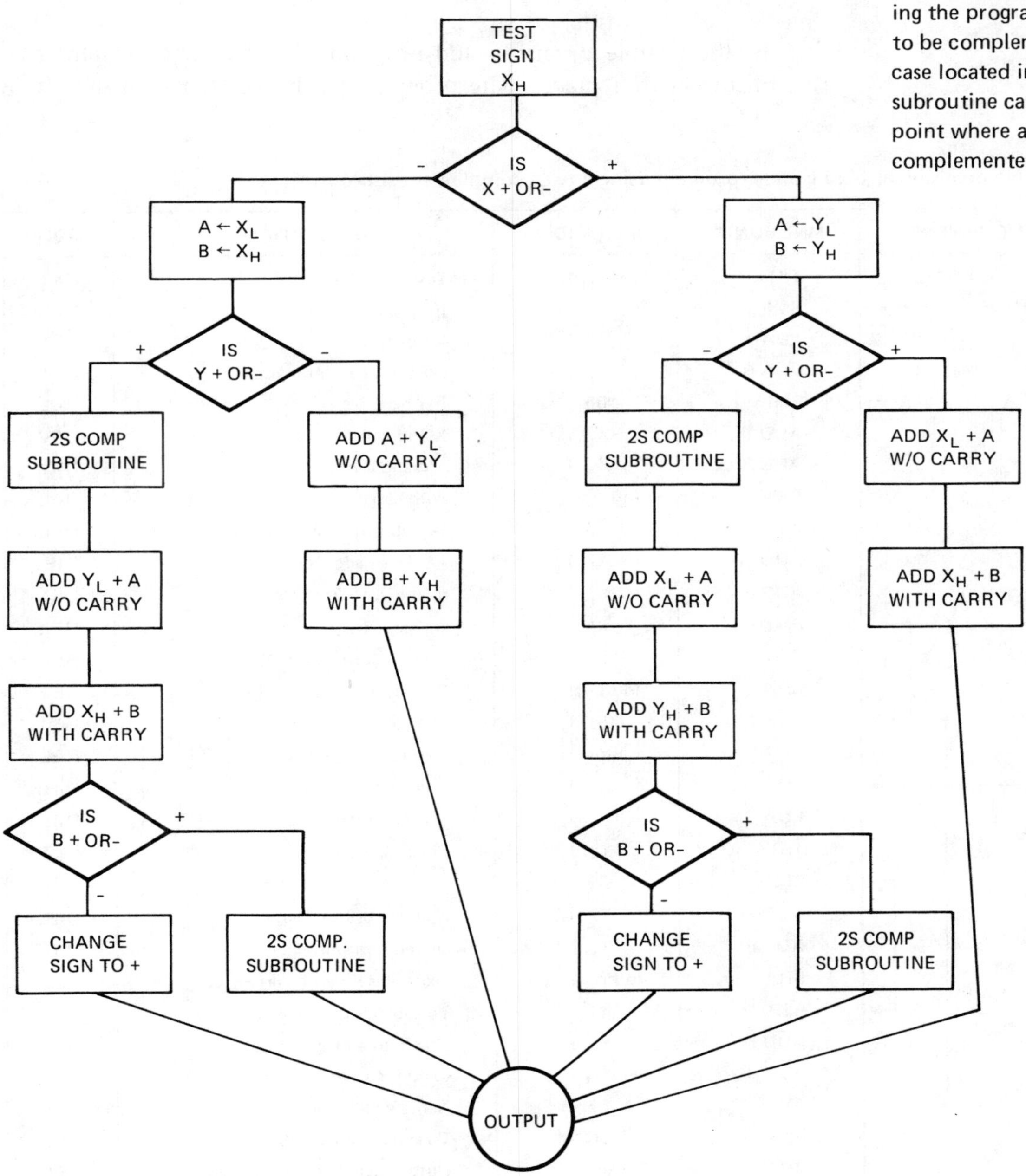

FIGURE 7.22 Flow diagram of a double precision adder. By arranging the program such that the bytes to be complemented are in every case located in the accumulators, a subroutine can be used at each point where a term needs to be complemented.

the complete microprocessor status. It is rare that the complete status need be saved. The more PSH and PUL instructions needed in the subroutine, the less advantageous the use of the subroutine. The routine must either be a lengthy one or must be called frequently to dwarf the need for PSH and PUL instructions. The need for saving status must be studied at each point in the program that the subroutine is called. If a subroutine is called in five places and the condition code register needs to be saved at only one of the five, it must still be pushed onto the stack during the subroutine.

Under certain conditions it may be advantageous to place the PUSH instructions in the main program preceding the Jump to subroutine and the PULL instruction in the main program following the jump to subroutine. This has the singular advantage of reducing the running time of the subroutine.

In the double precision add program, the twos complement routine occurs in four places. The program can be written with the use of

TABLE 7.10 (a) Double precision algebraic adder program using a twos complement subroutine.

ADDRESS	MOVEMENT	MNEMONIC	OPERAND	DESCRIPTION	MODE
060A		TST	(X_H)	Test sign of X	EXT.
0D		BMI	1C	If X negative	REL.
0F		LDA A	(X_L)	X positive	DIR.
11		LDA B	(Y_H)	store Y in accumulators	DIR.
13		BMI	06	If Y negative	REL.
15		ADD A	(X_L)	X and Y both positive	DIR.
17		ADC B	(X_H)	add and output	DIR.
19		BRA	(output)	With carry	REL.
1B		BSR	63	To subroutine at 0680	REL.
1D		ADD A	(X_L)	+X −Y so add 2s comp	DIR.
1F		ADC B	(X_H)	so add X to 2s comp of	DIR.
21		BMI	04	and check sign of sum	REL.
23		BSR	5B	To subroutine at 0680	REL.
25		BRA	(output)	Output negative sum (no carry)	REL.
27		SUB B	80_H	Change sign of sum to	IMM.
29		BRA	(output)	+ and output (no carry)	REL.
062B		LDA A	(X_L)	X is negative so store	DIR.
2D		LDA B	(X_H)	in accumulators	DIR.
2F		TST	(Y_H)	Check sign of Y	EXT.
32		BPL	06		REL.
34		ADD A	(Y_L)	X and Y both negative	DIR.
36		ADC B	(Y_H)	add and output	DIR.
38		BRA	(output)	negative sum with carry	REL.
3A		BSR	44	To subroutine at 0680	REL.
3C		ADD A	(Y_L)	−Y +Y so add 2s comp	DIR.
3E		ADC B	(Y_H)	so add Y to 2s comp of	DIR.
40		BMI	E5	X and check sign	REL.
42		BSR	3C	To subroutine at 0680	REL.
44		BRA	(output)	Output negative sum (no carry)	REL.

TABLE 7.10 (b) Twos complement subroutine low byte in accumulator A high byte in B.

ADDRESS	MOVEMENT	MNEMONIC	OPERAND	DESCRIPTION
0680		TST A		Check low byte for zero
81		BEQ	03	If zero begin 2s complement with high byte
83		NEG A		If low byte non zero, 2s complement low
84		COM B		byte. 1s complement high byte
85		RTS		
86		NEG B		2s complement high byte only
0687		RTS		

a subroutine called in these four places. A subroutine is of no value if even a slight difference must exist in the routines at different points in the program. As the flow diagram of Figure 7.21 shows, the twos complement routine differs at three of the four points in the program. The bytes to be complemented are X, Y, and in the case of the sum, the A and B accumulators. However, the twos complement routine precedes the add routines, each of which requires that one of the terms be stored in accumulators. If the move to A and B accumulators is inserted ahead of the twos complement routine, accumulators can be complemented in each case. This makes the twos complement routines identical at all four points allowing the use of a subroutine.

Figure 7.22 shows the flow diagram modified to allow the use of a subroutine. At each point that a value is to be complemented, that value is contained in the accumulators. This modification makes all four twos complement routines identical and suitable for use of a subroutine.

Table 7.10 shows the double precision add routine written with the use of a twos complement subroutine in four places. The saving of memory bytes in this example is small but where the subroutine is lengthy the savings can be considerable.

7.5.5 Binary Multiplication and Division

Figure 7.23 shows one example each of binary multiplication and division. Multiplication is a matter of add shift and add of the multiplicand. Division is more complicated in that it requires first a series of subtract and shift left of the divisor until either the result is negative or until the shift produces a negative.

```
                 1 1 0 1 1 1 0 0
shift
left  <--------  0 0 0 0 0 1 0 1
```

This locates the most significant 1 bit of the divisor in line with the most significant 1 bit of the dividend. Then we begin a series of: subtract; shift left and increment the quotient is positive; cancel and shift left the quotient if negative; shift right the divisor. This series is repeated until the shift right of the divisor results in a carry. This level of arithmetic obviously requires instructions that can shift numbers to either right or left. The 6800 shift and rotate instructions follow.

FIGURE 7.23 Examples of binary multiplication and division.

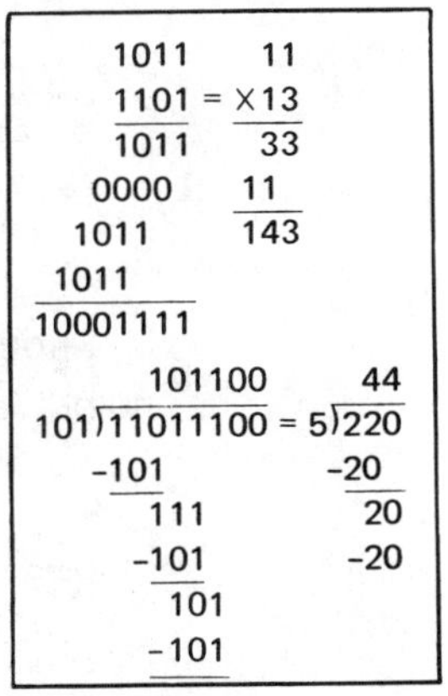

ASL = Arithmetic Shift Left Shifts all bits of ACCX or M one place to the left. Bit 7 shifts to the carry bit. A logic zero shifts into bit 0. See Figure 7.24(a). ASL repeated 8 times will shift the operand to all zeros.

ASR = Arithmetic Shift Right Shifts all bits of ACCX or M one place to the right. Bit 7 does not change. Bit 0 shifts to the carry. See Figure 7.24(b). Will shift to all zero or all ones depending on the level in Bit 7 at the beginning of a series of shifts.

FIGURE 7.24 6800 shift and rotate instructions.

a ASL Arithmetic Shift Left

Operation:

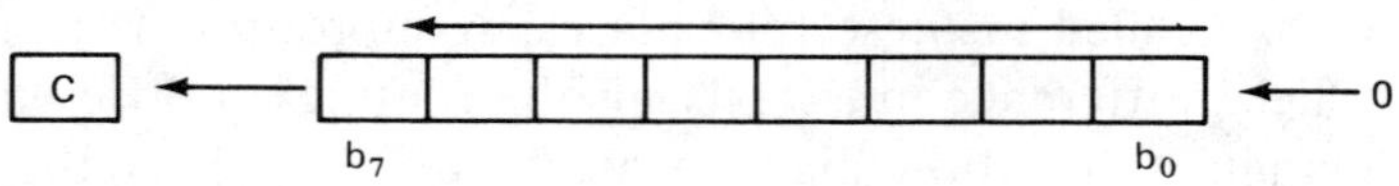

Description: Shifts all bits of the ACCX or M one place to the left. Bit 0 is loaded with a zero. The C bit is loaded from the most significant bit of ACCX or M.

b ASR Arithmetic Shift Right

Operation:

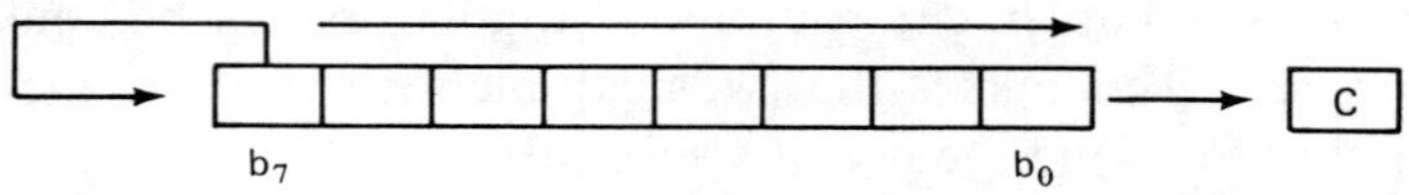

Description: Shifts all bits of ACCX or M one place to the right. Bit 7 is held constant. Bit 0 is loaded into the C bit.

c LSR Logical Shift Right

Operation:

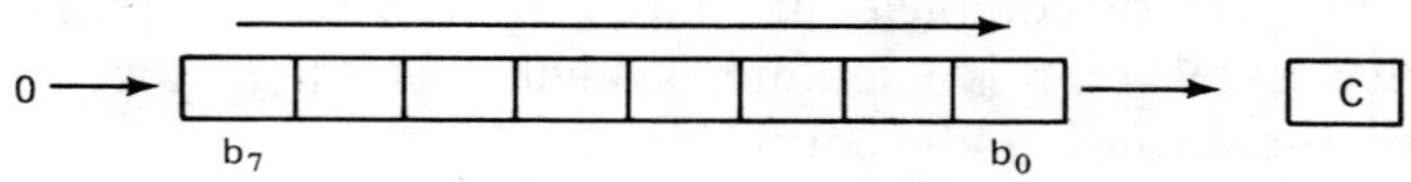

Description: Shifts all bits of ACCX or M one place to the right. Bit 7 is loaded with a zero. The C bit is loaded from the least significant bit of ACCX or M.

d ROL Rotate Left

Operation:

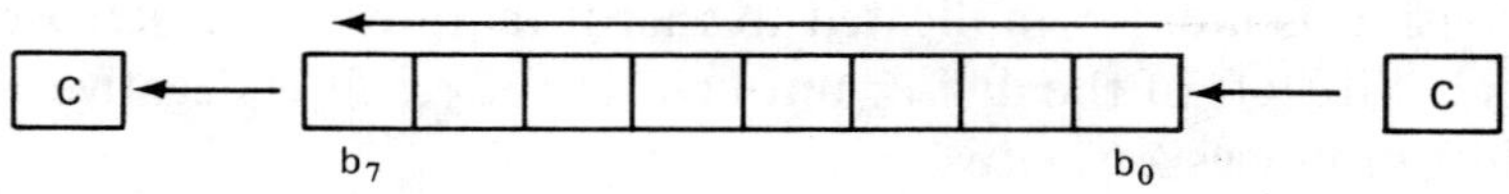

Description: Shifts all bits of ACCX or M one place to the left. Bit 0 is loaded from the C bit. The C bit is loaded from the most significant bit of ACCX or M.

e ROR Rotate Right

Operation:

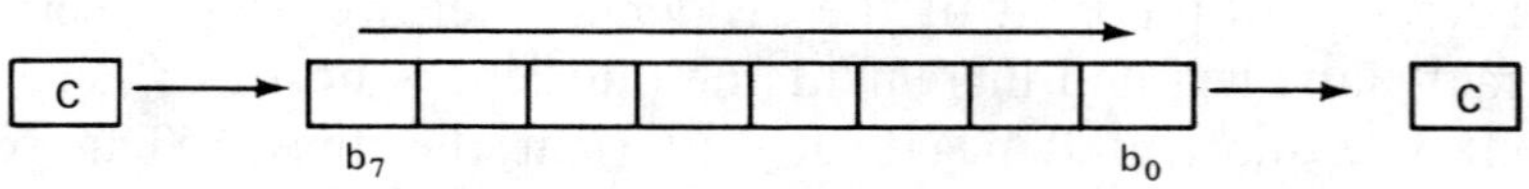

Description: Shifts all bits of ACCX or M one place to the right. Bit 7 is loaded from the C bit. The C bit is loaded from the least significant bit of ACCX or M.

LSR = Logical Shift Right Shifts all bits of ACCX or M one place to the right. Bit 7 is loaded with a zero. Bit 0 shifts to the carry. See Figure 7.24(c).

ROL = Rotate Left Shifts all bits of ACCX or M one place to the left. The carry bit shifts to bit 0. Bit 7 shifts to the carry. See Figure 7.24(d).

ROR = Rotate Right Shifts all bits of ACCX and M one place to the right. The carry bit shifts to bit 7. Bit 0 shifts to the carry. See Figure 7.24(e).

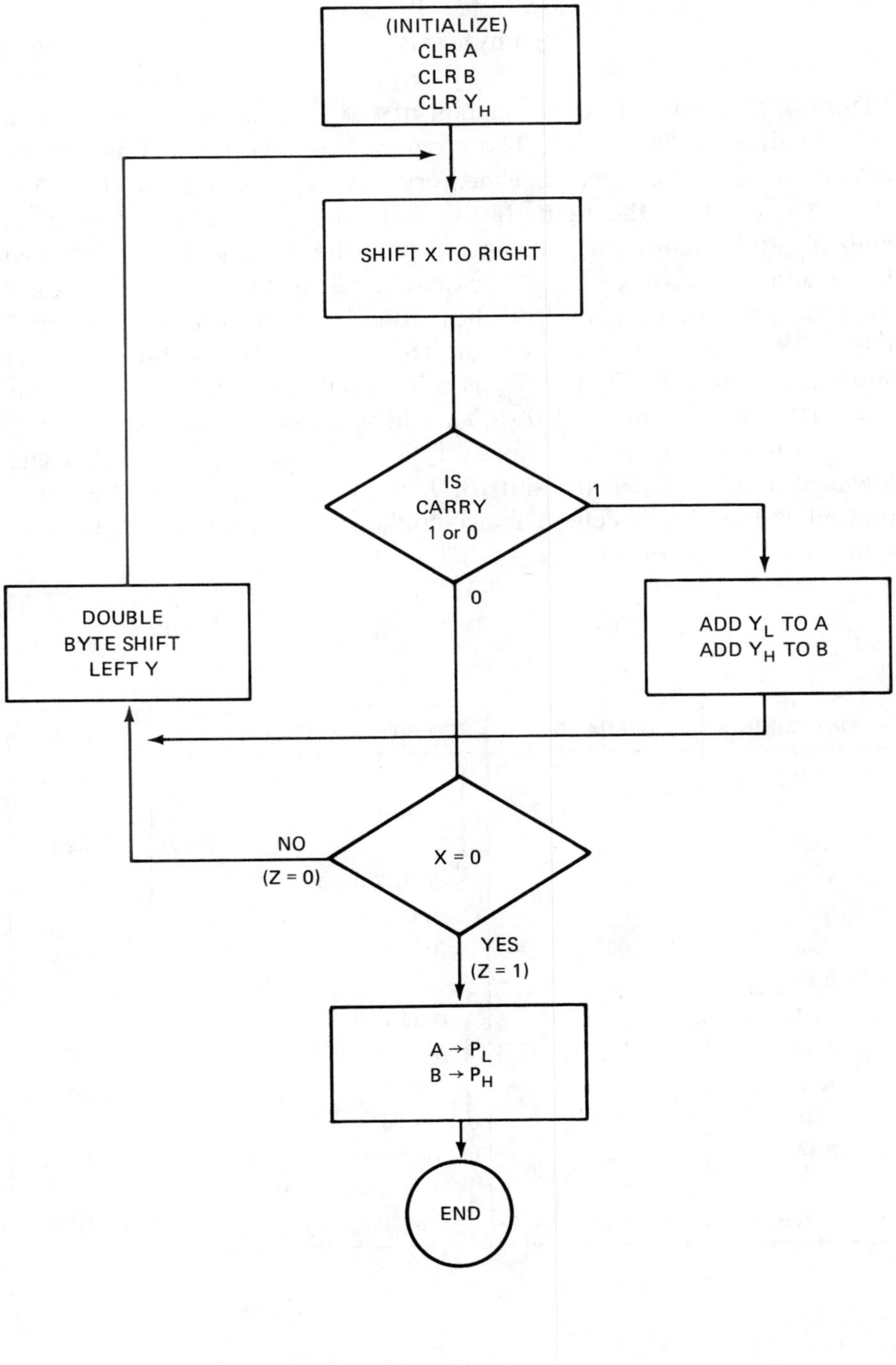

FIGURE 7.25 Flow diagram of a multiplication program.

7.5.6 Multiplication Program

To familiarize ourselves with these instructions let us program for multiplication of single byte binary numbers allowing for a product of two bytes. The following memory bytes must be assigned.

$P = X \cdot Y$ Multiplier = X

Multiplicand
low byte = Y_L
high byte = Y_H

Product
low byte = P_L
high byte = P_H

Figure 7.25 shows the flow diagram of the program. The written program is given in Table 7.11. The program starts with X and Y in memory. Accumulators, carry, and memory byte Y_H all must be clear. X is shifted one bit to the right. If this shifts a 1 into carry, the program adds Y_L to accumulator A using an add without carry. This is followed by an add with carry of Y_H to accumulator B. If the shift of X does not set the carry, the program branches around the add routines to a shift left of Y. Y_L is shifted left with an ASL which shifts bit 7 to carry and shifts a zero into bit 0. The Y_H is shifted left with an ROL; this shifts the carry from Y_L into bit 0 of Y_H and shifts the leftmost zero (bit 7) of Y_H into the carry. This effectively links the shift of the higher and lower byte of Y. When the shift of X produces a C = 0 and Z = 1, the multiplication is complete. The accumulators are stored in memory or transferred to an output port.

TABLE 7.11 6800 Multiplication program.

ADDRESS	MOVEMENT	MNEMONIC	OPERAND	DESCRIPTION	MODE
0301		CLR A			IMP.
0302		CLR B		Initialize	IMP.
0303		CLR	(Y_H)		EXT.
0306		LSR	(X)	Shift X to right	EXT.
0309		BCS	04	If C = 1 add Y to P	REL.
030B		BNE	06	If C = 0 Z = 0 don't add	REL.
030D		BRA	0C		REL.
030F		ADD A	(Y_L)	Add Y to P	DIR.
0311		ADC B	(Y_H)	And shift Y	DIR.
0313		ASL	(Y_L)	left	EXT.
0316		ROL	(Y_H)		EXT.
0319		BRA	EB	Return to shift left X	REL.
031B		STA A	(P_L)	X has shifted to 0	DIR.
031D		STA B	(P_H)	store the product	DIR.

7.6 The Dedicated 6800 Microprocessor Program

7.6.1 Counter Routines

Although microprocessor systems have some application as small scale general purpose computers, the majority of their applications are in control systems, which use only a trivial portion of the microprocessor's total capability. These dedicated applications use many simple routines such as counters, timers, and sequencers. A typical counter routine designates a memory byte or a register to be incremented or decremented until the desired count has been reached.

Table 7.12 shows a routine to be repeated five times. The instruction preceding the routine loads a count of 5 into accumulator B. At the completion of the routine, B is decremented. Until B reaches zero, the program branches back to repeat the routine. When B reaches zero the Z bit will be set and the program will move ahead. If accumulator B were needed within the routine, a memory byte could have been decremented instead of accumulator by inserting a STA B between the LDA B and the routine. The DEC B would change to a DEC memory.

Under some conditions it may be desirable to count to a number other than zero. This requires the use of the compare instructions.

CMP = Compare Compares the content of ACCX with the contents of memory.

$$(ACCX) - (M)$$

If they are the same the Z bit is set. If (M) is larger than (ACCX) C bit is set. If (M) is smaller than (ACCX) C and Z bits are reset.

The CMP instruction differs from the subtract instruction, SUB, in that the contents of neither memory nor accumulator are changed by the CMP instruction.

TABLE 7.12 Counter routine using a decrement to zero.

ADDRESS	MOVEMENT	MNEMONIC	OPERAND	DESCRIPTION
		LDA B	05	Load count into ACCB.
	→	Repeated Routine		First instruction of routine. (Routine to be repeated five times.)
		DEC B		Reduce count after each run of the routine.
		BNE	Offset in 2s complement	Program advances at B = Zero.

TABLE 7.13 Counter routine using an increment to five.

ADDRESS	MOVEMENT	MNEMONIC	OPERAND	DESCRIPTION
		CLR B		Start count at zero.
				First instruction of routine.
		Repeated Routine		(Routine to be repeated five times.)
		INC B		Count.
		CMP B	05	Has count reached 5.
		BNE	Offset in 2s complement	Program advances at count of 5.

CPX = Compare Index Register
(IXL) − (M + 1)
(IXH) − (M)

The contents of the index register is compared with the contents of two consecutive memory bytes.

The Z bit is set if the bytes are the same. (The N and V bits resulting from this instruction are not intended for use with branching instructions.)

Table 7.13 shows the count to 5 routine using the compare instruction. Accumulator B is incremented at the end of each repetition of the routine. When B reaches 5, the CMP B results in Z bit being set, and the branch instruction will cause a move ahead in the program.

7.6.2 The Timer Routine

Timer routines are a special application of counter routines. There are a definite number of machine cycles in the execution of an instruction. A machine cycle takes a precise period measured in microseconds (μsec). Between each increment of the counter there are an exact number of microseconds.

LDA B	(XX)	2 cycles
DECB		2 cycles
BNE FD		4 cycles

$$XX \leqslant 255$$

If the 6800 clock has a period of 1 μsec, then the routine above could provide time delays in increments of 2 μsec. Each count requires 6 machine cycles. The count to be loaded into B can be determined by

$$\text{Count} = (\text{Time} - 2\ \mu\text{sec}) \div 6$$

An additional 2 or 4 μsec per count may be added by inserting NOP instructions which do nothing, but they require two machine cycles to execute. A single count through the accumulator set to 255 will provide a time delay of 6 μsec X 255 = 1530 μsec.

In fact, if a maximum count is desired, a clear instruction can be used. This saves one memory byte and provides a count one higher than is obtained by loading 255. If a clear accumulator is used, the first decrement will bring the accumulator to 255.

If a memory byte is used as the counter, the decrement instruction increases to 6 cycles, thus increasing the time delay of a total count to 2550 μsec. The time can be multiplied manyfold by counting through two memory bytes. Figure 7.26 is a flow diagram of a timer using a

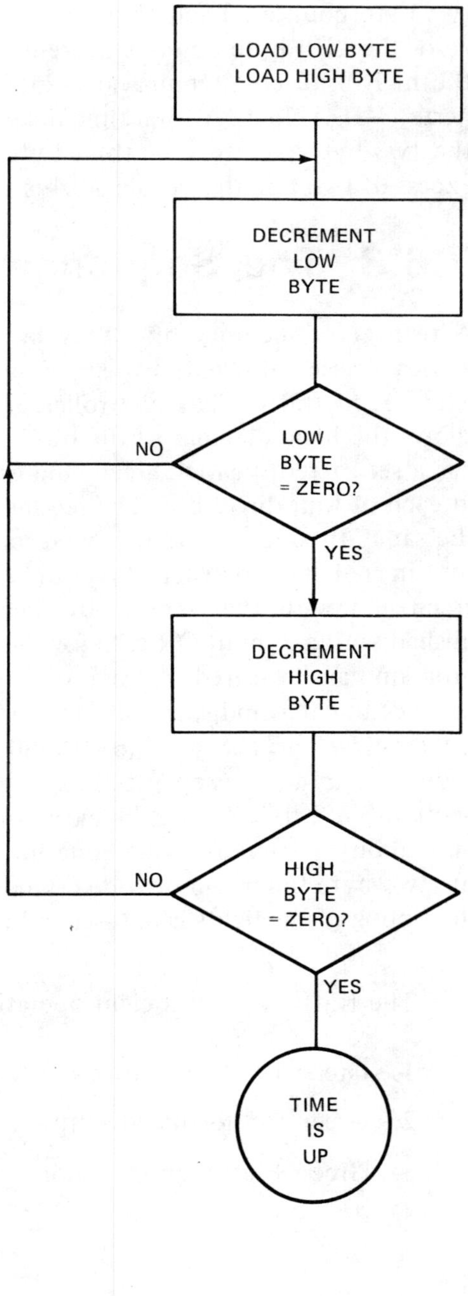

FIGURE 7.26 Flow diagram of a two byte timer. The low byte counter decrements 256 times for each decrement of the high byte counter.

TABLE 7.14 Two-byte timer.

ADDRESS	MOVEMENT	MNEMONIC	OPERAND	DESCRIPTION	MODE
0551		CLR	(1st Byte)	Clear the first counter byte.	EXT.
54		LDA A	Count	Load count for high byte.	IMM.
56		STA A	(High Byte)	Transfer count from ACCA to memory byte to be used as counter.	EXT.
59		DEC	(1st Byte)	Decrement memory byte-used as 1st counter.	EXT.
5C		BNE	FB	Is 1st byte zero?	REL.
5E		DEC	(2nd Byte)	Decrement memory byte used as 2nd counter.	EXT.
0561		BNE	F6	Is 2nd byte zero?	REL.

two-byte counter. Each time the low byte counter is decremented to zero, the high byte counter decrements once. Therefore, each count of the high byte counter provides 2560 μsec in a system with a 1 megahertz (MHZ) clock. A total time delay of 652,800 μsec is available from the two-byte counters. A three-byte timer can provide time delays in excess of two minutes. Table 7.14 is a program for a two-byte timer.

7.6.3 The Sequencer Routine

A register or memory byte may be used as a sequencer. A sequencer causes a series of events to happen in a specified order. Let us take, for example, a traffic light controller at a busy intersection. Figure 7.27 shows the logic diagram of the traffic light controller. The traffic signal has a set of red, yellow, green, and green arrow (left turn) lamps facing in each of four directions. The red light turns on when no other lamp in the same direction is lit. This is accomplished with a 2 input NOR gate for the red light of each direction. The green light turns on both for green and with the green arrow in a given direction. This is accomplished with a 2 input OR gate for the green light of each direction. The program can be stored in a pair of 256-X-4 PROMS. Very little RAM is needed, but it is indispensable for the functions of timer and synchronizer bytes. The 128-X-8 M6810 will more than fill the bill. Two memory bytes are to be used as timers employing the technique described in Section 7.6.2. If a 1-MHZ clock is used, a two-byte timer will provide only about 6/10-of-a-second time intervals. If a 100-KHZ clock is used, the two-byte timer will provide 6-second time intervals. For this reason, the timing of the lights is in 6-second multiples.

The traffic light has eight operating cycles in the sequence shown:

1. Green + left turn from south (18 sec.)
2. Green for north and south (24 sec.)
3. Green + left turn from north (18 sec.)

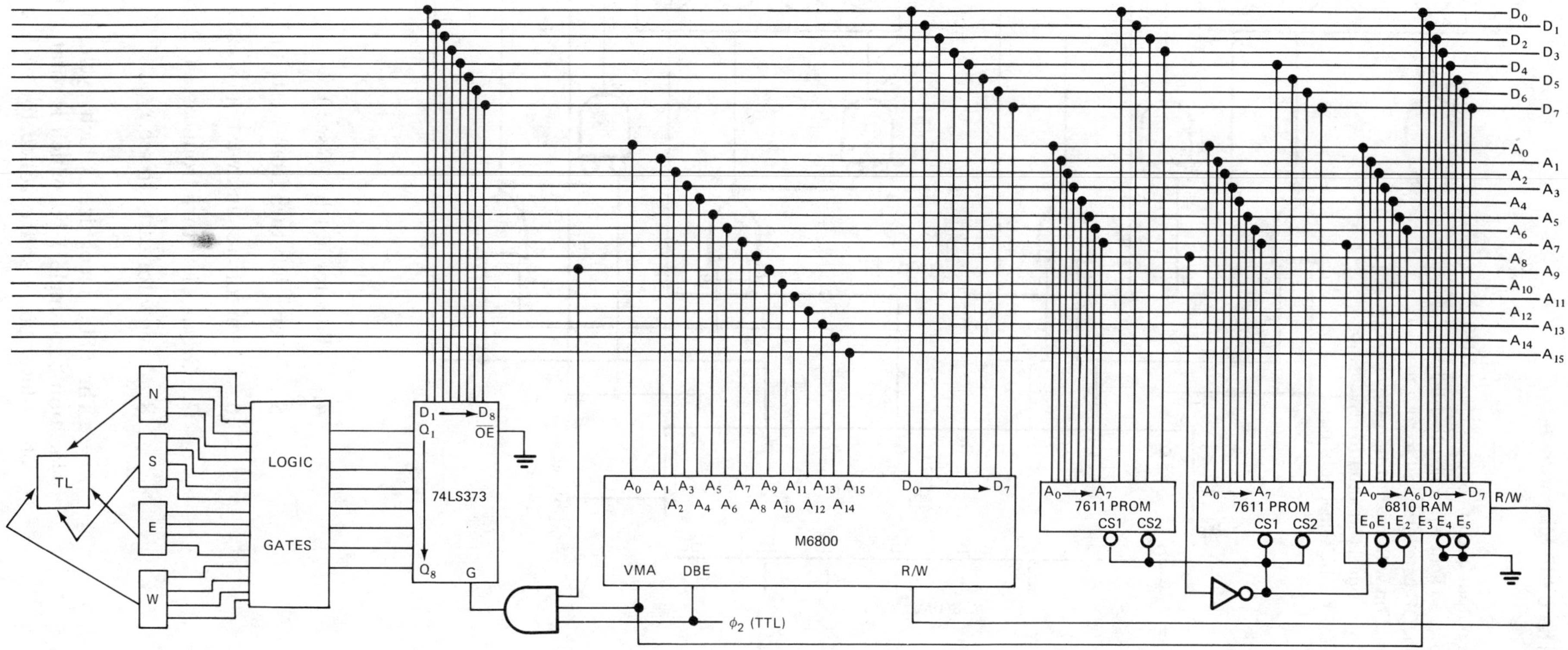

(a)

FIGURE 7.27 **(a)** Logic diagram of a 6800 traffic light controller. The program memory is composed of two 256-X-4 PROMS. The 6810 128-X-8 provides the random access memory. The output port function is supplied by a Quad latch, the 74LS373.

FIGURE 7.27(b) The output circuit contains Quad NOR gates used to turn on the red light when no other light in the same direction is on. OR gates are used to turn the green light on in conjunction with the left turn signal in a given direction. The logic signals are used to drive lamp or relay drivers within the traffic signal housing.

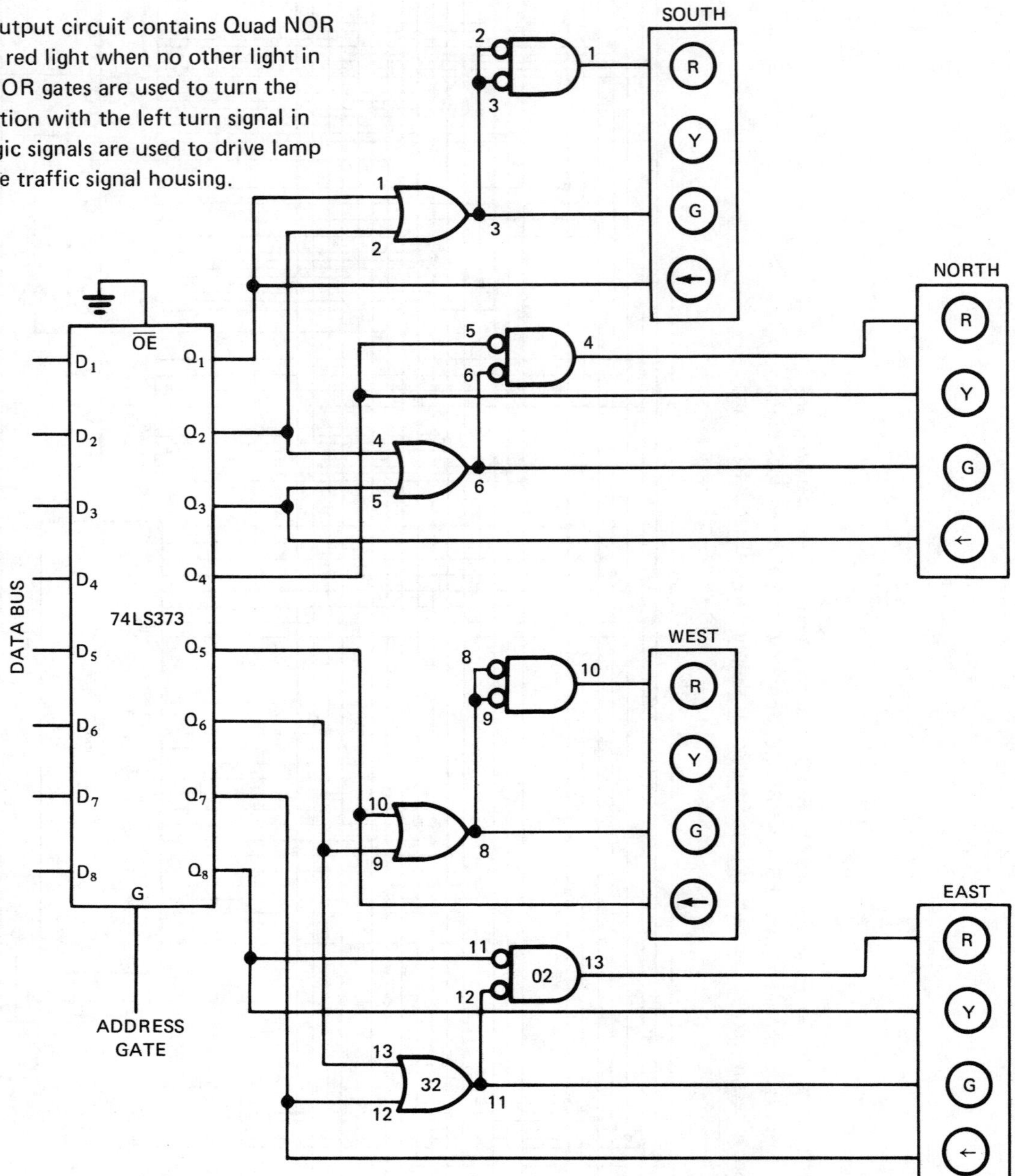

(b)

4. Yellow for north (6 sec.)
5. Green + left turn from west (12 sec.)
6. Green for east and west (18 sec.)
7. Green + left turn from east (12 sec.)
8. Yellow for east (6 sec.)

The 6800 recognizes which cycle of the sequence it is in by the location of a single 1 bit which is rotated through the sequencer byte. The 1-level bit is shifted once for each cycle of the sequence. Table

TABLE 7.15 Traffic signal cycles and the location of the 1 bit in the sequencer byte.

CYCLE	DIRECTION	SIGNAL	TIME (SECS)	D_7	D_6	D_5	D_4	D_3	D_2	D_1	D_0	DECIMAL VALUE	HEXA-DECIMAL VALUE
1	south	green + LT*	18	0	0	0	0	0	0	0	1	1	1
2	north and south	green	24	0	0	0	0	0	0	1	0	2	2
3	north	green + LT	18	0	0	0	0	0	1	0	0	4	4
4	north	yellow	6	0	0	0	0	1	0	0	0	8	8
5	west	green + LT	12	0	0	0	1	0	0	0	0	16	10
6	east and west	green	18	0	0	1	0	0	0	0	0	32	20
7	east	green + LT	12	0	1	0	0	0	0	0	0	64	40
8	east	yellow	6	1	0	0	0	0	0	0	0	128	80

*LT = left turn

7.15 shows the location of the bit in the sequencer byte for each cycle.

The traffic signal controller follows the steps shown in the flow diagram of Figure 7.28. Initialization occurs only after a power on or manual reset. Each cycle of the program begins with the sequencer rotating to the next light cycle. The sequencer byte is latched in the output port to change the signal lights. The program then jumps to a different memory segment for each cycle where it loads a time multiplier. With the time multiplier loaded in an accumulator, the program jumps to the 6-second timer routine and repeats that routine for the number of times called for by the multiplier. After the timer routine, the sequencer byte is examined. If the one bit in the sequencer byte has been rotated to the MSB, then the carry must be set to cause a repeat of the sequence. If the one bit is not in the MSB, the program returns to the rotate instruction with the carry clear. The sequencer byte is rotated and the next light cycle begins.

Table 7.16 lists the initialization instructions of the traffic light program. In the initialization of the program, which occurs only after a reset, a memory byte used for the sequencer is cleared. The carry is set in preparation for its rotation into the LSB of the sequencer byte. The index register is loaded with the address of the first "load multiplier" segment. Each cycle begins with the rotation of the sequencer memory byte. The sequencer byte is then transferred to the output where it causes the lights to change. This is followed by an indexed jump to the "load multiplier" segment for that cycle. Table 7.17 lists the rotate, output, and jump instructions used with each cycle.

The eight "load multiplier" segments are listed in Table 7.18. For each light cycle, the program is steered to one of the eight segments. The correct segment is selected by the indexed jump instruction and the fact that the address of the correct segment was loaded into the index register during the previous cycle. In each segment, the same functions occur. The time multiplier is loaded into the B accumulator.

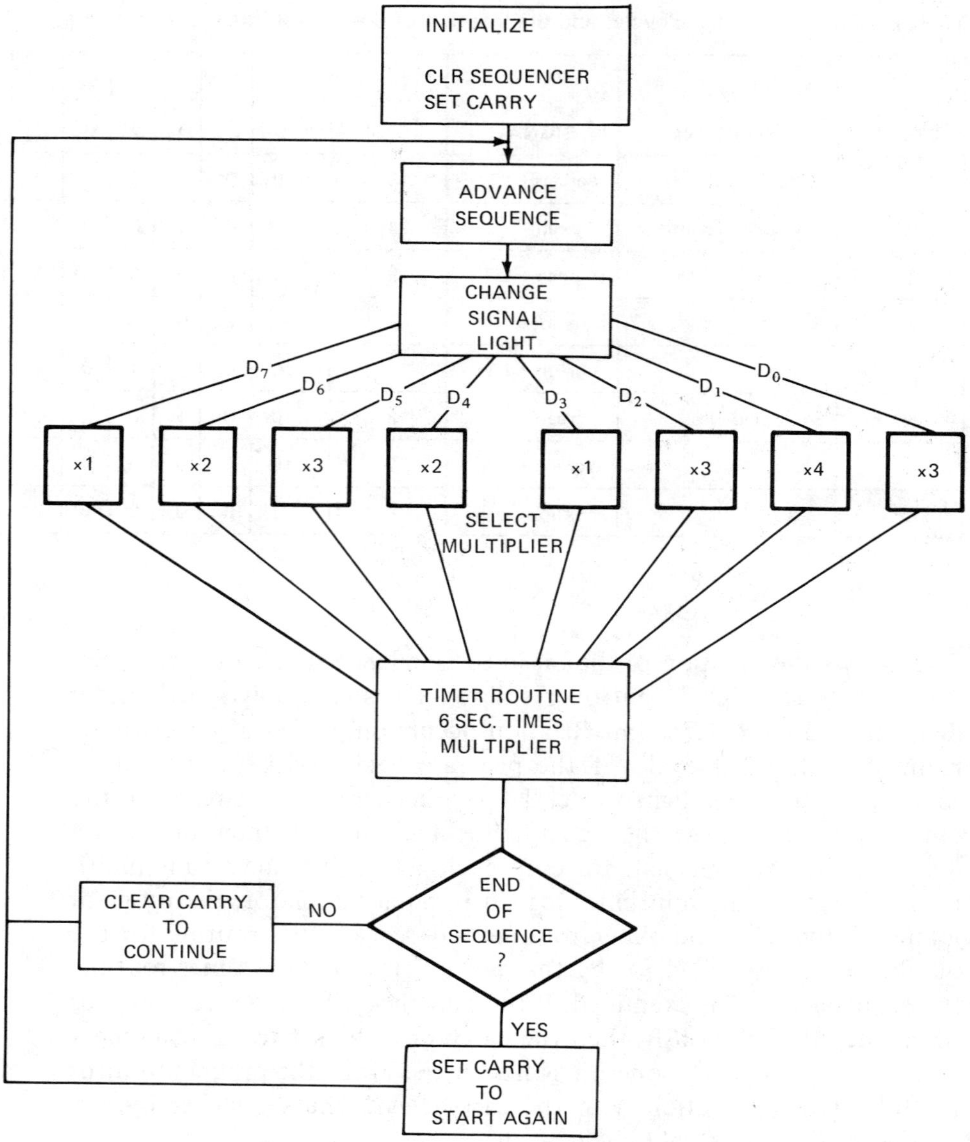

FIGURE 7.28 Flow diagram of traffic signal controller.

TABLE 7.16 Initializing instructions for 6800 traffic signal program.

ADDRESS	MOVEMENT	MNEMONIC	OPERAND	DESCRIPTION	MODE
0107		CLR	(0004)	Clear Sequencer	EXT
0A		SEC		Set Carry	INH
0B		LDX	0120	Address for first indexed jump to load multiplier segment at 0120	IMM

TABLE 7.17 Rotate sequencer output to change light; jump to select time multiplier segment.

ADDRESS	MOVEMENT	MNEMONIC	OPERAND	DESCRIPTION	MODE
010E		ROL	(0004)	Shift sequencer byte	EXT
11		LDA A	(04)	Output sequencer byte to select lights	DIR
13		STA A	(0200)		EXT
0116		JMP	00	Jump to load time multiplier segment (using address stored in index register)	IND

TABLE 7.18 Load multiplier segments for 6800 traffic signal program.

ADDRESS HEXADECIMAL	MOVEMENT	MNEMONIC	OPERAND (HEXADECIMAL)	DESCRIPTION	MODE
0120		LDA B	03	Load time multiplier	IMM
22		LDX	0128	Load address of next multiplier segment	IMM
25		BRA	39	Branch to timer	REL
0128		LDA B	04	Same as 0120 to 0126	
2A		LDX	0130		
2D		BRA	31		
0130		LDA B	03	Same as 0120 to 0126	
32		LDX	0138		
35		BRA	29		
0138		LDA B	01	Same as 0120 to 0126	
3A		LDX	0140		
3D		BRA	21		
0140		LDA B	02	Same as 0120 to 0126	
72		LDX	0148		
45		BRA	19		
0148		LDA B	03	Same as 0120 to 0126	
4A		LDX	0150		
4D		BRA	11		
0150		LDA B	02	Same as 0120 to 0126	
52		LDX	0158		
55		BRA	09		
0158		LDA B	01	Same as 0120 to 0126	
5A		LDX	0121		
5D		BRA	01		

The address of the load multiplier segment to be used in the next cycle is loaded into the index register. The program branches to the timer routine.

Table 7.19 is the timer routine. It is not a subroutine. A subroutine is used only when it is necessary to return to a *different* point in the main program each time the routine is used. In this case, the program returns to the *same* instruction each time the timer routine is used. In this application there is no need to save the return address on the

TABLE 7.19 Six-second timer routine for 6800 traffic signal program.

ADDRESS	MOVEMENT	MNEMONIC	OPERAND	DESCRIPTION	MODE
0160		DEC	(0001)	Timer routine 6-sec times, multiplier in ACC B.	EXT
63		BNE	FB		REL
65		DEC	(0002)		EXT
68		BNE	F6		REL
6A		DEC	B		EXT
6B		BNE	F3		REL
6D		TST	(0004)	Test sequencer byte.	EXT
70		BMI	03		REL
72		CLC		Clear carry to continue cycle.	IMP
73		BRA	99	Return to rotate sequencer.	REL
75		SEC		Set carry to start cycle over.	IMP
0176		BRA	96	Return to rotate sequencer.	REL
	To rotate instruction				

stack, so a subroutine is not needed. The first four instructions of the routine form a 2-byte counter providing 6-second time intervals (using a 100-KHZ clock). The 6-second time interval is repeated for as many times as the number in accumulator B. Once the time interval is completed, the sequencer is tested. If the 1 bit has been shifted to the MSB of the sequencer, the TST instruction will result in the N bit being set, and the program will set the carry so that the next ROL instruction will start the sequence over by shifting a 1 into the LSB of the sequencer. If the TST instruction does not result in the N bit being set, then a clear carry is used prior to the jump back to the ROL instruction.

Figure 7.29 shows a memory map of the traffic light controller. Only three bytes of RAM are used: two for the timer and one as the sequencer byte. A single output is used. The program requires less than a half page of PROM.

7.6.4 Use of Tables

The Advantage of Tables In many cases a program must respond to a set of conditions which occur at random or in a combination of sequences that make the program difficult to arrange. Under these conditions it is often convenient to use a table. The use of a table requires that each program condition have an exclusive numerical value that can be used as an address to the data in the table. The size of the memory needed for the table depends on the range of addresses generated. If the addresses are scattered over a large portion of the memory map, then the use of a table may not be economical. In the usual case, a table can be confined to a single page of ROM. Where the table does not densely populate the ROM, vacant segments can be used for other program routines.

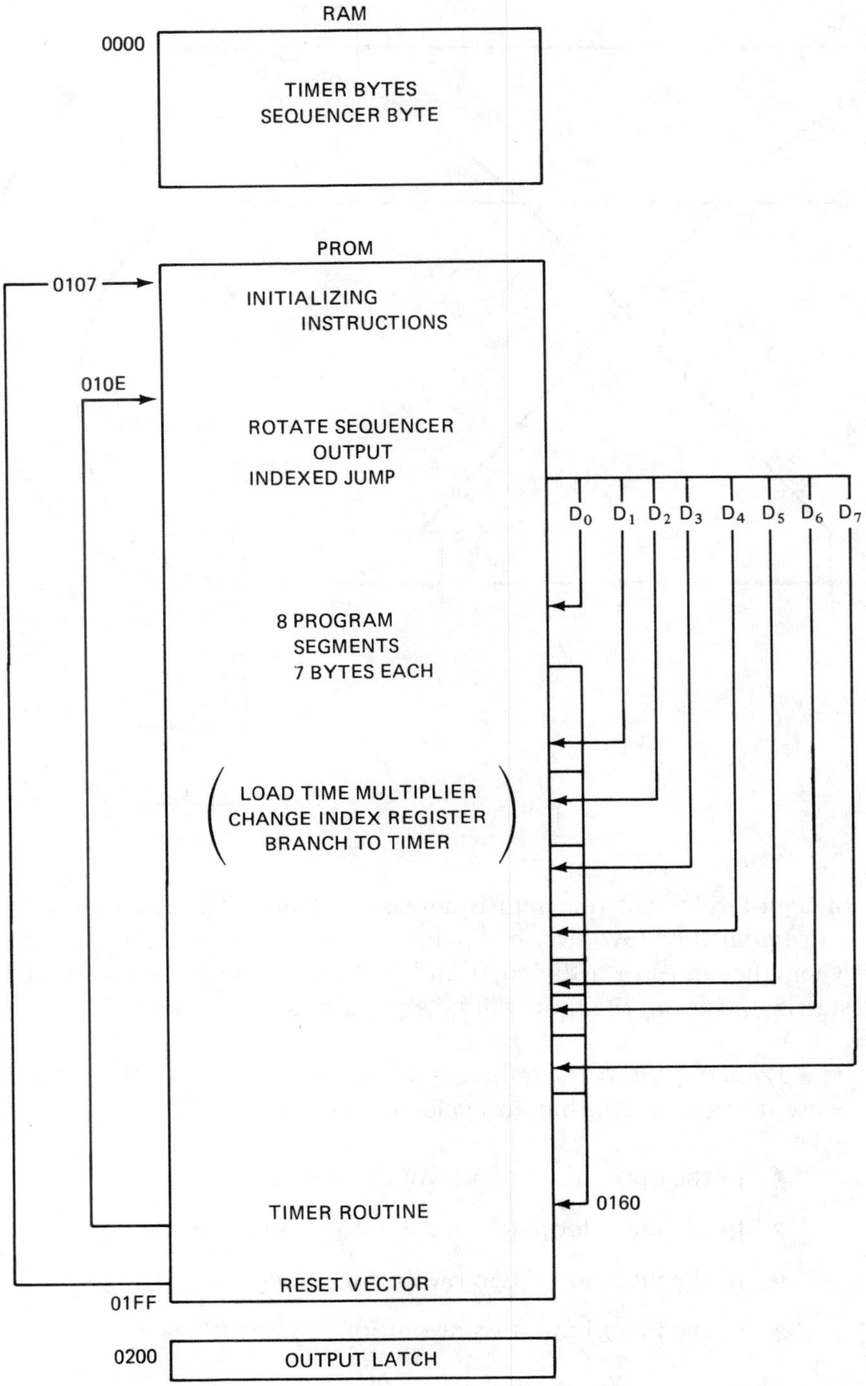

FIGURE 7.29 Memory map of traffic light controller.

The Model Railway Control Circuit As an example let us use a 6800 program for control of a model railway.

Situation: The model railway track is connected as shown in Figure 7.30. The track is connected to form an inner and an outer loop. Six switches are used to allow both changes in direction and changes from inner to outer loop. Six electronic sensors (three pairs) are used to sense the train's direction and location. The sensors transmit a digital 1

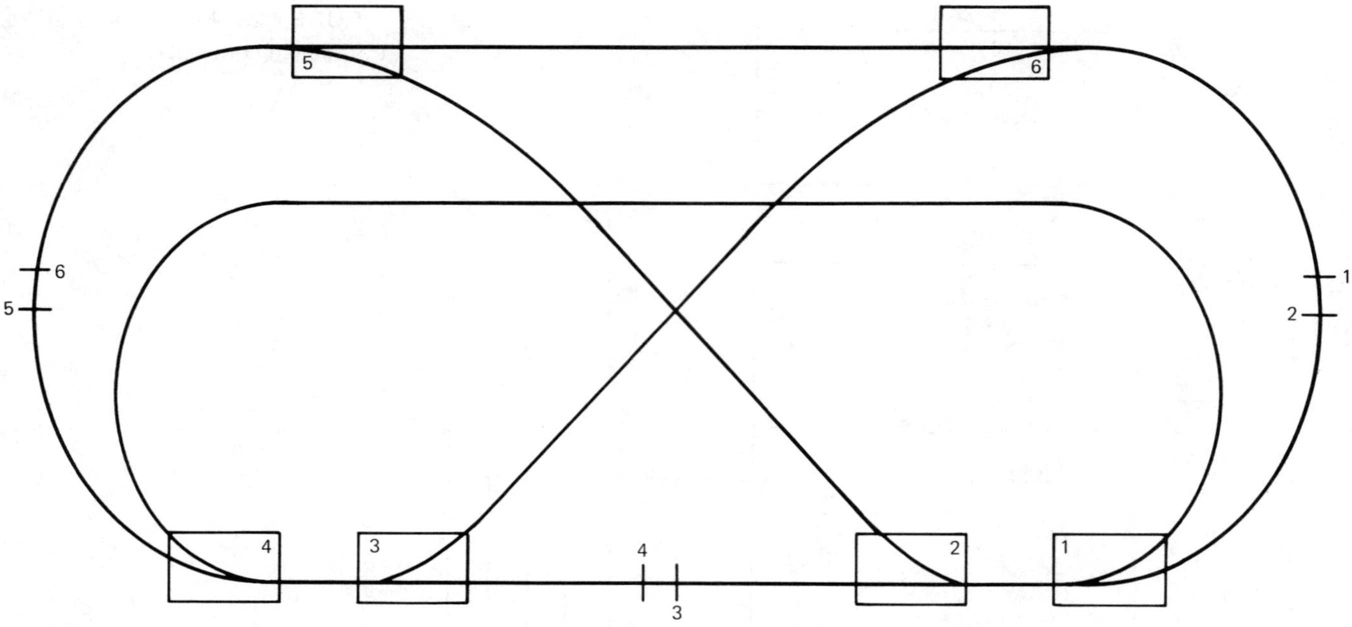

FIGURE 7.30 Model railway track connections.

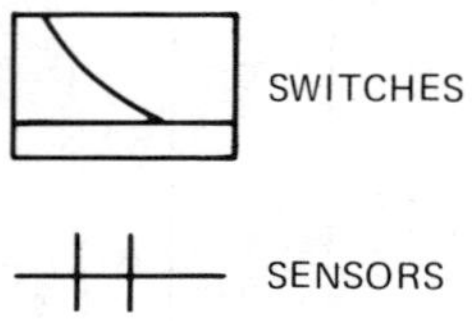

or high level when the train is abreast of the sensor. The sensors transmit digital 0 or low level in the inactive state. The switches are straight when they receive a digital 0 and will switch with a digital 1. In the starting position, the train will be abreast of sensors 3 and 4.

Problem: Start the train and, under control of the microprocessor, cause it to run in continuous cycles as follows:

- In the outer loop, two revolutions clockwise.
- In the outer loop, two revolutions counterclockwise.
- In the inner loop, two revolutions clockwise.
- In the inner loop, two revolutions counterclockwise.

Microprocessor Connections: The processor configuration is shown in Figure 7.31. The odd-numbered sensors are connected to the lower bits (D_0 through D_2) of the input port. The even-numbered sensors are connected to bits (D_4 through D_6) of the input port. To prevent overlap between odd and even input data, D_3 bit goes high with each even sensor input. The six switches are controlled through a single output port.

One ROM is used as a program memory, the second as a table to look up switch settings in response to each new sensor reading.

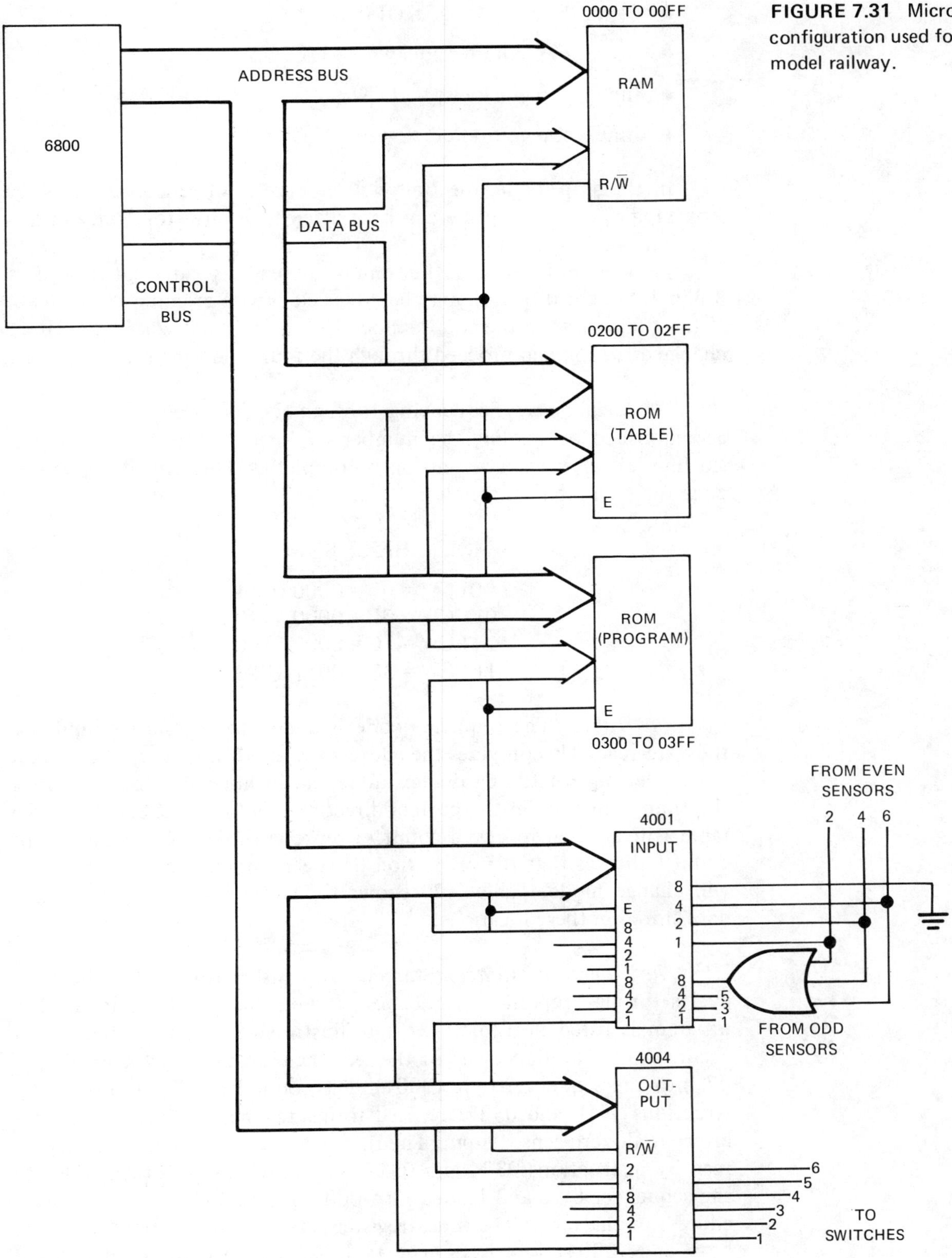

FIGURE 7.31 Microprocessor configuration used for control of model railway.

Operating Modes: There are four operating modes:

- Outer loop clockwise = OLCW
- Outer loop counterclockwise = OLCCW
- Inner loop clockwise = ILCW
- Inner loop counterclockwise = ILCCW

In the stop mode, the train will be abreast of sensors 3 and 4. A stop mode program routine can be written to insure stops only in this location. (See problem 7.21).

The starting location of the train is in every case adjacent to sensors 3 and 4, but the direction may be either clockwise or counterclockwise. If the train starts in the counterclockwise direction, it will immediately change direction and proceed through the four operating modes.

The Sequencer: Sequencing through the four operating modes is accomplished by loading the number 07 into a memory location and shifting left after each revolution is completed. This provides a unique code for each mode as follows:

MODE	HEX.	BINARY
OLCW =	07 =	0000 0111
OLCCW =	0E =	0000 1110
1LCW =	1C =	0001 1100
1LCCW =	38 =	0011 1000

The Table: The sequence code is added to the sensor inputs as they are read. This provides the address low used to look up the correct switch setting for the particular mode and location of the train. Once the train is moving in the correct direction and loop, the data from the table will be used to give a count of sensor readings. When the sensor count indicates that the revolution has been completed, the sequencer will change mode. Table 7.20 shows the addresses developed and the data stored in these locations.

The Operating Modes: Starting with instruction 0318, the train cycles through repetitive sequences of the four operating modes. The program is listed in Table 7.21 and illustrated in the flow diagram of Figure 7.32. The first cycle of the sequence is caused by the loading of 07 into the sequencer byte (0001). The counter (0002) is cleared. Instructions 031F and 0322 are used to insure that sensors are read only after an all zero sensor input. The first sensor to go high after all zero is read by instructions 0324 and 0327. The sensor input is then added to the sequencer byte and loaded into 0004. Byte 0003 contains the page address of the table. The index register is then loaded with (0003) high byte and (0004) low byte. The table is then read using an indexed mode instruction (LDA A). The value taken from the table is stored in

TABLE 7.20 Table of switch setting (addresses obtained by the sum of sensor inputs and sequencer code).

SEQUENCER ROUTINE →	LDA 07 STA 0000 0111	ASL 0000 1110	ASL 0001 1100	← JMP ASL 0011 1000
	OUTER LOOP		INNER LOOP	
(FROM INPUT) Sensor No.	Clockwise 07	Counter Clockwise 0E	Clockwise 1C	Counter Clockwise 38
01 (1)	08 (count) 00	0F (change direction) 12 [2+5]	1D (change loop) 08 [4]	39 (change direction) 12 [2+5]
02 (3)	09 (count) 00	10 (change direction) 12 [2+5]	1E (count) 09 [1+4]	3A (change direction) 12 [2+5]
04 (5)	0B (count) 00	12 (change direction) 12 [2+5]	20 (change loop) 08 [4]	3C (change direction) 12 [2+5]
18 (2)	1F (change direction) 24 [3+6]	26 (count) 00	34 (change direction) 24 [3+6]	50 (change loop) 01 [1]
28 (4)	2F (change direction) 24 [3+6]	36 (count) 00	44 (change direction) 24 [3+6]	60 (count) 09 [1+4]
48 (6)	4F (change direction 24 [3+6]	56 (count) 00	64 (change direction) 24 [3+6]	80 (change loop) 01 [1]

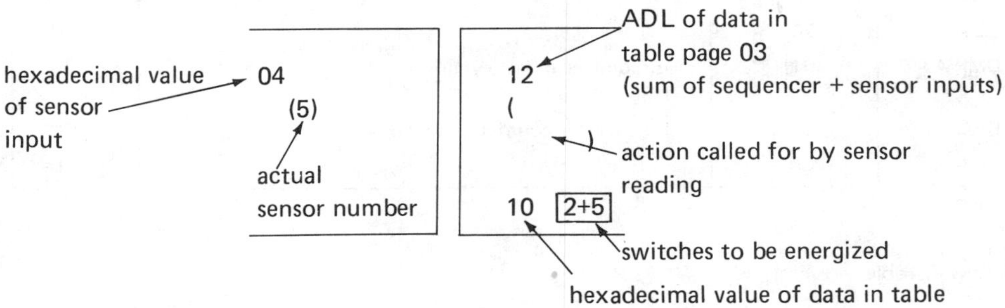

the output port causing the appropriate switches to be thrown. The switch setting is then tested to determine if it is time to count sensors. If accumulator A is zero, it indicates that the train is traveling in the outer loop and a count of sensor readings is begun in order to detect the completion of two revolutions. If the switches are set to 09, the train is traveling in the inner loop and a count of sensor readings (double count) is begun to detect the completion of two revolutions. After each

TABLE 7.21 Model railway control program (operating modes).

ADDRESS	MOVEMENT	MNEMONIC	OPERAND	DESCRIPTION	MODE
0314		LDA A	02	Store page address of table	IMM
16		STA A	(03)		DIR
18	→	LDA A	07	Load 07 into sequencer byte	IMM
1A		STA A	(01)		
1C	→	CLR	(0002)	Clear counter	EXT
031F	→	LDA A	(4001)	Continue to read sensor inputs till all zero	EXT
22		BNE	FB		REL
24	→	LDA A	(4001)	Continue to read sensor inputs till first bit goes high	EXT
27		BEQ	FB		REL
29		ADD A	(01)	Add sensor reading to sequencer value	DIR
2B		STA A	(04)	Store sum in preparation for transfer to index register	DIR
2D		LDX	(03)	Store table address in index register (content of memory 0003 and 0004)	DIR
2F		LDA A	00	Read table (switch settings)	IND
31		STA A	(4004)	Set switches	EXT
34		TST A		If switch setting is zero train is in outer loop	IMP
35		BNE	07		REL
37		INC	(0002)	Count sensor readings	EXT
3A		LDA A	06	(Outer loop)	
3C		BRA	09		
3E	→	CMP A	09	If switch setting is 09 train is in inner loop	IMM
0340		BNE	DD		REL
0342		INC	(0002)	Count sensor readings (inner loop)	EXT
45		LDA A	02	If count is two, revolutions are complete time to advance sequencer	IMM
47	→	CMP A	(02)		DIR
49		BNE	D4		REL
4B	TO 0318	ASL	(0001)		EXT
4E		LDA A	70		IMM
50		CMP A	(01)	Is sequence in last cycle? If so, reload 07.	DIR
52	TO 031C	BEQ	C4	If not, clear counter and read sensors.	REL
0354		BRA	C6		REL

4001 = Sensor Input
4004 = Switch Output

0001 = Sequencer Byte
0002 = Counter
0003 = Address High of Table
0004 = Address Low in Table

increment or double increment, there is a return to read sensors until the count of six. The count of six indicates the revolutions are complete and the sequencer is shifted to the next mode. The next sensor reading added to the new sequencer value will set switches for either a change in loop or change in direction or both. Once the change is completed, a count of sensor readings will begin again.

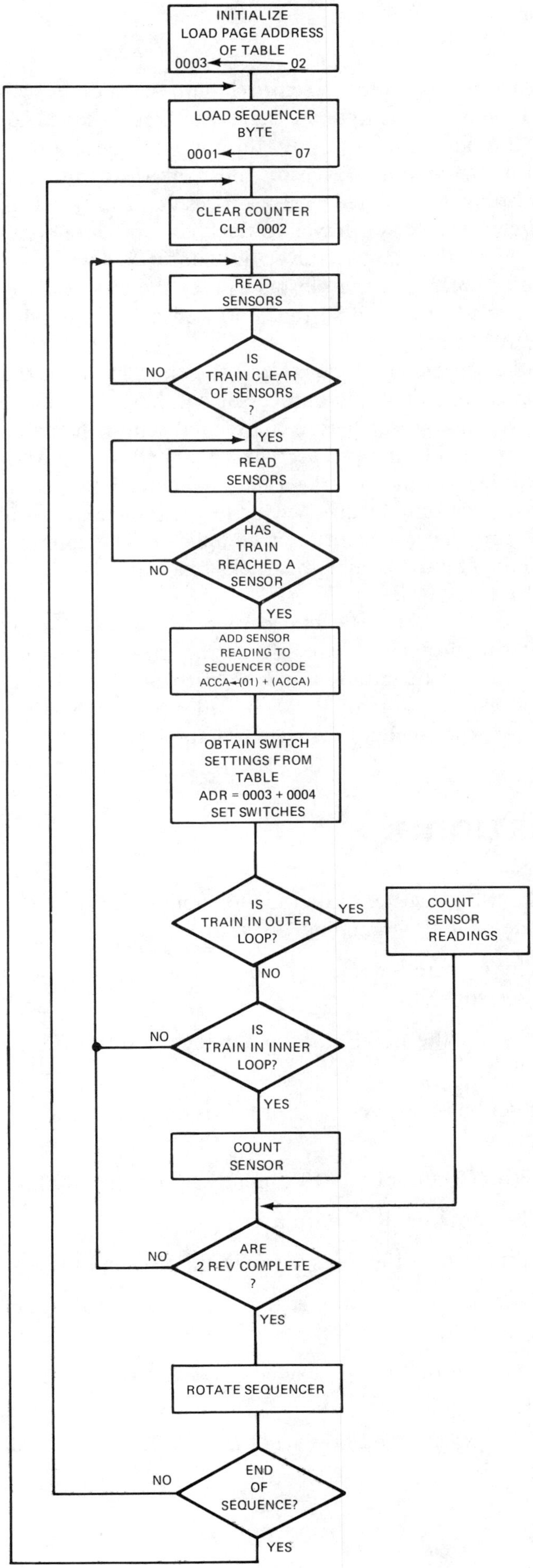

FIGURE 7.32 6800 model railway control program flow diagram.

Reading the Sensors: Sensor inputs will not be used until after both odd and even sensors are zero. The first sensor to go high after all zeros will produce an output. By this method, the second sensor in each pair will be ignored as all sensors must return to zero again before another reading is accepted. This will result in only odd sensors being recognized if the train is traveling clockwise and only even sensors being recognized if the train is traveling counterclockwise. As written, the program assumes that the sensors will see the train as a solid object and will be angled or spaced so that both sensors in the pair will not read zero between cars.

If the sensors are 1″ apart and the train has a maximum speed of 100″ per second, the microprocessor will have 10 milliseconds (msec) to read the first sensor before the second sensor in the pair goes high. Using a 500-KHZ clock (2 μsec per cycle) allows time for 5000 clock cycles, which are much more than adequate. If the sensors are set at truck level, the only change needed to the program is in the count used to determine that a revolution is completed. The count would need to be multiplied by the number of trucks to a train.

Use of Memory: The one page of RAM and two pages of ROM used for this problem is excessive. If no other chores are planned for this system, the operation could be performed with a single page of RAM and a single page of ROM. In order to preserve the clarity of the explanation, these economies were not applied.

Questions

7.1 Name six registers, counters, or pointers in the 6800 which must be considered in programming.

7.2 Why is there a minimum clock frequency specified for the 6800 microprocessor?

7.3 How do the 6800 clock input logic levels differ from standard TTL levels?

7.4 Describe the power on reset provisions used with the 6800 microprocessor.

7.5 What effect does the DBE input have on the 6800 output data?

7.6 When does the R/W output of the 6800 go low?

7.7 Explain the differences between the IRQ and the NMI inputs.

7.8 What interrupt vector is transferred to the program counter on receipt of an IRQ?

7.9 What information is loaded on the stack as the result of an interrupt request?

7.10 Under what condition will the 6800 not respond to an IRQ signal?

7.11 What changes occur in the contents of the stack pointer during an interrupt request routine?

7.12 What are the interrupt vectors and at what addresses are they located?

7.13 Which control input can be used to provide single instruction operation?

7.14 Why is it possible for some instruction mnemonics to have as many as four machine codes?

7.15 Describe six single-byte instructions. List their mnemonic, machine code in hexadecimal, function, and the clock periods required.

7.16 Describe six two-byte instructions. List their mnemonic, machine code in hexadecimal, function, and the clock periods required.

7.17 Describe six three-byte instructions. List their mnemonic, machine code in hexadecimal, function, and the clock periods required.

7.18 How does the operand differ between immediate mode and extended mode instructions?

7.19 On what page of memory is the operand of a direct mode instruction located?

7.20 How is the address of the operand obtained in the indexed addressing mode?

7.21 What type of instruction uses the relative addressing mode?

7.22 What are the primary differences between JMP and BRA instructions?

7.23 What is the function of a bootstrap loader?

7.24 What are the two operands of a data move instruction?

7.25 List and describe six data move instructions.

7.26 List the instructions that clear or set condition code register bits.

7.27 Which condition code register bits are affected by the CLR instruction?

7.28 Which instructions may be used in the handling of interrupts?

7.29 Explain how a 16-bit comparator can be used to provide a port with a switchable address.

7.30 Describe the state of a 6800 microprocessor after execution of a WAI instruction.

7.31 What initialization instructions are needed for the bootstrap loader routine?

7.32 Why is the indexed addressing mode so essential to the load and verify routines?

7.33 Explain the similarities and the differences between the load and verify routines of the bootstrap loader program.

7.34 What is the advantage of having both add with and add without carry instructions?

7.35 Explain the relationship between condition code register and the branch instructions.

7.36 What addressing mode is taken by all branch instructions?

7.37 What two instructions are used to complement numbers?

7.38 What difference exists in determining the sign of a number that is input to a signed arithmetic program as compared to determining sign of numbers generated by the program?

7.39 How many magnitude bits exist for numbers that input to a double precision signed arithmetic program?

7.40 When is it useful to use a TST instruction?

7.41 Explain a procedure used to twos complement a two-byte number.

7.42 Describe the relative advantages and disadvantages to selecting between BSR or JSR instruction.

7.43 What are the advantages of a subroutine?

7.44 What conditions in the program call for a subroutine rather than the use of an unconditional branch or jump instruction?

7.45 What differences exist between operation of the stack during a jump to subroutine and during interrupts? Why do these differences exist?

7.46 What instructions are used in saving the content of condition code register on the stack during a subroutine?

7.47 Which instructions begin with an increment of the stack pointer?

7.48 How may the contents of index registers be saved during a subroutine?

7.49 List five instructions which may be used to shift or rotate numbers. With what arithmetic programs are they used?

7.50 In the multiply program, Table 7.11, what is the purpose of shifting X to the right?

7.51 In the multiply program, Table 7.11, why is the LSR instruction used to shift X rather than the ROR?

7.52 In the multiply program, Table 7.11, why is the low byte shifted with ASL and the high byte with ROL?

7.53 What three instructions are used in a counter routine that ends at the count of zero?

7.54 What instructions are used in a counter routine that starts at the count of zero?

7.55 What is the relationship between timer and counter routines?

7.56 What is the fundamental increment of time in an 6800 timer routine?

7.57 If an accumulator or memory byte is cleared and then decremented, what will it contain?

7.58 How many clock cycles occur for each decrement of an accumulator used in a 6800 timer routine?

7.59 How many clock cycles are added to each decrement of an accumulator used in a timer routine for each NOP instruction added to the routine?

7.60 How many clock cycles occur for each decrement of a memory byte used in a timer routine?

7.61 In the traffic signal program, how are the lights in the traffic signals changed in accordance with the sequence?

7.62 In the traffic signal program, how are the various time intervals of the lights accomplished?

7.63 The traffic signal timing of Table 7.15 is to be modified so that East-West has the same 18-24-18 timing as North-South. Which instructions must be changed?

7.64 Under what conditions is the use of a look-up table advantageous?

7.65 How are the addresses of the look-up table generated during the running of the model railway control program?

Problems

7.1 Draw the interconnections to the components of Figure 7.33. The RAM is to occupy page 00. The PROM will occupy pages 01 and 02. The I/O ports will have address X8XX and X4XX. Add decoding gates where needed.

7.2 The following table lists unconditional jump instructions. Convert to a branch always instruction wherever such a conversion is valid.

ADDRESS	MNEMONIC	OPERAND
10F2	JMP	111A
018A	JMP	02FF
007F	JMP	003E
026C	JMP	013D
00F3	JMP	01A2

FIGURE 7.33 (Problem 7.1)

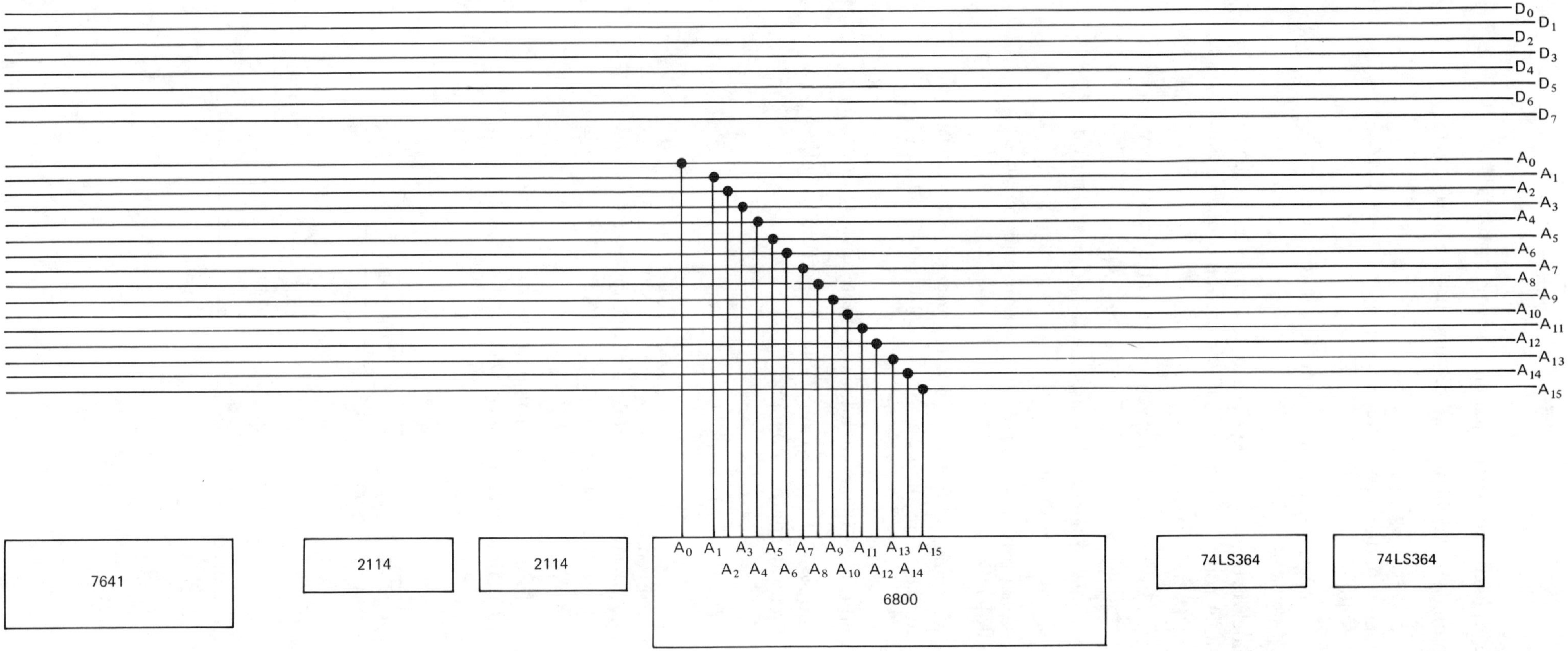

7.3 Convert the decimal numbers to binary and perform the algebraic additions listed using twos complement arithmetic:

124	124	68
+68	−68	−124
137	137	104
+104	−104	−137
92	92	116
+116	−116	−92

7.4 To the program of Table 7.7 add an output routine which outputs in hexadecimal to a pair of ports: one port to receive the sign, a second port to receive the lower 8 bits of the sum.

7.5 Appendix C gives a 6800 binary to BCD conversion program. Using this as a subroutine, modify the output routine called for in Problem 7.4 to output in BCD form.

7.6 Write a twos complement routine for a three-byte number.

7.7 Figure 7.34 shows the A accumulator and carry. Beginning with $5A_H$ in the accumulator and the carry set, determine the hexadecimal value of the accumulator and state of the carry after each of the following instructions:

Begin with A = $5A_H$, CY = 1 in each case	ASL A	A =	CY =
	ASR A	A =	CY =
	LSR A	A =	CY =
	ROL A	A =	CY =
	ROR A	A =	CY =

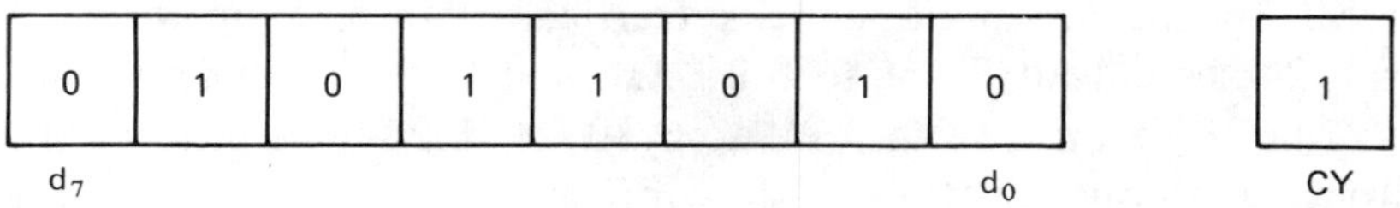

FIGURE 7.34 Accumulator containing the entry $5A_H$ with a set carry. (Problem 7.7)

7.8 Perform the following binary multiplications.

10010111	10110011
1001	10101
10001011	11011010
1001101	10110001

7.9 Write a routine that will convert the product of the multiplication program of Table 7.11 to BCD form. Store in three memory bytes.

7.10 Figure 4.20 is an output port which will demultiplex the output one BCD digit at a time into 4 quad latches. Write a program that will output the results of the program of Problem 7.9 into these latches.

TABLE 7.22 Input Ports 0800 0801 Starting Memory Address 0400

ADDRESS	MOVEMENT	MNEMONIC	OPERAND	DESCRIPTION	MODE
0110		LDX	0400	Load starting address in X register	IMM
13		LDA	0800	Read Port 00	EXT
16		STA	00	Store data in Mem address pointed to by the Index Reg.	IND
18		INX			IMP
19		LDA	0801	Read Port 0801	EXT
1C		STA	00	Store data in Mem address pointed to by the Index Reg.	IND
1E		INX			IMP
011F		BRA	F2	Return to read Port 0800	REL.

7.11 Table 7.22 is a segment of a routine which moves data from 2 adjacent input ports and stores it in adjacent memory addresses. Modify the program so that it will exit the routine after 100_{10} bytes have been stored.

7.12 Write the program routine of Table 7.22 such that the higher address port is read first and the memory addresses are decremented. Exit the routine after 40_H bytes are stored.

7.13 A 6800 is operating with a 420-KHZ clock. Write a timer routine for one millisecond ±1%.

7.14 A 6800 is operating with a 1-MHZ clock. Write a two-byte timer routine for 200 msec ±1%.

7.15 A 6800 is operating with a 110-KHZ clock. Write a two-byte timer routine for 1 second ±5%.

7.16 An industrial plant has a large amount of incoming traffic from 7 AM to 8:30 AM and a large amount of outgoing traffic from 4 PM to 6:30 PM. To accommodate this traffic, left turns from the east are to run 24 seconds at 7 AM to 8:30 AM, and left turns from the south are to run 36 seconds from 4 PM to 6:30 PM. A 24-hour timer in the signal housing supplies outputs as shown in Figure 7.35. To Table 7.23, add an input port for the timer and modify both hardware and software to change the timing.

FIGURE 7.35 Outputs from 24-hour timer cams. (Problem 7.16)

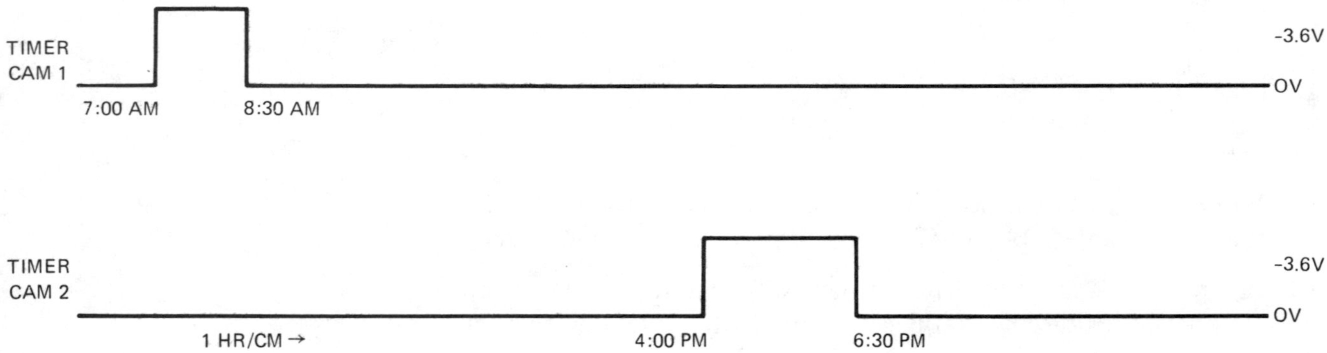

TABLE 7.23 Traffic signal timing and output byte.

CYCLE	DIRECTION	SIGNAL	TIME (SEC)	TIME (MULT)	S/W ←	S/W G	S/W Y	N/E ←	N/E G	N/E Y	O	M	HEXADECIMAL VALUE
1	south	green + left turn	18	3	1	1	0	0	0	0	0	1	C1
2	south	green	6	1	0	1	0	0	0	0	0	1	41
3	north and south	green	18	3	0	1	0	0	1	0	0	1	49
4	north south	green yellow	6	1	0	0	1	0	1	0	0	1	29
5	north	green + left turn	18	3	0	0	0	1	1	0	0	1	19
6	north	yellow	6	1	0	0	0	0	0	1	0	1	05
7	west	green + left turn	12	2	0	0	1	1	1	1	0	0	3C
8	west	green	6	1	1	0	1	1	1	1	0	0	BC
9	west and east	green	12	2	1	0	1	1	0	1	0	0	B4
10	west east	yellow green	6	1	1	1	0	1	0	1	0	0	D4
11	east	green + left turn	12	2	1	1	1	0	0	1	0	0	E4
12	east	yellow	6	1	1	1	1	1	1	0	0	0	F8

7.17 The traffic signal program of Table 7.17 makes only limited use of the yellow warning lights in changing signals from green to red. It would be adequate for only a slow speed intersection. For a high speed intersection, we would prefer to have the left turn arrow off for six seconds prior to the light turning green in the oncoming direction. The yellow light should be on for six seconds prior to any change from green to red. As Table 7.23 indicates, there are now twelve cycles to the sequence instead of the eight used in the previous program. In adapting this new technique to this program, we face the problem of the sequencer byte having only eight bits. There are any number of solutions to this problem. Considering that there are 256 unique states to an eight-bit output, we could definitely produce and decode at the output port some set of twelve. An ideal solution is to increment the sequencer byte rather than rotate it. The incremented byte can be used as an address to a table containing the bytes shown in Table 7.23. These bytes can be outputted to the port of Figure 7.36. Write a program for a traffic signal control that provides the timing of Table 7.23 using the output port of Figure 7.36.

FIGURE 7.36 Output port for expanded traffic light program. (Problem 7.17)

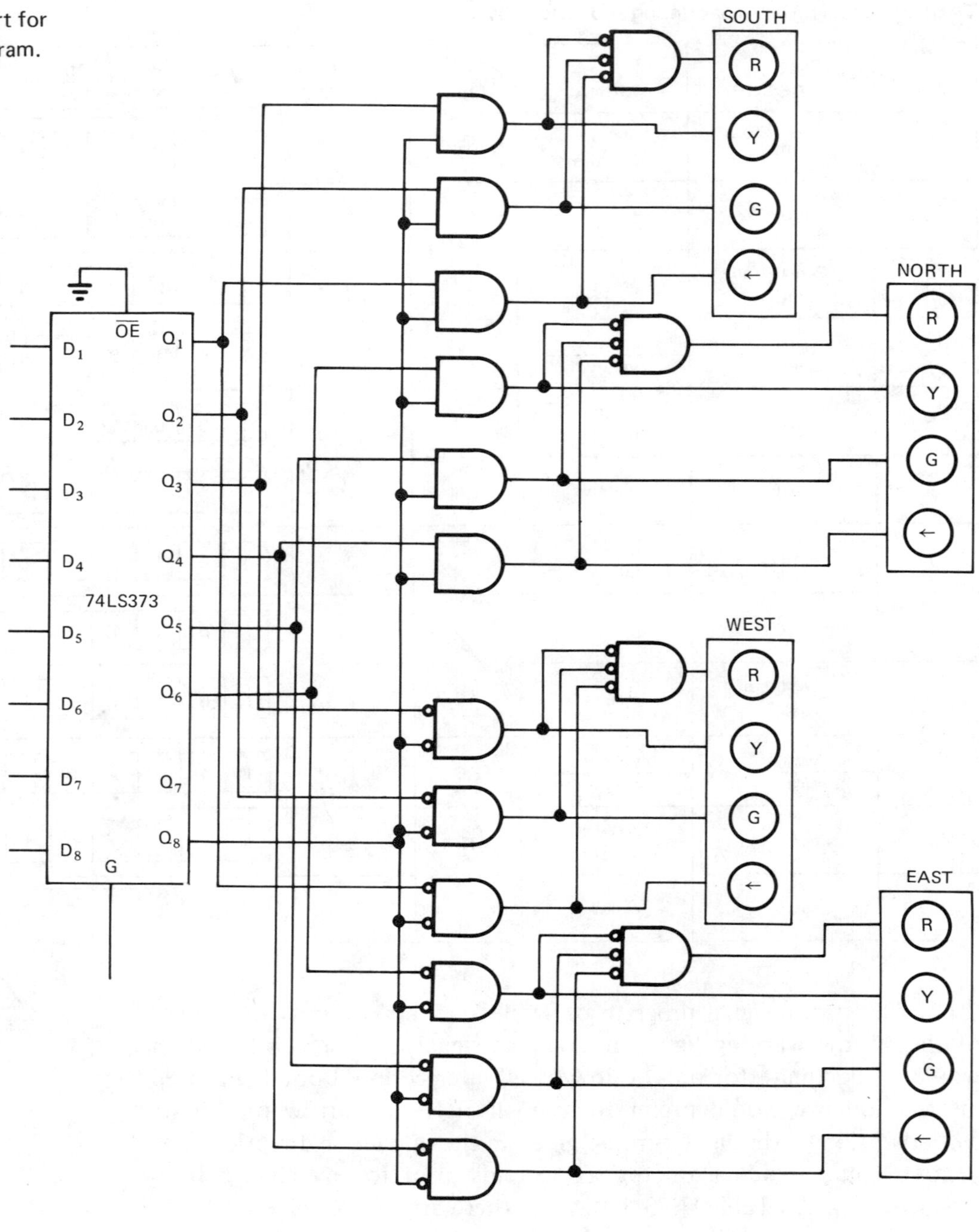

7.18 Modify the program of Table 7.24 and the hardware as needed so that the train changes modes as follows:

- In the outer loop four revolutions clockwise.
- In the inner loop four revolutions counterclockwise.
- In the outer loop four revolutions counterclockwise.
- In the inner loop four revolutions clockwise.

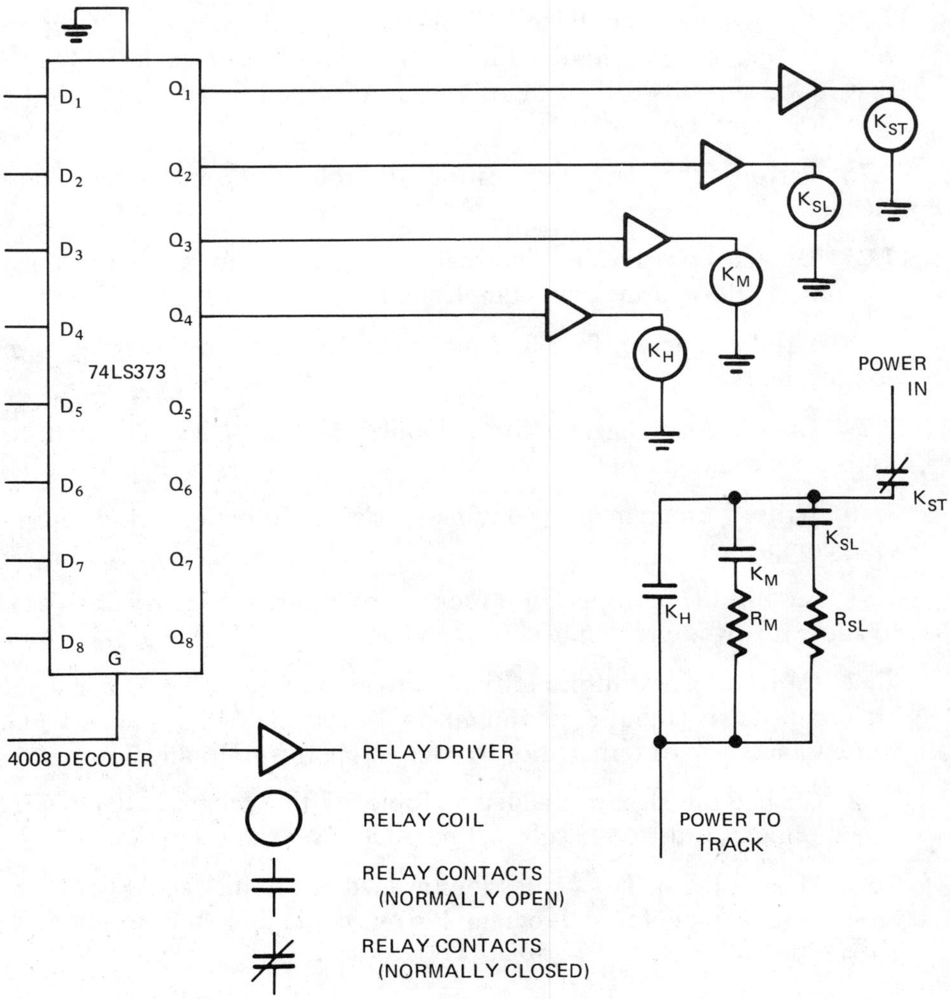

FIGURE 7.37 Speed control port for model railway. Address of port is 4008. (Problems 7.19 and 7.21)

7.19 Figure 7.37 is a speed control port to be added to the model railway. Modify the program such that the train starts at slow speed and after one revolution advances to medium speed in the inner loop and when in the outer loop, it travels at high speed.

7.20 Using the speed control port of Figure 7.37, modify the operating mode program of Table 7.21 so that the train will run at high speed in the outer loop, medium speed in the inner loop, and slow speed when switching modes.

7.21 Using the speed control port of Figure 7.37, write a stop mode program such that the train will reduce to slow speed and stop only when the train is adjacent to sensors 3 or 4.

7.22 Make a memory map of the look-up table, Table 7.20.

7.23 Show how the entire railway control program can be contained on the same page of ROM as the look-up table.

7.24 Write a program listing of a look-up table that converts two-digit BCD numbers to binary.

7.25 Using the look-up table of Problem 7.27 and the binary BCD program of Appendix C, modify the multiply program of Table 7.11 such that it will input two BCD digits and output the results in BCD to the port shown in Figure 4.20.

7.26 Perform the algebraic additions in Problem 7.6 using ones complement addition.

7.27 Draw a flow diagram like that of Figure 7.20 for single precision algebraic addition using ones complement.

7.28 Write a program for single precision algebraic addition using ones complement.

7.29 Draw a flow diagram for a double precision algebraic addition using ones complement.

7.30 Write a program for a double precision algebraic addition using ones complement.

7.31 Modify the multiplication program of Figure 7.25 and Table 7.11 to allow for two-byte numbers of X and Y.

7.32 Convert the eight-bit multiplier program of Table 7.11 to an algebraic multiplier. (Input signed numbers. Determine sign of product and store. Cancel sign of terms prior to completing the multiplication.)

7.33 Change the algebraic adder of Table 7.7 to a program that makes maximum use of the 6800 subtract instructions.

7.34 Make a list of key depressions needed to produce an ASCII-HEX programming tape for a Program PROM containing the program of Table 7.11.

7.35 The twos complement subroutine Table 7.10(b) must be relocated to beginning address at 05E0. Make the necessary corrections to the adder program of Table 7.10(a).

7.36 The twos complement subroutine Table 7.10(b) must be relocated to beginning address 0700. Make the necessary corrections to the adder program of Table 7.10(a).

7.37 Figure 7.38 is a circle of 8 LEDS which require 10 mA of forward current for light saturation. Draw an output latching port for connection to a 6800 bus. Show the connection of the 8 LEDS, including any drivers used to supply the needed current.

7.38 Write a program that will cause 4 of the 8 LEDS in Figure 7.38 to be lit. The 4 lit LEDS should rotate clockwise at a rate of about one revolution per second.

7.39 Write a program similar to that in Problem 7.38 but rotate the LEDS counterclockwise at 1 revolution every 3 seconds.

7.40 Table 6.4 shows a set of pulses needed to program a 7641 PROM. Write a program that will output that set of pulses to a latching output port.

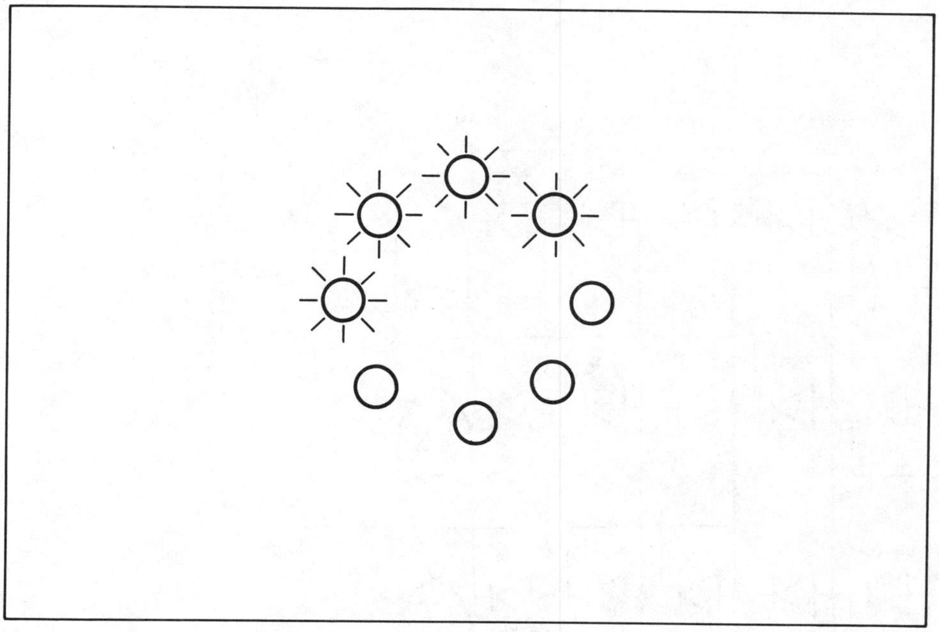

FIGURE 7.38 A circle of light emitting diodes. (Problems 7.37, 7.38, 7.39)

7.41 Modify the program of Problem 7.40 such that the program will look at a byte in memory and output fusing pulses only for those bits to be programmed as zeros.

7.42 Figure 7.39 is a set of LEDS connected to simulate a railroad track. Using the output circuits of Figure 7.40, write a program that will simulate the train by causing four LEDS to be lit. The set of four are to move clockwise around the track at 1 revolution every 3 seconds.

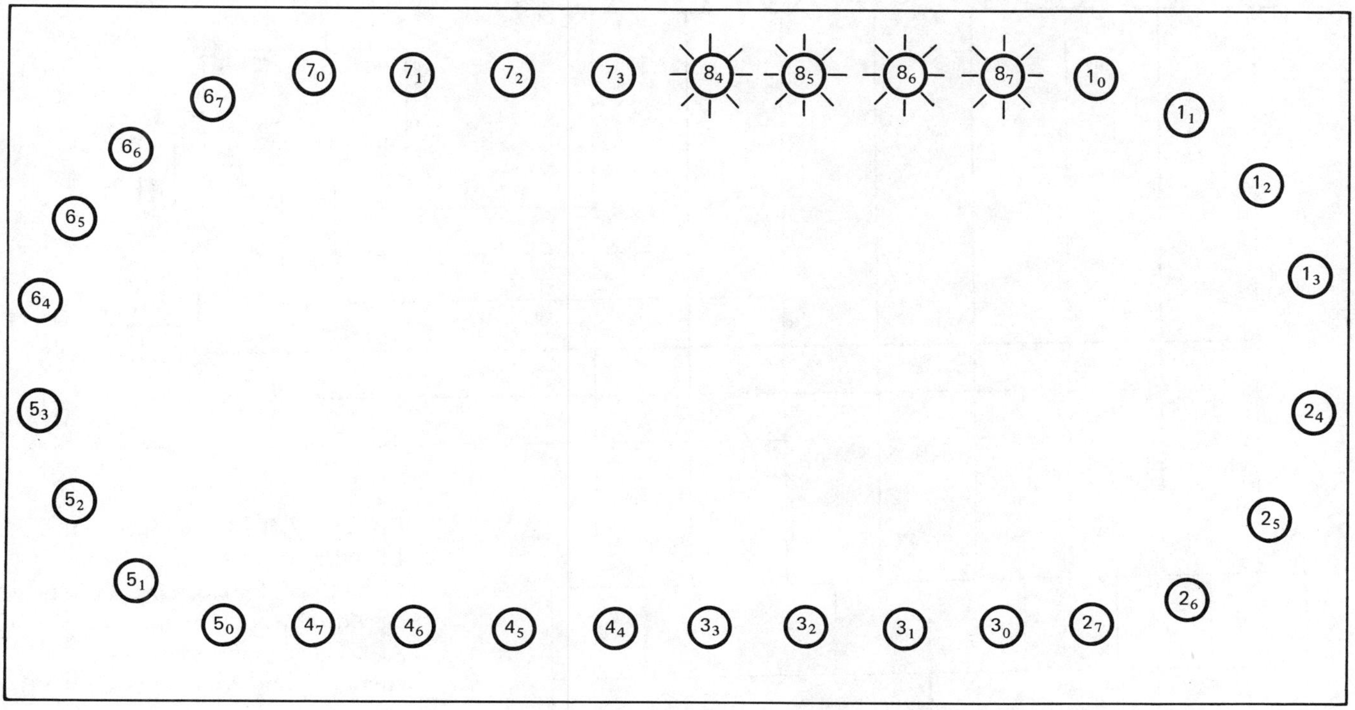

FIGURE 7.39 Model railway simulated with LEDS. (Problem 7.42)

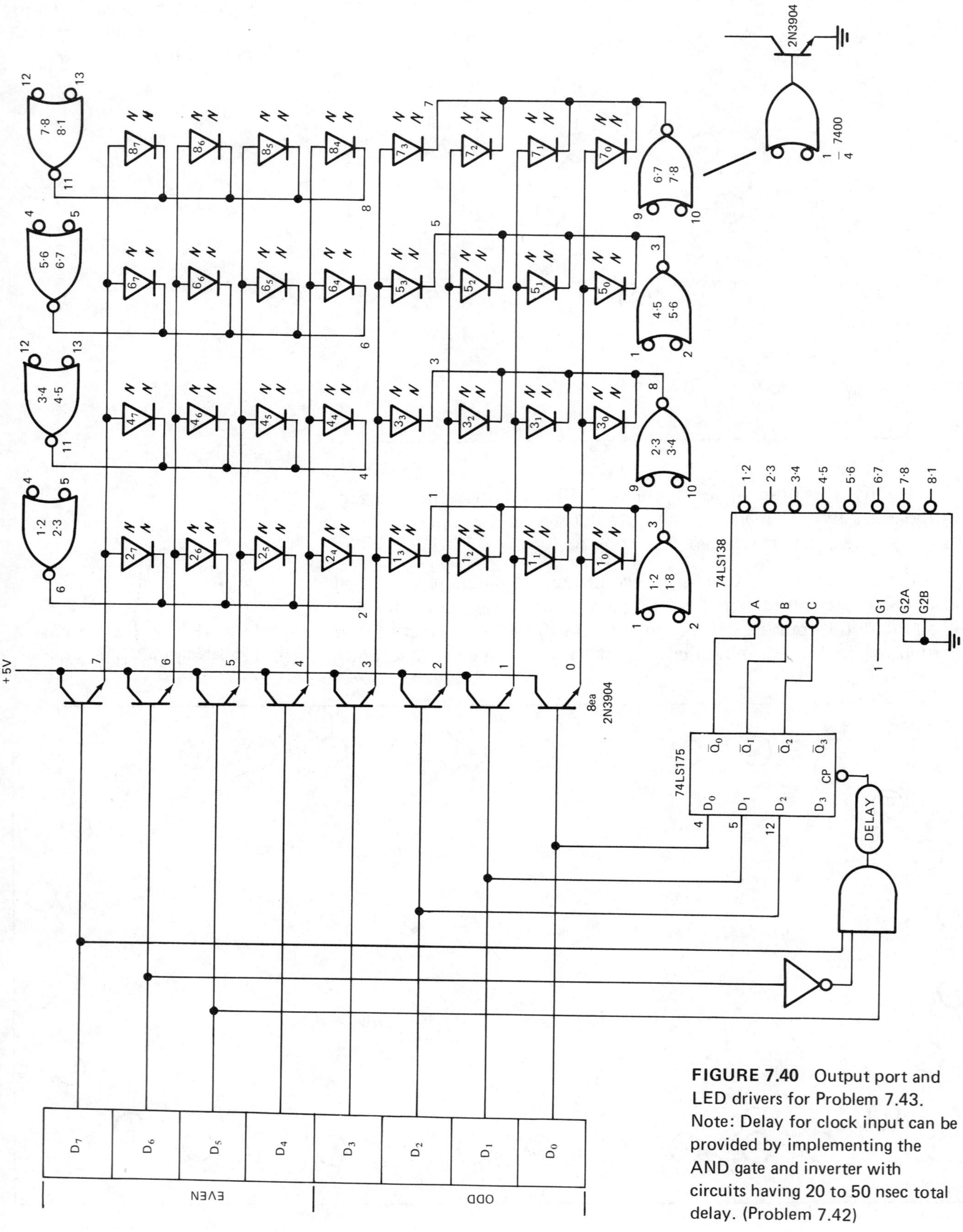

FIGURE 7.40 Output port and LED drivers for Problem 7.43. Note: Delay for clock input can be provided by implementing the AND gate and inverter with circuits having 20 to 50 nsec total delay. (Problem 7.42)

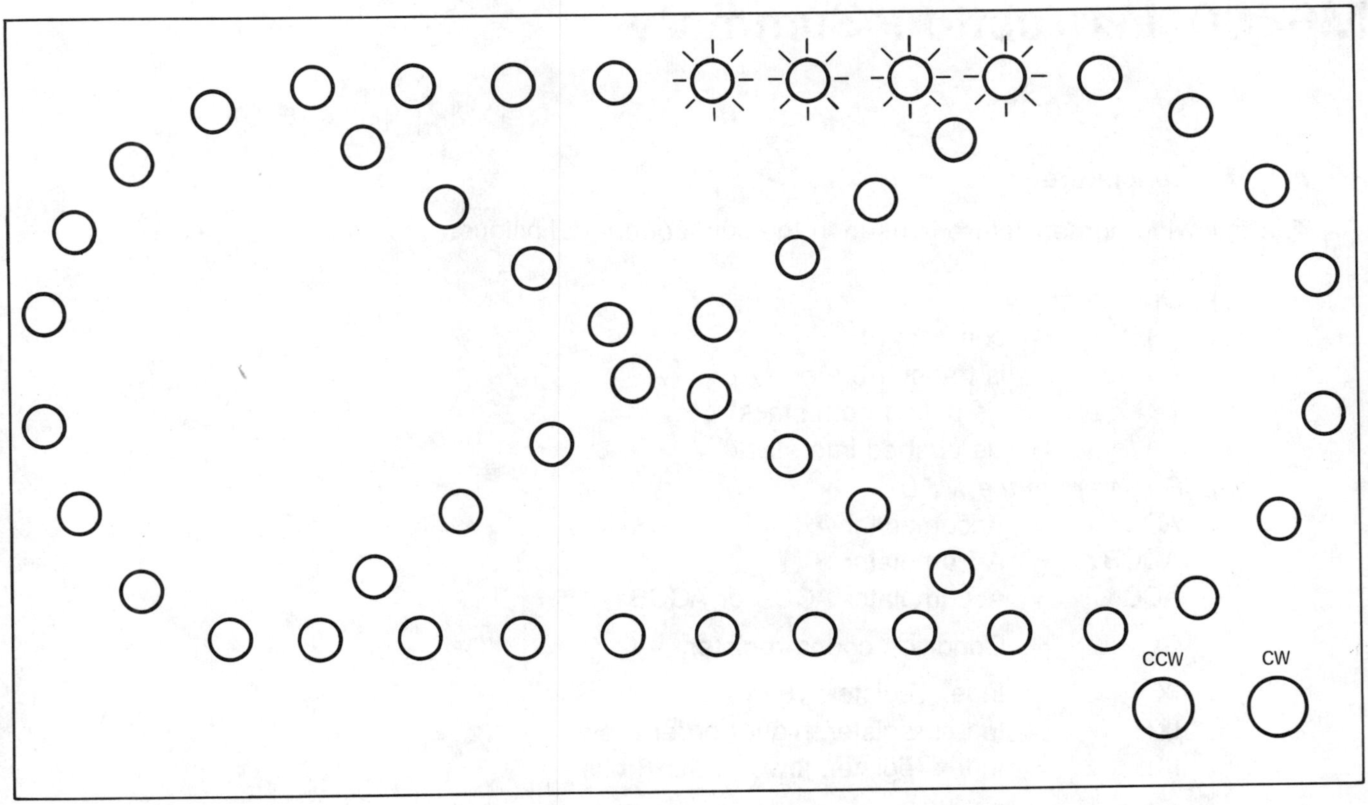

FIGURE 7.41 Simulated model railway with crossovers for changing direction. (Problem 7.44)

7.43 Revise the program of Problem 7.42 to have the train move counter clockwise around the track at 1 revolution every 5 seconds.

7.44 Figure 7.41 is a simulated railway with provisions for changing directions. Expand the hardware and software developed in Problems 7.42 and 7.43 to permit a change in direction by depressing the CW or CCW pushbutton.

M6800 Instruction Summary*

A.1 Nomenclature

The following nomenclature is used in the subsequent definitions.

(a) *Operators*

( )	=	contents of
←	=	is transferred to
↑	=	"is pulled from stack"
↓	=	"is pushed into stack"

(b) *Registers in the MPU*

ACCA	=	Accumulator A
ACCB	=	Accumulator B
ACCX	=	Accumulator ACCA or ACCB
CC	=	Condition codes register
IX	=	Index register, 16 bits
IXH	=	Index register, higher order 8 bits
IXL	=	Index register, lower order 8 bits
PC	=	Program counter, 16 bits
PCH	=	Program counter, higher order 8 bits
PCL	=	Program counter, lower order 8 bits
SP	=	Stack pointer
SPH	=	Stack pointer high
SPL	=	Stack pointer low

(c) *Memory and Addressing*

M	=	A memory location (one byte)
M +1	=	The byte of memory at 0001 plus the address of the memory location indicated by "M."
Rel	=	Relative address (i.e. the two's complement number stored in the second byte of machine code corresponding to a branch instruction).

(d) *Bits 0 thru 5 of the Condition Codes Register*

C	=	Carry — borrow	bit — 0
V	=	Two's complement overflow indicator	bit — 1
Z	=	Zero indicator	bit — 2
N	=	Negative indicator	bit — 3
I	=	Interrupt mask	bit — 4
H	=	Half carry	bit — 5

*(Courtesy of Motorola, Inc.)

Add Accumulator B to Accumulator A **ABA**

Operation: ACCA ← (ACCA) + (ACCB)

Description: Adds the contents of ACCB to the contents of ACCA and places the result in ACCA.

Condition Codes:
- H: Set if there was a carry from bit 3; cleared otherwise.
- I: Not affected.
- N: Set if most significant bit of the result is set; cleared otherwise.
- Z: Set if all bits of the result are cleared; cleared otherwise.
- V: Set if there was two's complement overflow as a result of the operation; cleared otherwise.
- C: Set if there was a carry from the most significant bit of the result; cleared otherwise.

Addressing Modes, Execution Time, and Machine Code (hexadecimal):

Addressing Modes	Execution Time (No. of cycles)	Number of bytes of machine code	Coding of First (or only) byte of machine code HEX.
Inherent	2	1	1B

ADC

Add with Carry

Operation: ACCX ← (ACCX) + (M) + (C)

Description: Adds the contents of the C bit to the sum of the contents of ACCX and M, and places the result in ACCX.

Condition Codes:
- H Set if there was a carry from bit 3; cleared otherwise.
- I: Not affected.
- N: Set if most significant bit of the result is set; cleared otherwise.
- Z: Set if all bits of the result are cleared; cleared otherwise.
- V: Set if there was two's complement overflow as a result of the operation; cleared otherwise.
- C: Set if there was a carry from the most significant bit of the result; cleared otherwise.

Addressing Modes, Execution Time, and Machine Code (hexadecimal):

(DUAL OPERAND)

Addressing Modes	**Execution Time (No. of cycles)**	**Number of bytes of machine code**	**Coding of First (or only) byte of machine code**
			HEX.
A IMM	2	2	89
A DIR	3	2	99
A EXT	4	3	B9
A IND	5	2	A9
B IMM	2	2	C9
B DIR	3	2	D9
B EXT	4	3	F9
B IND	5	2	E9

Add Without Carry

ADD

Operation: ACCX ← (ACCX) + (M)

Description: Adds the contents of ACCX and the contents of M and places the result in ACCX.

Condition Codes:
- H: Set if there was a carry from bit 3; cleared otherwise.
- I: Not affected.
- N: Set if most significant bit of the result is set; cleared otherwise.
- Z: Set if all bits of the result are cleared; cleared otherwise.
- V: Set if there was two's complement overflow as a result of the operation; cleared otherwise.
- C: Set if there was a carry from the most significant bit of the result; cleared otherwise.

Addressing Modes, Execution Time, and Machine Code (hexadecimal):
(DUAL OPERAND)

Addressing Modes	Execution Time (No. of cycles)	Number of bytes of machine code	Coding of First (or only) byte of machine code HEX.
A IMM	2	2	8B
A DIR	3	2	9B
A EXT	4	3	BB
A IND	5	2	AB
B IMM	2	2	CB
B DIR	3	2	DB
B EXT	4	3	FB
B IND	5	2	EB

AND

Logical AND

Operation: ACCX ← (ACCX) · (M)

Description: Performs logical "AND" between the contents of ACCX and the contents of M and places the result in ACCX. (Each bit of ACCX after the operation will be the logical "AND" of the corresponding bits of M and of ACCX before the operation.)

Condition Codes:
- H: Not affected.
- I: Not affected.
- N: Set if most significant bit of the result is set; cleared otherwise.
- Z: Set if all bits of the result are cleared; cleared otherwise.
- V: Cleared.
- C: Not affected.

Addressing Modes, Execution Time, and Machine Code (hexadecimal):

Addressing Modes	Execution Time (No. of cycles)	Number of bytes of machine code	Coding of First (or only) byte of machine code HEX.
A IMM	2	2	84
A DIR	3	2	94
A EXT	4	3	B4
A IND	5	2	A4
B IMM	2	2	C4
B DIR	3	2	D4
B EXT	4	3	F4
B IND	5	2	E4

Arithmetic Shift Left **ASL**

Operation:

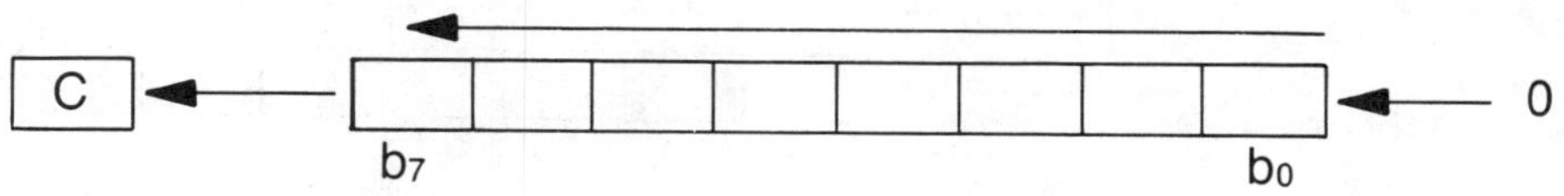

Description: Shifts all bits of the ACCX or M one place to the left. Bit 0 is loaded with a zero. The C bit is loaded from the most significant bit of ACCX or M.

Condition Codes:
- H: Not affected.
- I: Not affected.
- N: Set if most significant bit of the result is set; cleared otherwise.
- Z: Set if all bits of the result are cleared; cleared otherwise.
- V: Set if, after the completion of the shift operation, EITHER (N is set and C is cleared) OR (N is cleared and C is set); cleared otherwise.
- C: Set if, before the operation, the most significant bit of the ACCX or M was set; cleared otherwise.

Addressing Modes, Execution Time, and Machine Code (hexadecimal):

Addressing Modes	Execution Time (No. of cycles)	Number of bytes of machine code	Coding of First (or only) byte of machine code HEX.
A	2	1	48
B	2	1	58
EXT	6	3	78
IND	7	2	68

ASR

Arithmetic Shift Right

Operation:

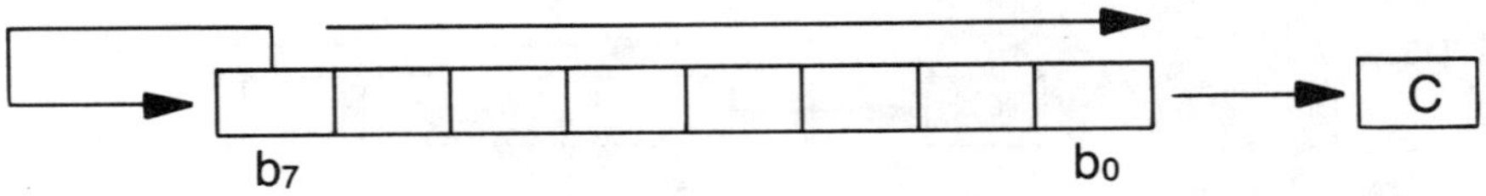

Description: Shifts all bits of ACCX or M one place to the right. Bit 7 is held constant. Bit 0 is loaded into the C bit.

Condition Codes:
- H: Not affected.
- I: Not affected.
- N: Set if the most significant bit of the result is set; cleared otherwise.
- Z: Set if all bits of the result are cleared; cleared otherwise.
- V: Set if, after the completion of the shift operation, EITHER (N is set and C is cleared) OR (N is cleared and C is set); cleared otherwise.
- C: Set if, before the operation, the least significant bit of the ACCX or M was set; cleared otherwise.

Addressing Modes, Execution Time, and Machine Code (hexadecimal):

Addressing Modes	Execution Time (No. of cycles)	Number of bytes of machine code	Coding of First (or only) byte of machine code
			HEX.
A	2	1	47
B	2	1	57
EXT	6	3	77
IND	7	2	67

Branch if Carry Clear **BCC**

Operation: PC ← (PC) + 0002 + Rel if (C)=0

Description: Tests the state of the C bit and causes a branch if C is clear.

See BRA instruction for further details of the execution of the branch.

Condition Codes: Not affected.

Addressing Modes, Execution Time, and Machine Code (hexadecimal):

Addressing Modes	Execution Time (No. of cycles)	Number of bytes of machine code	Coding of First (or only) byte of machine code HEX.
REL	4	2	24

Branch if Carry Set **BCS**

Operation: PC ← (PC) + 0002 + Rel if (C)=1

Description: Tests the state of the C bit and causes a branch if C is set.

See BRA instruction for further details of the execution of the branch.

Condition Codes: Not affected.

Addressing Modes, Execution Time, and Machine Code (hexadecimal):

Addressing Modes	Execution Time (No. of cycles)	Number of bytes of machine code	Coding of First (or only) byte of machine code HEX.
REL	4	2	25

BEQ

Branch if Equal

Operation: PC ← (PC) + 0002 + Rel if (Z)=1

Description: Tests the state of the Z bit and causes a branch if the Z bit is set.

See BRA instruction for further details of the execution of the branch.

Condition Codes: Not affected.

Addressing Modes, Execution Time, and Machine Code (hexadecimal):

Addressing Modes	Execution Time (No. of cycles)	Number of bytes of machine code	Coding of First (or only) byte of machine code HEX.
REL	4	2	27

BGE

Branch if Greater than or Equal to Zero

Operation: PC ← (PC) + 0002 + Rel if (N) $\oplus$ (V) = 0

i.e. if (ACCX) ⩾ (M)

(Two's complement numbers)

Description: Causes a branch if (N is set and V is set) OR (N is clear and V is clear).

If the BGE instruction is executed immediately after execution of any of the instructions CBA, CMP, SBA, or SUB, the branch will occur if and only if the two's complement number represented by the minuend (i.e. ACCX) was greater than or equal to the two's complement number represented by the subtrahend (i.e. M).

See BRA instruction for details of the branch.

Condition Codes: Not affected.

Addressing Modes, Execution Time, and Machine Code (hexadecimal):

Addressing Modes	Execution Time (No. of cycles)	Number of bytes of machine code	Coding of First (or only) byte of machine code HEX.
REL	4	2	2C

Branch if Greater than Zero **BGT**

Operation: $PC \leftarrow (PC) + 0002 + Rel$ if $(Z) \odot [(N) \oplus (V)] = 0$
i.e. if $(ACCX) > (M)$
(two's complement numbers)

Description: Causes a branch if [Z is clear] AND [(N is set and V is set) OR (N is clear and V is clear)].

If the BGT instruction is executed immediately after execution of any of the instructions CBA, CMP, SBA, or SUB, the branch will occur if and only if the two's complement number represented by the minuend (i.e. ACCX) was greater than the two's complement number represented by the subtrahend (i.e. M).

See BRA instruction for details of the branch.

Condition Codes: Not affected.

Addressing Modes, Execution Time, and Machine Code (hexadecimal):

Addressing Modes	Execution Time (No. of cycles)	Number of bytes of machine code	Coding of First (or only) byte of machine code
			HEX.
REL	4	2	2E

BHI

Branch if Higher

Operation: PC ← (PC) + 0002 + Rel if (C) · (Z)=0
i.e. if (ACCX) > (M)
(unsigned binary numbers)

Description: Causes a branch if (C is clear) AND (Z is clear).

If the BHI instruction is executed immediately after execution of any of the instructions CBA, CMP, SBA, or SUB, the branch will occur if and only if the unsigned binary number represented by the minuend (i.e. ACCX) was greater than the unsigned binary number represented by the subtrahend (i.e. M).

See BRA instruction for details of the execution of the branch.

Condition Codes: Not affected.

Addressing Modes, Execution Time, and Machine Code (hexadecimal):

Addressing Modes	Execution Time (No. of cycles)	Number of bytes of machine code	Coding of First (or only) byte of machine code
			HEX.
REL	4	2	22

Bit Test

BIT

Operation: (ACCX) · (M)

Description: Performs the logical "AND" comparison of the contents of ACCX and the contents of M and modifies condition codes accordingly. Neither the contents of ACCX or M operands are affected. (Each bit of the result of the "AND" would be the logical "AND" of the corresponding bits of M and ACCX.)

Condition Codes:
- H: Not affected.
- I: Not affected.
- N: Set if the most significant bit of the result of the "AND" would be set; cleared otherwise.
- Z: Set if all bits of the result of the "AND" would be cleared; cleared otherwise.
- V: Cleared.
- C: Not affected.

Addressing Modes, Execution Time, and Machine Code (hexadecimal/ octal/ decimal):

Addressing Modes	Execution Time (No. of cycles)	Number of bytes of machine code	Coding of First (or only) byte of machine code
			HEX.
A IMM	2	2	85
A DIR	3	2	95
A EXT	4	3	B5
A IND	5	2	A5
B IMM	2	2	C5
B DIR	3	2	D5
B EXT	4	3	F5
B IND	5	2	E5

BLE

Branch if Less than or Equal to Zero

Operation: PC ← (PC) + 0002 + Rel if $(Z) \odot [(N) \oplus (V)] = 1$

i.e. if (ACCX) ≤ (M)

(two's complement numbers)

Description: Causes a branch if [Z is set] OR [(N is set and V is clear) OR (N is clear and V is set)].

If the BLE instruction is executed immediately after execution of any of the instructions CBA, CMP, SBA, or SUB, the branch will occur if and only if the two's complement number represented by the minuend (i.e. ACCX) was less then or equal to the two's complement number represented by the subtrahend (i.e. M).

See BRA instruction for details of the branch.

Condition Codes: Not affected.

Addressing Modes, Execution Time, and Machine Code (hexadecimal):

Addressing Modes	Execution Time (No. of cycles)	Number of bytes of machine code	Coding of First (or only) byte of machine code
			HEX.
REL	4	2	2F

BLS

Branch if Lower or Same

Operation: PC ← (PC) + 0002 + Rel if $(C) \odot (Z) = 1$

i.e. if (ACCX) ≤ (M)

(unsigned binary numbers)

Description: Causes a branch if (C is set) OR (Z is set).

If the BLS instruction is executed immediately after execution of any of the instructions CBA, CMP, SBA, or SUB, the branch will occur if and only if the unsigned binary number represented by the minuend (i.e. ACCX) was less than or equal to the unsigned binary number represented by the subtrahend (i.e. M).

See BRA instruction for details of the execution of the branch.

Condition Codes: Not affected.

Addressing Modes, Execution Time, and Machine Code (hexadecimal):

Addressing Modes	Execution Time (No. of cycles)	Number of bytes of machine code	Coding of First (or only) byte of machine code
			HEX.
REL	4	2	23

Branch if Less than Zero — BLT

Operation: $PC \leftarrow (PC) + 0002 + Rel$ if $(N) \oplus (V) = 1$

i.e. if $(ACCX) < (M)$

(two's complement numbers)

Description: Causes a branch if (N is set and V is clear) OR (N is clear and V is set).

If the BLT instruction is executed immediately after execution of any of the instructions CBA, CMP, SBA, or SUB, the branch will occur if and only if the two's complement number represented by the minuend (i.e. ACCX) was less than the two's complement number represented by the subtrahend (i.e. M).

See BRA instruction for details of the branch.

Condition Codes: Not affected.

Addressing Modes, Execution Time, and Machine Code (hexadecimal):

Addressing Modes	Execution Time (No. of cycles)	Number of bytes of machine code	Coding of First (or only) byte of machine code
			HEX.
REL	4	2	2D

Branch if Minus — BMI

Operation: $PC \leftarrow (PC) + 0002 + Rel$ if $(N) = 1$

Description: Tests the state of the N bit and causes a branch if N is set.

See BRA instruction for details of the execution of the branch.

Condition Codes: Not affected.

Addressing Modes, Execution Time, and Machine Code (hexadecimal):

Addressing Modes	Execution Time (No. of cycles)	Number of bytes of machine code	Coding of First (or only) byte of machine code
			HEX.
REL	4	2	2B

BNE

Branch if Not Equal

Operation: PC ← (PC) + 0002 + Rel if (Z) = 0

Description: Tests the state of the Z bit and causes a branch if the Z bit is clear. See BRA instruction for details of the execution of the branch.

Condition Codes: Not affected.

Addressing Modes, Execution Time, and Machine Code (hexadecimal):

Addressing Modes	Execution Time (No. of cycles)	Number of bytes of machine code	Coding of First (or only) byte of machine code HEX.
REL	4	2	26

BPL

Branch if Plus

Operation: PC ← (PC) + 0002 + Rel if (N) =0

Description: Tests the state of the N bit and causes a branch if N is clear. See BRA instruction for details of the execution of the branch.

Condition Codes: Not affected.

Addressing Modes, Execution Time, and Machine Code (hexadecimal):

Addressing Modes	Execution Time (No. of cycles)	Number of bytes of machine code	Coding of First (or only) byte of machine code HEX.
REL	4	2	2A

Branch Always **BRA**

Operation: PC ← (PC) + 0002 + Rel

Description: Unconditional branch to the address given by the foregoing formula, in which R is the relative address stored as a two's complement number in the second byte of machine code corresponding to the branch instruction.

Note: The source program specifies the destination of any branch instruction by its absolute address, either as a numerical value or as a symbol or expression which can be numerically evaluated by the assembler. The assembler obtains the relative address R from the absolute address and the current value of the program counter PC.

Condition Codes: Not affected.

Addressing Modes, Execution Time, and Machine Code (hexadecimal):

Addressing Modes	Execution Time (No. of cycles)	Number of bytes of machine code	Coding of First (or only) byte of machine code
			HEX.
REL	4	2	20

BSR

Branch to Subroutine

Operation: PC ← (PC) + 0002
↓ (PCL)
SP ← (SP) − 0001
↓ (PCH)
SP ← (SP) − 0001
PC ← (PC) + Rel

Description: The program counter is incremented by 2. The less significant byte of the contents of the program counter is pushed into the stack. The stack pointer is then decremented (by 1). The more significant byte of the contents of the program counter is then pushed into the stack. The stack pointer is again decremented (by 1). A branch then occurs to the location specified by the program.

See BRA instruction for details of the execution of the branch.

Condition Codes: Not affected.

Addressing Modes, Execution Time, and Machine Code (hexadecimal):

Addressing Modes	Execution Time (No. of cycles)	Number of bytes of machine code	Coding of First (or only) byte of machine code HEX.
REL	8	2	8D

BVC

Branch if Overflow Clear

Operation: PC ← (PC) + 0002 + Rel if (V) = 0

Description: Tests the state of the V bit and causes a branch if the V bit is clear.

See BRA instruction for details of the execution of the branch.

Condition Codes: Not affected.

Addressing Modes, Execution Time, and Machine Code (hexadecimal):

Addressing Modes	Execution Time (No. of cycles)	Number of bytes of machine code	Coding of First (or only) byte of machine code HEX.
REL	4	2	28

Branch if Overflow Set **BVS**

Operation: PC ← (PC) + 0002 + Rel if (V) =1

Description: Tests the state of the V bit and causes a branch if the V bit is set.

See BRA instruction for details of the execution of the branch.

Condition Codes: Not affected.

Addressing Modes, Execution Time, and Machine Code (hexadecimal):

Addressing Modes	Execution Time (No. of cycles)	Number of bytes of machine code	Coding of First (or only) byte of machine code
			HEX.
REL	4	2	29

Compare Accumulators **CBA**

Operation: (ACCA) − (ACCB)

Description: Compares the contents of ACCA and the contents of ACCB and sets the condition codes, which may be used for arithmetic and logical conditional branches. Both operands are unaffected.

Condition Codes:
H: Not affected.
I: Not affected.
N: Set if the most significant bit of the result of the subtraction would be set; cleared otherwise.
Z: Set if all bits of the result of the subtraction would be cleared; cleared otherwise.
V: Set if the subtraction would cause two's complement overflow; cleared otherwise.
C: Set if the subtraction would require a borrow into the most significant bit of the result; clear otherwise.

Addressing Modes, Execution Time, and Machine Code (hexadecimal):

Addressing Modes	Execution Time (No. of cycles)	Number of bytes of machine code	Coding of First (or only) byte of machine code
			HEX.
INHERENT	2	1	11

CLC

Clear Carry

Operation: C bit ← 0

Description: Clears the carry bit in the processor condition codes register.

Condition Codes:
H: Not affected.
I: Not affected.
N: Not affected.
Z: Not affected.
V: Not affected.
C: Cleared

Addressing Modes, Execution Time, and Machine Code (hexadecimal):

Addressing Modes	Execution Time (No. of cycles)	Number of bytes of machine code	Coding of First (or only) byte of machine code HEX.
INHERENT	2	1	0C

CLI

Clear Interrupt Mask

Operation: I bit ← 0

Description: Clears the interrupt mask bit in the processor condition codes register. This enables the microprocessor to service an interrupt from a peripheral device if signalled by a high state of the "Interrupt Request" control input.

Condition Codes:
H: Not affected.
I: Cleared.
N: Not affected.
Z: Not affected.
V: Not affected.
C: Not affected.

Addressing Modes, Execution Time, and Machine Code (hexadecimal):

Addressing Modes	Execution Time (No. of cycles)	Number of bytes of machine code	Coding of First (or only) byte of machine code HEX.
INHERENT	2	1	0E

Clear **CLR**

Operation: ACCX ← 00
or: M ← 00

Description: The contents of ACCX or M are replaced with zeros.

Condition Codes:
H: Not affected.
I: Not affected.
N: Cleared
Z: Set
V: Cleared
C: Cleared

Addressing Modes, Execution Time, and Machine Code (hexadecimal):

Addressing Modes	Execution Time (No. of cycles)	Number of bytes of machine code	Coding of First (or only) byte of machine code HEX.
A	2	1	4F
B	2	1	5F
EXT	6	3	7F
IND	7	2	6F

Clear Two's Complement Overflow Bit **CLV**

Operation: V bit ← 0

Description: Clears the two's complement overflow bit in the processor condition codes register.

Condition Codes:
H: Not affected.
I: Not affected.
N: Not affected.
Z: Not affected.
V: Cleared.
C: Not affected.

Addressing Modes, Execution Time, and Machine Code (hexadecimal):

Addressing Modes	Execution Time (No. of cycles)	Number of bytes of machine code	Coding of First (or only) byte of machine code HEX.
INHERENT	2	1	0A

CMP

Compare

Operation: (ACCX) − (M)

Description: Compares the contents of ACCX and the contents of M and determines the condition codes, which may be used subsequently for controlling conditional branching. Both operands are unaffected.

Condition Codes:
- H: Not affected.
- I: Not affected.
- N: Set if the most significant bit of the result of the subtraction would be set; cleared otherwise.
- Z: Set if all bits of the result of the subtraction would be cleared; cleared otherwise.
- V: Set if the subtraction would cause two's complement overflow; cleared otherwise.
- C: Carry is set if the absolute value of the contents of memory is larger than the absolute value of the accumulator; reset otherwise.

Addressing Modes, Execution Time, and Machine Code (hexadecimal):

(DUAL OPERAND)

Addressing Modes	Execution Time (No. of cycles)	Number of bytes of machine code	Coding of First (or only) byte of machine code HEX.
A IMM	2	2	81
A DIR	3	2	91
A EXT	4	3	B1
A IND	5	2	A1
B IMM	2	2	C1
B DIR	3	2	D1
B EXT	4	3	F1
B IND	5	2	E1

Complement **COM**

Operation: ACCX ← ≈ (ACCX) = FF − (ACCX)
or: M ← ≈ (M) = FF − (M)

Description: Replaces the contents of ACCX or M with its one's complement. (Each bit of the contents of ACCX or M is replaced with the complement of that bit.)

Condition Codes:
- H: Not affected.
- I: Not affected.
- N: Set if most significant bit of the result is set; cleared otherwise.
- Z: Set if all bits of the result are cleared; cleared otherwise.
- V: Cleared.
- C: Set.

Addressing Modes, Execution Time, and Machine Code (hexadecimal):

Addressing Modes	Execution Time (No. of cycles)	Number of bytes of machine code	Coding of First (or only) byte of machine code HEX.
A	2	1	43
B	2	1	53
EXT	6	3	73
IND	7	2	63

CPX

Compare Index Register

Operation: (IXL) − (M+1)
(IXH) − (M)

Description: The more significant byte of the contents of the index register is compared with the contents of the byte of memory at the address specified by the program. The less significant byte of the contents of the index register is compared with the contents of the next byte of memory, at one plus the address specified by the program. The Z bit is set or reset according to the results of these comparisons, and may be used subsequently for conditional branching.

The N and V bits, though determined by this operation, are not intended for conditional branching.

The C bit is not affected by this operation.

Condition Codes:
- H: Not affected.
- I: Not affected.
- N: Set if the most significant bit of the result of the subtraction from the more significant byte of the index register would be set; cleared otherwise.
- Z: Set if all bits of the results of both subtractions would be cleared; cleared otherwise.
- V: Set if the subtraction from the more significant byte of the index register would cause two's complement overflow; cleared otherwise.
- C: Not affected.

Addressing Modes, Execution Time, and Machine Code (hexadecimal):

Addressing Modes	**Execution Time (No. of cycles)**	**Number of bytes of machine code**	**Coding of First (or only) byte of machine code**
			HEX.
IMM	3	3	8C
DIR	4	2	9C
EXT	5	3	BC
IND	6	2	AC

Decimal Adjust ACCA

DAA

Operation: Adds hexadecimal numbers 00, 06, 60, or 66 to ACCA, and may also set the carry bit, as indicated in the following table:

State of C-bit before DAA (Col. 1)	Upper Half-byte (bits 4-7) (Col. 2)	Initial Half-carry H-bit (Col.3)	Lower to ACCA (bits 0-3) (Col. 4)	Number Added after by DAA (Col. 5)	State of C-bit DAA (Col. 6)
0	0-9	0	0-9	00	0
0	0-8	0	A-F	06	0
0	0-9	1	0-3	06	0
0	A-F	0	0-9	60	1
0	9-F	0	A-F	66	1
0	A-F	1	0-3	66	1
1	0-2	0	0-9	60	1
1	0-2	0	A-F	66	1
1	0-3	1	0-3	66	1

Note: Columns (1) through (4) of the above table represent all possible cases which can result from any of the operations ABA, ADD, or ADC, with initial carry either set or clear, applied to two binary-coded-decimal operands. The table shows hexadecimal values.

Description: If the contents of ACCA and the state of the carry-borrow bit C and the half-carry bit H are all the result of applying any of the operations ABA, ADD, or ADC to binary-coded-decimal operands, with or without an initial carry, the DAA operation will function as follows.

Subject to the above condition, the DAA operation will adjust the contents of ACCA and the C bit to represent the correct binary-coded-decimal sum and the correct state of the carry.

Condition Codes:
- H: Not affected.
- I: Not affected.
- N: Set if most significant bit of the result is set; cleared otherwise.
- Z: Set if all bits of the result are cleared; cleared otherwise.
- V: Not defined.
- C: Set or reset according to the same rule as if the DAA and an immediately preceding ABA, ADD, or ADC were replaced by a hypothetical binary-coded-decimal addition.

Addressing Modes, Execution Time, and Machine Code (hexadecimal):

Addressing Modes	Execution Time (No. of cycles)	Number of bytes of machine code	Coding of First (or only) byte of machine code HEX.
INHERENT	2	1	19

DEC

Decrement

Operation: ACCX ← (ACCX) − 01

or: M ← (M) − 01

Description: Subtract one from the contents of ACCX or M.

The N, Z, and V condition codes are set or reset according to the results of this operation.

The C bit is not affected by the operation.

Condition Codes:
- H: Not affected.
- I: Not affected.
- N: Set if most significant bit of the result is set; cleared otherwise.
- Z: Set if all bits of the result are cleared; cleared otherwise.
- V: Set if there was two's complement overflow as a result of the operation; cleared otherwise. Two's complement overflow occurs if and only if (ACCX) or (M) was 80 before the operation.
- C: Not affected.

Addressing Modes, Execution Time, and Machine Code (hexadecimal):

Addressing Modes	Execution Time (No. of cycles)	Number of bytes of machine code	Coding of First (or only) byte of machine code HEX.
A	2	1	4A
B	2	1	5A
EXT	6	3	7A
IND	7	2	6A

Exclusive OR **EOR**

Operation: ACCX ← (ACCX) $\oplus$ (M)

Description: Perform logical "EXCLUSIVE OR" between the contents of ACCX and the contents of M, and place the result in ACCX. (Each bit of ACCX after the operation will be the logical "EXCLUSIVE OR" of the corresponding bit of M and ACCX before the operation.)

Condition Codes:
- H: Not affected.
- I: Not affected.
- N: Set if most significant bit of the result is set; cleared otherwise.
- Z: Set if all bits of the result are cleared; cleared otherwise.
- V: Cleared
- C: Not affected.

Addressing Modes, Execution Time, and Machine Code (hexadecimal):

Addressing Modes	Execution Time (No. of cycles)	Number of bytes of machine code	Coding of First (or only) byte of machine code HEX.
A IMM	2	2	88
A DIR	3	2	98
A EXT	4	3	B8
A IND	5	2	A8
B IMM	2	2	C8
B DIR	3	2	D8
B EXT	4	3	F8
B IND	5	2	E8

INC

Increment

Operation: ACCX ← (ACCX) + 01
or: M ← (M) + 01

Description: Add one to the contents of ACCX or M.

The N, Z, and V condition codes are set or reset according to the results of this operation.

The C bit is not affected by the operation.

Condition Codes:
- H: Not affected.
- I: Not affected.
- N: Set if most significant bit of the result is set; cleared otherwise.
- Z: Set if all bits of the result are cleared; cleared otherwise.
- V: Set if there was two's complement overflow as a result of the operation; cleared otherwise. Two's complement overflow will occur if and only if (ACCX) or (M) was 7F before the operation.
- C: Not affected.

Addressing Modes, Execution Time, and Machine Code (hexadecimal):

Addressing Modes	Execution Time (No. of cycles)	Number of bytes of machine code	Coding of First (or only) byte of machine code HEX.
A	2	1	4C
B	2	1	5C
EXT	6	3	7C
IND	7	2	6C

INS

Increment Stack Pointer

Operation: SP ← (SP) + 0001

Description: Add one to the stack pointer.

Condition Codes: Not affected.

Addressing Modes, Execution Time, and Machine Code (hexadecimal):

Addressing Modes	Execution Time (No. of cycles)	Number of bytes of machine code	Coding of First (or only) byte of machine code HEX.
INHERENT	4	1	31

Increment Index Register

INX

Operation: IX ← (IX) + 0001

Description: Add one to the index register.

Only the Z bit is set or reset according to the result of this operation.

Condition Codes:
- H: Not affected.
- I: Not affected.
- N: Not affected.
- Z: Set if all 16 bits of the result are cleared; cleared otherwise.
- V: Not affected.
- C: Not affected.

Addressing Modes, Execution Time, and Machine Code (hexadecimal):

Addressing Modes	Execution Time (No. of cycles)	Number of bytes of machine code	Coding of First (or only) byte of machine code
			HEX.
INHERENT	4	1	08

Jump

JMP

Operation: PC ← numerical address

Description: A jump occurs to the instruction stored at the numerical address. The numerical address is obtained according to the rules for EXTended or INDexed addressing.

Condition Codes: Not affected.

Addressing Modes, Execution Time, and Machine Code (hexadecimal):

Addressing Modes	Execution Time (No. of cycles)	Number of bytes of machine code	Coding of First (or only) byte of machine code
			HEX.
EXT	3	3	7E
IND	4	2	6E

JSR

Jump to Subroutine

Operation:

Either:	PC ← (PC) + 0003 (for EXTended addressing)
or:	PC ← (PC) + 0002 (for INDexed addressing)
Then:	↓ (PCL)
	SP ← (SP) − 0001
	↓ (PCH)
	SP ← (SP) − 0001
	PC ← numerical address

Description: The program counter is incremented by 3 or by 2, depending on the addressing mode, and is then pushed onto the stack, eight bits at a time. The stack pointer points to the next empty location in the stack. A jump occurs to the instruction stored at the numerical address. The numerical address is obtained according to the rules for EXTended or INDexed addressing.

Condition Codes: Not affected.

Addressing Modes, Execution Time, and Machine Code (hexadecimal):

Addressing Modes	Execution Time (No. of cycles)	Number of bytes of machine code	Coding of First (or only) byte of machine code HEX.
EXT	9	3	BD
IND	8	2	AD

Load Accumulator — LDA

Operation: ACCX ← (M)

Description: Loads the contents of memory into the accumulator. The condition codes are set according to the data.

Condition Codes:
- H: Not affected.
- I: Not affected.
- N: Set if most significant bit of the result is set; cleared otherwise.
- Z: Set if all bits of the result are cleared; cleared otherwise.
- V: Cleared.
- C: Not affected.

Addressing Modes, Execution Time, and Machine Code (hexadecimal):

(DUAL OPERAND)

Addressing Modes	Execution Time (No. of cycles)	Number of bytes of machine code	Coding of First (or only) byte of machine code
			HEX.
A IMM	2	2	86
A DIR	3	2	96
A EXT	4	3	B6
A IND	5	2	A6
B IMM	2	2	C6
B DIR	3	2	D6
B EXT	4	3	F6
B IND	5	2	E6

LDS

Load Stack Pointer

Operation: SPH ← (M)
SPL ← (M+1)

Description: Loads the more significant byte of the stack pointer from the byte of memory at the address specified by the program, and loads the less significant byte of the stack pointer from the next byte of memory, at one plus the address specified by the program.

Condition Codes:
H: Not affected.
I: Not affected.
N: Set if the most significant bit of the stack pointer is set by the operation; cleared otherwise.
Z: Set if all bits of the stack pointer are cleared by the operation; cleared otherwise.
V: Cleared.
C: Not affected.

Addressing Modes, Execution Time, and Machine Code (hexadecimal):

Addressing Modes	Execution Time (No. of cycles)	Number of bytes of machine code	Coding of First (or only) byte of machine code HEX.
IMM	3	3	8E
DIR	4	2	9E
EXT	5	3	BE
IND	6	2	AE

Load Index Register

LDX

Operation: IXH ← (M)
IXL ← (M+1)

Description: Loads the more significant byte of the index register from the byte of memory at the address specified by the program, and loads the less significant byte of the index register from the next byte of memory, at one plus the address specified by the program.

Condition Codes:
- H: Not affected.
- I: Not affected.
- N: Set if the most significant bit of the index register is set by the operation; cleared otherwise.
- Z: Set if all bits of the index register are cleared by the operation; cleared otherwise.
- V: Cleared.
- C: Not affected.

Addressing Modes, Execution Time, and Machine Code (hexadecimal/ octal/ decimal):

Addressing Modes	**Execution Time (No. of cycles)**	**Number of bytes of machine code**	**Coding of First (or only) byte of machine code**
			HEX.
IMM	3	3	CE
DIR	4	2	DE
EXT	5	3	FE
IND	6	2	EE

LSR

Logical Shift Right

Operation:

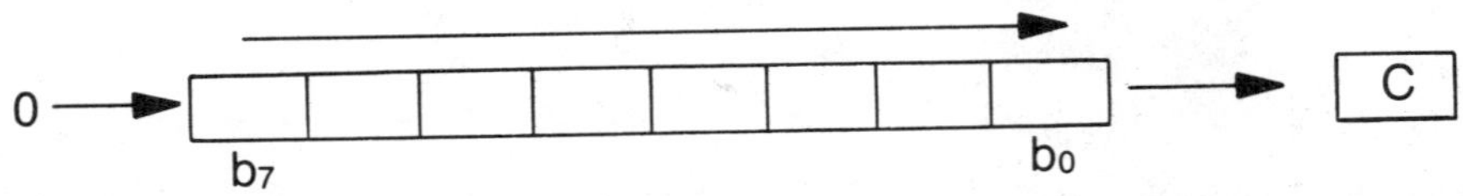

Description: Shifts all bits of ACCX or M one place to the right. Bit 7 is loaded with a zero. The C bit is loaded from the least significant bit of ACCX or M.

Condition Codes:
- H: Not affected.
- I: Not affected.
- N: Cleared.
- Z: Set if all bits of the result are cleared; cleared otherwise.
- V: Set if, after the completion of the shift operation, EITHER (N is set and C is cleared) OR (N is cleared and C is set); cleared otherwise.
- C: Set if, before the operation, the least significant bit of the ACCX or M was set; cleared otherwise.

Addressing Modes, Execution Time, and Machine Code (hexadecimal):

Addressing Modes	Execution Time (No. of cycles)	Number of bytes of machine code	Coding of First (or only) byte of machine code
			HEX.
A	2	1	44
B	2	1	54
EXT	6	3	74
IND	7	2	64

Negate

NEG

Operation: ACCX ← − (ACCX) = 00 − (ACCX)
or: M ← − (M) = 00 − (M)

Description: Replaces the contents of ACCX or M with its two's complement. Note that 80 is left unchanged.

Condition Codes:
- H: Not affected.
- I: Not affected.
- N: Set if most significant bit of the result is set; cleared otherwise.
- Z: Set if all bits of the result are cleared; cleared otherwise.
- V: Set if there would be two's complement overflow as a result of the implied subtraction from zero; this will occur if and only if the contents of ACCX or M is 80.
- C: Set if there would be a borrow in the implied subtraction from zero; the C bit will be set in all cases except when the contents of ACCX or M is 00.

Addressing Modes, Execution Time, and Machine Code (hexadecimal):

Addressing Modes	Execution Time (No. of cycles)	Number of bytes of machine code	Coding of First (or only) byte of machine code HEX.
A	2	1	40
B	2	1	50
EXT	6	3	70
IND	7	2	60

No Operation

NOP

Description: This is a single-word instruction which causes only the program counter to be incremented. No other registers are affected.

Condition Codes: Not affected.

Addressing Modes, Execution Time, and Machine Code (hexadecimal):

Addressing Modes	Execution Time (No. of cycles)	Number of bytes of machine code	Coding of First (or only) byte of machine code HEX.
INHERENT	2	1	01

ORA

Inclusive OR

Operation: ACCX ← (ACCX)⊙(M)

Description: Perform logical "OR" between the contents of ACCX and the contents of M and places the result in ACCX. (Each bit of ACCX after the operation will be the logical "OR" of the corresponding bits of M and of ACCX before the operation).

Condition Codes:
H: Not affected.
I: Not affected.
N: Set if most significant bit of the result is set; cleared otherwise.
Z: Set if all bits of the result are cleared; cleared otherwise.
V: Cleared.
C: Not affected.

Addressing Modes, Execution Time, and Machine Code (hexadecimal):
(DUAL OPERAND)

Addressing Modes	Execution Time (No. of cycles)	Number of bytes of machine code	Coding of First (or only) byte of machine code HEX.
A IMM	2	2	8A
A DIR	3	2	9A
A EXT	4	3	BA
A IND	5	2	AA
B IMM	2	2	CA
B DIR	3	2	DA
B EXT	4	3	FA
B IND	5	2	EA

Push Data Onto Stack **PSH**

Operation: ↓ (ACCX)
SP ← (SP) − 0001

Description: The contents of ACCX is stored in the stack at the address contained in the stack pointer. The stack pointer is then decremented.

Condition Codes: Not affected.

Addressing Modes, Execution Time, and Machine Code (hexadecimal):

Addressing Modes	Execution Time (No. of cycles)	Number of bytes of machine code	Coding of First (or only) byte of machine code HEX.
A	4	1	36
B	4	1	37

Pull Data from Stack **PUL**

Operation: SP ← (SP) + 0001
↑ ACCX

Description: The stack pointer is incremented. The ACCX is then loaded from the stack, from the address which is contained in the stack pointer.

Condition Codes: Not affected.

Addressing Modes, Execution Time, and Machine Code (hexadecimal):

Addressing Modes	Execution Time (No. of cycles)	Number of bytes of machine code	Coding of First (or only) byte of machine code HEX.
A	4	1	32
B	4	1	33

ROL

Rotate Left

Operation:

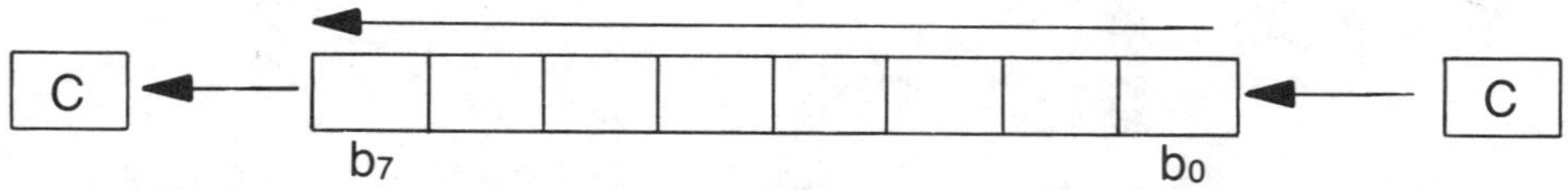

Description: Shifts all bits of ACCX or M one place to the left. Bit 0 is loaded from the C bit. The C bit is loaded from the most significant bit of ACCX or M.

Condition Codes:
- H: Not affected.
- I: Not affected.
- N: Set if most significant bit of the result is set; cleared otherwise.
- Z: Set if all bits of the result are cleared; cleared otherwise.
- V: Set if, after the completion of the operation, EITHER (N is set and C is cleared) OR (N is cleared and C is set); cleared otherwise.
- C: Set if, before the operation, the most significant bit of the ACCX or M was set; cleared otherwise.

Addressing Modes, Execution Time, and Machine Code (hexadecimal):

Addressing Modes	Execution Time (No. of cycles)	Number of bytes of machine code	Coding of First (or only) byte of machine code HEX.
A	2	1	49
B	2	1	59
EXT	6	3	79
IND	7	2	69

ROR

Rotate Right

Operation:

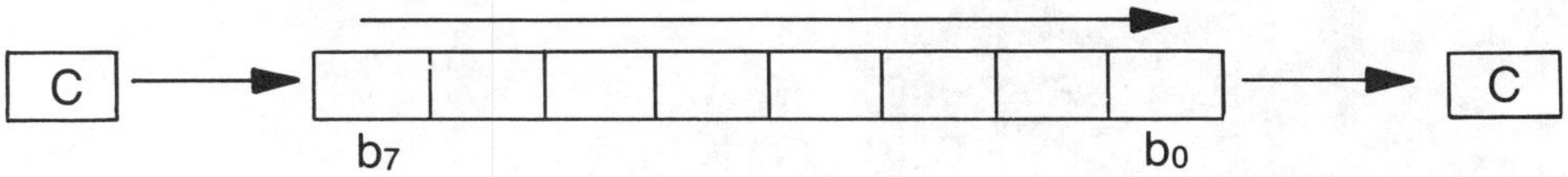

Description: Shifts all bits of ACCX or M one place to the right. Bit 7 is loaded from the C bit. The C bit is loaded from the least significant bit of ACCX or M.

Condition Codes:
- H: Not affected.
- I: Not affected.
- N: Set if most significant bit of the result is set; cleared otherwise.
- Z: Set if all bits of the result are cleared; cleared otherwise.
- V: Set if, after the completion of the operation, EITHER (N is set and C is cleared) OR (N is cleared and C is set); cleared otherwise.
- C: Set if, before the operation, the least significant bit of the ACCX or M was set; cleared otherwise.

Addressing Modes, Execution Time, and Machine Code (hexadecimal):

Addressing Modes	Execution Time (No. of cycles)	Number of bytes of machine code	Coding of First (or only) byte of machine code HEX.
A	2	1	46
B	2	1	56
EXT	6	3	76
IND	7	2	66

RTI

Return from Interrupt

Operation:

SP ← (SP) + 0001 , ↑CC
SP ← (SP) + 0001 , ↑ACCB
SP ← (SP) + 0001 , ↑ACCA
SP ← (SP) + 0001 , ↑IXH
SP ← (SP) + 0001 , ↑IXL
SP ← (SP) + 0001 , ↑PCH
SP ← (SP) + 0001 , ↑PCL

Description: The condition codes, accumulators B and A, the index register, and the program counter, will be restored to a state pulled from the stack. Note that the interrupt mask bit will be reset if and only if the corresponding bit stored in the stack is zero.

Condition Codes: Restored to the states pulled from the stack.

Addressing Modes, Execution Time, and Machine Code (hexadecimal):

Addressing Modes	Execution Time (No. of cycles)	Number of bytes of machine code	Coding of First (or only) byte of machine code HEX.
INHERENT	10	1	3B

RTS

Return from Subroutine

Operation:

SP ← (SP) + 0001
↑ PCH
SP ← (SP) + 0001
↑ PCL

Description: The stack pointer is incremented (by 1). The contents of the byte of memory, at the address now contained in the stack pointer, are loaded into the 8 bits of highest significance in the program counter. The stack pointer is again incremented (by 1). The contents of the byte of memory, at the address now contained in the stack pointer, are loaded into the 8 bits of lowest significiance in the program counter.

Condition Codes: Not affected.

Addressing Modes, Execution Time, and Machine Code (hexadecimal):

Addressing Modes	Execution Time (No. of cycles)	Number of bytes of machine code	Coding of First (or only) byte of machine code HEX.
INHERENT	5	1	39

Subtract Accumulators **SBA**

Operation: ACCA ← (ACCA) − (ACCB)

Description: Subtracts the contents of ACCB from the contents of ACCA and places the result in ACCA. The contents of ACCB are not affected.

Condition Codes:
- H: Not affected.
- I: Not affected.
- N: Set if most significant bit of the result is set; cleared otherwise.
- Z: Set if all bits of the result are cleared; cleared otherwise.
- V: Set if there was two's complement overflow as a result of the operation.
- C: Carry is set if the absolute value of accumulator B plus previous carry is larger than the absolute value of accumulator A; reset otherwise.

Addressing Modes, Execution Time, and Machine Code (hexadecimal):

Addressing Modes	Execution Time (No. of cycles)	Number of bytes of machine code	Coding of First (or only) byte of machine code
			HEX.
INHERENT	2	1	10

SBC

Subtract with Carry

Operation: ACCX ← (ACCX) − (M) − (C)

Description: Subtracts the contents of M and C from the contents of ACCX and places the result in ACCX.

Condition Codes:
- H: Not affected.
- I: Not affected.
- N: Set if most significant bit of the result is set; cleared otherwise.
- Z: Set if all bits of the result are cleared; cleared otherwise.
- V: Set if there was two's complement overflow as a result of the operation; cleared otherwise.
- C: Carry is set if the absolute value of the contents of memory plus previous carry is larger than the absolute value of the accumulator; reset otherwise.

Addressing Modes, Execution Time, and Machine Code (hexadecimal):
(DUAL OPERAND)

Addressing Modes	Execution Time (No. of cycles)	Number of bytes of machine code	Coding of First (or only) byte of machine code HEX.
A IMM	2	2	82
A DIR	3	2	92
A EXT	4	3	B2
A IND	5	2	A2
B IMM	2	2	C2
B DIR	3	2	D2
B EXT	4	3	F2
B IND	5	2	E2

SEC

Set Carry

Operation: C bit ← 1

Description: Sets the carry bit in the processor condition codes register.

Condition Codes:
- H: Not affected.
- I: Not affected.
- N: Not affected.
- Z: Not affected.
- V: Not affected.
- C: Set.

Addressing Modes, Execution Time, and Machine Code (hexadecimal):

Addressing Modes	Execution Time (No. of cycles)	Number of bytes of machine code	Coding of First (or only) byte of machine code HEX.
INHERENT	2	1	0D

Set Interrupt Mask **SEI**

Operation: I bit ← 1

Description: Sets the interrupt mask bit in the processor condition codes register. The microprocessor is inhibited from servicing an interrupt from a peripheral device, and will continue with execution of the instructions of the program, until the interrupt mask bit has been cleared.

Condition Codes:
H: Not affected.
I: Set.
N: Not affected.
Z: Not affected.
V: Not affected.
C: Not affected.

Addressing Modes, Execution Time, and Machine Code (hexadecimal):

Addressing Modes	Execution Time (No. of cycles)	Number of bytes of machine code	Coding of First (or only) byte of machine code
			HEX.
INHERENT	2	1	0F

Set Two's Complement Overflow Bit **SEV**

Operation: V bit ← 1

Description: Sets the two's complement overflow bit in the processor condition codes register.

Condition Codes:
H: Not affected.
I: Not affected.
N: Not affected.
Z: Not affected.
V: Set.
C: Not affected.

Addressing Modes, Execution Time, and Machine Code (hexadecimal):

Addressing Modes	Execution Time (No. of cycles)	Number of bytes of machine code	Coding of First (or only) byte of machine code
			HEX.
INHERENT	2	1	0B

STA

Store Accumulator

Operation: M ← (ACCX)

Description: Stores the contents of ACCX in memory. The contents of ACCX remains unchanged.

Condition Codes:
- H: Not affected.
- I: Not affected.
- N: Set if the most significant bit of the contents of ACCX is set; cleared otherwise.
- Z: Set if all bits of the contents of ACCX are cleared; cleared otherwise.
- V: Cleared.
- C: Not affected.

Addressing Modes, Execution Time, and Machine Code (hexadecimal):

Addressing Modes	Execution Time (No. of cycles)	Number of bytes of machine code	Coding of First (or only) byte of machine code HEX.
A DIR	4	2	97
A EXT	5	3	B7
A IND	6	2	A7
B DIR	4	2	D7
B EXT	5	3	F7
B IND	6	2	E7

STS

Store Stack Pointer

Operation: M ← (SPH)
M + 1 ← (SPL)

Description: Stores the more significant byte of the stack pointer in memory at the address specified by the program, and stores the less significant byte of the stack pointer at the next location in memory, at one plus the address specified by the program.

Condition Codes:
- H: Not affected.
- I: Not affected.
- N: Set if the most significant bit of the stack pointer is set; cleared otherwise.
- Z: Set if all bits of the stack pointer are cleared; cleared otherwise.
- V: Cleared.
- C: Not affected.

Addressing Modes, Execution Time, and Machine Code (hexadecimal):

Addressing Modes	Execution Time (No. of cycles)	Number of bytes of machine code	Coding of First (or only) byte of machine code HEX.
DIR	5	2	9F
EXT	6	3	BF
IND	7	2	AF

STX

Store Index Register

Operation: M ← (IXH)
M + 1 ← (IXL)

Description: Stores the more significant byte of the index register in memory at the address specified by the program, and stores the less significant byte of the index register at the next location in memory, at one plus the address specified by the program.

Condition Codes:
- H: Not affected.
- I: Not affected.
- N: Set if the most significant bite of the index register is set; cleared otherwise.
- Z: Set if all bits of the index register are cleared; cleared otherwise.
- V: Cleared.
- C: Not affected.

Addressing Modes, Execution Time, and Machine Code (hexadecimal):

Addressing Modes	Execution Time (No. of cycles)	Number of bytes of machine code	Coding of First (or only) byte of machine code HEX.
DIR	5	2	DF
EXT	6	3	FF
IND	7	2	EF

SUB

Subtract

Operation: ACCX ← (ACCX) − (M)

Description: Subtracts the contents of M from the contents of ACCX and places the result in ACCX.

Condition Codes:
- H: Not affected.
- I: Not affected.
- N: Set if most significant bit of the result is set; cleared otherwise.
- Z: Set if all bits of the result are cleared; cleared otherwise.
- V: Set if there was two's complement overflow as a result of the operation; cleared otherwise.
- C: Set if the absolute value of the contents of memory are larger than the absolute value of the accumulator; reset otherwise.

Addressing Modes, Execution Time, and Machine Code (hexadecimal):

(DUAL OPERAND)

Addressing Modes	Execution Time (No. of cycles)	Number of bytes of machine code	Coding of First (or only) byte of machine code
			HEX.
A IMM	2	2	80
A DIR	3	2	90
A EXT	4	3	B0
A IND	5	2	A0
B IMM	2	2	C0
B DIR	3	2	D0
B EXT	4	3	F0
B IND	5	2	E0

Software Interrupt

SWI

Operation:

PC ← (PC) + 0001
↓ (PCL) , SP ← (SP)-0001
↓ (PCH) , SP ← (SP)-0001
↓ (IXL) , SP ← (SP)-0001
↓ (IXH) , SP ← (SP)-0001
↓ (ACCA) , SP ← (SP)-0001
↓ (ACCB) , SP ← (SP)-0001
↓ (CC) , SP ← (SP)-0001
I ← 1
PCH ← (n-0005)
PCL ← (n-0004)

Description: The program counter is incremented (by 1). The program counter, index register, and accumulator A and B, are pushed into the stack. The condition codes register is then pushed into the stack, with condition codes H, I, N, Z, V, C going respectively into bit positions 5 thru 0, and the top two bits (in bit positions 7 and 6) are set (to the 1 state). The stack pointer is decremented (by 1) after each byte of data is stored in the stack.

The interrupt mask bit is then set. The program counter is then loaded with the address stored in the software interrupt pointer at memory locations (n-5) and (n-4), where n is the address corresponding to a high state on all lines of the address bus.

Condition Codes:

H: Not affected.
I: Set.
N: Not affected.
Z: Not affected.
V: Not affected.
C: Not affected.

Addressing Modes, Execution Time, and Machine Code (hexadecimal):

Addressing Modes	Execution Time (No. of cycles)	Number of bytes of machine code	Coding of First (or only) byte of machine code HEX.
INHERENT	12	1	3F

TAB

Transfer from Accumulator A to Accumulator B

Operation: ACCB ← (ACCA)

Description: Moves the contents of ACCA to ACCB. The former contents of ACCB are lost. The contents of ACCA are not affected.

Condition Codes:
- H: Not affected.
- I: Not affected.
- N: Set if the most significant bit of the contents of the accumulator is set; cleared otherwise.
- Z: Set if all bits of the contents of the accumulator are cleared; cleared otherwise.
- V: Cleared.
- C: Not affected.

Addressing Modes, Execution Time, and Machine Code (hexadecimal):

Addressing Modes	Execution Time (No. of cycles)	Number of bytes of machine code	Coding of First (or only) byte of machine code
			HEX.
INHERENT	2	1	16

Transfer from Accumulator A to Processor Condition Codes Register

TAP

Operation: CC ← (ACCA)

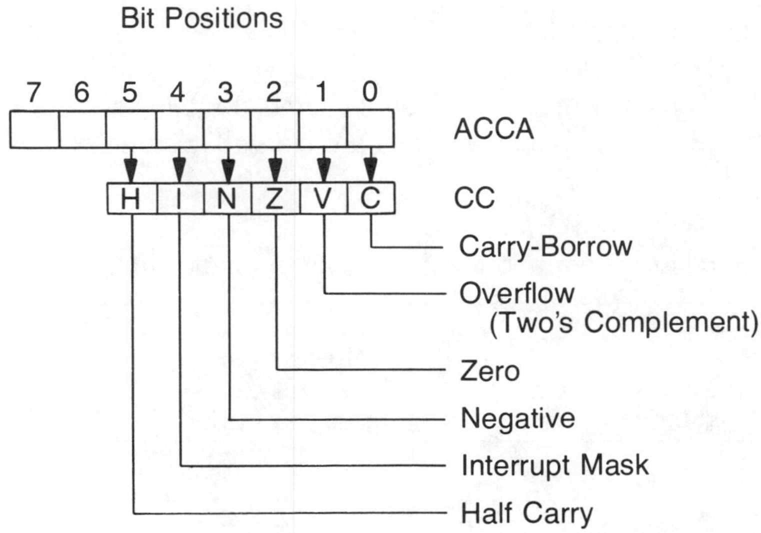

Description: Transfers the contents of bit positions 0 thru 5 of accumulator A to the corresponding bit positions of the processor condition codes register. The contents of accumulator A remain unchanged.

Condition Codes: Set or reset according to the contents of the respective bits 0 thru 5 of accumulator A.

Addressing Modes, Execution Time, and Machine Code (hexadecimal):

Addressing Modes	Execution Time (No. of cycles)	Number of bytes of machine code	Coding of First (or only) byte of machine code
			HEX.
INHERENT	2	1	06

TBA

Transfer from Accumulator B to Accumulator A

Operation: ACCA ← (ACCB)

Description: Moves the contents of ACCB to ACCA. The former contents of ACCA are lost. The contents of ACCB are not affected.

Condition Codes:
- H: Not affected.
- I: Not affected.
- N: Set if the most significant accumulator bit is set; cleared otherwise.
- Z: Set if all accumulator bits are cleared; cleared otherwise.
- V: Cleared.
- C: Not affected.

Addressing Modes, Execution Time, and Machine Code (hexadecimal):

Addressing Modes	Execution Time (No. of cycles)	Number of bytes of machine code	Coding of First (or only) byte of machine code
			HEX.
INHERENT	2	1	17

Transfer from Processor Condition Codes Register to Accumulator A

TPA

Operation: ACCA ← (CC)

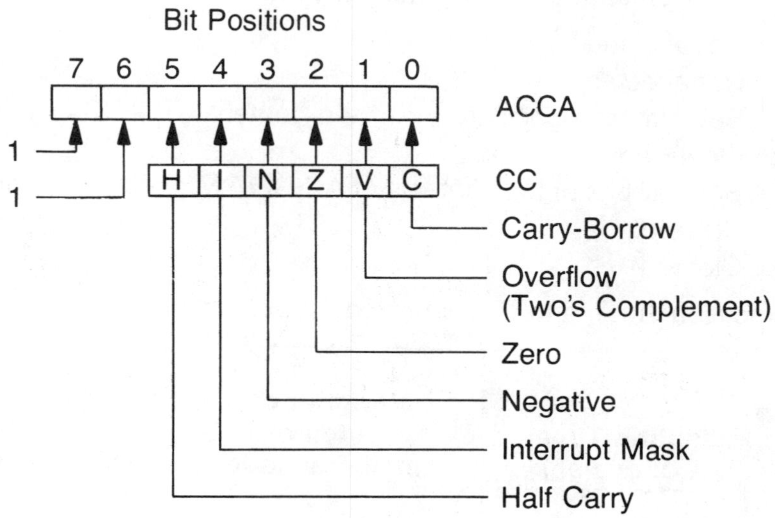

Description: Transfers the contents of the processor condition codes register to corresponding bit positions 0 thru 5 of accumulator A. Bit positions 6 and 7 of accumulator A are set (i.e. go to the "1" state). The processor condition codes register remains unchanged.

Condition Codes: Not affected.

Addressing Modes, Execution Time, and Machine Code (hexadecimal):

Addressing Modes	Execution Time (No. of cycles)	Number of bytes of machine code	Coding of First (or only) byte of machine code HEX.
INHERENT	2	1	07

TST

Test

Operation: (ACCX) − 00
(M) − 00

Description: Set condition codes N and Z according to the contents of ACCX or M.

Condition Codes:
- H: Not affected.
- I: Not affected.
- N: Set if most significant bit of the contents of ACCX or M is set; cleared otherwise.
- Z: Set if all bits of the contents of ACCX or M are cleared; cleared otherwise.
- V: Cleared.
- C: Cleared.

Addressing Modes, Execution Time, and Machine Code (hexadecimal):

Addressing Modes	Execution Time (No. of cycles)	Number of bytes of machine code	Coding of First (or only) byte of machine code HEX.
A	2	1	4D
B	2	1	5D
EXT	6	3	7D
IND	7	2	6D

TSX

Transfer from Stack Pointer to Index Register

Operation: IX ← (SP) + 0001

Description: Loads the index register with one plus the contents of the stack pointer. The contents of the stack pointer remain unchanged.

Condition Codes: Not affected.

Addressing Modes, Execution Time, and Machine Code (hexadecimal):

Addressing Modes	Execution Time (No. of cycles)	Number of bytes of machine code	Coding of First (or only) byte of machine code HEX.
INHERENT	4	1	30

Transfer From Index Register to Stack Pointer **TXS**

Operation: SP ← (IX) − 0001

Description: Loads the stack pointer with the contents of the index register, minus one. The contents of the index register remain unchanged.

Condition Codes: Not affected.

Addressing Modes, Execution Time, and Machine Code (hexadecimal):

Addressing Modes	Execution Time (No. of cycles)	Number of bytes of machine code	Coding of First (or only) byte of machine code
			HEX.
INHERENT	4	1	35

WAI

Wait for Interrupt

Operation: PC ← (PC) + 0001
↓ (PCL) , SP ← (SP)-0001
↓ (PCH) , SP ← (SP)-0001
↓ (IXL) , SP ← (SP)-0001
↓ (IXH) , SP ← (SP)-0001
↓ (ACCA) , SP ← (SP)-0001
↓ (ACCB) , SP ← (SP)-0001
↓ (CC) , SP ← (SP)-0001

Condition Codes: Not affected.

Description: The program counter is incremented (by 1). The program counter, index register, and accumulators A and B, are pushed into the stack. The condition codes register is then pushed into the stack, with condition codes H, I, N, Z, V, C going respectively into bit positions 5 thru 0, and the top two bits (in bit positions 7 and 6) are set (to the 1 state). The stack pointer is decremented (by 1) after each byte of data is stored in the stack.

Execution of the program is then suspended until an interrupt from a peripheral device is signalled, by the interrupt request control input going to a low state.

When an interrupt is signalled on the interrupt request line, and provided the I bit is clear, execution proceeds as follows. The interrupt mask bit is set. The program counter is then loaded with the address stored in the internal interrupt pointer at memory locations (n-7) and (n-6), where n is the address corresponding to a high state on all lines of the address bus.

Condition Codes:
H: Not affected.
I: Not affected until an interrupt request signal is detected on the interrupt request control line. When the interrupt request is received the I bit is set and further execution takes place, provided the I bit was initially clear.
N: Not affected.
Z: Not affected.
V: Not affected.
C: Not affected.

Addressing Modes, Execution Time, and Machine Code (hexadecimal):

Addressing Modes	Execution Time (No. of cycles)	Number of bytes of machine code	Coding of First (or only) byte of machine code
			HEX.
INHERENT	9	1	3E

Chapter 8

8080/8085 Microprocessor

Objectives

Upon the completion of this chapter, you will be able to:

- Connect an 8080 microprocessor to its supporting components to form a CPU set.
- Assemble the 8080 CPU set with RAM, ROM, and I/O ports to form a microcomputer system.
- Make the proper crystal and tank circuit connections to the 8224 clock generator.
- Make correct data and control bus connections between the 8228, systems controller, and the RAMS, ROMS, and I/O ports.
- Use the 8080 interrupt system.
- Write programs using the 8080 instruction set.
- Assemble an 8080 microprocessor system with a bootstrap loader.
- Write arithmetic programs with the 8080 instruction set.
- Write 8080 programs containing counter, timer, and sequencer routines.
- Construct dedicated 8080 microprocessor systems using lookup tables.

- Construct a microprocessor system using the 8085, 8755 PROM I/O and the 8155 RAM, I/O, Timer.
- Assemble an 8085 microprocessor system using an address latch.
- Use the special interrupt provisions of the 8085.
- Initialize the data direction registers of the 8355 I/O ports.
- Load the command status register of the 8155 to provide a variety of I/O port functions.
- Use the 2-byte timer of the 8155.

8.1 Description

The 8080 microprocessor is at present the most widely used 8-bit microprocessor. It owes this leading position primarily to the fact that it was the first microprocessor for which a complete software development system became available. Figure 8.1(a) shows the pin diagram of the 8080. It has 16 address outputs accommodating a 64K address bus. The 8-bit data bus is bidirectional. It requires two clock phases. Three power supplies are used as listed.

Pin 2	V_{SS}	0 volts	
Pin 11	V_{BB}	−5 volts	1 mA typical
Pin 20	V_{CC}	+5 volts	60 mA typical
Pin 28	V_{DD}	+12 volts	40 mA typical

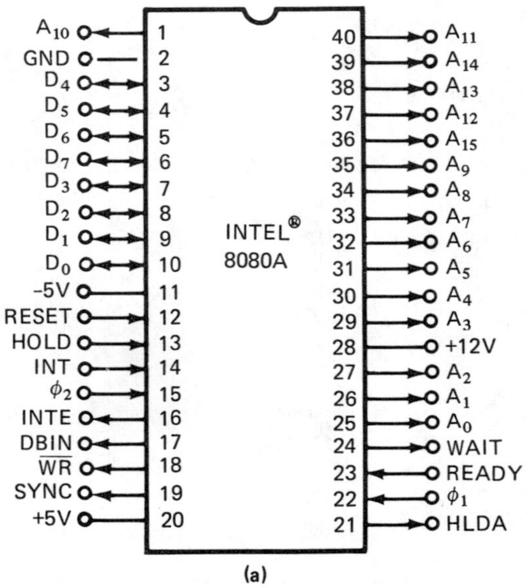

FIGURE 8.1 **(a)** Pin out diagram of 8080A Microprocessor. **(b)** Block diagram of 8080A Microprocessor. *(Courtesy of Intel Corporation)*

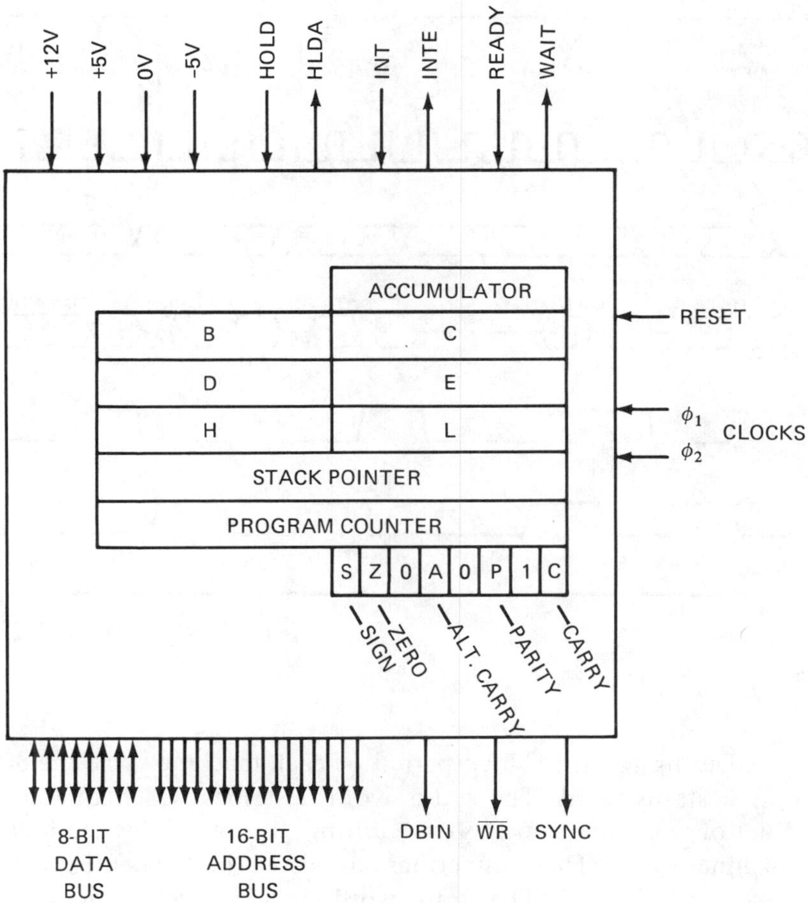

(b)

Four input and six output pins are used for control signals. All input and output signals are TTL voltage levels except ϕ_1 and ϕ_2 clocks which are 12 volts.

Figure 8.1(b) shows a block diagram of the 8080. It contains a single 8-bit accumulator, a 16-bit program counter, a 16-bit stack pointer, and three register pairs. The register pairs may be used as individual 8-bit registers or as 16-bit registers. The register pair H, L also functions as an address pointer. The status register contains five flag bits along with fixed levels in bits 1, 3, and 5.

8.2 The 8080 CPU Set

The 8080 microprocessor operates in machine cycles. There are two or more machine cycles to an instruction. Each machine cycle requires three or more clock periods. The timing for three consecutive instructions is shown in Figure 8.2.

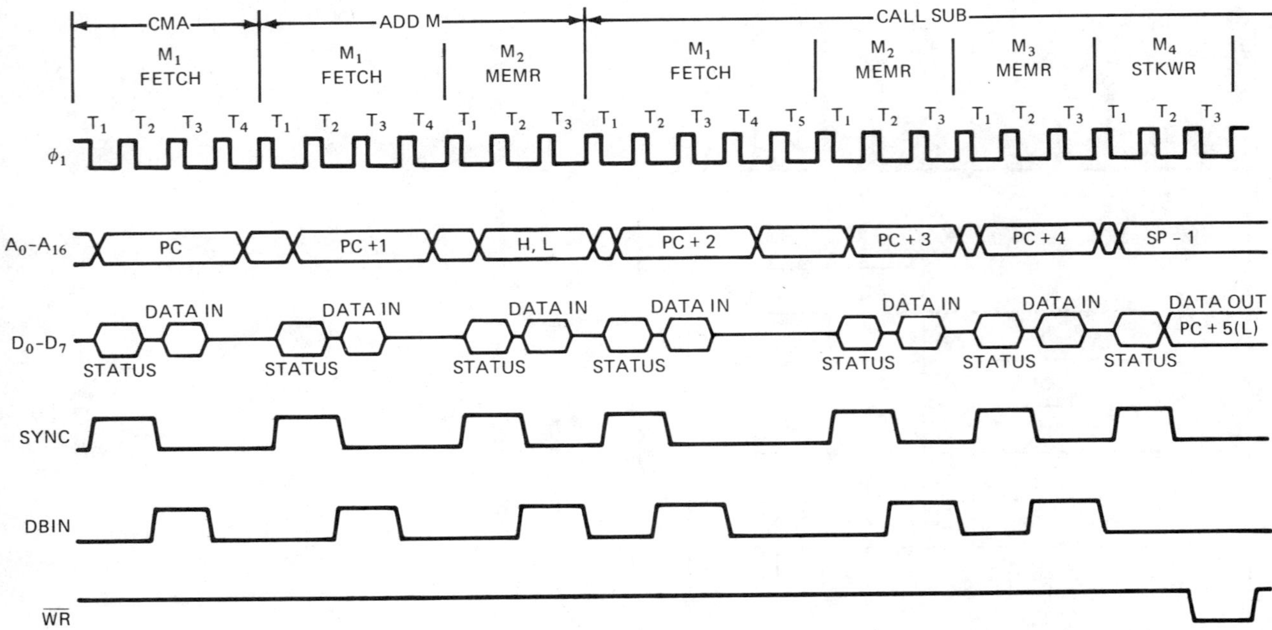

*M_5 of CALL instruction is another stack write.

FIGURE 8.2 Timing diagram of 8080 address, data bus, and control leads. The waveforms resulting from the execution of three consecutive instructions: CMA, ADD M, and CALL (subroutine). Each instruction requires one or more machine cycles (M_1 through M_5). Each machine cycle requires three or more clock states (T_1 through T_5). The 16-bit address is most often taken from the incrementing program counter (PC through P_C + 4). For some instructions, address is taken from address pointer register, registers (H & L). When reading or writing on the stack, address is taken from the stack pointer. The data bus outputs a status word at the beginning of each machine cycle. It receives data in during every fetch, memory read, I/O read or stack read machine cycle. It outputs data during every memory write, I/O write, or stack write machine cycle. The status output occurs in conjunction with the SYNC line going high. Data in occurs in conjunction with DBIN pulse. The WR goes low whenever the 8080 outputs a valid data word (not during a status word).

During the first clock period of each machine cycle the 8080 outputs a status word. The status word describes which of ten types of functions are being performed during the remaining periods of the machine cycle. These functions are listed in the status word chart shown in Table 8.1. The status word must be latched and used to generate control signals needed during the remainder of the machine cycle. This function is normally performed by the 8228, System Controller and Bus Driver. Figure 8.3 shows the 8080 CPU set. The three circuits shown are employed ideally together.

The 8224 clock generator and driver supplies the two clock phases needed by the 8080 CPU. The eight data bus leads and three control leads are connected between the 8080 and the 8228. The 8228 system controller recognizes a status word by the fact that it occurs in conjunction with a status strobe. The status strobe originates as a sync signal from the 8080 CPU. The sync signal is processed within the 8224 to form the status strobe. The 8228 converts the status word to control bus signals $\overline{\text{Mem R}}$, $\overline{\text{Mem W}}$, $\overline{\text{I/O R}}$, $\overline{\text{I/O W}}$, or $\overline{\text{INTA}}$.

Unlike most 8-bit microprocessors, the input and output ports of the 8080 system can be either memory mapped or can be handled with addressing different from the 64K memory system. Memory circuits and memory mapped I/O ports are addressed only when $\overline{\text{MEMR}}$ or $\overline{\text{MEMW}}$ signals are active. I/O ports may be separately addressed (by IN and OUT instructions) only when $\overline{\text{I/O R}}$ and $\overline{\text{I/O W}}$ signals are active. The separately addressed I/O system has only 256 addresses. The I/O addresses are duplicated on the lower 8 bits and upper 8 bits of the address bus. Address leads from either set can be connected to a given I/O port. In systems with large numbers of I/O ports the load can be divided.

TABLE 8.1 8080 Status words and control signals. There are twelve types of machine cycles indicative of the activity within the 8080 during the cycle. An external circuit must be used to latch the status word and generate the control signal listed in the right-hand column.

TYPE OF MACHINE CYCLE	STATUS BIT AND DATA BUS LOCATION								ACTIVE CONTROL SIGNAL GENERATED
	D7 MEMR	D6 INP	D5 M1	D4 OUT	D3 HLTA	D2 STACK	D1 $\overline{\text{WO}}$	D0 INTA	
Instruction Fetch	1	0	1	0	0	0	1	0	$\overline{\text{MEMR}}$
Memory Read	1	0	0	0	0	0	1	0	$\overline{\text{MEMR}}$
Memory Write	0	0	0	0	0	0	0	0	$\overline{\text{MEMW}}$
Stack Read	1	0	0	0	0	1	1	0	$\overline{\text{MEMR}}$
Stack Write	0	0	0	0	0	1	0	0	$\overline{\text{MEMW}}$
Input Read	0	1	0	0	0	0	1	0	$\overline{\text{I/OR}}$
Output Write	0	0	0	1	0	0	0	0	$\overline{\text{I/OW}}$
Interrupt Acknowledge	0	0	1	0	0	0	1	1	$\overline{\text{INTA}}$
Halt Acknowledge	1	0	0	0	1	0	1	0	NONE
Interrupt Acknowledge While Halted	0	0	1	0	1	0	1	1	$\overline{\text{INTA}}$

8.3 The 8224 Clock Generator

Figure 8.4 shows the 8224 clock generator interfaced to the 8080 CPU. A crystal connected to the 8224 clock input determines the oscillator frequency. The clock generator circuit in the 8224 counts down the oscillator frequency and produces the two clock phases, ϕ_1 and ϕ_2 as shown in Figure 8.5.

The clock frequency is 1/9 the oscillator frequency. An 18-MHZ oscillator frequency results in a 2-MHZ clock, typical for an 8080A operating speed. Either an 18-MHZ crystal with the tank input open circuited or a 6-MHZ crystal with an 18-MHZ tank circuit may be used. In addition, the 8224 can provide correct timing and wave shaping to the *reset* and *ready* signals. The 8080 *sync signal,* which indicates a status word output on the 8080 data bus, is also shaped and inverted in the 8224 before transmittal to the 8228 status latch as the $\overline{\text{STSTB}}$.

The reset signal to the 8080 is used to initialize the microprocessor by performing functions as follows:

- Suspends normal internal operation while reset is high
- Clears the program counter
- Clears the instruction register
- Clears the INTE flip-flop (interrupt is disabled)
- Clears the HLDA flip-flop (out of hold state)
- Clears the Halt state
- Sets timing generator to M_1 machine cycle, T_1 state when reset is removed.

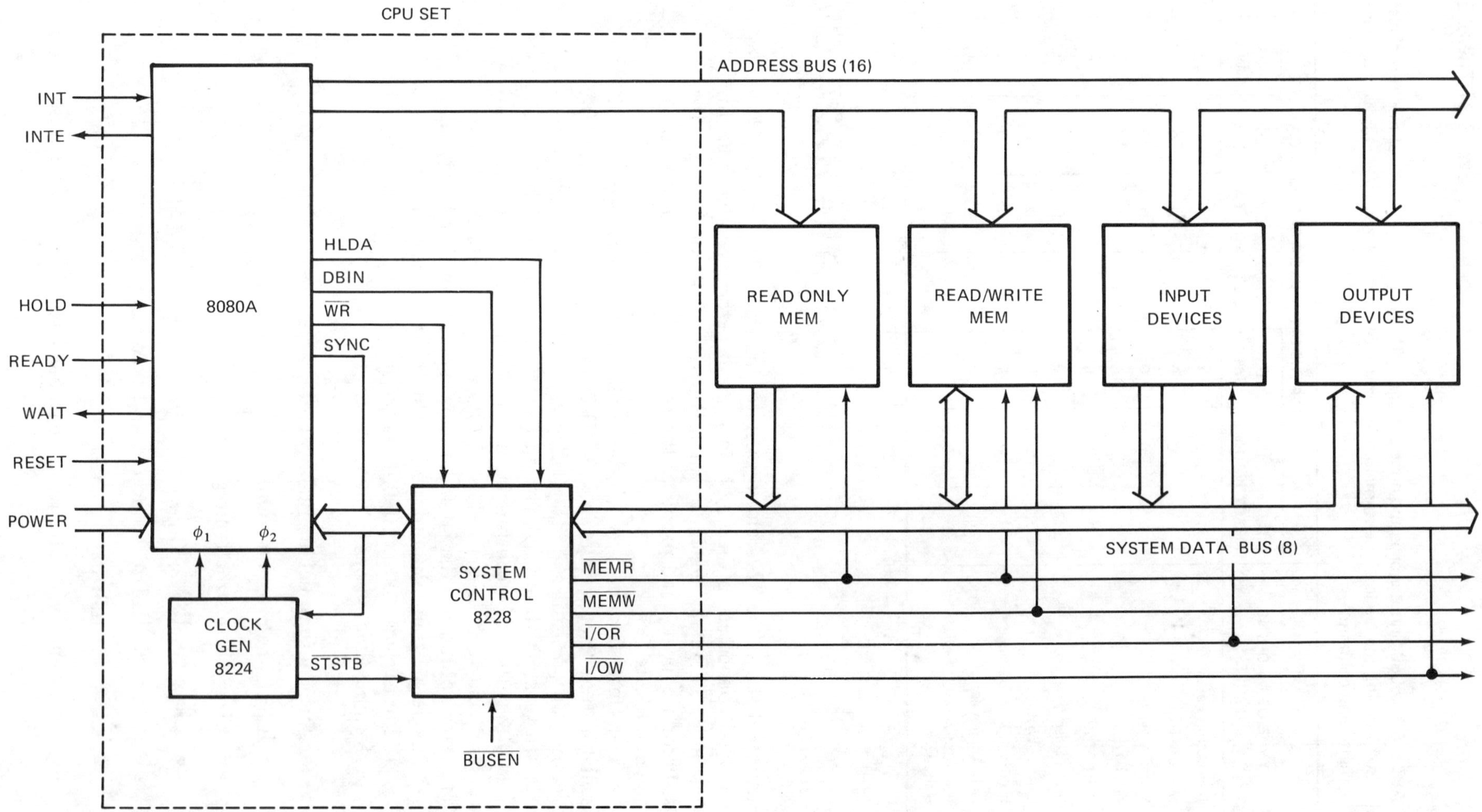

FIGURE 8.3 The 8080 CPU set. The 8080 is generally employed with two additional circuits to form a complete CPU set. The 8224 is needed to supply an ideal pair of clock signals. The 8228 is used to latch the status word and generate the five control signals. It also acts as a bus driver for the systems data bus.

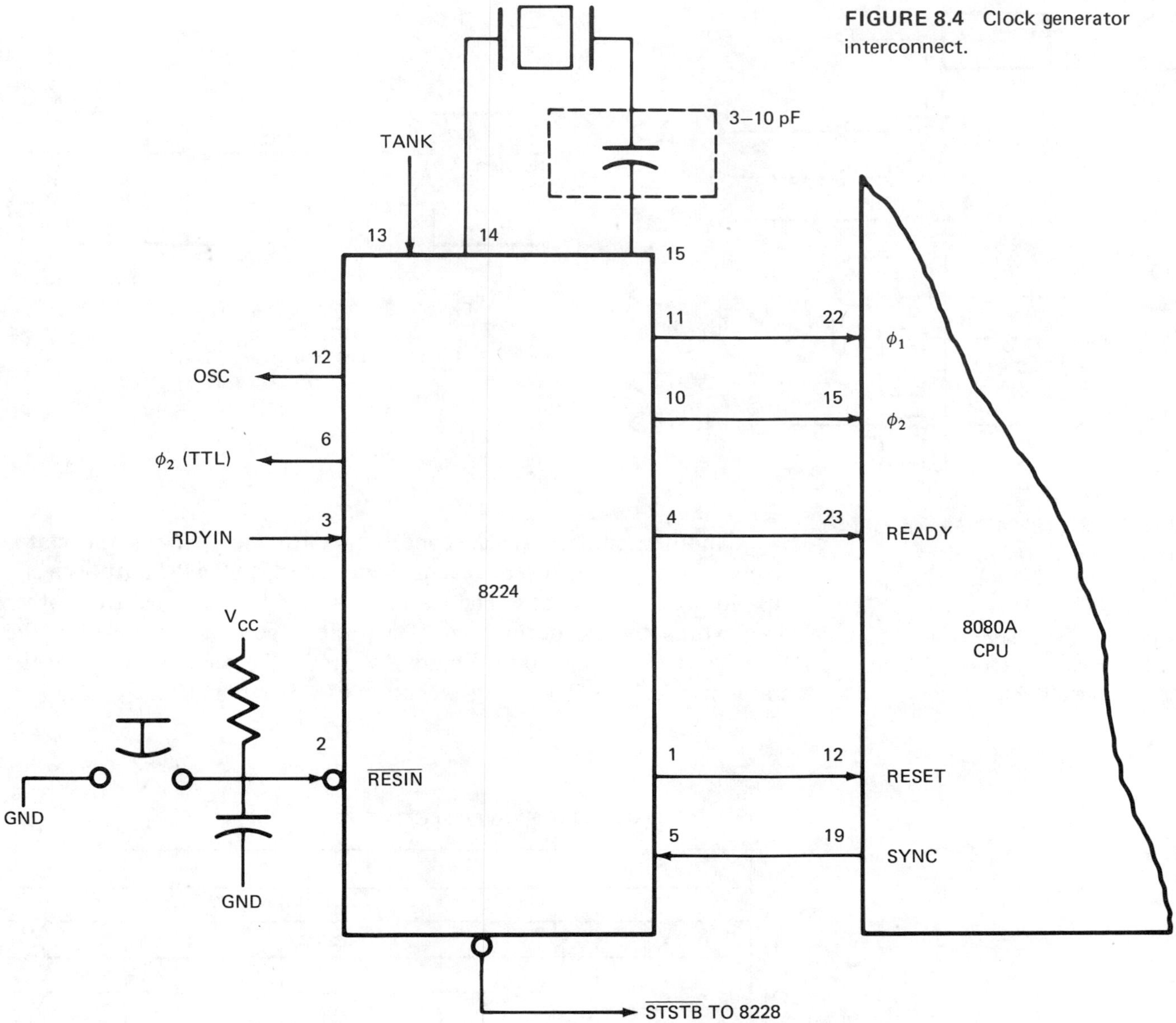

FIGURE 8.4 Clock generator interconnect.

As Figure 8.4 shows, a simple RC circuit can provide a reset after power on. The RC time constant must be high enough to insure that the $\overline{\text{RESIN}}$ remains low for several clock cycles after power up. A simple push button can be used to provide a reset without an interruption to system power.

When the READY input to the 8080 goes low, the microprocessor enters the wait state. The wait state makes it possible for the 8080 to work with memories or I/O devices which are too slow to accommodate the speed of the 8080. On being accessed, the slow speed device transmits a $\overline{\text{READY}}$ to the CPU causing it to enter the wait state. The 8224 insures that the $\overline{\text{READY}}$ goes low after the leading edge of ϕ_2 clock. Figure 8.6 shows the timing diagram of an I/O write cycle which results in a READY. The ready line can also be used to provide single cycle operation but as Figure 8.6 indicates, the wait (T_W) will occur after T_2, which is not the completion of the machine cycle.

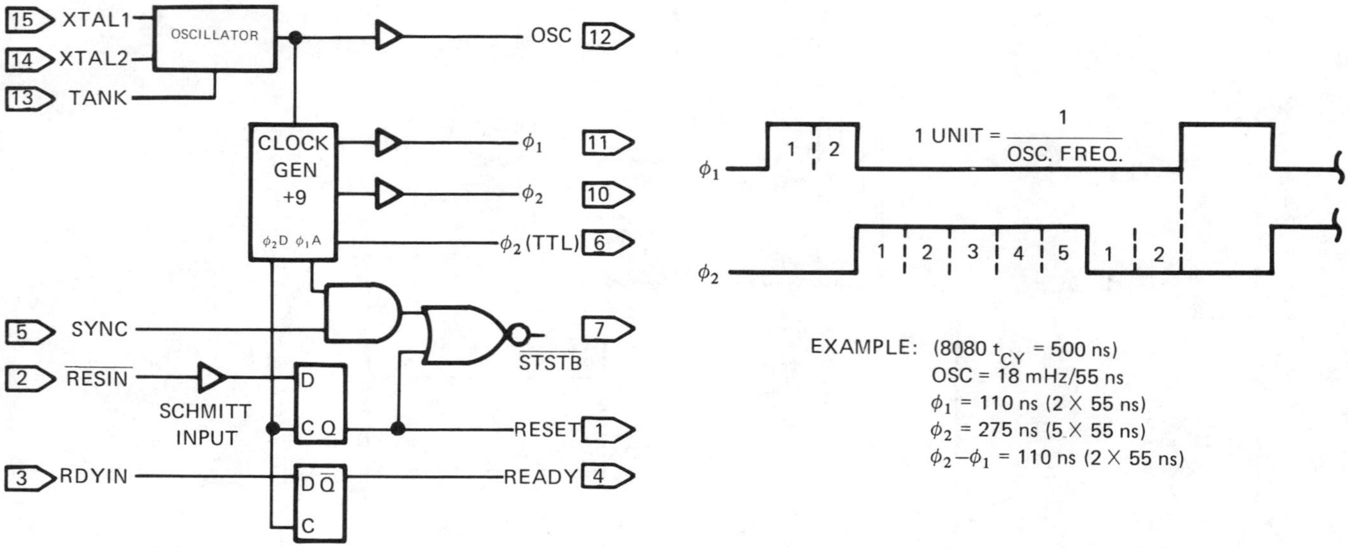

FIGURE 8.5 8224 Clock generator block diagram. The oscillator frequency is divided by 9 to produce the clock frequencies. Clock ϕ_1 goes high for two oscillator cycles. Clock ϕ_2 goes high after Clock ϕ_1 and remains high for 5 oscillator cycles.

Another control signal conditioned by the 8224 is the status strobe. During T_1 of every machine cycle, the 8080 CPU outputs a status word on its data bus. The status word can be identified from other data words by the occurrence of a positive going sync pulse on the SYNC output of the 8080. Figure 8.7 shows the relative timing of the status strobe ($\overline{\text{STSTB}}$) during execution of a 5-state machine cycle.

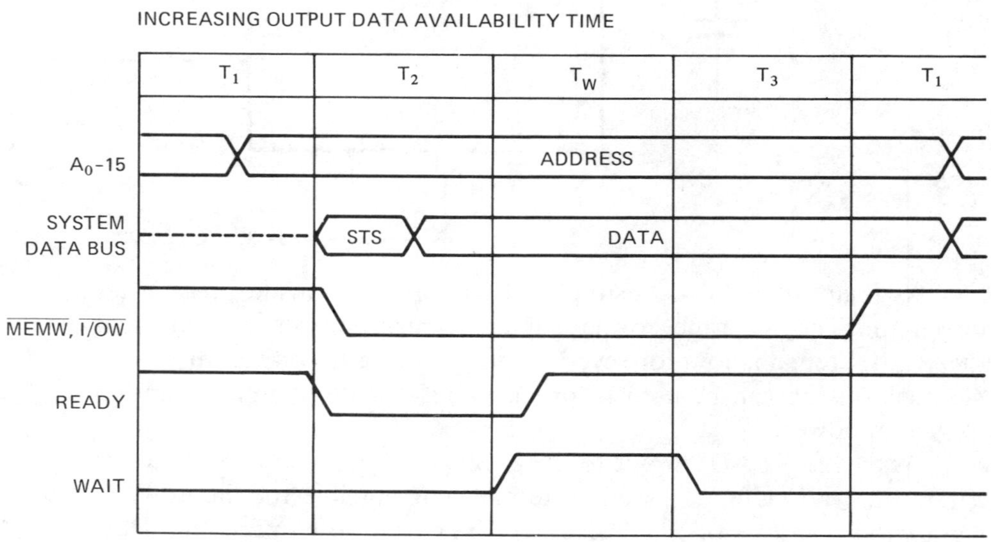

FIGURE 8.6 Ready line operation. A memory or I/O device which is too slow for the 8080 can cause the CPU to wait for an integral number of clock states (T_W) by holding the ready line low until it is ready to proceed.

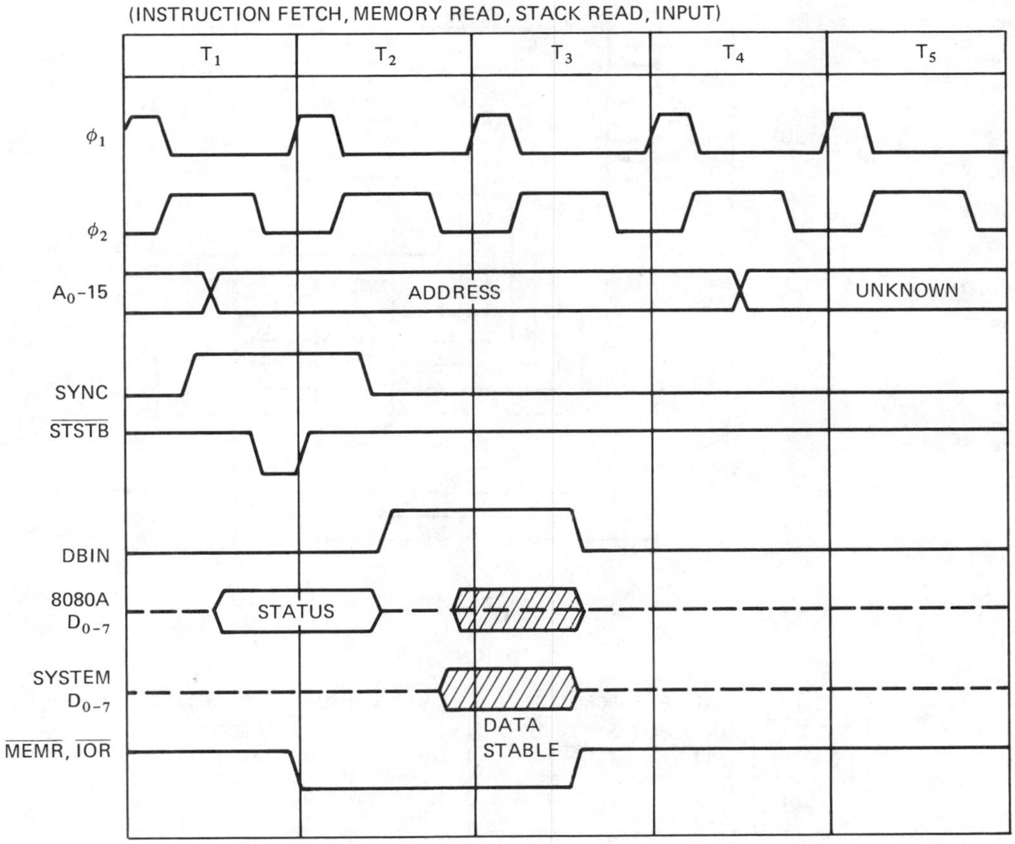

T_1 – ADDRESS BUS ← MEMORY ADDRESS OR I/O PORT #

T_2 – READY AND HOLD INPUTS SAMPLED
CHECK FOR HALT INSTRUCTION

T_3 – DATA BUS ← DATA FROM MEMORY OR INPUT PORT

$T_{4,5}$ – USED FOR INTERNAL OPERATIONS (IF NEEDED)

FIGURE 8.7 Typical read operation waveforms.

8.4 The 8228 System Controller and Bus Driver

The 8228 logic diagram is shown in Figure 8.8. During state one (T_1) of every machine cycle the 8228 receives the status word from the 8080. The status word is strobed into the status latch where in combination with other control inputs it produces the control bus outputs $\overline{MEMR}$, $\overline{MEMW}$, $\overline{I/OR}$, $\overline{I/OW}$, and $\overline{INTA}$. Figure 8.3 shows the 8228 control bus connections to memory and I/O ports.

Figures 8.7 and 8.9 show timing of signals on 8080 and 8228 busses during read and write cycles. There are three classes of signals on the 8080 data bus: status word, data in, and data out. Each is associated with a different 8080 control signal. Status word occurs with sync, data out occurs with a $\overline{WR}$, and DBIN occurs when the 8080 is ready to receive data. The DBIN line going high informs the systems controller that the 8080 is ready to receive data from the external data bus. The $\overline{WR}$ goes low indicating to the systems controller that the CPU is out-

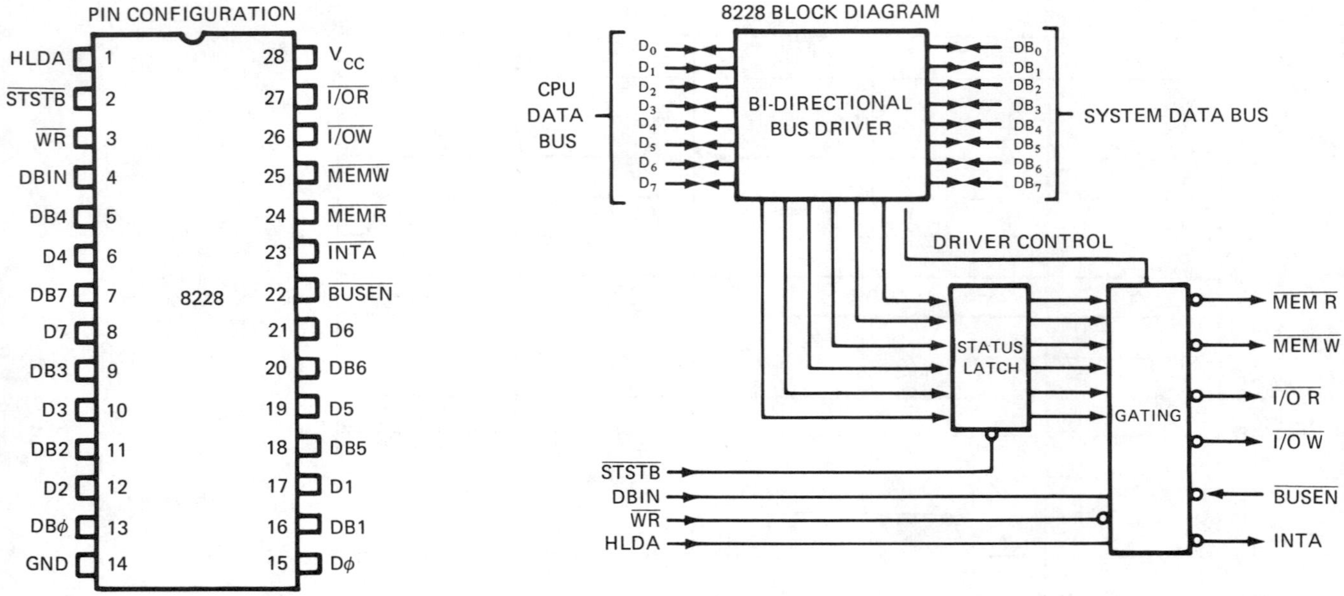

FIGURE 8.8 8228 Systems controller.

PIN NAMES

D7-D0	DATA BUS (8080 SIDE)
DB7-DB0	DATA BUS (SYSTEM SIDE)
$\overline{I/OR}$	I/O READ
$\overline{I/OW}$	I/O WRITE
$\overline{MEMR}$	MEMORY READ
$\overline{MEMW}$	MEMORY WRITE
DBIN	DBIN (FROM 8080)

HLDA	HLDA (FROM 8080)
$\overline{WR}$	WR (FROM 8080)
$\overline{BUSEN}$	BUS ENABLE INPUT
$\overline{STSTB}$	STATUS STROBE (FROM 8224)
V_{CC}	+5V
GND	0 VOLTS

putting a valid data word onto the data bus. As Figure 8.9 shows, the $\overline{WR}$ is not active (low) during the status word. For a short period during T_2, the status word will appear on the system bus in coincidence with a $\overline{MEMW}$ or $\overline{I/OW}$. If, in some unusual circumstance this presents a problem for a memory or I/O device, the $\overline{WR}$ can be ORed with the $\overline{MEMW}$ or $\overline{I/OW}$ to form the write control.

The HOLD, HLDA of the 8080 and the $\overline{BUSEN}$ of the 8228 are normally used with direct memory access (DMA) operations, which will not be discussed in this chapter. Where this function is not used, the HOLD and $\overline{BUSEN}$ should be tied low. The HLDA connection between pin 21 of the 8080 and pin 2 of the 8228 may be connected.

8.5 The 8080 Interrupt System

Like other 8-bit microprocessors, the 8080 is designed to allow I/O ports to interrupt the main program and divert the CPU to a routine that services the port. The interrupt system is an economical alternative to the periodic polling of the port to determine if and when it needs to be serviced. The 8080 has an interrupt input (INT.) through which the

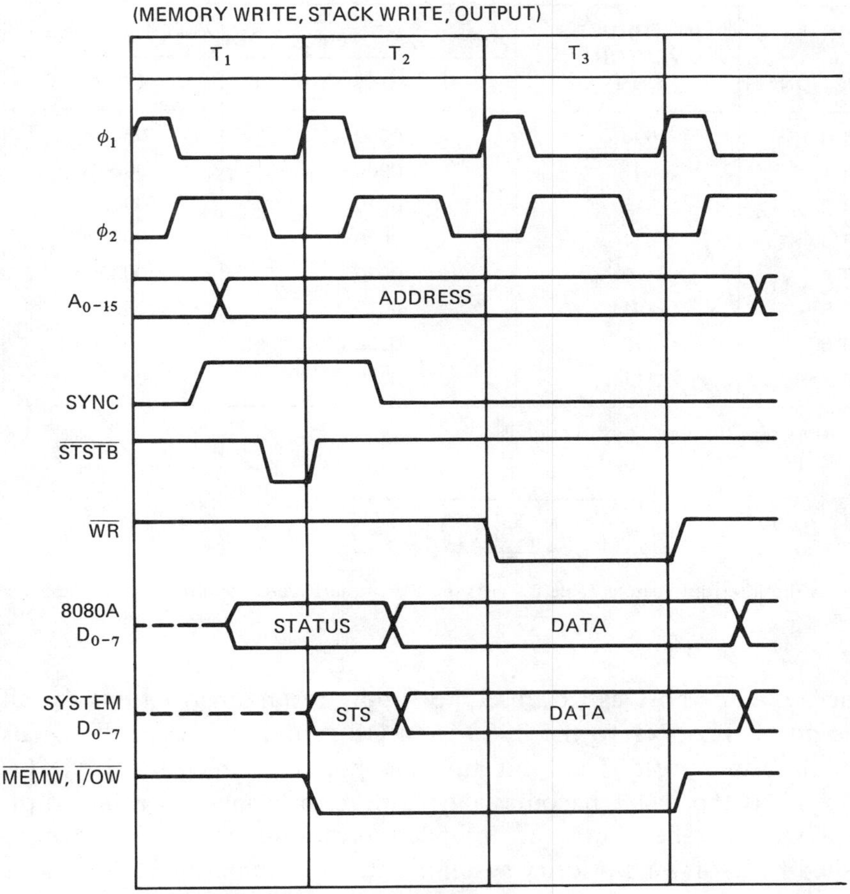

(1) FLOATING OR PREVIOUS DATA

T_1 – ADDRESS BUS ←MEMORY ADDRESS OR I/O PORT #

T_2 – READY AND HOLD INPUTS SAMPLED
CHECK FOR HALT INSTRUCTION

T_3 – DATA BUS ←DATA FROM CPU FOR MEMORY OR OUTPUT PORT

FIGURE 8.9 Typical write operation waveforms.

I/O port signals the microprocessor the instant it needs to be serviced. On receipt of a high level on the INT input, the 8080 finishes the instruction that is in process, the program counter is incremented, and the interrupt acknowledge machine cycle is executed. This generates an $\overline{\text{INTA}}$ control signal to the interrupting port informing it that the 8080 is ready to receive a restart or CALL instruction.

It is at this point that the 8080 interrupt system differs from other microprocessors. The interrupting port or an auxiliary port operating for it, must be designed to transmit a single byte restart instruction to the 8080 in response to the INTA signal. Table 8.2 lists the restart instructions and the address to which the 8080 is directed.

With the exception of RST7, each restart vector provides a memory space of only 8 bytes before an overlap occurs with the next higher vector. Eight bytes would rarely be enough memory for a complete service routine, but they are more than enough for a jump instruction to another memory block of adequate size.

Figure 8.10 shows a system of three I/O ports requiring different service routines. Each port must return a different restart instruction. A

TABLE 8.2 Restart instruction interrupt vector address.

INSTRUCTION	INTERRUPT VECTOR NNN	MEMORY ADDRESS	
		HEXADECIMAL	OCTAL
RST 0	000	0000	000000
RST 1	001	0008	000010
RST 2	010	0010	000020
RST 3	011	0018	000030
RST 4	100	0020	000040
RST 5	101	0028	000050
RST 6	110	0030	000060
RST 7	111	0038	000070

The binary format for the Restart instruction is:

7	6	5	4	3	2	1	0
1	1	N	N	N	1	1	1

where NNN is the interrupt vector. Table 8.2 lists the eight restart vectors and the corresponding addresses.

single auxiliary port can be used to supply restart instructions for all three ports. The INT to the 8080 is an OR function of the INT signals from the three ports. The 8-bit auxiliary port is enabled by the INTA signal. If, as the INTA becomes active, more than one port is interrupting, a restart other than the intended ones will occur. This can be handled by a software priority system. The programmer must determine which of the multiple ports interrupting should have priority and a jump instruction from the resulting memory segment to the segment of the priority port must be inserted. If the ports required priority in the order BAC, then the restart memory segments should contain programming as shown in Table 8.3.

FIGURE 8.10 Auxiliary input port used to supply restart instructions.

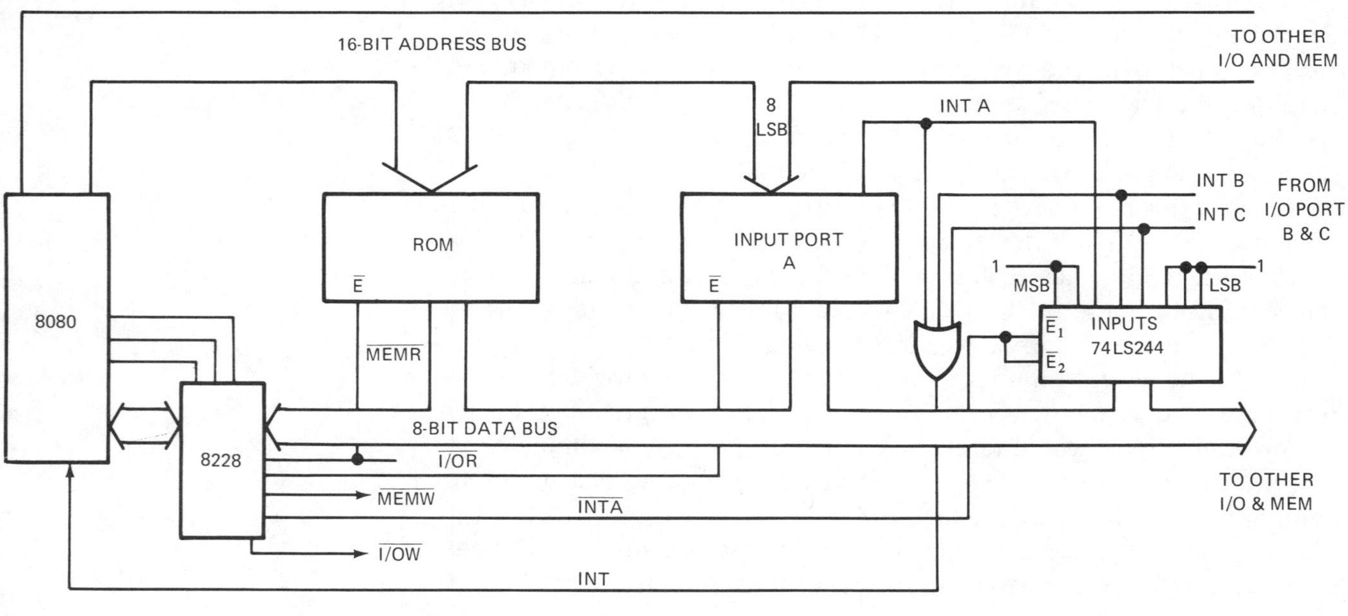

TABLE 8.3 Content of RESTART memory segments if the ports of Figure 8.10 are serviced in the priority B-A-C.

MEMORY CONTENT	INSTRUCTION	ADDRESS (HEX)
RESET JMP	RST 0	(0000)
PORT C (SVC ROUTINE OR JMP)	RST 1	(0008)
PORT B (SVC ROUTINE OR JMP)	RST 2	(0010
C + B (JMP TO B SVC ROUTINE)	RST 3	(0018)
PORT A (SVC ROUTINE OR JMP)	RST 4	(0020)
A + C (JMP TO A SVC ROUTINE)	RST 5	(0028)
A + B (JMP TO B SVC ROUTINE)	RST 6	(0030)
A + B + C (JMP TO B SVC ROUTINE)	RST 7	(0038)

If the system has ports requiring more than three service routines, OR gate encoders can be used provided it is not possible for interrupts to occur simultaneously. The software priority method will not work where the number of interrupts exceeds three. In a system requiring priority interrupts, the 8214 "Priority Interrupt Control" may be used. Figure 8.11 shows the 8214. The 8214 connects through an auxiliary port to provide restart instructions and priority control over multiple interrupts of seven I/O ports.

In addition to restart instructions, the 8080 will respond to subroutine CALL instructions as a response to an $\overline{\text{INTA}}$. On receipt of a CALL instruction, the program will proceed directly to the subroutine address instead of jumping to a restart memory segment. To do this the interrupting port must answer an INTA signal with a 3-byte instruction. The use of subroutine call by an interrupting port requires a relatively elaborate design, but this capability expands the capacity of the 8080 interrupt system considerably. A special peripheral device is available for this function, the 8259 "Interrupt Control". This device responds to an interrupt acknowledge by transmitting a 3-byte call instruction. The address bytes (bytes two and three) of the call instruction are written into the 8259 during the initialization sequence of the 8080 program. Interrupt systems of this complexity are not within the scope of this chapter. The introductory programs in this chapter will deal

PIN CONFIGURATION

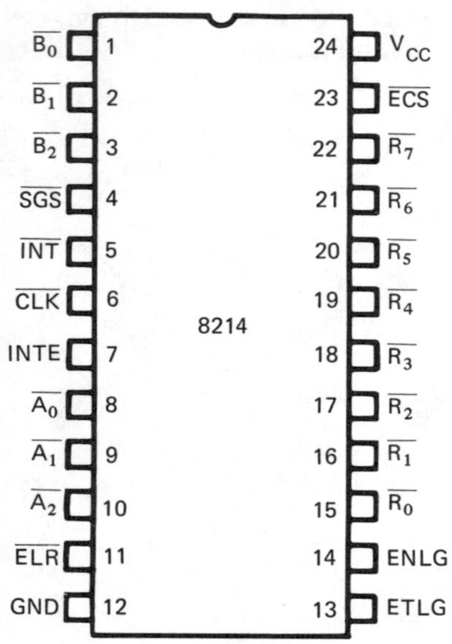

LOGIC DIAGRAM

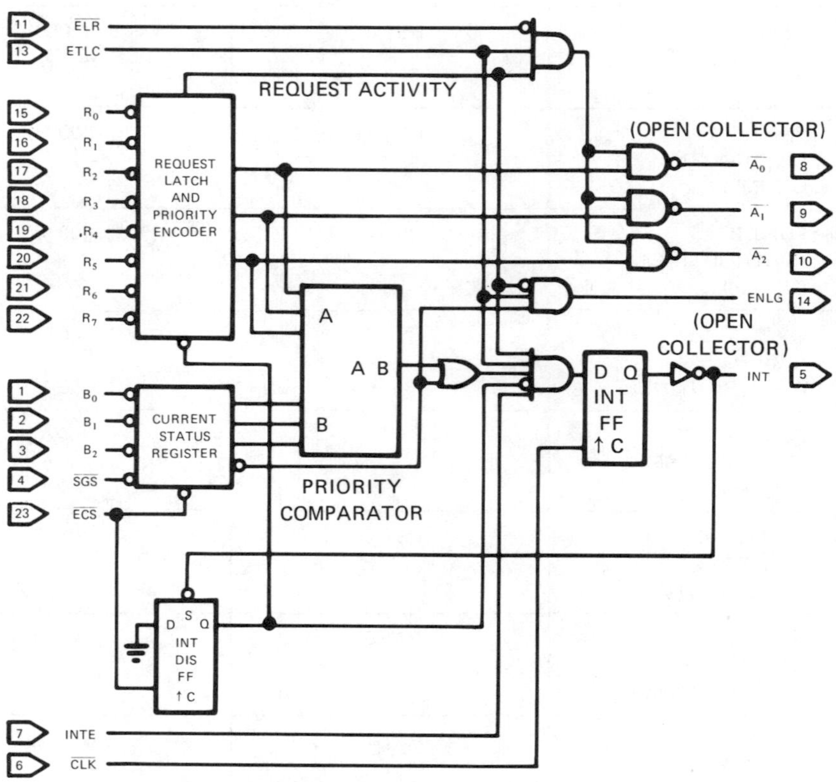

PIN NAMES

INPUTS		
$\overline{R_0}$-$\overline{R_7}$	REQUEST LEVELS (R_7 HIGHEST PRIORITY)	
$\overline{B_0}$-$\overline{B_2}$	CURRENT STATUS	
$\overline{SGS}$	STATUS GROUP SELECT	
$\overline{ECS}$	ENABLE CURRENT STATUS	
INTE	INTERRUPT ENABLE	
$\overline{CLK}$	CLOCK (INT F-F)	
$\overline{ELR}$	ENABLE LEVEL READ	
ETLG	ENABLE THIS LEVEL GROUP	
OUTPUTS		
$\overline{A_0}$-$\overline{A_2}$	REQUEST LEVELS	OPEN COLLECTOR
$\overline{INT}$	INTERRUPT (ACT LOW)	OPEN COLLECTOR
ENLG	ENABLE NEXT LEVEL GROUP	

FIGURE 8.11 8214 Priority interrupt control. This circuit may be used to supply restart instructions to eight separate I/O service routines. (*Courtesy Intel Corporation*)

with a single interrupt level. Where a single interrupt service routine is needed, the 8228 has a provision for generating a single restart instruction (RST 7). This is accomplished by connecting a 1K ohm resistor between the $\overline{INTA}$ pin and +12 volts. When this is done, the 8228 will automatically transmit an RST 7 to the 8080 in response to an interrupt acknowledge status word. The CPU then functions with a single interrupt vector to a service routine located at memory address 0038_H. The interrupt system then operates in the following steps.

Step 1 The 8080 in the process of executing main program instruction (PC) will have the INTE flip-flop set. Having the INTE flip-flop set results in a high level on the INTE line to the interrupting port informing the port that the processor is accepting interrupts.

Step 2 When the input device needs to be serviced it signals the processor with a high level on the INT line.

Step 3 On receipt of an active INT signal the processor completes execution of the instruction which is in process and increments the program counter.

$$PC \longleftarrow (PC + 1)$$

Step 4 The INTA machine cycle is executed causing the 8228 to transmit the RST 7 instruction to the 8080.

Step 5 The INTE flip-flop is reset inhibiting another interrupt routine from occurring prior to execution of the next EI instruction.

Step 6 The stack pointer is decremented, then the program counter content is stored on the stack. The restart vector address 0038_H is loaded into the program counter.

Step 7 The first instruction of the service routine is executed.

The initial instructions of the service routine must be push instructions to load the microprocessor status on the stack. Only the return to main program address is stored automatically. It is seldom possible to predict when or where an interrupt will occur in the execution of the main program. Because of this the content of the accumulator, status register, and any of the registers used in both main program and service routine must be loaded on the stack.

Step 8 On completion of the service routine, POP instructions must be included to transfer data from the stack and return the accumulator and registers to their original content. The POP instructions must precede the return from interrupt instruction.

Step 9 The return from interrupt instruction causes the transfer of the return to main program address from the stack to the program counter.

(*Note:* An interrupt request from an I/O port must somehow be reset prior to the return from interupt.)

Interrupts are not recognized by the 8080 unless the INTE flip-flop is set resulting in a high level on the INTE line. The INTE flip-flop is cleared during reset and anytime an INT input is received. INTE flip-flop is set by execution of an EI (enable interrupt) instruction. An EI must occur in main program before any interrupts can occur. An interrupt service routine can be interrupted by a second interrupt only after execution of an EI instruction during the first interrupt routine. To prevent a nested interrupt the EI instruction should not occur until just before return from interrupt instruction.

8.6 The 8080 Instruction Set

8.6.1 Number of Instructions

Of the 256 machine codes that are possible with an 8-bit word, the 8080 machine code set uses 244. The concept of address modes, although used in description of 8080 programs, has not been used to divide the machine code set into a smaller set of mnemonics. Table 8.4 is a listing of the instruction set in numerical order of the machine code with the equivalent mnemonic for each machine code. Note that many

TABLE 8.4 8080 CPU instructions in operation code sequence. The following is a summary of the instruction set:

OP CODE	MNEMONIC	OP CODE	MNEMONIC	OP CODE	MNEMONIC	OP CODE	MNEMONIC	OP CODE	MNEMONIC	OP CODE	MNEMONIC
00	NOP	2B	DCX H	56	MOV D,M	81	ADD C	AC	XRA H	D7	RST 2
01	LXI B,D16	2C	INR L	57	MOV D,A	82	ADD D	AD	XRA L	D8	RC
02	STAX B	2D	DCR L	58	MOV E,B	83	ADD E	AE	XRA M	D9	—
03	INX B	2E	MVI L,D8	59	MOV E,C	84	ADD H	AF	XRA A	DA	JC Adr
04	INR B	2F	CMA	5A	MOV E,D	85	ADD L	B0	ORA B	DB	IN D8
05	DCR B	30	SIM	5B	MOV E,E	86	ADD M	B1	ORA C	DC	CC Adr
06	MVI B,D8	31	LXI SPD16	5C	MOV E,H	87	ADD A	B2	ORA D	DD	—
07	RLC	32	STA Adr	5D	MOV E,L	88	ADC B	B3	ORA E	DE	SBI D8
08	—	33	INX SP	5E	MOV E,M	89	ADC C	B4	ORA H	DF	RST 3
09	DAD B	34	INR M	5F	MOV E,A	8A	ADC D	B5	ORA L	E0	RPO
0A	LDAXB	35	DCR M	60	MOV H,B	8B	ADC E	B6	ORA M	E1	POP H
0B	DCX B	36	MVI M,D8	61	MOV H,C	8C	ADC H	B7	ORA A	E2	JPO Adr
0C	INR C	37	STC	62	MOV H,D	8D	ADC L	B8	CMP B	E3	XTHL
0D	DCR C	38	——	63	MOV H,E	8E	ADC M	B9	CMP C	E4	CPO Adr
0E	MVI C,D8	39	DAD SP	64	MOV H,H	8F	ADC A	BA	CMP D	E5	PUSH H
0F	RRC	3A	LDA Adr	65	MOV H,L	8G	SUB B	BB	CMP E	E6	ANI D8
10	——	3B	DCX SP	66	MOV H,M	91	SUB C	BC	CMP H	E7	RST 4
11	LXI D,D16	3C	INR A	67	MOV H,A	92	SUB D	BD	CMP L	E8	RPE
12	STAX D	3D	DCR A	68	MOV L,B	93	SUB E	BE	CMP M	E9	PCHL
13	INX D	3E	MVI A,D8	69	MOV L,C	94	SUB H	BF	CMP A	EA	JPE Adr
14	INR D	3F	CMC	6A	MOV L,D	95	SUB L	C0	RNZ	EB	XCHG
15	DCR D	40	MOV B,B	6B	MOV L,E	96	SUB M	C1	POP B	EC	CPE Adr
16	MVI D,D8	41	MOV B,C	6C	MOV L,H	97	SUB A	C2	JNZ Adr	ED	——
17	RAL	42	MOV B,D	6D	MOV L,L	98	SBB B	C3	JMP Adr	EE	XRI D8
18	——	43	MOV B,E	6E	MOV L,M	99	SBB C	C4	CNZ Adr	EF	RST 5
19	DAD D	44	MOV B,H	6F	MOV L,A	9A	SBB D	C5	PUSH B	F0	RP
1A	LDAXD	45	MOV B,L	70	MOV M,B	9B	5BB E	C6	ADI D8	F1	POP PSW
1B	DCX D	46	MOV B,M	71	MOV M,C	9C	SBB H	C7	RST 0	F2	JP Adr
1C	INR E	47	MOV B,A	72	MOV M,D	9D	SBB L	C8	RZ	F3	DI
1D	DRC E	48	MOV C,B	73	MOV M,E	9E	SBB M	C9	RET Adr	F4	CP Adr
1E	MVI E,D8	49	MOV C,C	74	MOV M,H	9F	SBB A	CA	JZ	F5	PUSH PSW
1F	RAR	4A	MOV C,D	75	MOV M,L	A0	ANA B	CB	——	F6	ORI D8
20	RIM	4B	MOV C,E	76	HLT	A1	ANA C	CC	CZ Adr	F7	RST 6
21	LXI H,D16	4C	MOV C,H	77	MOV M,A	A2	ANA D	CD	CALL Adr	F8	RM
22	SHLD Adr	4D	MOV C,L	78	MOV A,B	A3	ANA E	CE	ACI D8	F9	SPHL
23	INX H	4E	MOV C,M	79	MOV A,C	A4	ANA H	CF	RST 1	FA	JM Adr
24	INR H	4F	MOV C,A	7A	MOV A,D	A5	ANA L	D0	RNC	FB	EI
25	DCR H	50	MOV D,B	7B	MOV A,E	A6	ANA M	D1	POP D	FC	CM Adr
26	MVI H,D8	51	MOV D,C	7C	MOV A,H	A7	ANA A	D2	JNC Adr	FD	——
27	DAA	52	MOV D,D	7D	MOV A,L	A8	XRA B	D3	OUT D8	FE	CPI D8
28	——	53	MOV D,E	7E	MOV A,M	A9	XRA C	D4	CNC Adr	FF	RST 7
29	DAD H	54	MOV D,H	7F	MOV A,A	AA	XRA D	D5	PUSH D		
2A	LHLD Adr	55	MOV D,L	80	ADD B	AB	XRA E	D6	SUI D8		

D8 = constant, or logical/arithmetic expression that evaluates to an 8-bit data quantity. D16 = constant, or logical/arithmetic expression that evaluates to a 16-bit data quantity. Adr = 16-bit address. *ALL MNEMONICS © 1974, 1975, 1976, 1977 INTEL CORPORATION.*

mnemonics differ only by one or two letters that specify operands. If some mnemonics are expressed in a general form, a more convenient list of reduced size can be used. This will become more evident as we examine the addressing modes and the format of the instructions.

8.6.2 Addressing Modes

Instructions may be from one byte to three bytes in length. In all cases the first byte of each instruction contains the opcode. In many instructions, the first byte may also identify one or more operands. For 2- and 3-byte instructions, the second and third bytes contain either the operand or the address of the operand. The addressing modes are: Implied, Register, Register Indirect, Immediate, and Direct. Most instructions have dual operands, the destination and source operands. Destination and source operands of the same instruction may take different addressing modes. In such cases, the instruction will be listed with the more complicated mode.

Implied Addressing Figure 8.12 illustrates the implied mode. The instruction is single byte and requires only a fetch of the opcode. The operand is implied by the opcode. Table 8.5 is a list of 8080 instructions which take the implied mode.

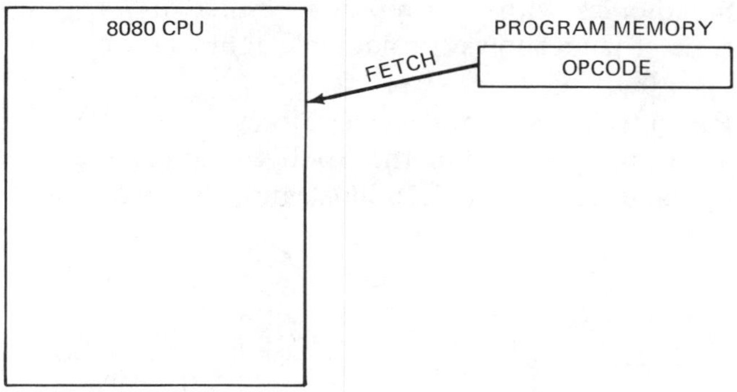

FIGURE 8.12 Implied addressing mode. The implied addressing mode is a single byte instruction containing the opcode only. The operand is the accumulator, status flag, or other element implied by the opcode.

TABLE 8.5 Instructions with implied addressing mode.

MNEMONIC	IMPLIED OPERAND	DESCRIPTION
CMA	ACC	Complement the accumulator $A \leftarrow \overline{A}$
DAA	ACC	Decimal adjust the accumulator
DI	I F/F	Disable interrupt
EI	I F/F	Enable interrupt
HLT	None	HALT
NOP	None	No operation
RAL	ACC	ROTATE left through carry
RAR	ACC	ROTATE right through carry
RRC	ACC	ROTATE ACC to right
SPHL	SP H&L	Move H, L to (SP) stack pointer
STC	C Flag	Set Carry
XTHL	H, L D, E	Exchange H, L with D, E

Register Addressing Register mode applies to instructions for which one of the 8080 internal registers is an operand. In the case of the MOV instructions, both destination and source operands may be registers. Figure 8.13 illustrates the register mode with the MOV instruction.

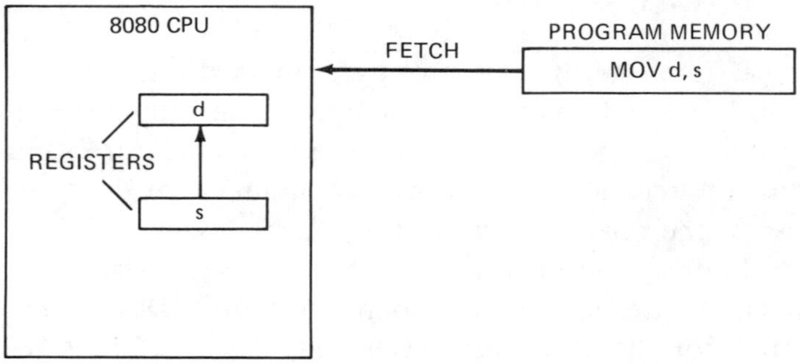

FIGURE 8.13 Register mode addressing. This mode requires a single byte instruction which contains in addition to the opcode, an operand field. The operand field identifies a register to be used as the destination, (d), or the source, (s).

These instructions are single byte and, as Figure 8.14 indicates, the machine code contains one or two operand fields that decode to identify which of seven registers is to be used as operands. (There is little need for the programmer to memorize the code.) The mode also applies to instructions using register pairs as 16-bit operands.

Table 8.6 lists the instructions that take the register mode. Using mnemonics with r to represent either of 7 registers or rp to represent register pairs allows considerable abbreviation of the instruction set.

Register Indirect Addressing Mode Register indirect addressing uses a register pair within the 8080 to supply the effective address of the operand. As Figure 8.15 illustrates, the instruction is single byte but re-

FIGURE 8.14 Register mode instruction formats. **(a)** The MOV instruction format contains both destination and source operand fields. Note: The MOV M,s and MOV d,M combine register and register indirect modes. **(b)** Some register mode instructions require only a source operand. **(c)** Register mode instructions that require 16-bit operands, use a format with a 2-bit register pair field.

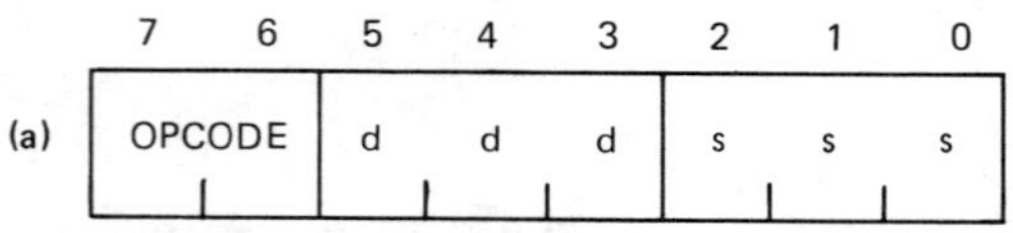

d d d s s s	LOCATION DESIGNATED
0 0 0	B REGISTER
0 0 1	C REGISTER
0 1 0	D REGISTER
0 1 1	E REGISTER
1 0 0	H REGISTER
1 0 1	L REGISTER
1 1 0	M (MEMORY LOCATION POINTED TO BY H AND L)
1 1 1	ACCUMULATOR

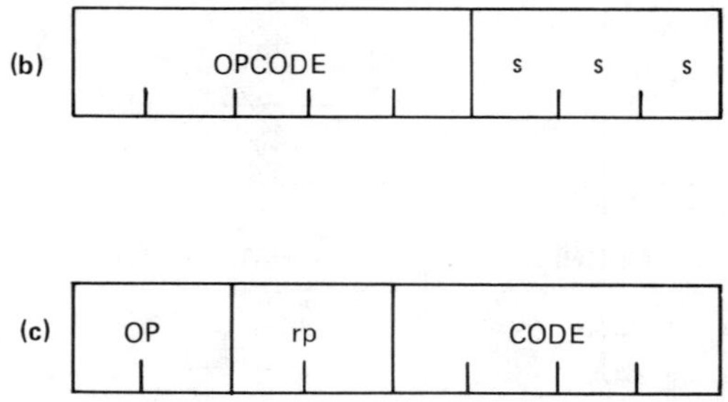

rp	LOCATION DESIGNATED
0 0	B AND C REGISTER PAIR
0 1	D " E " "
1 0	H " L " "
1 1	SP FOP DAD LXI INX AND DCX
1 1	ACC AND STATUS WORD FOR PSW PUSH AND POP

MNEMONIC	SPECIFIED OPERAND d	SPECIFIED OPERAND s	IMPLIED OPERAND	DESCRIPTION
MOV	r_d	r_s		Move contents of r_s to r_d
ADC		r_s	ACC	Add contents of r_s to ACC with carry
ADD		r_s	ACC	Add contents of r_s to ACC without
ANA		r_s	ACC	And carry contents of r_s to ACC
CMP		r_s	ACC	Compare register with ACC
DCR	r_d		ACC	Decrement r_d
INR	r_d			Increment r_d
ORA		r_s	ACC	OR contents of r_s with ACC
SBB		r_s	ACC	Subtract r_s from ACC with borrow
SUB		r_s	ACC	Subtract r_s from ACC without borrow
XRA		r_s	ACC	Exclusive OR r_s with ACC
DAD		r_p	H,L	Add r_p to H, L
INX	r_p			Increment r_p
POP	r_p		STACK	Pop contents of Stack to r_p
PUSH		r_p	STACK	Push r_p onto stack

TABLE 8.6 8080 Instructions which use register addressing mode. s = source operand. d = destination operand. r_s = register used as source operand. r_d = register used as destination operand. r_p = register pair.

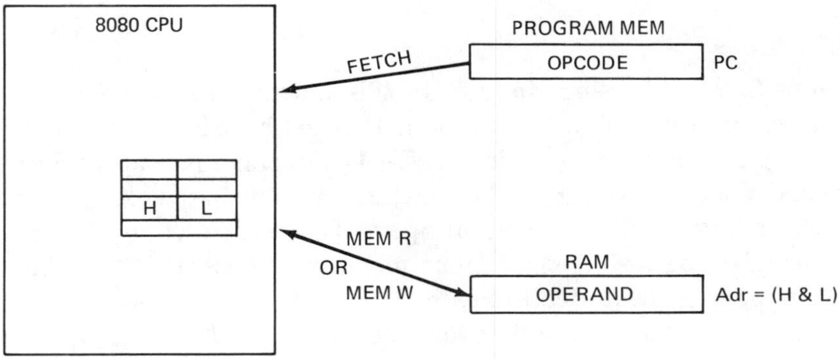

FIGURE 8.15 Register indirect address mode. The register indirect address mode has a format like that of Figure 8.15a with either a source or destination operand field containing 110 = M (Memory location pointed to by H and L). The LDAX instruction permits the use of B,C and D,E register pairs as pointers. Although the register indirect mode requires a single instruction to execute, it has the drawback that the pointer register pair must be loaded with the correct address prior to its use.

quires two or more machine cycles, one of which is the fetch of the opcode, another is a read or write of the operand. The operand is the contents of memory (designated M = 110). The operand memory address is taken from a register pair. In most cases the H, L register pair is used for this pointer function. The LDAX B loads the accumulator with the contents of a memory location at the address pointed to by the B, C register pairs. LDAX D is the same but uses the D, E register pairs as a pointer. However, the majority of these instructions use the letter M to indicate a memory address pointed to by H, L.

Table 8.7 lists the instructions that take register indirect mode. Register indirect is often combined with register and immediate modes in that instructions with both destination and source operands may have operands in each of two different modes.

TABLE 8.7 8080 Instructions which use register indirect addressing.
M = contents of a memory location whose address is the contents of the H, L register pair.

MNEMONIC	SPECIFIED OPERAND d	SPECIFIED OPERAND s	DESCRIPTION	IMPLIED OPERANDS
ADC		M	Add with carry the content of M to the ACC	ACC
ADD		M	Add without carry the contents of M to the ACC	ACC
ANA		M	And contents of M with the ACC	ACC
CMP		M	Compare contents of M with the ACC	ACC
DCR	M		Decrement M	
INR	M		Increment M	
LDAX		r_p	Load ACC with the contents of memory address pointed to by r_p.	ACC
MOV	r_d	M	Move contents of M to register r_d	
MOV	M	r_s	Move contents of register r_s to M	
SBB		M	Subtract from ACC with borrow the contents of M	ACC
SUB		M	Subtract from ACC without borrow the contents of M	ACC
XRA		M	Exclusive OR the contents of M with content of ACC	ACC

Immediate Addressing Mode In this addressing mode the operand is the second byte of the instruction. The first byte is the opcode fetched from program memory address (PC). The operand is read from program memory address (PC + 1). Although most immediate mode instructions are two bytes, a few have 16-bit operands and they require that an additional byte be read from program memory address (PC + 2). The immediate mode is illustrated in Figure 8.16. This mode is good for operands that are constant values known when the program is written. It does not apply for operands that must be computed and stored during the running of the program.

Table 8.8 lists those instructions which take the immediate mode. Note that the MVI instruction has destination operands in both register and register indirect mode.

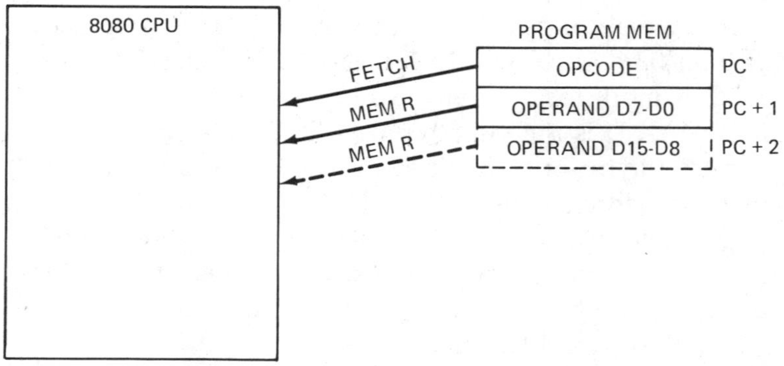

FIGURE 8.16 Immediate addressing mode. This mode is ideal for constant operands which can be written into the program. It cannot be used for variable operands that must be computed or changed during the run of the program. This mode may be combined with either register or register indirect mode in that the source operand has immediate addressing while the destination operand is register mode.

MNEMONIC	SPECIFIED DESTINATION OPERAND	IMPLIED DESTINATION OPERAND	DESCRIPTION
ACI		ACC	Add Immediate with carry to ACC
ADI		ACC	Add Immediate without carry to ACC
ANI		ACC	AND Immediate to ACC
CPI		ACC	Compare Immediate with ACC
LXI	r_p		Load a designated register pair with contents of (PC + 1) and (PC + 2)
MVI	r_d		Move Immediate to register
MVI	M		Move Immediate to memory address point to by (H, L)
ORI		ACC	OR Immediate with Accumulator
SBI		ACC	Subtract Immediate from ACC with borrow
SUI		ACC	Subtract Immediate from ACC without borrow
XRI		ACC	Exclusive OR Immediate with ACC
ACI		ACC	Add Immediate with carry to ACC

TABLE 8.8 8080 Instructions which use immediate addressing. For these instructions, the source operand is the contents of the second byte of the instruction. The first byte (PC) contains the opcode. The second byte (PC + 1) is the source operand.

Direct Addressing Mode The direct addressing mode may be used for variable operands that are computed during the program and stored in RAM. Instructions with direct addressing mode are 3-byte with the exception of the IN and OUT instructions. The first byte of the instruction is the opcode fetched from program memory address PC. The address of the operand is contained in the second and third bytes of the instruction. This instruction requires a minimum of four machine cycles. Figure 8.17 illustrates the direct addressing mode. Table 8.9 lists instructions that take the direct addressing mode.

8.6.3 Conditional Instructions

The call subroutine, return from subroutine, and the jump instruction can be unconditional or can occur conditionally dependent on one of eight conditions of the flags. The unconditional instructions are

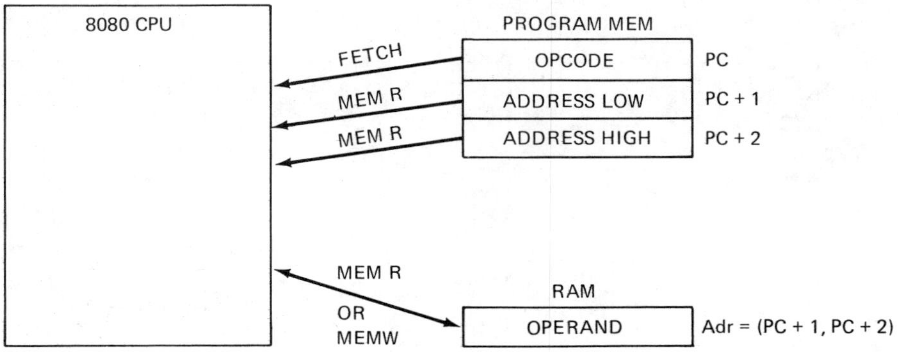

FIGURE 8.17 Direct addressing mode. With the exception of IN and OUT instructions this mode requires three bytes. The second and third byte contain the effective address of the operand. This is the most versatile addressing mode in that it can be used for variable operands and the address does not need to be loaded into a pointer register prior to its use. It requires a minimum of four machine cycles. As I/O ports are addressed by either the upper or lower half of the 16 address bits. The IN and OUT instructions require only a single address byte following the opcode.

TABLE 8.9 8080 Instructions which use direct addressing.

MNEMONIC (PC)	ADDRESS OF OPERAND (PC + 1)	(PC + 2)	DESCRIPTION
LDA	ADL	ADH	Load ACC from memory
LHLD	ADL	ADH	Load L Register from memory address specified in (PC + 1) and (PC + 2). Load H Register from next higher memory address.
SHLD	ADL	ADH	Store (L) Register in RAM address specified in (PC + 1) and (PC + 2). Store (H) Register in next higher RAM address.
STA	ADL	ADH	Store Accumulator in RAM address designated by (PC + 1) and (PC + 2).
IN	(EITHER HIGH OR LOW BYTE OF ADDRESS CAN BE USED)		Input DATA to the Accumulator from port designated by address (PC + 1).
OUT	(EITHER HIGH OR LOW BYTE OF ADDRESS CAN BE USED)		Output DATA from the Accumulator to port designated by address (PC + 1).

CALL = Jump to subroutine unconditionally

RET = Return from subroutine unconditionally

JMP = Jump unconditionally

The conditional forms of these instructions are coded in a machine code field as shown in Figure 8.18. The first letters of these conditional

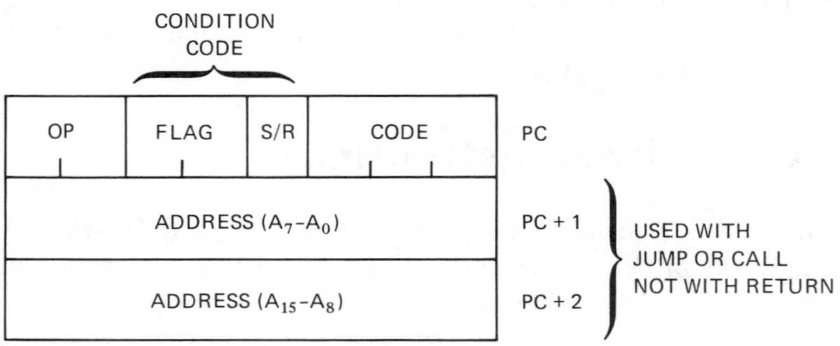

FIGURE 8.18 Conditional instruction format. Three instructions: the CALL, JUMP, and RETURN can be conditional. They are executed or not executed depending on condition of a flag. The first letter C, J, or R identifies the mnemonic as a call, jump or return instruction. The remaining letters identify the condition. The instruction format contains a field of the condition code. The CALL and JUMP instructions require address bytes (PC + 1) and (PC + 2). The return instruction obtains its address from the stack.

CALL MNEMONIC	JUMP MNEMONIC	RETURN MNEMONIC	CONDITION FLAG	S/R	CONDITION
CC	JC	RC	01	1	CY = 1: CARRY
CNC	JNC	RNC	01	0	CY = 0: NO CARRY
CP	JP	RP	11	0	S = 0: POSITIVE SIGN
CM	JM	RM	11	1	S = 1: NEGATIVE SIGN
CPE	JPE	RPE	10	1	P = 1: PARITY EVEN
CPO	JPO	RPO	10	0	P = 0: PARITY ODD
CZ	JZ	RZ	00	1	Z = 1: ZERO
CNZ	JNZ	RNZ	00	0	Z = 0: NOT ZERO

instructions are C, J, or R depending on whether it is a CALL, JUMP, or RETURN instruction. The suffix letters indicating the flag condition are the same for each of the three.

If the condition of the flag is correct, the instruction will be executed resulting in a change in the program count to the address written in (PC + 1) and (PC + 2), or SP in the case of a return. If the condition of the flag is not met, the program counter is incremented as usual.

8.7 The 8080 Bootstrap Loader

8.7.1 Function

Like other microprocessors the 8080 is useful only when it is under the control of a program. In usual applications the microprocessor is dedicated to a single task for which the program is the same each time it is executed. These dedicated programs are ideally stored in a ROM or PROM. The advantage of these memory devices is their nonvolatility. The program is not lost when the power is removed. In some systems, however, programs or short segments of program must be varied each time it is run. Under such conditions, programs must be loaded into RAM. The 8080 system has no built-in provisions for loading programs into RAM. This function must be controlled by a short dedicated program. A short program used to control the loading of larger programs is generally called a bootstrap loader. Our bootstrap loader will work in conjunction with a simple hexadecimal keyboard similar to that developed in Figure 5.18. As the hexadecimal digits are entered through the keyboard, they are first stored in the keyboard flip-flops, in pairs, to form the data bytes. It is the function of the loader program to move each byte from the keyboard flip-flops into the 8080 accumulator and from there to the desired RAM memory location.

8.7.2 Data Move Instructions

Before discussing the details of the bootstrap loader, let us take a more detailed look at the class of instructions used in this type of operation.

Instructions which move data form the largest group in the 8080 instruction set. There are the move, load, store, and transfer instructions which move data from register to register, from memory to register, and from register to memory. These instructions move data from a source operand to a destination operand.

$$d \longleftarrow (S)$$

After execution of a move instruction, destination and source operands both contain the same data. The most common of these instructions can be generalized as:

MOV d,s

The format of this instruction is given in Figure 8.14(a). There are 64 such instructions, (eight are of minor importance MOV A,A) 54 are register mode and they move data from one 8-bit register to another.

$$\text{MOV} \quad r_D, r_S \qquad r = \text{A,B,C,D,E,H,L}$$

The register letter is substituted for r_D and r_S.

The letter M signifies a memory byte located at an address which is taken from H, L register. This instruction moves a data byte from memory to the specified destination register.

$$\text{MOV} \quad r_D, \text{M} \qquad r_D \longleftarrow (\text{M})$$

The following instruction moves a data byte from the specified source register to a memory location pointed to by the H & L register.

$$\text{MOV} \quad \text{M}, r_S \qquad \text{M} \longleftarrow (r_S)$$

To use register indirect operand (M) the H & L register must be loaded with the desired address.

LHLD **LOAD H and L Register Direct** can be used to load the L register from a memory location. The address of the memory location is given in the second and third bytes of the instruction. The H register is loaded with the contents of the next higher memory address.

Load register pair immediate is used to load register pairs or stack pointer with data bytes taken from the second and third bytes of the instruction.

LXI rp Load Register Pair Immediate

$$rp \longleftarrow (PC + 2)$$

$$rp + 1 \longleftarrow (PC + 1)$$

rp = B, D, H or (Stack Pointer High Byte)

(rp + 1) = C, E, L or (Stack Pointer Low Byte)

Load accumulator direct moves a data byte from a memory location to the accumulator. The address of the memory location is given in the second and third bytes of the instruction.

LDA adr — Load Accumulator Direct

$$\text{ACC} \longleftarrow (\text{MEM})$$

Store accumulator direct moves a data byte from the accumulator to a memory location. The address of the memory location is given in the second and third bytes of the instruction.

STA	adr	Store Accumulator Direct

$$\text{MEM} \longleftarrow (\text{ACC})$$

Input is used to transfer data from an input port which is not memory mapped. The port uses not more than 8 address bits and must be enabled by the $\overline{\text{I/OR}}$ rather than $\overline{\text{MEMR}}$. The data is transferred from port to accumulator. The address of the port is given in the second byte of the instruction.

IN adr	Input

$$\text{ACC} \longleftarrow (\text{PORT})$$

Output is used to transfer data from accumulator to an output port which is not memory mapped. The port uses not more than 8 address bits and the $\overline{\text{I/OW}}$ is used rather than $\overline{\text{MEMW}}$. The address of the port is given in the second byte of the instruction.

OUT adr	Output

$$\text{PORT} \longleftarrow (\text{ACC})$$

8.7.3 Other Instructions Used with the Bootstrap Loader

Increment register pair is used to increase by one the value in a specified register pair or stack pointer.

INX	rp	Increment Register Pair

$$\text{rp} \longleftarrow (\text{rp} + 1)$$

rp = B, D, H, or SP

Decrement register pair is used to decrease by one the value in a specified register pair or stack pointer.

DCX	rp	Decrement Register Pair

$$\text{rp} \longleftarrow (\text{rp} - 1)$$

rp = B, D, H or SP

Jump unconditional is used to transfer the program to an address specified in the second and third bytes of the instruction. The program may be caused to jump either forward or backward with this instruction.

JMP adr Jump Unconditional

PCL ←—— (PC + 1)

PCH ←—— (PC + 2)

The halt instruction causes the 8080 to cease operation until it receives a reset or interrupt. On completion of the interrupt service routine, the program returns to the instruction immediately following the HLT instruction.

HLT Halt

8.7.4 Bootstrap Loader Hardware

A logic diagram of an 8080 microprocessor system with bootstrap loader is shown in Figure 8.19. A 16-bit comparator and 16 address switches are used to provide addressing for the keyboard circuit. The address bus connects to the comparator A inputs. The switches connect to the comparator B inputs. The A = B output connects to the enable input of the octal bus driver (74LS244). This circuit outputs the content of the keyboard flip-flops to the data bus only when enabled by the comparator. The A = B output or its complement A ≠ B also may be used to inhibit memory circuits that might output for the same address as is set on the switches. This feature allows the keyboard to supersede any single memory byte within the 64K memory map. The keyboard circuit should not be altered while a program is being executed. It should be changed prior to reset, in conjunction with a single instruction operation or during a wait (HLT).

8.7.5 Use of Restart Instructions

The bootstrap loader requires the use of interrupts for both loading and verifying data. For this reason the 32-word-by-8-bit PROM containing the bootstrap program can be ideally located between address 0000 and $001F_H$. This will allow for a jump instruction at the reset vector location 0000.

Figure 8.20 is a memory map of the lower 32 bytes of the 8080 memory map. Note that it includes 0000, the address to which the 8080 resets (otherwise called the reset vector RST0). It also covers RST1 at 0008_H, RST2 at 0010_H, and RST3 at 0018_H. It stops just short of RST4 at 0020_H.

FIGURE 8.19 (a) Microprocessor system with a bootstrap loader circuit.

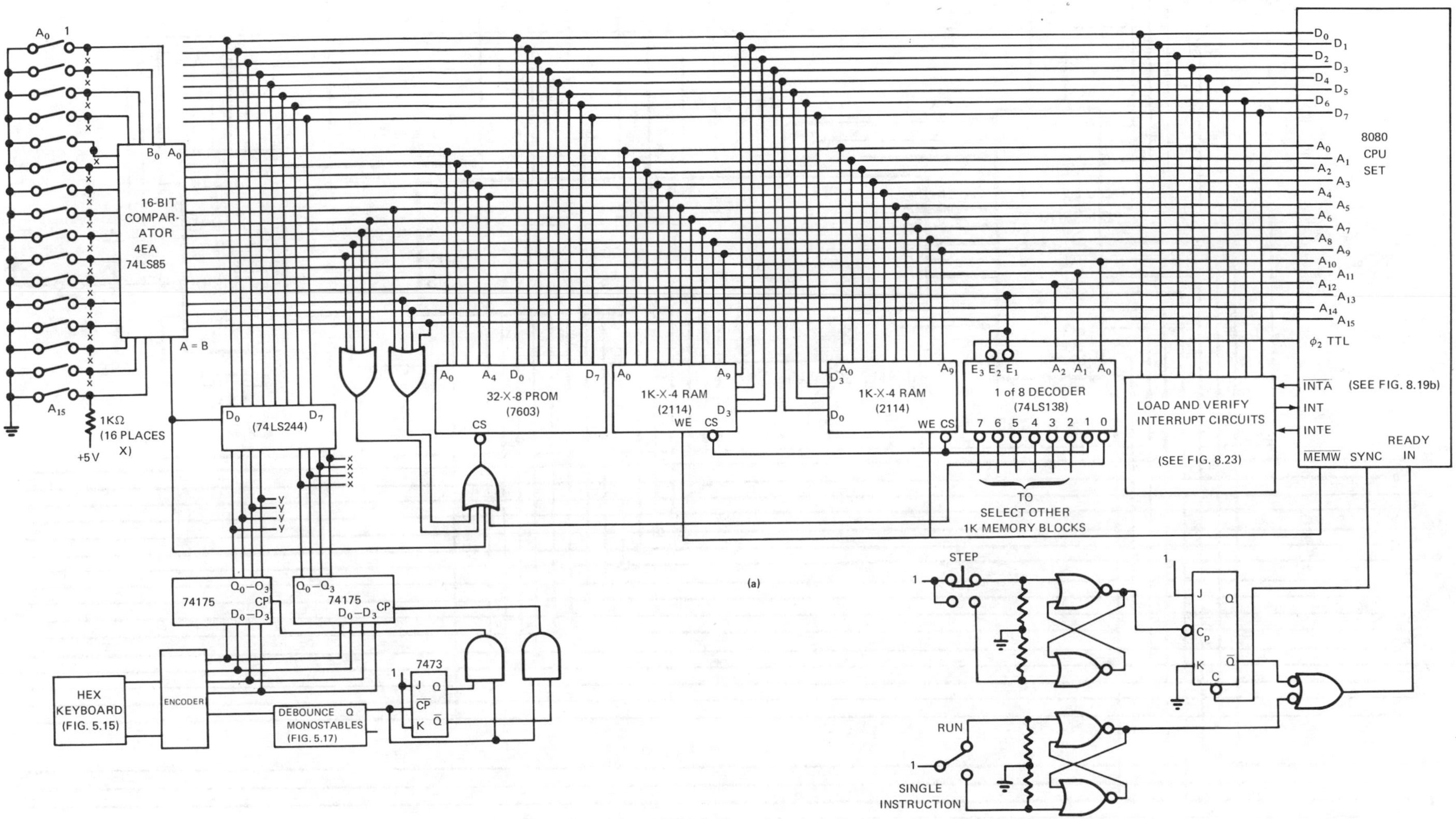

FIGURE 8.19 (b) 8080 CPU Set with connections to the address and data bus.

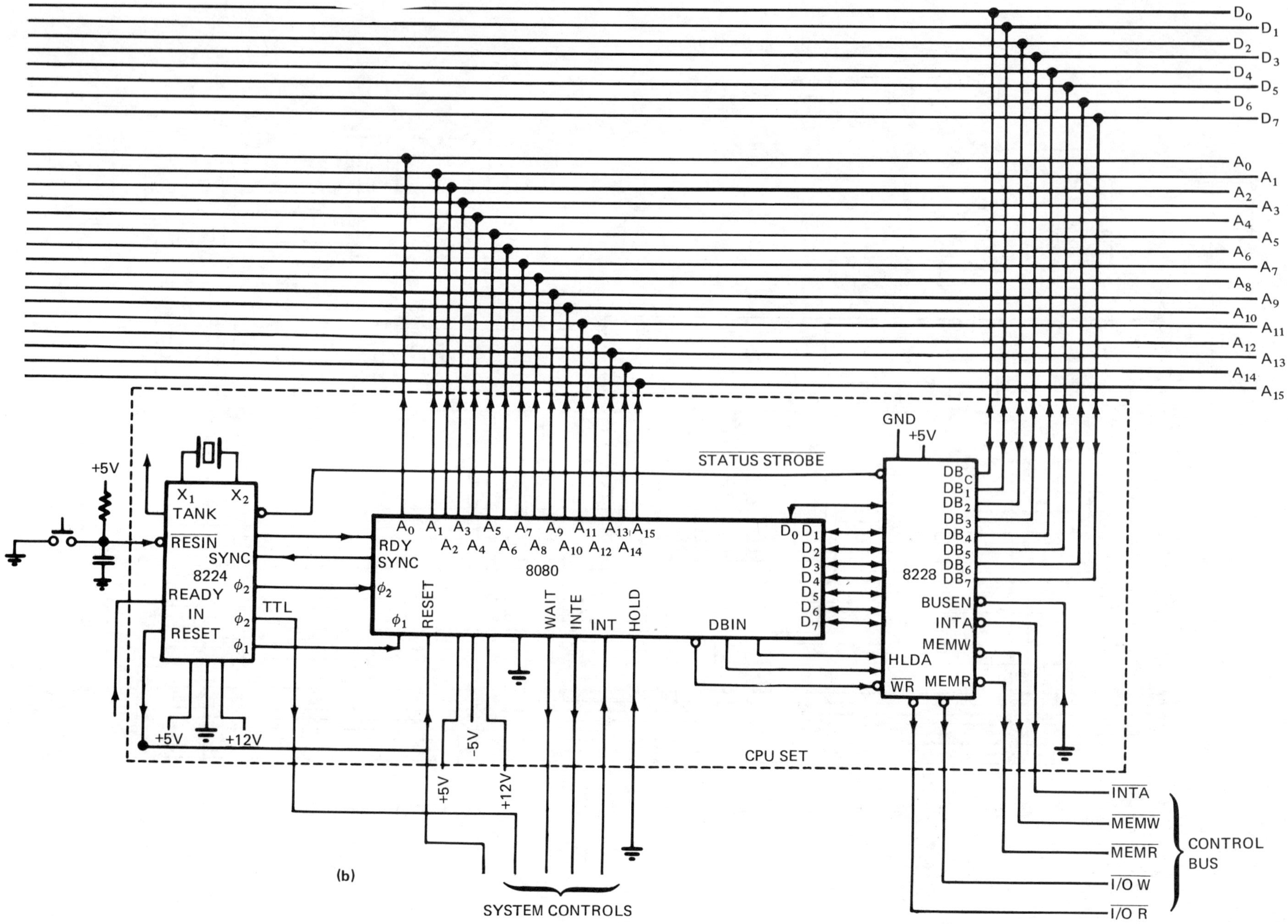

(b)

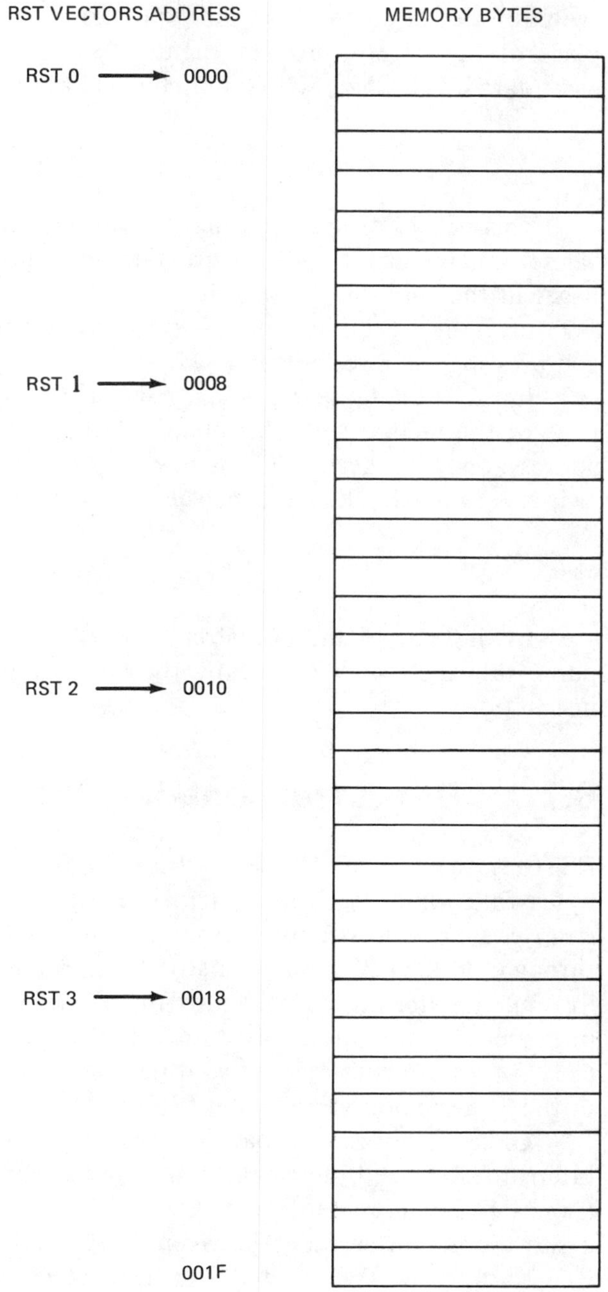

FIGURE 8.20 Memory map of lower 32-byte of the 8080 Microprocessor system. 32-byte PROM occupies memory area containing the lower four restart (RST) instructions.

8.7.6 The Reset Jump Instruction

The first three bytes of memory will contain an unconditional jump instruction. This instruction:

$$\text{JMP} \qquad 0000_H$$

will cause the 8080 to cycle continuously through the three lowest memory addresses. If, however, the keyboard comparator address switches are set to address 0002, the data in the keyboard will take the place of the data in program memory address 0002. Representing the eight data bits in the keyboard latches as kk, the result is

$$\text{JMP} \qquad \text{kk00}_H$$

This will be true only when the address switches are set to 0002. Therefore, we can cause the program to jump to any one of the 256 pages in the total memory system merely by loading the page number (kk) into the keyboard latches, setting the address switches to 0002, and pressing the reset button.

In addition to being able to select a program that starts on any page of the memory, the keyboard can be used to cause a jump to any address on page zero. This is done by setting the keyboard address switches to 0001. The reset instruction then becomes

$$\text{JMP} \qquad \text{00kk}_H$$

In the case of the bootstrap loader, the jump can be set to 0003 permitting the loader to occupy the memory just above the reset jump instruction.

8.7.7 Bootstrap Loader Memory Map

RST0 is the reset vector at address 0000. This address and the two bytes following it will be used for a reset jump instruction. The bootstrap loader will occupy memory just above this. Addresses 0003 through 000B will contain instructions for initializing the stack and loading the starting address into the H, L registers. The initialization program occupies the area of the RST1 vector and RST1 cannot be used for an interrupt service routine. Figure 8.21 shows a memory map of the 32-byte bootstrap loader PROM.

Once an address is loaded, the program will halt and wait for an interrupt. As each byte is loaded into the keyboard latches, an interrupt using RST2 will be generated. Each RST2 interrupt will be serviced by a short program segment between 0010 and 0014. The interrupt service routines RST2 initiated by the load push button and RST3 initiated by the memory read push button are interconnected by NOP instructions. Depressing the MEM READ push button causes the address and data of the next memory byte to be displayed (address H, L + 1). Depressing the load push button causes the contents of the keyboard latches to be stored in memory (address H, L) and proceeds with the display of the address and data of the next memory location (address H, L + 1). Address is incremented prior to a display and it must be kept in mind that during a load operation the address displayed is the one to be loaded rather than the one loaded previously. During a verify routine, the MEM READ push button is depressed. The address displayed is the current one and if the data is in error it can be corrected by entering the data into the keyboard latches and pressing the

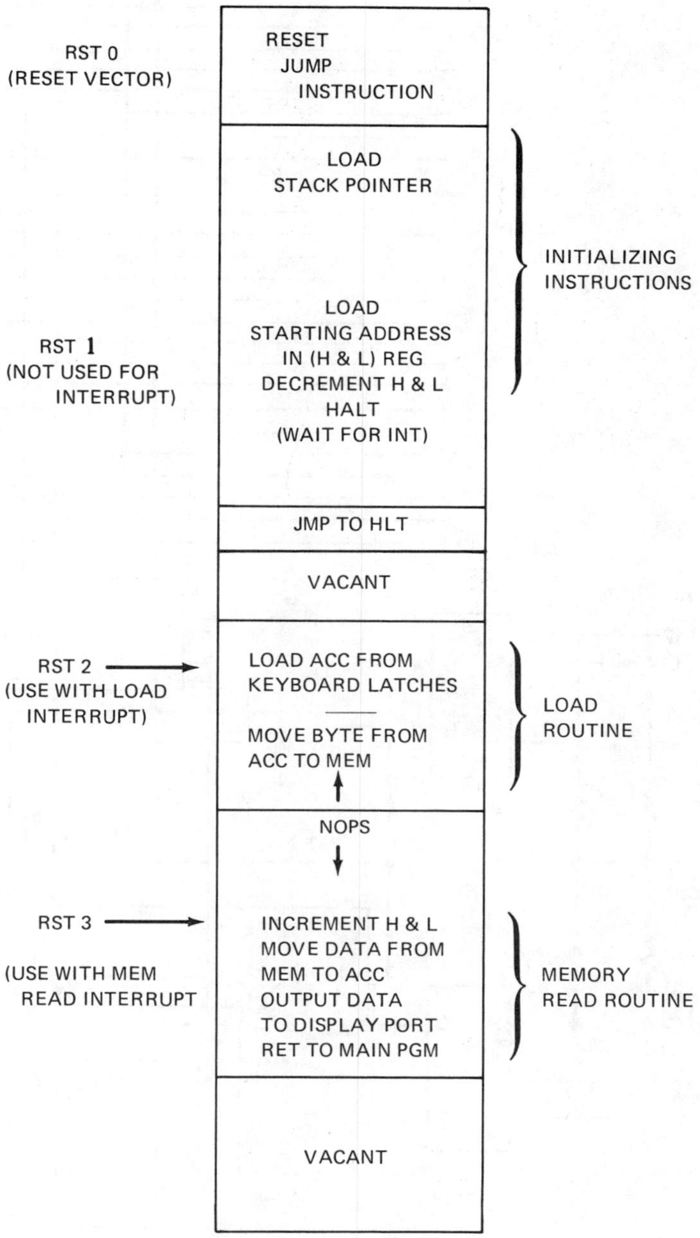

FIGURE 8.21 Memory map of bootstrap loader PROM showing the location of program functions.

load push button. After the correction is loaded the display will be of the next memory address.

An interrupt and restart instruction must be generated each time a data byte is loaded or verified. Figure 8.22 shows the circuit used to generate these signals. The load and MEM READ switches are debounced by a pair of crossed NOR flip-flops. Each flip-flop generates the necessary restart instruction which is gated onto the data bus when the bus driver (74LS244) is enabled by the $\overline{\text{INTA}}$ signal. The $\overline{\text{INTA}}$ is also used to remove the (INT) interrupt request insuring that multiple interrupts do not occur. Once set, the INT OFF flip-flop cannot be reset until both load and memory read switches are released.

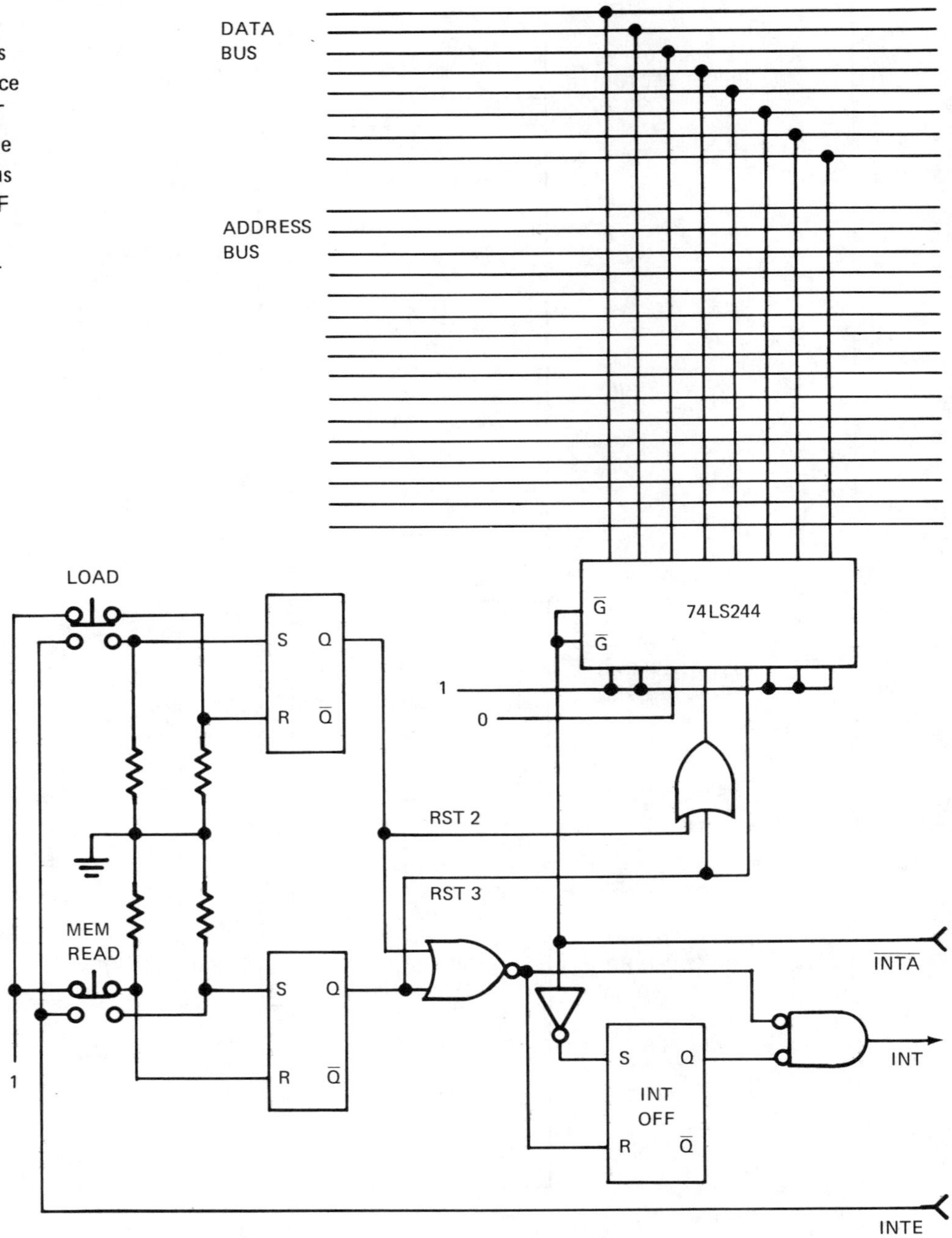

FIGURE 8.22 LOAD and VERIFY pushbutton circuits. Two cross NOR flip-flops are used to debounce the switches and generate the RST instructions. The INTA enables the RST instructions onto the data bus in addition to setting the INT OFF flip-flop. The INT-OFF flip-flop can only reset after both pushbuttons are released, thus preventing multiple interrupts from a single switch depression.

8.7.8 The 8080 Bootstrap Loader Program

Table 8.10 is a listing of the bootstrap loader program. Figure 8.23 is a memory map showing each data byte in the 32-X-8 PROM.

The steps taken by the operator in using the loader are as follows:

To Load Program

1. Processor in single instruction.

TABLE 8.10 8080 Bootstrap loader program listing.

ADDRESS	MOVEMENT	MNEMONIC	OPERAND	DESCRIPTION
0000	RST 0	JMP	0000	Reset jump instruction (either higher or lower digits of operand to be altered by keyboard)
03		LXI SP	01FF	LOAD STACK POINT INITIALIZES STACK at top of page 01
06		LXI H	kk00	LOAD H, L Register, kk is replaced by keyboard entry if address switches are set to 0008.
09		DCX H		
0A		EI		WAIT FOR INTERRUPT
0B		HLT		Jump back to halt and wait for interrupt.
0C		JMP	000A	
10	RST2 →	LDA	(FFFF)	Load Data byte from keyboard latches to accumulator. FFFF set on keyboard address switches.
13		MOV M, A		Move Data byte from ACC to MEM Address from (H, L).
14		NOP		
15		NOP		
16		NOP		
17		NOP		
18	RST 3 →	INX H		
19		MOV A, M		Move Data byte to ACC from MEM Address from (H, L).
1A		OUT	01	Output Data from ACC to display port.
001C		RET		Return to address on top of stack (000C).

2. Set keyboard address switches to 0001.
   Enter data 03.
3. Depress reset button.
4. Step processor to address 0003.
5. Set keyboard address switches to 0008.
   Enter data (page number of program to be loaded).
6. Processor to run.
   (Processor will advance to HLT instruction).
7. Set keyboard address switches to FFFF.
8. Depress memory read to verify correct starting address.
9. Enter Data (byte to be loaded at address currently pointed to by H, L).

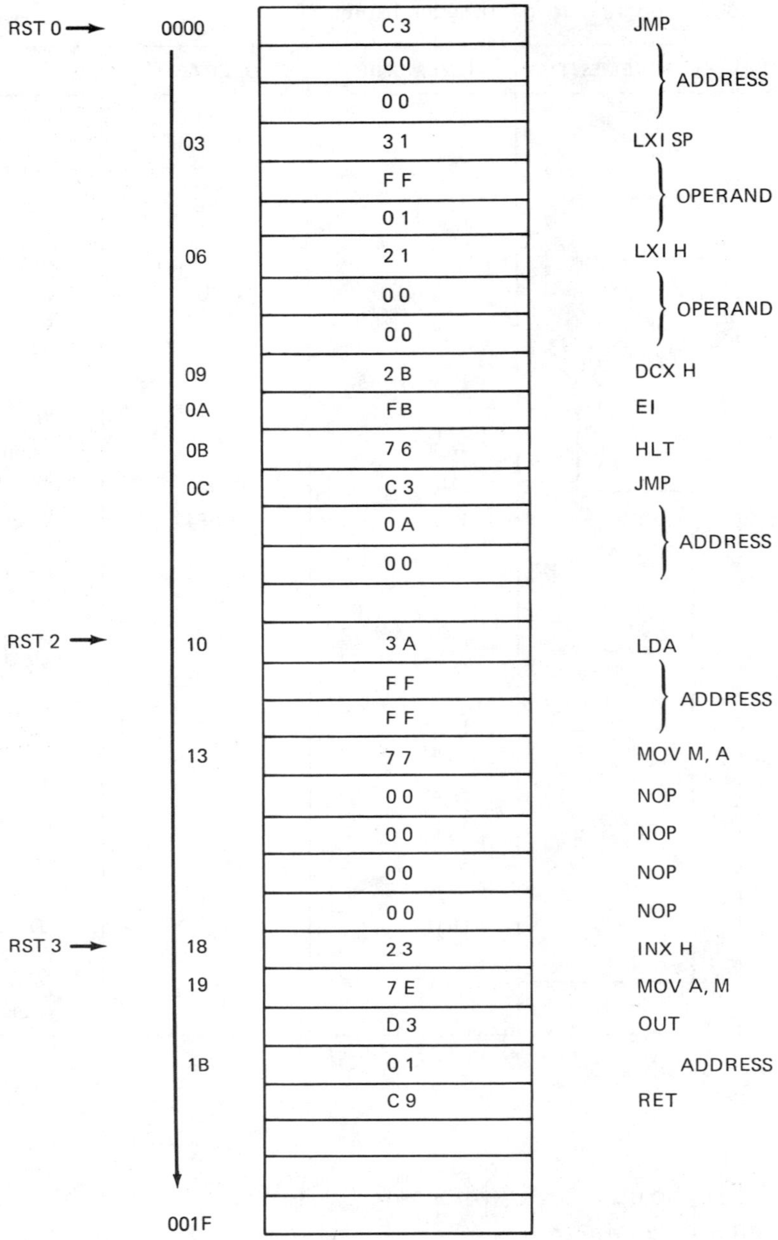

FIGURE 8.23 Bootstrap loader PROM content expressed in hexadecimal.

10. Depress load push button (RST 2).
11. Repeat Steps 9 and 10 until last program byte is loaded.

To Verify

12. Repeat Steps 1 through 7.
13. Depress MEM READ push button.
14. Observe that data and address displayed are correct.
15. Repeat Steps 13 and 14 until each program byte has been verified.

To Make Corrections

If during a verify routine an error is detected in the data stored at a given memory address, a correction can be made merely by entering the correct data into the keyboard latches and depressing the load push button. The correction will be loaded and the display will advance to the next memory address.

8.7.9 Displays

To accommodate the bootstrap loader, the display function should be alterable to display address only when it is the address taken from H, L register.

A 4-digit, 7-segment LED display may be used for the address and two digits to display the data. Both address and data to the displays must be latched. A separate data display may be used with the keyboard latches or a single data display can be used, switching between memory data and keyboard data on a last to be changed basis. Address and data cannot be latched with the same signal. The address from the H, L register pair are on the address bus only during the second machine

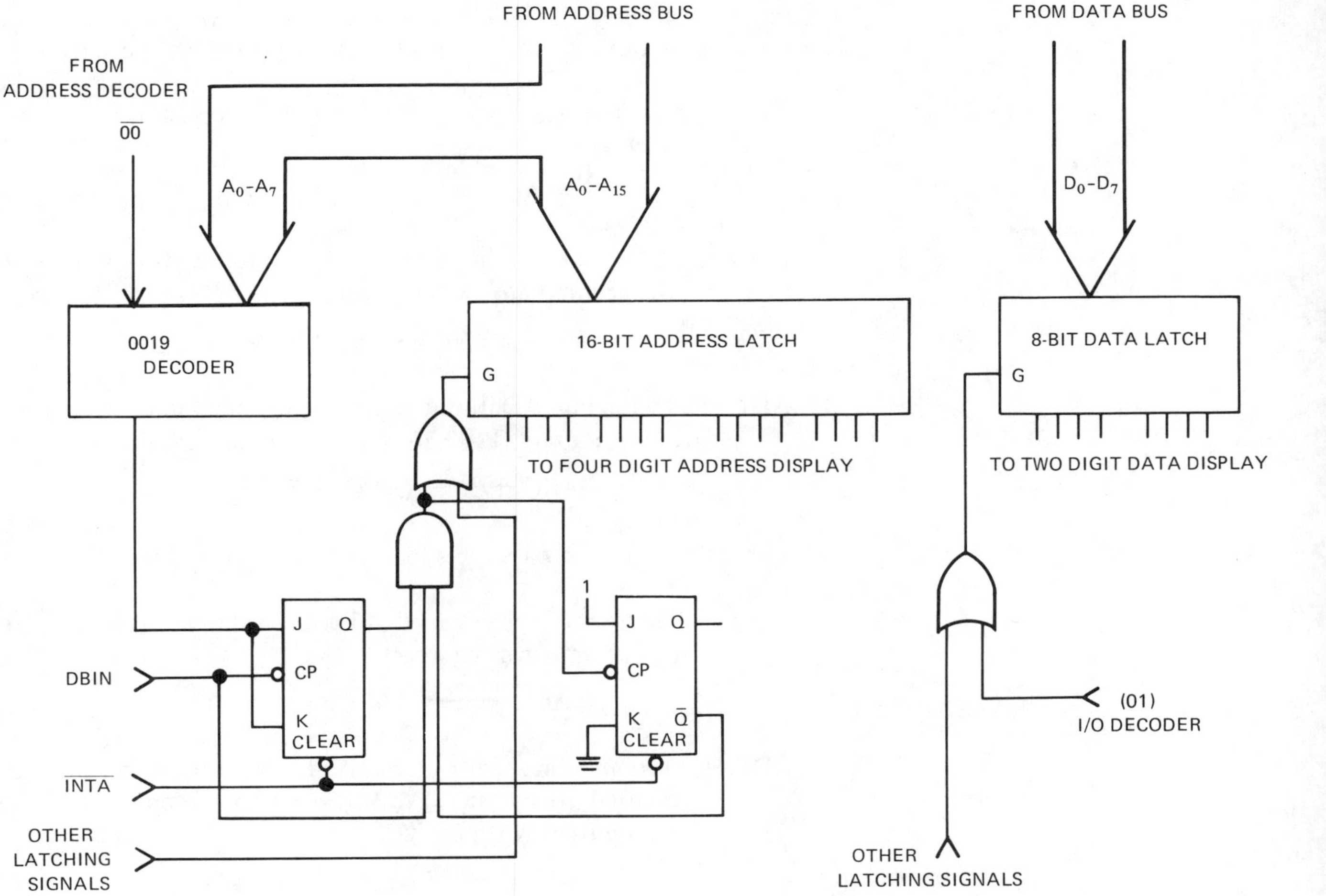

FIGURE 8.24 Decode and latch circuits for bootstrap loader displays. The AND gate is inhibited until the second DBIN occurring after a decode of 0019. The second DBIN pulse latches the address (content of H and L) into the 16-bit latch. The second J-K flip-flop sets on the trailing edge of the latch pulse inhibiting the AND gate so that subsequent DBIN pulses will not change the address display.

cycle of instruction 0019 (MOV A, M). Figure 8.24 shows the latch circuits for the displays. The data is latched during the OUT 01 instruction. The address is latched using the second DBIN pulse after a decode of instruction address 0019. The MOV A, M (like the ADD M instruction in Figure 8.2) has the content of H, L on the address bus in coincidence with second DBIN pulse of that instruction.

8.8 8080 Arithmetic Programs

8.8.1 Arithmetic Instructions

The arithmetic logic unit along with the sign and carry flag within the 8080 make possible all forms of binary arithmetic. Programs may be written for signed or unsigned arithmetic in either ones or twos complement. The auxiliary carry flag and the decimal adjust instruction facilitate arithmetic in binary coded decimal form.

Bytes may be added with or without carry. If add without carry is used for the addition of the least significant bytes of an add operation, it is not necessary to clear the carry flag. The state of the carry flag prior to an add without carry has no effect on the outcome. However, the state of the carry flag will be valid after the add without carry. The following instructions comprise the add without carry instructions

ADD r Add the value in register r to the accumulator without carry.

$$ACC \longleftarrow (ACC) + (r)$$

ADD M Add the value in memory address pointed to by H, L to the accumulator without carry.

$$ACC \longleftarrow (ACC) + (M)$$

ADI Add immediate without carry. Adds the value in program memory address (PC + 1) to the accumulator without carry.

$$ACC \longleftarrow (ACC) + (PC + 1)$$

The following comprises the add with carry instructions.

ADD r Add register with carry. Adds the value in register (r) to the accumulator with carry.

$$ACC \longleftarrow (ACC) + (r) + CY$$

ADC M Add memory with carry. Adds the content of memory pointed to by the H & L register to the content of the accumulator with carry.

$$ACC \longleftarrow (ACC) + (M) + CY$$

ACI Add immediate with carry. Adds contents of program memory immediately following the opcode to the contents of the accumulator with carry.

$$ACC \longleftarrow (ACC) + (PC + 1) + CY$$

For subtract instructions there is a choice of subtracting with or without borrow.

SUB r Subtract register from accumulator without borrow.

SUB M Subtract memory from accumulator without borrow.

SUI Subtract immediate from accumulator without borrow.

SBB r Subtract register from accumulator with borrow.

SBB M Subtract memory from accumulator with borrow.

SBI Subtract immediate from accumulator with borrow.

Although subtract instructions are available it is often desirable to handle algebraic addition by ones or twos complement. Ones complement can be accomplished by a single instruction:

CMA Complement the accumulator.

$$\overline{ACC} \longleftarrow (ACC)$$

The twos complement can be accomplished by following the CMA instruction with an INR A to add one to the accumulator after it has been complemented.

INR r Increment register.

$$r \longleftarrow (r) + 1$$

The conditional jump and call instructions play an important roll in multiplication, division, and in signed arithmetic. Branches in the program are chosen based on the condition of the flags. Table 8.11 shows the conditional jump instructions.

An important difference between the 8080 and other microprocessors is the fact that the flag register of the 8080 represents the condition of the accumulator only after an arithmetic or logic instruction. Instructions such as those which move, store, or transfer data have no effect on the condition flags. The only exception is the POP PSW which loads the flag register from the stack. If a jump, call, or return is to occur on the basis of the condition of the accumulator immediately following a non ALU instruction, a simple logic instruction must be inserted between the non ALU instruction and the conditional instruction. It must be a logic instruction which has no effect on the value in the accumulator and merely will cause the condition flags to reflect that which is in the accumulator. Table 8.12 shows four segments of

TABLE 8.11 Jump instructions. The program will jump to the address given in (PC + 1) and (PC + 2) only if the indicated flag is in the state specified. If the flag is not correct the program will increment to the instruction at (PC + 3).

JXX	(PC)
Address A_7 - A_0	(PC + 1)
Address A_{15} - A_8	(PC + 2)

MNEMONIC	NAME	CONDITION FLAG S	Z	P	CY	EQUATION
JMP	Jump Unconditional					None
JC	Jump if Carry Set				1	CY = 1
JNC	Jump if Carry Clear				0	CY = 0
JP	Jump if Positive	0				S = 0
JM	Jump if Minus	1				S = 1
JPE	Jump if Parity Even			1		P = 1
JPO	Jump if Parity Odd			0		P = 0
JZ	Jump if Zero		1			Z = 1
JNZ	Jump if not Zero		0			Z = 0

TABLE 8.12 Four program segments using conditional jump instructions. Segment (a) will work as conditional jump follows an arithmetic instruction. Segment (b) may not work as conditional jump is on condition of a non ALU instruction. Segment (c) will work as the ANA A affects the flags and does not change the accumulator. Segment (d) will work similar to segment (a). Inserting a non ALU instruction between an ALU instruction and a conditional instruction does not affect the flags. The condition of the flags is always based on the last ALU instruction executed, and the program will jump accordingly.

(a)	MOV A, B		Move B to Accumulator
	ADI A	04	Add 4 to Accumulator
	JNC	01A0	Jump to address 01A0 if CY = 0
(b)	MOV A, B		Move B to Accumulator
	JZ	011B	Jump if A = 0
(c)	MOV A, B		Move B to Accumulator
	ANA A		A A = A (Condition flags affected)
	JZ	011B	Jump if A = 0
(d)	MOV A, B		Move B to Accumulator
	ADI A	04	Add 4 to Accumulator
	MOV B, A		Move A (B + 4) back to B
	JNC	01A0	Jump to address 01A0 if CY = 0

program. Segment (b) will not work correctly because the MOV instruction does not change the status register. Inserting ANA A, as in segment (c), allows the accumulator value to remain unchanged ($A \cdot A = A$), but ANA is a logical function and the status register will reflect the value in the accumulator after a logical function. ORI 00_H could have been used ($A + 0 = A$), but ANA A is a better choice because it is single byte.

8.8.2 Twos Complement Algebraic Adder

As an example of an arithmetic routine, let us program for twos complement algebraic addition $S = X + Y$ for which both X and Y may have either positive or negative signs. By the rules of algebra, if the signs are the same we add the terms X and Y. If the signs differ, the sum will be the difference between X and Y and will take the sign of the greater. If we implement this program with twos complement arithmetic, only add instructions need be used. For single precision arithmetic (single byte), the first 7 bits represent the magnitude of the binary number. The eighth bit represents the sign. A one level in the eighth bit signifies a negative number. A zero level signifies a positive number. Figure 7.16

shows some examples of twos complement arithmetic with numbers having both positive and negative signs. The sign bits are true only as the numbers input to the microprocessor.

During manipulation within the microprocessor, the program must interpret the condition flags to determine if the sign is true or inverted. The program must also determine if a valid carry exists. The programmer must determine how the extra bit of information generated is to be handled in outputting the results. The input terms contain 8 bits of information, but because of the carry, 9 bits are needed to express the results. The 2-byte output format is another programmer's option.

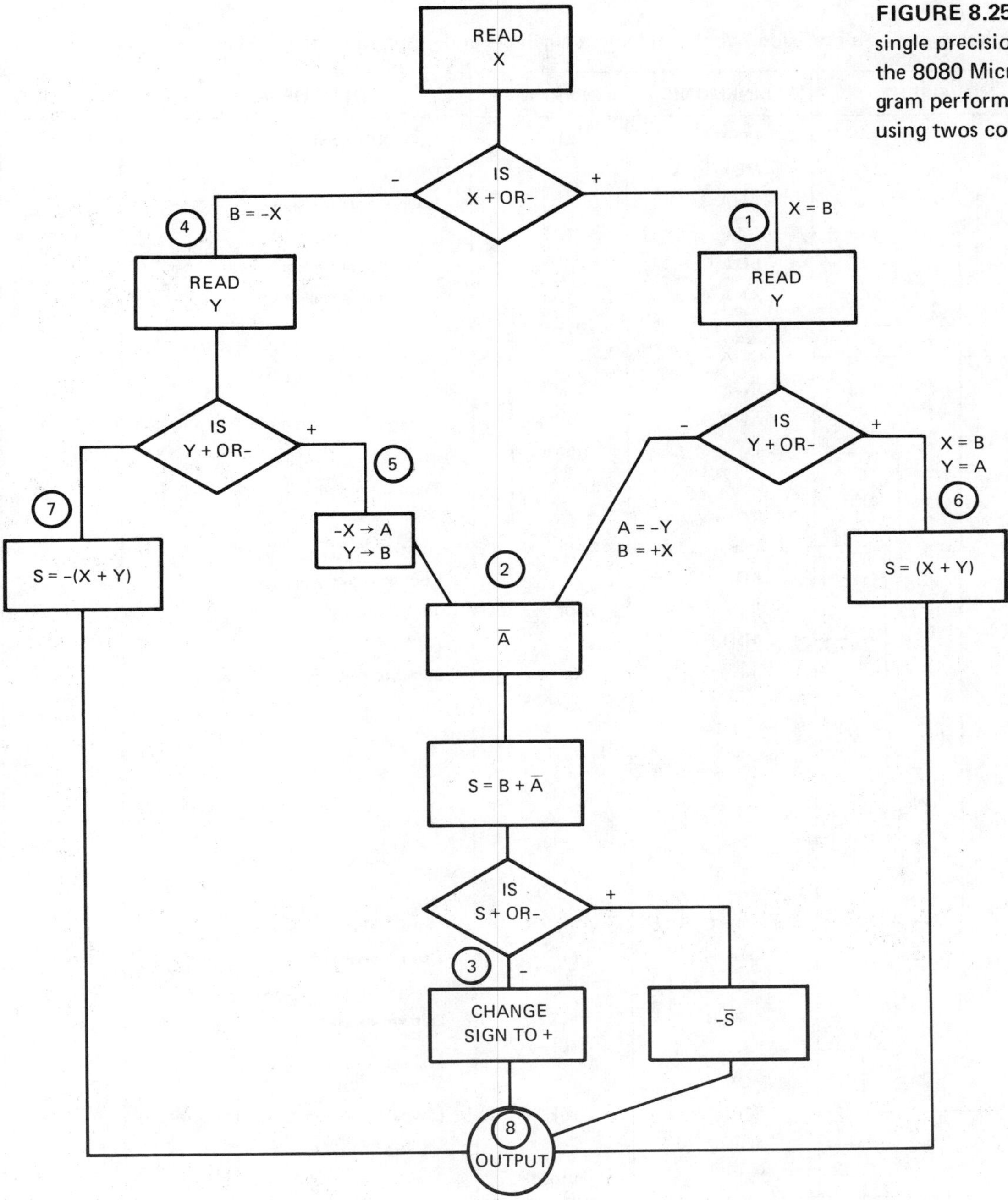

FIGURE 8.25 Flow diagram of a single precision adder program for the 8080 Microprocessor. The program performs algebraic addition using twos complement.

Figure 8.25 is a flow diagram of the twos complement algebraic adder program. The value X is read from memory. The program then branches on the basis of the sign. In each leg of the program, if X and Y have the same sign, there is a simple add and the correct sign of the output is used. If the sign of X and Y differ, the negative number is stored in A, the positive in B, and a subtraction by twos complement is performed. From the sign of the sum, the need for complementing the sum or changing the sign is determined. At the end is an output or storage routine not covered by this program.

Table 8.13 is the program listing. The value X is loaded from mem-

TABLE 8.13 Program listing of single precision twos complement algebraic adder program for the 8080 Microprocessor.

ADDRESS	MOVEMENT	MNEMONIC	OPERAND	DESCRIPTION	MODE
0180		LDA	(X)	Load X from mem	
83		MOV B, A		Move X to B	
84		ANA B		Load status for sign	
85		JM	01A3		
88		LDA	(Y)	Load Y from mem	
8B		ANA A		Load status for sign	
8C		JP	019F		
8F		CMA			
90		INR A		Twos complement A	
91		ADD B		B + (twos complement A)	
92		JM	019A		
95		CMA		Twos complement sum	
96		INR A			
97		JMP	Adr	Jump to output	
9A		ADI	80	Change sign by adding 80	
9C		JMP	Adr	Jump to output	
9F		ADD B		Add +X to +Y	
A0		JMP	Adr	Jump to output	
	TO OUTPUT PGM				
01A3		MOV C, B		Move – X to C	
A4		LDA	(Y)	Load Y from mem	
A7		MOV B, A		Move Y to B	
A8		ANA B		Determine status	
A9		JM	01B0		
AC		MOV A, C		Move –X to A	
AD		JMP	018F	(Twos complement add routine)	
B0		ADD C		S = (–X) + (–Y)	
01B1		JMP	Output		

ory. As the status register does not change with a load instruction, an ANA A instruction is inserted just prior to the jump on minus. The MOV B, A stores the value X in B so that Y can be moved to the accumulator where its sign can be checked. The number at the end of each arrow in the movement column represents the branches of the program as numbered on the flow diagram in Figure 8.25. Each branch of the program is explained as follows:

1. (+X) Load Y into accumulator and check sign. Jump if + Y.
2. (–A + B) Complement A and increment to produce 2s complement.

   Add $S = \bar{A} + B$. Jump if –S.

   (+S) Complement and increment sum to produce the correct –S. Jump to output.
3. (–S) Add 80_H to the sum which will change sign to positive.
4. (–X) Move –X to C. Load Y into accumulator and check sign. Jump if –Y.
5. (+Y–X) Move –X back to A and Jump to 2.
6. (+X+Y) Add without carry and jump to output.
7. (–X–Y) Add without carry and jump to output.
8. Output program: Because of the numerous options the output portion of the program is not listed. Where the signs of X and Y differ, there would be no carry and the sign of the sum would be valid prior to outputting. If the signs of X and Y are the same, a high level in the sign of the sum would actually be a carry. A high in the carry flag would occur only with a double negative. The output program would need to arrange these into a consistent format of sign and magnitude.

8.8.3 Double Precision Signed Arithmetic

Programs for either signed or unsigned arithmetic can be written to allow for the use of two bytes for each term. For unsigned arithmetic this permits terms of 16 bits in magnitude. For signed arithmetic only the higher byte contains a sign bit. This permits 15 magnitude bits. Let us compare the double precision arithmetic equivalent to the algebraic adder of Figure 8.25. For simplicity, we will begin the program with the values X and Y stored in four memory bytes we will identify as (X_L), (X_H), (Y_L), (Y_H). Figure 8.26 shows the flow diagram of this program. Only the high order bytes must be examined in determining the signs. This requires an ANA A instruction to be executed (at the time the high bytes are in the accumulator or register). The DAD r_p instruction provides for addition of two byte numbers in register pairs.

DAD rp Add register pair rp to the H, L register pair without carry.

FIGURE 8.26 Flow diagram of a double precision adder program. The program performs algebraic addition of two-byte numbers using twos complement.

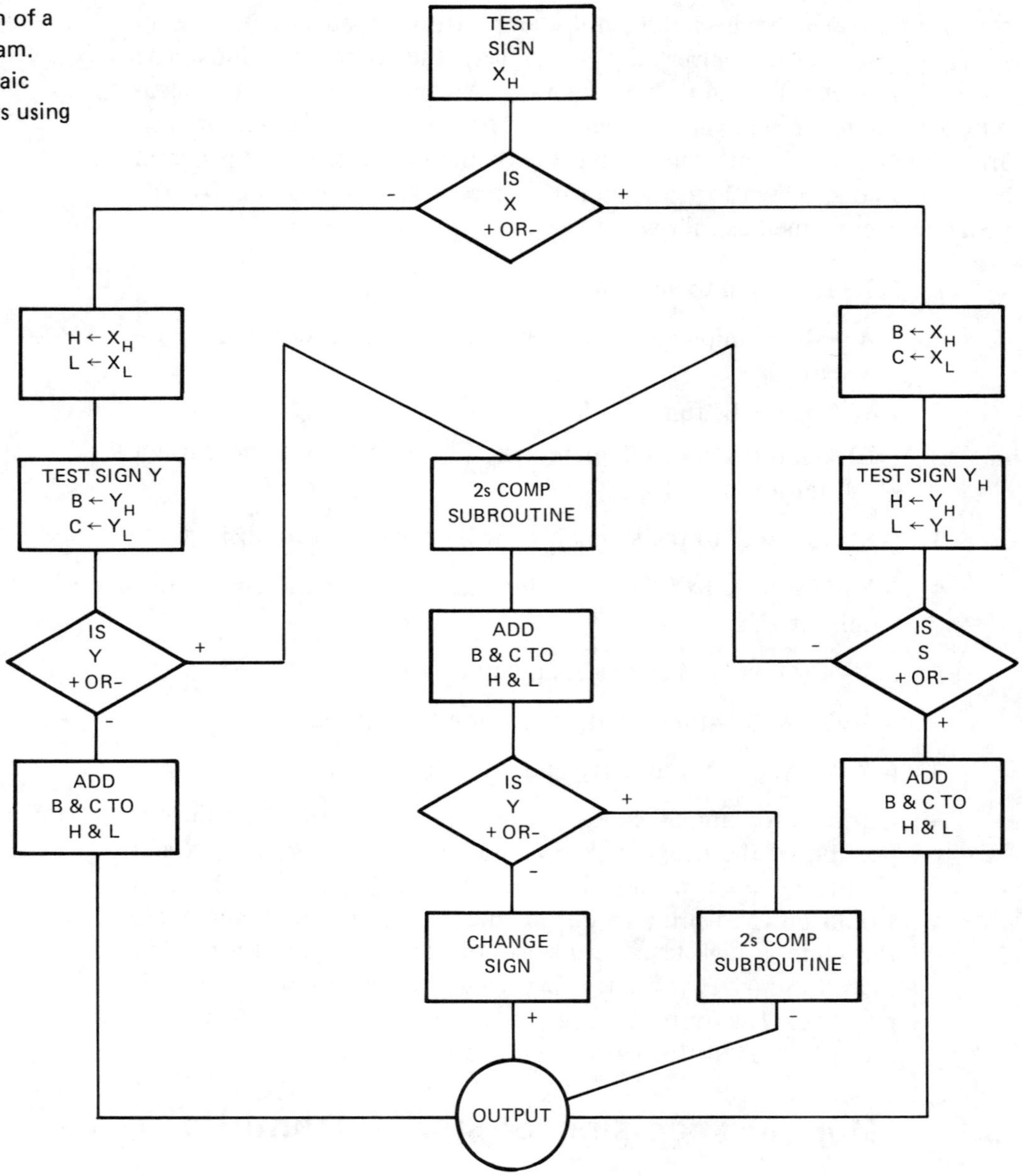

$$H, L \longleftarrow (H, L) + (rp)$$

rp { B (B and C) register pair
D (D and E) register pair
H (H and L) register pair
SP (Stack Pointer)

Unfortunately, other necessary functions such as complementing can be accomplished only when numbers are in the accumulator. To execute these functions on numbers stored in register pairs, each byte must be moved to and from the accumulator. Once the terms are correctly complemented and returned to register pairs, the addition itself is a simple one byte DAD rp instruction. As the flow diagram indicates, the high byte of X is checked for sign. If X is negative, it is moved to the H, L register pair. If X is positive, Y is moved to the H, L register pair. Using the same register pair for the negative value provides a program that complements the same register pair when signs differ. Selecting the H, L pair for the negative register pair rather than the B, C pair is advantageous because the DAD instruction stores the sum in H, L and the twos complement routine used on either augend or sum can be written as a complement of H, L. This makes them identical program segments, so it can be written once as a subroutine that can be called in both places thus reducing program storage. As the flow diagram shows, the twos complement of H, L occurs in two places. Once when H, L is an augend, and another when H, L is a sum.

8.8.4 Use of Subroutines

In many programs, there are portions of program which are repeated in two or more locations. A saving of memory bytes can be accomplished by writing it one time as a subroutine. Each point in the program at which the routine is needed, a subroutine call is inserted. The subroutine call differs from other branch instructions in that the program address jumped to is the same, but the address to which the program returns differs for each point in the program that the subroutine is called. Returning to the correct point in the program on completion of the subroutine is accomplished as the result of the return address being automatically pushed onto the stack when the subroutine is called and being popped back into the program counter as the result of a return from subroutine instruction. A subroutine call instruction may be unconditional or may occur based on the condition of one of the flags. Table 8.14 lists both the conditional and unconditional call instructions. As the memory format indicates, the call instruction is in direct addressing mode and the address at which the subroutine is located must be written immediately after the opcode in program memory.

MNEMONIC	NAME	CONDITION FLAG				EQUATION
		S	Z	P	C	
CXX	Call unconditional					None
CC	Call if carry set				1	C = 1
CNC	Call if carry clear				0	C = 0
CP	Call if positive	0				S = 0
CM	Call if minus	1				S = 1
CPE	Call if parity even			1		P = 1
CPO	Call if parity odd			0		P = 0
CZ	Call if zero		1			Z = 1
CNZ	Call if not zero		0			Z = 0

TABLE 8.14 Call instructions. The program will jump to subroutine at the address given in (PC + 1) and (PC + 2) only if the indicated flag is in the state specified. If the flag is not correct the program will increment to the instruction at (PC + 3).

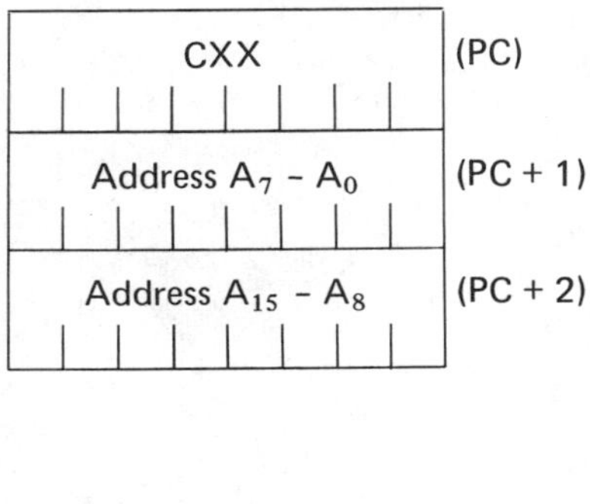

When a subroutine is called, the program count of the instruction immediately following the call instruction is written automatically on the stack. This is the address of the instruction in main program which will be executed immediately after the return from subroutine. The program count is the only microprocessor status that is saved automatically on the stack during the subroutine call. If the content of other registers must be saved, these can be stored on the stack using the push instructions.

PUSH rp Push register pair onto stack.

SP − 1 ⟵ (rph) Stack pointer is decremented from SP to SP − 1. High byte of the register pair is stored in SP − 1.

SP − 2 ⟵ (rpl) Stack pointer is decremented to SP − 2. Low byte of the register pair is stored in SP − 2.

The format and operand field of this instruction is given in Figure 8.14(c).

Push instructions are normally the initial instructions of the subroutine program. The content of a register pair need be pushed onto the stack only if two conditions exist.

- The content of the register pair is altered during the subroutine.
- The original content of the register pair is needed in the main program after the return from subroutine.

The last instruction executed in a subroutine is the return from subroutine instruction. This instruction can be conditional or unconditional. Table 8.15 lists the conditional and unconditional return instructions.

TABLE 8.15 Conditional and unconditional return instructions. Return instructions are single byte as the return address is taken from the stack.

MNEMONIC	NAME	CONDITION FLAG				EQUATION
		S	Z	P	C	
RET	Return unconditional					None
RC	Return if carry set				1	C = 1
RNC	Return if carry clear				0	C = 0
RP	Return if positive	0				S = 0
RM	Return if minus	1				S = 0
RPE	Return if parity even			1		P = 1
RPO	Return if parity odd			0		P = 0
RZ	Return if zero		1			Z = 1
RNZ	Return if not zero		0			Z = 0

The conditional return instructions allow for a subroutine or portion of it to be executed in a continuous loop, being repeated until the flag condition has been satisfied. The return instructions are single byte. They require no address as the return address is taken from the stack.

If push instructions were used at the beginning of a subroutine, corresponding POP instructions must be included prior to the return from subroutine. Failure to include them will not only lose essential register data, it will cause an incorrect return address to be loaded into the program counter.

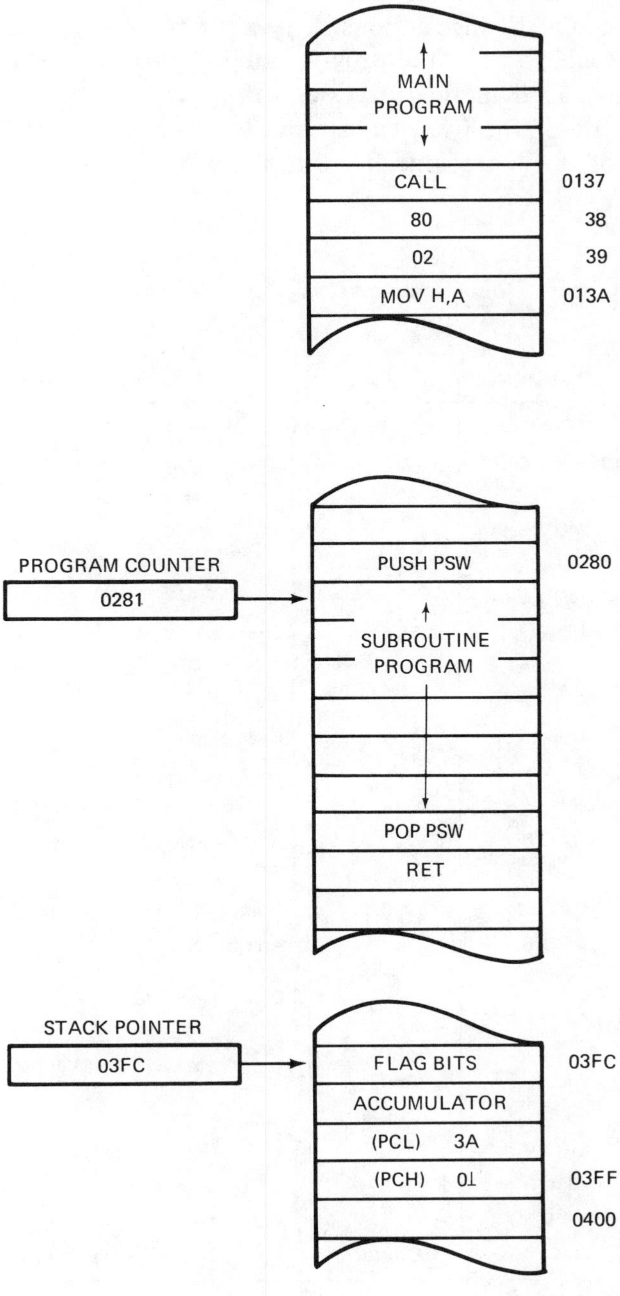

FIGURE 8.27 Segments of memory affected by a subroutine call. In the program shown the stack pointer was initialized to address 0400. A subroutine call was executed at address 0137. The return to main program address, 013A, was loaded on the stack using the locations pointed to by the decrementing stack pointer. After loading the return to main program address onto the stack, the 8080 jumped to the first instruction of the subroutine which pushed the accumulator content and flag bits onto the stack. During the execution of the subroutine the stack pointer content remains 03FC.

POP rp POP data off stack to register pair.

rpl ⟵ (SP)

rph ⟵ (SP + 1)

The contents of the stack memory location SP is loaded into the low byte of the register pair. Stack pointer is incremented to SP + 1. Contents of stack memory (SP + 1) is loaded into the high byte of the register pair. Stack pointer is incremented.

Format and operand field of this instruction is shown in Figure 8.15(c).

The more PSH and POP instructions needed in the subroutine the less advantageous the use of the subroutine. The routine must either be a lengthy one or must be called frequently to dwarf the need for PSH and PUL instructions. The need for saving status must be studied at each point in the program that the subroutine is called. If a subroutine is called in five places and the accumulator needs to be saved at only one of the five, it must still be pushed onto the stack during each call of the subroutine. The stack and stack pointer are key elements in both

TABLE 8.16(a) 8080 Program listing. Double precision, twos complement, algebraic adder (X Positive). Memory Addresses = ( )

ADDRESS	MOVEMENT	MNEMONIC	OPERAND	DESCRIPTION
0200		LDA	(X_H)	
03		ANA A		Check X for sign
04		JM	(0232)	
07		MOV B, A		
08		LDA	(X_L)	X Positive Move to B, C
0B		MOV C, A		
0C		LDA	(Y_H)	Check sign Y
0F		ANA A		
10		MOV H, A		
13		LDA	(Y_L)	Load Y in H, L
14		MOV L, A		
15		JM	021C	If Y negative call twos complement subroutine
18		DAD B		If Y Positive add and output
19		JMP	(Output)	
1C		CALL	0260_H	Jump to twos complement subroutine
1F		DAD B		Add S = X + Y
20		MOV A, H		Check sign of sum
21		ANA A		
22		JN	022B	Jump to twos complement subroutine if positive
25		CALL	0260	
28		JMP	(Output)	
2B		MOV A, H		
2C		ADI	80	Change sign of sum
2E		MOV H, A		
022F		JMP	(Output)	

TABLE 8.16(b) X negative.

ADDRESS	MOVEMENT	MNEMONIC	OPERAND	DESCRIPTION
0232		MOV H, A		Store X in (H, L)
33		LDA	(X_L)	
36		MOV L, A		
37		LDA	(Y_H)	Check sign Y
3A		ANA A		
3B		MOV B, A		Store Y in B, C
3C		LDA	(Y_L)	
3F		MOV C, A		
40		JP	0247	If Y negative add −X to −Y
43		DAD B		
44		JMP	(Output)	
47		CALL	0260	If + Y jump to twos complement subroutine of X
4A		DAD B		Add S = X + Y
4B		MOV A, H		Check sign of sum
4C		ANA A		
4D		JM	0256	
50		CALL	0260	If sum positive jump to twos complement subroutine
53		JMP	(Output)	
56		ADI	80	Change sign if sum is positive
58		MOV H, A		
0259		JMP	(Output)	

TABLE 8.16(c) Twos complement subroutine.

ADDRESS	MOVEMENT	MNEMONIC	OPERAND	DESCRIPTION
0260		MOV A, L		Complement L (low byte)
61		CMA		
62		MOV L, A		
63		MOV A, H		Complement H (low byte)
64		CMA		
65		MOV H, A		
66		INX H		(Add 1 to change ones complement to twos complement)
0267		RET		

interrupt and subroutine operations. Figure 8.27 shows memory map segments of main program memory, memory containing subroutine, and the stack memory. Note that the stack pointer **decrements prior to** the write in the stack and **increments after** each read of the stack memory.

Table 8.16 is a program listing of the double precision twos complement algebraic adder. A subroutine call is used in both locations that call for the twos complement of the H, L register pair. Table 8.16(c) shows the twos complement subroutine. There are no registers used during the subroutine that must be returned to original state after return from subroutine so no PSH or POP instructions are included. There is no instruction for complementing H and L so first L is moved to the accumulator to be complemented. The low byte is returned to L. The high byte is moved to the accumulator, complemented, and returned to H. At that point the H, L register pair has been ones complemented and an increment of the H, L register pair results in a twos complement.

8.8.5 Multiplication and Division with the 8080 Microprocessor

Figure 7.19 gives examples of binary multiplication and division. Multiplication is a matter of add shift and add of the multiplicand. Division is more complicated because it requires first a series of subtract and shift left of the divisor until either the result is negative or until the shift produces a negative.

```
                 1 1 0 1 1 1 0 0
shift left ←——
                 0 0 0 0 0 1 0 1
```

This locates the most significant 1 bit of the divisor in line with the most significant 1 bit of the dividend. Then begins a series of subtract, shift left, and increment the quotient if positive; cancel and shift left the quotient if negative; shift right the divisor. This series is repeated until the shift right of the divisor results in a carry. This level of arithmetic obviously requires instructions that can shift numbers to either right or left.

The 8080 has four rotate instructions which shift binary numbers through the accumulator.

RAL Rotate accumulator left through carry. Each bit of the accumulator is shifted left. The carry bit shifts into A_0. The A_7 (MSB) shifts into the carry. See Figure 8.28(a).

RAR Rotate accumulator right through carry. Each bit of the accumulator is shifted right. The carry bit shifts into A_7. The A_0 bit shifts into the carry. See Figure 8.28(b).

RLC Rotate accumulator left. Each bit of the accumulator is shifted left. The A_7 (MSB) bit is shifted into A_0 and into the carry. See Figure 8.28(c).

RRC Rotate accumulator right. Each bit of the accumulator is shifted right. The A_0 bit is shifted into A_7 and into the carry. See Figure 8.28(d).

The rotate instructions affect the carry flag only.

8.8.6 Multiplication Program

To familiarize ourselves with these instructions let us program for multiplication of single byte binary numbers allowing for a product of two

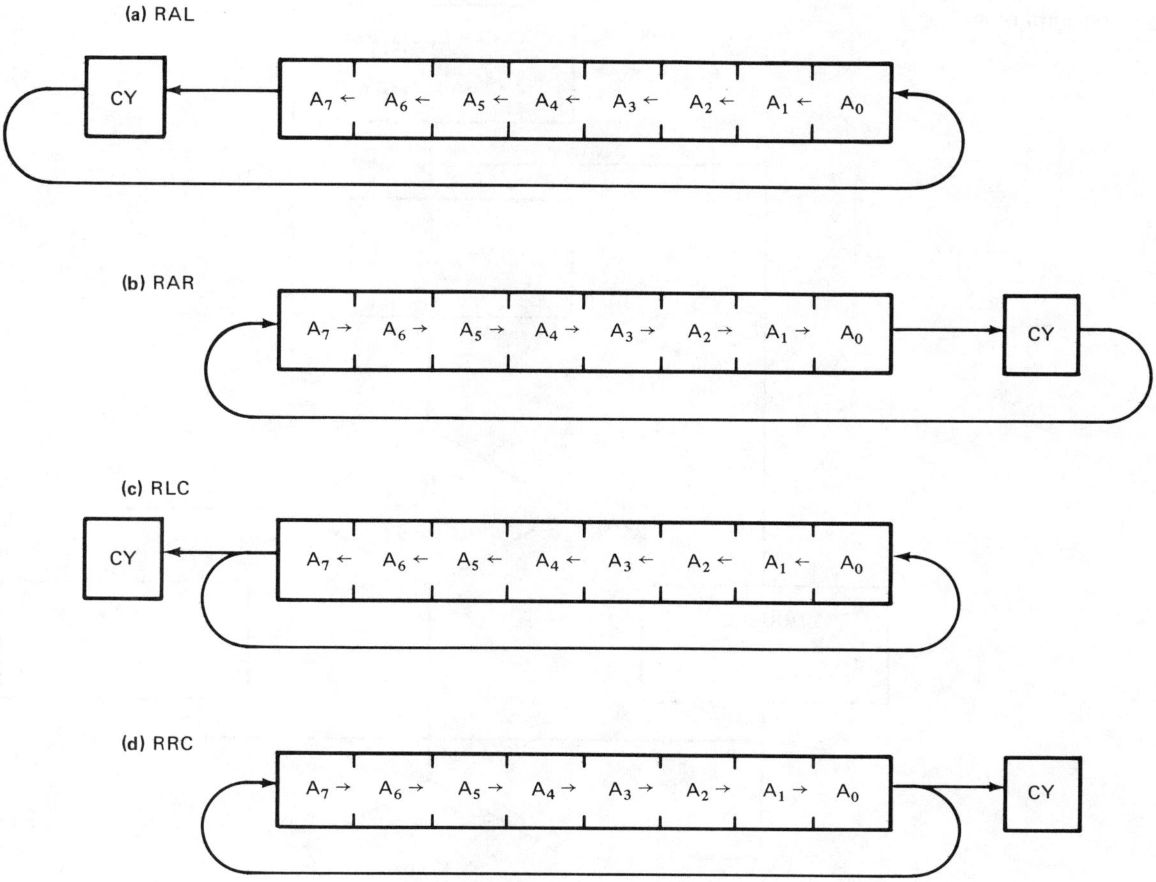

FIGURE 8.28 Movement of bits through the accumulator and carry as a result of a rotate instruction. **(a)** RAL—Rotate Accumulator Left through carry. **(b)** RAR—Rotate Accumulator Right through carry. **(c)** RLC—Rotate Accumulator Left. **(d)** RRC—Rotate Accumulator Right.

bytes. The following register bytes must be assigned.

Multiplier = X $\quad P = X \circ Y$

Multiplicand
low byte = Y_L
high byte = Y_H

Product
low byte = P_L
high byte = P_H

Figure 8.29 shows the flow diagram of the program. The program starts with X and Y in memory. Accumulator, carry, and register byte Y_H must all be clear. X is shifted to the right. If this shifts a 1 into carry, the program adds Y_L to P_L using an add without carry. This is followed by an add with carry of Y_H to P_H. If the shift of X does not set the carry, the program branches around the add routines to a shift left of Y. Y is shift left.

This multiply operation is a typical example of the work horse nature of the single accumulator. The numerous other registers within the 8080 can serve only as holding registers for the five bytes of information that must be operated on. The many functions required to complete the total operation can be performed only on the accumulator.

FIGURE 8.29 Flow diagram of an 8080 multiply program: P = XY.

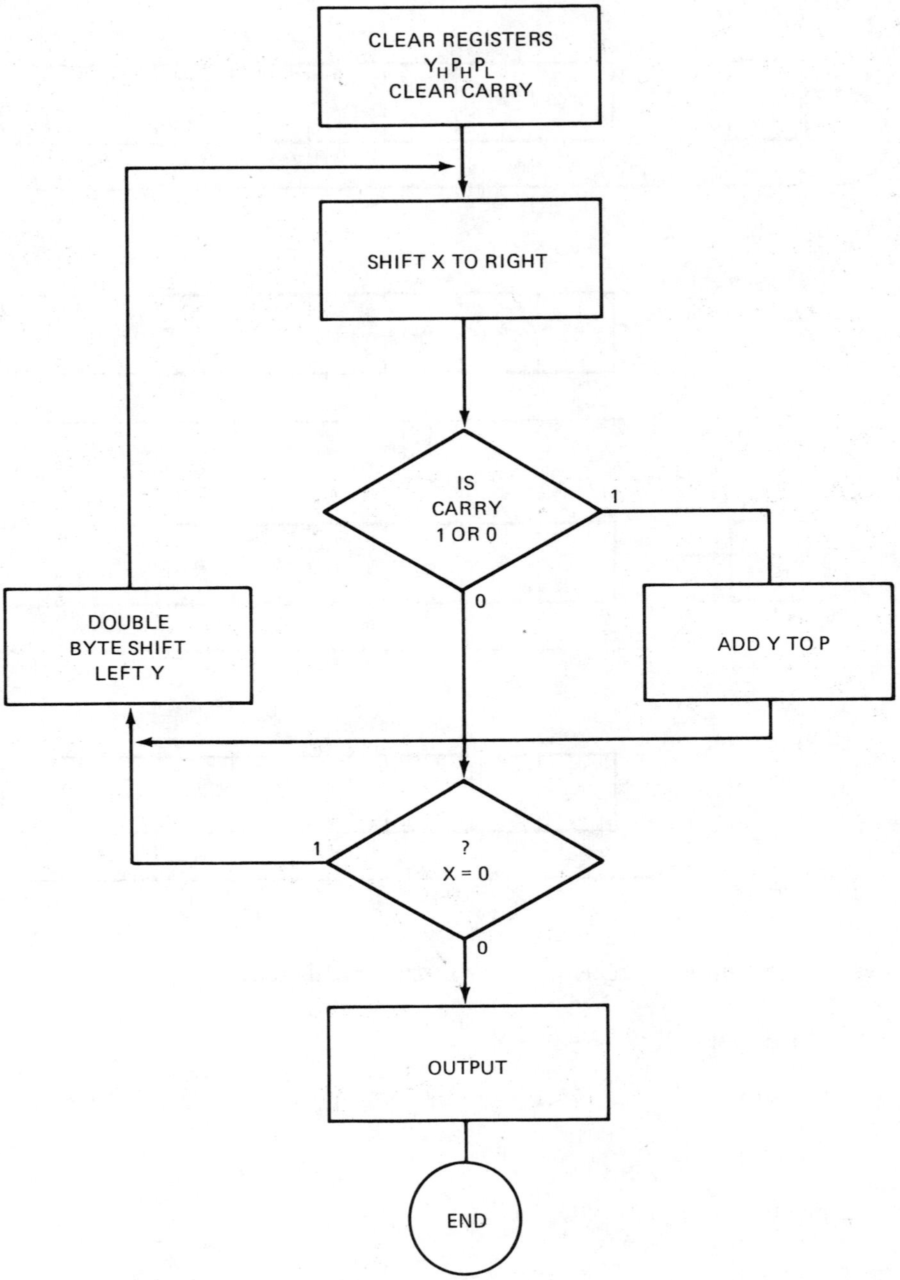

The key to the program is the correct series of move to accumulator, modify, and return the byte to register storage. Let us assume that the five bytes (X, Y_L, Y_H, P_L, P_H) are each assigned 8-bit registers. X is the multiplier. We examine each bit of X, one per cycle, to determine if there should be an add or do not add of the multiplicand. This is done as shown in Figure 8.30 after the carry is cleared, X is moved to the accumulator and rotated right (RAR). If this places a 1 in carry, Y is added to P. If the RAR places a 0 in carry, Y is not added to P. Shifted X is checked for 0 to determine if multiplication is complete.

Figure 8.30 gives a typical program technique for this operation. The manipulation of Y is more complex in that four bytes and both

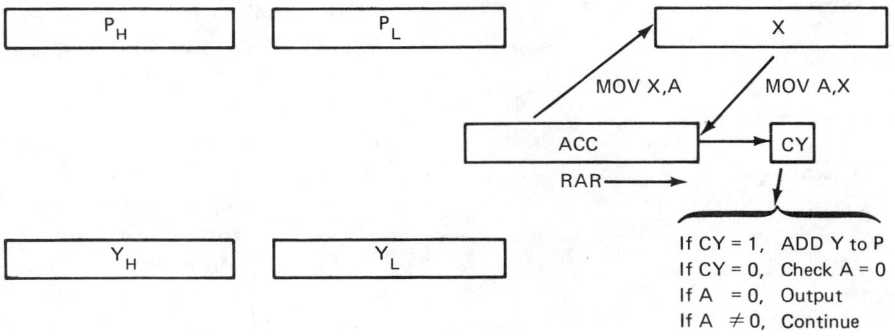

FIGURE 8.30 Register operation for multiply program manipulation of multiplier (X)
Program segment for manipulating multiplier X.

```
SEC      } Clear carry so X
CMC      } will shift to zero.
MOV A, X } Move X to
RAR      } accumulator
MOV X, A } Rotate.
JC    → To Program adding Y to P
ANA A
JZ    → To Program outputting P
JMP   → To Program Shift Y without Add
```

shift and add operations are involved. Y begins life as a single byte, but it is shifted left as many bits as there are in X and thus becomes a 2-byte number. Let us first examine the addition of Y to P.

Figure 8.31 shows the movement between the accumulator and the four registers containing P and Y. First P_L is moved to the accumulator for an add without carry of Y_L. The sum is returned to P_L. P_H is moved to the accumulator for an add with carry of Y_H. The sum is returned to P_H. Figure 8.31 gives a typical program for this operation.

The double byte shift left operation of Y_L and Y_H is shown in Figure 8.32. The carry must be cleared at the start of shift. Y_L is moved to the accumulator. A shift left through carry places zero in A_0, and A_7 shifts into carry. The shifted Y_L is moved back to its register. Y_H is moved to accumulator. A shift left through carry shifts the carry (A_7 of the previous Y_L) into A_0 of Y_H. Throughout the shifts of Y_H the MSB (A_7) is always zero. This eliminates any need to clear carry for the next operation. Figure 8.32 gives a typical program for this operation.

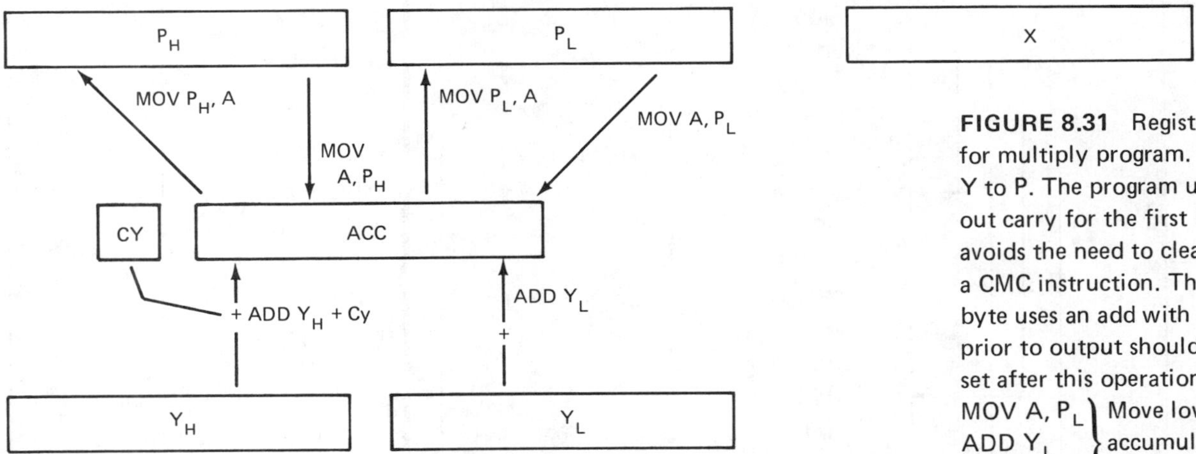

FIGURE 8.31 Register operation for multiply program. Addition of Y to P. The program uses add without carry for the first byte. This avoids the need to clear carry with a CMC instruction. The second byte uses an add with carry. Only prior to output should a carry be set after this operation.

```
MOV A, PL } Move low byte of P to
ADD YL    } accumulator and add
MOV PL, A } low byte of Y. Store
            sum in PL register.
MOV A, PH } Move high byte of P
ADC YH    } to accumulator and
MOV PH, A } ADD with carry the
            high byte of Y. Store
            the sum in PH register.
```

The complete program is a matter of assembling the segments given in Figures 8.29 through 8.32 assigning the registers and inserting the necessary jump and initializing instructions. Table 8.17 is a complete program listing for the 8080 multiply program described by flow diagram Figure 8.28.

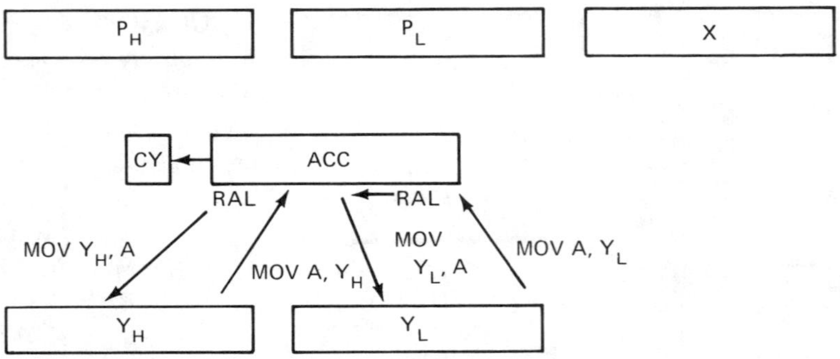

FIGURE 8.32 Register operation for multiply program shift Y left. Beginning with carry clear.

MOV A, Y_L
RAL
MOV Y_L, A
} Move low byte of Y from its register to accumulator. Shift left one bit and return to register.

MOV A, Y_H
RAL
MOV Y_H, A
} Move high byte of Y from its register to accumulator. Shift left through carry one bit and return to register.

The MSB of Y_H is zero each time this operation is performed, therefore, the operation ends with a clear carry.

TABLE 8.17 8080 Microprocessor program to multiply two 8-bit numbers.

P = X · Y.

X = B Y_H = D

P_H = H Y_L = E

P_L = L

ADDRESS	MOVEMENT	MNEMONIC	OPERAND	DESCRIPTION	MODE
0210		MVI D	00	Clear Y_H	
12		MOV H, D		Clear P_H	
13		MOV L, D		Clear P_L	
14		STC		Clear carry	
15		CMC			
16		MOV A,B		Shift X right See Figure 8.30 B = X	
17		RAR			
18		MOV B,A			
19		JC	0223		
1C		ANA A			
1D		JNZ	0229		
20		JMP	OUTPUT		
23		MOV A, L		ADD Y to P See Figure 8.31 L = P_L H = P_H E = Y_L D = Y_H	
24		ADD E			
25		MOV L, A			
26		MOV A, H			
27		ADC D			
28		MOV H, A			
29		MOV A, E		Shift Y to left See Figure 8.32	
2A		RAL			
2B		MOV E, A			
2C		MOV A, D			
2D		RAL			
2E		MOV D, A			
022F	To Output Program	JMP	0216		

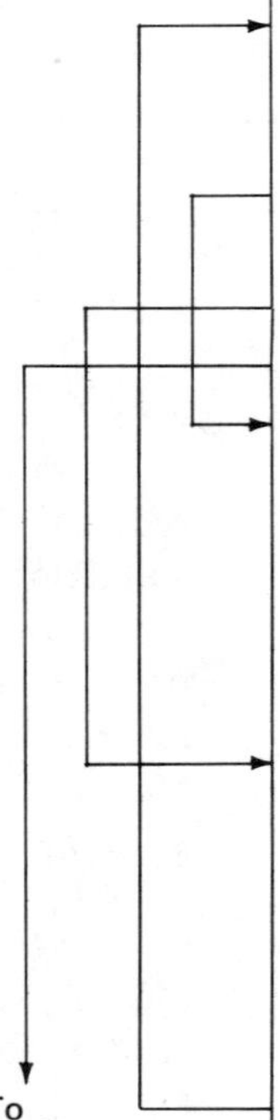

8.9 Dedicated 8080 Microprocessor Programs

8.9.1 Counter Routines

Although microprocessor systems have some application as small-scale general purpose computers, the majority of their applications are in control systems which use only a trivial portion of the microprocessor's total capability. These dedicated applications use many simple routines such as counters, timers, and sequencers. A typical counter routine designates a memory byte or a register to be incremented or decremented until the desired count has been reached.

Figure 8.33 shows a routine to be repeated five times. The instruction preceding the routine loads a count of 5 into register B. At the completion of the routine, B is decremented. Until B reaches zero, the program branches back to repeat the routine. When B reaches zero, the Z flag will be set and the program will move ahead. The accumulator would be the ideal register for use as a counter, but in the usual routine, the accumulator is an essential register. The register used as the counter must be one which is not needed during the routine. If all registers are needed during the routine, a memory byte can be used to hold the count. Table 8.18 is a listing of a routine which stores the count in memory at the beginning and returns it to the accumulator at the end of each run of the routine. Under some conditions it may be desirable

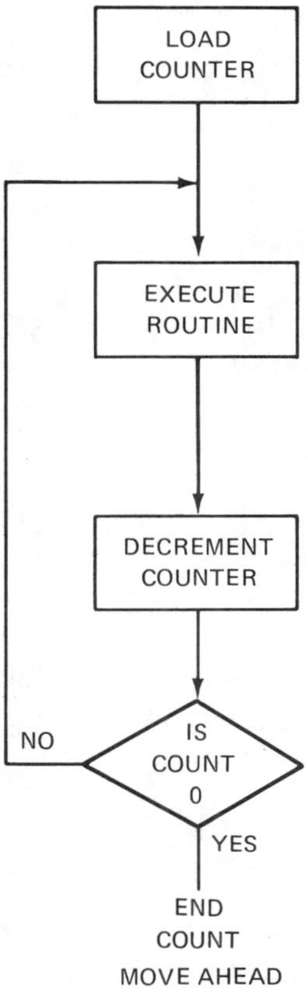

ADDRESS	OPCODE	OPERAND	DESCRIPTION
0210	MVI B	05	LOAD COUNT
12	↑ ROUTINE TO BE REPEATED 5 TIMES ↓		EXECUTE ROUTINE
	DCR B		DECREMENT COUNT
	JNZ	0212_H	IS COUNT COMPLETE

FIGURE 8.33 8080 Program of a routine to be executed five times. Register B is used as a counter. The counter is decremented each time the routine is executed. Until the counter register is decremented to zero the program will jump back and repeat the routine.

TABLE 8.18 Counter routine in which counter byte must be stored in memory during the execution of a program segment that requires the use of all registers.

ADDRESS	MOVEMENT	MNEMONIC	OPERAND	DESCRIPTION
0210		MVI A	05	Load counter
12	→	STA	(02FF)	Store counter in memory
		Routine To Be Repeated 5 Times		Execute Routine
		LDA	(02FF)	Load counter in accumulator
		DCR A		Decrement counter
		JNZ	0212	Advance if count zero
		↓		Additional program ↓

to count to a number other than zero. This requires the use of compare instructions.

CMP r Compare register with accumulator.

$$CY, Z \longleftarrow (ACC) - (r)$$

Compares the content of accumulator with the content of r and sets the flag bits accordingly.
Z flag is set if A = r.
CY flag is set if A < r.

CMP M Compare register with memory.

$$CY, Z \longleftarrow (ACC) - (M)$$

Compares the content of the accumulator with a memory byte pointed to by H and L and sets the flag bits accordingly.
Z flag is set if A = (M).
CY flag is set if A < (M).

CPI Compare immediate with accumulator.

$$CY, Z \longleftarrow (ACC) - (PC + 1)$$

Compares the content of the accumulator with a memory byte immediately following the opcode in program memory (PC + 1) and sets the flag bits accordingly.
Z flag is set if (A) = (PC + 1).
CY flag is set if (A) < (PC + 1).

The compare instructions differ from subtract instructions in that the contents of accumulator, register, and memory bytes involved in the

TABLE 8.19 Count routine using an incremented counter and compare instruction to detect the end of count.

ADDRESS	MOVEMENT	MNEMONIC	OPERAND	DESCRIPTION
0180		MVI B	00	Clear counter
82	→	Routine To Be Repeated 5 Times		Execute Routine
		INR B		Increment counter
		MVI A	05	Load final count in A
		CMP B		Compare counter for final count (5)
	←	JNZ	0182	Advance if count complete
		↓		

compare are left unchanged. Table 8.19 lists a count to 5 routine using a compare instruction. The counter register is started at zero. At the end of the program segment, the counter is incremented and compared with a 5. The routine will be repeated until B reaches 5 at which time a set Z flag after compare will cause the program to move ahead.

8.9.2 The Timer Routine

Timer routines are a special application of counter routines. There are a definite number of clock periods in the execution of an instruction. A clock period takes a precise time measured in microseconds (μsec). Between each increment of the counter there are an exact number of microseconds. The timer routines in Table 8.20 merely count from the number in B to zero. This requires 7 clock periods to set the count and 15 clock periods for each count. In a system with a 500-nanosecond clock period, each count requires 7½ microseconds. As the calculations in Table 8.20 indicate, a count of 133_{10} (85_H) results in a 1-msec timer with an error of only 1 μsec. An error of ½ count is the largest that need be accepted. The time period per count can be extended by decrementing more than once per cycle or by inserting NOP instructions.

NOP No operation. No operation is performed. Requires 4 clock periods.

The NOP inserted between the DCR B and JNZ results in 19 clock periods per count. The maximum count possible from a single byte counter is 256 accomplished by decrementing from zero back to zero. With 15 clock periods per count, the maximum time interval obtainable with a 500-nanosecond clock period would be 256 × 15 × ½ microsecond = 1920 microseconds or 1.92 milliseconds. Each NOP instruction will expand this time interval by 512 microseconds or slightly over half a millisecond. The use of NOP to expand the time period more than a few milliseconds will require an excessive num-

TABLE 8.20 Timer routines showing clock periods required per count. Count period can be altered by using a double count. Count period can be expanded by inserting NOP instructions between decrement and jump instructions.

ADDRESS	MOVEMENT	MNEMONIC	OPERAND	DESCRIPTION
0130		MVI B	(h h)	Load count
32		DCR B		5 clock periods
0133		JNZ	0132	10 clock periods
				(15 clock periods per count) + 7
				$hh \leqslant 225_{10}$
0130		MVI B	(h h)	Load count
32		DCR B		5 clock periods
33		DCR B		5 clock periods
0134		JNZ	0132	10 clock periods
				(20 clock periods per count) + 7
0130		MVI B	(h h)	Load count
32		DCR B		5 clock periods
33		NOP		4 clock periods
0134		JNZ	0132	10 clock periods
				(19 clock periods per count) + 7

(hh) Two-digit hexadecimal number

ber of program memory bytes. At that point a two byte timer becomes more practical. Figure 8.34 is a flow diagram and program for a two byte timer routine. The high byte is incremented only once for each 256 counts of the low byte. This amounts to 1.92 microseconds for each count of the high byte in a system with a 500-nanosecond cycle time. A total time of nearly a half second for a full count of both bytes. The 8080 has instructions for incrementing and decrementing register pairs. However, these do not affect the flags and there is no instruction for comparing register pairs. But the use of register pair instructions may be advantageous for timers of three bytes or more.

8.9.3 The Sequencer Routine

A register or memory byte may be used as a sequencer. A sequencer causes a series of events to happen in specific order. For example, let us take a traffic light controller at a busy intersection. Figure 8.35 shows the logic diagram of the traffic light controller. The traffic signal has red, yellow, green, and green arrow (left turn) lamps facing in each of four directions. The red light turns on when no other lamp in the same direction is lit. This is accomplished with a 2-input NOR gate for the red light of each direction. The green light turns on both for green and with the green arrow in a given direction. This is accomplished with a 2-input OR gate for the green light of each direction. The program can be stored in a pair of 256-X-4 PROM. RAM is not needed because there are sufficient registers within the 8080 for the functions of timer and

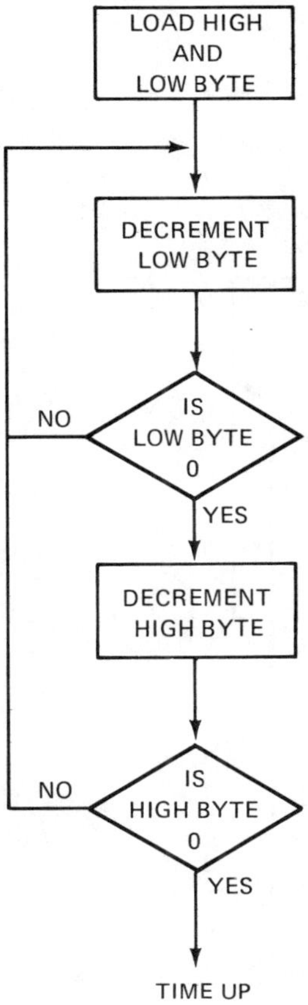

ADDRESS	OPCODE	OPERAND	DESCRIPTION
0220	MVI B	40	LOAD HIGH BYTE
22	MVI C	00	LOAD LOW BYTE
24	DCR C		DECREMENT LOW BYTE
25	JNZ	0224	IS LOW BYTE ZERO
28	DCR B		DECREMENT HIGH BYTE
0229	JNZ	0224	IS HIGH BYTE ZERO

FIGURE 8.34 Flow diagram and 8080 program for a 2-byte timer. The high byte counter is decremented only once each time the low byte decrements to zero (Note: Decrementing a counter which is at zero produces a count of 255).

sequencer bytes. Two register bytes are to be used as timers employing the technique described in Section 8.9.2. If a 2-MHZ clock is used, a 2-byte timer will provide only 0.5-second time intervals.

By using the readily available television crystal of approximately 3.58 MHZ with the 8224 clock generator, a clock cycle time of about 2.51 microseconds is provided as follows:

$$\frac{3.58\text{MHZ}}{9} = 398\text{KHZ} \quad \frac{1}{398\text{ KHZ}} = 2.51\ \mu\text{sec}$$

(The 8224 clock generator divides crystal frequency by 9.)

The traffic signal operates in time intervals that are multiples of 6 seconds.

$$6\text{ sec} = \frac{6{,}000{,}000\ \mu\text{sec}}{2.51\ \mu\text{sec per clock cycle}} = 2{,}390{,}438\text{ clock cycles}$$

A 2-byte timer counts to 65,536

$$\frac{2{,}390{,}438\text{ clock cycles}}{65{,}536\text{ counts}} = 36.5\text{ clock cycles/count}$$

As Table 8.20 indicates, a count takes 15 clock cycles adding

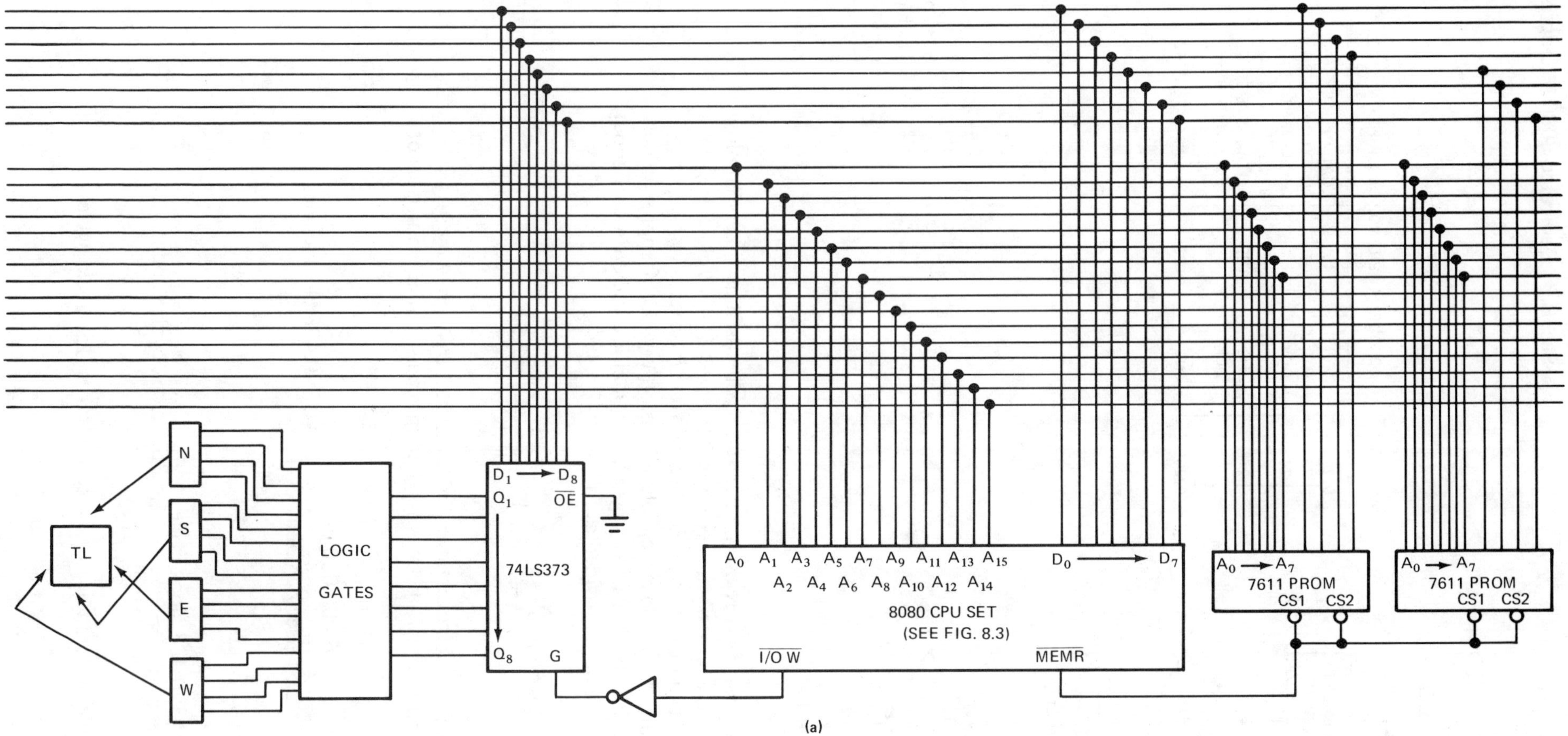

(a)

FIGURE 8.35 (a) Logic diagram of an 8080 traffic light controller. The program memory is composed of two 256-X-4 PROMS. The output circuit is a quad D latch which is enabled by the I/OW control signal. Being the only output circuit, it requires no address line connections. The output enable is kept grounded so that the output is continuously active.

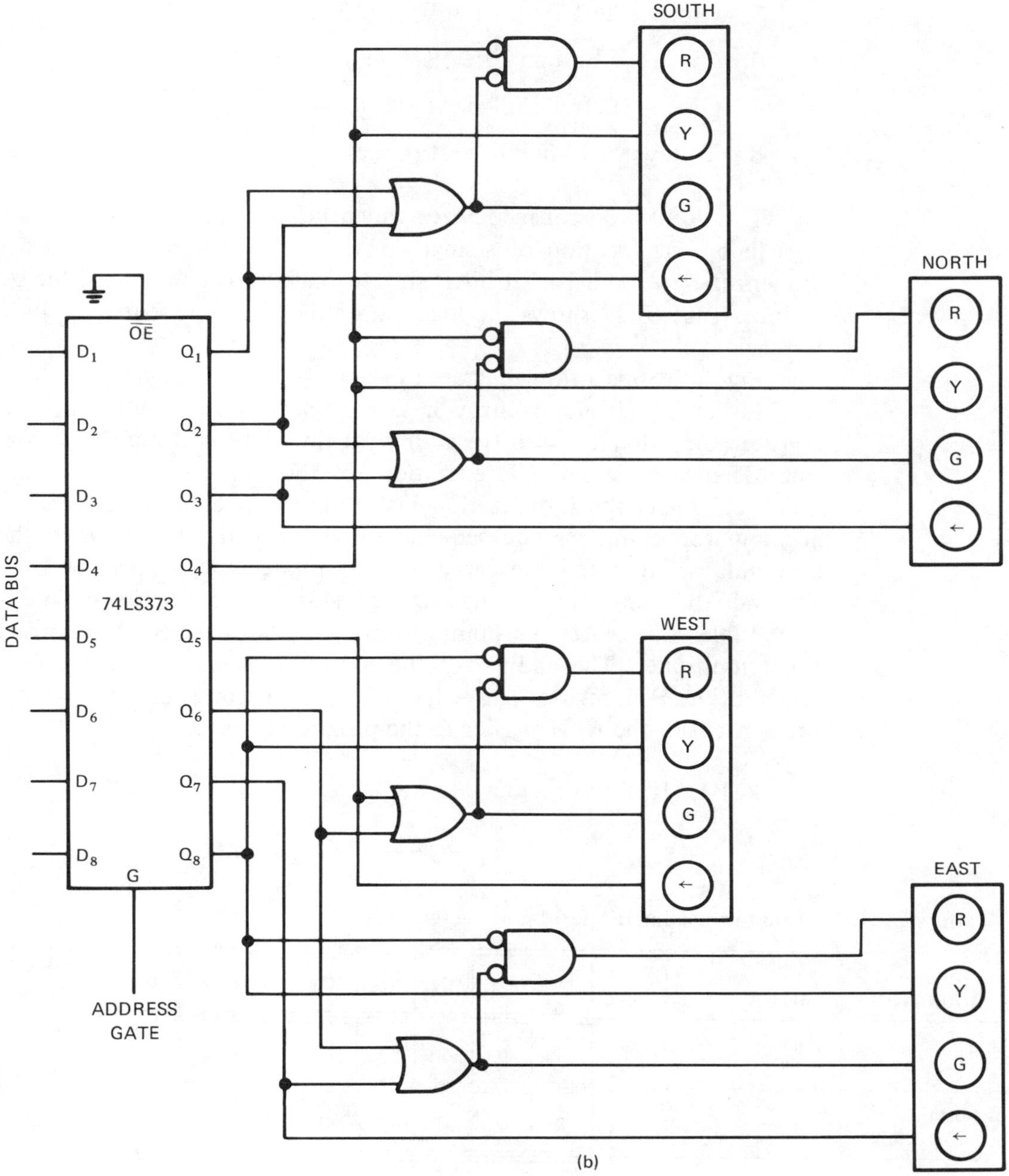

(b)

(36.5 - 15) = 21.5 cycles needed

five NOP instructions of 4 clock cycles each will expand each count to 35 clock cycles which is sufficiently accurate for the 6 second timer.

The traffic light has eight operating modes in the sequence shown:

1. Green + Left Turn from South (18 sec)
2. Green for North and South (24 sec)
3. Green + Left Turn from North (18 sec)
4. Yellow for North and South (6 sec)

FIGURE 8.35 (b) The output circuit contains quad NOR gates used to turn on the red light when no other light of the same direction is on. OR gates are used to turn the green lights on in conjunction with the left turn signals of a given direction. The logic signals are used to activate lamp or relay drivers within the traffic signal housing.

5. Green + Left Turn from West (12 sec)
6. Green for East and West (18 sec)
7. Green + Left Turn from East (12 sec)
8. Yellow for East and West (6 sec)

The 8080 program recognizes which mode of the above sequence it is in by the location of a single 1 bit which is rotated through the sequencer byte. The 1-level bit is shifted once for each mode of the sequence. Table 8.21 shows the location of the bit in the sequencer byte for each cycle.

Figure 8.36 is a flow diagram of the traffic signal program.

Initially registers A through D are loaded with zero. The H, L register pair is loaded with the address of the first select multiplier routine. The carry is set in preparation for the first rotate instruction. Table 8.22 lists the initialization instructions. After initialization the accumulator acting as the sequencer byte is rotated left. With the accumulator clear and the carry set, the rotate left produces an 01_H. This value is transferred to the output resulting in the lights of cycle 1 (see Table 8.21). At this point the program must select the correct timer multiplier. The address of the multiplier select segment is contained in the H, L register pair. The PCHL instruction is used to transfer the content of the H, L register to the program counter.

PCHL H, L to program counter.

$$PC \longleftarrow (H, L)$$

TABLE 8.21 Traffic signal cycles and the location of the 1 bit in the sequencer byte.

CYCLE	DIRECTION	SIGNAL	TIME (SECS)	D_7	D_6	D_5	D_4	D_3	D_2	D_1	D_0	HEX VALUE
1	South	green + LT	18	0	0	0	0	0	0	0	1	1
2	North and South	green	24	0	0	0	0	0	0	1	0	2
3	North	green + LT	18	0	0	0	0	0	1	0	0	4
4	North	yellow	6	0	0	0	0	1	0	0	0	8
5	West	green + LT	12	0	0	0	1	0	0	0	0	16
6	East and West	green	18	0	0	1	0	0	0	0	0	32
7	East	green + LT	12	0	1	0	0	0	0	0	0	64
8	East	yellow	6	1	0	0	0	0	0	0	0	128

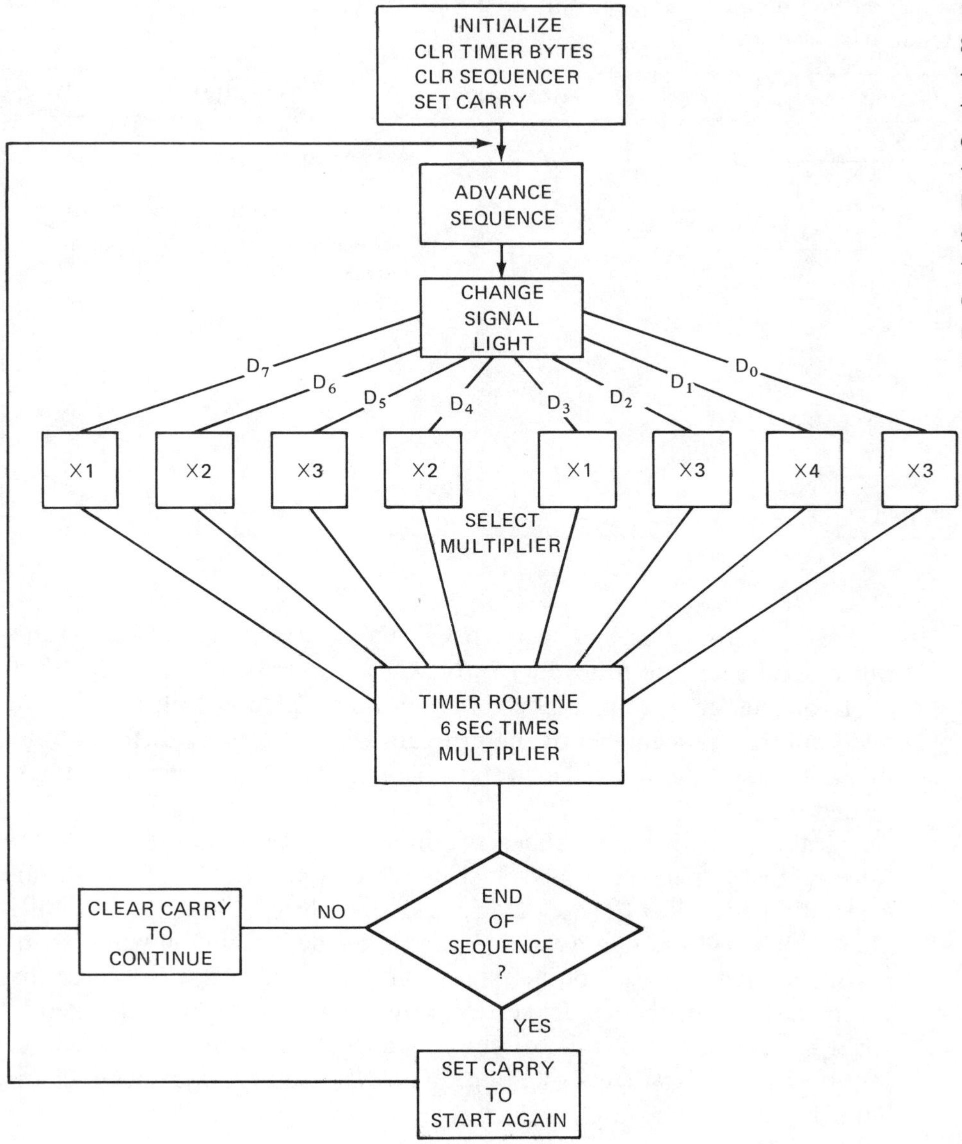

FIGURE 8.36 Flow diagram of an 8080 traffic control program. Initialization occurs when power is turned on. At the beginning of each cycle the sequencer is rotated. Traffic lights are changed based on the location of the one bit in the sequencer. Program jumps to a different select multiplier routine with each cycle. The 6-second timer is repeated as often as the multiplier indicates.

TABLE 8.22 Initialization instructions for 8080 traffic light control program. Initialization occurs only when power is applied to the microprocessor circuit.

ADDRESS	MOVEMENT	MNEMONIC	OPERAND	DESCRIPTION
0004		MVI A	00	
05		LXI H	0010	Load address of first multiplier select
08		STC		Set carry

Has effect of an unconditional jump instruction except that address jumped to is taken from the H, L pair.

Table 8.23 is the rotate and output segment of the traffic light program. At the end of each timer interval the program returns to this segment to start the next light cycle in the sequence.

TABLE 8.23 Rotate sequencer and output to change lights occurs in two instructions. The third instruction jumps program to select multiplier segment.

ADDRESS	MOVEMENT	MNEMONIC	OPERAND	DESCRIPTION
09	FROM TIMER ROUTINE →	RAL		Rotate sequencer
0A		OUT	01	Output sequencer to change lights
0C	↓ TO ADDRESS IN (H, L)	PCHL		Jump to select multiplier segment address in H, L

The multiplier select segments of the program perform three functions: load the time multiplier into D, load address of the next multiplier routine, and jump to the timer routine. Table 8.24 lists the eight select multiplier segments of the program. Note that they differ only by the multiplier number loaded into D and the next segment address loaded into L.

Table 8.25 lists the timer routine. The timer routine is a 2-byte timer with the necessary NOP instructions to produce a 6-second time interval when a 400-KHZ clock is used. The third byte, D, is the multiplier which will contain a value 1 through 4 depending on whether the particular light cycle should remain on for 6, 12, 18, or 24 seconds. When time is up, the sequencer byte in the accumulator is checked to see if it is on the last cycle of the sequence. If it is, the N flag will be set. If it is the last cycle of the sequence, the carry is set prior to the jump back to the rotate instruction. If not, the carry is cleared prior to the jump to rotate instruction.

Figure 8.37 is a memory map of the 256-byte memory.

8.9.4 Use of Tables

The Advantage of Tables In many cases, a program must respond to a set of conditions which occur at random or in a combination of sequences that make the program difficult to arrange. Under these conditions it is often convenient to use a table. The use of a table requires that each program condition have an exclusive numerical value that can be used as an address to the data in the table. The size of the memory needed for the table depends on the range of addresses generated. If the addresses are scattered over a large portion of the memory map, the use of a table may not be economical. In the usual case, a table can be confined to a single page of ROM. Where the table does not densely populate the ROM, vacant segments can be used for other program routines.

TABLE 8.24 8080 Traffic light control program select multiplier segments. The program jumps to a different segment for each of the eight light cycles. Each segment loads a multiplier number to provide the correct timing for the light (multiple of 6 sec). Then the address of the next select multiplier segment is moved to L register. Finally the program jumps to the timer routine.

ADDRESS	MOVEMENT	MNEMONIC	OPERAND	DESCRIPTION
0010	→	MVI D	03	Load multiplier (18 sec)
0012		MVI L	18	Load address of next select multiplier segment
0014		JMP	0080	Jump to timer
0018		MVI D	04	(24 sec)
001A		MVI L	20	
001C		JMP	0080	
0020		MVI D	03	(18 sec)
0022		MVI L	28	
0024		JMP	0080	
0028		MVI D	01	(6 sec)
002A		MVI L	30	
002C		JMP	0080	
0030		MVI D	02	(12 sec)
0032		MVI L	38	
0034		JMP	0080	
0038		MVI D	03	(18 sec)
003A		MVI L	40	
003C		JMP	0080	
0040		MVI D	02	(12 sec)
0042		MVI L	48	
0044		JMP	0080	
0048		MVI D	01	(6 sec)
004A		MVI L	10	Return to cycle 1
004C		JMP	0080	

8.9.5 The Model Railway Control Circuit

As an example let us use an 8080 program for control of a model railway.

Situation The model railway track is connected as shown in Figure 8.38. The track is connected to form an inner and outer loop. Six switches are used to allow both changes in direction and changes from inner to outer loop. Six electronic sensors (three pairs) are used to sense the train's direction and location. The sensors transmit a digital

TABLE 8.25 8080 Traffic light controller program timer routine. A 2-byte timer with five NOP instructions provides a 6-second time interval. A multiplier loaded into register D repeats the 6-second interval as many times as required to give the correct timing for the light cycle. After cycle 8, the 1 bit in the sequencer is in the MSB (bit 7). The carry must be set prior to returning to the RAL instruction.

ADDRESS	MOVEMENT	MNEMONIC	OPERAND	DESCRIPTION
0080	From multiplier select	DCR C		6 sec timer
81		NOP		
82		NOP		
83		NOP		
84		NOP		
85		NOP		
86		JNZ	0080	
89		DCR B		
90		JNZ	0080	
8D		DCR D		Timer Multiplier
8E	To	JNZ	0080	
91	0009	ANA A		Test Sequencer
92		JM	0099	
95		STC		
96		CMC		If minus set carry — jump to rotate instruction
97		JMP	0009	If plus clear carry — jump to rotate instruction
9A		STC		
009B		JMP	0009	

1 or high level when the train is abreast of the sensor. The sensors transmit digital 0 or low level in the inactive state. The switches are straight when they receive a digital 0 and will switch when they receive a 1 level. In the starting position, the train will not be on the switches or crossovers. If stopped on the inner loop, it will be abreast of sensors 9 and 10.

Problem Start the train and under control of the microprocessor cause it to run in continuous cycles as follows:

- In the outer loop two revolutions clockwise.
- In the outer loop two revolutions counterclockwise.
- In the inner loop two revolutions clockwise.
- In the inner loop two revolutions counterclockwise.

Microprocessor Connections The microprocessor configuration is shown in Figure 8.39. The odd-numbered sensors are connected to the lower bits (D_0 through D_2) of the input port. The even sensors are connected to D_4 through D_6 of the input port. To prevent overlap between odd and even input data, D_3 bit goes high with each even

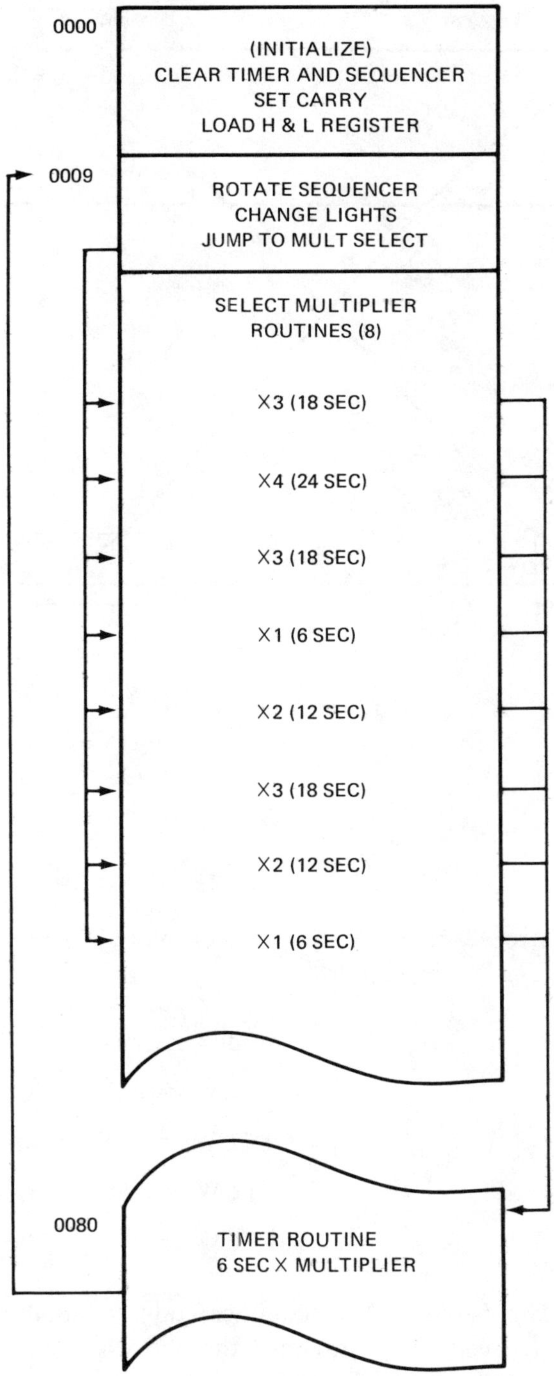

FIGURE 8.37 Memory map of 8080 traffic light controller program. After rotating the sequencer and changing the light, the program jumps to one of eight select multiplier segments then to the time and back to rotating the sequencer.

sensor input. The six switches are controlled through a single output port. One ROM is used as a program memory, the second as a table to look up switch settings in response to each new sensor reading.

The Sequencer Sequencing through the four operating modes is accomplished by loading the number 07 into a register and shifting left

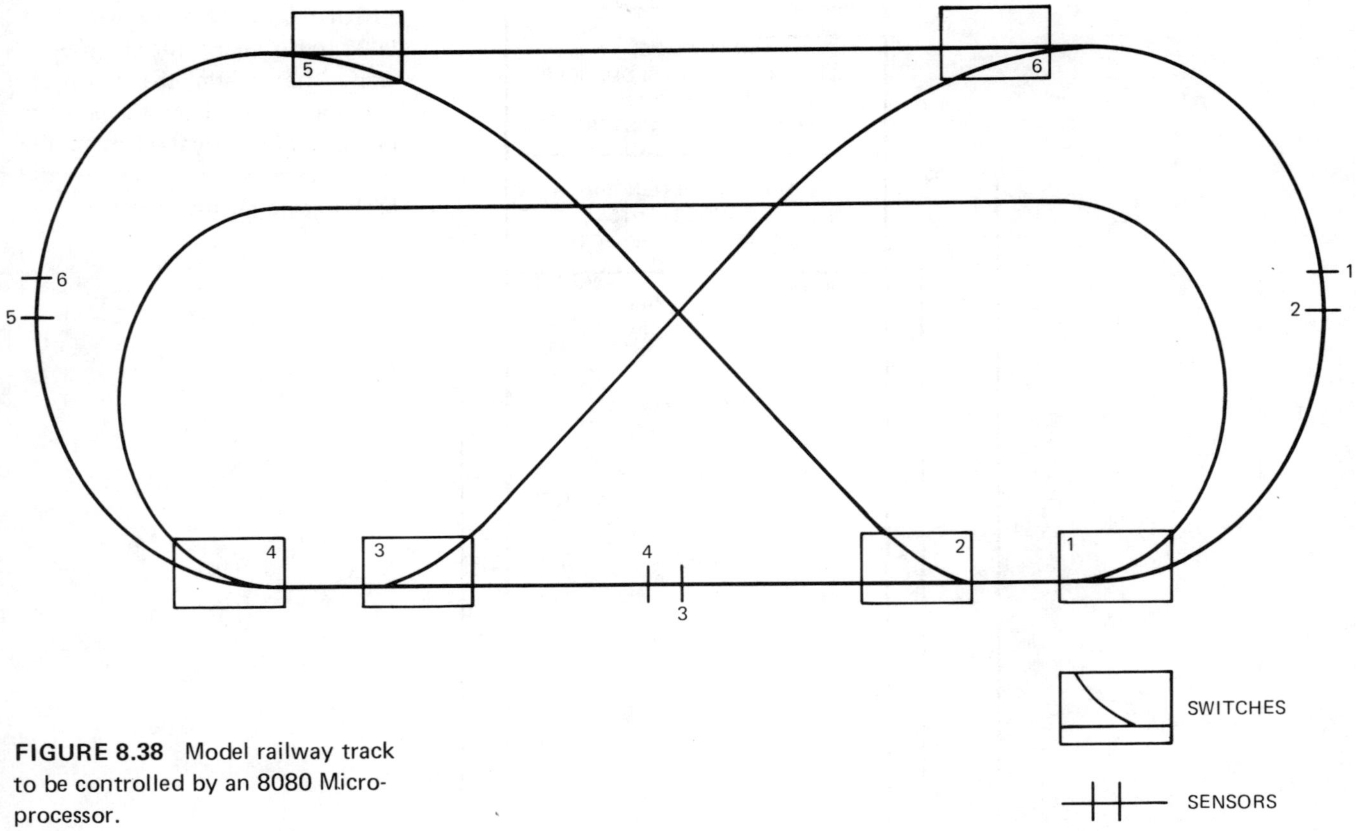

FIGURE 8.38 Model railway track to be controlled by an 8080 Microprocessor.

after each revolution is completed. This provides a unique code for each mode as follows:

mode		hex.		binary
OLCW	=	07	=	0000 0111
OLCCW	=	0E	=	0000 1110
ILCW	=	1C	=	0001 1100
ILCCW	=	38	=	0011 1000

The Table The sequence code is added to the sensor inputs as they are read. This provides the address low used to look up the correct switch setting for the particular mode and location of the train. Once the train is moving in the correct direction and loop, the data from the table will be used to give a count of sensor readings. When the sensor count indicates that two revolutions have been completed, the sequencer will change mode. Table 8.26 shows the addresses developed and the data stored in these locations.

The Operating Modes There are four operating modes:

- Outer loop clockwise = OLCW

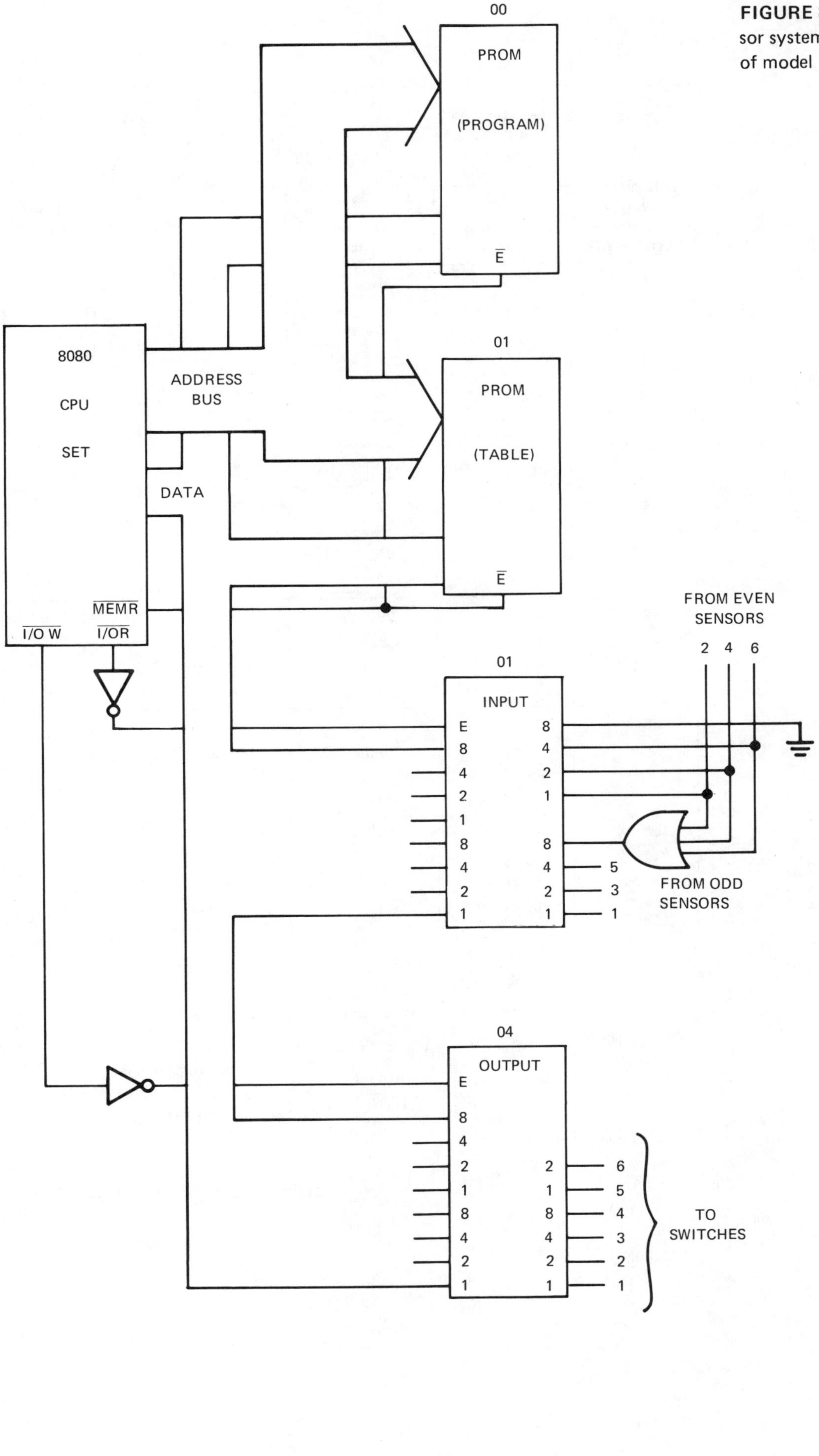

FIGURE 8.39 8080 Microprocessor system to be used for control of model railway.

TABLE 8.26 Table of switch setting (addresses obtained by the sum of sensor inputs and sequencer code).

SEQUENCER ROUTINE: MVI A 07 (0000 0111) → RLC (0000 1110) → RLC (0001 1100) → RLC (0011 1000) → JMP

(FROM INPUT) SENSOR NO.	OUTER LOOP CLOCKWISE 07	OUTER LOOP COUNTER CLOCKWISE 0E	INNER LOOP CLOCKWISE 1C	INNER LOOP COUNTER CLOCKWISE 38
01 (1)	08 (count) 00	0F (change direction) 12 [2 + 5]	1D (change loop) 09 [1 + 4]	39 (change direction) 12 [2 + 5]
02 (3)	09 (count) 00	10 (change direction) 12 [2 + 5]	1E (count) 09 [1 + 4]	3A (change direction) 12 [2 + 5]
04 (5)	0B (count) 00	12 (change direction) 12 [2 + 5]	20 (change loop) 09 [1 + 4]	3C (change direction) 12 [2 + 5]
18 (2)	1F (change direction) 24 [3 + 6]	26 (count) 00	34 (change direction) 24 [3 + 6]	50 (change loop) 09 [1 + 4]
28 (4)	2F (change direction) 24 [3 + 6]	36 (count) 00	44 (change direction) 24 [3 + 6]	60 (count) 09 [1 + 4]
48 (6)	4F (change direction) 24 [3 + 6]	56 (count) 00	64 (change direction) 24 [3 + 6]	80 (change loop) 09 [1 + 4]

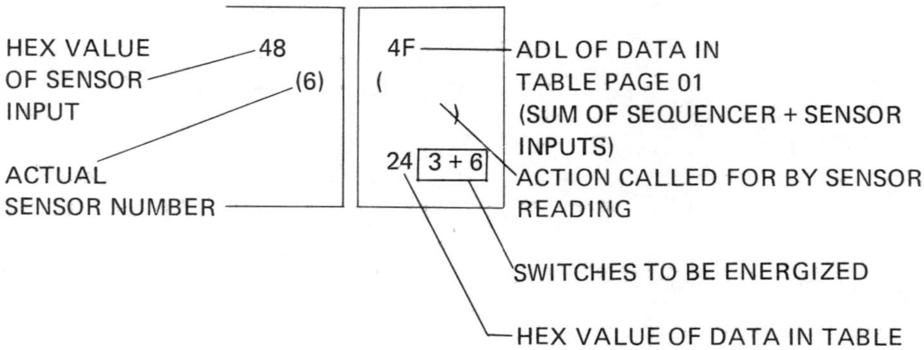

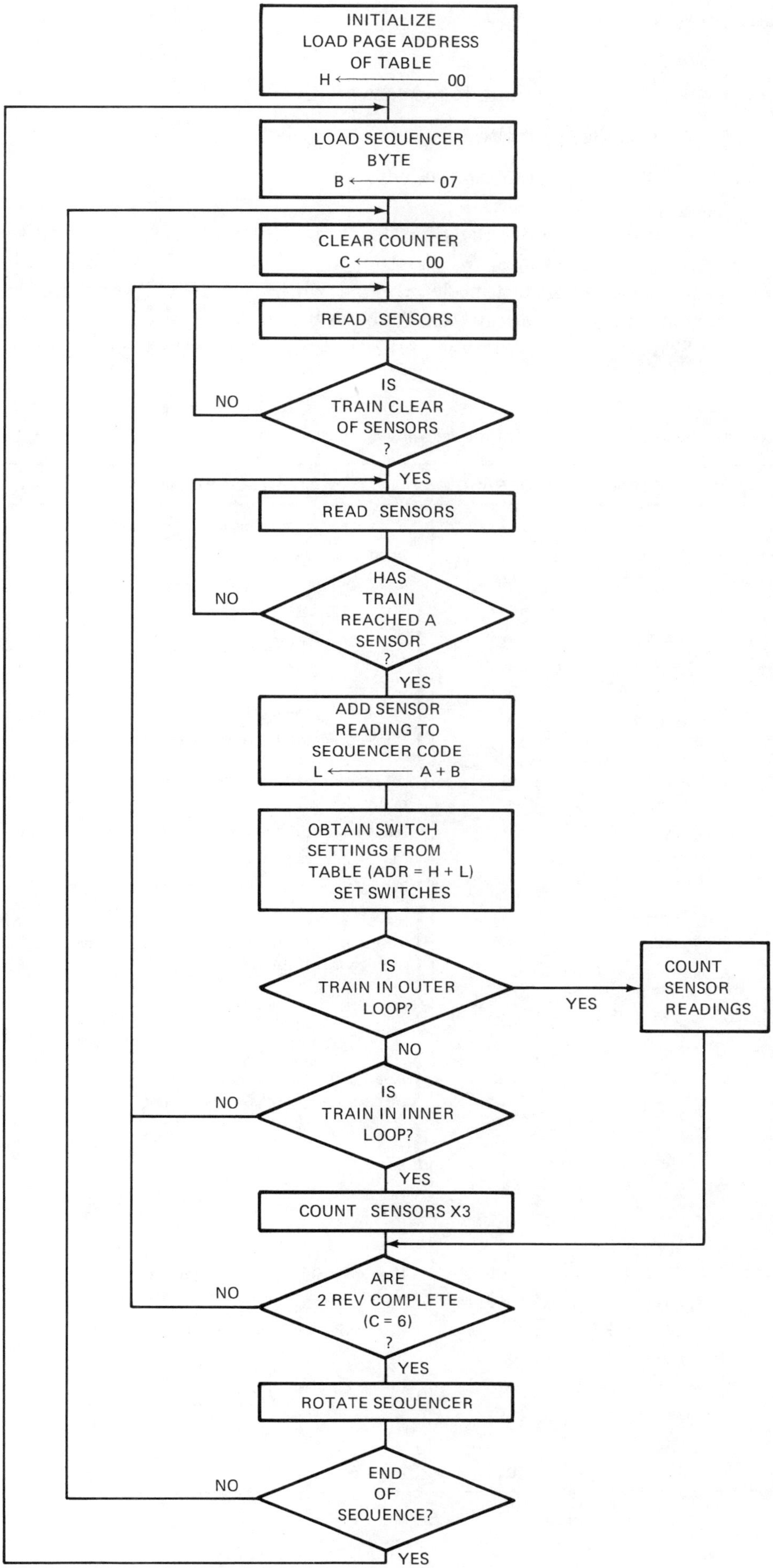

FIGURE 8.40 8080 model railway control program flow diagram.

- Outer loop counterclockwise = OLCCW
- Inner loop clockwise = ILCW
- Inner loop counterclockwise = ILCCW

Figure 8.40 shows the flow diagram with the decisions needed to change between modes. When stopped, the train will be abreast of sensors 3 and 4. A stop mode program routine can be written to insure stops only in this location. (See Problem 8.26).

Starting with instruction 0012, the train cycles through repetitive

TABLE 8.27 8080 Microprocessor program for control of model railway.

ADDRESS	MOVEMENT	MNEMONIC	OPERAND	DESCRIPTION
0010		MVI H	01	Initialize H to table page address
0012		MVI B	07	Load sequencer byte
0014		MVI C	00	Clear counter
0016		IN	(01)	Check sensors for zero
0018		ANA A		
0019		JNZ	0016	
1C		IN	(01)	Has sensor gone high?
1E		ANA A		If yes, program. If no, check sensors
1F		JNZ	001C	
22		ADD B		Add sensor reading to sequencer to form table address
23		MOV L, A		Move table address to L
24		MOV A, M		Move table reading to accumulator
25		OUT	04	Set switches in accordance with table reading
27		ANA A		Test switch setting. If zero, train is in outer loop-count sensor readings
28		JNZ	002F	
2B		INR C		
2C		JMP	0037	
2F		CPI	09	Are switches set for inner loop? If so, count each sensor reading 3 times. If not, read sensors
31		JNZ	0016	
34		INR C		
35		INR C		
0036		INR C		
0037		MOV A, C		
0038		CPI C	06	If count is 6, revolution is complete time to change mode. If not, read sensors
3A	TO 0016	JNZ	0016	
3D		MOV A, B		Shift sequencer to next mode
3E		RLC		
3F		CPI	70	Check for end of sequence
41	TO 0012	JZ	0012	Reload sequencer
44		MOV B, A		
0045	TO 0014	JMP	0014	Reset count

sequences of the four operating modes. Table 8.27 is the operating mode section of the program. The first cycle of the sequence is caused by the loading of 07 into the sequencer byte, (Register B). The counter, (Register C), is cleared. This is followed by a sensor reading routine (instructions 0016 through 001F).

Reading the Sensors Sensor inputs will not be used until after both odd and even sensors are zero. The first sensor to go high after all zeros will produce an active input. By this method, the second sensor in each pair will be ignored as all sensors must return to zero again before another reading is accepted. This will result in only odd sensors being recognized if the train is traveling clockwise and only even sensors being recognized if the train is traveling counterclockwise. The program as written assumes the sensors will see the train as a solid object and will be angled or spaced so that both sensors in pair will not read zero between cars.

On completion of the sensor reading routine, the value of the sensor reading is in accumulator A. It is then added to the sequencer byte and loaded into Register L. Register H contains the page address of the table. The H, L register then contains the appropriate table address. The table is read using a register indirect MOV A, M instruction. The value taken from the table is stored in the output port causing the correct switches to be thrown. The switch setting is then tested to determine if it is time to count sensors. If accumulator A is zero, it indicates the train is traveling in the outer loop and a count of sensor readings is begun in order to detect the completion of 2 revolutions. If the switches are set to 09, the train is traveling in the inner loop and a count of sensor readings (triple count) is begun to detect the completion of 2 revolutions. After each increment or triple increment, there is a return to read sensors until the count of six. The count of six indicates that 2 revolutions are complete and the sequencer is shifted to the next mode. The next sensor reading added to the new sequencer value will set switches for either a change in loop or a change in direction, or both. Once the change is completed, a count of sensor readings will begin again.

If the sensors are 1″ apart and the train has a maximum speed of 100″ per second, the microprocessor will have 10 milliseconds to read the first sensor before the second sensor in the pair goes high. Using a 500-KHZ clock (2 microseconds per cycle) allows time for 5000 clock cycles, which are more than adequate. If the sensors are set at truck level, the only change needed to the program is in the count used to determine that a revolution is completed. The count would need to be multiplied by the number of trucks to a train.

Use of Memory The 2 pages of PROM used for this problem are excessive. If no other chores are planned for this system the operation could be performed with a single PROM. These economics were not applied here in order to preserve the clarity of the explanation.

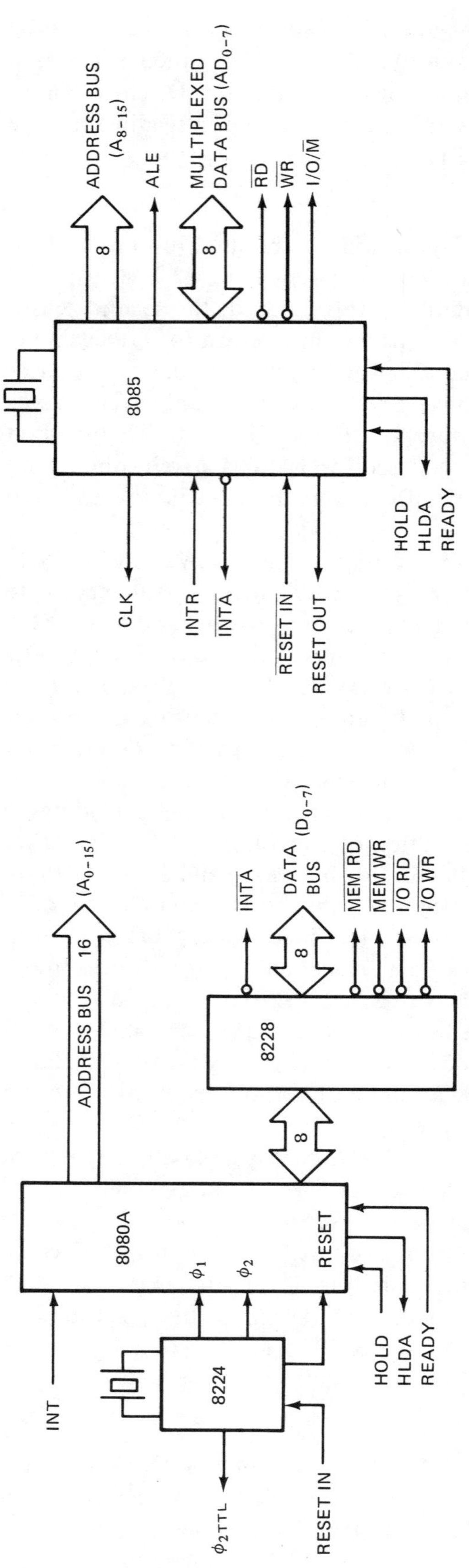

FIGURE 8.41 The 8085 MPU compared with the 8080A CPU set. The 8085 supplies from a single 40-pin circuit the equivalent functions of the three circuits in the 8080A CPU set. An economy of pins is accomplished by multiplexing the data bus with the lower 8 bits of the address bus. (*Courtesy Intel Corporation*)

8.10 The 8085 Microprocessor

8.10.1 Comparison of 8080 and 8085 Microprocessor

The 8085 is an 8-bit microprocessor that has the same instruction set as the 8080A. Programs written for the 8080A can be executed in an 8085 microprocessor system. The 8085 is more convenient to use for several reasons. Figure 8.41 compares the 8080 CPU set with the 8085. The 8085 has an on-board clock and requires only a crystal. The 8228 system controller is no longer needed. A single 5-volt power supply is used instead of the three voltages used with the 8080A. As an added convenience for interrupt handling, a number of RST inputs have been added to allow the 8085 to jump to a service routine without the need for an externally generated CALL or RST instruction. A serial in (SID) and serial out (SOD) are also added features. The instruction pertaining to serial in and out (SIM, RIM) are the only instructions that appear in 8085 instruction set that are not also present in the 8080A instruction set.

8.10.2 Bus Organization

To accommodate the added features within a 40-pin package, the 8085 microprocessor economizes on pinout by using a multiplexed address and data bus. As Figure 8.41 shows, the lower byte of the address A_0 through A_7 is transmitted through the same output leads as the data bus D_0 through D_7 and are appropriately designated AD_0 through AD_7. Figure 8.42 shows the relative timing of the address and address-data bus. Note also the ALE (address latch enable) signal generated by the 8085. The ALE signal is used to latch the lower address byte into

FIGURE 8.42 Timing of the address and address data bus. The address bus A_8–A_{15} remains valid through three states of the machine cycle. The address data bus AD_0–AD_7 becomes a valid address during clock state T_1 of each machine cycle. During clock state T_2 of each machine cycle, the AD bus becomes a bus for either data in (from memory or I/O) or data out (from 8085). The address latch enable (ALE) from the 8085 is used to latch the low order byte of the address into memory, I/O or bus latches prior to the AD bus changing to data. *(Courtesy Intel Corporation)*

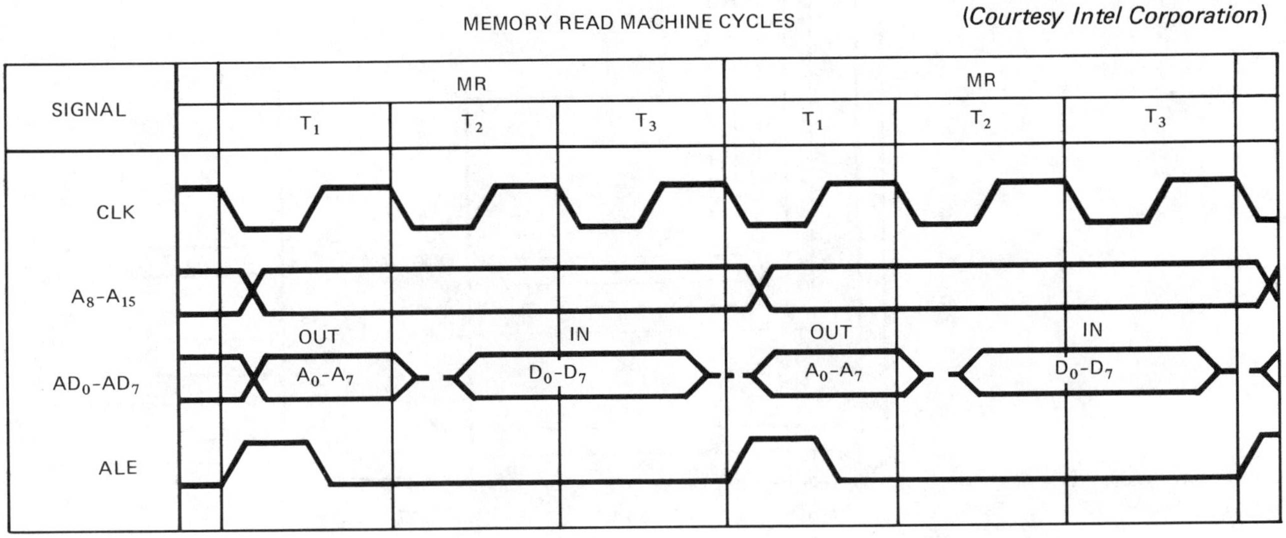

FIGURE 8.43 Minimum 8085 system requiring only three 40-pin circuits. The 8355 ROM contains on-board address latches and is designed to work directly with the 8085. It supplies 2K-X-8 ROM and two I/O ports. The 8755 is the EPROM equivalent of the 8355. The 8156 RAM also contains address latches and is designed for direct connection to the 8085. It supplies 256-X-8 RAM, three I/O ports, and a 14-bit timer. (*Courtesy Intel Corporation*)

holding latches prior to the time the AD bus changes to data. A number of RAM, ROM, and I/O devices that contain on-board address latches have been developed. This makes them ideal for use with the 8085. Figure 8.43 shows the interconnection of these devices with the 8085 to form a minimum system. The microcomputer system shown provides 2K bytes of ROM, 256 bytes of RAM, and 5 I/O ports. In comparison with an equivalent 8080A system, there is a saving in number of circuits and in the required interconnections. To allow the use of conventional memory circuits without address latches, the low order byte of the address can be latched using an 8212 or equivalent octal latch circuit to form a separate low order address bus. An 8085 system using an address latch is shown in Figure 8.44.

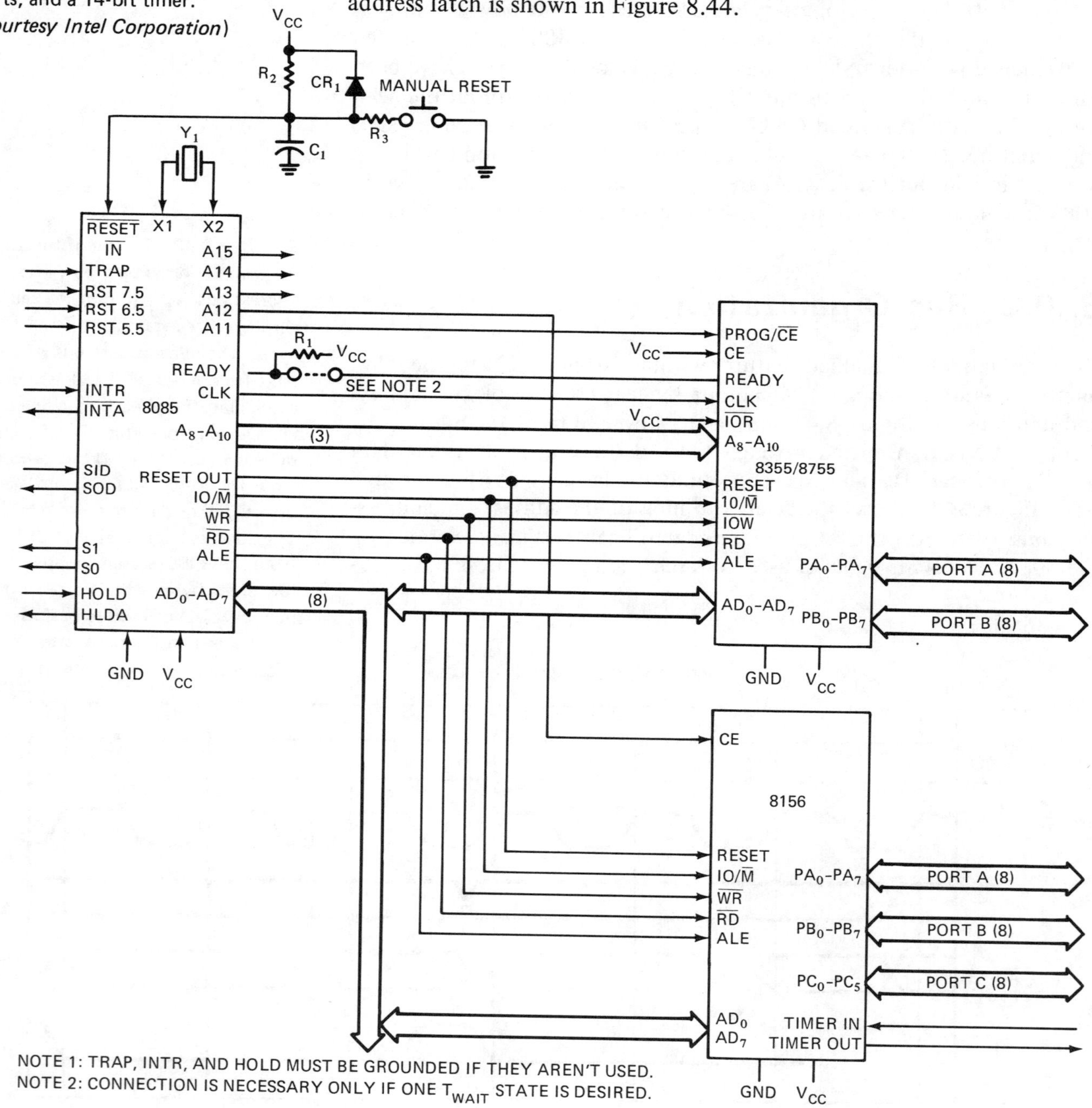

NOTE 1: TRAP, INTR, AND HOLD MUST BE GROUNDED IF THEY AREN'T USED.
NOTE 2: CONNECTION IS NECESSARY ONLY IF ONE T_{WAIT} STATE IS DESIRED.

FIGURE 8.44 Demultiplexing the 8085 address bus. The 8212 or equivalent 8-bit latch can be used to latch the lower byte of the address to form a 16-bit address bus which remains valid during the period that $\overline{WR}$ and $\overline{RD}$ are active. The AD bus is in the data period during the active period of $\overline{WR}$ and $\overline{RD}$ and therefore the data need not be latched. (*Courtesy Intel Corporation*)

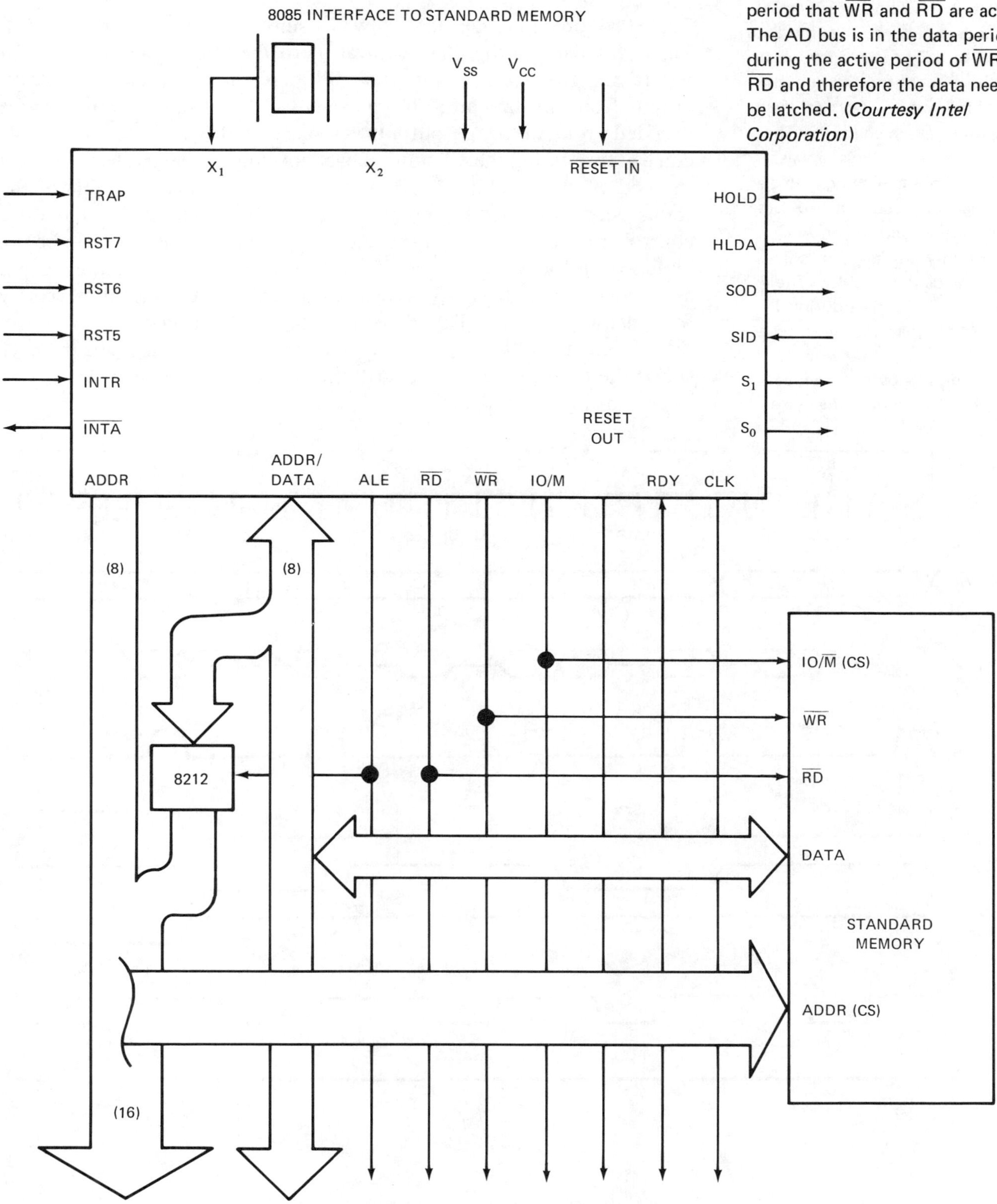

8212 is necessary because 8085 data/address bus is multiplexed.
8212 also provides "buffered" output drive capability.

8.10.3 Machine Cycles (Status and Control Signals)

The 8085 operates in machine cycles similar to those of the 8080A. Figure 8.45 shows the 8085 equivalent to the 8080 machine cycles of Figure 8.2. However, an important difference is the absence of a status output from the data bus. The equivalent status bus information can be decoded from the three outputs IO/$\overline{M}$, S_0, and S_1. These outputs become active during the T1 state of each machine cycle and lasts through the end of the machine cycle. Figure 8.46a is the truth table of the status outputs. In a system requiring an 8080 type control bus, the five controls previously supplied by the 8228 systems controller can be obtained from the 8085 status and control outputs using decoding gates, as shown in Figure 8.46b. The decoding of status signals is not necessary for most applications. The use of IO/$\overline{M}$ in conjunction with the control signals $\overline{RD}$ and $\overline{WR}$ may be adequate for most systems. Figure 8.47 shows the timing of these signals during a typical machine cycle.

FIGURE 8.45 Timing diagram of 8085 address, address-data bus and control leads. The waveforms result from the execution of instructions ADD M followed by OUT 02 beginning with program count PC. The high byte of each address appears on A8-A15 bus beginning with T_1 of the machine cycle. The low byte of each address appears on AD_0-AD_7 bus only during T_1 machine cycle coincident with ALE. The AD bus is available for data during T_2 and T_3 of the machine cycle. IO/$\overline{M}$, S_0, and S_1 change state with T_1. The $\overline{RD}$ and $\overline{WR}$ becomes active during T_2 of each machine cycle.

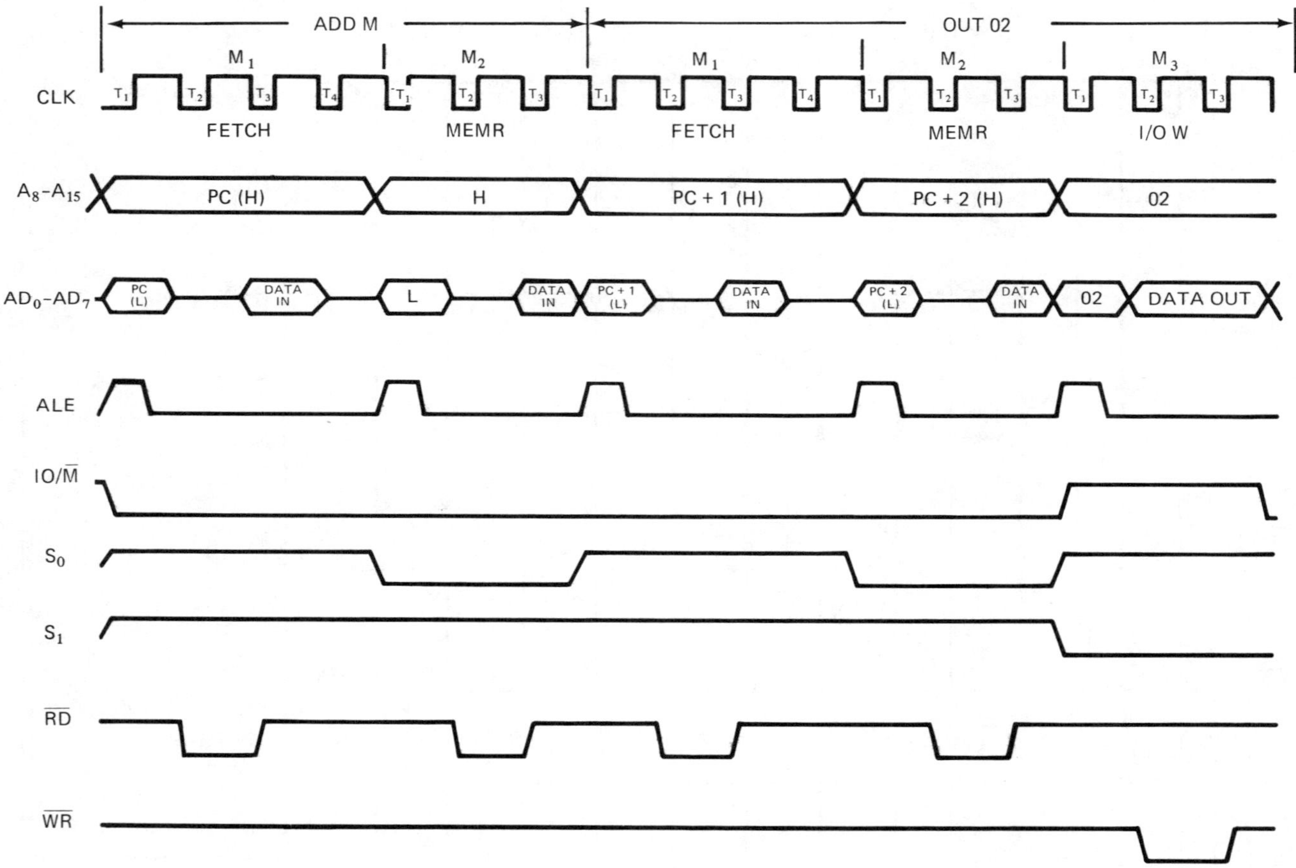

TRUTH TABLE SHOWING ALL
THE TIMING SIGNALS TOGETHER

	STATUS			CONTROL		
MACHINE CYCLE	IO/M	S_1	S_0	RD	WR	INTA
OPCODE FETCH	0	1	1	0	1	1
MEMORY READ	0	1	0	0	1	1
MEMORY WRITE	0	0	1	1	0	1
I/O READ	1	1	0	0	1	1
I/O WRITE	1	0	1	1	0	1

0 = LOGIC "0" 1 = LOGIC "1"

(a)

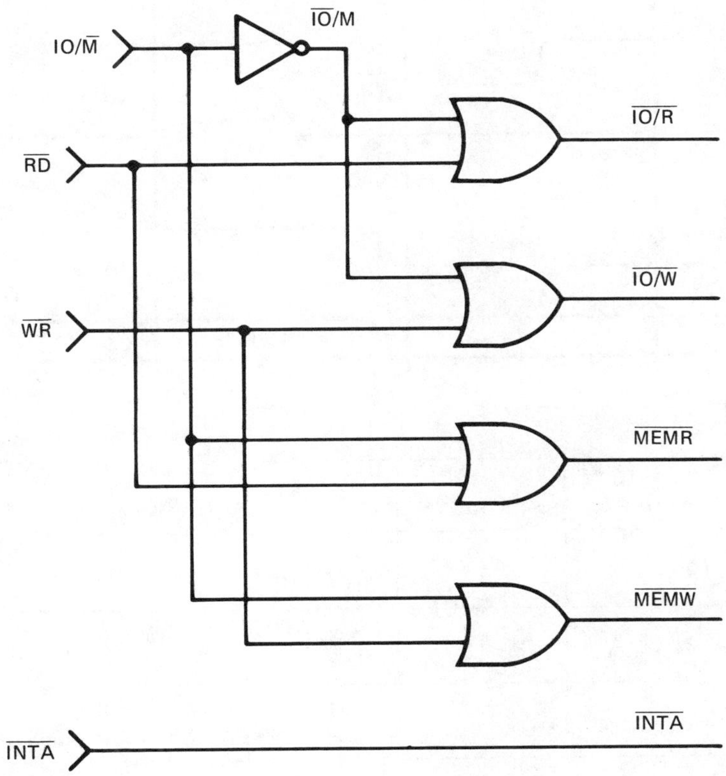

(b)

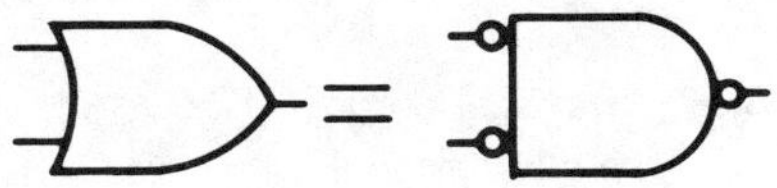

FIGURE 8.46 Status and control signals. **(a)** The 8085 has six status and control signal outputs not all of which need be used in a given system. **(b)** An 8080 style control bus can be decoded from the IO/$\overline{M}$ and three control outputs.

8.10.4 The 8085 Interrupt System

The 8085 has an interrupt system that allows the input of either RST or CALL instructions as a response to an INTA (interrupt acknowledge). This system operates as described in Section 8.5 for the 8080A except that INTR input of the 8085 functions identically to the INT input of the 8080A and the INTA outputs directly from the 8085 instead of being decoded from the status output.

The 8085 has a number of interrupt provisions in addition to those incorporated in the 8080A. These are the direct, vectored interrupt inputs listed in Table 8.28. When one of these inputs is activated rather than INTR, the program count is immediately changed to the address

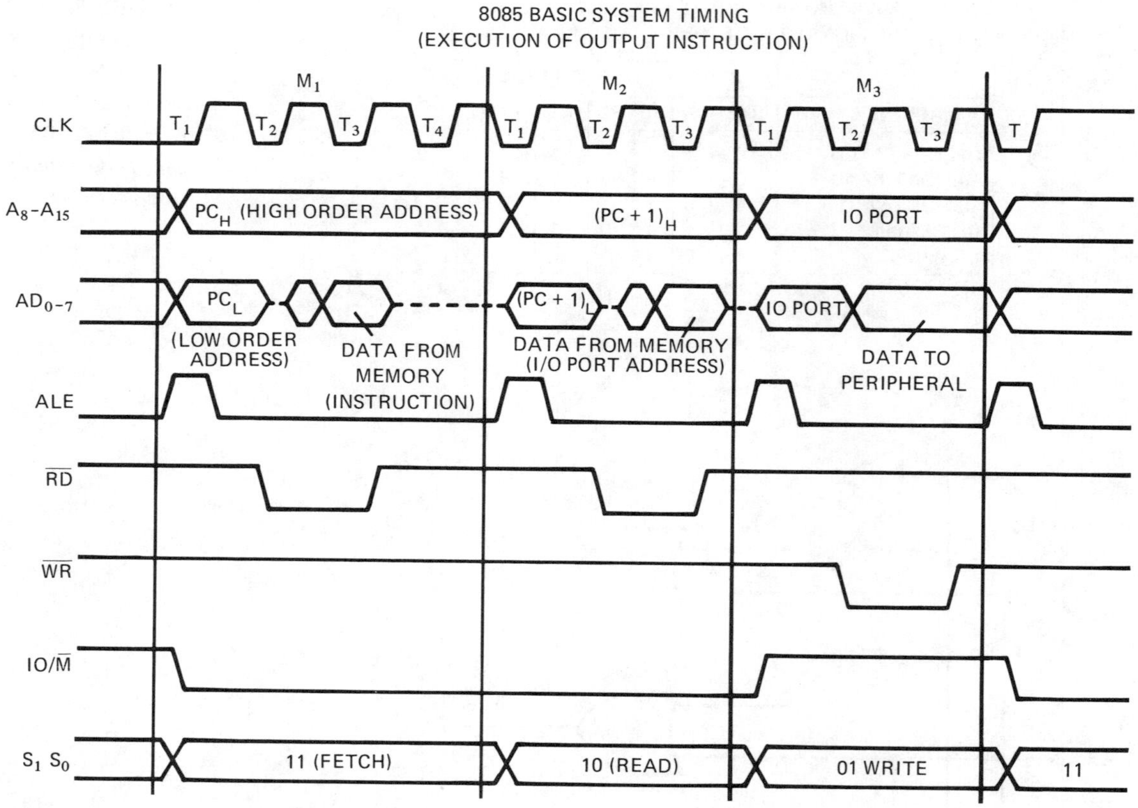

FIGURE 8.47 Status and control signal timing. The status signals ($IO/\overline{M}$, S_0, S_1) change during T_1 of each machine cycle and remain active through T_2 and T_3 clock states (T_W also if one occurs). In the machine cycles for which they occur, the control signals become active during clock state 2 and remain active into clock state 3. (*Courtesy Intel Corporation*)

TABLE 8.28 Vectored interrupts. In addition to the INTR interrupt which requires either restart or call instructions in response to an interrupt acknowledge, the 8085 has four vectored interrupts.

NAME	ADDRESS	PRIORITY*	ACTIVE INPUT	REMARKS
TRAP	24_H	1	high level	nonmaskable
RST 5.5	$2C_H$	4	high level	maskable by SIM instruction
RST 6.5	34_H	3	high level	maskable by SIM instruction
RST 7.5	$3C_H$	2	pulse (rising edge)	maskable and resetable by SIM instruction
INTR	Restart or call instruction dependent	5	high level	same as 8080 INT

*An interrupt service routine cannot be interrupted by an interrupt of higher priority other than TRAP unless an EI has occurred during the service routine. If an EI has occurred then the routine can be interrupted by interrupts of higher or lower priority.

of the particular vector. In the usual case, a jump to service routine is located at the vector address. No RST or CALL instruction need be transmitted through the data bus by an interrupting port. The restart instructions RST 5.5, RST 6.5, RST 7.5, and TRAP are all handled internally by the 8085. The TRAP interrupt takes priority over all RST inputs, and will interrupt other service routines. The TRAP instruction is nonmaskable and, therefore, it is ideal for routines to be executed on detection of catastrophic errors or power failure. The memory map of the 8085 restart instructions is shown in Figure 8.48.

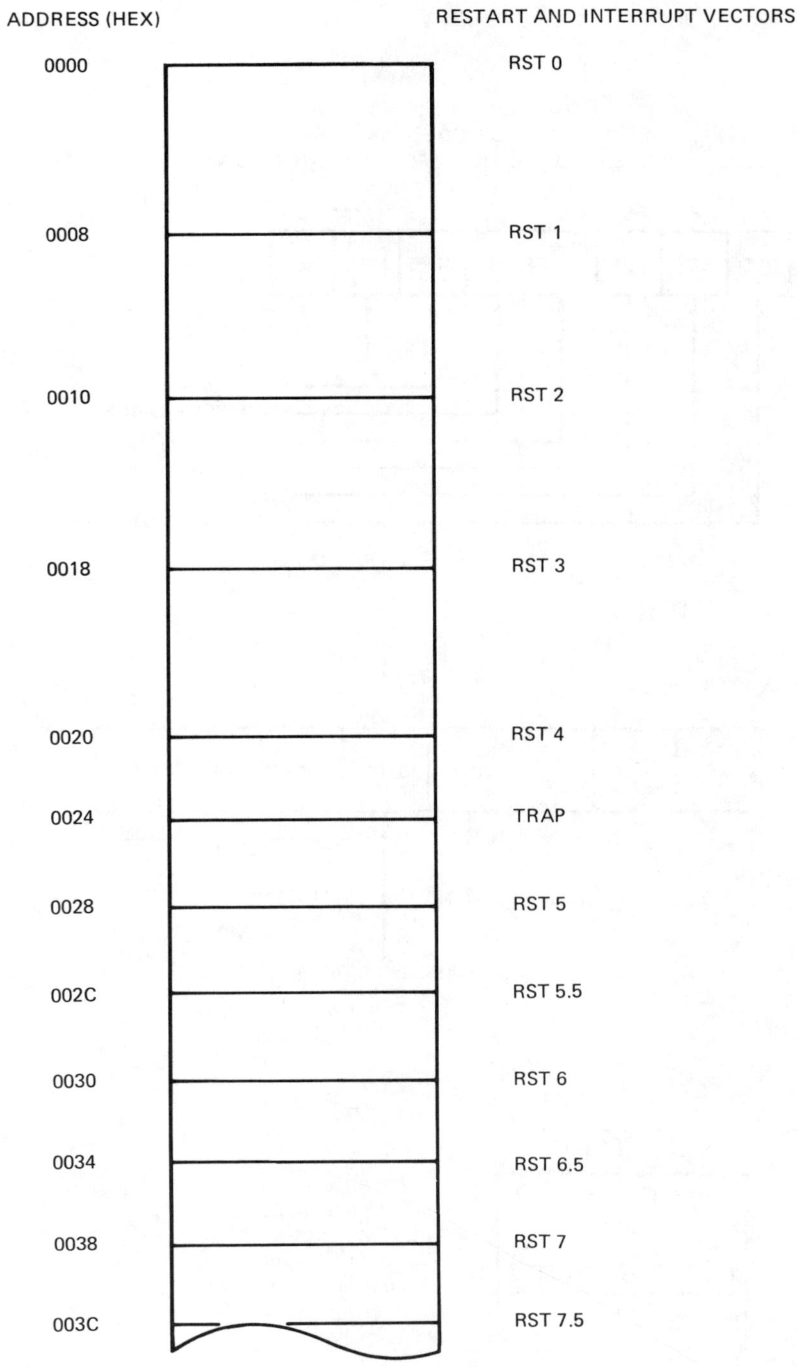

FIGURE 8.48 Memory map of restart and vectored interrupt addresses. There are only four bytes of memory for a vectored interrupt before an overlap occurs with the next interrupt memory segment. This is enough for a JMP instruction that will jump the program to the interrupt service routine. The direct vectored interrupts do not require the interrupting port to issue a restart instruction.

8.10.5 Interrupt Enabling, Priorities, Masking

With the exception of the TRAP interrupt, interrupts are not recognized unless the interrupt enable flip-flop is set. The interrupt enable flip-flop is cleared during reset and during an interrupt acknowledge. It can be set only with an EI (enable interrupt) instruction. If enabled, the interrupts are recognized in order of priority, TRAP (highest), RST 7.5, RST 6.5, RST 5.5, and INTR (lowest). A service routine started by a

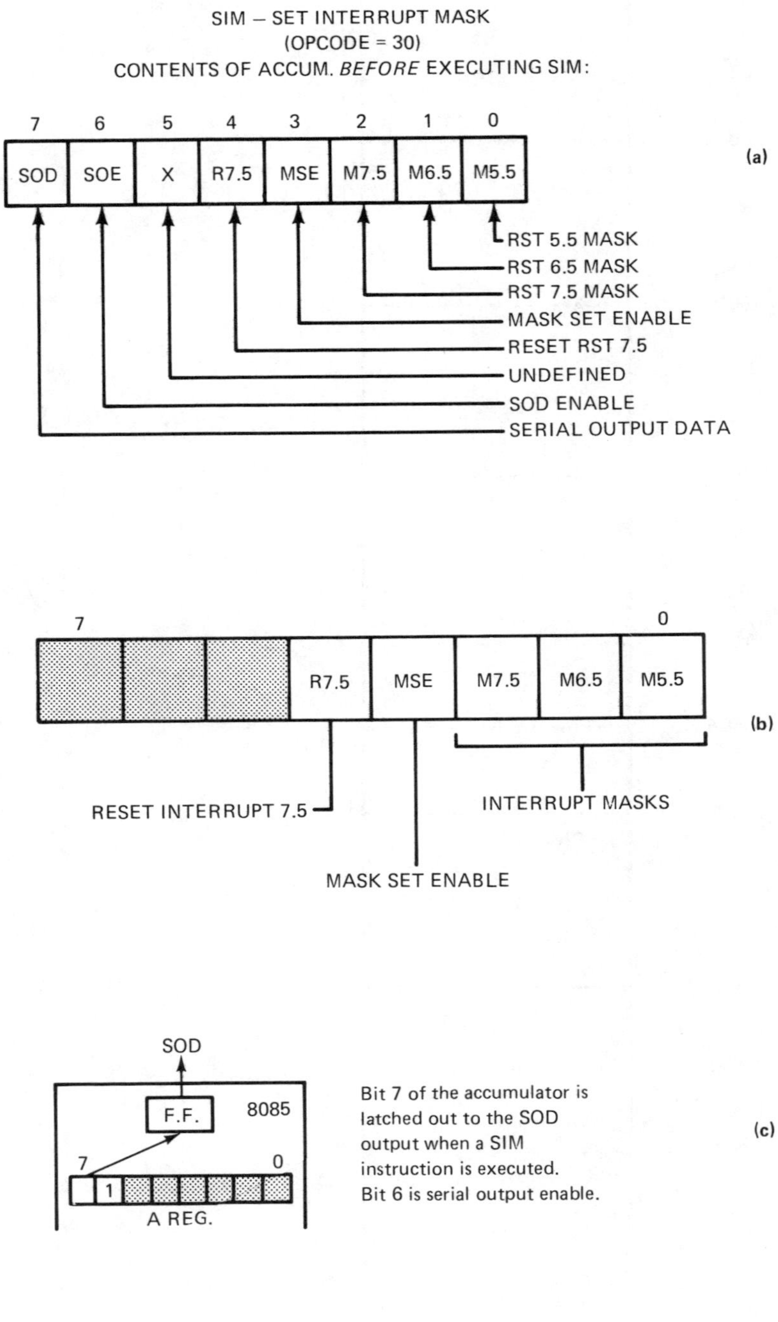

FIGURE 8.49 The SIM Instruction. SIM instruction serves a dual role. It is used to control the enabling and masking of three vectored interrupts. Its other role is to transfer bit 7 of the accumulator to the serial output port. The accumulator must be loaded with the correct control word prior to the SIM instruction. **(a)** Each accumulator bit except bit 5 has a function as shown. **(b)** 5 accumulator bits which affect the interrupt flip-flops. MSE must be high for any SIM instruction used to change mask bits and should be low for any SIM instruction used in serial output. **(c)** To transfer bit 7 of accumulator to serial output flip-flop. Serial out data must be in accumulator bit 7 and bit six must be high. (*Courtesy Intel Corporation*)

higher priority interrupt can be interrupted by a lower priority interrupt after an EI instruction occurs during the service routine. Interrupt inputs with the exception of RST 7.5 must remain high until acknowledged in order to be serviced. RST 7.5 requires only a pulse, the rising edge of which sets an internal flip-flop that remains set until the service routine is completed. On completion of the RST 7.5 service routine, the flip-flop is automatically reset. In addition to the RST 7.5 enable flip-flop, there are mask flip-flops which can be set anytime during a program to prevent interrupts from RST 7.5, RST 6.5, or RST 5.5. These mask flip-flops can be set only with the use of a SIM instruction. Prior to the execution of a SIM instruction, the correct mask word must be entered into the accumulator. The SIM instruction has a dual function. The two most significant bits pertain to serial output. When using SIM to alter the interrupt masks, bit 6 being "0" zero will prevent changes on the serial output flip-flop. Figure 8.49 shows the location of the interrupt mask bits. In addition to setting mask bits, SIM instruction can also be used to reset the RST 7.5 flip-flop.

RIM is another dual role instruction. It can be used to transfer serial input data to bit 7 of the accumulator. In addition, it transfers the state of the interrupt system to the other 7 bits of the accumulator as shown in Figure 8.50.

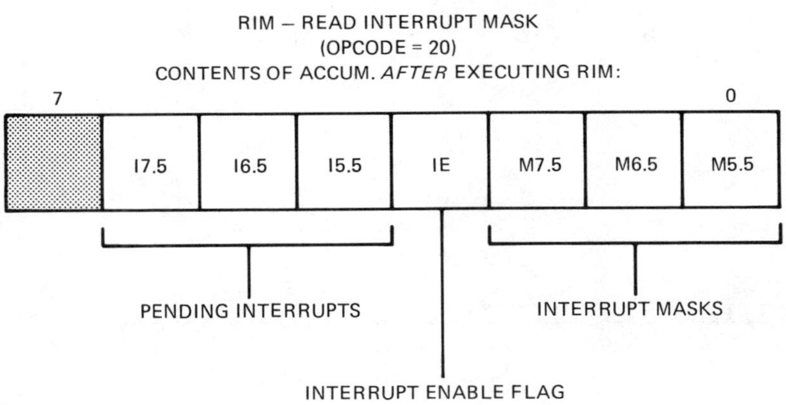

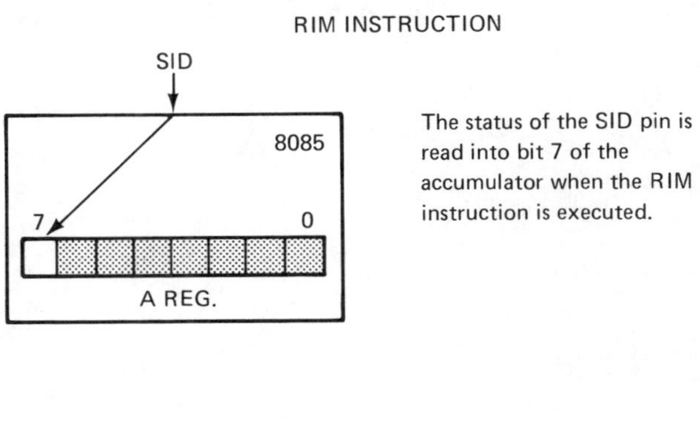

FIGURE 8.50 The RIM instruction. The RIM instruction serves a dual role. The status of interrupts, interrupt enable, and interrupt masks are transferred to the accumulator with each RIM instruction. **(a)** Interpretation of first seven bits of the accumulator after a RIM instruction. **(b)** For serial input, each RIM instruction transfers the state of SID (serial input pin) to bit 7 of the accumulator. (*Courtesy Intel Corporation*)

FIGURE 8.51 8355 2K-X-8 ROM with 2 I/O ports. (*Courtesy Intel Corporation*)

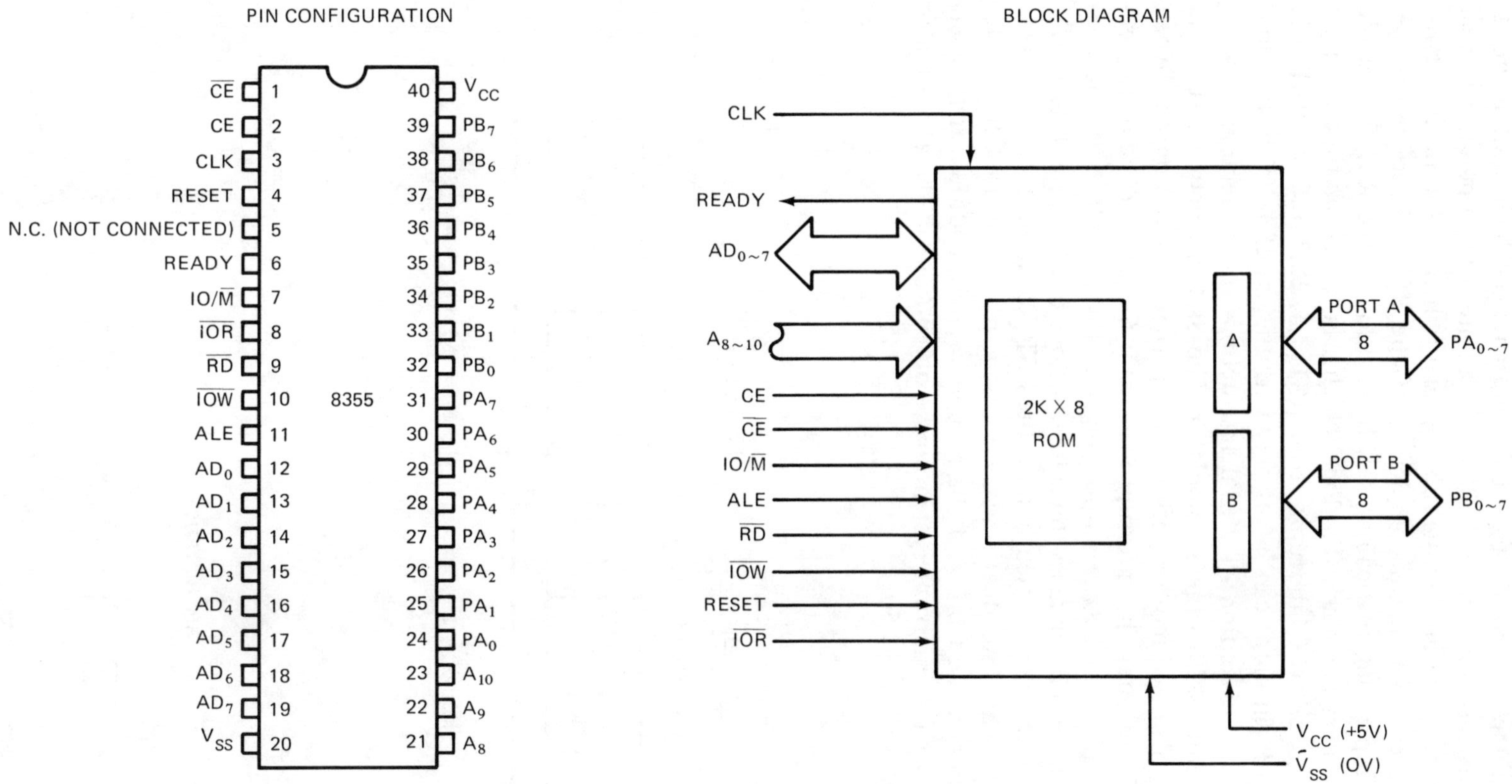

8.10.6 8085 Compatible ROM/EPROM (8355/8755)

Use of ROM The 8355 contains a 2K-X-8 ROM with on-board address latches. Figure 8.51 shows the pin diagram and block diagram of this device. It connects to the 8085 address and control bus as shown in Figure 8.52. The AD_{0-7}, $IO/\overline{M}$, CE, and $\overline{CE}$ inputs are latched internally by the ALE pulse.

Figure 8.53 shows the relative timing of the memory bus and control signals during a memory read cycle. Note that the AD_{0-7} bus returns to high impedance after clock period 1, and the data from the ROM occupies the AD_{0-7} bus during a portion of clock periods 2 and 3. The READY output of the 8355 can be used to cause a wait state in an 8085 system which is operating at too rapid a clock frequency for the 8355 (in excess of 3 MHZ). The 8755 is an EPROM version of the 8355. It has identical pin-out and can be erased by ultraviolet light.

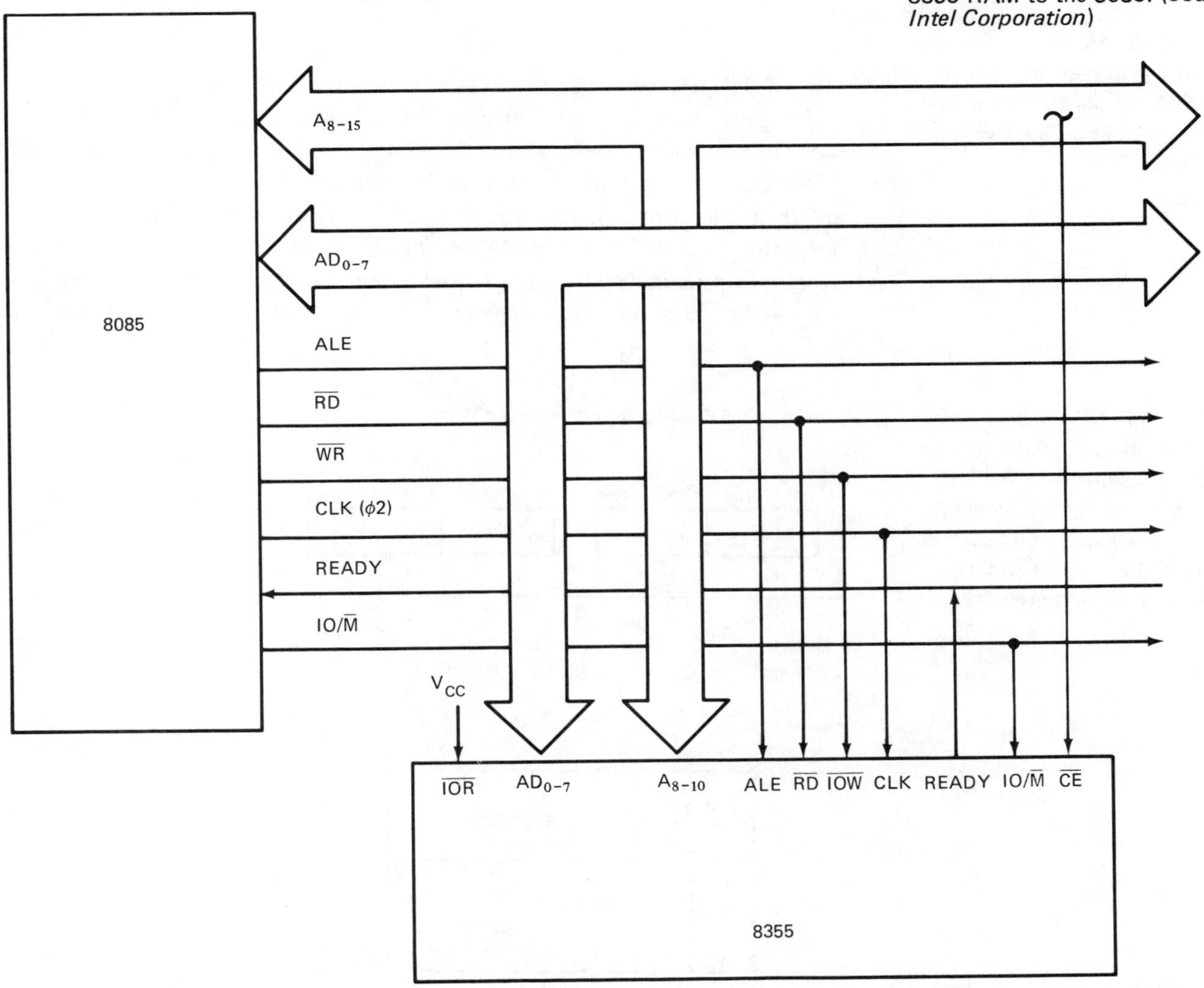

FIGURE 8.52 Connection of 8355 RAM to the 8085. (*Courtesy Intel Corporation*)

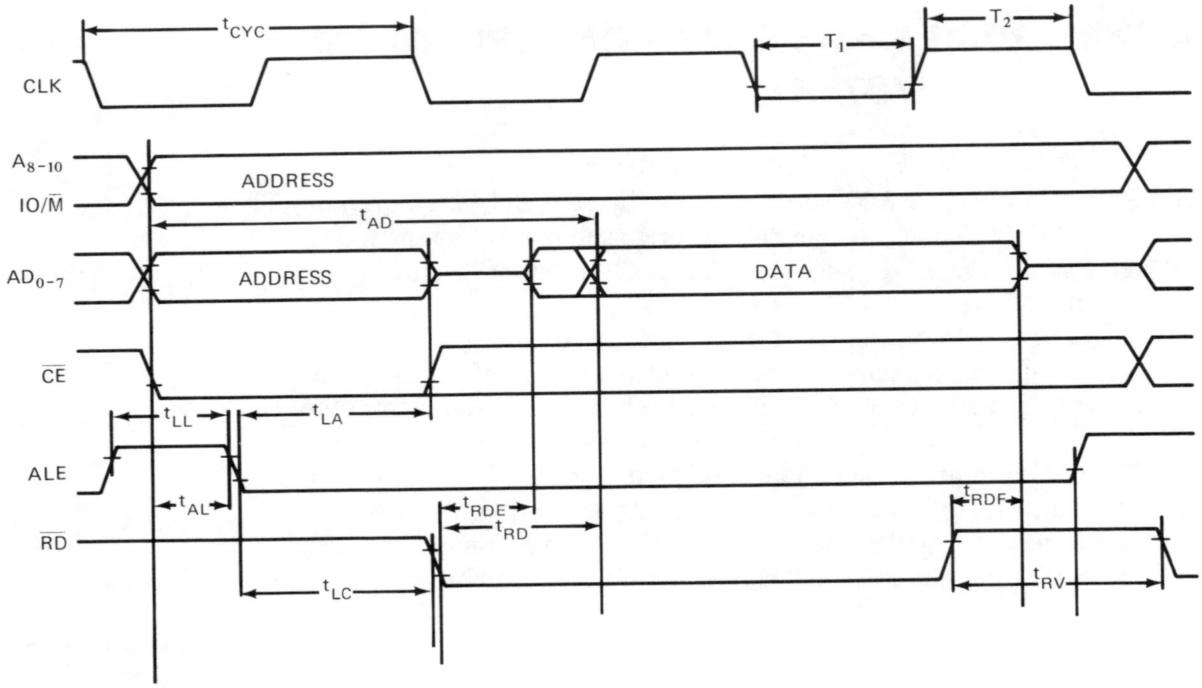

FIGURE 8.53 Memory read cycle timing of signals between 8085 and 8355 ROM. All signals except data are from the 8085. (*Courtesy Intel Corporation*)

Use of I/O Ports As the block diagram of Figure 8.51 shows, the 8355 contains two 8-bit I/O ports in addition to the ROM. These ports have 8 pins each. They are labeled $PA_{0\text{-}7}$ and $PB_{0\text{-}7}$, respectively. The ports must be initialized during the program to specify whether they are to act as input or output. A set of registers within the 8355 called data direction registers (DDR) are addressed and loaded with either 0 to designate pins as inputs or 1 to designate them as outputs. Figure 8.54 shows the data direction registers and their addresses with respect to

FIGURE 8.54 I/O Ports of the 8355/8755. **(a)** The registers of the 8355/8755 include both the I/O port latches and the data direction registers (DDR) each of which has an address. **(b)** I/O port and data direction register addresses.

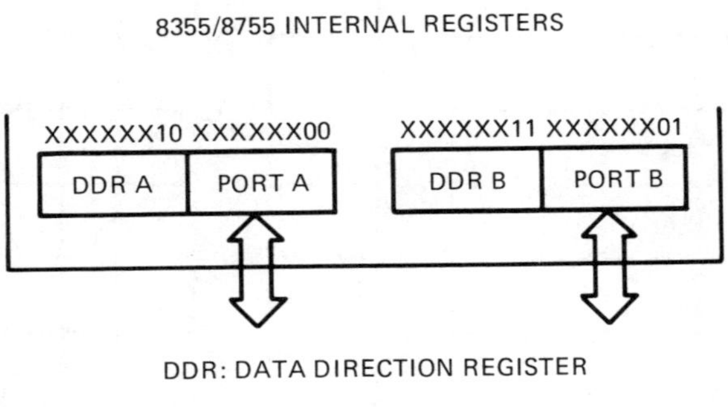

(a)

I/O ADDRESS		SELECTION
A_1	A_0	
0	0	I/O Port A
0	1	I/O Port B
1	0	Port A Direction Register
1	1	Port B Direction Register

(b)

the ports they control. The data direction registers are loaded using an OUT instruction. Normally, a port is used as all 8 bits being output or all 8 bits as inputs. In such cases, the accumulator is loaded with 00 prior to the OUT to DDR instruction used to initialize a port as an input. The accumulator is loaded with FF prior to the OUT to DDR instruction used to initialize the port as an output. It is not necessary that all 8 pins of a port be designated as input or all 8 as output. Any

FIGURE 8.55 256-X-8-Bit RAM (8155) connected to the 8085 Microprocessor. (*Courtesy Intel Corporation*)

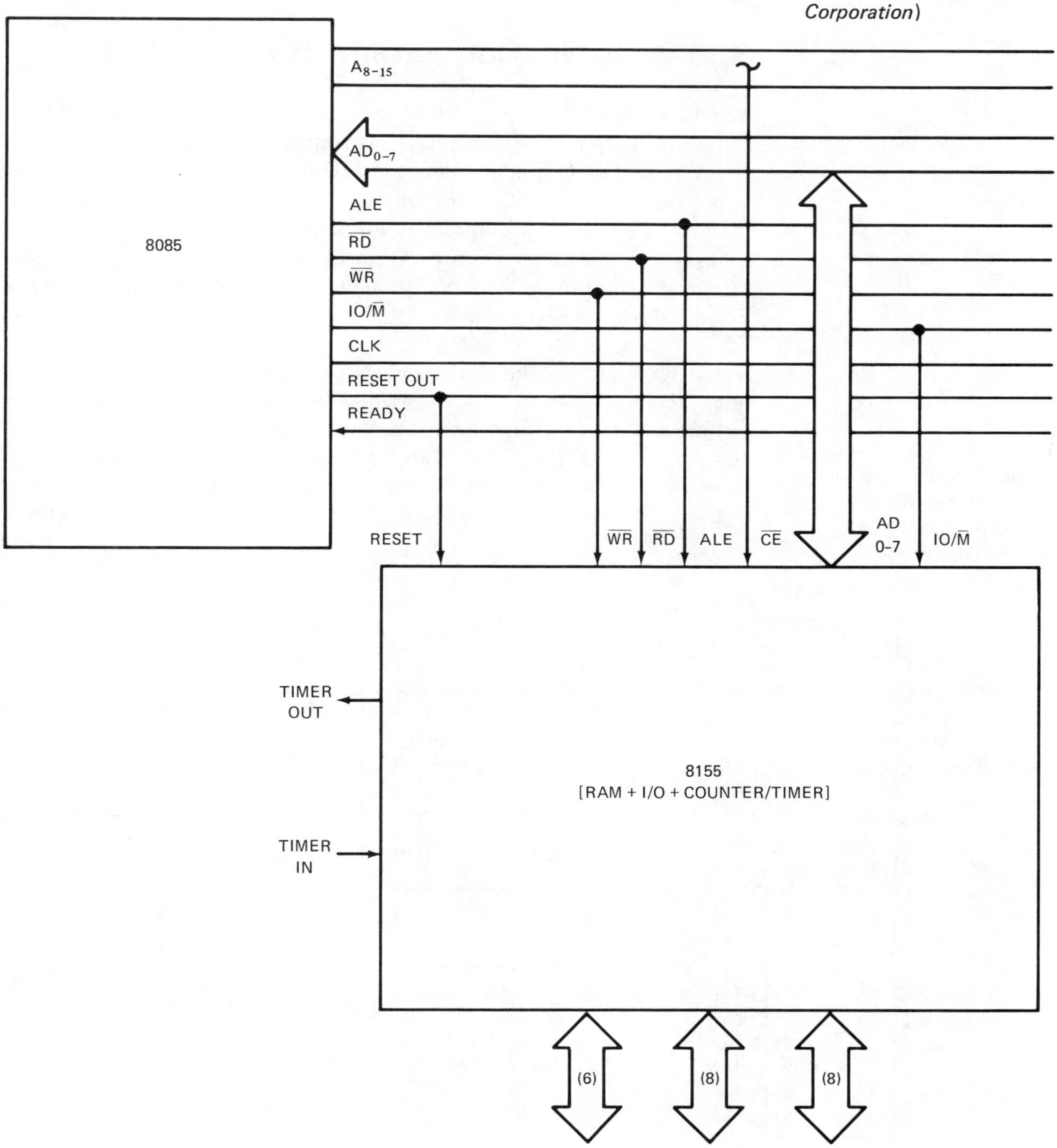

bit for which the accumulator contains a 0 prior to loading a DDR will serve as an input. Any bit for which the accumulator contains a 1 prior to loading the DDR will serve as an output. When reading a port for which some bits have been designated outputs, the pins designated output will read whatever state was last outputted to those pins. When outputting to a port for which some pins have been designated inputs, the pins designated inputs will remain in the high impedance state. The DDR need not be loaded prior to each OUT instruction. It is normally loaded in the initialization of a program or routine, but may be changed at any point in a program.

8.10.7 8085 Compatible RAM (8155)

The 8155 RAM The 8155 is another circuit designed for use with the 8085. It is a 256-X-8 bit RAM. It contains on-board address latches for $AD_{0\text{-}7}$. The CE, chip enable, and IO/$\overline{M}$ are also latched. The device is connected to the 8085 bus as shown in Figure 8.55. It is a 40-pin integrated circuit and contains additional features as shown in Figure 8.56. These include two 8-bit I/O ports, one 6-bit I/O port, and a 14-bit timer. The timing for a typical memory read cycle or memory write cycle is shown in Figure 8.57.

8155 I/O Ports Like the I/O ports of the 8355, the 8155 I/O ports must be initialized to designate whether they are to serve as input or output ports. This function is accomplished by loading a command status register (C/S register). Table 8.29 shows the addresses assigned to the C/S register and the three ports. To initialize the ports the appropriate control word is loaded into the accumulator followed by an OUT

FIGURE 8.56 8155 Pinout and block diagram. In addition to the 256-X-8-bit RAM, the 8155 provides three I/O ports and a timer. (*Courtesy Intel Corporation*)

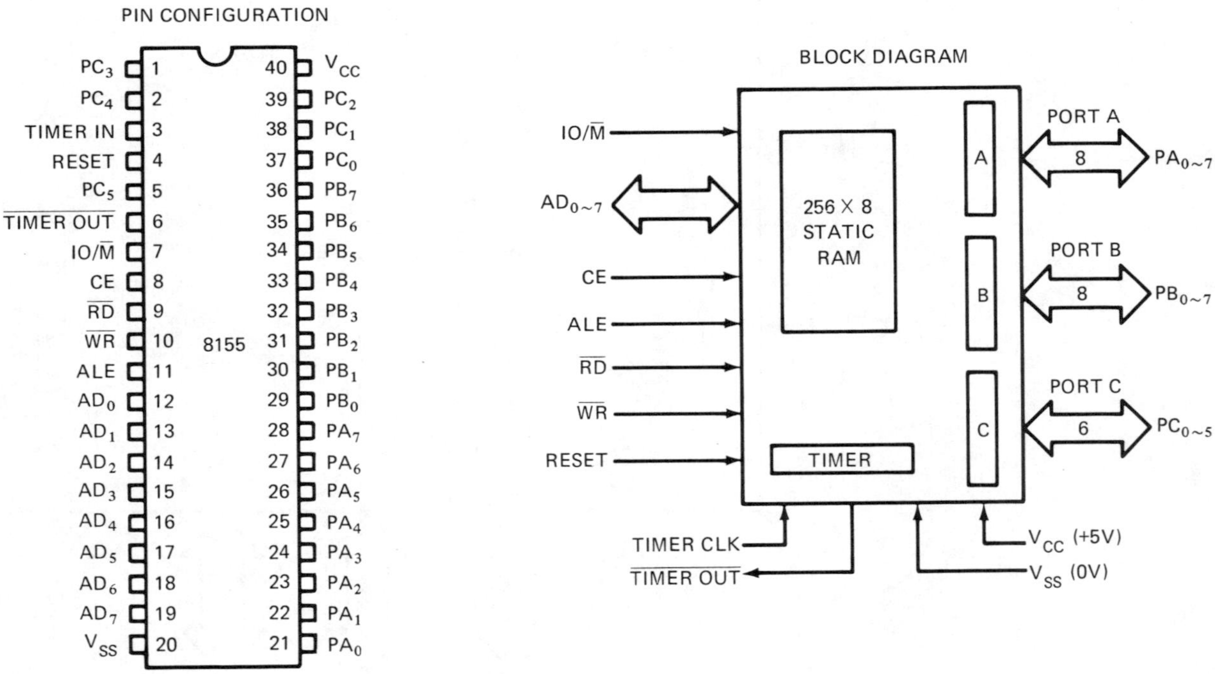

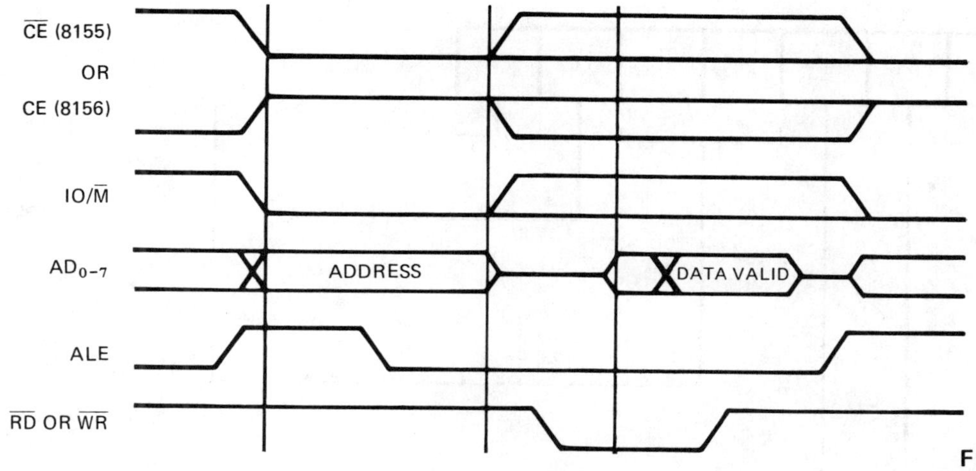

FIGURE 8.57 Waveforms for memory read or write timing for the 8155/8156. Because IO/M and chip enables are latched, these signals need be valid only during the trailing edge of ALE. (Note: The 8156 is identical to the 8155 with the exception of a CE in place of CE). *(Courtesy Intel Corporation)*

TABLE 8.29 I/O Address assigned to the C/S register I/O ports and timer bytes of the 8155.

I/O PORT AND TIMER ADDRESSING SCHEME			
I/O ADDRESS			
A2	A1	A0	SELECTION
0	0	0	Internal Command/Status Register
0	0	1	General Purpose I/O Port A
0	1	0	General Purpose I/O Port B
0	1	1	Port C—General Purpose I/O or Control
1	0	0	Low-Order 8-bits of Timer Count
1	0	1	High 6-bits of Timer Count and 2-bits of Timer Mode

instruction to the C/S register address. Figure 8.58 shows the command status register bit assignment. The lower two bits designate whether Port A and Port B are either input or output. Bits 2 and 3 determine whether the 6 pins of Port C will act as input, output, or as control signals for the other two ports. The four alternatives for Port C are listed in Table 8.30. Of the 3-bit control functions provided by Port C, the STB and BF function together. For a simple input mode, an IN instruction will transfer to the accumulator whatever data is on the port pins at the time the IN instruction is executed. Using the strobed input, the data can be strobed into the port buffers at some time prior to the IN instruction. This is done by applying a properly timed strobe to the appropriate Port C input pin. When the input port buffers are strobed, the BF lead goes high to indicate to the external circuits that the port buffers have been loaded and are not ready for additional data. When the IN instruction is executed, the BF automatically returns to the inactive state (low). Figure 8.59 shows the block diagram for a single bit of Ports A or B. The timing diagram for a strobed input mode is shown in Figure 8.60. The Port C control leads also make possible the

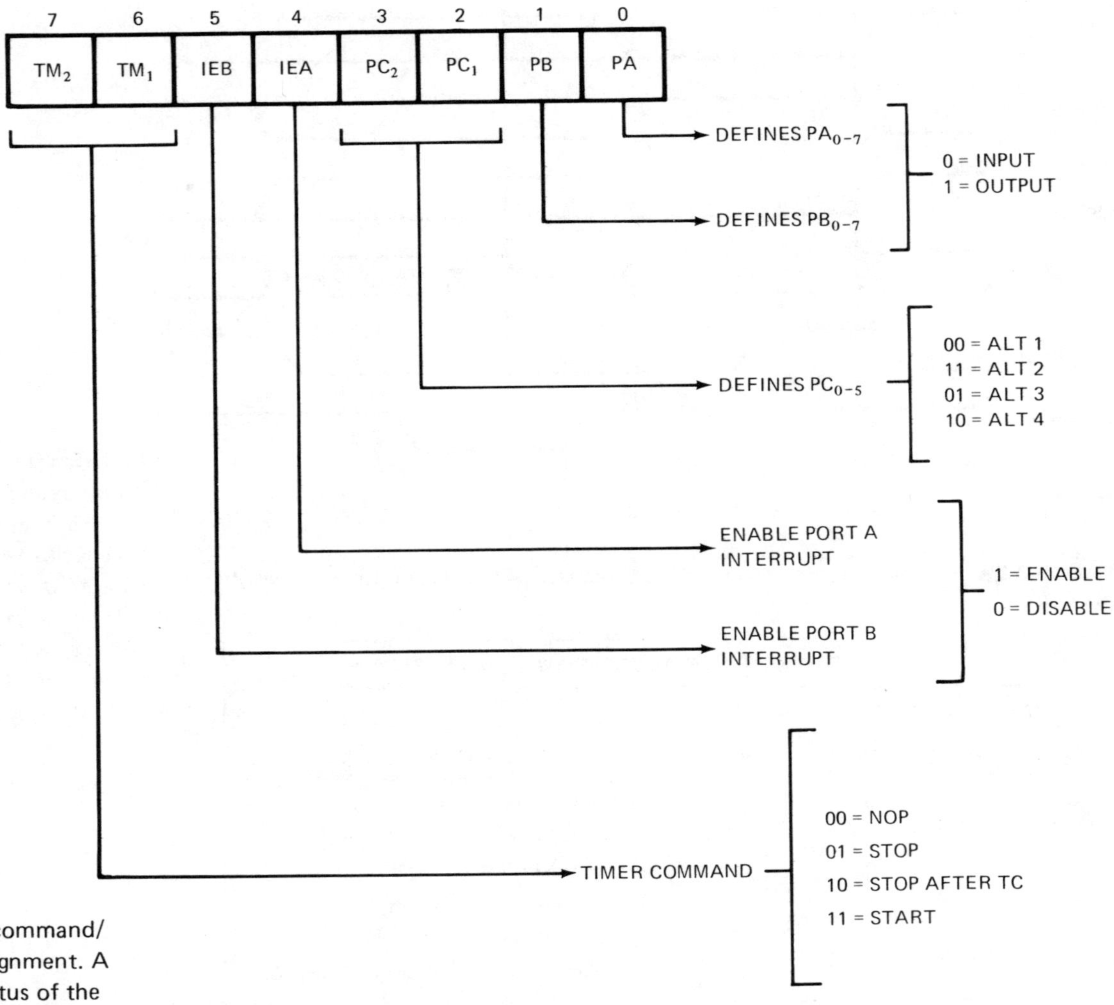

FIGURE 8.58 The command/status register bit assignment. A word defining the status of the timer and I/O ports is loaded into the accumulator. This is followed by an OUT instruction to the command/status register. (*Courtesy Intel Corporation*)

TABLE 8.30 The four alternative functions of Port C. These functions are defined by bits 2 and 3 of the command status register.

PORT C BIT ASSIGNMENTS				
PIN	**ALT1**	**ALT2**	**ALT3**	**ALT4**
PC0	Input Port	Output Port	A INTR (Port A Interrupt)	A INTR (Port A Interrupt)
PC1	Input Port	Output Port	A BF (Port A Buffer Full)	A BF (Port A Buffer Full)
PC2	Input Port	Output Port	A $\overline{STB}$ (Port A Strobe)	A $\overline{STB}$ (Port A Strobe)
PC3	Input Port	Output Port	Output Port	B INTR (Port B Interrupt)
PC4	Input Port	Output Port	Output Port	B BF (Port B Buffer Full)
PC5	Input Port	Output Port	Output Port	B $\overline{STB}$ (Port B Strobe)

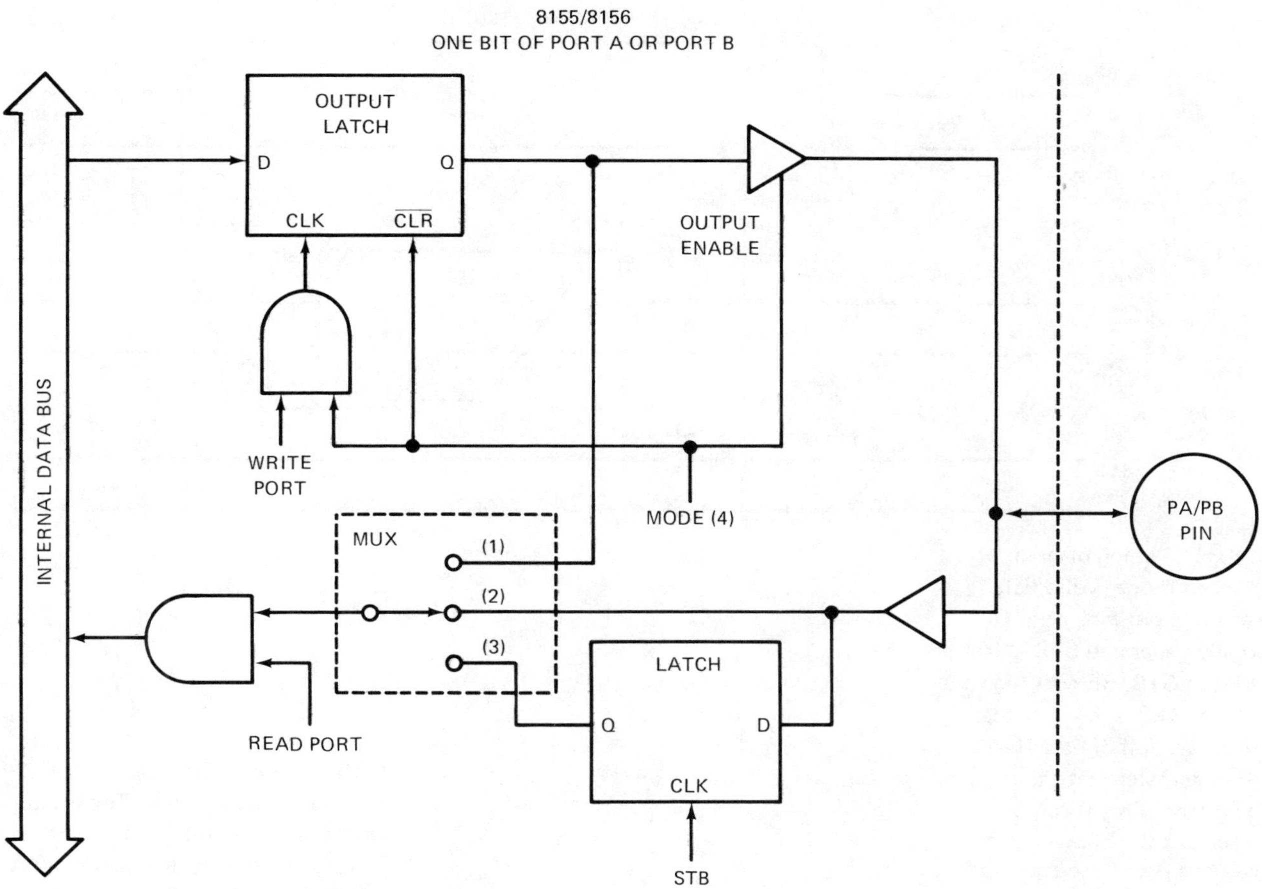

NOTES:
(1) OUTPUT MODE
(2) SIMPLE INPUT
(3) STROBED INPUT
MULTIPLEXER CONTROL

(4) = 1 FOR OUTPUT MODE
= 0 FOR INPUT MODE

READ PORT = (IO/$\overline{M}$ = 1) · ($\overline{RD}$ = 0) · (CE ACTIVE) · (PORT ADDRESS SELECTED)
WRITE PORT = (IO/$\overline{M}$ = 1) · ($\overline{WR}$ = 0) · (CE ACTIVE) · (PORT ADDRESS SELECTED)

FIGURE 8.59 Logic diagram of a single bit of Port A or Port B. (*Courtesy Intel Corporation*)

use of strobed output mode. In this mode the output latches are loaded from the AD bus during the execution of an OUT instruction. The execution of the OUT instruction causes the BF pin to go low indicating to the external circuits that the port has a data byte ready to be transferred. When the external circuit is ready to use the data stored in the output latches, it sends a strobe to the appropriate Port C pin and receives the output in the form of parallel pulses. When the output is strobed, the BF returns to the inactive state. Figure 8.61 shows the timing diagram for a strobed output mode.

The external circuit can be given even greater control of either input or output ports by employing the interrupt. When an input is strobed, the Port C INTR output associated with it goes high. This lead can be connected to the INTR or RST interrupt inputs of the 8085. (The INTE output of the 8085 may be used to enable the strobe.) Therefore, the Port C INTR will cause a service routine to be executed

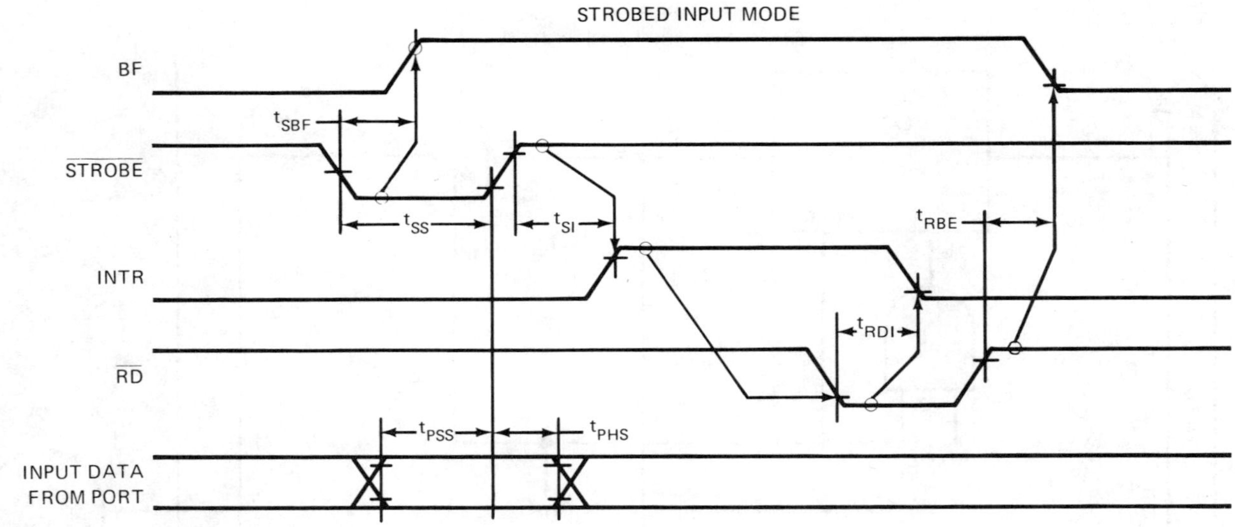

FIGURE 8.60 Timing diagram of a strobed input mode. Valid data must be at the input pins prior to the externally generated STB. After leading edge of STB, BF goes high to indicate to external circuits that input buffers are full of data that has yet to be transferred to the 8085. INTR from Port C can be used to interrupt the 8085 causing it to service the port. Once the port is read the BF goes low. (*Courtesy Intel Corporation*)

FIGURE 8.61 Timing diagram of a strobed output mode. The 8085 writes the data into the port latches. The output pins of the port are not affected. The BF goes high notifying the external circuits that a data byte is in the port. The external circuits read the output port by transmitting a STB to the appropriate pin of Port C. An interrupt from Port C may be useful in multiprocessor operation. (*Courtesy Intel Corporation*)

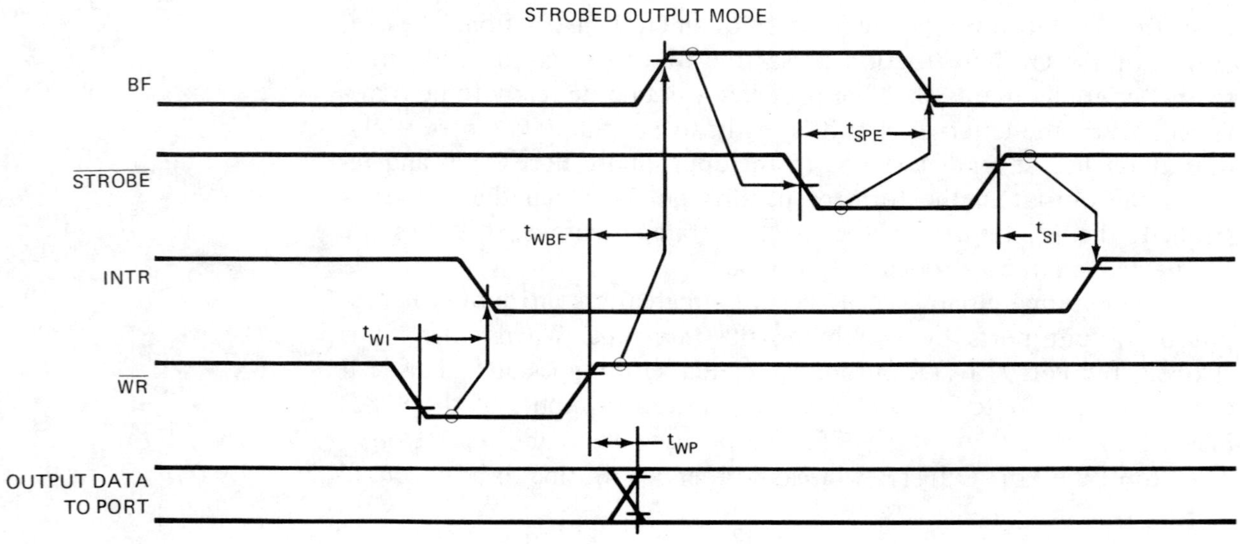

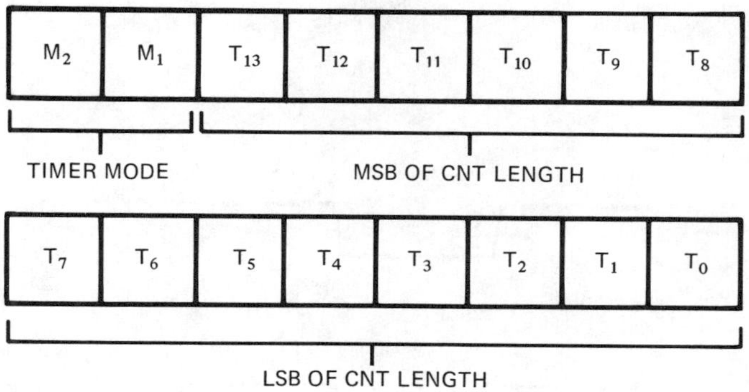

TIMER FORMAT

M2 M1 defines the timer mode as follows:

M2	M1	
0	0	Puts out low during second half of count.
0	1	Square wave, i.e., the period of the square wave equals the count length programmed with automatic reload at terminal count.
1	0	Single pulse upon TC being reached.
1	1	Automatic reload, i.e., single pulse everytime TC is reached.

Note: In case of an asymmetric count, i.e. 9, larger half of the count will be high, the larger count will stay active.

FIGURE 8.62 Count length register format. The length of the count is determined by the value loaded in the lower 14 bits of the count length register. This provides a count range of from 2_H to $3FFF_H$. The counter counts pulses occurring on the TIMER IN. (*Courtesy Intel Corporation*)

to service the port. If the interrupting port is being used to generate a RST or CALL instruction for the service of another operating port, the interrupting port can use the INTA signal rather than the RD. Note that the interrupt remains active until after the falling edge of an RD or INTA signal.

The 14-Bit Timer The counter contains two bytes that must be loaded. These are called the count length registers and are initialized first by loading the accumulator with the correct value and then transferring it to the count length register (CLR) with an OUT instruction to address XXXXX100 for the low byte or address XXXXX101 for the high byte. The content of these registers is shown in Figure 8.62. Once the two bytes of CLR are loaded, the counter will decrement once for each pulse that occurs on the TIMER IN lead but not until it receives a start. The STOP and START of the counter are controlled by bit 6 and 7 of the command/status register. The four commands are listed in Figure 8.58. When the terminal count is reached, the TIMER OUT can provide a square wave or pulse depending on the content of the two M bits of the count length register. The four output modes are described in Figure 8.63.

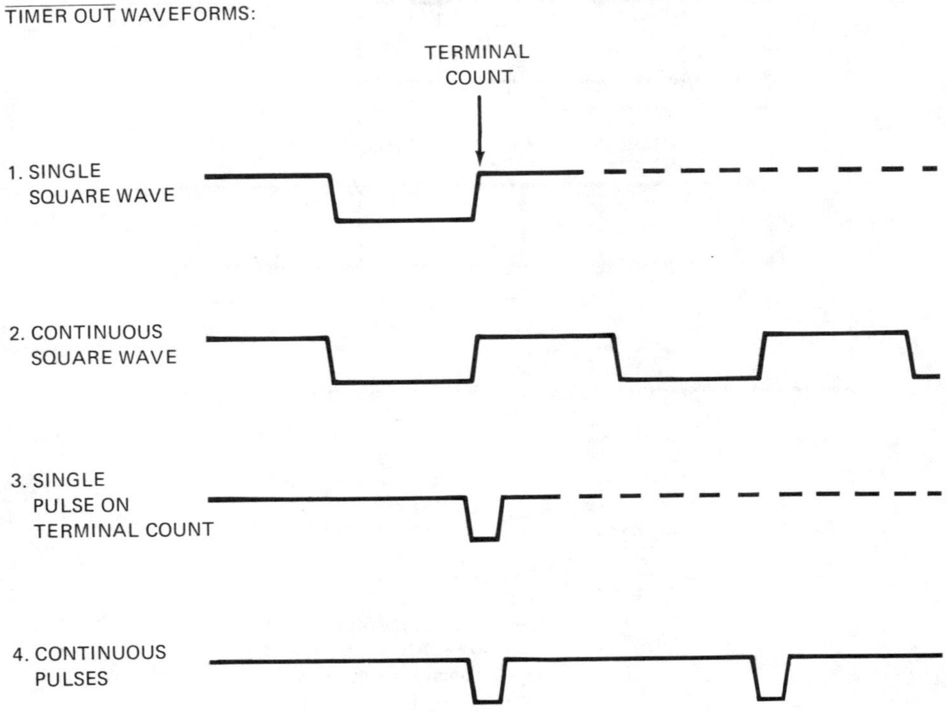

FIGURE 8.63 Counter output modes. The four output modes are determined by the content of M1 and M2 of the count length register. *(Courtesy Intel Corporation)*

Questions

8.1 List the internal registers, counters, and pointers used in the programs of the 8080 microprocessor.

8.2 Which bus leads of the 8080 are bidirectional?

8.3 What is the total addressing capacity of the 8080 microprocessor?

8.4 What circuit is ideally suited for supplying clock signals to the 8080?

8.5 What are the eleven basic machine cycles of the 8080 microprocessor?

8.6 What is the first machine cycle in each instruction cycle?

8.7 What output occurs with the first clock state of each machine cycle?

8.8 What circuits are typically used to form a CPU set?

8.9 What are the minimum number of clock states per machine cycle?

8.10 An instruction that moves a data byte from ROM to an 8080 register will have at least what two machine cycles?

8.11 An instruction that moves a data byte from an 8080 register to a RAM address will have at least what two machine cycles?

8.12 What instruction will require a stack write machine cycle?

8.13 What instruction will require a stack read machine cycle?

8.14 What is the function of the status strobe? Where does it originate?

8.15 What information from the 8080 bus is not used on the systems bus?

8.16 What is the ratio between the oscillator frequency of the 8224 and the clock frequency of the 8080?

8.17 Which outputs of the 8224 do not have short circuit capability?

8.18 During what portion of the time is the ϕ_1 clock from the 8224 high?

8.19 During what portion of the time is the ϕ_2 clock from the 8224 high?

8.20 During what portion of the time are both ϕ_1 and ϕ_2 clocks from the 8224 low?

8.21 A memory or I/O device that is too slow for the 8080 (high access time) can use what control signal to cause the 8080 to wait?

8.22 What control bus signals are generated by the 8228 systems controller following the status strobe?

8.23 What type of information should occur on the 8080 data bus in conjunction with each of the following control signals: SYNC, DBIN, WR?

8.24 What output from the 8080 informs an I/O port that the 8080 will accept an interrupt? Through what input of the 8080 does an I/O port signal the 8080 that it is in need of being serviced?

8.25 What machine cycle results from an interrupt signal?

8.26 What two types of instructions should the 8080 receive in response to an INTA? Do these instructions come from program memory?

8.27 How many restart instructions are there?

8.28 If a restart instruction were expressed in octal, what would the MSD and LSD be for all RST instructions?

8.29 How many memory bytes exist for each RST instruction? If a service routine will not fit in this space what must the programmer do?

8.30 What is special about RST 0?

8.31 The auxiliary port in Figure 8.10 provides RST instructions for three I/O ports. List the instructions and the address of the vectors.

PORT	RST	ADDRESS
A		
B		
C		

8.32 If in the system shown in Figure 8.10, several ports interrupted simultaneously, how may the priority be established?

8.33 If more than three interrupt ports must be handled on a priority basis, what circuits can be used?

8.34 For a system with a single interrupt service routine, what special provision does the 8228 have for generating a restart instruction?

8.35 In what state is the INTE output at the time an interrupt service routine is being executed?

8.36 How does the stack and the stack pointer function during an interrupt?

8.37 How are the accumulator, flags, and register contents saved during an interrupt?

8.38 The 8080 instruction set includes how many machine codes?

8.39 List the addressing modes of the 8080 and the number of bytes per instruction for each mode.

8.40 Which addressing mode requires that an address pointer be prepared in advance of the use of the instruction?

8.41 The letter M refers to what address pointers?

8.42 From where is the source operand obtained in the immediate mode?

8.43 In the direct addressing mode the effective address of the operand is obtained from what part of the memory?

8.44 For which two instructions is direct addressing only 2-byte?

8.45 What do the machine codes of conditional call, jump, and return instructions have in common?

8.46 For an MOV r_1, r_2 instruction, which r is the destination operand?

8.47 Explain the difference between instructions MOV r, M and MOV M, r.

8.48 Compare the advantages and disadvantages of loading the accumulator with either of the following three instructions:

MOV A, M
LDA adr
MVI A data

8.49 Which instruction is ideal for initializing the stack pointer?

8.50 Describe the two I/O instructions. Why do they require only two bytes?

8.51 What is the result of a HLT instruction? How is the halt terminated?

8.52 Explain how the comparator circuit in Figure 8.19 permits the keyboard to supersede any single address in the microprocessor memory map.

8.53 Explain how the reset jump instruction can be altered by the keyboard to supersede any single address in the microprocessor memory

8.54 In Figure 8.22, how long does the INT signal continue from the time a pushbutton is depressed?

8.55 In Figure 8.22, how long is the RST instruction on the data bus?

8.56 Figure 8.23 shows the reset vector program beginning with a JMP 0000. What will occur if the keyboard is not used to supersede one of these addresses?

8.57 If a program to be run is located on page 04 of the memory, how should the address switches of the keyboard be set and what should be entered into the keyboard latches?

8.58 If a program is to be loaded, how should the address switches of the keyboard be set and what should be entered into the keyboard latches prior to reset?

8.59 Explain the extent to which load and verify programs of the bootstrap loader are the same or different.

8.60 List three add without carry instructions of the 8080 (one each in register, register indirect, and immediate modes).

8.61 List three add with carry instructions of the 8080 (one each in register, register indirect, and immediate modes).

8.62 What 8080 instructions are used to ones complement and 2s complement numbers?

8.63 What class of 8080 instruction causes a change in the flags?

8.64 What instruction can be used to obtain the status of the accumulator after a non-ALU instruction?

8.65 For single-byte arithmetic, which register must contain both an augend and the sum?

8.66 For double-byte arithmetic, which register pair must contain both an augend and the sum?

8.67 What adjustment must be made to the arithmetic program in order that a twos complement subroutine may be used?

8.68 In double precision signed arithmetic, why is the high byte of each term examined first?

8.69 Which functions in the double precision signed arithmetic can be accomplished only in the accumulator?

8.70 What two existing conditions require that register pairs be saved on the stack during a subroutine call?

8.71 List the 8080 instructions that shift or rotate numbers.

8.72 To which register must a byte be moved in order to shift or rotate it?

8.73 In the 8080 multiplication program, what is the purpose of shifting X?

8.74 In the multiplication of single-byte numbers X and Y, why is a high order byte needed for Y?

8.75 In Figure 8.27, if an interrupt occurs during the execution of a two byte instruction at addresses 0291 and 0292, what changes will occur to the stack and the stack pointer?

8.76 A number in register B is to be shifted to the left once each time a routine is executed, the right hand bits must shift to zero. The program moves ahead when B shifts to zero. List the instructions used to shift and test B.

8.77 In Figure 8.30, what condition of the flag register causes Y to shift without adding? Does this agree with the operation for binary multiplication?

8.78 What changes must be added to the counter of Figure 8.33 to accommodate the fact that all registers of the 8080 must be used in the routine being counted?

8.79 How does the compare instruction (CMP) differ from the subtract instruction?

8.80 What flags are effected by the CMP instruction?

8.81 In the traffic signal control program of Figure 8.36, what controls the state of the lights?

8.82 Using a 6-second 2-byte timer, how does the program produce the variety of time intervals called for in Table 8.21?

8.83 In the 8080 traffic signal controller, what controls the turn on of the red lights?

8.84 In the timer routine, why is the machine cycle time not used as the element of time?

8.85 In the 8080 traffic light controller, how does the program choose the correct select multiplier routine for a given cycle in the sequence?

8.86 The traffic signal timing of Table 8.21 is to be modified so that North-South timing has the same 12-18-12 timing as East-West. Which instructions must be changed?

8.87 Explain the need for initialization instruction in Table 8.22.

8.88 Under what conditions is the use of a lookup table advantageous?

8.89 How are the addresses of the lookup table generated during the running of the 8080 model railway control program?

8.90 What signal is used in separating address and data information from the AD bus of the 8085?

8.91 What are three major advantages of the 8085 in comparison to the 8080?

8.92 RST 5.5, RST 6.5, and RST 7.5 differ from the INT input of the 8080 in what way?

8.93 Which input to the 8085 functions identically to the INT input of the 8080?

8.94 List the priority of interrupts of the 8085 microprocessor.

8.95 Under what condition can a RST 7.5 service routine be interrupted by an RST 5.5 interrupt?

8.96 How does an RST 7.5 interrupt signal differ from that of an RST 6.5?

8.97 When is an octal latch circuit like the 8212 needed in an 8085 microprocessor system?

8.98 What signals of the 8085 can be used to replace the status information normally supplied by the 8228 in the 8080 CPU set?

8.99 What are the dual functions of the SIM and RIM instructions?

8.100 What function must occur prior to a SIM instruction?

8.101 What special features of the 8355 and 8155 make them ideal for use with the 8085?

8.102 How is an I/O port of the 8355 initialized as an input port?

8.103 What initialization procedure is needed to designate port B of an 8155 as a strobed input port?

Problems

8.1 In the circuit of Figure 7.33, substitute the 8080 CPU set for the microprocessor and draw the component connections to Address Data and control buses needed to form a microcomputer. The PROM will occupy pages 00 and 02. The RAM will occupy page 03. An input port will have address of XX81. An output port will have address of XX41. (I/O not memory mapped). Use decoding gates where needed.

8.2 Draw the equivalent microprocessor system to that of Problem 8.1, but use the 8085, 8155, and the 8355.

8.3 Draw the equivalent microprocessor system to that of Problem 8.2, but use the 8085 and 8212 latch. RAM, ROM, and I/O to be the same as in Problem 8.1.

8.4 From the hexadecimal displays of the flag register listed below, determine whether sign zero or carry bits are set.

12	53
47	96
D3	C2
86	D7

8.5 Draw an 8080 timing diagram like Figure 8.2 for the following instructions.

```
LDA 0080
MOV M, C
```

8.6 Draw an auxiliary port used to provide both RST 1 and RST 4 restart vectors. Use an 8212 I/O port shown in Figure 4.13. Label all connections.

8.7 Convert the decimal numbers to binary and perform the algebraic additions listed using twos complement arithmetic.

113 + 59	113 - 59	59 -113
146 + 95	146 - 95	95 -146
83 +125	83 -125	125 - 83

8.8 Add to the program of Table 8.16 an output routine which outputs in hexadecimal to a pair of ports: one port to receive the sign and 7 high bits, a second to receive the 8 lower bits of the sum. For a sum in excess of 15 bits magnitude, output FFFF to indicate an overflow.

8.9 Write the double precision adder program of Table 8.16 without using the DAD instruction.

8.10 Beginning with a $C3_H$ in the accumulator and the carry clear, determine the hexadecimal value of the accumulator and state of the carry after each of the following instructions.

Begin with	RAL	A =	CY =
$A = C3_H$ CY = 0	RAR	A =	CY =
in each	RLC	A =	CY =
case.	RRC	A =	CY =

8.11 Do the single precision algebraic adder program like that of Figure 8.25 taking advantage of the 8080 subtract instructions.

8.12 Write an 8080 routine for the twos complement of a 3-byte number.

8.13 Draw a flow diagram and write an 8080 program for a double precision algebraic adder using 1s complement.

8.14 Table 8.31 is a segment of a routine that moves data from 2 adjacent input ports and stores it in adjacent memory addresses. Modify the program so that it will exit the routine after 100_{10} bytes have been stored.

TABLE 8.31

ADDRESS	MOVEMENT	MNEMONIC	OPERAND	DESCRIPTION
2010		LXI H	2040	Load first MEM ADR
2013		IN	00	Input to ACC
2015		MOV M,A		ACC to MEM
2016		DCX H		DEC to next ADR
2017		IN	01	Input to ACC
2019		MOV M,A		ACC to MEM
2020		DCX H		DEC to next ADR
2021		JMP	2013	LOOP

8.15 Write the program routine of Table 8.31 such that the higher address port is read first and the memory addresses are incremented. Exit the routine after 40_H bytes are stored.

8.16 Perform the following binary multiplications.

```
10001011        10101011
    1101           11011
--------        --------

10010111        10011010
 1001001        10011001
--------        --------
```

8.17 Convert the multiplication program of Table 8.17 to that of an algebraic multiplier. (Input signed numbers. Determine sign of product and store. Cancel sign of terms prior to proceeding with the multiplication of the magnitude bits).

8.18 Modify the multiply program of Table 8.17 to provide for two bytes of X and Y.

8.19 An 8080A is operating with a 2-MHZ clock. Write a timer routine for 500 msec ± 1%.

8.20 An 8080 CPU set is operating with a 3.8-MHZ oscillator frequency. Write a timer routine for one second ± 5%.

8.21 An industrial plant on the south side of town has a large amount of incoming traffic from 7 A.M. to 8:30 A.M. and a large amount of outgoing traffic from 4 P.M. to 6:30 P.M. To accommodate this traffic, left turns from the east are to run 24 seconds at 7 A.M. to 8:30 A.M., and left turns from the south are to run 36 seconds from 4 P.M. to 6:30 P.M. A 24-hour timer in the signal housing supplies outputs as shown in Figure 7.35. Add to Figure 8.35 an input port for the timer and modify both hardware and software to change the timing.

8.22 The traffic signal program of Table 8.21 makes only limited use of the yellow warning lights in changing signals from green to red. It would be adequate for only a slow speed intersection. For a high speed intersection, we would prefer to have the left turn arrow off for six seconds prior to the light turning green in the oncoming direction. The yellow light should be on for six seconds prior to any change from green to red. As Table 7.23 indicates there are now twelve cycles to the sequence instead of the eight used in the previous program. In adapting this new technique to this program, we face the problem of the sequencer byte having only eight bits. There are any number of solutions to this problem. Considering that there are 256 unique states to an 8-bit output we could definitely produce and decode at the output port some set of twelve. An ideal solution is to increment the sequencer byte rather than rotate it. The incremented byte can be used as an address to a table containing the bytes shown in Table 7.23. These bytes can be outputted to the port of Figure 7.36. Write an 8080 program for a traffic signal control that provides the timing of Table 7.23 using the output port of Figure 7.36.

8.23 Modify the program of Table 8.27 and the hardware as needed so that the train changes modes as follows:

- In the outer loop four revolutions clockwise,
- In the inner loop four revolutions counterclockwise,
- In the outer loop four revolutions counterclockwise,
- In the inner loop four revolutions clockwise.

8.24 Figure 7.37 is a speed control port to be added to the model railway. Modify the program of Table 8.27 such that the train starts at slow speed and after one revolution advances to medium speed in the inner loop. When in the outer loop, it travels at high speed.

8.25 Using the speed control port of Figure 7.37, modify the operating mode program of Table 8.27 so that the train will run at high speed in the outer loop, medium speed in the inner loop, and slow speed when switching modes.

8.26 Using the speed control port of Figure 7.37, write a stop mode program such that the train will reduce to slow speed and stop only when the train is adjacent to sensors 3 and 4.

8.27 Make a memory map of the lookup table, Table 8.26.

8.28 Show how the entire 8080 railway control program can be contained on the same page of ROM as the lookup table.

8.29 Figure 7.38 is a circle of 8 LEDS which require 10 mA of forward current for light saturation. Draw an output latching port for connection to an 8080 bus. Show the connection of the 8 LEDS, including any drivers used to supply the needed current.

8.30 Write an 8080 program that will cause 4 of the 8 LEDS in Figure 7.38 to be lit. The 4 lit LEDS will rotate clockwise at a rate of about one revolution per second.

8.31 Write a program similar to that in Problem 8.30 but rotate the LEDS counterclockwise at 1 revolution every 3 seconds.

8.32 Table 6.4 shows a set of pulses needed to program a 7641 PROM. Write an 8080 program that will output that set of pulses to a latching output port.

8.33 Modify the program of Problem 8.32 such that the program will look at a byte in memory and output fusing pulses only for those bits to be programmed as zeros.

8.34 Figure 7.39 is a set of LEDS connected to simulate a railroad track. Using the output circuits of Figure 7.40, write a program that will simulate the train by causing four LEDS to be lit. The set of four are to move clockwise around the track at 1 revolution every 3 seconds.

Appendix A

Execution of M6800 Programs

A.1 The MEK6800D2 Microcomputer

The MEK6800D2 is a microcomputer which uses the M6800 as a central processing unit. The kit is assembled on two circuit boards as Figure A.1 shows. The microcomputer module board contains the M6800 plus the ROM, RAM, and interface adaptor circuits. The keyboard/display module board is mounted with a 6-digit display, a keyboard, and the necessary circuits for interfacing to an audio cassette. Figure A.2 shows a memory map of the minimum system. The user RAM extends from address 0000 through address 00FF. This allows for user programs requiring 256 bytes or less for program, data storage, and stack. The JBUG and monitor program are contained in ROM addresses between E000 through E3FF. The JBUG and monitor use 128 bytes of RAM between address A000 and A07F. The user available I/O ports are addressed between 8004 and 8008. The PIA for keyboard interface is

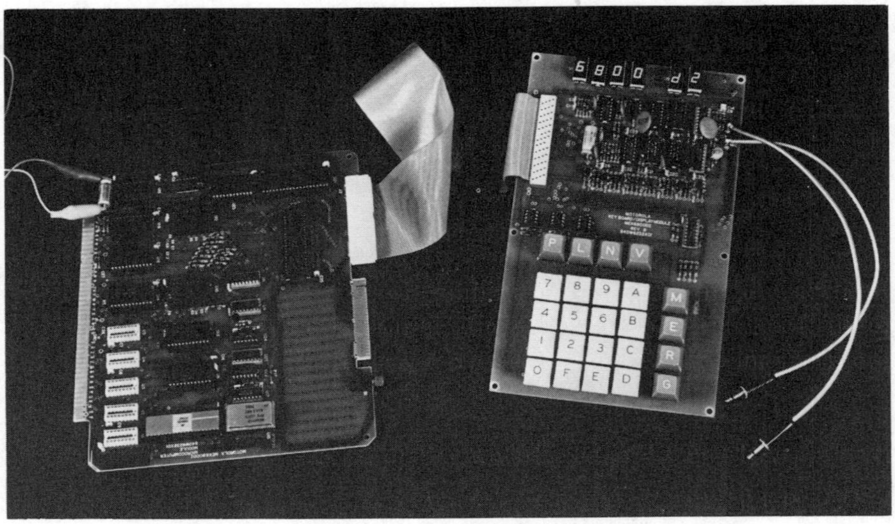

FIGURE A.1 MEK6800D2. A two-board microcomputer which employs the M6800 as an MPU. (*Courtesy of Motorola, Inc.*)

addressed at 8020 and 8024. Additional 6810S (128–X–8 RAM) may be installed to provide an added 256 byte of RAM. Figure A.3 shows the memory map of expansion RAM, PROM, or ROM addresses. If the 2708 (1K-X-8 EPROM is used for added program storage then the additional voltages (–5V, +12V) must be applied.

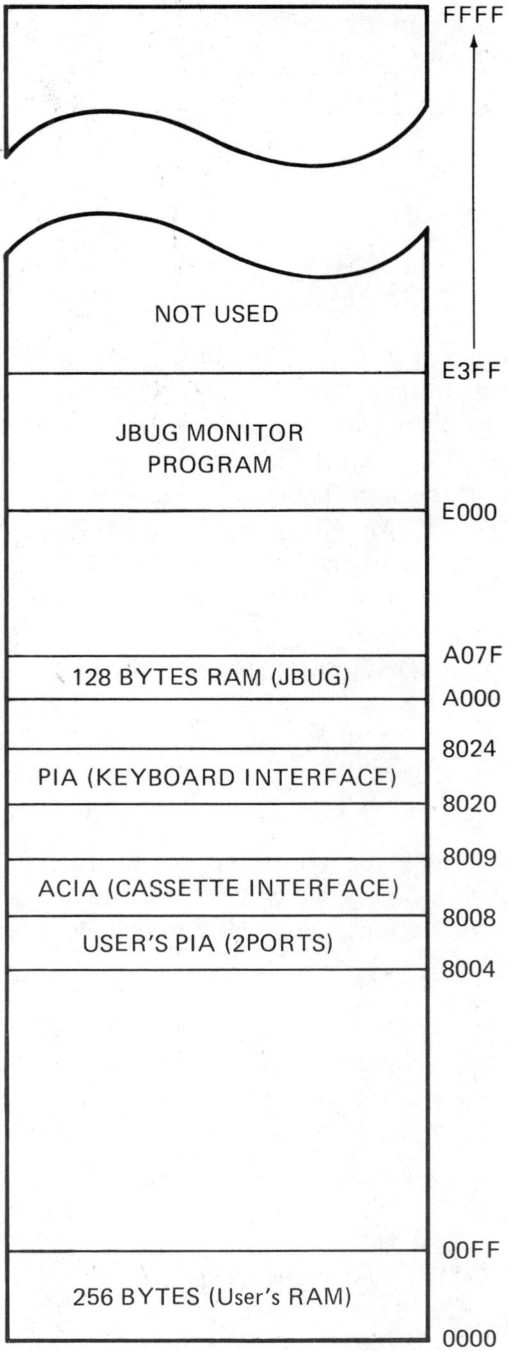

FIGURE A.2 Memory map of MEK6800D2 minimum system.

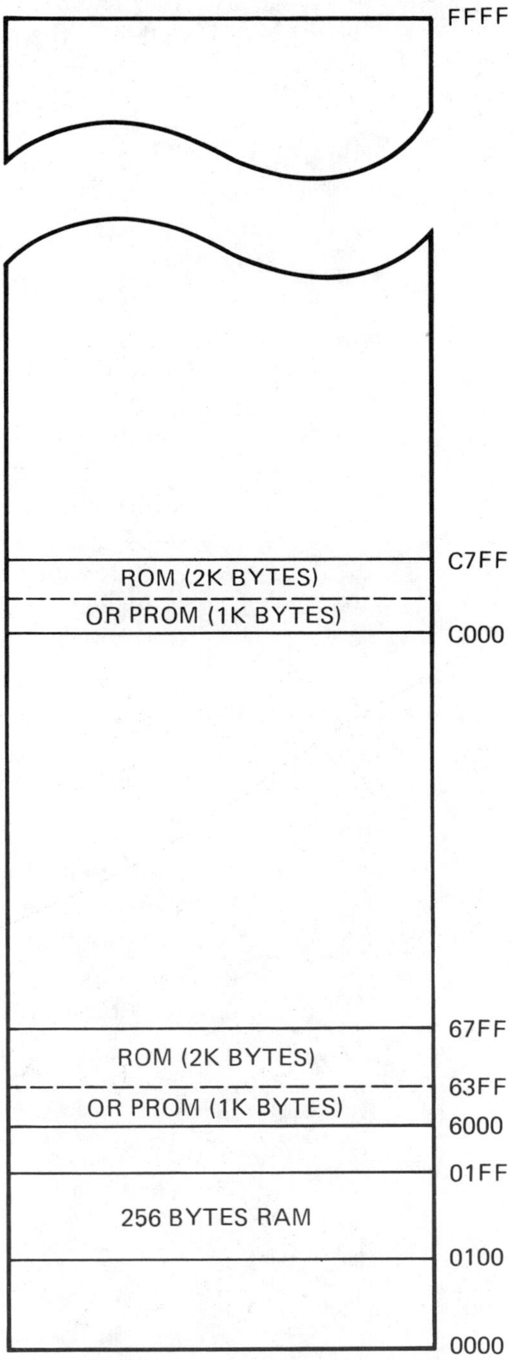

FIGURE A.3 Memory map of MEK6800D2 expansion provisions.

A.2 The Single Precision Algebraic Adder

Using the minimum 6800D2 system, the single precision adder routine of Table 7.7 can be run. To allow for the entry of values of X and Y and the examination of the sum and sign, memory addresses must be assigned for each of these bytes. Also a short output routine must be added to the program as it appears in Table 7.7.

Memory bytes are assigned as follows:

0080 = X

0081 = Y

007F = SUM

007E = sign of SUM
(FF = negative, 00 = positive)

Note that the main program is designed such that the MSD of the sum is the sign. The output routine, however, uses a separate byte for the sign. For this reason the output routine must, in addition to storing FF or 00 in memory byte 007E, cancel the negative sign where it exists as a one in data bit seven of the sum. Table 7.7 uses a beginning address of 0401. To run on the D2 kit, we will translate this to 0001. The added output routine will occupy memory from 0082 to 0093. The program is loaded as given in the address and data columns of Table A.1 (p. 390).

To execute the program, let's use an example of adding:

-47_{10}	$-2F_H$ $(+80_H)$	AF_H
$+56_{10}$	$+38_H$	$+38_H$
+9	+9	+9

Note that the numbers must be converted to hexadecimal and the sign (making data bit 7 a binary 1) is accomplished by adding 80_H $= 10000000_2$. (These operations could be handled by a short input routine).

First load the data.

0080 = 38

0081 = AF

Then run the program.

E
0001 (starting address)
G

The program will halt at either 008C or 0093. To determine the results type E, then 007E followed by M. It will read 00 indicating positive. Type G and address 007F will read 09.

A.3 The Double Precision Algebraic Adder

To execute the double precision add program of Figure 7.10 on the M6800D2 kit, the addresses must be translated to the RAM address between 0000 and 00FF. Memory bytes are assigned for input and output as follows:

0080	=	X_L
0081	=	X_H
0082	=	Y_L
0083	=	Y_H
007E	=	SUM (high byte)
007D	=	SUM (low byte)
007F	=	sign of SUM (FF = negative, 00 = positive)

An input and output routine must be added. The main program which begins at 060A in Table 7.10 is moved to address 000A. Because this program uses a subroutine, the stack pointer must be initialized. This is performed by the LDS instruction 0007. The listing for this program is given in address and data columns of Table A.2 (p. 391).

Again a short output routine is added. This is located between 0085 and 0098.

To check the execution of the program let's use the example:

-29361_{10}	$-72B1_H$	$F2B1_H$
$+23572_{10}$	$+5C14_H$	$5C14_H$
-5789_{10}	$-169D_H$	$-169D_H$

The decimal values must be converted to hexadecimal and 8000_H is added to negative values to provide the sign. Load the data:

0080	=	B1
0081	=	F2
0082	=	14
0083	=	5C

Then execute the program.

E
0007 (starting address)
G

The program will halt at 0094 or 0098. Examine memory at 007D by typing E then 007D followed by M. It will read 9D.

Next (G) 007E = 16

Next (G) 007F = FF

A.4 The Multiply Program

The multiply program of Table 7.11 is run by translating the program to between addresses 0013 and 0035. Memory bytes are assigned for data as follows:

$X = 0081$

$Y_L = 0082$

$P_L = 007D$ (product low byte)

$P_H = 007E$ (product high byte)

Load the program as listed in the address and data columns of Table A.3 (p. 392).

A check of the multiply program operation is accomplished by attempting the highest value multiplication.

$$255_{10} \times 255_{10} = 65025_{10}$$

or

$$FF_H \times FF_H = FE01$$

Load X and Y.

0081 = FF

0082 = FF

Then execute the program.

E
0013 (starting address)
G

The program will halt at address 0035. Examine Memory at 007D and 007E by typing E then 007D followed by M. It will read 01.

Next (G) 007E = FF

A.5 Traffic Signal Program

The traffic signal program of Tables 7.16 through 7.19 requires the use of an output port. Either of the 8-bit ports from the user's PIA can be used conveniently in place of the 74LS373 shown in Figure 7.27. The eight pins of port B can be wired to the logic gates in place of the Q_1 to Q_8 outputs. Use of this port requires that it be initialized as an output. This is accomplished by outputting FF to the port 0 data direction register at address 8006. Each of the ports of the 6800D2 kit has three registers but only two addresses.

Table A.4 (p. 392) shows the address and register combinations to be considered in initializing an output port for address 8006. After reset, address 8006 will write data to the data direction register. Storing FF will designate that address as an output port, but a high level must be stored in bit 2 of the control register (address 8007) to convert address 8006 from a DDR address to the port address. This is done by instruction 000A through 000C. The listing in Table A.5 (p. 393) is the same as Tables 7.16 to 7.19 except for the initialization of the port at address 0005 through 000E. A COM instruction precedes the outputting of the sequencer byte to cancel the inversion by the output port.

The program is run by the following steps.

E
0005 (beginning address)
G

From the time G is depressed, the signal will continue through the light sequence until E is depressed. The timing of the signals can be adjusted by changing the time multipliers (the operands of the LDA B instructions).

A. 6 Loading Programs

Programs are loaded into the memory of the MEK6800D2 using the following steps:

STEP	DEPRESS	DISPLAY
1	E	
2	Key in 4 digits of address	AAAA
3	M	AAAA XX
4	Key in 2 digits of data	AAAA DD
5	G	(AAAA+1)XX
6	Repeat 4 and 5	

AAAA = selected address digits XX = existing data
DD = selected data

TABLE A.1 M6800 Machine code listing for algebraic adder. (See Table 7.7.)

MEMORY		INSTRUCTION		
ADDRESS	DATA	MNEMONIC	OPERAND	REMARKS
0001	B6	LDA A	0080	See Table 7.7
0002	00			
0003	80			
0004	2B	BMI	12	
0005	12			
0006	F6	LDA B	0081	
0007	00			
0008	81			
0009	2A	BPL	09	
000A	09			
000B	50	NEG B		
000C	1B	ABA		
000D	2B	BMI	16	
000E	16			
000F	40	NEG A		
0010	7E	JMP	0082	
0011	00			
0012	82			
0014	1B	ABA		
0015	7E	JMP	008D	
0016	00			
0017	8D			
0018	F6	LDA B	0081	
0019	00			
001A	81			
001B	2B	BMI	0D	
001C	0D			
001D	40	NEG A		
001E	1B	ABA		
001F	2B	BMI	04	
0020	04			
0021	40	NEG A		
0022	7E	JMP	0082	
0023	00			See Table 7.7
0024	82			
0025	8B	ADD A	80	
0026	80			
0027	7E	JMP	008D	
0028	00			
0029	8D			
002A	1B	ABA		
002B	7E	JMP	0084	
002C	00			
002D	84			
0082	8B	ADD A	80_H	Output Routine
0083	80			
0084	B7	STA A	007F	
0085	00			
0086	7F			
0087	B6	LDA A	FF	
0088	FF			
0089	B7	STA A	007E	
008A	00			
008B	7E			
008C	3F	SWI		
008D	B7	STA A	007F	
008E	00			
008F	7F			
0090	7F	CLR	007E	
0091	00			
0092	7E			
0093	3F	SWI		

TABLE A.2 M6800 Machine code listing for double precision algebraic adder. (See Table 7.10.)

MEMORY ADDRESS	MEMORY DATA	INSTRUCTION MNEMONIC	INSTRUCTION OPERAND	REMARKS
0007	8E	LDS	00F0	Load
0008	00			Stack
0009	F0			Pointer
000A	7D	TST	0081	See
000B	00			Table
000C	81			7.10
000D	2B	BMI	22	
000E	22			
000F	B6	LDA A	0082	
0010	00			
0011	82			
0012	F6	LDA B	0083	
0013	00			
0014	83			
0015	2B	BMI	08	
0016	08			
0017	BB	ADD A	0080	
0018	00			
0019	80			
001A	F9	ADC B	0081	
001B	00			
001C	81			
001D	20	BRA	68	
001E	66			
001F	8D	BSR	7F	
0020	7F			
0021	BB	ADD A	0080	
0022	00			
0023	80			
0024	F9	ADC B	0081	
0025	00			
0026	81			
0027	2B	BMI	04	
0028	04			
0029	8D	BSR	75	
002A	75			
002B	20	BRA	57	See
002C	57			Table
002D	C0	SUB B	80	7.10
002E	80			
002F	20	BRA	56	
0030	54			
0031	B6	LDA A	0080	
0032	00			
0033	80			
0034	F6	LDA B	0081	
0035	00			
0036	81			
0037	7D	TST	0083	
0038	00			
0039	83			

MEMORY ADDRESS	MEMORY DATA	INSTRUCTION MNEMONIC	INSTRUCTION OPERAND	REMARKS
003A	2A	BPL	08	See
003B	08			Table
003C	BB	ADD A	0082	7.10
003D	00			
003E	82			
003F	F9	ADC B	0083	
0040	00			
0041	83			
0042	20	BRA 41	87	
0043	41			
0044	8D	BSR	5A	
0045	5A			
0046	BB	ADD A	0082	
0047	00			
0048	82			
0049	F9	ADC B	0083	
004A	00			
004B	83			
004C	2B	BMI	DF	
004D	DF			
004E	8D	BSR	50	
004F	50			
0050	20	BRA	33	
0051	33			
0085	C8	ADD B	80	Output Routine
0086	80			
0087	B7	STA A	007D	
0088	00			
0089	7D			
008A	F7	STA B	007E	
008B	00			
008C	7E			
008D	24	BCC	06	
008E	05			
008F	86	LDA A	FF	
0090	FF			
0091	B7	STA A	007F	
0092	00			
0093	7F			
0094	3F	SWI		
0095	7F	CLR	007F	
0096	00			
0097	7F			
0098	3F	SWI		
00A0	4D	TST A		twos comp. subroutine
00A1	27	BEQ	03	
00A2	03			
00A3	40	NEG A		
00A4	53	COM B		
00A5	39	RTS		
00A6	50	NEG B		
00A7	39	RTS		

TABLE A.3 M6800 Machine code listing for multiply program. (See Table 7.11.)

MEMORY		INSTRUCTION		
ADDRESS	DATA	MNEMONIC	OPERAND	REMARKS
0013	4F	CLR A		See Table 7.11
0014	5F	CLR B		
0015	7F	CLR	0083	
0016	00			
0017	83			
0018	74	LSR	0081	
0019	00			
001A	81			
001B	25	BCS	04	
001C	04			
001D	26	BNE	08	
001E	08			
001F	20	BRA	0E	
0020	0E			
0021	BB	ADD A	0082	
0022	00			
0023	82			
0024	F9	ADC B	0083	
0025	00			
0026	83			
0027	78	ASL	0082	
0028	00			
0029	82			
002A	79	ROL	0083	
002B	00			
002C	83			
002D	20	BRA	E9	
002E	E9			
002F	B7	STA A	007D	
0030	00			
0031	7D			
0032	F7	STA B	007E	
0033	00			
0034	7E			
0035	3F	SWI		

TABLE A.4 6820 PIA (Port B initializing).

ADDRESS	REGISTER	OTHER ADDRESS REQUIRED
8006	Port Output if DDR = FF Input if DDR = 00	CR2 = 1
	Data Direction Register	After Reset or CR2 = 0
8007	Control Register	

DDR = Data Direction Register
CR = Control Register

TABLE A.5 M6800 Machine code listing for traffic signal program. (See Tables 7.16 through 7.19.)

MEMORY		INSTRUCTION		
ADDRESS	DATA	MNEMONIC	OPERAND	REMARKS
0005	96	LDA A	FF	Initialize
0006	FF			Output
0007	B7	STA A	8006	Port
0008	80			
0009	06			
000A	96	LDA A	04	
000B	04			
000C	B7	STA A	8007	CR2=1
000D	80			
000E	07			
000F	7F	CLR	0004	Initialize
0010	00			See
0011	04			Table
0012	0D	SEC		7.16
0013	CE	LDX	0021	
0014	00			
0015	21			
0016	79	ROL	0004	
0017	00			
0018	04			
0019	96	LDA A	04	
001A	04			See
001B	43	COM A		Table
001C	B7	STA A	8006	7.17
001D	80			
001E	06			
001F	6E	JMP	00	
0020	00			
0021	C6	LDA B	06	See
0022	06			Table
0023	CE	LDX	0028	7.18
0024	00			
0025	28			
0026	20	BRA	38	
0027	38			
0028	C6	LDA B	08	
0029	08			
002A	CE	LDX	0030	
002B	00			
002C	30			
002D	20	BRA	31	
002E	31			
0030	C6	LDA B	06	
0031	06			
0032	CE	LDX	0038	
0033	00			
0034	38			
0035	20	BRA	29	
0036	29			
0038	C6	LDA B	02	
0039	02			
003A	CE	LDX	0040	

MEMORY		INSTRUCTION		
ADDRESS	DATA	MNEMONIC	OPERAND	REMARKS
003B	00			See
003C	40			Table
003D	20	BRA	21	7.18
003E	21			
0040	C6	LDA B	04	
0041	04			
0042	CE	LDX	0048	
0043	00			
0044	48			
0045	20	BRA	19	
0046	19			
0048	C6	LDA B	06	
0049	06			
004A	CE	LDX	0050	
004B	00			
004C	50			
004D	20	BRA	11	
004E	11			
0050	C6	LDA B	04	
0051	04			
0052	CE	LDX	0058	
0053	00			
0054	58			
0055	20	BRA	09	
0056	09			
0058	C6	LDA B	02	
0059	02			
005A	CE	LDX	0021	
005B	00			
005C	21			
005D	20	BRA	01	
005E	01			
0060	7A	DEC	0001	See
0061	00			Table
0062	01			7.19
0063	26	BNE	FB	
0064	FB			
0065	7A	DEC	0002	
0066	00			
0067	02			
0068	26	BNE	F6	
0069	F6			
006A	5A	DEC B		
006B	26	BNE	F2	Timer
006C	F2			Routine
006D	7D	TST	0004	
006E	00			
006F	04			
0070	2B	BMI	03	
0071	03			
0072	0C	CLC		
0073	20	BRA	A1	
0074	A1			
0075	OD	SEC		
0076	20	BRA	9E	
0077	9E			

Appendix B

Execution of 8080/8085 Programs

B.1 The SDK-85 Microcomputer

The SDK-85 (MCS-85 Systems Design Kit) shown in Figure B.1 is a single-board microcomputer which uses the 8085 as an MPU. It contains an ROM which provides a monitor program that supervises the loading and execution of instructions and, in addition, provides features which aid in the debugging of programs. The operator loads programs through a hexadecimal keyboard and controls execution with eight additional control keys. The keyboard is shown in Figure B.2. A 6-digit LED display provides a 4-digit address display on the left. The right two digits serve as a data display. The keyboard and display are controlled through both the program in the 8355, ROM, and the 40-pin 8279, (keyboard/display interface). The operator can address either memory or MPU registers and observe or modify the data contained in them.

FIGURE B.1 SDK-85. A single-board computer which employs the 8085 as an MPU. (*Courtesy of Intel Corporation*)

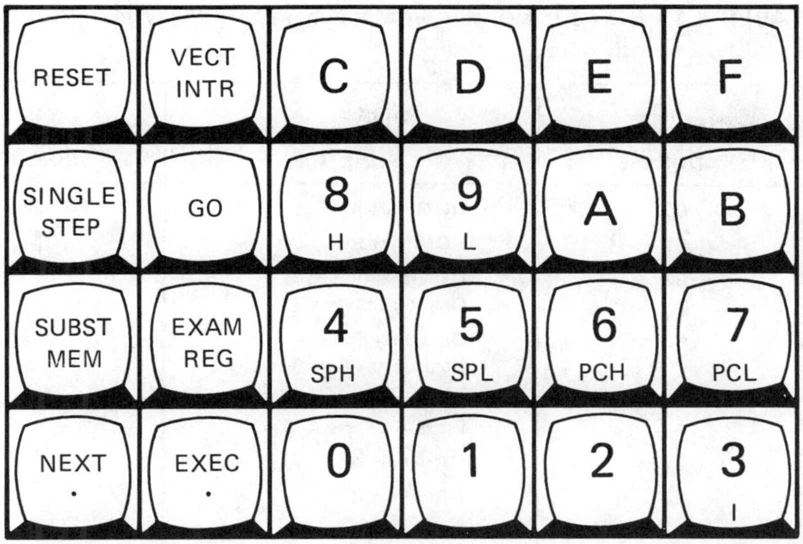

FIGURE B.2 Keyboard of the SDK-85 Microcomputer.

The SDK-85 can be used to run most of the programs used in the explanations of Chapter 8 and many of the problems. Figure B.3 shows the memory map of a minimum SDK-85 system. Note that the monitor program requires the use of a portion of the 256-byte RAM. This limits the user to the RAM from address 2000 to 20C1. Programs requiring a total of 194 bytes or less of instructions stack and data memory can be run on a minimum system. In addition to the RAM, four 8-bit and one 6-bit I/O ports plus a programmable timer are provided. These are addressed as shown in Table B.1.

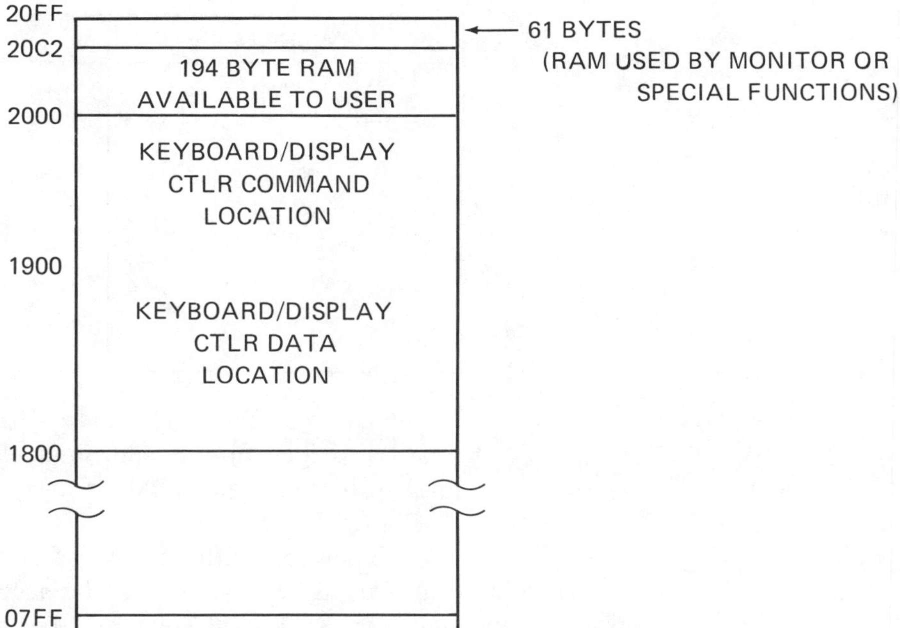

FIGURE B.3 Memory Map of SDK-85 Minimum System. The 194 bytes available to the user are at address 2000 to 20C2.

TABLE B.1. I/O Ports available with minimum SDK-85 system. (Note: I/O port addresses are single byte.)

I/O PORT ADDRESS	FUNCTION	CIRCUIT
00	ROM Port A	8355
01	ROM Port B	"
02	Data direction Register for Port A	"
03	Data direction Register for Port B	"
20	Command status register for RAM Ports A, B, C	8155
21	RAM Port A	"
22	RAM Port B	"
23	RAM Port C	"
24	Low order byte of timer	"
25	High order byte of timer	"

Systems Expansion

A full 256 bytes of RAM, three I/O ports, and a timer are added by simply installing an additional 8155. The circuit board already provides for this connection. The addresses of this device are given in Table B.2.

TABLE B.2 I/O Ports and RAM available to the user after the installation of the second 8155 to the SDK-85 system.

ADDRESS	FUNCTION
2800 through 28FF	256 Bytes of user available RAM
28	Command status register
29	Port A
2A	Port B
2B	Port C
2C	Low order byte of timer
2D	High order byte of timer

Expansion by ROM is more difficult for the small user. The circuit board provides for an additional 2K bytes by installing either 8355 mask programmable ROM or an equivalent 8755 ultra violet erasable PROM (EPROM).

Expansion with the use of standard memory products that lack onboard address latches can be accomplished by activating the expansion bus. To do this requires the installation of two 8212 octal latch circuits and five 8216 quad buffers along with a 74LS74 and a 74S00. These are provided for in the bus expansion driver section of the board. Once this is done, standard PROMS and RAM can be wired into the wire wrap area of the board and controlled from the expansion bus.

B.2 The Single Precision Algebraic Adder

Using the minimum SDK-85 system, the single precision adder routine of Table 8.13 can be run. To allow for the entry of values of X and Y and the examination of the sum and sign, memory addresses must be assigned for each of these bytes and a short output routine must be added to the program as it appears in Table 8.13.

Memory bytes are assigned as follows:

2020 = X

2021 = Y

2022 = SUM

2023 = sign of SUM
(FF = negative, 00 = positive)

Table 8.13 uses addresses 0180. We will use the same low byte numbering beginning at 2080. There is insufficient space in RAM following the main program so the output routine is in addresses preceding the main program. In addition, a three byte initialization instruction precedes the main program. The program is loaded as given in the address and data columns of Table B.3 (p. 401).

To execute the program, let's use an example of adding.

-47_{10}	$-2F_H$ $(+80_H)$	AF_H
$+56_{10}$	$+38_H$	$+38_H$
+9	+9	+9

Note that the numbers must be converted to hexadecimal and the sign (making data bit 7 a binary 1) is accomplished by adding 80_H $= 10000000_2$. (These operations can be handled by a short input routine-see Problem 8.8). First load the data.

2020 = 38

2021 = AF

Then run the program.

RESET
GO
207D
EXECUTE

The program will halt at either 2047 or 2050. To determine the results examine memory at 2022. It will read 09. Depress next and address 2023 should read 00 indicating positive.

B.3 The Double Precision Algebraic Adder

To execute the double precision add program of Figure 8.16 on the SDK-85 again the addresses must be translated to the RAM address between 2000 and 20C1. Memory bytes are assigned for input and output as follows:

2080 = X_L

2081 = X_H

2082 = Y_L

2083 = Y_H

2084 = SUM (high byte)

2085 = SUM (low byte)

2086 = sign of SUM
(FF = negative, 00 = positive)

A subroutine is used, therefore, the stack must be initialized and an input and output routine must be added. The main program which begins at 0200 in Table 8.16 is moved to address 2010. The stack pointer is initialized by the LXI SP instruction, 200D. The listing for this program is given in address and data columns of Table B.4 (p. 402).

Again a short output routine is added. This is located between 2090 and 20A9.

To check the execution of the program let's use the example:

$$\begin{array}{r} -29361_{10} \\ +23572_{10} \\ \hline -5789_{10} \end{array} \longrightarrow \begin{array}{r} -72B1_H \\ +5C14_H \\ \hline -169D_H \end{array} \longrightarrow \begin{array}{r} F2B1_H \\ 5C14_H \\ \hline 169D_H \end{array}$$

The decimal values must be converted to hexadecimal, and 8000_H is added to negative values to provide the sign. First load the data.

2080 = B1

2081 = F2

2082 = 14

2083 = 5C

Then execute the program.

RESET
GO
200D (starting address)
EXECUTE

The program will Halt at 20A9.

Examine memory at 2084 = 9D
Next 2085 = 16
Next 2086 = FF

B.4 The Multiply Program

The multiply program of Table 8.17 is run by translating the program to between addresses 2008 and 2031. A short output routine is added at 2032 to 203A. Memory bytes are assigned for data as follows:

X = 2080
Y = 2081
P_L = 2082 (product low byte)
P_H = 2083 (product high byte)

Load the program as listed in the address and data columns of Table B.5 (p. 403).

A check of the multiply program operation is accomplished by attempting the highest value multiplication:

$$255_{10} \times 255_{10} = 65025_{10}$$

or

$$FF_H \times FF_H = FE01$$

First load X and Y.

2080 = FF
2081 = FF

Then execute the program.

RESET
GO
2008 (starting address)
EXECUTE

The program will halt at address 203A.

Examine memory at 2082 = 01
Next 2082 = FE

B.5 The Traffic Signal Program

The traffic signal program of Tables 8.22 through 8.25 requires the use of an output port. Either of the two ports from the 8355 can be used conveniently. Port 0 will be used in place of the 74LS373. The eight pins of port 0 can be wired to the logic gates in place of the Q_1 to Q_8 outputs. Use of this port requires that it be initialized as an output. This is accomplished by outputting FF to the port 0 data direction register at address 02. The listing in Table B.6 (p. 404) is the same as Tables 8.22 through 8.25 except for the initialization of the port at address 2000 through 2003. The program is run by the following steps:

RESET
GO
2000 (starting address)
EXECUTE

From the time execute is depressed, the signal will continue through the light sequence until reset is depressed. The timing of the signals can be adjusted by changing the time multipliers (the operands of the MVI D instructions.)

B. 6 Loading Programs

Programs are loaded into the memory of the SDK85 using the following steps:

STEP	DEPRESS	DISPLAY
1	RESET	8085
2	SUBSTITUTE MEMORY	
3	Key in 4 digits of address	AAAA
4	NEXT	AAAA XX
5	Key in 2 digits of data	AAAA DD
6	NEXT	(AAAA+1) XX
7	Repeat 5 and 6 until all data is loaded	

AAAA = selected address digits XX = existing data
DD = selected data

Steps 1 through 4 are repeated when a discontinuity in memory addresses exists.

To verify the loading of a program, use the procedure outlined above, but include step 5 only when a correction is to be made.

TABLE B.3 Machine Code Listing for Single Precision Algebraic Adder (See Table 8.13.)

MEMORY		INSTRUCTION		
ADDRESS	DATA	MNEMONIC	OPERAND	REMARKS
207D	21	LXI H	2023	Load H&L for output routine
207E	23			
207F	22			
2080	3A	LDA	2020	See Table 8.13
2081	20			
2082	20			
2083	47	MOV B,A		
2084	A0	ANA B		
2085	FA	JM	20A3	
2086	A3			
2087	20			
2088	3A	LDA	2021	
2089	21			
208A	20			
208B	A7	ANA A		
208C	F2	JP	209F	
208D	9F			
208E	20			
208F	2F	CMA		
2090	3C	INR A		
2091	80	ADD B		
2092	FA	JM	209A	
2093	9A			
2094	20			
2095	2F	CMA		
2096	3C	INR A		
2097	C3	JMP	2040	
2098	40			
2099	20			
209A	C6	ADI	80_H	
209B	80			
209C	C3	JMP	204B	
209D	4B			
209E	20			
209F	80	ADD B		

MEMORY		INSTRUCTION		
ADDRESS	DATA	MNEMONIC	OPERAND	REMARKS
20A0	C3	JMP	204B	See Table 8.13
20A1	4B			
20A2	20			
20A3	48	MOV C,B		
20A4	3A	LDA	2021	
20A5	21			
20A6	20			
20A7	47	MOV B, A		
20A8	A0	ANA B		
20A9	FA	JM	20B0	
20AA	B0			
20AB	20			
20AC	79	MOV A,C		
20AD	C3	JMP	208F	
20AE	8F			
20AF	20			
20B0	81	ADD C		
20B1	C3	JMP	2042	
20B2	42			
20B3	20			
2040	C6	ADI	80_H	Output Routine
2041	80			
2042	32	STA	2022	
2043	22			
2044	20			
2045	36	MVI M	FF	
2046	FF			
2047	76	HLT		
2048				
2049				
204A				
204B	32	STA	2022	
204C	22			
204D	20			
204E	36	MVI M	00	
204F	00			
2050	76	HLT		

TABLE B.4 Machine code listing for double precision 2s complement algebraic adder. (See Table 8.16.)

MEMORY		INSTRUCTION		
ADDRESS	DATA	MNEMONIC	OPERAND	REMARKS
200D	31	LXI SP	20B0	Load
200E	B0			Stack
200F	20			Pointer
2010	3A	LDA	2081	See
2011	81			Table
2012	20			8.16
2013	A7	ANA A		
2014	FA	JM	2042	
2015	42			
2016	20			
2017	47	MOV B,A		
2018	3A	LDA	2080	
2019	80			
201A	20			
201B	4F	MOV C,A		
201C	3A	LDA	2083	
201D	83			
201E	20			
201F	A7	ANA A		
2020	67	MOV H,A		
2021	3A	LDA	2082	
2022	82			
2023	20			
2024	6F	MOV L,A		
2025	FA	JM	202C	
2026	2C			
2027	20			
2028	09	DAD B		
2029	C3	JMP	209C	
202A	9C			
202B	20			
202C	CD	CALL	2070	
202D	70			
202E	20			
202F	09	DAD B		
2030	7C	MOV A,H		
2031	A7	ANA A		
2032	FA	JM	203B	
2033	3B			
2034	20			
2035	CD	CALL	2070	
2036	70			
2037	20			
2038	C3	JMP	2090	
2039	90			
203A	20			
203B	7C	MOV A,H		
203C	C6	ADI	80_H	
203D	80			
203E	67	MOV H,A		
203F	C3	JMP	209C	See
2040	9C			Table
2041	20			8.16
2042	67	MOV H,A		
2043	3A	LDA	2080	
2044	80			
2045	20			
2046	6F	MOV L,A		
2047	3A	LDA	2083	
2048	83			
2049	20			
204A	A7	ANA A		
204B	47	MOV B,A		
204C	3A	LDA	2082	
204D	82			
204E	20			
204F	4F	MOV C,A		
2050	F2	JP	2057	
2051	57			
2052	20			
2053	09	DAD B		
2054	C3	JMP	2094	
2055	94			
2056	20			
2057	CD	CALL	2070	
2058	70			
2059	20			
205A	09	DAD B		
205B	7C	MOV A,H		
205C	A7	ANA A		
205D	FA	JM	2066	
205E	66			
205F	20			
2060	CD	CALL	2070	
2061	70			
2062	20			
2063	C3	JMP	2090	
2064	90			
2065	20			
2066	C6	ADI	80	
2067	80			
2068	67	MOV H,A		
2069	C3	JMP	209C	
206A	9C			
206B	20			
2070	7D	MOV A,L		Twos
2071	2F	CMA		Compliment
2072	6F	MOV L,A		Subroutine
2073	7C	MOV A,H		

TABLE B.4 Continued.

MEMORY		INSTRUCTION		
ADDRESS	DATA	MNEMONIC	OPERAND	REMARKS
2074	2F	CMA		2s Comp Sub. Cont.
2075	67	MOV H,A		
2076	23	INX H		
2077	C9	RET		
2090	7C	MOV A,H		Output Routine
2091	C6	ADI	80	
2092	80			
2093	67	MOV H,A		
2094	3E	MVI A	FF	
2095	FF			
2096	32	STA	2086	
2097	86			
2098	20			
2099	C3	JMP	20A1	
209A	A1			
209B	20			

MEMORY		INSTRUCTION		
ADDRESS	DATA	MNEMONIC	OPERAND	REMARKS
209C	3E	MVI A	00	Output Routine
209D	00			
209E	32	STA	2086	
209F	86			
20A0	20			
20A1	7C	MOV A,H		
20A2	32	STA	2085	
20A3	85			
20A4	20			
20A5	7D	MOV A,L		
20A6	32	STA	2084	
20A7	84			
20A8	20			
20A9	76	HLT		

TABLE B.5 Machine code listing for multiply program. (See Table 8.17.)

MEMORY		INSTRUCTION		
ADDRESS	DATA	MNEMONIC	OPERAND	REMARKS
2008	3A	LDA	2080	See Table 8.17
2009	80			
200A	20			
200B	47	MOV B,A		
200C	3A	LDA	2081	
200D	81			
200E	20			
200F	5F	MOV E,A		
2010	16	MVI D	00	
2011	00			
2012	62	MOV H,D		
2013	6A	MOV L,D		
2014	37	STC		
2015	3F	CMC		
2016	78	MOV A,B		
2017	1F	RAR		
2018	47	MOV B,A		
2019	DA	JC	2023	
201A	23			
201B	20			
201C	A7	ANA A		
201D	C2	JNZ	0229	
201E	29			
201F	20			
2020	C3	JMP	2032	
2021	32			
2022	20			

MEMORY		INSTRUCTION		
ADDRESS	DATA	MNEMONIC	OPERAND	REMARKS
2023	7D	MOV A,L		See Table 8.17
2024	83	ADD E		
2025	6F	MOV L,A		
2026	7C	MOV A,H		
2027	8A	ADC D		
2028	67	MOV H,A		
2029	7B	MOV A,E		
202A	17	RAL		
202B	5F	MOV E,A		
202C	7A	MOV A,D		
202D	17	RAL		
202E	57	MOV D,A		
202F	C3	JMP	2016	
2030	16			
2031	20			
2032	7C	MOV A,H		
2033	32	STA	2083	
2034	83			
2035	20			
2036	7D	MOV A,L		
2037	32	STA	2082	
2038	82			
2039	20			
203A	76	HLT		

TABLE B.6 Machine code listing for traffic signal program. (See Tables 8.22 through 8.25.)

MEMORY		INSTRUCTION		
ADDRESS	DATA	MNEMONIC	OPERAND	REMARKS
2000	3E	MVI A	FF	Initialize
2001	FF			Output
2002	D3	OUT	02	Port
2003	02			
2004	3E	MVI A	00	
2005	00			Table
2006	21	LXI H	2010	8.22
2007	10			
2008	BB			
2009	37	STC		
200A	17	RAL		
200B	D3	OUT	00	Table
200C	00			8.23
200D	E9	PCHL		
2010	16	MVI D	09	See
2011	09			Table
2012	2E	MVI L	18	8.24
2013	18			
2014	C3	JMP	2080	
2015	80			
2016	BB			
2018	16	MVI E	24	
2019	12		12	
201A	2E	MVI L	20	
201B	20			
201C	C3	JMP	2080	
201D	80			
201E	BB			
2020	16	MVI D	9	
2021	09			
2022	2E	MVI L	28	
2023	28			
2024	C3	JMP	2080	
2025	80			
2026	BB			
2028	16	MVI D	03	
2029	03			
202A	2E	MVI L	30	
202B	30			
202C	C3	JMP	2080	
202D	80			
202E	BB			
2030	16	MVI D	06	
2031	06			
2032	2E	MVI L	38	
2033	38			
2034	C3	JMP	2080	
2035	80			
2036	BB			
2038	16	MVI D	09	
2039	09			

MEMORY		INSTRUCTION		
ADDRESS	DATA	MNEMONIC	OPERAND	REMARKS
203A	2E	MVI L	40	See
203B	40			Table
203C	C3	JMP	2080	8.24
203D	80			
203E	BB			
2040	16	MVI D	06	
2041	06			
2042	2E	MVI L	48	
2043	48			
2044	C3	JMP	2080	
2045	80			
2046	BB			
2048	16	MVI D	03	
2049	03			
204A	2E	MVI L	10	
204B	10			
204C	C3	JMP	2080	
204D	80			
204E	BB			
2080	00	DCR C		See
2081	00	NOP		Table
2082	00	NOP		8.25
2083	00	NOP		
2084	00	NOP		
2085	C2	JNZ	2080	
2086	80			
2087	BB			
2088	05	DCR B		
2089	C2	JNZ	2080	
208A	80			
208B	BB			
208C	15	DCR D		
208D	C2	JNZ	2080	Timer
208E	80			Routine
208F	BB			
2090	A7	ANA A		
2091	FA	JM	2099	
2092	99			
2093	BB			
2094	37	STC		
2095	3F	CMC		
2096	C3	JMP	200A	
2097	0A			
2098	BB			
2099	37	STC		
209A	C3	JMP	200A	
209B	0A			
209C	BB			

Appendix C

Binary-To-BCD Conversion Using the MC6800*

A standard technique for binary-to-BCD conversion is that of the Add 3 algorithm. Figures C.1 and C.2 show a flow diagram and example of this algorithm. The technique requires a register containing the N-bit binary number and enough 4-bit BCD registers to contain the maximum equivalent BCD number for the initial binary number. The conversion starts by checking each BCD register for a value of 5 or greater. If this condition exists in one or all of these registers (initially this condition cannot exist), then a 3 is added to those registers where this condition exists. Next the registers are shifted left with the carry out of the previous register being the carry in to the next register. Again each BCD register is checked for values of 5 or greater. This sequence continues until the registers have been shifted N times, where N is the number of bits in the initial binary word. The BCD registers then contain the resulting BCD equivalent to the initial binary word. The example in Figure C.2 starts with an 8-bit binary word consisting of all "1's." This word is converted to the BCD equivalent of 255 by this technique. After 8 shifts the last binary bit has been shifted out of the binary register and the hundreds, tens, and units registers contain a 255.

Figure C.3 shows an MC6800 software routine for performing this technique of binary to BCD conversion. The initial binary number is a 16-bit number and occupies memory locations MSB and LSB; this binary number is converted to the equivalent BCD number in memory locations TENTSD, HNDTHD and UNTTEN. Each of these memory locations contains two BCD digits. Eighty-three memory locations are required for program storage with a maximum conversion taking 1.8 ms.

---

*(From Application note AN-757, Courtesy of Motorola, Inc.)

FIGURE C.1 Binary to BCD Conversion Flow Diagram

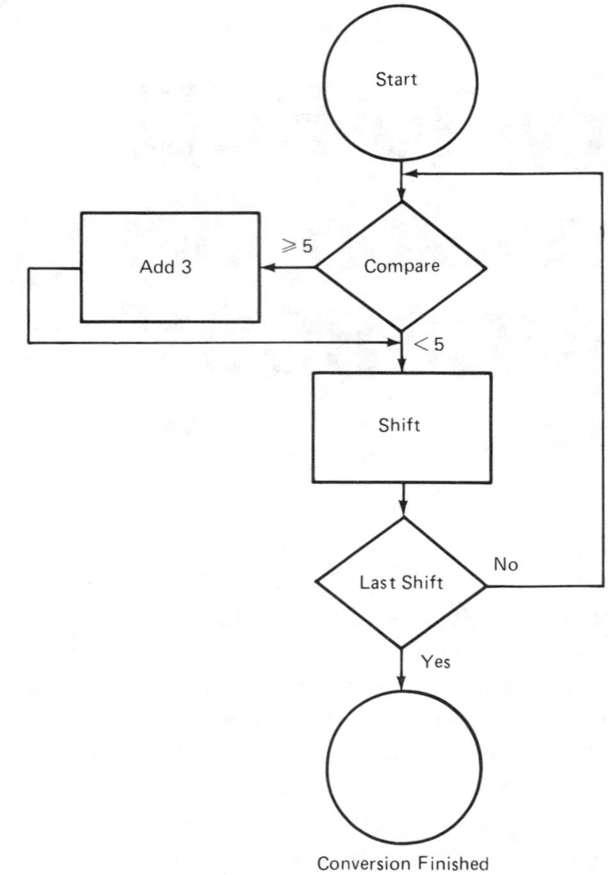

FIGURE C.2 Binary to BCD Conversion.

Hundreds	Tens	Units	8 Bit Binary	
			1 1 1 1 1 1 1 1	
		1	1 1 1 1 1 1 1	Shift 2
		1 1	1 1 1 1 1 1	Shift 2
		1 1 1	1 1 1 1 1	Shift 3
		1 0 1 0	1 1 1 1 1	Add 3 to Units
	1	0 1 0 1	1 1 1 1	Shift 4
	1	1 0 0 0	1 1 1 1	Add 3 to Units
	1 1	0 0 0 1	1 1 1	Shift 5
	1 1 0	0 0 1 1	1 1	Shift 6
	1 0 0 1	0 0 1 1	1 1	Add 3 to Tens
1	0 0 1 0	0 1 1 1	1	Shift 7
1	0 0 1 0	1 0 1 0	1	Add 3 to Units
1 0	0 1 0 1	0 1 0 1		Shift 8
2	5	5		

Figure C.3 is an assembly listing. This would be converted to a machine code listing prior to use. For the reader with access to the MEK6800D2 kit, Table C.1 provides a machine code listing for a two byte binary to BCD conversion. The numbers to be converted are entered into memory as:

0070 = LSB (least significant byte)

0071 = MSB (most significant byte)

The converted digits are assigned memory bytes:

0080 = UNTTEN

0081 = HNDTHD

0082 = TENTSD

Take note of the identity of program segments between the instructions LDA A and STA B. The program is shortened by the use of a subroutine at these points. The AND instructions are used to blank out one digit in the byte while the other is being checked. The index register is used as a counter to insure the correct number of shifts. The example in Figure C.2 is for a single byte conversion. The program; however, is for a two byte conversion and therefore, the index register is initialized for a count of 16.

FIGURE C.3 Binary-to-BCD Conversion Software

```
  NAM DWA21
  OPT MEM
♦
♦♦♦♦♦♦♦♦♦♦♦♦♦♦♦♦♦♦♦♦♦♦♦♦♦♦♦♦♦♦♦♦♦♦♦♦♦♦♦♦♦♦♦♦♦♦♦♦♦♦♦♦♦♦♦♦♦♦♦♦♦♦♦♦♦♦♦♦♦♦
♦                                                                      ♦
♦                    BINARY TO BCD CONVERSION                          ♦
♦                         ADD 3 ALGORITHM                              ♦
♦                              16 BIT                                  ♦
♦♦♦♦♦♦♦♦♦♦♦♦♦♦♦♦♦♦♦♦♦♦♦♦♦♦♦♦♦♦♦♦♦♦♦♦♦♦♦♦♦♦♦♦♦♦♦♦♦♦♦♦♦♦♦♦♦♦♦♦♦♦♦♦♦♦♦♦♦♦
♦
  ORG 0                      INITIAL BINARY NUMBER
MSB RMB 1                      MOST SIGNIFICANT 8 BITS
LSB RMB 1                      LEAST SIGNIFICANT 8 BITS
♦
♦
♦
  ORG $0010                  BCD RESULTS
UNTTEN RMB 1                   UNITS AND TENS DIGITS
HNDTHD RMB 1                   HUNDREDS AND THOUSANDS
TENTSD RMB 1                   TENS OF THOUSANDS DIGIT
♦
♦
♦
  ORG $0F00           ♦♦ BEGINNING OF PROGRAM ♦♦
  CLR UNTTEN
  CLR HNDTHD
  CLR TENTSD
  LDX   $0010
BEGIN LDA A UNTTEN           UNITS COMPARISON
  TAB
  AND A   $0F
  SUB A   $05
  BMI AT
  ADD B   $03
AT TBA                       TENS COMPARISON
```

Continued

FIGURE C.3 Continued

```
   AND A  $0F0
   SUB A  $50
   BMI BT
   ADD B  $30
BT STA B UNTTEN
♦
   LDA A HNDTHD                HUNDREDS COMPARISON
   TAB
   AND A  $0F
   SUB A  $05
   BMI CT
   ADD B  $03
CT TBA
   AND A  $0F0
   SUB A  $50
   BMI DT
   ADD B  $30
DT STA B HNDTHD
♦
   LDA A TENTSD                TENS OF THOUSANDS COMPARISON
   TAB
   SUB A  $05
   BMI ET
   ADD B  $03
ET STA B TENTSD
♦
♦
   ASL LSB
   ROL MSB
   ROL UNTTEN
   ROL HNDTHD
   ROL TENTSD
   DEX
   BNE BEGIN                   END OF CONVERSION CHECK
♦
♦
♦
♦
   END
   MON
```

TABLE C.1 Machine Code Listing for MC6800 Binary to BCD Conversion

MEMORY		INSTRUCTION		REMARKS
ADDRESS	DATA	MNEMONIC	OPERAND	
0010	7F	CLR	UNITEN	
0011	00			
0012	80			
0013	7F	CLR	HNDTHD	
0014	00			
0015	81			
0016	7F	CLR	TENTSD	
0017	00			Initialize
0018	82			
0019	CE	LDX	0010	
001A	00			
001B	10			
001C	8E	LDS	00E0	
001D	00			
001E	E0			
001F	96	LDA A	80	
0020	80			
0021	8D	BSR	6D	UNITEN
0022	6D			
0023	D7	STA B	80	
0024	8D			
0025	96	LDA A	81	
0026	81			
0027	80	BSR	67	HNDTHD
0028	67			
0029	D7	STA B	81	
002A	81			
002B	96	LDA A	82	
002C	82			
002D	8D	BSR	61	TENTSD
002E	61			
002F	D7	STA B	82	
0030	82			
0031	78	ASL	0070	
0032	00			
0033	70			
0034	79	ROL	0071	
0035	00			
0036	71			
0037	79	ROL	0080	
0038	00			5 byte
0039	80			shift
003A	79	ROL	0081	left
003B	00			
003C	81			
003D	79	ROL	0082	
003E	00			
003F	82			
0040	09	DEX		16 bits
0041	26	BNE	DC	completed
0042	DC			return to
0043	3F	SWI		monitor

MEMORY		INSTRUCTION		REMARKS
ADDRESS	DATA	MNEMONIC	OPERAND	
0090	16	TAB		
0091	84	AND A	0F	
0092	0F			
0093	80	SUB A	05	
0094	05			1st Digit
0095	2B	BMI	02	
0096	02			
0097	CB	ADD B	03	
0098	03			Sub
0099	17	TBA		routine
009A	84	AND A	F0	
009B	F0			2nd
009C	80	SUB A	50	Digit
009D	50			
009E	2B	BMI	02	
009F	02			
00A0	CB	ADD B	30	
00A1	30			
00A2	39	RTS		

Index